Heroes, Rascals, and the Law

Heroes, Rascals, and the Law

Constitutional Encounters in Mississippi History

JAMES L. ROBERTSON

University Press of Mississippi / Jackson

The University Press of Mississippi is the scholarly publishing agency of
the Mississippi Institutions of Higher Learning: Alcorn State University,
Delta State University, Jackson State University, Mississippi State University,
Mississippi University for Women, Mississippi Valley State University,
University of Mississippi, and University of Southern Mississippi.

www.upress.state.ms.us

The University Press of Mississippi is a member of
the Association of University Presses.

First printing 2019

∞

Library of Congress Cataloging-in-Publication Data

Names: Robertson, James L. 1940– author.
Title: Heroes, rascals, and the law : constitutional encounters in
Mississippi history / James L. Robertson.
Description: Jackson : University Press of Mississippi, [2019] | Includes
bibliographical references and index. |
Identifiers: LCCN 2018031162 (print) | LCCN 2018036815 (ebook) | ISBN
9781496819956 (epub single) | ISBN 9781496819963 (epub institutional) |
ISBN 9781496819970 (pdf single) | ISBN 9781496819987 (pdf institutional)
| ISBN 9781496819949 (hardcover : alk. paper)
Subjects: LCSH: Law—Mississippi—History. | Mississippi—History—Anecdotes.
| Mississippi—Social life and customs—Anecdotes. | Mississippi—Politics
and government. | Mississippi—Constitution.
Classification: LCC F341.6 (ebook) | LCC F341.6 .R624 2019 (print) | DDC
976.2—dc23
LC record available at https://lccn.loc.gov/2018031162

British Library Cataloging-in-Publication Data available

FOR LINDA
who said I should write a book

Contents

VII | Preface

3 | CHAPTER 1
We the People, the Courthouse, and the Constitution

15 | CHAPTER 2
Only People Were Slaves

57 | CHAPTER 3
Judicial Review Comes to Mississippi

95 | CHAPTER 4
Mississippi Bank Wars

151 | CHAPTER 5
Agricultural Liens and Related Policy Products of Police Power

203 | CHAPTER 6
Advent of the Regulatory State in Mississippi

257 | CHAPTER 7
The Police Power of the State Moves to the Piney Woods

301 | CHAPTER 8
The Coming of the Common Law in Mississippi

371 | CHAPTER 9
The Governor and the "Gold Coast"

423 | CHAPTER 10
Balancing Industry with the Constitution

477 | Epilogue

491 | Index

Preface

Stories are found on the pages that follow of people who had substantial encounters with the state of Mississippi and its constitutional processes. Some moved here. Others made their mark and then left. Some were just passing through. Others lived their whole lives here and left descendants. A few wound up wishing they'd never heard of Mississippi. More could not imagine life anywhere except Mississippi, its frustrations and foibles just a part of day-to-day comings and goings. The tales of these people hop, skip, and jump among the calendars from times before December 1817 and statehood up through and including the Great Depression and then the era of World War II in the 1940s. These men and women by and large have three things in common: their encounters with some power, protection, or act of the State arguably in the name of its constitution du jour, trips to the courthouse where they experienced a constitutional creation or effect, and their humanity. What follow are but variations on these themes and their inherent commonality.

A DIFFERENT APPROACH

Justice George H. Ethridge's *Mississippi Constitutions*, published in 1928, remains useful. "Citizenship is an important affair and to fill the requirements satisfactorily requires a full knowledge of at least the fundamental laws of the state." Ethridge hoped that his work would "be read not only by lawyers, but be found by all citizens an interesting study, and especially do I hope that it will find its way into the high schools and colleges and in the libraries of all who teach the subject of constitutional government." Ethridge took the familiar top-down approach. "It is my purpose to explain briefly, the separate provisions, as well as give the substance of such decisions as we have construing these several sections."

Prof. John W. Winkle III has published *The Mississippi State Constitution*, 2nd ed. (2014), a useful book of fewer than two hundred pages, a once-over-lightly top-down effort, touching every section of the state constitution today, with in-depth treatment of few. There are out-of-print or just hard-to-find works such as Prof. Huey B. Howerton's *Yesterday's Constitution Today*, first published in 1960. Two sometimes useful works in process are accessible online, viz., "Mississippi Constitutions," *Mississippi College School of Law* website, law.mc.edu/lmr/constitutions; and Wikipedia's "Constitution of Mississippi," en.wikipedia.org/wiki/Constitution of Mississippi. In 1986, Governor Bill Allain convened a special commission and charged it to draft a new constitution for Mississippi. The product was published as "A Draft of a New Constitution for the State of Mississippi, Constitutional Study Commission," 7 Miss. Coll. L. Rev. 1–45 (Fall 1986). More than thirty years later, this noble though never-enacted effort remains worthy of study and reflection.

Lately I have authored with annual updates a 500-plus-page exposition on Mississippi constitutional law and its practice, more or less top-down in form. See *Encyclopedia of Mississippi Law*, Vol. 3, *Constitutional Law* (Jeffrey Jackson et al. eds., Thomson Reuters, 2d ed. Supp., 2018). I expect that project to continue for the foreseeable future, each year's update enriched by new developments, reactions, critiques, and other comments upon the work du jour.

My approach today is the inverse of that taken by others. It is the inverse of the encyclopedia chapter that I have produced and updated, revised and extended, and directed primarily to lawyers, judges, and perhaps political scientists and other professionals who find profit in thinking hard about particular ins and outs of constitutional law, theory, and practice.

Arguably, the meaning and effect and worth of a constitution is better understood through the experiences of people—men and women who have encountered it and the activities it authorizes, the powers people practice, and the rights it protects. Some have sought to evade and avoid their constitution, others to use and abuse it, and still others to respect or sneer. There are those who proceed blithely. What's a constitution among friends? Or so the saying goes. All add humanity to an otherwise sterile parchment or an organized complex of electrons, depending on one's point of view. We can learn from the fates and fears and dreams of people who have found themselves at odds with one another or with the State, and who—because of their disagreements, their social dilemmas, their legitimate needs, their faults, and their blunders—have found themselves in the courthouse and at times in other governmental offices, calling forth an exposition on the meaning, application, and practical effects of some constitutional principle or prerogative. Or in the mere exercise of powerful processes such as legislating, regulating, litigating, or judging, processes often benign until some person or entity comes to the courthouse, the capitol, or the regulator's office and asks for help.

One hundred thirty years of stories of humanity with constitutional components are told below. More recent, post–World War II era happenings are mentioned where those may aid understanding. No doubt there are other cogent encounters whose importance and capacity for teaching future generations could justify treatment here. A case could be made that the ones I have selected are not the best, the most illustrative or important. Still, each has something to say, and in its own right. A good cross section, the whole hopefully greater by orders of magnitude than the sum of its parts. Each tells of substantial circumstances and people and relationships and consequences—and spins—that have not been readily accessible in the work to date. A chapter on the common law in Mississippi, its history and its processes, provides glue, affords a gravitational interaction that gives body to the whole, though it includes a few tall tales of its own. Collectively, the stories are diverse and afford a complex and full flavor of what it has meant—in fact and in practice to Mississippi and the people who have passed through—to live and act and encounter one or more of the four constitutions the State has enacted as a part of, though not an altogether loyal partner in, that federal union called the United States of America.

Without people, without our social existence, no constitution would be necessary. And so I have by and large turned to narrative form, emphasizing human qualities and experiences of those involved and affected, who they were, when they lived, what they did and said without my unnecessary paraphrasing, what they felt and what they feared, when they succeeded or when they failed—often a bit of each—and at times just how they struggled from day to day in the times in which each lived. On most days, no constitution has seemed to matter, though one has always been there. Then there are the times when we have to struggle with the counsel of our better angels, who whisper and remind us of the inexorable reality that taxes really are the price we pay for civilization, and a price worth paying.

In the end, I propose a day-in-the-life-of quiz to see if—and to what extent—awareness may have been raised, understanding enhanced. That we may have learned more of how and just how often, and in ways how diverse, lives do intersect with—encounter—some power or right or responsibility traceable to the state or federal constitution, and no doubt on occasions far beyond this work.

In these narratives I reject one of the well-known perspectives of Oliver Wendell Holmes, from his latter days as a state supreme court justice, viz.

> The reason why a lawyer does not mention that his client wore a white hat when he made a contract, while Mrs. Quickly would be sure to dwell upon it along with the parcel gilt goblet and the sea-coal fire, is that he foresees that the public force will act in the same way whatever his client had upon his head.

See Oliver Wendell Holmes, *The Path of the Law*, 10 Harv. L. Rev. 457, 458 (1897). But we want Mrs. Quickly to find the adjudication and its lesson human and informative and reliable, too. Reliability and understanding are enhanced when we see those affected as three-dimensional, living, breathing, and often quite quirky people we have met, know, or see on the streets, or wonder about through electronic or social media. Mundane data about men and women who cross the stage add reality—if also everydayness—to lives lived and human worth. If you do not take an interest in people and their foibles, this book may not be for you.

I have organized these few particular "encounters" in part chronologically, in other parts functionally, in still other parts simply bowing to the importance of times past that ought to mean something. At least one chapter focuses on events and travails under each of Mississippi's four constitutions. Several chapters overlap at least two of those constitutions. Chapter 8 concerning common law has concerns with all four and the state's full life of two hundred years and counting.

Overall, attention has been paid to practical concerns that have arisen. There is no necessary connection between one "constitutional encounter" and the next, nor should there be. Each is one or another angle on one or more generations of the same elephant family being inspected by the same blind man. All are connected by the fact that each is a story of something that mattered (and, hopefully, is interesting) in lives lived, something that probably would not have happened had there been no constitution or courthouse, or at least would not have turned out as it did. Whether a given encounter led to good or bad or just the next day will be a matter on which reasonable minds may not agree. That we may have become more informed, reflective, tolerant, and reliably reactive will be enough.

THE GREAT FIELDS OF CONSTITUTIONAL PRACTICE

There are at least six great general fields of constitutional law and practice. It may be helpful to mention these, that they be kept in mind in parsing the encounters in the stories that follow. Most stories implicate two or three of these fields, some all six. In no particular order of prominence or practical effects, but at a high level of generality, these are:

1. The Legislative Power, including Eminent Domain, the Police Power and more recently the Regulatory State, each of which is administered through Executive Power and is subject to Judicial Review;
2. The Executive Power and Responsibilities;
3. The Judicial Power and Responsibilities;
4. Individual Rights of human dignity, Responsibilities, and Remedies versus and vis-à-vis the Eminent Domain and Police Power of the Regulatory State;
5. The rights and freedoms of speech, assembly, petition and of the press, which shall be held "sacred" and shall never be impaired, and
6. The Separation of Powers and Responsibilities.

The dividers separating these fields are porous, as well they should be, with overlaps and shades of gray. Still, the fields are discernible. Some would build walls, but experience teaches that those seldom last and wouldn't do much good if they did. Good public officials do not need arbitrary powers, much less walls. Bad public officials shouldn't have them.

Overarching all is the social compact, found in one form or another in each Mississippi constitution

1. Miss. Const. art. 1, §§ 1, 2 (1817);

2. Miss. Const. Preamble and art. 1, §§ 1, 2 (1832);

3. Miss. Const. Preamble and art. 1, §§ 1, 2 (1869); and

4. Miss. Const. art. 3, §§ 5–7, 11, 13, 32 (1890).

In its first great case in its very first term, the Supreme Court of Mississippi embraced the "social compact" political theory of Jean-Jacques Rousseau: *Harry and Others v. Decker & Hopkins*, Walker (1 Miss.) 36, 40, 1818 WL 1235 (1818). The story of this case is told in chapter 2 below. Three subsequent sets of constitution makers have carried the compact forward.

Horizontal and vertical interactions attend our social compact. It is horizontal among the people, vertical between the people and their State. It is vertical between the United States and the States and the peoples of both. And at each dimension We the People have evolved within continuous and dynamic processes of becoming, in the course of which, "every year if not every day we have to wager our salvation upon some prophecy based upon imperfect knowledge" *Abrams v. United States*, 250 U.S. 616, 630 (1919) (Holmes, J., dissenting). Along the way humility is that quality of life that we have found least dispensable. The higher the office, the more imperative that humility attend the discharge of its duties and the exercise of its functions. In this vein, it takes a hardened heart not to cherish the humanity in Barack Obama's 2015 colloquy with Marylynne Robinson, set in Iowa, whence it flows southerly with Ol' Man River and readily washes ashore at all points from Memphis, capital of the apocryphal state of North Mississippi, to the southernmost tip of Wilkinson County, Mississippi, just above Louisiana's infamous Angola State Penitentiary. See Barack Obama and Marylynne Robinson, "A Conversation in Iowa" (pts. I & II), *New York Review of Books*, Nov. 5 and Nov. 19, 2015), www .nybooks.com/articles/2015.

Encounters in the six fields are important parts of the stories that follow. Diverse and in many ways complex and controversy-filled categories of constitutional experience or collections of experiences are presented. In each, powers and prerogatives have been exercised in the courthouse, wherever else they may have been practiced. Forward-looking legislation and daily leadership, regulation, and administration have taken place in the state capitol and hundreds of other places. And as for all things past, the courthouse has never been far away as the day of judgment approached. Justice, fairness, and humanity in all of their ambiguity take hits, emerge, and endure.

WORDS OF CAUTION AND PERSPECTIVE

Overall, my approach to the legal process and constitutional practice in the place where I was born and raised is a work in process (hopefully, "progress" is also a credible descriptor). The experiences of producing my published work from the mid-1980s and the decades that followed have advanced my thinking and understanding considerably.

More than ever, I have learned that we must be careful with labels. For starters, "liberal" and "conservative" are nonsensical labels in intelligent legal parlance. "Living constitution" means different things to different people. To some, these are fighting words. Constitutional law should not be made up on the fly, according to the whims of the times. "Originalism" and "original understanding" are equally offensive, particularly for those who find textual bases within our constitutions and their history for believing that our constitutions were meant for peoples and times and understandings beyond the prescience of their draftsmen.

Then there is legal pragmatism that at times pushes meaning and effect as far as texts may permit, in practical directions, with a sensitive regard for reasonable reliance interests and an informed regard for the fairly doable and the aggregate effects of doing, impacts likely experienced in the foreseeable future, costs probably incurred. These ostensible points of view are hardly mutually exclusive. I would like to think that mechanical jurisprudence and its poor cousin, mere wooden legal thinking, are a thing of the past, but they are not. Of late and for the foreseeable future, I see myself a nonideological pragmatic instrumentalist, insofar as the rule of law will allow. Reliability is the foremost imperative of adjudication, constitutional or lesser exercises of the judicial power.

For the moment I can only add a cautionary note disclaiming the loaded meaning at times associated with "labels" that have slipped by my edits. I concur that we should try to agree on ground rules for our discussions. I deny that there are hard-and-fast rules of historical certainty or geometric—much less legal—precision that may guide our efforts. Absolutes are destined to disappoint. Refusal to bring a touch of humility to the project strips people of any real or imagined standing to get mad over some constitutional encounter contrary to their druthers. With a little luck, I have kept these tales of encounters sufficiently in the past that we do not get bogged down in the less-than-helpful rhetoric that has been trotted out with each post-Bork nomination of a new justice for the US Supreme Court. A public order of human dignity remains our goal.

I am concerned that people who have lived in decades and centuries past be cut a little slack when it comes to the mores of their times that today might seem out of line or just quaint. Lincoln soared into history at Gettysburg and in his Second Inaugural, but that does not mean his every other thought, utterance, and action should be fly-specked according to some latter-day standard of political correctness. It was outrageous that not long ago some at Princeton wanted to distance the school from Woodrow Wilson because his racial views seem to have been a bit short of standards more accepted a century after Wilson lived. Just condemnation of *post hoc* judgments regarding our fellow human beings is hardly limited to views and actions regarding race, creed, religion, national origin, sexual orientation, and the like. Men and women should not be pilloried by reference to the mores, understandings, and opportunities of centuries after they were dead and buried, lest few among us might escape hanging at the hands of some future generation.

IF ONLY MORE EVIDENCE COULD BE FOUND

In a more accessible world, if I had another decade to work on this demanding project, more could no doubt be found and told about many of the players who appear herein. Foremost, the stories in chapter 2 about Harry, Bob, Anthony, Rachel, and many other slaves the Deckers purported to sell in Natchez circa 1816 would be enriched if only more of their personal stories would come to light. If only we knew more about Sylvia Brooks, Jesse Christian, and some thirty-eight other farm workers—freedmen all—who worked the land, cultivated the fields, and harvested the crops in one of the stories in chapter 5. Or about Bohlen Lucas, Drew Whitley, and fifteen other African American freedmen who at about the same time were tenant farmers on a plantation in Washington County, Mississippi. Not even a name is known of the slave Isaac Jones murdered, for which he was hanged. It would be nice to know a bit about Jones, too.

We'd love to have the full story on how Governor Alexander G. McNutt evolved—personally and politically—from supporter of the Mississippi Union Bank, signatory on the guaranty bonds, and then to arch enemy who wished that in time his friends would mark his grave "Here lies McNutt the Repudiator." Was it more than just weakness of character or lack of intelligence—or what—that led Mississippi's leaders and followers to think that, in a constitutional state subject to the rule of law, compliance with the unanimous final judgment in *State of Mississippi v. Hezron A. Johnson*, 3 Cushm. (25 Miss.) 625 (1853), and the holding of that case, coupled with *Beasley Campbell v. Mississippi Union Bank*, 6 Howard (7 Miss.) 625 (1842) as controlling legal precedent—really was optional?

On the other hand, diligent search has failed to unearth the full story of W. S. Allbritton, who came forward in 1937 and—for reasons to this day not clear—mounted a constitutional challenge to the viability of Governor Hugh White's Balance Agriculture with Industry Act. Or even whether the spelling of Allbritton's name on his tombstone is correct. What was veteran Chief Justice Sydney McCain Smith really thinking when he rose to address a law school audience in the fall of 1936 concerning the State and the social process, knowing that only a couple of weeks earlier the legislature had passed the BAWI bill and that its constitutionality was sure to be challenged before the state supreme court in the near future? And what he was thinking when he said,

If the state is to promote the happiness of its citizens, it must abandon *laissez-faire*—a doctrine that is an anachronism in a state that exists to make life good, and which the American states have already partially abandoned—and secure to all of its citizens an equal opportunity to obtain a fair share of economic fruits.

We can be sure that we do not know the full stories of the what's and why's of Rankin County constable Norris Overby or kingpin of vice Samuel Alvin Seaney, each of whom died at the hands and gun of the other in the early minutes of Wednesday, August 28, 1946, at the Shady Rest nightclub on the Gold Coast. But can we be sure that Virgil A. Griffith really was taking us back to Magna Carta in those last three paragraphs of his fine legal essay that became *State v. McPhail*, 180 So. 387, 392 (Miss. April 18, 1938)? And what was in his mind as he did so? Hopefully, in chapter 9 we scratch the surface.

A JUDGMENT CALL ABOUT PRESENTING THE PLAYERS

Where it has seemed practicable and would not unduly interrupt the narrative, a bit about each player is presented as he or she comes onto the stage. With some, a bit more of a complete biographical sketch seems in order, and for a variety of reasons. For example, in chapter 4, three Yerger brothers—George, Jacob, and William—and George's brother-in-law Charles Scott seem almost four horsemen defending the Mississippi Union Bank bonds against the repudiators. They are presented as a family. In chapter 9, Alexander Alvin Seaney and his very complex extended family are also presented as the colorful and troubled and tragedy-prone troupe that they were. Other major players are sometimes grouped by function and by the constitutional encounters in which they played a part.

The reader encountering a cast of characters on pages that follow should feel free to fast-forward to the next part of the particular chapter. A character's appearance in the story may be a better time to circle back and learn a bit more about Volney E. Howard or Horatio F. Simrall, to name but two among many not known so well today. Most are interesting in their own right, and to the extent reasonably available, end notes are provided where the reader may learn more about this player or that who may not have been a household name. The Internet is there as well. At press time, at least ten players in these chapters had had their names enshrined in the Mississippi Hall of Fame. While only one had been hanged, more than a few had died violently.

THE BUILDING BLOCKS

My research for this work has been extensive. It has included works with which I have not been heretofore familiar. It has included a re-review of works I knew of and which I had not found congenial with my views, which remain evolving if I am to achieve any part of my fervent wish. Because I know my views are not universally shared (whose are?), I have tried to consider and cite responsible discussions from differing perspectives. This seems appropriate to make it a little easier for critical readers to pick my points apart. Not only have I changed my mind from time to time over the years, I have lived long enough to have realized that in times past, I have been just plain wrong!

Still the thought struggles and processes leading to my prior published work inform the present effort. These will include articles I authored and published circa 1988–1998.

1. *Discovering Rule 11 of the Mississippi Rules of Civil Procedure,* 8 Miss. Coll. L. Rev. 111 (1988).

2. *Post-Custody Pre-Indictment Problems of Fundamental Fairness and Access to Counsel: Mississippi Opportunity,* 13 Vt. L. Rev. 249 (1988) (with Amy D. Whitten).

3. *Of Bork and Basics,* 60 Miss. L. Journ. 439 (1990).

4. *Myth and Reality—Or, Is It "Perception and Taste"?—In The Reading of Donative Documents,* 61 Fordham L. Rev. 1045 (April, 1993).

5. *The Law of Business Torts in Mississippi, Part I,* 15 Miss. Coll. L. Rev. 13, 331 (1994–1995) (with David W. Clark).

6. *The Law of Corporate Governance: Coming of Age in Mississippi?* 65 Miss. L. Journ. 477 (1996).

7. *Judge William C. Keady and the Bill of Rights* (1991) (Annual Keady Memorial Lecture, Mississippi Humanities Council), reprinted in 68 Miss. L. Journ. 3 (1998).

Particularly important has been the hard study and reflection that led to two articles that I published in 2015 and 2016, my *Variations on a Theme by Posner: Facing the Factual Component of the Reliability Imperative in the Process of Adjudication,* 84 Miss. L. Journ. 471–683 (2015), followed in short order by my *Practical Benefits of Literature in Law, and Their Limits,* 35 Miss. Coll. L. Rev. 266–342 (2016), as well as the updated *Encyclopedia of Mississippi Law,* chapter 19 of Vol. 3, *Constitutional Law* (Jeffrey Jackson et al. eds., Thomson Reuters, 2d ed. Supp. 2018).

Of course, there are nuggets and slip-ups that abound between volumes 427 and 608 of the Southern Reporter (2d series) (Mississippi Cases, 1983–1992), and essays published online over the last fifteen years or so at www.caba.ms/articles, and at times under the pseudonym of The Road Lawyer.

WORDS ABOUT FORM AND SOURCES

I have provided sources and citations for each chapter that, hopefully, will give the curious or skeptical reader ready access to materials consulted in most of my assertions in this work. Where I may have fallen short, computer research programs such as Lexis/Nexis, Westlaw, and, of course, the Internet can take you as far as you care to go.

Without apology, and joining most rational people that I know, I hate *The Bluebook*, that damnable guide to form and citations in legal writing that ruins the communication abilities of so many good law students who somehow allow themselves to be brainwashed that it must be their slave master. Those who insist upon sentence-by-sentence, line-by-line citations are deserving of the fate suffered by Isaac Jones, the only point for debate being whether they should thereafter be resurrected and flogged. And *The Chicago Manual of Style* is a useful guide, nothing more.

At the end of this work and on a chapter-by-chapter basis, I provide two resources that may be helpful. First are endnotes. Not every word and thought encountered from a public source or the work of another is documented. Still, I try to give credit where it is due. The pages in *Harry and Others* decided by the Supreme Court of Mississippi in 1818 and *State v. McPhail* decided in 1938 and many others—on each page—have double-digit thoughts worthy of individualized endnotes. You get a healthy fraction below. Only minimal effort should enable the reader to call me to account where I may have slipped.

The same goes for ideas and inimitable phrases found in narrative works such as W. J. Cash's *The Mind of the South* (1941, 1991), David L. Cohn's several books of insights drawn from growing up in the Mississippi Delta, and, of course, William Faulkner. I know of no one over forty with an excuse not to have read *The Flush Times of Alabama and Mississippi*, originally published by country lawyer and later judge Joseph G. Baldwin, in 1853. The insights of these works have been supplemented, and valuably so. They have not been replaced.

One's understanding of chapter 2 and the ideas behind freedom-by-residence would be enhanced by perusing *Redemption Songs, Suing for Freedom before Dred Scott*, by Lea VanderVelde (2014), and the more Mississippi-focused articles of US District Judge Michael P. Mills, found in the *Mississippi Law Journal*. It is special that we have papers prepared by the great-great-great-grandson of Judge Joshua G. Clarke, telling the story of his family in those early days in *The Life of Joshua G. Clarke: Mississippi's First Chancellor*, FCH Annals (May 2013), and *A Path Not Taken: Joshua Giles Clarke of Mississippi, Supreme Court Judge and Chancellor*, https://www.academia .edu/5660628 (from a reading of this article, its title should be "What Passes as a Humanist").

Alexander v. State by and through Allain, 441 So. 2d 1329 (1983) is the finest fruit of chapter 3 concerning judicial review and separation of powers. US Circuit Judge Leslie H. Southwick's careful published writings enrich understanding and challenge us to think.

Much has been written about the stories told in chapter 4 and the Union Bank bond mess and the state's more general war on banks. In 1969, William L. Coker published the now hard-to-find *Repudiation and Reaction: Tilghman M. Tucker and the Mississippi Bond Question*. It's a good read. The author gives no hint that he understands much about the law, legal reasoning, or the meaning of a final judgment in a state constitutionally committed to the rule of law. "The New Nation of Mississippi," published in the *New York Times* on January 29, 1861, and Clifford Thies, "Repudiation in Antebellum Mississippi," *Independent Review* 191 (Fall 2014), are two very different articles that informed chapter 4. Meredith Lang's *Defender of the Faith*, first published in 1977, has a valuable chapter on that part of Mississippi's "war on banks" that did not concern bank bonds. Each of these works is worth reading in its entirety.

The work prior hereto concerning Mississippi's postbellum crop lien laws and practice is scattered and a mixed bag. I proffer Cash and Cohn as observers who set the stage for chapter 5. Roger L. Ransom and Richard Sutch's volume *One Kind of Freedom: The Economic Consequences of Emancipation* (1977) is a valuable resource. So is the work of Harold D. Woodman, particularly *New South— New Law: The Legal Foundations of Credit and Labor Relations in the Postbellum Agricultural South* (1995). After surveying the work in the field, I see no substitute for a summary review of the differing stages of legislation from 1867 through 1880 or so, followed by a review of the work done in the courthouses and really reading most of the fifty-three or more opinions of judges in endnote 112.

Chapter 6 tells the story of the regulatory state coming to Mississippi. In this sense, the essential work is Mississippi native Tom McCraw's Pulitzer Prize–winning work called *Prophets of Regulation* (1984). But this chapter also humanizes the rise and decline of the railroads, and our century-long romance with that wonderful form and means of transportation. An objective telling of the stories of the Y&MV Railroad and its parent company, the Illinois Central Railroad, is hard to find. Noel Workman's "Stopped in Its Tracks," *Delta Magazine* (May 12, 2012) is enjoyable.

Gilbert H. Hoffman, *Steam Whistles in the Piney Woods* (1998), is the must-read regarding chapter 7, for the facts humanized. James E. Fickle, *Mississippi Forests and Forestry* (2001), and Nollie W. Hickman, *Mississippi Harvest: Lumbering in the Longleaf Pine Belt, 1840–1915* (1962), are worthy as well. Justice Holmes's dissenting opinion in *Lochner v. New York*, 198 U.S. 46, 75–76 (1904) complements Hoffman, though Holmes spoke almost a century before. More recently, Judge Richard A. Posner has extended his analysis and critique of Holmes's *Lochner* dissent, concluding, "It is merely the greatest judicial opinion of the last hundred years" (Posner, *Law and Literature* 346 [3d ed. 2009]). Chapter 7 opens with a barbed insight from Robert Penn Warren, *All the King's Men* (1946). It completes the circle and closes with a poignant passage from Faulkner's *Light in August* (1932).

Regarding chapter 8 and the common law, well, read *The Common Law* by Oliver Wendell Holmes, circa 1881. And then Holmes's famous article published sixteen years later, *The Path of the Law*, 10 Harv. L. Rev. 457 (1897), mentioned above. A more recent article by a native Mississippian is of particular interest and value: Evelyn Keyes, *Hedgehogs and Foxes: The Case for the Common Law Judge*, 67 Hastings Law Journal 749, 774 (2016). Players appearing in chapter 8 have also appeared in other chapters. Josiah A. P. Campbell is one. Perhaps more colorful are senator, and later representative, Gordon Boyd's lengthy orations in legislative chambers, though the one supporting the Married Women's Property Law (chapter 8) may have had more merit than his attack on the Planters' Bank bonds (chapter 4).

If there is one go-to piece regarding chapter 9 and the Gold Coast, it is Craddock Goins's article "Hooch and Homicide in Mississippi," *American Mercury*, Vol. XLVIII (October 1939). In 2015, Janice Branch Tracy published *Mississippi Moonshine Politics*, which provides a perspective beyond the Gold Coast and its heyday, though her legal research is lacking. More so than with other chapters, original information was found in the court files kept by the chancery clerk of Rankin County—God bless public officials who preserve records with no clue of the tales they may someday tell for latter-day history hunters! Praises be to Justice Virgil Griffith for his fine legal essay, and to those who have preserved it for posterity. May the unknown and unnamed person responsible for losing the court file and appellate record for *State v. McPhail* (1938) spend eternity in the infernal regions!

Regarding chapter 10, much better records may be accessed regarding Governor Hugh White's Balance Agriculture With Industry program. One cannot put a value on "Mississippi's BAWI Plan," published by Federal Reserve Bank of Atlanta in its Thirty-Fifth Annual Report (1949), http://fraser.stlouisfed.org/. Yet mystery remains around the full story behind Chief Justice Sydney McCain Smith's address at the University of Mississippi School of Law, *The State and the Social Process*, published and still available at 9 Miss. L. Journ. 147 (December 1936). It is enough that we have this brief paper, which is both unique and wonderful. Past that, surely at some point someone will come forth and tell us the story of W. S. Allbritton, and why he became the plaintiff challenging the BAWI program, and why he spelled his last name with two ells, or if he really did.

One more prefacing thought. You do not have to be a lawyer to appreciate the must-read status of judicial decisions such as *Harry and Others v. Decker & Hopkins*, Walker (1 Miss.) 36 (1818), and *State of Mississippi v. Hezron A. Johnson*, 3 Cushm. (25 Miss.) 625 (1853) (despite its considerable length), or *State vs. McPhail*, 182 Miss. 360, 180 So. 360 (1938). Just do it. And also many other primary resources invoked. That the quotations may be brief, and the citations fewer than one expects from a lawyer, should be taken as publisher's insistence on some limits, not the author's view of the lack of worth of the ideas contained in the work listed. By all means, consult the bibliography appended after the endnotes to each chapter.

ACKNOWLEDGMENTS

My sincerest appreciation to the many people who helped in so many ways, from research assistance, reading partial drafts, offering comments and critiques, discussions—you name it. Fearful that I have left some out who helped, thanks are due to Kay T. Allen, Reuben V. Anderson, Clinton Bagley, Fred L. Banks, Marshall Bennett, Robert E. Bobo, John Robin and Laura Bradley, David Bramlette, Trevor Brown, Mack Cameron, Hodding Carter III, Eric C. Clark, J. Calvitt Clarke, Madison Coburn, Thomas A. Coleman, Gordon A. Cotton, Lucius B. Dabney, Charles Eagles, Andrew T. Fede, Matthew Freedman, Virgil G. Gillespie, Christopher Grillis IV, John Grisham, Daniel Hammett, William H. Hammett, Tom Henderson, Gilbert H. Hoffman, Beverly Wade Hogan, Lamar Hooker, Clara W. Joorfetz, James B. Kelly, Evelyn V. Keyes, Sidney E. Lampton, Cindy Lawler and other staff of the University of Southern Mississippi Special Collections including Jennifer Brannock, William and Patty Lewis, Roy Noble Lee Jr., Tom S. Lee, John Clark Love, Virginia Magee, Kaitlyn McMellon, Howard McMillan, Stephen Middleton, Mimi Miller, Michael P. Mills, Geoffrey Morgan, Genie Nussbaum, Stephen J. Parks, Donald B. Patterson, Irl Dean Rhodes, R. David Sanders, David G. Sansing, Lemuel A. Smith, III, Leslie H. Southwick, Joshua Stover, James C. Sumner, Michael M. Taylor, Andy Thaggard, Michael B. Wallace, William L. Waller Jr., Jenae Ward, Bill Wardlaw, J. Lott Warren, the Eudora Welty Library and its staff, William F. Winter, Dan M. Woodliff, W. Swan Yerger, and two anonymous peer review readers provided by University Press of Mississippi. The work could not have been done without the resources and assistance of Katie Blount and the highly professional staff of Mississippi Department of Archives and History. Thanks, Katie, and to all others.

Special thanks are due my legal assistants Wanda Fisher and Karen McDonald, in particular, and to Wise Carter Child & Caraway, P. A., more generally, for support and patience in ways too numerous to count.

Without Craig Gill and staff at the University Press of Mississippi, the work would never have seen ffruition. Copyeditor Lisa Williams's patience, stamina, and attention to detail were amazing.

My wife, Linda Thompson Robertson, and my sister Lucie Robertson Bridgforth provided advice, assistance, and support—and caring critiques—far above and beyond the call of duty.

Each person listed above has enabled the work in some important way. Alone I am responsible for its shortcomings.

Heroes, Rascals, and the Law

CHAPTER 1

We the People, the Courthouse, and the Constitution

A BROODING OMNIPRESENCE

In the antebellum frontier, "everywhere [the southerner] built his courthouse almost before he built anything else." That is what keen-eyed journalist W. J. Cash saw when he studied the story of his native land, and that is what he said. William Faulkner elaborated a decade later. He spoke of the symbolic, mystical, and practical role of the courthouse in a community—a jurisdiction—and of its brooding omnipresence.

> But above all, the courthouse; the center, the focus, the hub; sitting looming in the center of the county's circumference like a single cloud in its ring of horizon, laying its vast shadow to the uttermost rim of horizon; musing, brooding, symbolic and ponderable, tall as cloud, solid as rock, dominating all; protector of the weak, judiciate and curb of the passions and lusts, repository and guardian of the aspirations and the hopes;....

• • •

> ...Because it was theirs, bigger than any because it was the sum of all, it must raise all of their hopes and aspirations level with its own aspirant and soaring cupola, so that, sweating and tireless and unflagging, they would look about at one another a little shyly, a little amazed, with something like humility too, as if they were realising, or were for a moment at least capable of believing, that men, all men, including themselves, were a little better, purer maybe even, than they had thought, expected, or even needed to be.[1]

Cash and Faulkner weighed well in mind as I began this work, on this and other fronts, and as the work has proceeded. I have found myself thinking, wondering, reflecting—"constitution" in lieu of "courthouse"? Perhaps these thoughts from Cash and Faulkner bear repeating altogether, with "constitution" replacing "courthouse." The US Congress had said that adopting a constitution creating a republican form of government was Mississippi's ticket for admission to the Union, one of several to be sure, but still before its people did almost anything else. As Faulkner understood, "We the People" in the presence of the courthouse on the high ground—or high-minded men and women just thinking of their constitution—every so often experience awe and humility, pride and thankfulness, and make a silent self-promise to do better.

Inside, the courthouse endures mischief, greed and shenanigans and disingenuousness. It is not hard to find adjudications of doubtful reliability, men's mistakes, shabby streaks of meanness, active narcissism, crude approximations of justice that people practice there, and, above all, raw power politics. And yet the courthouse stands, stoic, impervious, defiant, enduring, ready for come what may. So often it seems the mundane and the self-centered office holder, the meat grinder, the glad-hander, and the administrator, the collision of interests and the limits of practical reality, are what and all there is. So much everydayness. Papers filed. Taxes paid. Orders entered. Promises made. Ambitions shared. Fibs told. Behind-the-back assessments of others. Bragging rights claimed. Every day. Then suddenly comes a burst of justice and good, of humanizing power and civilizing practice. Though the functioning courthouse is a continuous and often bumpy process of becoming, some embracing new technologies more eagerly than others, it makes us citizens and not just residents. We could not do without it.

And so of our constitution. One at a time, Mississippi has had four. The courthouse is a place where the promises and the powers of the constitution become real in the lives of flawed and fearful and yet hopeful human beings. An eighteen-year-old registers to vote. The circuit clerk issues a marriage license to a young couple. The new family files the deed to its first home in the chancery clerk's office. Loan papers are filed there so a man or woman can start up a new business in this still pretty free enterprise system we have. The board of supervisors approves widening the old road and reinforcing that damn bridge. The school board struggles to find the funds and quality staffing to provide more than merely an adequate education for the thousands of youngsters in the public schools, and to fend off the political clout of those who would defund the public schools tomorrow if they could. A jury returns a verdict that really does approach the truth. A judge rules, and that ruling embodies—and shows judicial understanding of—the wisdom of Solomon, the patience of Job, and the humanity of Shakespeare. An executor files a deceased's will for probate, pays all legacies and debts, and enables a bit of the future, as time goes by. And yet the courthouse is a place where so often we deny that same constitution that makes so many good things possible. We ease past it sitting on the shelf, unnoticed or unheeded, scared of its spirit because it asks of us too much. The constitution makes possible more than any one of us can understand or control, or knows is happening, or is even there. A local public order of human dignity.

The courthouse is where we encounter the constitution at its most paradoxical, at once expressing a people's hope for freedom and for order, for majority rule and yet protecting each of us from the majority's momentary madness, allowing us to do as we please while at once allowing space for others who please to do otherwise. Above all, in the courthouse we realize that the constitution is somehow so much more perfect than the people who made it. We cannot escape the vexing question of whether and to what extent the people who work with the constitution and the laws made thereunder are up to the task—of using it reliably, at once boldly and humbly, doing more good than harm. As with religion, so many of us turn to it only when we are afraid of something, when we want something for ourselves or something to be done to or about somebody else, to pass judgment on other people or some threat or circumstance. We trot out the constitution to justify or bolster some posture we are already sure is right on other grounds. We put ourselves, our families—those most dear or just most like us—first and foremost. We turn to the constitution to vanquish doubt, to disarm or ward off the opposition. It is the bible of our civic religion. In its otherness, it is our mirror. It is always there, silent as we come and go, too much in a hurry—or is it too much afraid to look up and see and be seen?

On its merits, the 1844 case of *Morgan v. Reading*[2] is a for-instance, one of thousands. It concerned people with conflicting rights and interests in navigable waterways and the lands those waters ran through over in Warren County. What practical needs did the riparian landowners have to exclude other people's use of the waterways? What rights did the law afford each of them in that regard? What were the prerogatives of third persons who so desperately needed the waters as a means of transportation and commerce? And whence the law that, in the exercise of his constitutional "judicial power," the judge in Faulkner's courthouse[3] would apply? With what level of care, reliability, fairness, practicability, and promptness did the judge rule? When was it reasonable to expect the judge to have ruled? How was social activity affected the next day? In the next decade? What can we learn from these tales about lives lived under our constitution-based "rule of law"? And in hundreds of settings beyond the rivers that run through our little part of the world?

In the late 1930s, the governor called out the state militia in the face of widespread vice and a breakdown in law and order in western Rankin County involving hundreds of participants and conflicts. In time, trial and appellate courts were called into service.[4] Chapter 9 tells that tale of rich and rowdy life and tragedy—over a decade or more—and lets you judge whether and how and to what extent the constitution and the courthouse helped. When more recently, albeit over time, the legislature arrogated unto itself great executive and high-level administrative powers until 1983, judgment under the constitution came, and in the courthouse.[5] W. J. Cash's finding regarding the priority of the court-house[6] and Faulkner's sense of its brooding omnipresence, as well as the articu-lation of a social compact grounded in humanity,[7] are threads that weave a web through and over the whole of the work that follows.

In more than two or three chapters, we ponder other words from Faulkner, in *The Town* (1957), and we wonder whether and with what profit the constitu-tion enables the State

> to preside unanguished and immune above this miniature of man's passions and hopes and disasters—ambition and fear and lust and courage and abnegation and pity and honor and sin and pride—all bound, precarious and ramshackle, held together by the web, the iron-thin warp and woof of his rapacity but withal yet dedicated to his dreams.

Mississippians get riled up over their state constitution every now and then. Often this is so when a particular amendment is proposed. Some group or faction wants to control or at least inhibit some other group or faction. We cannot or will not summon the faith of our fathers to speak in grand gen-eral phrases, for fear that some judge will come along and find meaning and effect that some of us may not like, that won't let us be quite as petty as is our penchant. Few of us can hold at bay that urge to control. Most of us cannot imagine that we should even try. Joseph Baldwin—sage of the antebellum Southwest, and a lawyer, to boot—was on target that neither he nor the rest of us, recalling times past, remembered in *The Flush Times of Alabama and Mississippi* (1853)

> hearing any question debated that did not resolve itself into a question of consti-tution—strict construction, &c.,—the constitution being a thing of that curious virtue that its chief excellency consisted in not allowing the government to do anything; or in being a regular prize fighter that knocked all laws and legislators into a cocked hat, except those of the objector's party.

We bristle when a court construes the constitution and applies it in ways at odds with our perhaps ill-informed but surely self-centered druthers. It enables us to elevate fear into belief and into righteousness, then to self-righteousness, then to law. A century ago a wise judge saw this flaw—common among so many of us—and said that

> if you have no doubt of your premises or your power and want a certain result with all your heart, you naturally express your wishes in law and sweep away all opposition. To allow opposition by speech seems to indicate that . . . you doubt either your premises or your power.[8]

We demand in the name of the constitution that others accept our particular paramount and paradoxical insistence that a Bible and a gun are our birthright, and woe to the wicked. We can't seem to see that an eye for an eye soon makes the whole world blind. Those brought up in the Judeo-Christian tradition so often forget the fifth chapter of the Gospel According to St. Matthew, wherein lies what just might be the greatest repealer clause ever written for a society accepting that the behavior of its people should be regulated by rules.

To so many, the constitution is like the weather. Better forecasts would help, but that's about all one should hope for, except of course on a given day when all wish for a fair advantage over one's adversaries. And over those whose life circumstances and experiences or skin color or nationality or basic beliefs and preferred practices have not been quite the same as ours, or those who do not see the world—and what should be done—as we do. It is enough that we have friends who share our prejudices, and neighbors who don't disagree too often.

In the practical world of getting and spending—that is otherwise so much with us—people bump into one another. We have disputes, among ourselves and with our state and local governments, and some of these implicate the constitution directly. Almost all are dealt with by the exercise of some constitutional power. Some state and local officials exercise legislative and executive powers in funny ways. Mississippi's constitution adds that "the exercise of the police powers of the State shall never be abridged," that is, until some clause in the bill of rights stands firm and says, not so fast. The judicial power!

NO ARBITRARY POWER

We are blessed that every now and then some judge comes along and reminds us that "under our form of government there is no arbitrary power, that is to say, no power above the law; but every unlawful power is the subject of scrutiny by the courts, where it operates to the legal hurt of any citizen, however humble." These words of Justice Virgil Griffith give pause. In this lesson grounded in the collective reading of Sections 14, 21, and 24 of Mississippi's much-maligned constitution du jour, we have just been reminded of the cornerstone of our positive law, the best that was ever in—and about all that remains of—that parchment signed by King John under great duress on June 15, 1215 AD. This "no arbitrary power" injunction activates and informs and enriches the foremost duty of judges facing the facts and circumstances in the stories that follow, in this work and tomorrow. In 1938, Griffith added that "these sections guard and protect against unwarranted action on the part of any officer, however great." Unwarranted? So says the constitution, but as who reads it?

And yet each state court—and each circuit court, and the supreme court in particular—really is charged to facilitate practical justice, to face down any tendency toward arbitrary power. Aggregated, these courts are an intrinsic part of the government of Mississippi that each person may of right petition "on any subject." From Magna Carta comes the notion that each person's petition and its response should be adjudged according to due process and the law of the land. Each state court "shall be open … [that] right and justice shall be administered without sale, denial or delay." Though penned first at Runnymede—and under dubious circumstances—these practical ideals have been stated more fully and without much change at all in each of Mississippi's four constitutions. In those three final paragraphs of his *McPhail* opinion (starting with the "but whenever" clause halfway down the third paragraph from the end), Justice Griffith elaborated the still-extant core that remains available for the asking by each of us.[9] Who has said it better?

In a sense, this was nothing new. As long ago as 1844, Justice Joseph S. B. Thacher saw that Mississippi's second constitution had recognized "Magna Charta which declared that no freeman shall be taken or imprisoned, but by the lawful judgment of his equals, or by the law of the land (Mag. Chart. C. 29)." "Judicial proceedings according to the course of the common law" were embedded among those rights that history traces back eight hundred years and are the core of Article the Second of the Northwest Ordinance of 1787. The stories that follow tell of what we thought of that at differing times, and under varying circumstances, yesterday. So many tomorrows lie ahead.

WORDS MATTER

State courts are creatures of the same constitution and parts of the same state government as other state-level officials. The constitution gives no notice that judges are entitled, that they can and should put on airs—particularly when enrobed. Yet it is a fact of history and constitutional practice that officials of the judicial department of state government do claim prerogatives not available to one another—legislators and executive department officials. The proceedings of judges are not so open as those of officials in the other two departments. Strict time, place, and manner rules constrain opportunities to petition a court, to communicate with judges—formally, that is. No open meetings laws like those that govern others. Neither of the other two departments gets to make up rules—from whole cloth—that block access, like standing to sue or the so-called political question doctrine and other atextual constraints on justiciability.

Most problematic are the times when judges won't answer questions of public interest when people really do need answers and where the circumstances are such that answers from any other source aren't worth a plug nickel. Judges get the final say on what the constitution means and what the laws mean, how each is applied, and with what consequences. But that doesn't mean the judge's say always has to come last. Or after the parties have jumped through every hoop the courts can imagine as prerequisites to their doing their job of judging. How long did sensible citizens struggle to gain a declaratory judgment procedure in their courts, and how hard have so many judges fought to evade and avoid the meaningful use of that procedure? Judges claim immunity from being questioned as to their special privileges. Given these, one would think that at the very least judges should point to something in the constitution that really does afford them the privilege of being a bit less accessible to people with problems, and to the public at large, than are officials of other departments of government. A cumbersome elective judiciary ameliorates these penchants to some extent, but by no means completely. It is arguable that this creates more problems than it solves. The judicial system and the legal process are so mysterious, so misunderstood, in so many instances.

Judges are on their honor to accept that the state constitution accepts the judicial power, and then vests all of it in a supreme court and several lower courts. Nothing in the constitution lets on that judicial power is lesser or greater—qualitatively or quantitatively—than the legislative power or the executive power. That the three powers are different more or less—each from the other two—is apparent, but that doesn't take us far. The judicial power enables—no, charges—state judges collectively to perform that core function of adjudicating all matters on any subject, challenging them to adjudge each matter reliably and fairly, and with humility and humanity. Any constrictions past these are but a contrivance of men to take themselves seriously. Still some demur, confusing the familiar with the necessary. The importance of the point cannot be overstated, for the work that follows, and for the understanding and candid critique of that work. And for our daily lives. So we take it by the numbers.

The constitution extends state judicial power to "matters." We speak of subject *matter* jurisdiction. Chancery courts are trial courts. They have "full jurisdiction" of certain "matters and cases, viz; (a) All matters in equity; . . . [and] Matters testamentary and of administration." Chancery courts are courts of limited jurisdiction. Circuit courts are also trial-level courts, sometimes called common law courts. Their authority is stated in the negative. Circuit courts "shall have original jurisdiction in all matters [that word again!] civil and criminal in this state not vested by this Constitution is some other court." Circuit courts are courts of general jurisdiction. They possess residual jurisdiction.

Words matter. The active verb "matter" means that particular words cause something to occur. But "matter" can also be a noun. The constitution uses the plural noun "matters" and captures the breadth and essence of the many kinds of petitions and other proceedings that the two constitutionally created trial-level courts are authorized to consider. "Matters" means something broader than just "cases" or "controversies" or these two combined, though in the context of legal practice it often includes one or both of them, and at times more. A matter need not be a case, sometimes called a lawsuit or an action or a prosecution, though it often includes those. A matter need not involve a controversy of any particular magnitude, though controversy commonly attends matters that people petition judges to consider. The authority of the state courts to adjudge "all matters" is broader than—means more than—all mere cases or controversies. We know this because the constitution uses a word—"matters"—that tells us so.

As we proceed, keep in mind that—because of Miss. Const. art. 6, §156 (1890)—the state trial courts aggregated have no authority not to decide as reliably as may be each matter properly presented by a person or legal entity. Particularly is this so in the face of any pretense toward arbitrary power. In the practical world, not to decide is to decide. As early as 1821, in *Cohens v. Virginia*, US Chief Justice John Marshall declared that it "would be treason to the constitution" for a court of the United States "to decline the exercise of jurisdiction which is given . . ." Any such evasion or avoidance of duty at the state level is worse. State governments are not nearly so limited as the federal government.

It's a sin, a civic sin, for a state (or federal) court not to decide every matter within its jurisdiction—every single one—according to law reasonably elaborated, reliably applied to the relevant facts found, practicably, and taking account as best may be of reasonable reliance interests and foreseeable effects that the adjudication may have. But the duty to adjudge includes more than that. The court should consider reasonably relevant legislative facts as well as judicially known and other adjudicative facts, "the felt necessities of the times," that is, all the while using those time-tested tools that through the years have enabled courts to make law that we still call common law. All of this will be fleshed out in chapter 8 below, and with a variety of examples and illustrations.

Once is not enough for a point as important as the one Article 6 of the constitution just made. And so it is our great good fortune that the constitution says it all again, more simply, another way, a second way, and with the same practical effect. Look at Article 3, §11. Consider the state's petition clause: "The right of the people . . . to petition the government on any subject shall never be impaired." Earlier the constitution has recognized that civil government consists of the aggregation of three powers of government. Judicial power is one of these. The judicial department is a distinct department, "a separate magistracy" within which the judicial power over matters has been "confided." "The judicial power of the State shall be vested in a Supreme Court and such other courts as are provided for in this Constitution." There is no way around the constitutional fact that each person may of right petition one or more judges on any subject arising in the context of any matter, and if none is found with specific authority to act, section 156 says that person, petitioner, plaintiff, or other applicant may not be turned away from a circuit court of proper venue. That this right is subject to reasonable regulation as to time, place and manner[10] hardly waters it down. For such regulation, the opportunities of a person or firm to approach the judges becomes efficient, effective, practical, productive, and altogether real. These may not be begrudged consistent with the judge's oath.

Through its history, the state's highest court has often been in need of a good old-fashioned seventh-grade English teacher, armed with a ruler and saying quietly and firmly, "Now, what part of 'every person' do you not understand? And of 'all matters' and 'on any subject' and 'shall not be impaired'? And what part of 'not vested by this Constitution in some other court' do you not understand?" It is a relevant question of constitutional dimensions in each of the stories that follows, whether and to what extent the mind of the court and not just the door to the courthouse has been opened. And whether the judicial mind has been duly engaged so that it may adjudge, with optimal reliability according to law applied to the facts, each petition it receives from any person regarding any matter on any subject. In the end, it is important that the rest of us be ever vigilant that right and justice, in the full and complete sense the constitution provides, have—in practical reality—been administered without sale, denial, or delay.[11]

Fortunately, we haven't had many cases over the years where right and justice were thought for sale.[12] We have certainly seen denials, when the court has hidden behind some judge-made dodge to avoid a duty, refuses to rule on the merits of a matter, or otherwise begrudges access to its jurisdiction. Or just did not make time to face serious arguments advanced, dig deeply enough, and articulate reliably and with reasoned elaboration why the argument failed.[13] Past that, we need only recall that Prince Hamlet listed "the law's delay [and] the insolence of office"[14] as two of seven trials of living so hard to bear that a person might decide in favor of suicide. There are dimensions of life in organized society that have not improved much in more than four centuries.

THE EFFECTS OF FEDERALISM, AND OF LOCAL GOVERNMENT

There remain those who are mystified a bit by the clauses used in the courthouse that form the architecture enabling and guiding state courts in what they do regarding matters they are charged to consider. Another source of this mystery is the difference between the state and federal judiciaries.

The Mississippi Constitution and the courts it has created are different in fundamental ways from their federal counterparts, and not just in that state courts are so relatively underfunded, understaffed, and less elaborately housed and equipped. Legislative and executive officials—federal and state—always have the constitutionally permissible option of doing nothing, hoping for the best in the next election. There are times when the federal judiciary is supposed to do nothing, except dismiss a would-be case or controversy for want of subject matter jurisdiction. The state judiciary as a whole, however, is constitutionally expected to act every time a person or entity, public or private, approaches and presents a matter involving any subject. Every time.[15] Not as with the federal judiciary, where all courts are courts of limited jurisdiction, sometimes very limited. State judges get paid to adjudge matters, not to look for excuses not to adjudge some matters. That doesn't mean the plaintiff should always win. It does mean that judges are supposed to know—and to understand—that a defendant in whose favor a final judgment is entered seldom gives a hoot what the ground may have been. That he escaped hanging is what matters. The incentives sent to the community—for good or for ill—are essentially the same, maybe even more deleterious where the judges check the merits and decide on so-called non-justiciability grounds. The insolence of office.

The federal government, by way of contrast, is a government of limited powers. Similarly, all federal courts are courts of limited jurisdiction. But conceptually and practicably the matter is different at the state level. That's what the Tenth Amendment is all about. The residuum remains with the states. All powers not conferred by the US Constitution upon the federal government or some officer(s) or department thereof are reserved to the respective states and to the people.

At the state level and vertically downward, the converse is so. Local governments such as counties and municipalities are governments of limited powers. They have only the political powers that have been granted them by the state consistent with its constitution.[16] Again, the residuum remains with the state. All powers not conferred by the state constitution upon local government or by the legislature within its powers are reserved to the state. Of course, the state gets its political powers from the people. Not many strings attached there, as the people can—and sometimes do—amend the state constitution.

At the federal level, government officials in general and judges in particular have to be mindful of the Tenth Amendment at all times. The same is so in the case of local government officials as well. But not so as to state level officials. These should stay within their bounds more or less vis-à-vis each other as explained above, but those horizontal boundaries are not nearly so clear as the vertical ones. In the state judicial department, there is at the trial level a court of general jurisdiction, as we have seen. No trial court jurisdiction of "matters" that may arise on any subject has been withheld. None. While there is no constitutional right of appeal, as a practical matter, the state supreme court has the authority to—and does—hear appeals in all matters on any subject adjudged by an arguably proper trial court. Vertical distinction between trial and appellate courts, properly understood, is another of those areas where so many judges just cannot wait for their next opportunity to confuse the familiar with the necessary.

A familiar baseball metaphor paraphrased may round out understanding. In the context of reasonably disputed matters of federal vs. state constitutional power, the tie goes to the state. The same is so for reasonably disputed matters between the state and local government. Tie goes to the state.

At the state level we have learned to live with federal supremacy. White southerners fought a war over that one and lost. Before that, Mississippi's courts were at times defiant, and not just regarding slavery. After the War, regarding the newly freed slaves, the United States amended its Constitution in major respects, ostensibly to keep the former rebels in line going forward. In 1890, Mississippi's constitution makers tested the limits of those postbellum federal amendments with nefarious restraints on the right to vote. Then, a few years later, the US Supreme Court gave the political leaders of Mississippi and other southern states a helping hand with *Plessy v. Ferguson* and its "separate but equal" promise, both flawed and false.

Through it all, the principle of federal supremacy—not quite so limited as before the War—has remained intact. It is our umbrella, broad and forever, or at least well past our ability to see what lies ahead. Since January 1, 1869, the Mississippi constitution has enjoined that the State may make no law "in derogation of the paramount allegiance of the citizens of this state to the government of the United States." And while "[t]he people of this state shall have the inherent, sole, and exclusive right . . . to alter or abolish their constitution and form of government whenever they deem it necessary to their safety and happiness," that right is qualified. "Such change [may not be] repugnant to the Constitution of the United States." Nor may it place any arbitrary power beyond the reach of the law or the scrutiny of some court—every time—somewhere, sometimes even looking inward.

Note taking is allowed as you plow through the stories that follow. Corrections and elaborations communicated to the author or publisher will be cherished.

ENDNOTES

1. *Requiem for a Nun* (1950). The body of Faulkner's work is a rich minefield of twisted, at times tortured, and at other times uplifting tales of humanity caught in legal conundrums. *See, e.g., The Law and Southern Literature Symposium*, 4 Miss. Coll. L. Rev. 165–329 (Spring 1984), devoted almost entirely to Faulkner's work; Michael Allan Wolf, *William Faulkner, Legal Commentator: Humanity and Endurance in Hollywood's Yoknapatawpha*, 77 Miss. L. Journ. 957 (Summer 2008). More generally, this entire work is informed by—and flows from—the ideas and approach of my article *Practical Benefits of Literature in Law, and Their Limits*, 35 Miss. Coll. L. Rev. 266–342 (Spring 2016).

2. *Morgan v. Reading*, 3 Smedes & M. (11 Miss.) 366, 1844 WL 3217 (1844), discussed in chapter 8 below.

3. William Faulkner, *Requiem for a Nun* 35, 37 (1950).

4. *State v. McPhail*, 182 Miss. 360, 180 So. 387 (April 18, 1938), discussed in chapter 9 below.

5. *Alexander v. State by and through Allain*, 441 So. 2d 1329 (1983).

6. W. J. Cash, *The Mind of the South* 33 (1941, 1991).

7. *Harry and Others v. Decker & Hopkins*, Walker (1 Miss.) 36, 1818 WL 1235 (1818).

8. *Abrams v. United States*, 250 U.S. 61 6, 630 (1919 (Holmes, J., dissenting, joined by Brandeis, J.).

9. *State v. McPhail*, 182 Miss. 360, 180 So. 387, 392 (April 18, 1938), elaborating Miss. Const. art. 3, §§ 14, 21, and 24 (1890).

10. Examples of such reasonable regulations include the Mississippi Rules of Civil Procedure, the Mississippi Rules of Criminal Procedure, and the Mississippi Rules of Evidence, among others regularly found in the annually published *Mississippi Rules of Court—State*.

11. See the last clause in Miss. Const. art. 3, § 24 (1890); in Miss. Const. art. 1, § 28 (1869); in Miss. Const. art. 1, § 14 (1832); and in Miss. Const. art. 1, § 14 (1817).

12. Maybe some of this is depicted in Curtis Wilkie, *Fall of the House of Zeus* (2010). Chapter 4 below tells of the State's failure and refusal to honor its solemn pledge of faith and credit guaranteeing payment of Union Bank bonds and Planters' Bank bonds. *See* Miss. Const. art. 14, § 258 (1890).

13. Regarding my ten years of appellate judicial service, I place myself at the top of the list of those whose work deserved further scrutiny. *See, e.g.,* my "A Life Sentence Served by an Innocent Man," *Capital Area Bar Ass'n Newsletter*, June 2011 8, 10, available at http://www.caba.ms/newsletter/caba-newsletter-june2011.pdf.

14. William Shakespeare, *Hamlet*, act 3, scene 1, lines 72–73.

15. This proposition was articulated in 1843 by Chief Justice William L. Sharkey in *Houston v. Royston*, 7 Howard (8 Miss.) 543, 548–49, 1843 WL 2035 (1843) (construing constitution of 1832). Sharkey's view was accepted and followed in *State ex rel. Knox v. Speakes*, 144 Miss. 125, 109 So. 129, 133 (1926) (Anderson, J.) and *Farrar v. State*, 191 Miss. 1, 2 So.2d 146, 147 (1941) (Griffith, J., construing substantially similar constitution of 1890). *See* Robertson, Subject Matter Jurisdiction, § 1:23, in *Mississippi Civil Procedure* (Jackson, Campbell, and Matheney eds., 2018).

16. *See, e.g.,* Hemphill Constr. Co. v. City of Laurel, 760 So.2d 720, 723 (2000) (municipality); *Delta Electric Power Ass'n v. Mississippi Power & Light Co.,* 149 So.2d 504, 510–511 (1963) (municipality); *Smith v. Dorsey,* 599 So. 2d 529, 535 (1992) (school board); *City of Belmont v. Mississippi State Tax Com'n,* 860 So.2d 289, 306 (2003) (Municipality); *City of Jackson v. Freeman-Howie, Inc.,* 121 So. 2d 120, 123 (1960) (Municipality); *Lee County Bd. of Sup'rs v. Scott,* 909 So.2d 1223, 1226 (Miss. App. 2005) (Board of Supervisors/County Authority); *Adams v. First Nat. Bank,* 103 Miss. 744, 60 So. 770, 772 (1913) (powers of Board of Supervisors limited to those conferred by statute).

BIBLIOGRAPHY

Baldwin, Joseph G., *The Flush Times of Alabama and Mississippi* (1853, 1974).
Cash, W. J., *The Mind of the South* (1941, 1991).
Faulkner, William, *Requiem for a Nun* (1950).
Faulkner, William, *The Town* (1957).
Gospel According to St. Matthew, chapter 5 (King James Version).
Magna Carta (1215, Blackstone edition).
Mississippi Constitution of January 1, 1869.
Mississippi Constitution of November 1, 1890.
Robertson, James L., *Encyclopedia of Mississippi Law*, Vol. 3, *Constitutional Law* (Jeffrey Jackson et al., eds. 2nd ed. Supp. 2018).
Robertson, James L., *Practical Benefits of Literature in Law, and Their Limits*, 35 Miss. Coll. L. Rev. 266 (2016).
Robertson, James L., "Subject Matter Jurisdiction," in *Mississippi Civil Procedure* (Jackson, Campbell, and Matheney eds., 2018).
Robertson, James L., *Variations on a Theme by Posner: Facing the Factual Component of the Reliability Imperative of the Process of Adjudication*, 84 Miss. L. Journ. 471 (2015).

CHAPTER 2

Only People Were Slaves

How should the Court decide if construction was really
to determine it? I presume it would be in favour of liberty.
—JUDGE JOSHUA GILES CLARKE (1818)

Harry and Others v. Decker & Hopkins[1] is one of the earliest known opinions
of the Supreme Court of Mississippi. It is remarkable in many ways. Freedom-
by-residence cases brought by slaves seeking freedom were not uncommon
in the years leading into the 1850s. *Harry and Others* was the first known case
where at the end of the day the court of last resort in a southern slave state
had ruled that the slaves were free. Likely from a very early age, perhaps from
birth, Harry and two others whose gender is not known had been enslaved
in Virginia. In 1784 their owner took them to lands that—three years later—
became "free soil" as a matter of federal law. The Northwest Ordinance of
1787 governed the lands that would become the southwestern area of Indiana,
admitted to the Union as a free state the year before Mississippi was admitted
as a slave state.

The core ground for the claims for freedom made by Harry and many more
than two others was that their owner had settled and lived with his family and
possessions, including his slaves, in a part of the country where as a matter of
positive law slavery was prohibited. The owner and his extended family built
homes, established businesses—usually related to farming and agriculture—
and otherwise sought their fortunes there. They weren't just passing through.
They enjoyed the benefits and protections of the law of their new home area.
Conversely, these new citizens of the Northwest Territory were deemed to
accept the burdens of that law, including laws made after they arrived, the same
as settlers everywhere in the new nation.

Particularly was this so when such settlers did not leave after a reasonable time had passed, and after the passage of said-to-be-offensive new laws.
Such a settled new residence rent the ties that had bound the slaves to their
masters. Those ties were not resurrected where a former slave found himself or herself in another slave state. "Once free, forever free." But would this

argument prevail where slavery was not only legal but was also regulated by the new state's constitution?

Three years after Harry and his fellow slaves won their freedom in a Mississippi court, a white man killed a slave—a black man who was a stranger to the white man. Isaac Jones was that white man, and he had acted with malice aforethought. "The taking away the life of a reasonable creature, under the king's peace, with malice aforethought, . . . is murder at common law."[2] And so on July 27, 1821, the sheriff of Adams County, Mississippi, had Isaac Jones hanged—the fourth man to be executed by the new state of Mississippi. The humanity of the slave, whose name is not known, and who was not so fortunate as Harry and the others, was vindicated posthumously.

Thirty-five years later, what little was left of the courage and hope of men and women who had been enslaved came crashing down when the US Supreme Court decided the *Dred Scott* case and fanned the flames that led to war. Mississippi had backpedaled in the 1830s. Its holdings were checkered for the next several decades. *Harry and Others* in 1818—and the trial that preceded it— are all the more memorable as a major constitutional encounter in Mississippi history. In the fullness of time, a Natchez reporter told the nation of

> a decision alike honorable in our state and in humanity. It appeared that, some time in the spring of 1816, twenty-eight black persons, who were slaves for a cer- tain period of time, were brought by the defendants from Indiana, and sold in this state as slaves for life. By the decision of the Court and Jury they were restored to entire freedom.[3]

THE DECKERS IN THE NEIGHBORHOOD OF VINCENNES

The story that led to the summer of 1818 in southwest Mississippi began in Virginia at a time when the ink was barely dry on the Treaty of Paris. Soon after Cornwallis refused to meet Washington at Yorktown, settlers from Virginia began moving into the lands north and west of the Ohio River, more than a few bringing slaves with them. John Decker (ca. 1719–1790) and his family were among such settlers.

The Deckers had come from Kingston in the Dutch country in New York, and into Hampshire County on the inverted shin of what is now northern West Virginia, adjacent to the mother state. They are thought to have had at least eight children, five sons and three daughters. The sons had biblical names like Abraham, Isaac, Jacob, Moses, and Luke. All fought with the Indiana mili- tia. John Decker also owned a number of slaves, male and female. In 1783, the Decker family picked up and left Hampshire County, stopping briefly in Kentucky before making a new home in 1784 in what in time became Knox

County, Indiana. They settled in "the neighborhood of Vincennes," bringing with them Harry, Bob, Anthony, Rachel, and many other slaves. They established Decker Township, no doubt benefiting from the hard labor of their slaves, some acquired after they arrived in their new home. In time, John Decker lived below Deckertown, now just the small town of Decker, south of White River. He was said to have been one of the first sheriffs of Knox County.

Decker Township was southerly but still in the neighborhood of Vincennes, on the lower Wabash River—in time the boundary between southwestern Indiana and southeastern Illinois—until it flows into the Ohio River, ending to the south against northwestern Kentucky. People settling in the area enjoyed ready access to the navigable inland waterways. John Decker's son Isaac occasionally ran flatboats to Natchez and New Orleans. Because he had no practical alternative, Isaac would walk home along the Natchez Trace. Southerly flowing tributaries and then the mighty Mississippi itself would become avenues for transportation quite important to the slaveholding Deckers over the years to come.

John Decker is believed to have died in 1790 or possibly 1791, leaving four female slaves to his wife and children. Luke Decker (1760–1825), one of John's sons, became leader and spokesman for the family. Farmer, judge, and militia officer, Luke owned and traded slaves in the Northwest Territory, the Indiana Territory, and the State of Indiana. Col. Luke Decker was said to have fought with William Henry Harrison in 1811 at the Battle of Tippecanoe against Tecumseh's American Indian Federation. Coincident with Indiana's imminent statehood, Decker suffered two slave escapes, one in his home area, and the other near Natchez, in Mississippi. Between 1816 and 1822, Luke was the proslavery protagonist in constitutional wars fought on two jurisdictional fronts. But this is getting ahead of the story.

Soon after Decker Township was established, the Congress enacted the aforesaid Northwest Ordinance of 1787. Article the Sixth read, "There shall be neither slavery nor involuntary servitude in the said territory, otherwise than in punishment of crimes whereof the party shall have been duly convicted." To most who are familiar with the King's English, these words are straightforward. If Article 6 had said, "There shall be neither whiskey, vinous nor otherwise spirituous or intoxicating liquors in said territory," its meaning would have been clear, though likely few would have obeyed. Self-interest leads people to make funny arguments. This is particularly so when that self-interest is informed by prejudice and familiar practice, and where financial interests are substantial and at risk. Of course, declaring free soil in the Northwest Territory was only the first step.

John Decker had been well aware of the problem this new federal ordinance posed for his family's slaveholdings. Likely with the help of a lawyer, the Deckers found it easy to convince themselves that the new 1787 ban on slavery had no retroactive effect. John and likeminded men could not be expected to dispense with valuable slaves they had brought to the neighborhood in Vincennes, all acquired before there was an Ordinance of 1787. They didn't think much more of the notion that they could not acquire as many new slaves as they liked. After the death of his father John circa September of 1790, Luke Decker became an outspoken leader of the proslavery faction in what would become the free state of Indiana. In 1794, his brother Moses Decker assisted another New York Dutch country immigrant in kidnapping a slave and his wife so that they could not appear in a federal territorial court to present their petition for freedom.

In 1793, in his capacity as judge of the Court of Common Pleas in Knox County, Luke Decker received an opinion letter from Arthur St. Clair, governor of the Northwest Territory. St. Clair advised that Article 6 had no retroactive effect. In December of 1794, St. Clair reiterated his position, refusing to enforce an order of Territorial Judge George Turner that a slave be freed. The territorial governor went further and joined forces with proslavery forces in Knox County in forcing the judge's resignation on threat of impeachment based on trumped-up charges of "demanding bribes and levying fines without trial."

Slavery had found a firm foothold in Knox County and nearby areas along the northern banks of the Ohio River, including counties in the Illinois Territory to the west. Luke Decker's group persisted—and was persistently unsuccessful—in petitioning the Congress that it should repeal Article 6 of the Northwest Ordinance. It would be hard to argue that John Decker, then Luke and their family, acquiesced in the notion that the family's slaves—and particularly those in being before the Ordinance of 1787—were eligible for freedom by their residence. It would be equally hard to argue that the Deckers were unaware of what their continued residence and extended roots in the neighborhood of Vincennes might portend for their slaveholdings.

On December 11, 1816, Indiana became the nineteenth state admitted to the Union. The Indiana Constitution drafted the summer before was more elaborate and specific than the Northwest Ordinance. Article I, Section 1, in practical effect enshrined the "inalienable rights" clause in the Declaration of Independence in Indiana constitutional law. This new Indiana constitution came to the attention of the Supreme Court of Mississippi in summer of 1818, and at its very first term. Judge Joshua Giles Clarke authored the opinion handed down in that summer and reported as *Harry and Others v. Decker & Hopkins*. The court read Indiana's new constitutional Section 1 thusly: "Does not the first article of the constitution declare the condition of the people of Indiana free, and this condition, by the last article, is likewise declared to be out of the control of government, or to be a right reserved to the people."

Completed on June 29, 1816, the new Indiana Constitution had been a shot across the bow to men like those of the Decker clan. Statehood lay ahead, and it was almost certain to arrive in the not-too-distant future.[4] Theretofore, the Deckers and others had enjoyed the advantages of practical inaccessibility from Washington and of sympathetic officials like Governor St. Clair and future president William Henry Harrison. In the nation's capital, men from slave states like

Virginia and South Carolina still wielded great political power. The federal government had not appointed a territorial judge until 1791, and that judge made no appearance in Vincennes until 1794. Proslavery forces benefited from the not-always-benign neglect of sympathetic officials like St. Clair and Harrison. The Indiana constitutional convention suggested that life was about to change for the slaveholders in the southern part of the soon-to-become new state.

With appropriate dispatch, Luke Decker and others gathered Harry and at least twenty-seven other slaves and began navigating downstream. There are no known records of the voyage. Luke put his son, Hiram Decker (1794–1863), in charge, along with other hands who knew the down-river course. As noted above, Luke had other and similar fish to fry at home in Indiana. Harry and the other slaves were removed from Indiana soil in July of 1816. Luke was calling the shots. Ownership papers on Harry and at least the older of the others may still have been in the name of John Decker, who had brought them to the neighborhood of Vincennes in the first place. As the Decker vessel headed south, those in charge had but one purpose—to sell Harry and the others as soon as practicable and for the best price they could get.

The Deckers' destination was almost certainly Natchez, maybe New Orleans if the market opportunities in Natchez were not satisfactory. As early as 1801 Natchez was becoming known as a slave trading center. Slavers were purchasing people cheaply in the old tobacco states and selling them at a premium in markets such as Natchez and New Orleans. "The Natchez slave market, along with [one other], became the most active in the whole South" in the years after the War of 1812. This is consistent with Judge Michael P. Mills's relatively recent showing that "[f]rom the beginning, the new state [of Mississippi] would be a major destination point for human cargo 'sold down' the river' from border states." Nothing suggests this activity was not well under way prior to the formality of Mississippi's statehood on December 10, 1817.

FRANCIS HOPKINS[5]

Everything known about Francis Hopkins (1770–1821) of McIntosh County, Georgia, suggests he was the sort of southern entrepreneur who in the second decade of the nineteenth century could and—if the price was right—would buy twenty-eight slaves at a market like that in Natchez. Likely, he was the buyer of Harry and the other twenty-seven. The 1820 census records that Hopkins owned 183 slaves.[6] Other records show that in the decade prior to his death, on May 5, 1821, Hopkins was dealing in slaves as often as in land.

Francis Hopkins was born in Beaufort County, South Carolina, on November 10, 1770. The family later moved to McIntosh County, a coastal county in Southeast Georgia, below Savannah and today near Brunswick. In time, Francis Hopkins owned as many five plantations in the McIntosh County area, along with a large number of slaves. Likely, that number would have been larger by twenty-eight had it not been for the judicial proceedings in Mississippi between and including 1816 and 1818.

Twenty-nine-year-old Francis Hopkins was commissioned as a lieutenant in the Georgia state militia in 1810. With the advent of the War of 1812, Hopkins was promoted to captain and then to major in the McIntosh County Battalion. In 1817, the war relegated to history, Hopkins was commissioned a brigadier general in command of the militia for eight Georgia counties, including Chatham and Savannah. This was a year before his eldest son's slave buying and legal appearance in Adams County, Mississippi. Between 1807 and 1816, General Hopkins served as a representative and one term as a senator in the Georgia legislature. He also served as a justice of the McIntosh Inferior Court from 1813 until his death in 1821.

John L. Hopkins (1795–1828), a lawyer and the eldest son of Francis Hopkins, would have been about twenty-one years old in 1816. That John dealt in slaves in Mississippi is suggested by a March 1819 transaction. A man named Thomas C. Vaughan bought two slaves from Elijah Morton, in exchange for Morton's $1,775 note payable and negotiable at the Bank of the State of Mississippi on March 6, 1819. John Hopkins and another, Andrew Montgomery, guaranteed the note. Before the note was due, Vaughan published notice on March 2, 1819, in the Natchez newspaper (*Mississippi Republican*) that he would not pay the note unless compelled by law, as the slaves had "proved unsound."

Francis Hopkins and his son were otherwise not strangers to lawless adventures. On March 27, 1819, not long after the problematic slave transactions near the Natchez area, John and his father became engaged in Darien, Georgia, in a verbal altercation with a family friend named McQueen McIntosh, a volatile member of the first family of McIntosh County. Long story short, John assaulted McIntosh with a cane and pistols and killed him. In due course, John was tried and found guilty of manslaughter. He was sentenced to three years' imprisonment. In time, he escaped (or through family influence made a civil exit) from the prison. John then fled to England, returning to southeast Georgia a few years later to set matters straight. The governor granted a full pardon, whereupon John Hopkins moved to Tennessee to open a new law office, and in time to become a judge and establish a new family. As fate would have it, the Georgia governor's grant of peace was short-lived. John made it only to the age of thirty-three, whereupon he was shot and fatally wounded by a party aggrieved by one of Judge Hopkins's rulings.[7]

THE VOYAGE TO NATCHEZ

By 1811, there were the beginnings of steamboat traffic from Pittsburgh down the Ohio River, then to the Mississippi River, and on to New Orleans. Flatboats or "broad-horns" were in use for transporting a variety of cargoes, including a large number of slaves. Downstream navigation usually meant a float rate of about four miles per hour. Approximately six hundred river miles lie between Cairo, Illinois, and Natchez. Commonly, the slaves were confined by chains in steerage or on the decks. In the latter instance, Ronald Davis reports, slaves would be "forced to sit on open decks, usually surrounded by boxes of cargo and supplies." One report has fourteen large broad-horns docking in Natchez in 1817 with cargoes of slaves to be marketed.

No known documentation describes the vessel Luke Decker sent south in the summer of 1816. Decker's human-cargo-laden vessel likely arrived in Natchez in the late summer of 1816. Once the boat was disembarked and offloaded in Natchez, Decker sold to Francis Hopkins at least twenty-eight slaves "as slaves for life." The sale and then escape[8] of Harry and his companions were surely in the late summer or early fall of 1816. These were men of practical reason, a point Judge Joshua G. Clarke would make with eloquence a few years later on behalf of a less fortunate slave.

Careful investigators have reported that lawyers found southwest Mississippi—territory and then state—an attractive place to establish a practice. Title and other land disputes are often mentioned. On the other hand, in the early 1820s, New Jersey immigrant lawyer Richard Stockton Jr. (1791–1827) found that "nobody ever paid a circuit rider; only in Natchez was it possible to build up a lucrative practice."[9] Still, finding a lawyer to help Harry and the others may have presented problems. There are many unanswered questions of how the Decker-sold slaves got to the courthouse. As a practical matter, they must have had assistance from white persons in the area. The fact that in time a jury found that Harry and the others should be granted their freedom is strong evidence that there were white persons in the area ready and willing to help.

The circumstantial evidence leaves little doubt that at some timely point these slaves escaped and found counsel at the hands of lawyers like Lyman Harding and Tully Robinson. By late October of 1816, their case was formally before a trial court of the Mississippi Territory, called "a superior court holden at the court house in and for the county of Adams." This wording comes from a printed form in use in October of 1816 by way of which witnesses were subpoenaed and thus commanded to appear and testify. The presiding officer was ten-year veteran territorial judge Walter Leake, who had held that office since 1807.[10] Judge Leake would later become a delegate to the 1817 constitutional convention, representing Claiborne County. After statehood, Leake served briefly as a US senator and was then elected the third governor of Mississippi. Governor Leake held office from January 1822, until his death in late 1825 cut short his life and public service. See chapter 3, "Judicial Review," below, where Governor Leake was significantly involved.

Witness subpoenas were issued for a trial set in Natchez for the third week in October of 1816. By their form these subpoenas were issued by the clerk of the superior court for a trial of the case brought by the Mississippi Territory against Hiram Decker and Francis Hopkins. This form suggests a prosecution in the public interest, that Decker and Hopkins were charged with committing an offense against the peace and dignity of the territory. The charge is not specified in records that have surfaced to date. The known facts suggest that the prosecution may have been commenced under the territorial law of 1808 regulating the importation of slaves.

At least five witnesses were subpoenaed by the prosecution. These included John Routh, one of the largest cotton planters in the world at the time. Another witness subpoenaed to testify against Decker and Hopkins was Natchez merchant Christopher H. Kyle, known to have freed his slaves. Court records reflect subpoenas issued at the instance of Decker and Hopkins for ten witnesses, including brothers Abraham Decker and Luke Decker.[11] Keep in mind that Hiram was the son of Luke Decker and the grandson of John Decker. Known facts and circumstances leave little doubt this earlier case involved the same persons and arose from the same events as gave rise to the petition for freedom-by-residence, the appellate version of which we know as *Harry and Others.*

Records available to date do not confirm whether the trial was held as scheduled. Then as now, trial settings were often cancelled, with the case continued and a new trial date set at some point in the future. A news report from Natchez published in Washington, DC, and in Boston almost three years later, suggests a trial "during the late term of our Superior Court." The dateline on both known published versions of the story reads "Natchez, June 20." June 20 of what year? We know that in the late summer of its June term, 1818, the Supreme Court of Mississippi decided the case of *Harry and Others v. Decker & Hopkins.* But that was the appeal. The news reports describe a trial and jury verdict granting the slaves their freedom. By the calendar, this means the Natchez news story was authored on June 20, 1817, referring to a trial at the most recent term of superior court prior thereto. A second puzzle is that the news reports refer to "the case of Harry et al. vs. Decker & Hopkins," not Mississippi Territory vs. Decker & Hopkins. This fits with the opinion of the Supreme Court in *Harry and Others,* which in its very first sentence says the court is considering the "motion for a new trial" filed by Decker and Hopkins. A territorial proceeding naming Hiram Decker, the person in charge of the slaves brought from the "neighborhood of Vincennes," suggests a criminal or other public interest prosecution. The case in the Supreme Court naming the long-deceased John Decker suggests that the legal ownership and title were involved in that case.

But how and why did the case get from the form of a territorial prosecution, which it was in October of 1816, to become a civil action, petitions for freedom of slaves, by the "late term of our Superior Court" prior to June 20, 1817? A not unreasonable hypothesis here is that, once in the hands of lawyers like Harding and Robinson, the tactical decision was made to seek only freedom for the slaves. Sympathetic and savvy lawyers would have known of the substance and procedure for petitions for freedom by slaves. Any claim of illegal trafficking in slaves may have seemed problematic; besides, freeing Harry and the others was much more important than sticking Decker and Hopkins with the monetary penalties authorized under the act of 1808.

There is another question. *Harry and Others* decides the appeal brought by Decker and Hopkins regarding only three slaves, Harry and two others. What happened to the other twenty-five slaves who "by the decision of the court and jury were restored to entire freedom"?[12] Here the likely answer turns on a technical legal point. Harry and the two others had been Decker's slaves for three years before the July 13, 1787, effective date of the Northwest Territory Ordinance. This gave Decker a stronger position for his non-retroactivity objection, uncomplicated by the fact that the other twenty-five slaves had all been acquired after 1787, and after the anti-slavery clause of the ordinance was in full force and effect. New buyer Francis Hopkins was a necessary party, but almost certainly the laboring oar and expense of the appeal was borne by Decker, who in law was obliged to defend the title to the slaves that he had conveyed to Hopkins.

As much as we hope that these puzzles may at some point be answered definitively, by records of authenticity and detail, they cause no concerns for the central premise and achievement of this important constitutional encounter in Mississippi's early history.

THE SUMMER OF 1818

The Supreme Court of Mississippi was still a gleam in the eye—an imminent gleam, to be sure—when Harry and his companions were force fed into the Natchez slave market in the southwestern Mississippi Territory. That court formally sat in the late spring and then through the summer of 1818. Statehood had been formally accomplished on December 10, 1817. Four judges served in that first term and year. They also served as circuit judges (trial judges, sometimes known as superior court judges).[13]

Presiding Judge John Taylor (1783–1820) of Adams County served from the Second District. Taylor was born in West Chester, Pennsylvania. His father had been a deputy sheriff, and John assisted him at the courthouse. By age eighteen John had begun to read law. In St. Louis in 1804, Taylor obtained his first license to practice law. In 1805, he came south to New Orleans but soon moved back upriver to Natchez. Taylor's first case in Natchez was a criminal case of some notoriety, and he won an acquittal. Within a matter of weeks, he had a busy practice. He served as a delegate to the constitutional convention in the late summer of 1817. Taylor won his legislative election as Second District Judge in 1818. He died in 1820 while still on the bench.

Judge John P. Hampton (d. 1827) of Wilkinson County served from the Third District (Wilkinson County east to the Pearl River). A native of South Carolina, Hampton became Presiding Judge Hampton in 1820, succeeding John Taylor. Hampton was reported to have been learned, and his decisions were marked by a lofty, purely moral, and diligent regard for equity and justice. Altogether, John Hampton served for almost ten years, 1818–1827.

Judge Joshua G. Clarke (1780–1828) of Claiborne County served from the First District (Warren, Claiborne, and Jefferson Counties) until late November of 1821. Judge Clarke was front and center for an exquisite constitutional experience in the summer of 1818, and for another in June of 1821.

Judge Powhatan Ellis[14] (1790–1863) of Wayne County, and a native of Virginia, served from the Fourth District from 1818 until September of 1825, when he resigned to accept an appointment to represent Mississippi in the United States Senate. We will meet Judge Ellis again in chapter 3, as he played a substantial role in establishing the State's constitutional practice of judicial review.

THE MAN OF THE CONSTITUTIONAL MOMENT

Little is known about the early life of Joshua Giles Clarke. It is believed that he was born in Maryland in 1780.[15] In time the family moved to Pennsylvania, where Clarke is said to have "received a competent education." At some point Clarke came to Mississippi. In 1807, he married Martha "Patsy" Calvit of Jefferson County. The Calvit family had come to the southwestern corner of the Mississippi Territory after the American Revolution and had become regarded not only as political figures but as plantation owners. An admiring descendant reported that Clarke's immediate and some extended family were slaveholders, and that he was a relatively small slave owner himself. In 1810, six slaves lived in Joshua Clarke's household in Claiborne County, and also in 1816.

Politically, Clarke was a Jeffersonian Republican. In July 1817, he became a founding member and first secretary of the Washington Lodge of the Freemasons in Port Gibson, in time the county seat of Claiborne County. In 1826, Chancellor Joshua G. Clarke played a leading role in establishing Mississippi's first Episcopal diocese, connecting with the Protestant Episcopal Church in the United States. In these latter years of his all-too-short life, Clarke built Claremont, one of the larger homes in the area. In 1979, the National Register of Historic Places added Claremont.

In the summer of 1818, this man, this brand-new first-term-of-court judge, in the first term of the court as well, would be called upon to adjudge the claims and defenses of three recently sold slaves from Indiana and their would-be masters of more than thirty years. This is the story of an early practical experience in the judicial aspect of constitutional government in the new state of

Mississippi, and of the light it shone that had not quite been extinguished by 1857 when it was cited by US Supreme Court Justice John McLean in dissent from the judgment in a case that lives in infamy.[16]

Joshua G. Clarke had a varied professional career. His lawyering days date back at least to January 7, 1804, when he was admitted to practice by Judge Peter Bryan Bruin in Claiborne County. In late November 1804, he made a filing in an estate matter. One historian described him as "a lawyer of ability, and a man of sterling qualities." Another, writing in 1891, said, "Judge Clarke was not a brilliant lawyer, but was careful, well-read and solid. He was patient and amiable, and his opinions quite creditable."[17] In time, he began to represent parties with land title claims, often complicated by purported sovereign grants from Spain or France. As late as 1817, Clarke appeared as counsel for defendant in a case that came before the formally brand-new state supreme court in the following year.[18]

Clarke represented Claiborne County in the Mississippi Territorial Legislature.[19] In the summer of 1817, he served as a delegate to the constitutional convention along with his future judicial colleague John Taylor. Dunbar Rowland deemed Clarke "one of the best legal minds in the convention [who] did faithful service by his wise advice and counsel." In short order, Clarke would be called upon to construe and apply and lead the people in understanding the respect for humanity embedded within the constitution he helped draft.

In January of 1818, the general assembly considered Clarke for the office of judge of the First District. He was defeated, however, by William Bayard Shields, by a vote of 21 to 11. Before the new state supreme court could do much at its first term, which began in mid-June of 1818, President James Monroe had appointed Judge Shields as the trial court judge for District Court of the United States for the district of Mississippi. On July 2, 1818, Shields formally resigned his state judgeship. On July 9, 1818, Clarke accepted a commission from Gov. David Holmes to replace Judge Shields.[20] Almost three and a half years later—in late November of 1821—Clarke resigned his dual trial/appellate state judgeship to become the first chancellor for the State of Mississippi. In time, one of the state's preeminent chancellors would comment that "fortunately [Clarke] was selected as the first chancellor, the position being regarded as preferable to a place on the supreme court bench."

Historian James D. Lynch, in Bench and Bar, had great praise for Clarke the judge. "He possessed in a high degree that placid temper and amiable patience which comport so compatibly with the requisite character of a good chancellor and a just judge." And "[h]is career upon the supreme bench, though short, gave eminence to his judicial character. His opinions are marked with learning, dignity, and force."

Professionally, Clarke's last six and a half years were spent in service as chancellor of Mississippi. "His learning and integrity first directed our system of equity jurisprudence into those channels through which it has flowed with increasing volume and utility." One latter-day observer says of Chancellor Clarke that "he presided for years with signal ability, purity of character and dignity." In 1833 a new county in southern east central Mississippi along the Alabama state line was organized and given the name of Clarke County.[21]

The *Harry and Others* opinion was released by the Supreme Court of Mississippi in its very first term Then as now, as a practical matter, formal "terms" extended well beyond the month in which by law they should be convened. Word of Judge Shields's imminent appointment as federal judge was out at least as early as April of 1818. There is no reason to doubt that the first term of the state supreme court extended well past July 9, when Judge Clarke was commissioned and sworn in.

Adams County was a fortuitous venue. Warren, Claiborne, and Jefferson Counties may have been excluded if the suit had been brought after Judge Clarke took office. As the judge for the First District, he would have almost certainly served as the trial judge, which would have precluded his sitting on the appeal. Practical realities plus the calendar, however, show this to have been impossible. The case first reached a territorial judicial docket before Mississippi's statehood and before there was a formal First District. As noted, Hiram Decker's human-cargo-laden vessel would almost certainly have reached and passed Vicksburg on its downriver voyage by the late summer of 1816.

The opinion issued by the state supreme court in the summer of 1818 says John Decker and a man named Hopkins were the defendants in the suit filed by Harry and the others. But John Decker had been dead for twenty-eight years. Luke had inherited the bulk of his father's estate. In his opinion, Judge Clarke makes a reference to "old Decker," and then to "those who claim under him." The October 1816 witness subpoenas suggest that Hiram—son of Luke Decker and grandson of John Decker—was in fact the Decker defendant in Harry and Others' petition for freedom suit.

THE LEGAL LANDSCAPE

Mississippi was formally admitted to the Union on December 10, 1817. The twentieth state reached this goal one day short of a year after Indiana had achieved its statehood. Harry and his companions filed their petition for freedom before Mississippi became a state. What is known beyond any reasonable doubt is that writing a final decision on Decker and Hopkins's appeal ultimately fell to the lot of Judge Joshua G. Clarke.[22] Because "[t]he facts in this case are not controverted," Judge Clarke spent little time with the factual or procedural details. He said enough that, with all else that is known, what happened is clear in its broad strokes.

The legal landscape in Mississippi recognized the practice of slavery, before and after statehood. A discrete but unnumbered article labeled "Slaves," and containing two numbered sections, was included in the constitution drafted in the late summer of 1817.[23] Section 1 treats slaves as property in the eyes of the law in any number of contexts. Slaveholders were protected from legislative emancipations. No law granting slaves their freedom could be passed "without the consent of their owners, unless where a slave shall have rendered to the State some distinguished service, in which case the owner shall be paid a full equivalent of the slaves so emancipated." What is more, the general assembly was without power to prevent new settlers coming to Mississippi from bringing their slaves with them. These "slaves" included "such persons as are deemed slaves by the laws of any one of the United States, so long as any person of the same age or description shall be continued in slavery by the laws of this state." After all, it was the loud and clear public policy of the new state that settlers from older parts of the country be encouraged to emigrate, bringing their slaves with them, and make their homes and fortunes in Mississippi.

There was no Northwest Ordinance for slaves in pre-statehood Mississippi to turn to for help. The Georgia Compact of 1798 established the Mississippi Territory and declared applicable the first five articles of the Northwest Ordinance. Article 6, however, was omitted. The Georgia Compact limited slavery only in the sense that the foreign slave trade was declared illegal in the Mississippi Territory. Mississippi was still a territory at the time Decker's vessel descended the River until Hiram reached what he thought were the more amenable territorial waters of the not-quite-yet twentieth state. In time the state constitution would grant the general assembly of Mississippi "full power to prevent slaves from being brought into this State as merchandise." At that moment, however, Luke Decker was more concerned with the constitution of the nineteenth state when his vessel—his son Hiram at the helm—embarked from Knox County, Indiana, for more friendly waters, his valuable cargo and merchandise including Harry and the other slaves.

FREEDOM IN THE TRIAL COURT

Harry and twenty-seven others sued for their freedom in a territorial trial court. The Supreme Court concludes "that the petitioners are entitled to have the verdict confirmed." Judge Clarke's second sentence refers to "the court below."[24] There is every good reason to take the word "verdict" at face value.[25] Though not in effect at the time of trial, such common law practices were hardly a controversial aspect of the case. The Natchez-based news reporter said it was a "court and jury" that granted the slaves' petition for freedom. Lawyer and historian Andrew

Fede, in "Judging against the Grain," has reasonably assumed "[a] jury verdict favored the plaintiffs." *Harry and Others'* dual references to "motion for a new trial" are consistent with a jury having returned a verdict favorable to those who had petitioned for their freedom. Knowing that Mississippi Territory vs. Hiram Decker and Francis Hopkins was on the trial docket in Adams County in October of 1816 makes it almost certain that the trial preceding *Harry and Others* was held in Adams County, such that the jury hearing the case can be scrutinized against the backdrop of the particular mores and idiosyncrasies of the eligible jurors and the people of Adams County at large.

The reported opinion in *Harry and Others* opens with a puzzle. Judge Clarke said that in what was to follow he would confine himself to those issues "as have occasioned a difference of opinion." He added "that it is and always will be a source of regret, to me, when I am so unfortunate as to differ from my brethren of the bench." This suggested that there was a dissenting judge.[26] Judge Clarke wrote as though he were expecting one of his colleagues to dissent. Yet no dissenting opinion, or other indicia of a formal dissent, has been found. In a more modern appellate court, this would likely mean that, when the judges discussed the case in conference, one judge disagreed with the majority, but, when the majority opinion was circulated, for one reason or another that judge changed his mind and decided not to dissent. All that the record published by official reporter Robert J. Walker reflects is that no judge dissented.[27]

JUDGE CLARKE'S LEGAL ANALYSIS

Cases like *Harry and Others* are difficult to discuss today. Slavery was a monstrous evil. The level of moral wrong and harm from slavery in the antebellum United States is such that saying anything positive about participants in the practice invites opprobrium—from within the speaker and from without. Harry and his companions are the heroes of this story, if only more could be known about *their* stories.[28] We know even less about the unfortunate slave whose loss of life led to *Jones v. State*. These are like unknown soldiers. Indeed, it is not even known whether or how many of the "others" who accompanied Harry may have been women. As with Bob and Anthony back in Indiana, it took courage "to confront a man of [Luke] Decker's reputation." All have earned a unique place of honor in history.

The story of Harry and the others brings to mind an insight of Justice Evelyn Keyes of Texas. "[T]he study of the humanities by lawyers and judges . . . acquaints us with different modes of perception and understanding of human predicaments and of the essential dignity and worth (or evil [or ambiguity]) of those caught within those predicaments. . . ."[29] Keyes points to "revelations of the dehumanizing experience of slavery captured by Toni Morrison's *Beloved*." The constitutional experiences are presented here with every reasonable effort made that they be understood in the practical and legal and *human* contexts of the times.

In the summer of 1818 the Supreme Court of Mississippi affirmed the territorial court's verdict and judgment granting freedom to Harry and his companions. Clarke began his opinion for the court with the fact that "the three negroes were slaves in Virginia." He never denied that slavery was lawful in Mississippi. Clarke's subsequent opinion three years later in *State v. Jones*,[30] decided in June of 1821, equally accepted the legality of slavery in Mississippi. The constitution emerging from the Washington, Mississippi, convention in the late summer of 1817 never affirmatively said, "Slavery is legally permissible in this state," but it assumed as much. The lack of an affirmative and positive constitutional blessing for slavery left room for Clarke's natural law argument that followed.

Clarke never suggested that Decker could not have legally owned Harry and the others in Mississippi, or that he could not have sold them in the state, if Decker had brought them to Mississippi by some strategy appropriate to their status as slaves. If in 1784 John Decker and his family had left Hampshire County, Virginia, for example, and traveled directly to the Mississippi Territory,[31] never leaving slave states, and then settled in the territory, the legal premises of *Harry and Others* would have required a judgment for Decker. And, if the Decker family had stopped in the Mississippi territory, as sojourners in Mobile or at some settlement in what is now Alabama, and had lived there with family and slaves uninterruptedly until 1816, then moved on and resettled in Natchez, the same legal outcome would follow. Had any of these been the facts "not controverted," judgment would have had to be rendered for the Deckers who had taken under "old Decker's" will. If the 1816 voyage down the River had been a part of a bona fide effort by the Decker clan to resettle in Mississippi, the case for Harry and the others would have been harder, though the Deckers' knowing continued residence in the Indiana Territory from 1787 until 1816 would have provided a strong ground for freedom-by-residence.

Clarke accepted the above premises, albeit *sub silentio*. He had to. He argued, however, that these were not the facts and certainly not the outcome-determinative facts before the court in the summer of 1818.

A CASE OF FIRST IMPRESSION

There are always cases that have never arisen in a given jurisdiction in the precise form presented by a particular case at hand, cases where there is no clearly controlling rule of the positive law, yet the case must be decided.[32] In the summer of 1818, and the years that ensued, practically every case that came before the brand-new Supreme Court of Mississippi was in some sense a case of first impression.[33] There was the common law to the extent it might apply.[34]

The judges had been directed that the territorial law be followed, except to the extent displaced by the new constitution.[35] More so than today,[36] early statehood judges of practical necessity relied in substantial part on their personal experiences, general learning and intuition. They had to. The appeal brought by Decker and Hopkins presented such a case of first impression. In *Harry and Others,* Judge Clarke relied on his experience as a delegate to the constitutional convention in the late summer of 1817. His discussion of Rousseau's "social compact" political theory was almost certainly a product of his own education and general reading, rather than argument presented by counsel. He likely relied as well on what in his view were "considerations of what [wa]s expedient for the community concerned."[37]

While freedom-by-residence cases became familiar in time, Joshua Clarke had no such precedent to guide him in the summer of 1818. Border slave state Kentucky would grant such a claim for freedom in October of 1820.[38] Virginia so held two months after that.[39] Louisiana's judicial acceptance of freedom-by-residence lay six years in the future.[40] The important Missouri jurisdiction—it wasn't even a state at the time *Harry* was decided—was more than six years away from formally recognizing freedom-by-residence.[41] In the summer of 1818, Clarke was on his own. Still, he made it clear that he understood his responsibility to decide the case according to accepted legal methods, considering only legal premises known in those times and applied to the relevant facts. Clarke well knew that "the importance of the question is great." While the outcome-determinative facts may have been undisputed, the proper reading and decision of the controlling legal question were very much "controverted."

The basic rationale of freedom-by-residence cases was that if, with the consent of his owner, the slave lived, resided on "free soil" for a significant period of time, the legal bonds of slavery were deemed expunged.[42] These bonds did not reattach if the former slave was later found in a slave state. This theme is found in *Harry and Others.* No one moving to a new state or territory, establishing a new home and means of livelihood there, bringing his possessions with him, had a reasonable expectation that the laws of that state or territory would not someday be changed to his personal disadvantage. A new citizen was deemed to acquiesce in the law-making and law-altering processes of his new home jurisdiction. All were subject to what in time became familiar and known colloquially as the petty larceny of the police power.

Because Harry and the others were not just present but had in fact—and under the authority and direction of the Deckers—lived on free soil in the southwestern Indiana Territory for a substantial period of time, they had become free men in the eyes of the law. Their former legal subjugation to the Deckers was not resurrected in 1816 when they were brought into the Mississippi Territory against their will. This is particularly so here, as Decker's undisguised purpose was to liquidate his assets that were threatened by the "free soil" clause in the looming new Indiana Constitution.

Clarke's reasoning was meticulous, elegant, philosophical, and in the end practical and humane. Again, he began with the "facts . . . not controverted."

> [T]he three negroes were slaves in Virginia; that in seventeen hundred and eighty four they were taken by John Decker to the neighborhood of Vincennes, that they remained there from that time until the month of July, 1816; that the ordinance of Congress [was] passed in the month of July of 1787,[43] and that the constitution of the state of Indiana was adopted on the 29th of June, 1816.

The lands lying north and west of the Ohio River included "the neighborhood of Vincennes."

In 1787, Virginia granted its rights in these lands to the United States. Clarke looked carefully at Virginia's treaty of cession. Although these lands had been "conquered by the arms of Virginia, [he found] nothing to show that the laws of Virginia [authorizing slavery] were ever extended to that country after its conquest." Clarke then asked whether "the clause in the [Northwest] ordinance [Article 6] prohibiting slavery, or involuntary servitude, [is] a violation of the treaty of cession." Clarke was "endeavor[ing] to show, in what condition these people were after the conquest by Virginia, what rights they possessed, and the rights they acquired under the treaty of cession." Judge Clarke viewed the Northwest Ordinance "as a compact between the original states, and the people and states of said territory." He concluded that the "'titles, possessions, rights and liberties' . . . [these people] enjoyed, prior to the conquest, the 'lex loci,' [were] not as citizens of Virginia, but as a provincial appendage."

Then Clarke turned to Article 6. He noted Decker's argument that "those who were slaves at the passing of the ordinance, must continue in the same situation." Clarke then responded: Can this construction be correct? Would it not defeat the great object of the general government? It is obvious that it would, and it is inadmissible upon every principle of legal construction.

A pause is in order. Common sense suggests a reader of a legal (or most any other kind of) exposition should be careful when confronted with phrases such as "it is obvious," particularly when the question is so controversial and controverted. Such rhetoric—and even more dramatic flourishes—was common two hundred years ago, particularly in constitutional contexts. Still, Clarke's discussion would have been less provocative had he moved directly to his point that if Article 6 were unenforceable, that might well mean that all other terms and provisions of the Ordinance were similarly unenforceable. "Considering the six articles of compact equally obligatory and binding, made upon sufficient consideration, all the objection to the want of power in congress to make the compact with the people of the said territory must vanish."

THE PROBLEMATIC INDIANA CONSTITUTION

The newly adopted constitution of the state of Indiana was then called up and considered by Clarke as an independent and alternative ground on which Harry and the others may have become emancipated. But there was a problem here. The Indiana Constitution had—and could have—no legal force or effect until the state was formally admitted to the Union on December 11, 1816.[44] Adopting a constitution was on the checklist of qualifications the applicant for statehood had to meet.[45] Indiana checked this one off as done on June 29, 1816, but that constitution remained inchoate until the other conditions of statehood— practical requisites such as surveying state boundaries, taking a census—had been met and formally accepted by the United States.[46]

Of course, we do not know the exact date that Decker's vessel left the territorial waters of Indiana headed south on its nefarious venture. Clarke suggested it left the Indiana Territory in "the month of July, 1816." Newspaper articles had said "spring of 1816," which, of course, ended nine days before July 1. We do know that all were in Adams County, Mississippi Territory, in early October of 1816. The present point, of course, is that Decker's human-cargo-carrying vessel had long been far south of Indiana soil when statehood arrived on December 11, 1816.

The formal enforceability point aside, Clarke presented the case for state authority "to effect a general emancipation." *Harry and Others* may have been the first time the courts of the new state of Mississippi would be called upon to adjudge a freedom-by-residence suit, but it certainly would not be the last. Lots of slaveholding men like Luke Decker lived in other states north of the Ohio River (or the Mason-Dixon Line). With improved technology in river navigation and transportation, any number of such men could be expected to use a Decker-like strategy to liquidate their assets on advantageous terms. To be sure, points the court might make on an issue, not properly justiciable in the case du jour, could be treated as dicta and not binding precedents. An exposition of the law on the effect *vel non* of freedom-by-residence emancipation could nonetheless be useful in future cases if that discussion were well reasoned and persuasive. And not only future Mississippi cases. The soon-to-follow decisions in Kentucky, Virginia, Missouri, and adjacent Louisiana lay in the future.

In the years not too long after 1818, judges might see practical comity considerations for recognizing freedom granted to slaves in other states, and on a variety of particular grounds. It is not clear that Clarke foresaw this practice. He did see the need to engage the legal logic of freedom-by-residence by reason of constitutional emancipation in another state or elsewhere. He explained that and why other sovereigns just might have the authority to declare and really mean that all men were born free and possessed of unalienable human rights. At a time when men were exultant at having been accepted into the diverse and

complex Union, the more broadminded among them likely sensed that respect
for the laws of older states—not necessarily congruent with Mississippi law—
was an obvious and practical step toward winning acceptance of Mississippi's
law by other states.

According to Clarke, to engage this ground for a freedom-by-residence suit,
"we must first inquire into the source of sovereignty, as understood in these
United States, to reside in the people." The constitution that less than a year
earlier he had helped write declared,

> that all political power is inherent in the people, and all free governments are
> founded on their authority, and instituted for their benefit; and, therefore, they
> have, at all times, an unalienable and indefeasible right to alter or abolish their
> form of government, in such manner as they may think expedient.[47]

This was not airy rhetoric to Joshua Clarke. Real, substantive, and practical
on-the-ground meaning flowed from this declaration, which he would proceed
to explain.

POLITICAL THEORIST AND PRACTITIONER

Clarke's inquiry began with the premise that, in any society that has been
organized to the point where it has a government, there is an absolute power
existing somewhere within it. This is so as a matter of social fact. As a practical
matter, that power may be identified. "In all governments whatsoever there
must be of necessity, and in the nature of things, a supreme irresistible
absolute and uncontrolled authority, in which the *jura summi imperii*," or the
rights of sovereignty reside."[48] This absolute authority is to be understood "in
contradistinction of the powers given under a constitution, or the powers of a
limited government." The power of the people is conceptually separate from a
constitution. It precedes the existence of any constitution that might emerge.

> The people restrain the power under a delegated authority, but put no restraint
> upon themselves; the acts of the supreme power, though contrary to natural
> rights, are nevertheless binding. In every case under the social compact there
> must be an inequality to destroy the validity of the surrender. Among an ignorant
> and uninstructed people, what are the rights surrendered?

Clarke answers with the teachings of Jean-Jacques Rousseau: each person gives
"all his rights and privileges to the whole community." "[A]ll are in the same
circumstances, so that no one can be interested in rendering burthensome their
common connection." Clarke qua Rousseau follows with an incisive insight.

If anyone had a right distinct from another, which he pretended had not been surrendered, each individual might question the acts of the social compact, and if this were permitted, it would destroy itself, as there would be no common umpire to appeal to, a state of nature would exist, and the social compact would be a splendid bauble.

We read these words, and they immediately call to mind the first section in the Declaration of Rights in then new Mississippi Constitution: "That all freemen, when they form a social compact, are equal in rights, and that no man or set of men, are entitled to exclusive, separate, public emoluments or privileges, from the community, but in consideration of public services."[49] Read together with section 2, little doubt is left that Clarke had not been just a delegate to the convention held in little Washington, Mississippi. He had in fact played a substantial drafting role at the convention. With or without the awareness of his fellow delegates, Clarke had infused the core political ideology of Jean-Jacques Rousseau at the heart of the new constitution.

A year later in *Harry and Others*, Clarke summarized and then applied Rousseau's thought. In doing so he may also have left another calling card that he was the author of the formally anonymous opinion in *Harry and Others*.[50] The Indiana constitutional convention had been "delegated by the people" with the power to adopt "articles of compact." Effective date aside, one of those articles abolished slavery.

Does not the first article of the constitution declare the condition of the people of Indiana free, and this condition, by the last section of the first article, is likewise declared to be out of the control of government, or to be a right reserved to the people.

Clarke then described a "similar provision" in the Massachusetts Constitution that abolished slavery, the concluding clause of that constitution declaring that "all laws conflicting with the provision of the constitution are repealed." As this was so,

[c]an it be that slavery exists in Indiana? If it does, language loses its force, and a constitution intended to protect rights, would be illusory and insecure, indeed. If the language is plain, saying there shall be neither slavery nor involuntary servitude, does it comport with the constitution to say that *there shall* be slavery? This dilemma cannot be got over, by those who give it a construction, that would make the petitioners slaves.

Below the constitutional level were several state statutory enactments regarding slavery. Clarke noted that Pennsylvania, Delaware, New Jersey, New

York, and the New England states—Massachusetts excepted—had legislated on the subject. These enactments were proper, because there was no state constitutional clause denying that power to the state legislature. By way of contrast, Judge (and former Mississippi constitutional convention delegate) Clarke noted that on the matter of slavery, "so guarded was our convention upon this subject, that they inhibited the legislature from the exercise of the power." Legislation regarding slavery was proper "when not constrained by the constitution, (as) is evident by the caution of our convention."

CASES OF DOUBT

Legal questions of retroactivity remained. The Deckers argued that any such new laws could apply prospectively only. Otherwise, vested property rights would be disturbed. This required the court to face a question of constitutional dimensions.[51] No one doubted that Harry and at least two of the others were in slave legal status before they were ever brought to land "in the neighborhood of Vincennes." And before there was an Ordinance of 1787. As this was so, neither the federal Northwest Ordinance, much less the pending—three decades later— new Indiana Constitution, could change their status, or so the argument would go. When *Harry and Others* reached the Supreme Court of Mississippi in the summer of 1818, the meaning and effect of the positive law on retroactivity *vel non* was disputed, subject to differing constructions and applications.

In this setting Clarke answered,

> But it is contended that the provisions of the constitution admit of a different construction—that it is prospective, and to give it the meaning its language imports, would violate vested rights. What are these vested rights, are they derived from nature, or from the [positive] municipal law? Slavery is condemned by reason and the laws of nature. It exists and can only exist through [positive] municipal regulations, and in matters of doubt, is it not an unquestioned rule, that courts must lean "*in favorem vitae et libertatis*." ... How should the Court decide, if construction was really to determine it? I presume it would be in favour of liberty.

It is easy to applaud Clarke's decision. Earlier in the opinion, he had articulated his understanding of the law of nature, providing the Mississippi Supreme Court's first and only discussion (to date) of Jean-Jacques Rousseau's social contract. Such talk was still in the air in 1818, revered by many, though its heyday in Jefferson's introductory clauses of the Declaration of Independence was almost forty years in the past.

Judge Clarke implicitly followed the 1772 King's Bench opinion of Lord Mansfield in *Somerset v. Stewart*.[52] Slavery, according to Lord Mansfield, was "incapable of being introduced on any reasons, moral or political; but only [by] positive law[.]"[53] Harry and the others had lived on lands that in 1787 had been declared by the positive law of the United States to be free soil. Whatever de facto form of submission Harry and others may have endured after 1787, legally they had become free men. Whether the positive law may have reattached the bonds of slavery once Harry and the others entered Mississippi waters was sufficiently open to question that the case was controlled by the maxim "*in favorem vitae et libertatis. . . .* How should the Court decide . . . ? I presume it would be in favour of liberty."

A SLAVE RETAINED HIS HUMANITY

Three years later, in the spring of 1821, Judge Clarke drew another slave case. Isaac Jones, a white man, murdered an unnamed man who was a slave. Over the years, *Jones v. State* has drawn considerable attention.[54] All seem to agree that Isaac Jones was a stranger to his victim. What else might Clarke have meant when in context he wrote "giving even to a master, much less to a *stranger*, power over the life of a slave"? Jones was not the owner or master or overseer of the slave he killed.

The question of law before the court was whether a slave was a human being, such that his death from an otherwise felonious homicide constituted the crime of murder. No statute addressed the point. Judge Clarke turned to the English common law. "The taking away the life of a reasonable creature, under the king's peace, with malice aforethought, express or implied, is murder at common law." There is a constitutional encounter in *Jones* in the sense that there is always the question whether the court has the judicial power to adjudge a particular case,[55] and whether the state has the authority to have a man hanged, once he has been found guilty of murder.[56] In adjudging *Jones*, Clarke held that the law extended to slaves a measure of humanity that others might have denied. His a priori legal premise—that a slave is a "reasonable creature" such that his death is murder when he is killed by another acting with malice aforethought—arguably stood in sharp relief juxtaposed aside the constitutional premise that "all freemen" and only "freemen" enjoy the protection and benefits of Mississippi's not quite five years old Declaration of Rights.[57]

As in the summer of 1818, Clarke's weapons were his powers of reason and expression. "Reason is the life of the law" Sir Edward Coke had declared, "nay, the common law is nothing else but reason."[58] Clarke understood that the common law was as much a process as it was a not altogether written body of law. He understood as well his authority and responsibility as a judge speaking with the acquiescence of his three colleagues. He began, "Because individuals may have been deprived of many of their rights by society, it does not follow, that they have been deprived of all of their rights."

> In some respects, slaves may be considered as chattels, but in others, they are regarded as men. The law views them as capable of committing crimes. This can only be upon the principle, that they are men and rational beings. In this state, the Legislature have considered slaves as reasonable and accountable beings and it would be a stigma upon the character of the state, and a reproach to the administration of justice, if the life of a slave could be taken with impunity, or if he could be murdered in cold blood, without subjecting the offender to the highest penalty known . . . ."

Speaking for the Supreme Court, Clarke continued, explaining that the slave

> is still a human being, and possesses all those rights, of which he is not deprived by the positive provisions of the law, but in vain shall we look for any law passed by the enlightened and philanthropic legislature of this state, giving even to the master, much less a stranger, power over the life of a slave.[59]

From this Clarke invoked the human sense of fair play where the stakes are the highest, reasoning that "[b]y the provisions of our law, a slave may commit murder, and be punished with death; why then is it not murder to kill a slave?"

Recurring to the backdrop of natural law as he had in *Harry and Others*, Clarke reiterated that "[t]he right of the master exists not by the force of the law of nature or of nations, but by virtue only of the positive law of the state." The positive law of the state included the common law of crimes, limited only as necessary to accommodate the practice of slavery as it was permitted by the constitution and laws of the state. But the positive law of the state of Mississippi did not declare any right in a master, much less a stranger, to feloniously harm or kill a man who also happened to be a slave. To the contrary, the general assembly was constitutionally vested with the authority "to oblige the owners of slaves to treat them with humanity, . . . to abstain from all injuries to them extending to life or limb . . ."[60]

A century later a wise judge would remind us that "[t]he common law is not a brooding omnipresence in the sky but the articulate voice of some sovereign or quasi-sovereign that can be identified."[61] The sovereign state of Mississippi, speaking through the articulate and authorized voice of Judge Joshua Clarke, in relevant part, declared that,

> The taking away the life of a reasonable creature, under the king's peace, with malice aforethought, express or implied, is murder at common law. Is not the slave a reasonable creature, is he not a human being, and the meaning of this phrase

reasonable creature is a human being, for the killing a lunatic, an idiot, or even an unborn child, is murder, as much as the killing a philosopher, and has not the slave as much reason as a lunatic, an idiot, or an unborn child?

Through the articulate *and authorized* voice of Joshua Clarke, the Supreme Court of Mississippi had declared that Harry and his fellow slaves were free. As a matter of elementary legal understanding, that declaration thereby became a part of the positive law of the state. These three former slaves were free by operation of the positive law of the state of Mississippi, which recognized, honored, and applied further federally obligatory positive law, Article 6 of the Northwest Ordinance of 1787.[62] Three years later, this same articulate *and authorized* voice declared that, as a matter of the positive law of the state, as a reasonable creature in fact, a slave was within the protection of common law of homicide.

THE "OUGHT" VERSUS THE "IS"

There are legal problems—realities, if you will—within Judge Clarke's most famous utterance. Does he have a defense to the acrid criticism: "That's just your opinion"? To the question "What makes you think you really have rendered a judgment which emanated from a reasoned application of premises that satisfied the criteria for legal validity?"

In fairness, Clarke reasoned through the points in his opinion in the summer of 1818 more carefully than many appellate judges do today. But he found himself stuck in the end with the choice for which he is celebrated, "that courts must lean *in favorem vitae et libertatis....* How should the Court decide, if construction was really to determine it? I presume it would be in favour of liberty." Clarke decided and adjudged in favor of what he thought the law ought to have been. Does this differ from *Olmstead v. United States*, more than a century later, an exclusionary rule search and seizure case, where Justice Holmes faced up to the fact that no law mandated this result or that, and then famously said, "We have to choose, and for my part I think it a less evil that some criminals should escape than that the government should play an ignoble part."[63]

Considered today, was Clarke's reasoning any more acceptable to those who disagreed than are *Roe v. Wade*[64] and progeny[65] acceptable to those who believe abortion to be a great moral wrong? Conversely, a ruling that Harry and the others were still Decker's slaves—or Hopkins's after their sale—would have been just as outrageous as overruling *Roe v. Wade* would be to those who believe that it would be a great moral wrong to deny a pregnant woman the right to make the terrible choice whether to have an abortion. A more recent exemplar was provided on June 26, 2015. A person wishing to marry another of the same sex was held to have a right to do so. *Obergefell v. Hodges*[66] created a firestorm. Is it not likely, if not probable, that a hundred years from now most will honor Justice Anthony Kennedy for what he did in *Obergefell*[67] as we honor Judge Joshua Clarke for what he did two hundred years ago in *Harry and Others*? Each had the courage to decide.

In the early years of Mississippi's statehood, Clarke looked to what many enlightened men considered the law of nations regarding slavery. A generation later, Chief Justice William L. Sharkey took a very different view.[68] By the late 1850s the person of African descent had no standing under any law of nations that Mississippi thought it had to honor.[69] The last time the Supreme Court of Mississippi took note of a law of nations was in 1912. On that occasion, Justice Richard F. Reed "look[ed] back through the ages . . . to the laws of nations" and found "law regulating the time when men shall labor."[70] Of late, there has been passionate argument in the United States whether and to what extent we should regard the law of other nations. US Supreme Court Justices Stephen Breyer and the late Antonin Scalia recently engaged in a high-profile and public debate on the point.[71]

There are dozens of issues that divide people by reference to moral or religious scruples. Convincing a man or woman that he or she is wrong on one of these issues is next to impossible. Such is arguably none of our business vis-à-vis each other, except that we must find some way to get along. Sometimes, however, even when men disagree strongly at the pre-legal level, a socially helpful acceptance follows a final judgment entered by a court of competent jurisdiction, reliably applied positive law that satisfies the criteria for legal validity.[72] Is this not necessary in a democratic society committed to the rule of law, however fuzzy, unmathematical, and otherwise problematic those criteria may be? If your answer is yes, hold that until you get to chapter 4 and the question of whether the final judgment decision in *State of Mississippi v. Hezron A. Johnson*, 3 Cushm. (25 Miss.) 625, 1853 WL 3667 (1853), foreclosed those who passionately believed that the State should not honor its guaranty of five million dollars in Mississippi Union Bank bonds.

With twenty-twenty hindsight, there may have been such a somewhat more neutral and reliable adjudicative route to the ultimate decision and judgment of the court in *Harry and Others*.

A FIRMER FOUNDATION

There is an elementary point that has not been considered. Article the Sixth of the Northwest Ordinance had been enacted by the Congress on July 13, 1787. No one suggests that the processes by which the original thirteen states so agreed were improper. To be sure, all of this was done under the Articles of Confederation. The work that George Washington and the others had under way behind closed doors in Philadelphia was not completed until September of 1787, and ratification lay several years in the future. But once the Constitution had been ratified, "among the earliest laws passed under the new Government, is one reviving the ordinance of 1787." All of this is set out and well explained in *Dred Scott*. The new Supreme Court of Mississippi did not have Chief Justice Taney's exposition available in 1818. Still the records that Taney used in *Dred Scott* to explain the continued enforceability of the Northwest Ordinance of 1787 were extant and available in 1818, had it been thought appropriate to consult them.

In those early days of the country, there was nothing to limit the coverage of the due process clause of the Fifth Amendment to the processes of a court of competent jurisdiction. The Congress had readopted and reenacted the ordinance governing the lands "North-West of the River Ohio." Assume *arguendo* that Harry and the others (who had been born) were slaves prior to July 13, 1787. On that day the core premise of freedom-by-residence claims became law. It became law and in due course was applied to John and then Luke and then Hiram Decker (and no doubt many other slave owners in southwest Indiana and other parts of the Northwest Territory). This was due process of law as men knew it at the time. To be sure, the Mississippi due process clause[73] did not become effective until December 10, 1817. That clause conferred a right that necessarily required the court to look backwards to when the person says his property was improperly taken. The eminent domain clause did not require that Decker be paid "just compensation," because Decker's property rights, if any, in Harry and each of the others were not "taken or applied to public use."[74]

This was an answer that Judge Clarke and the Supreme Court of Mississippi could have given Decker, that he was shorn of his said-to-be vested property rights by due process of law. The court could have said all of this in 1818. Had its successors had the courage to stay the course, "freedom-by-residence" for men such as Harry and the others may have even survived *Dred Scott*. In the summer of 1818, this would have been a firmer legal foundation—grounded in solid positive law—for the freedom granted the former slaves, than that set out in the *Harry and Others* opinion.

There was a second firmer foundation on which Harry and the others may have been adjudged to be free. In the eyes of the law Harry and the others had been kidnapped by Decker prior to—and certainly at—the moment they were involuntarily taken from the neighborhood of Vincennes and loaded on board, headed southerly down the Wabash River. The Deckers had learned a thing or two about kidnapping slaves as far back as 1794 when Moses Decker, as noted above, lent a helping hand to a fellow New York Dutch country immigrant in making sure that a slave and his wife could not appear in a federal territorial court to present their petition for freedom. In 1821, Clarke taught us that a slave was within the protections of the positive common law of homicide. Nothing in that exposition excluded other crimes that a slave was legally protected from, consistent with the practical requisites of slavery. After all, in the eyes of the law, slaves were property with economic value to the largely agricultural communities where slavery was so prevalent. Of course, the legal grounds on which Harry and the others had ceased to be slaves were established at some time shortly after 1787. That these de jure grounds had not yet been converted into a de facto reality only goes to show that Harry and the others were more clearly entitled to the protection of the laws of kidnapping than was the unfortunate unnamed slave slain by Isaac Jones. Nor did it matter whether Decker's crime was committed before or after December 10, 1817, or when the trial was held, or the appeal adjudged.

We know that the Constitution of 1817 granted the general assembly "full power . . . to oblige the owners of slaves to treat them with humanity, to provide them with necessary clothing and provision, to abstain from all injuries to them extending to life and limb."[75] So what, that the general assembly had not yet acted. Or that this clause was not in effect in the latter part of 1816 when Decker's vessel brought Harry and the others—against their will—down the River. The constitution mandated a smooth transition from territorial status to statehood.[76] The common law was in full force and effect in those territorial years and "continue[d] in full force as the laws of this State, until they . . . shall be altered or repealed by the Legislature thereof."[77] Nothing had repealed the common law of kidnapping. Article 6 of the Northwest Ordinance may not have been positive law in Mississippi. But it certainly was in the "neighborhood of Vincennes" where for the twenty-nine years—knowing well what the law was— the Deckers kept Harry and the others under their thumb, all the while sending regular petitions to Washington, DC. demanding that Article 6 be repealed.

At its legal core, a property right has always included a right to exclude.[78] Given the known facts, beginning at some point reasonably after July 13, 1787, no rule of positive law[79] authorized the Deckers to exclude others from enjoying the benefits of the labor or services of Harry or any of the others. Nothing suggests there may have been any privately made law—such as a (written or oral) indentured servitude or a contract for employment—binding the Deckers and these former de facto slaves. Luke Decker and the others moved from false imprisonment to the more aggravated offense of kidnapping in July of 1816 when—with Harry and the others in tow, Hiram Decker at the helm—their vessel left the neighborhood of Vincennes, navigating southerly.

Hiram Decker entered the Mississippi Territory with Harry and the others under his ostensible control, and involuntarily so. The individual members of this human cargo were persons within the common law. They were "person[s]" within the contemplation of the constitution[80] that had become effective by the time the case reached the Supreme Court of Mississippi. On the facts presented, there could be no objective basis—grounded in the applicable positive law—for anyone believing that in the latter months of 1816 Harry and the others were "the *bona fide* property" of Decker, or of Hopkins after their sale, though Hopkins may have had a right to recover what he paid Decker in the defective sale.

The Constitution of 1817 encouraged immigrants to come to Mississippi, and, if they wished, to bring their slaves with them. After December 10, 1817, such immigrants were required to show that "such person or slave" as was brought here was "the *bona fide* property of such immigrants." This changed nothing in the laws that were in force in the Mississippi Territory in 1816.[81] Nothing known suggests that Luke Decker or his son Hiram could have qualified as immigrants. Nothing in the known facts suggested that Deckers had any plans to settle in Mississippi. The Decker family's presence in Knox County, Indiana—rooted, built, and enhanced since 1784—strongly suggested to the contrary. Luke Decker's undisguised motive to evade the consequences of the new constitution in his homeland further eviscerated any hint of good faith in his actions. On the known facts, Decker could never have shown to a court of competent jurisdiction in Mississippi that Harry and the others were his property.

It follows that putative slave owners like the Deckers, proposing to sell any "such person or slave" at any time between 1816 and through 1818, had to make a strong showing in court of a right to exclude. Kidnappers like the Deckers could not show any rights at all. The common law of kidnapping was available, had Judge Clarke chosen to use it.[82] More readily than the common law of murder that he chose to apply in 1821, because Harry, his two companions in appellate litigation, and the other twenty-five enjoyed a de jure free status before they ever reached the courthouse. The Deckers—and later Francis Hopkins—could hardly have complained that the court used the lesser included common law tort of false imprisonment to free their captives, and not for their own conviction and imprisonment for the crime of kidnapping.

Moreover, the constitution had a no-merchandise clause. The general assembly was granted "full power to prevent slaves from being brought into this State as merchandise."[83] There can be little doubt that—while Harry and the others were in Mississippi—the Deckers regarded them as property to be sold, and in that sense they were "merchandise." A common law court in 1818 had the authority to fashion a rule within the no-merchandise clause, and to apply that rule given the case before it, albeit the general assembly had the prerogative at a future session of modifying, extending, or restricting that rule as it saw fit within the constitution. If the state was empowered to prevent enslaved persons being brought into Mississippi as "merchandise," it was certainly empowered to respond appropriately to kidnap victims brought there, particularly after finding that they had been de jure free men for almost thirty years already.

There can be no reasonable doubt but that in July of 1816 and thereafter, Decker was—without authority of law—seeking to enlarge and exercise his legal rights, if any, regarding Harry and the others. And that Decker—and in turn Hopkins—were acting to this nefarious end within the jurisdiction of the Mississippi Territory. The court would have been well within its prerogatives to draw upon the common law of kidnapping, so long as that use and application did not impair the rights of bona fide slave owners residing in, immigrating to, or traveling though Mississippi. Luke Decker back in Indiana held no such rights, nor did Hiram Decker at the time his vessel entered the waters of the Mississippi Territory.

Given these premises, including all available and applicable positive law, before and after December 10, 1817, the Deckers and Hopkins had no legally defensible arguments that they may have marshalled to the end of a judgment against Harry and his fellow putative slaves.

DOES NATURAL LAW HAVE A PLACE?

Thoughts of natural law or the law of nature have long been interesting and at times uplifting, but no man may be hanged or enslaved by virtue of the natural law alone, nor may he be acquitted or freed. To be sure, we wish to celebrate Judge Clarke and in particular *Harry and Others*, as its two-hundredth anniversary has come and passed. A barely known human being named Harry—and two others utterly unknown—were found and placed on the side of the angels by Justice John McLean in 1857 in his dissenting opinion in the *Dred Scott* case.[84] But time has taught that constitutional constructions "when the importance of the question is great" should be made of sterner stuff than Clarke brought to bear, if that is at all possible.

Clarke exposed the point in *Jones*. "Because individuals may have been deprived of many of their rights by society, it does not follow, that they have been deprived of all of their rights."[85] What other "rights"? Either of two views grounded in positive law and presented above may well have carried the day for Harry and the others. But suppose those were not there, or that there might be some flaw in the positive legal logic leading to the two results explained above. "There is no mystic over law to which even the United States must bow."[86] Nor has there ever been a "mystic over law" enforceable in the state of Mississippi, except it satisfied the criteria for legal validity via legislation or judge-made law. What source of valid and enforceable rights of reasonable creatures is there, except the positive law made by the authorized constitutional organs of organized society? That the philosopher might see each of us—that we might see ourselves—as free moral agents possessing a dignity and worth by virtue of our being affords us no claims against the state that may be enforced. The values articulated so well in the opening sentences of the Declaration of Independence cannot be proved, much less may they—without more—be enforced. We fight fiercely over what the words mean and particularly how they may be applied. These values have force and effect when men understand them, believe them, and are willing to act on those beliefs. It is the sobering lesson of history that all too often these values have only been declared.

There is a limited place for the idea of natural law[87] in a constitutional democracy. When the positive legal materials play out, without producing a reliable decision, a judge has no choice but to look elsewhere. In *Jones* the positive legal materials were the common law of homicide as accepted in Mississippi, any superseding statutory law, and ultimately the constitution of 1817,[88] reliably applied, of course, to the relevant, credibly found facts of the case, and according to the common law adjudicative process of reasoned elaboration (which is not to be confused with some imaginary process of mathematical or mechanical elaboration). Three years earlier in *Harry and Others*, the positive legal materials included the Northwest Ordinance of 1787, and implicitly the Supremacy Clause of the Constitution of the United States.[89] Judge Clarke thought it included the Indiana Constitution of 1816, although he may have erred in this. And the positive law of Mississippi included the "judicial power" identified and authorized in its constitution[90] and laws.[91] Within these, the court was charged to consider the legislative facts of "what was expedient for the community concerned."[92] Without arguable doubt, the legislative facts include the humanity of the affected community, the fears and prejudices that cause men to fail, the objectively foreseeable consequences of the case, and the reasonable reliance interests, if any, of persons affected.

The legal materials became scant when the court came to the retroactivity issue in *Harry and Others*, excluding the two firmer foundation points found via Monday-morning quarterbacking and set out above. Luke Decker's defense was that he and his predecessor in title—his father—held property rights that had vested well prior to the Ordinance of 1787. A careful reading of the opinion of the court suggests that Clarke saw the seriousness of this defense, perhaps more so than do sympathetic readers two hundred years later. He had tried to head this one off. Early in his opinion, Clarke analyzed the treaty of cession whereby Virginia has surrendered the Northwest Territory to the United States. Nothing that happened before July of 1787, Clarke argued, stood as an impediment to the confederated states enacting and the United States later recognizing and enforcing the Northwest Ordinance. A thinking lawyer reading this argument might find it a bit iffy. That slavery had never been imposed by positive law in the lands Virginia ceded in 1784 did not mean that, prior to their removal, Harry and the other two had not been slaves in Virginia proper. Remember, at that time, the lands we now know as the state of West Virginia were—until 1863—a part of Virginia proper. Clarke was smart enough to see this. So in the end he turned to the maxim "in matters of doubt, is it not an unquestioned rule, that courts must lean '*in favorem vitae et libertatis.*' . . . How should the Court decide, if construction was really to determine it? I presume it would be in favour of liberty."

Recall that just prior to presenting the maxim, Clarke had exclaimed, "Slavery is condemned by reason and the laws of nature." As a matter of fact, he was surely correct, so long as he limited the source of condemnation to civilized men of reason and moral understanding. As a matter of enforceable positive law, something very different was happening in this penultimate paragraph of the opinion. Clarke had to decide the case. Judges have no authority not to decide cases within their jurisdiction.[93] Judge Clarke had to adjudge Decker's vested rights defense, and to do so forthrightly. There was no legal premise of speed limit precision and application available to help. So he turned to the maxim "in matters of doubt, . . . that courts must lean '*in favorem vitae et libertatis.*' . . ." Perhaps he gilded the lily with "is it not an unquestioned rule." No matter. Clarke had to decide, and he decided well and legitimately. He honored his duty in exercising the constitutional judicial power to draw on the best premises he could find.

Lest the point be overlooked, in doing so, "*in favorem vitae et libertatis*" as a rule of construction became incorporated into the positive law of Mississippi. Judge Clarke did this and more, first and before any other state. Nothing the Supreme Court of Mississippi has done overrules *Harry and Others*, should some trial or appellate court today find it persuasive or otherwise helpful in some pending or future matter.

REFLECTIONS

History tells us that Judge Clarke's tour de force did not last. Judge Mills has told that sad story. Others have placed Mississippi's story in the context of the hell-bent-on-self-destruction and practicably blinded South as a whole.[94]

First, recall that *Harry and Others* was not published until Walker's volume of *Mississippi Reports*, dated 1832, hit the streets in 1834.[95] The new Jacksonian-democracy-influenced constitution of 1832 was already in place. Joshua G. Clarke had become the first chancellor of Mississippi in late 1821 and had served with distinction until he died on July 23, 1828. Leading up to 1833 and the organization and naming of Clarke County along the Alabama state line just south of Meridian, no record confirms that much of anyone even knew of *Harry and Others* decided back in 1818 or of *Isaac Jones v. State* decided in 1821.

Fear and isolationism and their alter ego, southern nationalism, grew. And more fear, as Armageddon approached. *Dred Scott* in 1857 only accelerated the pace. The nation's survival of the fiery trial through which it passed, plus the Reconstruction Amendments to the US Constitution, rendered *Harry and Others* unnecessary. As we approached the millennium, the early work of Joshua

Clarke was virtually unknown. *Harry* was decided in the very first term of the Supreme Court of Mississippi, which has cited it for nothing since. A mark worth a pause. Judge Mills, a former justice of that court, turned the tide with his 2001 article in the *Mississippi Law Journal*. Still, a few phone calls to friends in Clarke County as this was being written leave doubts whether anyone there knew anything of *Harry* and *Jones* as the calendar turned toward the year 2018.

Joshua Clarke set a standard. Coming across Clarke's citation of Rousseau in *Harry and Others* brings to the mind Judge Learned Hand's jewel offered years ago in this context.

> I venture to believe that it is as important to a judge called to pass on a question of constitutional law, to have at least a bowing acquaintance with Acton and Maitland, with Thucydides, Gibbon and Carlyle, with Homer, Dante, Shakespeare, and Milton, with Machiavelli, Montaigne and Rabelais, with Plato, Bacon, Hume and Kant, as with the books which have been specifically written on the subject.[96]

With little doubt, that gentle man would have assented to the addition of Rousseau, probably placed between David Hume and Immanuel Kant, and with an apology for his omission.

A few years back, Justice Evelyn Keyes argued that one can never become "a great judge without a thorough grounding in what the humanities, including literature, as well as the law itself, really do have to teach us." She closed with a more elaborate version of the same provocative point, viz., with these "he has at least the possibility of becoming a great judge, which, without these attributes, he can never be." The more modest "a very good judge" might taste better. That aside, the positive points made are persuasive. The law and its centerpiece, the exercise of the judicial power, most assuredly are an inexorable dimension of the humanities. These have arisen from human experience and govern human behavior. Their end is nothing less than a society in which we should want to live. Keyes also notes the other side of the coin: "[O]nly a morally literate and humanistically informed people can maintain a free society against the dehumanizing forces of totalitarian ideology and destructiveness that constantly assail it, for only then will they know what is at stake."[97] Ay, there's the rub. Now, as it was two hundred years ago.

Regarding Joshua Clarke, it would be hard to improve on what Judge Mills has had to offer. "Great-souled men and women must occasionally fret their hours on the stage and steer institutions aright. . . . Joshua G. Clarke possessed the courage, idealism and will to" do what was needed in 1818 and again in 1821. "Clarke establishes that men of good will and fair minds can speak the truth, even in the worst of times." In the end, there can be no serious doubt but that "the high point of antebellum Mississippi judicial sentiments supporting universal freedom and human compassion was clothed in the robe of one Joshua G. Clarke."

There is a place for humanity in the use and application of our constitution and laws, albeit a limited one. Judge Clarke provided two instances—*Harry and Others* and *Jones*—where a court has turned to the humanities, ideas of our fleeting existence as well as insights from Rousseau, to enrich the quality of its adjudications. He enriched the quality of our history, and our lives. His lessons endure.

As does Hamlet's advice to the fearful Horatio: "there are more things in heaven and earth than are dreamt of in your philosophy,"[98] with a respectful reminder that law and judging occupy but a practical and service-oriented corner of our philosophy, properly understood. We have little or no authority outside that practical corner and should confine ourselves thereto, except, of course, for the aspirational value and power of the constitution and laws. We should never forget that this practical and aspirational corner includes John Marshall's counsel that judges should never "decline the exercise of the jurisdiction which is given," lest they commit "treason to the constitution."[99] And that this is and always has been true in Mississippi and in all states with a constitution that has created and upon a chosen few has conferred the judicial power. Men and women, lawyers and judges and jurors, citizens all, do have an opportunity that the proverbial blunt instrument—the process of adjudication—which they work with daily be made and seen a bit more discerning. With hopeful hearts, people pursue optimal permissible levels of humanity in adjudication, their opportunities for good legal practice made richer.

ENDNOTES

1. *Harry and Others v. Decker & Hopkins*, Walker (1 Miss.) 36, 1818 WL 1235 (1818).

2. *State v. Isaac Jones*, Walker (1 Miss.) 83, 1820 WL 1414 (1821).

3. The news reports published in 1819 say that there were "twenty-eight black persons" involved in the trial "in the case of Harry et al. vs. Decker & Hopkins." *Daily National Intelligencer* (Washington, DC), Tues., July 20, 1819, Vol. 7, No. 2034, page 2; *see* http://www/genealogybank.com; and *New-England Palladium* (Boston, Mass.), Fri., July 30, 1819, Vol. XLIX, No. 9, page 1, see http://www/genealogybank.com

4. Some thoughtful observers have argued that the Indiana Constitution became effective immediately, or at least by July of 1816. *See* Andrew Fede, *Roadblocks to Freedom* 297, fn. 68 (2011), and accompanying text. As a matter of federal law, this seems unlikely. Nothing the people of Indiana did had legal effect under federal law until statehood was formally bestowed by President Madison's signature on December 11, 1816. Of course, the Congress could have granted the Indiana Constitution effect on December 11, 1816, *nunc pro tunc* June 29, 1816, or any other date prior to December 11, 1816. No evidence of such congressional action has been produced. *State v. Laselle*, 1 Blackf. 60, 1820 WL 868 (Ind. 1820) does not embarrass the point. The slaves freed in *Laselle* were all present on Indiana's free soil after statehood in December of

1816. For present purposes, the point is a nonlegal one. By early July of 1816, Luke Decker and his family quite reasonably foresaw that their slaveholdings were in great and imminent legal jeopardy, particularly so long as their slaves remained on Indiana soil.

5. Five witness subpoena forms completed by hand in mid-October 1816 name Francis Hopkins as the codefendant in a prosecution brought in the Territorial Court of Adams County, Mississippi, wherein Hiram Decker is the first-named defendant. Diligent search and inquiry suggests no one from the vicinity of Knox County, Indiana, named "Francis Hopkins" who might have been associated with Luke Decker or his son Hiram at the time. The circumstantial evidence suggests Francis Hopkins of McIntosh County, Georgia, as the buyer, coupled with the absence of evidence of any other substantial slave owner or trader of the time named Francis Hopkins.

6. 1820 US census, Census Place, McIntosh County, Georgia, page 26; NARA Roll $M33\_9$, Image 47; *see* Ancestry.com, "Francis Hophens in the 1820 United State Federal Census." *See also* David Hopkins, "Slaves of Francis Hopkins" (April 30, 2007), at http://www.genealogy.com/forum/surnames/topics/hopkins/6049/.

7. Betsey Fancher, "The Duel They Still Talk About," *Atlanta Journal Constitution* (Nov. 2, 1964), page 21.

8. Historian J. F. H. Claiborne has reported that "when the territory of Indiana became a State, with a Constitution prohibiting slavery, Decker immediately brought his negroes to Mississippi, and sold them. They instituted a suit for their freedom," leading to the decision in *Harry and Others*. J. F. H. Claiborne, *Mississippi, as a Province, Territory and State* 470 (1880; reprinted by LSU Press, 1964). Claiborne cites nothing. The fact that [Hiram] Decker is the lead named defendant suggests that Decker still had an ownership interest that had to be extinguished before Harry and the others could be free. If title had passed to Hopkins, he likely had a claim over against Decker, should that title be held defective. As a practical matter, the lawyer for Harry and the others thought it prudent to join as defendants both the prior owner and master of the slave vessel that docked in Natchez and the buyer, quite likely Francis Hopkins.

9. Alfred Hoyt Bill, *A House Called Morven: Its Role in American History, 1701–1954* 84–85 (2015).

10. Judge Leake would later become a delegate to the 1817 constitutional convention, representing Claiborne County. See "Walter Leake" in David G. Sansing, *Mississippi Governors: Soldiers, Statesmen, Scholars, Scoundrels: A Bicentennial Edition* 26–29 (2016); "Walter Leake," in *Mississippi Encyclopedia* 718–719 (Ownby and Wilson eds., 2017).

11. Court records show that Abraham Decker was served with the subpoena compelling his attendance as a witness in the Circuit Court of Adams County in October of 1816. Luke Decker, however, was not served. Presumably, this was because Luke was otherwise occupied back in Indiana with the escape of his slaves named Anthony and Bob.

12. *Daily National Intelligencer* (Washington, DC), Tues., July 20, 1819, Vol. 7, No. 2034, page 2, see http://www/genealogybank.com; and *New-England Palladium* (Boston, Mass.), Fri., July 30, 1819, Vol. XLIX, No. 9, page 1; *see* http://www/genealogybank.com.

13. A more complete explanation of the legal architecture of the original Supreme Court of Mississippi and the civil court system in general is set out in chapter 3. See particularly, Michael H. Hoffheimer, *Mississippi Courts: 1790–1868*, 65 Miss. L. Journ. 99, 113–117 (Fall 1995).

14. Further biographical information concerning Judge Powhatan Ellis may be found below in chapter 3 on judicial review. *See, e.g.*, "Ellis, Powhatan," in *Mississippi Encyclopedia* 386–387 (Ownby & Wilson eds., 2017).

15. *Statesman and Gazette* (Natchez, Miss.), July 6, 1831.

16. *Dred Scott v. Sanford*, 19 Howard (60 U.S.) 393, 561, ** 124, 15 L. Ed. 691, 765, 1856 WL 8721 (1857) (McLean, J., dissenting).

17. Goodspeed Brothers, *Biographical and Historical Memoirs of Mississippi*, Vol. 1, 112 (1891).

18. *Holt v. Briscoe*, Walker (1 Miss.) 19, 1818 WL 1240 (1818).

19. Andrew T. Fede, "Judging against the Grain? Reading Mississippi Supreme Court Judge Joshua G. Clarke's Views on Slavery in Context," *FCH Annals* 12 (May 2013), http://fch.ju.edu/fch_vol_20.pdf.

20. Governor Holmes acted in accordance with his authority whenever "a vacancy shall happen in any office." Miss. Const. art. 4, § 13 (1817). Clarke's formal acceptance of the commission issued by Holmes is dated and signed July 9, 1818.

21. James Daniel Lynch, *The Bench and Bar of Mississippi* (1880); https://en.wikipedia.org/wiki/Clarke_County_Mississippi; Lowry and McCardle, *History of Mississippi*, pages 460–461.

22. Judge Clarke's name does not appear on the official report of the opinion. Circumstantial evidence shows beyond a reasonable doubt that Judge Clarke authored the opinion. Preliminarily, in those early years, most opinions were delivered orally. In that first year 1818, there were twenty published decisions by the Supreme Court. The author of only three of these is identified. One delivered by Judge Powhatan Ellis is a lengthy opinion concerning auditors' accounts, having nothing in common with *Harry and Others*. Judge John Taylor delivered a short opinion in December 1818 concerning issues of pleadings and process. He followed with a more lengthy opinion presenting a jurisdictional question and another concerning a substantive controversy regarding public roads. Chief Judge John P. Hampton of Wilkinson County never authored an opinion of the style, substance, or level of legal reasoning found in *Harry and Others*. The unsigned opinions delivered in 1818 include *Harry and Others*. The strongest evidence that Judge Clarke authored *Harry and Others* is his 1821 opinion in *State v. Isaac Jones*, Walker (1 Miss.) 83, 1820 WL 1414 (1821), concerning the murder of a slave by a white man not the slave's master. The humanity and style of reasoning manifest in *Jones* are consistent with *Harry and Others*.

Three others have considered the authorship of *Harry and Others*. After a careful analysis, US District Judge Michael P. Mills concluded that the *Harry and Others* opinion "rendered anonymously . . . in 1818, could only have been penned by Justice Clarke." Mills, *Slave Law in Mississippi from 1817–1861: Constitutions, Codes and Cases*, 71 Miss. L. Journ. 153, 178 (Fall 2001). Lawyer/historian Andrew T. Fede has come around to this view after an appropriate initial reluctance. Andrew T. Fede, *Roadblocks to Freedom: Slavery and Manumission in the United States South* 298 (2011); also, Andrew T. Fede, "Judging against the Grain? Reading Mississippi Supreme Court Judge Joshua G. Clarke's Views on Slavery in Context," *FCH Annals* 11, 18 (May 2013), http://fch.ju.edu/fch_vol_20.pdf. Judge Clarke's great-great-great grandson has persuasively argued that Clarke authored *Harry and Others*.

23. The unnumbered article regarding slaves in the constitution of 1817 bears a marked similarity to the Constitution of Kentucky, Article 9 (1792). At many points, the texts of the two are verbatim identical.

24. *Harry and Others v. Decker & Hopkins*, Walker (1 Miss.) 36, **1, 1818 WL 1235 (1818). This reference should be understood in the context of the "fully developed, multi-level court system in the [Mississippi] territory" in place immediately prior to statehood. *See* Michael H. Hoffheimer, *Mississippi Courts: 1790–1868*, 65 Miss. L. Journ. 99, 116 (Fall 1995).

25. Two years later, this same terminology was used with its still-customary meaning and effect. In *Hinds v. Terry*, Walker (1 Miss.) 80, 1820 WL 949 (June 1820), as in *Harry and Others*, the matter came before the supreme court "on a motion for a new trial." The procedural question was whether, after a trial, the "verdict" should have been set aside. The term "verdict" is correctly used a number of times, in contradistinction from the term "judgment," also used correctly. *Hinds v. Terry*, Walker (1 Miss.) 80, 81, 82, 83 ("verdict") and 83 ("judgment"), 1820 WL 949 (June 1820). There is no reason to believe that in *Harry and Others*, Judge Clarke was using

these terms in a different sense than that Judge Powhatan Ellis had in mind two years later in *Hinds*. Given that the term "jury" appears at least six times in *Hinds*, there is every good reason to take *Hinds v. Terry* to confirm that "motion for a new trial" and the other terms used in *Harry and Others* collectively and equally connote a verdict at the end of a jury trial. After all, Judge Clarke was still on the court at the time of *Hinds* in 1820.

26. Some might think it odd that Judge Powhatan Ellis approved the opinion in *Harry and Others*. The reason this might be so is found in Judge Ellis's opinion in *Hinds v. Terry*, Walker (1 Miss.) 80, 1820 WL 949 (1820). *Hinds* arose from a dispute over property rights in an unnamed slave. The decision is governed by the common law rules governing tenants in common and the common law action of trover against another. To be sure, the opinion coldly treats the slave as property and nothing more. Nothing in *Harry and Others* suggests any judge approving that opinion should have legal objections to anything in *Hinds*, or vice versa. The two cases are about two distinct dimensions of the existence of slaves in Mississippi in 1818–1820.

27. The earliest dissents Walker noted were in 1824. One is recorded as simply "Judge Turner dissented," in *Bolls v. Duncan*, Walker (1 Miss.) 161, 165, 1824 WL 1310 (1824); the other, as "Judge Stockton dissented," in *Stark's Heirs v. Mather*, Walker (1 Miss.) 181, 193, 1824 WL 46 (1824).

28. Lea VanderVelde has told the story of Dred Scott and his wife in *Mrs. Dred Scott: A Life on Slavery's Frontier* (2009); *see also* Lea VanderVelde, "The Dred Scott Case in Context," *Journal of Supreme Court History* 40, no. 3, pages 263–281 (2015). It would be a great good fortune to history and humanity if someday something approaching that level of personal information is found, so that Harry's story and the stories of his companions may be told, at least as fully as the stories of the Decker family or Dred Scott's family are known.

29. Evelyn Keyes, *The Literary Judge: The Judge as Novelist and Critic*, 44 Houston L. Rev. 679, 699 (2007). Justice Keyes sits on the Texas Court of Appeals, First District. Keyes spent her early childhood and adolescent years in Greenville, Mississippi, *sub nom.* Evelyn Vincent.

30. *Jones v. State*, Walker (1 Miss.) 83, 1821 WL 1413 (1821).

31. Paul Finkelman had employed four categories of presence on "free soil" to assist in analyzing freedom-by-residence cases. These categories are "transient, visitor, sojourner or resident." Finkelman, *Imperfect Union*, quoted and discussed in Andrew Fede's "Freedom Suits Based on the Movement of Slaves," in his *Roadblocks to Freedom: Slavery and Manumission in the United States South* 289, 326, fn. 9 (2011), and accompanying text.

32. See my discussion in Robertson, *Variations on a Theme by Posner: The Factual Component of the Reliability Imperative in the Process of Adjudication*, 84 Miss. L. Journ. 471, 520 (2015).

33. *See, e.g., Bolls v. Duncan*, Walker (1 Miss.) 161, **1, 1824 WL 1310 (1824), a decision regarding the law of escheat and the administration of estates, where Chief Judge Hampton began, "It is a case of the first impression, arising under our own municipal laws, in the adjudication of which we are not to expect lights and precedents from abroad."

34. The inhabitants of all new states coming into the Union were entitled to "judicial proceedings according to the common law," guaranteed by Article the Second in the Northwest Territory Ordinance of July 13, 1787. See Michael H. Hoffheimer, *Mississippi Courts: 1790–1868*, 65 Miss. L. Journ. 99, 103 fn. 12 and accompanying text (Fall 1995). This ordinance established the Equal Footings Doctrine, under which all new states were admitted "into the Union on an equal footing with the original States." See act of March 1, 1817, 3 Stat. 348 (1817); act of December 10, 1817, formally admitting Mississippi to the Union, 3 Stat. 472, 473 (1817). The new state accepted these terms in the preamble to the Mississippi Constitution of 1817. See chapter 8 re the common law in Mississippi, presented below.

35. Miss. Const., Schedule § 5 (1817).

36. Even today, judges are from time to time charged to decide cases of first impression. In cases where the legal materials are plentiful, "[i]t is a rare case on appeal when the judges

are not influenced by some point not in the record, e.g., something remembered from prior similar cases, cases found by the judge or a law clerk on independent research (and not just on updating the research after the briefs have been filed), a point the judge remembers from prior practice of law, a lesson remembered from law school, etc. . . . At times judges are influenced by political, religious or moral beliefs, no matter how hard the judge may try to play it straight." Robertson, *Variations on a Theme by Posner: The Factual Component of the Reliability Imperative in the Process of Adjudication*, 84 Miss. L. Journ. 471, 531 fn. 249 (2015).

37. Oliver Wendell Holmes, *The Common Law*, 35 (1881). This Holmes passage, give or take a few lines above or below, enjoys almost biblical authority.

38. *Rankin v. Lydia, a Pauper*, 2 A.K.Marsh 467, 9 Ky. 467, 1820 WL 1098 (Oct. 1820).

39. *Griffith v. Fanny*, Gilmer (21 Va.) 143, 1820 WL 809 (Dec. 1820).

40. *Lunsford v. Coquillon*, 2 Mart. (n.s.) (La.) 401, 1824 WL 1649 (May 1824).

41. *Winny v. Whitesides Alias Prewitt*, 1 Mo. 472, 1824 WL 1839 (Nov. 1824).

42. For a full discussion of this point of slavery law in all of its complexities, and over time until *Dred Scott* in 1857, see Andrew T. Fede, "Freedom Suits Based on the Movement of Slaves" in his *Roadblocks to Freedom: Slavery and Manumission in the United States South* 287–337 (2011).

43. An Ordinance for the Government of the Territory of the United States, North-west of the River Ohio, effective July 13, 1787, 1 Statutes at Large 475. The US Supreme Court held the ordinance unenforceable consistent with the US Constitution in *Dred Scott v. Sanford*, 19 Howard (60 U.S.) 393, 15 L.Ed. 691, 1856 WL 8721 (1857). No state supreme court acting in 1818 should be faulted for not anticipating this ultimately tragic ruling.

44. On December 6, 1816, the US Senate approved the act to admit Indiana as a state. On December 9, 1816, the US House of Representatives approved the same bill. On December 11, 1816, President James Madison signed the act formally admitting Indiana as the nineteenth state of the United States of America. See U.S. Const. art. 4, § 3(1).

45. On April 19, 1816, President Madison approved the Indiana statehood Enabling Act of 1816. Section 4 of that Enabling Act required Indiana to adopt a constitution, with two caveats. First, the new state constitution had to provide for a "republican form of government," U.S. Const. art. 4, § 4. Second, no clause in the new state constitution could be repugnant to the Northwest Ordinance of July 13, 1787.

46. It appears that Indiana tried to make its constitution effective from its approval at the convention on June 29, 1816. *See* William P. McLauchlan, *The Indiana State Constitution: A Reference Guide* (1996), see Andrew T. Fede, "Freedom Suits Based on the Movement of Slaves," in his *Roadblocks to Freedom: Slavery and Manumission in the United States South* 297, 330, fn. 68 and accompanying text (2011). But Indiana could not have accomplished this without authorization from the Congress of the United States. This point of constitutional law is noted, though it does not detract (a) from Decker's strong incentive to remove his slaves from Indiana immediately so that he could sell them "down the river," or (b) from the reasonableness of Judge Clarke's course of discussing state sovereignty in *Harry and Others* to explain the point for judges likely to face the question in the future, if not for other practical reasons as well.

47. Miss. Const. art. 1, § 2 (1817). These sections of the constitution of 1817 bear a marked similarity to Sections 1–3 of the Virginia Bill of Rights, June 12, 1776, and to the Kentucky Constitution art. 12 (1792).

48. *Harry and Others v. Decker & Hopkins*, Walker (1 Miss.) 36, 40 **1, 1818 WL 1235 (1818). Extracts immediately following also refer to this opinion, 39–43. *See also* Meredith Lang, *Defender of the Faith: The High Court of Mississippi 1817–1875*, 11–12 (1977) for a further exposition of this text, published before some of the more recent findings regarding the facts and circumstances that have given rise to *Harry and Others*.

49. Miss. Const. art. 1, § 1 (1817).

50. *Harry and Others v. Decker & Hopkins,* Walker (1 Miss.) 36, 40 **1, 1818 WL 1235 (1818). Note the use of "social compact" in Miss. Const. art. 1, § 1 (1817), and in *Harry and Others,* and on multiple occasions in the judicial opinion merely "compact." Most translate the title of Rousseau's famous work as "The Social Contract" (published in 1762). Past this, the *Harry and Others* opinion misspells the great French political philosopher's name "Rosseau," *Harry and Others v. Decker & Hopkins,* Walker (1 Miss.) 36, 40 **1, 1818 WL 1235 (1818), omitting the first "u" which is otherwise universally used. Of course, the blame here may lie with Robert J. Walker, the first official reporter of decisions of the Supreme Court, who did not produce his volume of decisions until sometime in 1834, with *Harry and Others* being printed at pages 36–43. Accounts of Walker's service are told in Griffith, *Mississippi Reports and Reporters,* 22 Miss. L. Journ. 37, 37–39 (1950); John Ray Skates Jr., *A History of the Mississippi Supreme Court, 1817–1948* (1973).

51. Decker and Hopkins's particular constitutional argument is not articulated in the opinion. Given the times and the brand-new Constitution of Mississippi, one can easily see an argument based on one or more of the following: Miss. Const. art. 1, § 10 (1817) (no person "can be deprived of his . . . property, but by due course of law"); Miss. Const. art. 1, § 13 (1817) ("nor shall any person's property be taken or applied to public use . . . without just compensation being made therefor; and/or Miss. Const. art. 1, § 19 (1817) ("that no ex post facto law . . . shall be made").

52. *Somerset v. Stewart,* Lofft 1, 98 Eng. Rep. 499, 20 Howard St. T. 1 (K. B. 1772). Lawyer and historian Andrew T. Fede presents a helpful explanation of Lord Mansfield's opinion in *Somerset* and its use and influence in the United States, including Mississippi, in his *Roadblocks to Freedom: Slavery and Manumission in the United States South* 289–308 (2011).

53. *See Somerset v. Stewart,* Lofft 19. Judge Clarke would repeat this point three years later in *Jones v. State,* Walker (1 Miss.) 83, 85, **1, 1821 WL 1413 (1821). *See also* Andrew T. Fede, "Judging against the Grain? Reading Mississippi Supreme Court Judge Joshua G. Clarke's Views on Slavery in Context," *FCH Annals,* page 16, fn. 38 and accompanying text (May 2013), http://fch. ju.edu/fch_vol_20.pdf.

54. *See, e.g.,* Andrew Fede, *People without Rights: An Interpretation of the Fundamentals of the Law of Slavery in the U.S. South,* 73–75 (1992); Ruth Wedgwood, *The South Condemning Itself: Humanity and Property in American Slavery,* Chicago-Kent L. Rev. 1392–1398 (1992–1993).

55. Miss. Const. art. 5, §§ 1, 4 (1817).

56. *See* Miss. Const. art. 1, §§ 10, 16, 17 (1817).

57. Miss. Const. art. 1, § 1 (1817).

58. Edward Coke, *The First Part of the Institutes of the Laws of England, or, A Commentary on Littleton* (1628).

59. *Jones v. State,* Walker (1 Miss.) 83, 84, **1, 1821 WL 1413 (1821); *see* William C. Davis, *A Way through the Wilderness: The Natchez Trace and the Civilization of the Southern Frontier* 76–79 (1995), for a broader summary view of the practice of slavery in southwest Mississippi at the time.

60. Miss. Const. Slaves, § 1 (1817).

61. *Southern Pacific Co. v. Jensen,* 244 U.S. 205, 222 (1917) (Holmes, J., dissenting).

62. An Ordinance for the Government of the Territory of the United States, North-west of the River Ohio, effective July 13, 1787, 1 Statutes at Large 475.

63. *Olmstead v. United States,* 277 U.S. 438, 469–471 (1928) (Holmes, J., dissenting).

64. *Roe v. Wade,* 410 U.S. 113 (1971).

65. *See, e.g., Casey v. Planned Parenthood of Southeastern Pennsylvania,* 505 U.S. 833 (1992).

66. *Obergefell v. Hodges,* 135 S. Ct. 2584 (2015).

67. For a cogent analysis of *Obergefell,* see Richard A. Posner, *Divergent Paths: The Academy and the Judiciary* 390–400 (2016). I offer a Mississippi-based historical perspective in my

"The Confession of Justice Thomas Pickens Brady," *CABA Newsletter*, www.caba.ms/articles/
October2015.

68. *Hinds v. Brazealle*, 2 Howard (3 Miss.) 837, 1838 WL 1199 (1838).

69. *See Heirn v. Bridault*, 8 George (37 Miss.) 209, 1859 WL 3633 (1859); *Mitchell v. Wells*, 8
George (37 Miss.) 235, 1859 WL 3634 (1859).

70. *State v. J. J. Newman Lumber Co.*, 102 Miss. 802, 59 So. 923, 929 (1912), discussed in chapter 7 below. In context, Justice Reed's reference is an argumentative ploy, not a source of law
with precedential or other controlling force.

71. *See, e.g.*, https://www.wcl.american.edu/secle/founders/2005/ . . . /050113.cf . . .

72. *See, e.g.*, H. L. A. Hart, *The Concept of Law* 100–110 (2d ed., 1964); *see also* James L.
Robertson and David W. Clark, "An Interpretive Stratagem," in *The Law of Business Torts in
Mississippi*, 15 Miss. Coll. L. Rev. 13, 27–30 (1994); Robertson, "Myth and Reality—Or Is It
'Perception and Taste'?"—*In the Reading of Donative Documents*, 61 Fordham L. Rev. 1045,
1056–1059 (1993).

73. Miss. Const. art. 1, § 10 (1817).

74. Miss. Const. art. 1, § 13 (1817).

75. Miss. Const. Slaves, §1 (1817).

76. Miss. Const. Schedule, §§ 1–5 (1817).

77. Miss. Const. Schedule, § 5 (1817). See chapter 8 below concerning the origins and practice of the common law in Mississippi.

78. William Blackstone, *Commentaries*, book 2, ch. 1; *Curry v. State*, 710 So.2d 853, 856 (¶9)
(1998) (right to exclude others from land an incidence of title or possession); *Crenshaw v. Gray-
beal*, 597 So.2d 650, 652 (1992) (right to exclude others from manmade body of water); *eBay,
Inc. v. MercExchange, LLC*, 547 U.S. 388, 392 (2006) (patents); *College Savings Bank v. Florida
Prepaid Postsecondary Ed. Exp. Bd.*, 527 U.S. 666, 673 (1999) ("hallmark of a protected property
interest is the right to exclude others"); *Int'l News Serv. v. Associated Press*, 248 U.S. 215, 246
(Holmes, J.) and 250 (Brandeis, J.) (1918) (copyrights).

79. Law is a social fact, albeit proof of such a fact is made by processes differing from those
used for proving such evidentiary facts as that the Decker family settled in "the neighborhood
of Vincennes" in 1784, bringing slaves with them.

80. Miss. Const., Slaves, § 1 (1817), viz., "provided, that such person or slave be the bona fide
property of such immigrants."

81. Miss. Const., Schedule, § 5 (1817).

82. *See Cuevas v. State*, 338 So.2d 1236, 1238 (1976) (common law of kidnapping); *Aikerson
v. State*, 274 So.2d 124, 126 (1973); 51 C. J. S., *Kidnapping* § 1 (2003), explaining the elements of
kidnapping at common law.

83. Miss. Const., Slaves, § 1 (1817).

84. *Dred Scott v. Sanford*, 19 Howard (60 U.S.) 393, 561, ** 124, 15 L.Ed. 691, 765, 1856 WL 8721
(1857) (McLean, J., dissenting).

85. *Jones v. State*, Walker (1 Miss.) 83–84, **1, 1821 WL 1413 (1821).

86. *The Western Maid*, 257 U.S. 419, 432 (1922) (Holmes, J.).

87. *See* John Finnis, *Natural Law and Natural Rights* (2d ed., 2011), explaining that there is so
much more that is rich and complex in the idea of natural law than Joshua Clarke and so many
others ever thought.

88. See Miss. Const., Schedule, § 5 (1817).

89. U.S. Const. art. 6, §2.

90. Miss. Const. art. 2, § 1, and art. 5, §§ 1, 2 (1817), and the statutes creating and empowering
the supreme court.

91. *See* Michael H. Hoffheimer, *Mississippi Courts: 1790–1868*, 65 Miss. L. Journ. 99, 113–117
(Fall 1995).

92. Oliver Wendell Holmes, *The Common Law*, 35 (1881).

93. *Shewbrooks v. A. C. & S., Inc.*, 529 So. 2d 557, 560 (Miss. 1988); *See also Lexmark Int'l, Inc. v. State Control Components, Inc.*, 134 S.Ct. 1377, 1386 (2014) ("court's [duty] to hear and decide cases within its jurisdiction is virtually unflagging") (citing and quoting *Sprint Communications, Inc. v. Jacobs*, 134 S.Ct. 584, 591 (2013)); *Cohens v. Virginia*, 6 Wheat. (19 U.S.) 264, 404, 5 L.Ed. 257, 291 (1821) ("treason to the constitution"). The federal cases are summarized in *New Orleans Public Service, Inc. v. Council of City of New Orleans*, 491 U.S. 350, 358–359 (1989). The supreme court has recognized this judicial duty in civil actions against churches and their officials, e.g., *Roman Catholic Diocese of Jackson v. Morrison*, 905 So.2d 1213, 1223 (¶23) (Miss. 2005).

94. Lawyer and historian Andrew T. Fede has told this story well and often, particularly in his *Roadblocks to Freedom: Slavery and Manumission in the United States South* 147–150 (2011).

95. Robert J. Walker of Natchez became the first official reporter of decisions of the supreme court but did not produce his volume of decisions until sometime in 1834.

96. Learned Hand, "Sources of Tolerance," in Hand, *The Spirit of Liberty: Papers and Addresses of Learned Hand* 66, 81 (Irving Dillard ed., 1952).

97. Evelyn Keyes, *The Literary Judge: The Judge as Novelist and Critic*, 44 Houston L. Rev. 679 (2007).

98. Shakespeare, *Hamlet*, act 1, scene 5, lines 166–167.

99. *Cohens v. Virginia*, 6 Wheat. (19 U.S.) 264, 404, 5 L.Ed. 257, 291 (1821).

BIBLIOGRAPHY

Allen, Michael, "Mississippi Broadhorn or New Orleans Boat," in *Western Rivermen,1763–1861*; see *Steamboat Times*, http://steamboattimes.com/flatboats/html.

Berwanger, Eugene H., *The Frontier against Slavery; Western Anti-Negro Prejudice and the Slavery Extension Controversy* (1967).

The Mary Bateman Clark Project, http://www.marybatemanclark.org/biography.

Barnett, Jim, and H. Clark Burkett, "The Forks of the Road Slave Market at Natchez," Vol. 63, *Journal of Mississippi History* (2001).

Claiborne, J. F. H., *Mississippi, as a Province, Territory and State* (1880; reprinted by LSU Press, 1964).

Clarke, J. Calvitt III, "The Life of Joshua G. Clarke: Mississippi's First Chancellor," *FCH Annals* (May 2013).

Clarke, J. Calvitt III, *A Path Not Taken: Joshua Giles Clarke of Mississippi, Supreme Court Judge and Chancellor*, https://www.academia.edu/5660628.

Daily National Intelligencer (Washington, D.C.), Tues., July 20, 1819, Vol. 7, No. 2034.

Davis, Ronald L. F., *Black Experience in Natchez: 1720–1880* (April 1993), https://archive.org/ stream/blackexperienceioodavi/blackexperienceioodavi_djvu.txt.

Davis, William C., *A Way through the Wilderness: The Natchez Trace and the Civilization of the Southern Frontier* (1995).

Fede, Andrew T., "Judging against the Grain? Reading Mississippi Supreme Court Judge Joshua G. Clarke's Views on Slavery in Context," *FCH Annals* (May 2013), http://fch.ju.edu /fch_vol_20.pdf.

Fede, Andrew T., *Roadblocks to Freedom: Slavery and Manumission in the United States South* (2011).

Gamble, Thomas, "Political Feuds and Resulting Duels," in *Savannah Duels and Duelists, 1733– 1877* (1923), available at http://files.usgwarchives.net/ga/chatham/history/other /gms414savannah.txt.

Gray, Ralph D., *Indiana History: A Book of Readings* (1994).

Griffith, Virgil A., *Mississippi Chancery Practice* (2d ed., 1950).

Griffith, Virgil A., *Mississippi Reports and Reporters*, 22 Miss. L. Journ. 37 (1950).

Hemleben, Sylvester John, and Richard T. Bennett, *Beginnings of the Legal Profession in Mississippi*, 36 Miss L. Journ. 155 (1965).

Hoffheimer, Michael H., *Mississippi Courts: 1790–1868*, 65 Miss. L. Journ. 99 (Fall 1995).

"Hopkins, Gen. Francis," *Find A Grave*.

"Gravesite of General Francis Hopkins, Crescent," *Vanishing Coastal Georgia*, https://vanishingcoastalgeorgia.com/2014/06/23/gravesite-of-general-francis-hopkins-crescent.

"Jones, Isaac," *Genealogy Trails*, http://genealogytrails.com/miss/executions.html; *Death Penalty USA*, http://deathpenaltyusa.org/usa1/date/1821.htm #2022.

Keyes, Evelyn. *The Literary Judge: The Judge as Novelist and Critic*, 44 Houston L. Rev. 679 (2007).

Knox and Daviess County, Indiana, History of: From Earliest Time to the Present," Etc. (Goodspeed, 1886).

"Leake, Walter," in David G. Sansing, *Mississippi Governors: Soldiers, Statesmen, Scholars, Scoundrels: A Bicentennial Edition* 26–29 (2016).

"Leake, Walter," in *Mississippi Encyclopedia* 718–719 (Ownby and Wilson eds., 2017).

Lynch, James Daniel, *The Bench and Bar of Mississippi* (1880).

Margolis, Kate, "A Brief History of Mississippi's Chancery Court," posted May 2010, http://www.caba.ms/feature3.html.

Mills, Michael P., *Slave Law in Mississippi from 1817–1861: Constitutions, Codes and Cases*, 71 Miss. L. Journ. 153 (Fall 2001).

New-England Palladium (Boston, Mass.), Friday, July 30, 1819, Vol. XLIX, No. 9; *see* http://www/genealogybank.com.

Pierce, Merrily, "Luke Decker and Slavery: His Cases with Bob and Anthony, 1817–1822," *Indiana Magazine of History* (1989).

Pittman, Anna, HAMPTON, JOHN P., on file at the State Law Library, Supreme Court Building, Jackson, Mississippi.

Pittman, Anna, undated report of "amf" or by Anna Pittman re Joshua Giles Clarke, on file at the State Law Library, Supreme Court Building, Jackson, Mississippi.

Robertson, James L., Book Excerpt, *Only People Were Slaves*, 87 Miss. L. Journ. 383 (2018).

"Rough, John," https://en.wikipedia.org/wiki/Dunleith; https://en.wikipedia.org/wiki/Routhland.

Rowland, Dunbar, "Mississippi's First Constitution and Its Makers," in *Publications of the Mississippi Historical Society* (Riley ed., 1902), Vol. 6.

Skates, John Ray, Jr., *A History of the Mississippi Supreme Court, 1817–1948* (1973).

Statesman and Gazette (Natchez, Mississippi), July 6, 1831.

VanderVelde, Lea, "The Dred Scott Case in Context," *Journal of Supreme Court History* 40, no. 3 (2015).

VanderVelde, Lea, *Redemption Songs: Suing for Freedom before Dred Scott* (2014).

CHAPTER 3

Judicial Review
Comes to Mississippi

It "would be treason to the constitution" for the court
to "decline the exercise of jurisdiction which is given."
—JOHN MARSHALL (1821)

No clause in the Mississippi Constitution du jour confers upon the judiciary the authority to declare legislative enactments unconstitutional, and thus unenforceable. Or to engage in any other practice of judicial review. There was no such authorizing clause in the constitutions of 1817, of 1832, or 1869, nor, for that matter, is there such a clause in the US Constitution. Yet the practice of state constitutional judicial review has been bedrock for almost two hundred years. The quality of state government has been enhanced, as our judges have displayed courage and applied practical wisdom.

Aggressive and restrained exercises of judicial review have substantially impacted the lives of many Mississippians who have come and gone. How beneficial those impacts have been has been a function of how well our judges have understood that judicial review is just a special instance of the process of adjudication itself. No particular outcome is foreordained, though the court may wisely decide that the action of some officer or department is a proper occasion for review and, on the merits, was altogether prudent and permissible.

Approaching the bicentennial of judicial review is an appropriate time to take stock. For those here, now, and in the future, the sword remains. How well has it been wielded over the decades, and what sort of folk have done the wielding? With what legitimacy and discretion? For what reasons, and with what practical effects? How can we apply what experience has taught for the general welfare of humanity—within the State's reach—at least for the foreseeable future? These are questions worthy of reflection, and always will be.

It is one of the lessons of Western political history that the judicial review prerogative is not essential to a successful and flourishing democracy, or a republic, as Americans once called their country. Oliver Wendell Holmes said as much, and more than once. Until recently, the parliamentary democracy of the United Kingdom was exhibit A. Have we not long been told that the Parliament of England can pass any law, however it may violate first principles, and the courts would be bound to enforce it? Whether a people enjoyed "a republican form of government" so as to qualify for statehood has never turned on the extent to which judicial review would be practiced there. London's rethinking of late has the United Kingdom tending toward our approach, and not vice versa. How Mississippians came to practice constitutional judicial review—to honor that practice, though at times to shy away from its awesome responsibility—is a story worth telling.

Men of diverse interests and backgrounds and responsibilities—leading up to December of 1823, their work done by early February of 1825—walked the path to this early constitutional encounter. The men who took the first step included a court clerk, son of a political kingfish in Southwest Mississippi who had fought in the Revolutionary War, and a judge from Virginia with an Indian tribal affinity. The second step began with hard-nosed creditors pursuing a struggling debtor with a wife and five children, his only nonexempt assets being three yoke of oxen, a wagon, and a mare and a colt. It included an enigmatic judge from New Jersey whose grandfather had signed the Declaration of Independence, the governor who had appointed this judge and whose veto had been overridden, a River county sheriff who served in territorial times as well as two terms after statehood, and legislators with differing views, levels of awareness and approaches. Together, these worthies presented a two-act play. The first act began with a scene in Lawrence County, and a second scene in Natchez. The second act opened in Claiborne County but climaxed in the new capital city of Jackson. A variety of characters appeared, featuring many players—at times unwitting—in sensing, denying, establishing, and constraining the practice of state constitutional judicial review.

In time, each player moved on to address other matters, to face new challenges, to pursue other and diverse interests. The fates were not kind to all. The powerful effects of what they did in the early 1820s—at times collectively, at other times seriatim—are felt today and will remain formidable and beneficial for the foreseeable future, if only we are up to the task.

FIRST FORAYS SUMMARIZED

In 1982, Attorney General Bill Allain went to court. He attacked a massive, years-in-the-making legislative usurpation of executive powers. Seldom has a public official so summoned political courage and bit the hand that fed him, and scored such a telling knockout. Many features of the litigation are remarkable. The Supreme Court of Mississippi traced its authority to adjudge this intrastate constitutional crisis back to an otherwise obscure decision made in 1823.[1] It was one of those nice fortuities of fate and history that, in deciding the *Alexander* case in 1983,[2] Chief Justice Neville Patterson of Lawrence County found his footing in a less momentous Lawrence County case—*Runnels v. State*—that was approaching its 160th birthday.

The core practical issue in *Runnels* was whether a bottom-rung court appointee could keep his job. This was fitting. Twenty years earlier, another appointee's struggle to keep his bottom-rung judicial job in the District of Columbia had set the stage for John Marshall's finest moment. In his justly famous opinion in *Marbury v. Madison*, delivered in 1803,[3] Chief Justice Marshall made the federal case for judicial review. The federal judiciary was held to have the authority—nay, the duty—to scrutinize acts of the Congress for whether they may be inconsistent with the Constitution.

Straddling the turn of the years 1824 to 1825, Mississippi had a second and less elegant clash over the intrastate practice of judicial review. The case was a sidebar in the social, political, and humanitarian struggle to relieve insolvent debtors of the pains of imprisonment and worse. A number of men played out problematic roles in the never-formally-reported *Cochrane & Murdock v. Kitchens* and its aftermath, each in his way fueling, controlling and putting out the fire. The case had been commenced in early April of 1822. It had percolated in fits and starts through the processes of the Circuit Court of Claiborne County for several years. *Cochrane & Murdock* reached the Supreme Court at its June term, 1824. What happened then was only prelude to the contentious proceedings in the house of representatives in January of 1825. A month later, the *Runnels* principle of judicial review and supremacy in state constitutional law had not only endured; it had prevailed.

THE CONSTITUTIONAL ARCHITECTURE, 1822–1825

The separation of political powers received no express mention in the work done at the federal constitutional convention in Philadelphia in the summer of 1787. It had to be implied. Thirty summers later, Mississippi's constitution makers convened in the little town of Washington—six miles east of Natchez—preliminary to the twentieth state's qualifying for admission to the Union, and reduced that great separation principle to written form. Within the wisdom and customs of the times, they created the constitutional architecture for a representative majoritarian republic. The state was to function within such familiar strictures as the tripartite separation of the powers of government, a comprehensive and quite exemplary (for the times) bill of rights,[4] and other limitations less honored but equally enforceable.

Mississippi's 1817 Declaration of Rights, Article 1, concluded with a clause that merits mention in telling the story of the rise of state judicial review.

> To guard against transgression of the high powers, herein delegated, We Declare
> that everything in this article is excepted out of the general powers of govern-
> ment, and shall forever remain inviolate; and that all laws contrary thereto, *or to
> the following provisions*, shall be void.

This clause was clear. The State had no power to transgress upon the rights or
powers that were so declared. State government was stripped of any authority
as it might otherwise have been thought to have in these regards. But the
constitution writers stopped short of saying who was to do the guarding against
transgression. That authority had to be inferred from what came later.

The phrase "or [contrary] to the following provisions," was important.
Curiously, no one seems to have mentioned it in the stories of the *Runnels* or
Cochrane & Murdock cases told below. Still it was there. The "following provisions" were nothing less than the rest of the constitution of 1817 in its entirety.
The best reading of that phrase was that all laws contrary to the rights secured
or to the limitations on the powers granted anywhere in the whole constitution were excepted out of the general powers of state government. That is, the
government and the officials that did its bidding had no authority to do anything inconsistent with the constitution. Not a thing!

The most immediate "following provision" was Article 2, entitled "Distribution
of Powers." Section 1 recognized that there were three kinds of political powers
that governments practiced—legislative, executive, and judicial. It divided the government into three distinct departments, a separate department to exercise each
of the powers. Prior to 1787 and the ratification that followed, all of this had been
political theory in the then-untested works of Locke and Montesquieu.[5] By 1817,
six new states had worked off of the federal experience and the models of the original states. In the summer of that year, Mississippi's constitution makers put their
own spin on separation of powers. Section 1 declared the three kinds of political
power of the state, a separate department to exercise each of the three conceptually and practicably distinct powers. Articles 3, 4, and 5 spelled out the elements of
structure, top personnel, and authorized power for each of the departments.

The constitution vested the legislative power in a general assembly to con-
sist of two distinct branches, the senate and the house of representatives. What
made up the legislative power was left to a number of "you-mays" and "you-
may-nots" set out later, and any reasonable inferences that might follow from
these. The supreme executive power was vested in a governor elected for a two-
year term. The constitution provided as well for an elected lieutenant-gover-
nor. A secretary of state, treasurer, and auditor of public accounts were to be
appointed. The judicial power was vested in "one supreme court, and such superior and inferior courts of law and equity as the Legislature may, from time to
time, direct and establish."

To ensure that the officials in each department of government functioned only within the limits constitutionally prescribed, Article 2 included the following proviso: "No person or collection of persons, being of one of those departments, shall exercise any power properly belonging to either of the others, except in the instances hereinafter expressly directed or permitted." Article 2 added a level of clarity and precision not found in the federal constitution, though stopping short of a mechanical jurisprudence of separation of powers. "Properly belonging" is one of those grand general phrases that enable good constitutions to serve the people but not enslave them.

As with Article 1, Article 2 stopped short of setting out how—in case of dispute—it should be decided whether a particular exercise of political power "properly belonged" to one department or to another. More pointedly, how should it be decided whether court consideration of the constitutional enforceability of a statute were a bona fide judicial power, or if it were the judicial usurpation of a power granted to the legislative department? If there be a transgression, what should be done? To complicate matters, the constitution did not say who would decide whether an encroachment, if one be found, had been "expressly directed or permitted." It could have been anybody. After all, each officeholder—legislative, executive, and judicial—took and was bound by the same oath to support the same constitution.

THE JUDICIARY'S FIRST DECADE

Shortly after statehood in December of 1817, the general assembly created four judicial districts, with a circuit judge for each. These judges served as trial judges within their respective districts. Jefferson, Claiborne, Warren, and later Hinds Counties as they were then configured made up the First District. Judge Richard Stockton Jr. (1791–1827), of Claiborne County and before that of New Jersey, served the First District in 1822–1825, and into the years of the first practice of constitutional judicial review in Mississippi.[6] The Second District included Adams, Franklin, Lawrence, and Covington Counties and was served by Judge Louis Winston (1784–1824) of Natchez, who had been secretary of the constitutional convention in the summer of 1817. Judge Winston died in August of 1824. Shortly thereafter, Judge Edward Turner (1778–1860), also of Natchez, began a long term of service in District Two.

Southernmost counties of Wilkinson, Amite, Pike, Marion, and Hancock—each bordering the state of Louisiana—composed the Third District. Chief Judge John P. Hampton, a native of South Carolina, and a resident of Wilkinson County, served the Third District through the early years of statehood until 1827. Judge Powhatan Ellis (1790–1863) came from Virginia and rode circuit in the Fourth District, which consisted of the eastern counties of Jackson, Greene, Perry, Wayne, and Monroe as their boundaries were then configured.

The general assembly had directed, "The Supreme Court shall be held at the City of Natchez, on the second Monday of June and the second Monday of December in each year, and may continue until the business therein depending shall be disposed of." No doubt for practical and logistical reasons, the law at the time provided that "any two of them shall constitute a court." Understandably, a judge whose decision at the trial level was under review was disqualified from sitting with the supreme court when it heard an appeal in that case.

HARMON M. RUNNELS JR. AND THE FAMILY

Harmon M. Runnels Jr. of Lawrence County was one of four brothers, but their father ran the family and much more. In or about 1810 or 1811, Harmon M. Runnels Sr. (1749–1839) abandoned the state of Georgia, headed west, and in short order, as a river-county Mississippian observed, "ruled the Pearl River Country as long as he lived." This sage of a later era would also note, "Everyone who came here came to improve his economic or social condition or because he was run out of town where he lived."[7] No evidence excludes Harmon Runnels Sr. from either element of this depiction. Once in Mississippi, Runnels established his reputation as a hardshell Baptist and was said to have been even more aggressive in politics. He "had four sons to back him, as ready to fight as he was."[8]

Just before Christmas of 1814, Runnels convinced the territorial legislature to excise the northern half of Marion County and create a new Lawrence County. He laid out the town of Monticello and donated the lots for the public square. Monticello became the county seat. In the summer of 1817, Runnels and another spoke for Lawrence County at the constitutional convention. Along with Charles B. Green and future judge Edward Turner, Runnels served on a committee entrusted with the organization of the judicial system. Runnels argued that judges should serve for limited terms, the same as other constitutional officers. His effort failed by a vote of 24 to 20. As finally written, Mississippi's first constitution provided that judges "shall hold their offices during good behavior," although they could not continue in office after they "shall have arrived at the age of sixty-five years."[9] Runnels made a similar proposal that court clerks serve only a term of years, a proposal similarly defeated.[10] A touch of fortuity attended this one, as Runnels's namesake son would later take advantage of his father's defeat at the convention.

At and shortly after statehood, the Runnels sons and brothers held assorted public positions, beginning in Lawrence County. Hiram George Runnels was the first postmaster, then state auditor of public accounts, and later served a term as governor of Mississippi. In 1838, he served as president of the Mississippi Union

Bank and was caught up in the bank bond controversy that is the centerpiece of chapter 4 below. Hardin R. Runnels was the sheriff, and later a state legislator. A generation later, Hardin was in Texas and in politics, where he served as governor, 1857–1859, the only man ever to defeat Sam Houston at the ballot box. Howell W. Runnels, the lawyer in the family, served in the state senate. Harmon M. Runnels Jr. served as court clerk. Harmon Sr., the father, was "a kind of kingfish over them all."[11]

Runnels legends abound. Capt. Harmon Runnels Sr. was said to have fought with Daniel Morgan at Cowpens, South Carolina, in January of 1781. Future governor Hiram G. Runnels fought several duels. In the end, modest Harmon M. Jr., the clerk, may have left on his home state the most lasting mark of all. In 1823, his will to stay on as a court clerk, notwithstanding the legislature's act to abolish the office, gave Judge Powhatan Ellis and his colleagues the opportunity to light the torch of judicial review, for others to defend, practice, and nourish ever since. In the *Alexander* case 160 years later, resolving arguably the greatest constitutional crisis in the state's history, the Supreme Court of Mississippi cited *Runnels* as having given birth to the cardinal principle of the state's constitutional practice. Later in that same 1983 case, it was made clear that "if the system be found efficient and nevertheless in violation of the constitution, our duty is clear. See *Runnels v. State*, Walker (1 Miss.) 146 (1823)."

POWHATAN ELLIS

The future judicial author of *Runnels v. State* was born in 1790 and raised in Virginia. The Powhatan Indians occupied the lands in coastal Virginia where the English landed and settled as Jamestown. Pocahontas is said to have been the daughter of a Powhatan chief. A bit more—albeit less apocryphal—should be known of the man before proceeding to the 1823 constitutional moment when he found himself front and center. Ellis was educated at what is now Washington & Lee University and Dickinson College in Pennsylvania, and he studied law at William and Mary College. He moved to Natchez to practice law in 1816 but in short order moved easterly to Winchester, now a ghost town in Wayne County. Judge for the Fourth Mississippi District from 1818 until late September of 1825, including simultaneous service on the state supreme court, was the first of many offices Ellis held.

Ellis was an avid follower of Andrew Jackson. It is reported that he knew Jackson at an early age. In 1816, Ellis set out for the southwest part of the Mississippi Territory, carrying letters of introduction from Jackson, who had so recently won fame at New Orleans in January of 1815.

Beginning in late September 1825, Ellis served the four remaining months of a term in the US Senate but was defeated when he ran for a full term.[12] In

1827, Ellis was elected to the Senate and served until July of 1832, when Old Hickory appointed him as US District Judge for the District of Mississippi. President Jackson later named Ellis as chargé d'affaires of the United States to Mexico. In time, Ellis served as minister plenipotentiary to Mexico under President Martin Van Buren.

Powhatan Ellis's first public service is the matter at hand. In September of 1817, after the constitution had been approved, but pending Mississippi's admission to the Union, Gov. David Holmes appointed Ellis a judge. After statehood, the general assembly elected Ellis as judge for the Fourth District, defeating William J. Minton.

Originally, District Four was by far the largest of the four districts, reaching from Alabama west to the Pearl River, from the Gulf Coast to the northern boundaries of what are now Jefferson Davis, Covington, Jones, and Wayne Counties. Much later, a eulogist recalled Ellis telling of "his journeys, as he and the lawyers practicing before him traveled on horseback from court to court, through a region in its primitive state, but thinly settled, and partly occupied by Indians—many of whom became his warm friends."[13]

Ellis produced his fair share of the published opinions during his seven plus years of service on the state supreme court. Effective September 28, 1825, Gov. Walter Leake appointed Ellis to fill the vacancy created by the resignation of US senator David Holmes, the same David Holmes who as governor had brought Ellis to judicial service in the several months leading to December 10, 1817. Writing several generations after the fact, historian James D. Lynch reported that "Ellis was a pure and upright judge, and a popular and useful member of society; true to his friends and devoted to his official duties." Lynch added that Ellis's "decisions are illuminated by his integrity, and his conclusions are just and correct."[14] More or less.

Two early decisions reflect the flavor of the jurist who would formally bring constitutional judicial review to Mississippi. In *State v. Moor*, decided in 1823, Ellis correctly held that in a criminal case a hung jury did not give the accused a double jeopardy defense to being retried on the original indictment. En route, he wrote that the Double Jeopardy Clause "of the [federal] constitution was binding in the . . . state courts of the Union."[15] But at the time that was not so at all regarding the federal Bill of Rights. Not until the Due Process Clause of the Fourteenth Amendment came along after the War and—even then—not until 1969 did the US Supreme Court find "incorporation theory" embedded within the Fourteenth Amendment, thus binding the states to this clause of the federal Bill of Rights. Judge Ellis deserves credit for his 1823 insight "that the constitution of the United States is the paramount law, of the land, any law usage or custom of the several states to the contrary notwithstanding," albeit his context was wrong, his particular application more than 145 years premature.

Still, Ellis's general exhortation regarding the US Constitution did not surprise, as his constituents and fellow citizens—almost all transplants from some other and older state—were justly proud of Mississippi's statehood secured only a few years earlier. What is curious is that Ellis made no mention of the state double jeopardy clause, which should have controlled and, what is more, was susceptible of the same legal and practical meaning and application he saw in the federal Double Jeopardy Clause. In a more important case decided that same year, Ellis would show that he well knew his way around the new state constitution. Before turning to that case, a centerpiece of this chapter, note should be taken of another dimension of Ellis's pragmatism when approaching controversial, high-voltage legal issues.

In 1824, the court was faced with the legal question of whether Mississippi law would recognize a husband's ancient right of chastisement of his wife. Calvin Bradley had been charged with criminal assault and battery of his wife, Lydia. Calvin argued that he acted within his fundamental right, which barred the prosecution. Ellis wrote an opinion, rejecting the argument in practical effect. Like judges then and now, he did not want to appear an activist. The unknowing people would not approve. And so Ellis recognized that the husband may practice chastisement, and to that end he may "use a whip or rattan, no bigger than my thumb, in order to enforce the salutary restrains of domestic discipline."[16] The rule of thumb, some might say. Any purported chastisement less moderate might be prosecuted. Formally, Ellis had remained within the judicial role. Substantively, practicably and slyly, he had watered down an old fashioned rule the humanity of which was well in doubt among thoughtful persons at the time.

All in all, Ellis's judicial product has drawn scant if not faint praise. US District Judge Michael P. Mills cites the view of Ellis as "extremely indolent" to exclude him as the possible author of an unsigned opinion showing an enlightened (for the times) view of the rights and humanity of slaves. (See chapter 2 above.) Another commentator said Ellis's "opinions are dry and workmanlike, showing little flamboyance and heavy regard for the established law." Of course, this was a bit of an exaggeration as at the time there wasn't much established law. The remark no doubt referred to the English common law and similar judge-made law gleaned from early decisions of the more established state judiciaries, as that is all there was in Mississippi's first few years. Some might regard as delightful Ellis's strategy for showing respect for traditional law in the *Bradley* case. Others would regard it as unwarranted sexism, even for the times. In sentiment, Federalists and Republicans approved when "[h]e proclaimed the paramountcy of the US Constitution over the laws and customs of the states."[17] In his 1823 opinion in the *Moor* case, however, he gave the US Constitution more paramountcy than it then deserved.

THE SECOND RICHARD STOCKTON JR.

Mississippi's Richard Stockton Jr. (1791–1827) grew up in New Jersey. His grandfather signed the Declaration of Independence. Richard Stockton, the signer, was born October 1, 1730 and died February 28, 1781. His son, the first Richard Stockton Jr. (1764–1828), represented New Jersey in the US Senate and later served a term as a congressman from New Jersey. He was known as "the Old Duke" and was a close friend of the silver-tongued orator Daniel Webster. He suffered a stroke and died at the age of sixty-three, a year after the death of his ill-starred eldest son, who only a few years earlier had played a pivotal role in establishing the constitutional practice of judicial review amidst the political growing pains of the still fairly new state of Mississippi.

The second Richard Stockton Jr. was a complex man. Bipolar might be a likely diagnosis today. He was prone to conflict and controversy for most of his life. He pursued as many dubious activities as he did honorable paths. It is hard to know whether he had more enemies than friends, numbers that seem to have varied from time to time. The future Judge Stockton was educated at Princeton, A.B., 1810, where he graduated with "first honors." While still in his home state of New Jersey, Stockton was described as "charming in manner, an able lawyer, when he chose to work, but more given to enjoying the advantages of his position than to accepting its responsibilities."[18] Other bad habits included gambling and, in time, dueling, though the sometimes high-strung Stockton no doubt believed firmly that dueling was an honorable response to challenges to a man's character.

In his young adulthood, Richard Stockton Jr. and his father are known to have quarreled bitterly. The father was concerned for the son's gambling and other problematic personal propensities. In his late twenties, the second Richard Jr. abandoned his law practice and home in New Jersey—likely because of his father's disapproval of his wastrel habits—and moved to Mississippi. Before and during these times, many from New Jersey moved to the Natchez area. Stockton appears not to have been among those, at least not at first. In January of 1821 he bought a small residential property on Farmer Street in downtown Port Gibson,[19] and by 1822 he had acquired a couple of slaves. Stockton became a circuit-riding lawyer based in Claiborne County. He appeared in a case tried in Warren County, the appeal of which was decided in December 1821. In time, he learned, as he admitted in a letter to his father, that "nobody ever paid a circuit rider; only in Natchez was it possible to build up a lucrative practice." In early December of 1826, by then Attorney General Stockton sold his Farmer Street property, delivering a deed that identified him as "Richard Stockton of Natchez."

Several generations after the fact, James D. Lynch reported in *Bench and Bar* that "Judge Stockton was an eminent lawyer and a man of ability. He was remarkably modest and unassuming in his manners." Stockton had been a colonel on the staff of Governor Walter Leake, who appointed him judge for the First

District in August 1822, succeeding Judge Joshua G. Clarke, who had resigned to become the state's first chancellor. On December 13, 1822, Judge Stockton was one of thirty-eight members attending the semi-annual meeting of the Mississippi Bar Association held at Mr. Parker's Tavern in Natchez. In the following year, the general assembly elected Stockton to fill the judicial seat Clarke had vacated.

By 1823, he may have reconciled with "the Old Duke," his father back in New Jersey. According to one account, he wrote to his father and promised, "The name I bear shall never again be tarnished in my person." His report that he was "on circuit" no doubt referred to his holding court in trial-level proceedings in District One, Warren, Claiborne, Jefferson, and by then Hinds Counties. Judge Stockton told his father that he had "the friendship of some of the best gentlemen in the state [of Mississippi]." One may need to read between the lines in a later report to his father "[t]hat the lawyers in that part of the country were so ignorant . . . that his attainments were 'superior' to theirs." [20] Such views from a "first honors" Princeton graduate—little in what is known suggests Stockton could or would have kept such a distinction to himself—were likely received by the lawyers in the four-county First District about as warmly as similar views from an Ivy League graduate today would be received, even though his grandfather had led the New Jersey delegation that supported and signed the Declaration of Independence.

THE *RUNNELS* CASE PLAYS OUT

The general assembly, at times called "the legislature," was empowered to establish a court of probate in each county. The constitution of 1817 set out a number of powers that a probate court could be given, such as "the granting of letters testamentary, and of administration, or orphan's business, for county police, and for the trial of slaves." In due course, the general assembly acted on this authority. An 1821 enactment provided that "in the manner directed by the constitution a suitable person [shall] be appointed Register [or clerk] of the Orphans [and Probate] court, in each county within this State." [21]

Harmon M. Runnels Jr. was appointed register of the Court of Probate for Lawrence County, shortly after the creation of that office. The appointment was made by Judge—and future governor—Charles Lynch, a farmer, not a lawyer, and yet judge of probate of that county. A few years earlier, the Mississippi Constitution had been formally enacted and provided that, in relevant part, "[e]ach court shall appoint its own clerk, who shall hold his office during good behaviour, but shall be removable therefrom for neglect of duty, or misdemeanor in office, by the supreme court, which court shall determine both the law and fact." [22] In 1822, Runnels was "regularly inducted into office, under all of the requirements of the act of 1821."

On June 30, 1822, the general assembly modified its then only seven months' old action. The probate court remained, but a new law declared and enacted that "[t]he Office of Register [Clerk] of the Orphans' [and Probate] Court shall be, and the same is hereby abolished." The new bill provided that the judge of the probate court would take over the chores of clerk. The probate judge himself would thenceforth "enjoy all the rights, privileges and emoluments, and discharge all the duties which were of right appertaining to, and required of the clerk."[23] No doubt the legislative justification for this action was that experience was making clear that there wasn't enough to be done to justify two men on the taxpayers' payroll.

In time, the circuit court ordered Clerk Runnels to turn over to Judge Lynch, the probate judge, all papers, books, and records that as clerk he held. Without surprise, Harmon M. Jr. had within him a bit of his father's bullheadedness. He refused and filed suit. His case reached the Supreme Court in its December term of 1823. At the time, the court was composed of Judges John P. Hampton, Louis Winston, Powhatan Ellis, and Richard Stockton Jr. Runnels pointed to the constitution and said it limited the circumstances under which the State might dispense with his services as clerk.

There seems to be no doubt but that Runnels had taken his office—call it register or clerk—and along with it the protections set out in Article 5, Section 11, of the constitution of 1817. He was to "hold his office during good behaviour." His service was subject to no term of years. He could be ousted only "for neglect of duty, or misdemeanor in office." No one suggested that Clerk Runnels had neglected the duties of his office or that he had committed a misdemeanor in office. Nor does there appear a charge that—while clerk—Runnels's behavior was anything but exemplary.

THE A PRIORI QUESTION

This led to the a priori question in American constitutional practice. Does a court of otherwise competent jurisdiction have the authority—and, perhaps, the duty—to declare unenforceable an act of the legislature that does not square with the constitution of that jurisdiction? In 1803, John Marshall had faced that question at the federal level in *Marbury v. Madison* and had answered it in the affirmative. Each state was within its prerogative to approach the intrastate dimensions of the point as it pleased, either through an explicit clause in its constitution or through an adjudication of the highest court of the state. The point had drawn interest and discussion at the constitutional convention in August of 1817. Several proposals failed. The promulgated constitution that became effective December 10, 1817, was silent on the subject.

Runnels presented what today is known as an "as applied" challenge. No one was questioning the legislative prerogative of passing a law abolishing the office of probate clerk and conferring those clerk duties on the probate judge himself. Runnels, however, was in office. The constitution spoke to the terms of his service and possible discharge. The question was whether Runnels could be ousted from the office he held other than by the constitutional criteria. The Supreme Court answered, "No." To so hold, and to establish that the general assembly had no power to oust a clerk except as provided in Article 5, §11, the Supreme Court had to find in the constitution the authority—"the judicial power"—to review the enforceability of acts of the general assembly, on their face or as applied in particular discrete circumstances.

Judge Ellis called the matter before the court "this momentous question"— not so much whether Clerk Runnels may be sent home, but whether he may be so sent for reasons other than those found in Article 5, § 11. And whether under the constitution the Supreme Court of Mississippi had a say in the matter. On the latter view, Judge Ellis and the Supreme Court could "not feel insensible either as it regards the 'magnitude of the case,' or the delicacy of our situation." Regarding the constitutionality of a legislative act, Ellis said he had "on occasions more than one . . . expressed the diffidence and reluctance, and consequently 'the caution and circumspection,' with which I approach such investigations. I have repeatedly said it was unwise and inexpedient to declare law unconstitutional, where there is any doubt, and when they might be reconciled to the spirit, if not the letter of the constitution." No specifics are provided for these "occasions more than one," nor is it known when Ellis "repeatedly said" such things. No such expressions are found in the first 145 prior pages of Walker's Reports of Supreme Court decisions, or in any other record that has been found after diligent search and inquiry.

Caution and circumspection would be appropriate were the authority for judicial review conferred expressly in the constitution. These are appropriate the more so, given that judicial review was and remains at best an implied prerogative. Ellis suggests that the constitutional text is clear enough, adding "[b]ut, the people of this state have formed a paramount rule of action for themselves, and they have declared"[24] the now familiar tripartite separation of legislative, executive, and judicial powers. Still, not only does Ellis never mention *Marbury v. Madison*, he "provides no argument comparable to that of [John] Marshall's . . . to support the imperative of judicial scrutiny of legislative acts."[25]

To be sure, the Supreme Court of Mississippi had been empowered to act in each case with a court of only two judges. *Hackler's Heirs v. Cabel*[26] seems to have been such a case, given that the Opinion of the Court was delivered by Judge Ellis, Fourth District, and Judge John P. Hampton, Third District. Ellis's home in Wayne County was on the other side of the state from Stockton's home in Claiborne County. Travel was difficult in those days. Still, there were times when all judges participated in cases of arguably much less significance than *Runnels* or *Cochrane & Murdock v. Kitchens*. At the December Term, 1822, the Supreme Court had decided *Lee, Adm'r v. Montgomery*[27] with an opinion authored by Judge Ellis, concluding with a notation—"Judges HAMPTON, WINSTON and STOCKTON concurred." There is no reason to doubt that a full court had considered both *Runnels* and *Cochrane & Murdock*, and that no judge had disagreed with either judgment of the court.

A VERBAL NUGGET

Regarding the manner in which Clerk Runnels was being discharged as probate clerk, Ellis had this to say: "If the Legislature in the exercise of an unlimited discretionary power, can overleap the barriers of the constitution, . . . then, . . . we shall, in the language of a distinguished statesman, 'be called upon to curse our revolution as a great fountain of discord, violence and injustice.'"[28] Such verbal exuberance was common in these early years. The quotation may tell us a bit about Ellis and the way he interacted with his fellow judges, beyond the fact that he liked (and distorted) the words of the "distinguished statesman." Particularly, this affords insights into Ellis's relationship with his judicial colleague Richard Stockton Jr.

The "language of a distinguished statesman" is found near the end of an unofficial report of the argument made only a few years earlier before the US Supreme Court in the *Dartmouth College* case. The full text reads,[29]

> Can this court, can this country hear such pretensions without shuddering? Shall we be called upon to curse our revolution as a great fountain of discord, violence and injustice; instead of looking to it with reverence and gratitude; as the means of establishing an immense empire, in which the freedom and rights of man shall be understood and maintained; the government of the law only acknowledged and the eternal principles of justice secured to all.

These words had been uttered by Joseph Hopkinson, who was associated with Daniel Webster as counsel for the Trustees of Dartmouth College before the US Supreme Court. Hopkinson had served as a member of the US House of Representatives from Pennsylvania's First District from March 4, 1815, through March 3, 1819. Most of Hopkinson's argument in reply appears verbatim in the official report of the case, *Trustees of Dartmouth College v. Woodward*, and in an unofficial report published by Dartmouth College. Curiously, two long paragraphs—concluding Hopkinson's argument in reply—are omitted from all other reproductions of his argument. These begin in the middle of the unofficial Dartmouth College version, with "Some observations have been made upon our clients" and continuing for two long paragraphs ending three pages later.

Judge Powhatan Ellis picked the words he liked and presented them with a slant. What is of interest is how Ellis happened upon "the language of a distinguished statesman" in the first place. The facts and circumstances we know reasonably suggest several possibilities. Counsel for Harmon M. Runnels Jr. may have supplied them, though there is no known record of the name or argument of counsel. Copies of the argument and *Dartmouth College* decision may have made their way to Wayne County (or was it Lawrence County or Natchez?) in the four years before Ellis undertook to write his *Runnels* opinion. That makes a certain amount of practical sense. Publishing the arguments of counsel was common at the time and for years thereafter, but this does not explain how Ellis gained access to the two paragraphs missing from all official versions of the reply argument.

There are two more likely, albeit related, hypotheses. Each is a function of circumstantial evidence. Under each, Ellis learned of the words he quoted from his colleague Richard Stockton Jr. We know that Daniel Webster[30] was a friend of Judge Stockton's father. Webster surely had access to Dartmouth's unofficial version of the arguments, including those last two paragraphs. He may well have thought this version of Joseph Hopkinson's reply argument the correct one. Webster could have shared this version of the case he thought so important with the Old Duke, who passed it on to his son, newly a judge in Mississippi. The second Richard Stockton Jr., becoming a judge in his adopted state many miles from New Jersey, may well have enhanced the reconciliation of father and son, putting their troubled past further in the past.

There is another reasonable hypothesis. Joseph Hopkinson was the son of Francis Hopkinson, who, like his fellow New Jersey delegate Richard Stockton Sr. had signed the Declaration of Independence. By the calendar, forty-five years had elapsed since Francis Hopkinson and Judge Stockton's grandfather served together in 1776 in the New Jersey delegation to the Continental Congress. Their descendants likely knew and respected each other, although the "distinguished statesman" was some twenty years older than Judge Stockton. Besides, Joseph Hopkinson served with Luther Martin as counsel for Justice Samuel Chase, securing an acquittal in the latter's impeachment trial before the US Senate in 1804 and 1805. In late February of 1819, Hopkinson argued against Daniel Webster in the case, now known as *McCulloch v. Maryland*. It is easy enough to see Richard Stockton Jr. having been taken with the distinguished elder statesman of the bar, having followed the latter's career through the Dartmouth College version of the argument. Imbued with his family's prestige and being an almost certain name dropper, Judge Stockton likely told his Mississippi judicial colleague Judge Powhatan Ellis of Hopkinson's standing and shared with Judge Ellis a copy of Hopkinson's argument.

At the end of the day at the December term, 1823, Runnels won his case. In *Runnels*, the Supreme Court had not only provided a constitutional articulation of the doctrine of judicial review. The court had also practiced judicial review by holding that—as applied to Harmon M. Runnels Jr.—insofar as it abolished the office of probate clerk, legislative action was constitutionally infirm and thus unenforceable.

The precise manner of Ellis's access to "the language of a distinguished statesman" may never be known with certainty. What is known is the practical and fraternal cooperation between Richard Stockton Jr., from a River county to the west, and Powhatan Ellis, from a hard-to-get-to county along the Alabama state line. Each was also a strong proponent of judicial review, a fact surely known to the other at the time of the *Runnels* decision at the December 1823 term. A little over a year later, Judge Stockton had the occasion to present and defend his view rather publicly, to address a problem he had played a role in creating, a story to which we turn below.

COCHRANE & MURDOCK V. BENJAMIN KITCHENS, THE PARTIES

Robert and George Cochrane[31] had come from Ireland and settled in the Natchez area during the Spanish era, before the turn of the new century. Soon they established a substantial business that involved extensions of credit. John Murdock,[32] a native of Ireland and related to the Cochranes, had amassed a large fortune. In 1804, Murdock came to visit the Cochranes in Natchez, and they established a partnership. Shortly thereafter, George Cochrane died. On September 14, 1807, Robert Cochrane and Murdock published an offer "TO RENT THAT large and commodious Dwelling HOUSE (lately repaired) in South Second Street, formerly occupied by George Cochran, deceased."[33] In 1809, Murdock went back to Ireland to acquire a wife and wind up his affairs there, before returning to Mississippi for good. The Cochranes and Murdock were men of considerable standing during the territorial period leading up to Mississippi's statehood in December of 1817. Family lore has it that the Murdocks referred to Robert as "Uncle Cochrane." In addition to running other businesses, they were lending money in the days before banks.

They also had public squabbles with those with whom they did business. For example, in 1819, Robert Cochrane of Bayou-Pierre warned the public against paying any money due him or in which he may be interested to one Mr. John Lombard, whom Cochrane had dismissed as his agent due to "difficulties between them." Lombard replied publicly and in kind, stating that he had rendered important services from October 1815 to February 1819, for which Cochrane refused to compensate him in accordance with the contract.

In 1808, Cochrane and Murdock had dissolved their partnership.[34] Yet in time, they were again in business together and were engaged in a substantial real estate brokerage and lending business, based in Claiborne County. In a published notice dated September 16, 1820, they offered for sale or rent the 1,100 acre La Cache Plantation, with 120 acres under cultivation, plus thirteen slaves. "Application to be made to the subscribers, who are the owners, or at their store in Port Gibson. ROBERT COCHRAN, JOHN MURDOCK."[35]

Meet Benjamin Kitchens (1781–1855), born in Georgia. While still a teenager, he married a woman of similar age. By 1800, Kitchens and his wife had moved to the Mississippi Territory. At some point prior to 1820, the family moved to Claiborne County. Kitchens and his wife had five children.[36] He was never a man of financial substance.

COCHRANE & MURDOCK VS. KITCHENS, THE CASE

During his lean years Benjamin Kitchens borrowed money from Cochrane & Murdock. His demand promissory note read as follows:

> One day after date, I promise to pay to Cochrane & Murdock, or order, eighty one dollars and forty seven cents, for value received, with interest from 1st January, 1821.
> (Signed) BENJAMIN KITCHENS
> Test, William Young.

The rate of interest is not given. When Cochrane & Murdock presented the note and demanded payment, Kitchens could not comply. At that point, Cochrane & Murdock brought suit in the Circuit Court of Claiborne County to enforce the note and collect what Kitchens owed them. On April 4, 1822, the trial court entered judgment on the note in favor of Cochrane & Murdock and against Kitchens. The amount of the judgment is not known, but presumably it included unpaid principal with interest accruing daily, plus court costs.

Joseph L. Briggs (1780–1830) had been sheriff of Claiborne County prior to statehood. He conducted sheriff's sales to satisfy court-issued writs of execution on July 15, 1814, and on August 24, 1814. He made a personal conveyance of real property on May 2, 1815. Public records show that in August 1813, Daniel Burnett brought charges against Sheriff Briggs, alleging negligence in office and favoritism toward friends. Territorial Governor David Holmes made an extensive investigation and exonerated the sheriff. In 1821, Claiborne County voters elected Briggs for a two-year term as sheriff, and on August 7, 1823, reelected him for a like term. He was a man to be dealt with in Claiborne County. In 1820, Briggs owned twenty-one slaves,[37] suggesting he was a man of some wealth. In 1821, the general assembly created the first fire company in Port Gibson, with Joseph Briggs as a charter member. To the point, he knew how to conduct a sheriff's sale under a court-issued writ when a judgment debtor for whatever reason did not pay.

In due course, on application of Cochrane & Murdock, the circuit court issued a writ of execution to enforce the judgment they had secured. Sheriff Briggs was required to report back to the court at its October term of 1822. The sheriff reported that he had taken a bond from Kitchens, with Richard Armstrong and Bates Dorsey as sureties. By operation of law, this bond—not having been honored—was converted into a judgment against Kitchens, Armstrong, and Dorsey. By the time the calendar showed the turn of the new year 1824, however, Cochrane & Murdock still had received no money on the judgment debt, either from Benjamin Kitchens, his sureties, or a sheriff's sale of the judgment debtor's assets.

THE DEBTORS' RELIEF ACT

On January 23, 1824, "An Act, further to extend relief to Debtors," became law in Mississippi.[38] The new law was a comprehensive effort to ameliorate the hardships of the traditional view that debtors should be imprisoned until they paid their debts. Enacting such a law was within the legislative power vested in the general assembly. It implemented and gave specificity to debtors' rights declared secure in the constitution. The tenor of the new law is apparent in its text. It prohibited the imprisonment of women—white women, that is—for debt: "[N]or shall any free white woman, be in any manner imprisoned, or detained in prison, for debt, within this state, any law, usage, or custom, to the contrary notwithstanding." As for men, "the prison bounds of each County within this State, shall be extended to the entire limits thereof." Such men "shall hereafter only be bound to give bond and security, to keep within the limits of the County within which he may reside, at the time of his imprisonment."

Governor Walter Leake had vetoed the bill when it was originally passed on grounds it impaired the obligations of contracts existing at the time. The veto was then overridden by the requisite two-thirds vote in each house of the general assembly.

Section 7 of the new law set out the process the sheriff should follow when a judgment debtor's unliquidated "lands and tenements, or any other property" had to be seized in order to satisfy his debts. First was an appraisal process. "[T]hree respectable disinterested freeholders of his county" were to view the property and certify "the fair value thereof in ready money." If the sheriff's public sale yielded a bid equal to or in excess of the fair value so appraised, fine, well and good. But, if the property could not be sold at least "for two thirds of the said valuation," the new law authorized the sheriff to "sell the same, to the highest bidder on a credit of twelve months, taking bond with good and sufficient security."[39] In other words, the judgment creditor would hold a secured debt payable in one year.

Back to *Cochrane & Murdock*. On February 11, 1824, a month after the new Debtors' Relief Act took effect, a new writ of execution had issued upon the old judgment held by Cochrane & Murdock. This time Sheriff Briggs reported that he had seized the following property: three yoke of oxen, one wagon, and one mare and colt—the only assets Kitchens had. When no bidder made a cash offer to purchase these assets for two-thirds of their appraised value, the sheriff then sold the property on one year's credit, three yoke of oxen to George Lake for $100, one wagon to Joshua Rundell for $39.50, and one mare and colt to Thomas M. Cogan for $22.

COCHRANE & MURDOCK START A RUCKUS

Cochrane & Murdock were not pleased with this turn of events. The firm had been trying to collect the sums Kitchens owed before and since April 4, 1822, the date of the original civil judgment entered by the Circuit Court of Claiborne County. The firm was most unhappy that in all likelihood it remained a year away from receiving any money. Cochrane & Murdock complained as well of the new sureties on its still uncollected judgment debt. In legalese, the firm argued that this was enough of a change that it impaired enforceable obligations of the Cochrane & Murdock contract with Kitchens.

At its June Term, 1824—the next term after the court decided *Runnels v. State*—at the instance of Cochrane & Murdock, the Supreme Court again undertook judicial review of recent legislation. Now sitting on the court was Judge Richard Stockton Jr., a Claiborne County appointee of the same Governor Leake who had vetoed the Debtors' Relief Act. Cochrane & Murdock filed a post-judgment motion, asking the court to fine the sheriff for making an improper sale.[40] As the case had been brought in Claiborne County, it fell to Judge Stockton to handle the matter. But Stockton did not call Cochrane & Murdock's motion for hearing. Rather, he invoked a sensible and then accepted procedure. He asked the Supreme Court to consider and answer the questions of law needed to decide whether Cochrane & Murdock's motion had merit. This move allowed Stockton to remain eligible to participate as the fourth judge of the Supreme Court. No decision by him was under consideration. The matter was not considered a "cause wherein he is directly or indirectly interested."[41]

With Stockton participating, the Supreme Court held that the act was indeed unconstitutional and unenforceable because it impaired the obligations of a contract, contrary to both the US Constitution and the Mississippi Constitution.[42] The court then fined the sheriff one hundred dollars,[43] because he had made a "false and untrue return" on the writ of execution that the circuit court had issued, ordering him to seize and sell Kitchens's property to satisfy the judgment debt. In practical effect, the Supreme Court told Sheriff Briggs he should have foreseen that the secured credit sale process in "the act further to extend relief of debtors" was unenforceable.

THE FIRESTORM BREAKS

Some legislators were outraged. They had overridden Governor Leake's veto of "the act further to extend relief of debtors." Now Stockton, the governor's appointee, appeared to be overriding the general assembly, and on the same grounds the governor had relied on, unpersuasively. The fine imposed on a veteran sheriff was certain to be received as a dagger penetrating common sense. The then-recent death of Sheriff Briggs's wife may have inclined many toward his side of the issue. Ann Briggs died April 8, 1823. This part of the court's ruling called for a written and public explanation, if nothing else did. The legislative reaction in substantial part may well have been that the Supreme Court published no written opinion so that the public might see the grounds for the court's actions. At the time, most decisions of the Supreme Court were delivered orally. On appeal, only the judgment of the court had to be reduced to writing and certified to the clerk of the court in which the case had originated.[44]

The reports reflect that, though not required to do so, at times some of the judges wrote opinions explaining their decisions. During the Supreme Court's June term, 1824, Judge Hampton authored one short opinion. Judge Powhatan Ellis had released four written opinions. No opinions had been written by Judges Winston or Stockton. At the December term, 1824, Hampton wrote six opinions, three of which recite that Ellis concurred. Judge Ellis wrote eight opinions, three of which recite that Hampton concurred. Newly appointed Judge Edward Turner is shown concurring in two of Hampton's opinions, and dissenting as to one.

Stockton is mentioned but twice in the known reports from the December term, 1824. He dissented without opinion from one of Hampton's decisions, regarding a Spanish land grant and the equitable law of trusts. In another, Ellis wrote an opinion reversing a judgment entered by Stockton at the trial-court level. "We think our brother Stockton . . . was mistaken."[45]

The *Runnels* decision affected only the handful of persons who may have been in office when the general assembly abolished the office of probate clerk. *Cochrane & Murdock* portended a broader effect. The court vitiated a practical course for the likely common circumstance where a debtor's assets did not bring their so-called appraised value at sheriff's sale, at least for all contracts made before the law was passed.

On Monday, January 3, 1825, the general assembly convened in the new capital city of Jackson. Rep. William Haile (1800–1837) was the first to act. Haile was a prominent lawyer in Wilkinson County. He would later become an at-large congressman from Mississippi from July 10, 1826, until September 12, 1828. He became a staunch supporter of Andrew Jackson, but was defeated for reelection to Congress. Haile "was actively engaged in politics at the time of his death at the age of thirty-seven. Many people felt at the time that, had he lived, he would have been a popular candidate for governor of Mississippi."[46]

Right away, Haile moved that "the Judges of the Supreme Court" be requested to forward to the house of representatives "immediately" a copy of their ruling in the *Cochrane & Murdock* case, together with "a statement of the facts in relation to a cause recently decided in the Supreme Court, wherein the operation and constitutionality of said law [for the further relief of debtors] came into question." Rep. Christopher H. Williams of Monroe County went further. He offered a resolution that the judges be required to show cause why they "should not be removed from office." Both motions were tabled. A few days later, however, the house appointed a committee to investigate the matter. That committee in turn summoned Stockton, as judge of the First District and of the Supreme Court, to appear before it. The case had originated in Claiborne County within the First District, where Stockton served.

JUDGE STOCKTON'S DEFT RESPONSE

Judge Stockton honored the house committee's summons. He sought to reframe the question. He suggested to the committee that its proper question should be "whether the judges, in rendering their opinion, had been governed by impure motives, or had decided according to established law."[47]

Stockton then explained in writing why the Supreme Court found that the Debtors' Relief Act was unconstitutional. He meticulously presented the facts of the case and the proceedings in the circuit court. Judge Stockton cited the texts of the contracts clauses of the federal and state constitutions. He then told the committee about cases decided by the US Supreme Court and the Court of Appeals of Kentucky, the only two cases Stockton was able to identify from "my memory, or the limited libraries in this town [Jackson] has [*sic*] enabled me to obtain." In other words, Stockton provided the house committee with the written opinion that the state supreme court should have issued in the first place. All in all, he was acting consistent with the reputation he had back in New Jersey, that he "was charming, and able ... when he chose to work."

The committee pressed Judge Stockton on two points. First was the fine assessed against the sheriff. What was the legal basis for that action? Second,

Was it the opinion of the Supreme Court that the Court had the power and right to declare an act of the Legislature unconstitutional—if so, from whence does the Court derive its power—was it expressly delegated or implied, or was it from common usage?

Addressing the committee chairman in response, Judge Stockton began by thanking the committee "for the very handsome and delicate manner with which they have treated me throughout the whole of this investigations." He continued throughout the hearing to show courtesy, deference and respect for the house committee and the course upon which it had embarked, mistaken though he thought it was.

Judge Stockton gave assurances to the committee that "[t]he motion to fine the sheriff was in strict conformity to the statutes, and the committee have, already, the opinion of the court in writing." On the second question, he equivocated: "The question is an abstract one, and was not agitated; unless the Committee consider the principle to be embraced in the opinion of Cochrane & Murdock against Kitchens and others, already before them, all of which is most respectfully submitted."[48] He added, "The opinion of the Supreme Court, which is in possession of the committee, was that ... [the statute] was unconstitutional as to all contracts made previous to the passage of the law." Though this latter question had not formally be placed before the court, he continued, and although "he was the junior member of the bench, he would give [his opinion] with great cheerfulness, and assure them that the other members of the bench joined him in [this] opinion."[49]

THE HOUSE COMMITTEE TAKES ITS STAND

Rep. Joseph Johnson (1776–1848) of Wilkinson County served as chairman of this house committee. Historians of the era report that Johnson possessed a keen intellect and great magnetism. His father, Isaac Johnson (1744–1832), who fought in the Revolutionary War, moved the family to Wilkinson County in 1802. He had acquired large tracts of land in the area through Spanish land grants. Joseph Johnson "quickly established himself in the cultural and political affairs of the Mississippi Territory." He was the first president of the West Feliciana Railroad. Johnson became a lawyer of some standing. In 1811, Joseph Emory Davis, older brother of Jefferson Davis, had read law in Johnson's law office. Johnson had been a delegate to the constitutional convention in the summer of 1817. In time, his brother Henry became the fifth governor of Louisiana and represented the state for three terms in the US Senate and three terms in the US House of Representatives. Still younger brother, William Johnson (1792–1854), became active in local politics. He practiced law for many years, then gave full attention to his plantations.

Preliminarily, Chairman Johnson praised Stockton for his "frank and candid manner" and for providing the Committee with "what information was in his power." Johnson's committee then reported to the full house of representatives, criticizing the Supreme Court on both points. Substantively, the committee found no fault with Sheriff Briggs for the way he handled the sale of Kitchens's property.

> As respects the fine imposed upon the Sheriff, the committee do not hesitate to say it was unjust and illegal—for they cannot believe that any subordinate officer ought to be punished for executing any process which emanates from any competent authority—*it is his duty to execute it, and not to judge of its legality.*[50]

In separation-of-powers parlance, the sheriff was exercising executive powers when he was called upon to conduct a sheriff's sale. It was not his place to consider whether the writ—the court order he was directed to carry out— was consistent with the law and had been procedurally properly issued. The Supreme Court was out of line ordering that the sheriff be fined for discharging the facially proper order to sell Kitchens's property in accordance with the Debtors' Relief Act.

On the second and more serious question, the house committee rejected the constitutional principle of judicial review.

> The committee knows of no power, either delegated or implied from the constitution, that authorizes the Supreme Court to make such a declaration of the unconstitutionality of any Law to suspend its operations; but must believe such power assumed and maintained on the grounds of Judiciary precedents alone.[51]

The committee's position on this point, of course, was arguable. A state legislative committee circa 1825 could hardly be faulted for its failure to understand the legal status and power of "judiciary precedents alone." Nor could the committee be blamed for not understanding the legitimacy of the power of judicial review Chief Justice Marshall had found in *Marbury v. Madison*. It is curious, however, that no mention is made of the *Runnels* decision, which had been rendered a little over a year earlier,[52] especially since Judge Ellis (who wrote the *Runnels* opinion) was still on the high court at the time of *Cochrane & Murdock*.

Of interest is the apparent failure of the house committee to consider the two-step nature of the second question. Judge Stockton's legal analysis of the particular question presented in *Cochrane & Murdock* may have been faulty, even if the constitutional practice of judicial review should be accepted. But the committee chose not to match wits with Judge Stockton on the point of law, for whatever reason. In point of fact, the committee told the full House that "they could not, for a moment, entertain an idea that the Supreme Court were

influenced in their decisions by any impure motive." To this extent, the committee accepted Stockton's rephrasing of the question. It then urged the house

> to determine the question [of the legitimacy of the practice of judicial review]
> with such firmness as should forever secure the rights and interests of the com-
> munity, and, at the same time, with that justice, liberality, and respect which is due
> to those to whom was committed the administration of the laws.[53]

These proceedings before the house committee and its report aid understanding of what happened next. Chairman Johnson suggested amending the
report so that it took issue only with the fine imposed on the sheriff. Instead
of rejecting the practice of judicial review, Johnson proposed that the house
merely reaffirm the principle of separation of powers. The house voted to table
both the committee report and Johnson's proposed amendment. In accordance
with customary practice, it also ordered the printing of a hundred copies of
each for the use of members of the house.

LEVEL HEADS EMERGE

On January 10, 1825, without stating his reasons, Judge Stockton tendered to
the general assembly his resignation as judge of the First Judicial District.[54]
This further defused any hostilities within the house that may have been latent
beneath the surface courtesies that had been exchanged by all parties. Stockton's
resignation seemed to confirm that he was a man of principle with proper
respect and humility in the face of his coequal department of state government.
After all, his grandfather had signed the Declaration of Independence, legislative
reverence for which is formally manifest in the opening clause of the *House
Journal*—the house convened in Jackson on Monday, January 3, 1825, "in the
forty-ninth year of the Independence of the United States of North America."
Nationalistic fervor had been growing in Mississippi, formalized by a house
resolution submitted on January 8, 1825, and leading to April 18 and 19, 1825,
when the Marquis de Lafayette's visited Natchez "as a part of his triumphant
tour of an appreciative America." In short order thereafter, the same general
assembly elected Stockton as attorney general of Mississippi.

Still, political exigencies suggested that some legislative action was needed.
Cochrane & Murdock had been the most substantial matter considered in
January of 1825, at least in the house of representatives. On February 4, 1825, the
general assembly passed "an act relative to the Supreme Court, and to prescribe
the duties of the Judges therein." Section 1 required that the court appoint one
of its members "to deliver the opinion of the supreme court in writing, upon
any suit, controversy, matter or thing, whatsoever, which may be brought in

or presented for adjudication in said court." No quarrel could be had with this one. The court should have been doing this anyway. It is likely that the *Cochrane & Murdock* controversy may have been avoided, or at least ameliorated, if the court's reasoning had been more quickly reduced to writing and made public, as Judge Ellis had done in the *Runnels* case.

Section 2 of the Act of February 4, 1825 is more focused.

> The judges of this state, when in the supreme or circuit courts, where they shall make any decision affecting the constitutionality of any law passed by the legislature, shall make out a full report of the case and decision thereon, and sign the same, and within twenty days thereafter, transmit a copy thereof, to the governor of this state, who shall immediately have the same published in some public newspaper, printed within the state for the information of the citizens thereof.[55]

Again, there could have been no quarrel with Section 2. In 1825, as today, public dissemination of the court's ruling and the reasoning said to support it could only have a salutary effect in two ways. First, the court would likely be more disciplined and discreet in its constitutional rulings if it knew those rulings in their entirety would be published and available for interested and affected officials and persons, other judges, lawyers, and the public at large. Conversely, these same persons could be expected to become better-informed officials and citizens, to the extent that they partook of the chance to read and study the rulings of the court.

Yet there was a larger point in Section 2 of the act of February 4, 1825. The constitutional practice of judicial review had survived. Assurance of its proper judicial stewardship was left to extralegal human and public forces.

Governor Walter Leake had become ill in 1824. He died in office on November 17, 1825, in the town now known as Clinton, Mississippi.

A TRAGIC AFTERMATH

Whatever honeymoon Richard Stockton enjoyed as attorney general did not last long. For one thing, Stockton left Port Gibson and moved to Natchez. No longer a judge, and the office of attorney general not then being a full-time job, Stockton immediately offered his services as a privately practicing lawyer.[56] In May of 1826, Stockton announced his candidacy for an at-large seat as US representative in the Twentieth Congress.[57] He received only 447 votes, some 5.5 percent of all votes case, finishing fifth and last in an election won by William Haile, Stockton's state legislative adversary of eighteen months earlier.[58]

Less than two years after he assumed the office of attorney general, Stockton was subjected to a legislative investigation for allegedly having challenged others to duels. A house resolution filed January 10, 1827, charged that in recent months Stockton had "challenged Andrew Turnbull, in Marion County, and Alison Ross, in Claiborne County, to duels. Further, he had carried a challenge from John H. Esty to Alison Ross." He survived legislature censure, the house sensibly having decided that the matter was for the courts, not the general assembly.[59]

There are clouds surrounding the last days of Richard Stockton Jr., continuing evidence that he was indeed his own worst enemy. We know that on December 8, 1826, Stockton sold his home in Port Gibson to Peter Sloan of New Orleans for $500. The deed was executed in Claiborne County, but the grantor is identified as "Richard Stockton, Jr., of Natchez," confirming that prior thereto Stockton had moved to Natchez. That he took a one-third loss on the property he had purchased almost six years earlier suggests that Stockton's financial circumstances may have been problematic.[60] We know nothing of Peter Sloan, but Stockton's sale suggests business dealings in New Orleans. We know that Stockton was in New Orleans in early February of 1827. The reason we know that with certainty is that then and there—on February 6, 1827—Richard Stockton Jr. died in a duel.[61]

Apparently, the fateful duel stemmed from a quarrel with John P. Parson while the two were vacationing at Columbia Springs, a then-popular resort in Marion County, Mississippi, sometimes known as Stovall's Springs for its politically well-connected proprietor, Charles Stovall. Family archives hold a report that Stockton "had been 'grossly in the wrong' in the quarrel." The basic facts are undisputed. Parson shot and killed Stockton, then thirty-six years of age. Purposely, Stockton did not fire at Parson. A letter found in his pocket explained why. One version of the story quotes Stockton as admitting his "'own conduct had been rash and wrong from the beginning,' and it was his intention upon surviving the first fire to acknowledge his error and make amends with Payson [sic]."[62] Others report that Stockton's note simply said he was not married.[63]

Three evenings later, numerous and respectable men of Natchez, legal dignitaries and others, friend and foe alike, assembled at the Mississippi Hotel in Natchez, to show "in a suitable manner their respect" for the memory of Richard Stockton, Jun., Esq. It was fitting that Judge Powhatan Ellis, lead player in act 1 of the advent of judicial review in Mississippi, should preside over an occasion memorializing his fallen colleague, who had played such a crucial part in act 2. Ellis no doubt recalled Stockton's role and support in the *Runnels* case, and his own support for Stockton in *Cochrane & Murdock v. Kitchens*. Ellis called on prominent Natchez lawyer William B. Griffith for remarks. Griffith began,

> He fell the victim of a mistaken though a chivalric sense of honor. He conceived
> himself bound to afford an opportunity of satisfaction to one whom he had

offended—and he went into the field with the determination to risk his own life, without seeking that of his adversary.

Griffith pulled few punches in his brief remarks.

> Naturally of a most ardent and sanguine temperament, with an open hand and an open heart, even these most praiseworthy qualities and accomplishments led him into errors of which he most bitterly repented. But of Mr. Stockton it may truly be said that all his errors were errors of the head and not of the heart.

He extolled Stockton's learning and eloquence: "A rich and copious flow of language, with a highly cultivated taste, gave brilliancy to his diction . . . and his prodigious memory placed within his reach the stories of ancient and modern learning." In the end, "[a]s a man, Mr. Stockton was generous, frank and high minded."[64]

Six months after the fatal duel, George Winchester—prominent Natchez lawyer, almost simultaneously appointed as justice, Mississippi Supreme Court—publicly offered a $100 reward for the capture and return of a runaway slave, a twenty-five-year-old Negro named Elijah, who "formerly belonged to the Honorable Richard Stockton."[65] His enigmatic personality, melancholy mind, and troubled life aside, Judge Richard Stockton Jr. remains an important figure in Mississippi judicial history because of the role he played in securing the constitutional practice of judicial review, the second act of the events that played out from December of 1823 through February of 1825.

REFLECTIONS

There are a number of takeaway points from this constitutional encounter in early Mississippi history, aside from the obvious—constitutional adjudications by the Supreme Court of Mississippi need to be written, well grounded, reliable, timely, and readily available to the public.

The reaction to the *Cochrane & Murdock* case may well have been a function—in substantial part—of the intuitive injustice of tagging Sheriff Joseph Briggs with what in those days was a substantial fine of one hundred dollars for doing what he reasonably saw as his duty. The Circuit Court of Claiborne County had entered a judgment against Kitchens and in favor of Cochrane & Murdock. The proper writ had issued from the court directing the sheriff to seize Kitchens's nonexempt property and hold a sheriff's sale, with the proceeds of the sale to go to Kitchens's judgment creditors. Sheriff Briggs knew and understood the relevant clauses of the new Debtors' Relief Act. When no bid was received equal to at least two-thirds of its appraised value, Sheriff Briggs sold the Kitchens property on one year's credit, taking the required "bond [of the credit purchasers] with good and sufficient security." One would think a longtime sheriff who followed a new legal procedure to a T would be commended, not fined. It was patently unfair to hold that the sheriff should have foreseen that Section 7 of the multifaceted new act "further to extend relief to debtors" would be found unconstitutional. The Supreme Court's order that Sheriff Briggs pay the fine may have been seen as so improper that the credibility of the rest of its ruling was undermined.

Judge Stockton's grounds for striking the new statute—the no-impairment-of-obligations-of-contracts clauses of the state and federal constitutions—could well have been doubted. First was the politics of the matter. Governor Walter Leake had vetoed the Debtors' Relief Act on the grounds that it would impair the obligations of contracts already in existence. That veto overridden, here was Governor Leake's judicial appointee in practical effect reinstating the veto. If judicial review were a valid constitutional practice, there was no apparent override option short of impeachment of the judges. Even then the new judges would have a hard time finding a way around a final judgment. Bottom line: a judge in Richard Stockton's position is charged with extra prudence, judicial care, and adjudicative articulation before he rises to defend a political position taken by the governor who appointed him to office.

Such extra prudence is particularly mandated in a case like *Cochrane & Murdock*. The Mississippi Constitution did indeed enjoin that "no[] law impairing the obligation of a contract shall be made." The US Constitution said so as well: "No State shall . . . pass any . . . Law impairing the Obligation of Contracts." No facts suggest that any contractual obligation owed by Kitchens to Cochrane & Murdock was legally impaired. To the contrary, the circuit court had entered a judgment that Kitchens must perform his obligations owed to Cochrane & Murdock, failing which his nonexempt property would be seized and sold at a sheriff's sale. It does not take much understanding of bankruptcy law and policy to know that there is a difference between the legal validity of a promise to pay, on the one hand, and whether as a practical matter that same contractually valid debt is collectible, on the other hand. That the judgment debt may in substantial part have been uncollectible did not mean the contractual obligations that Cochrane & Murdock held from Kitchens had been illegally impaired.

In any event, Section 7 regarding sheriff's sales was hardly the most important part of the new comprehensive Debtors' Relief Act. Foremost, the act provided that "hereafter no citizen of this state shall be imprisoned for debt, upon his complying with the provisions hereinafter provided." Even for those "imprisoned," many of the teeth in that traditional penalty were effectively extracted. Judge Stockton never answered the house committee's pointed question, was the entirety of Section 7 unconstitutional, or if only a part of the Section, what part? Still, there should have been no problem as to contracts made after the act was passed. The more important protections provided in the act were almost certain to survive any challenge on judicial review if for no other reason than that they implemented rights secured by Article I, Section 18, authorizing the general assembly to "prescribe by law" how and on what terms "the person of a debtor . . . shall not be detained in prison."

The record does suggest that Judge Stockton "fell back on precedent, calling forth decisions by the US Supreme Court and other state courts in which similar laws had been held unconstitutional." A quick look at the cases cited suggests they may well have confirmed Judge Stockton's bona fides to the house committee. Still, commonsense reasoning from the two constitutional texts to the known facts of *Cochrane & Murdock v. Kitchens* suggests the Supreme Court's ruling on its merits was doubtful. That being so, one not schooled in the niceties of the law might reasonably have paused before blessing Judge Stockton's practice of judicial review. Stockton did not approach judicial review with the restraint and deference Judge Ellis sets out in his *Runnels* opinion. Stockton did not even write an opinion explaining the case until pressed to do so by the house committee. The committee's deference and respect for Stockton notwithstanding, some house members may not unreasonably have wondered whether he was trying to pull a fast one.

Sober reflection on the men involved, the judges and the legislators, suggests a hard-to-miss purpose behind the publication act of February 4, 1825. A matter such as the act further to extend relief to debtors was well within the legislative power of the State that the Constitution vested in the general assembly. The legislative exercise of such a power was subject to the strictures of the Declaration of Rights, in this instance the contracts clause, as well as the federal Contracts Clause, which expressly began "No State shall . . ." Necessarily, the existence of the power of judicial review at all was independent of and preceded its practical exercise by the court. The house of representatives had chosen not to lock horns with the Supreme Court on either the constitutional practice of the power or of its exercise in the particular case. So seen, the act of February 4, 1825, could only mean that judicial review was here to stay. Judges should just tell the public when they find they should exercise it and, as in *Runnels*, explain their grounds when and why a statute should be held unenforceable, on its face or only as applied in a particular circumstance.

There is no evidence that anyone considered what may have been the strongest argument under the constitution of 1817 for the practice of judicial review (as distinguished from the application of the statute, after jurisdiction and judicial review authority has been accepted). The declaration that no "law impairing the obligation of a contract, shall be made" is one of those rights within the Conclusion to Article 1 of the Declaration of Rights. If one accepts that the "act to extend further relief to debtors" did in law impair the obligation of contracts made prior to its enactment, that law "shall be void." Such power as the general assembly had purported to exercise had been "excepted out of the general powers of government" so that it could not be exercised by anyone acting on behalf of the government. The right secured by Section 19 was among those that "shall forever remain inviolate; and all laws contrary thereto . . . shall be void."

With or without *Runnels* serving as a binding precedent, the question whether the act "shall be void" was surely one within the "judicial power" constitutionally conferred upon the state supreme court. Members of the general assembly were duty-bound to "support the Constitution of the United States, and the Constitution of the State of Mississippi," the same as were the judges of the state supreme court. There had to be some authority and process within the government for addressing and remedying such violations by the legislators, when an affected or potentially affected person or firm made a colorable claim that this had occurred. Impeachment would be inadequate, as those within the protection of Section 19 would still have suffered the loss of their supposedly "inviolate" rights. Hence, authority for the practice of judicial review was impliedly, if not necessarily or even inherently, within the judicial power that Article 5 had vested in the state supreme court.

In time, other nuances of the practice of judicial review would be contested and fleshed out. For one, it has become accepted that the actions of the governor are subject to judicial review.[66] This judicial prerogative extends to the actions of other officials exercising executive or administrative powers. Of late, for reasons not entirely clear, the court has been reluctant to accept that the power of judicial review has no limits or prerequisites outside the existence of a viable controverted "matter" otherwise subject to the power and the practice of adjudication.[67] In these instances it is crucial to keep in mind the sharp conceptual and practical distinction between the power so nearly unlimited, and its reliable and otherwise proper exercise. And that a major element of proper exercise is always prudence, which includes a comity-based partial deference to others who have taken the same oath as judges. For some reason, one of the core lessons of *Cochrane & Murdock v. Kitchens* is forgotten from time to time.

The propriety of the constitutional practice of judicial review does not seem to have been a matter of concern after February of 1825 and for the remainder of the life of the Mississippi Constitution of 1817. First, the judicial power had become accepted as including the power of judicial review. How that power was exercised came to be seen as a separate and sequentially subsequent step in the process. Harmon M. Runnels Jr. set the stage for Powhatan Ellis's reasonable exposition of judicial review. *Cochrane & Murdock* provoked Richard Stockton Jr. to a ruling, both parts of which are subject to reasonable doubt on their merits—but not the authority to decide each point on its legal merits. Surely this latter authority is sound. The practical mind can see that someone must be authorized to decide these questions. From the record available,

Richard Stockton Jr.'s stature and professional respect for the house committee that was after his hide, followed by his resignation from the bench, may well—as a practical matter—have saved and secured acceptance of the practice of judicial review. To be sure, soon after his selection as attorney general, Stockton was in hot water again. Some have seen these new issues as continuing the judicial review brouhaha.

There was a point that lay a-smoldering. It was implicit in *Cochrane & Murdock*. There are times when governmental entities and officials need to know where they stand vis-à-vis the constitution. There are times when the people need to know where they stand vis-à-vis their government and their constitution. The practical importance of the exercise of judicial review presumes nothing as to how a given matter should be resolved. In this setting, it is important to keep in mind the commonsense proposition that there are no matters not within the subject matter jurisdiction of some court, if only the circuit court by default. This point would be recognized in *Houston v. Royston*, decided under the constitution of 1832. It would arise in later days under the constitution du jour. In time, it would become clear even more so that in the federal courts not to decide is to decide, that it would be treason to the state constitution du jour for the court to decline to exercise jurisdiction which is given, and to close its eyes to the fact that authority to decide all matters is constitutionally placed in some court. The *only* question is, In which state court?

Judge Stockton's family has retained its prominence as one of America's first families. The signature of Richard Stockton sits atop the five-member delegation from New Jersey that signed the Declaration of Independence. The first Richard Stockton Jr. served in the US Senate and later the US House of Representatives and remains highly regarded. Among the grandchildren of the Signer, Commodore Robert Field Stockton wrote several pages of American history as a naval officer, was the first military governor of California, and later a US senator from his native New Jersey. The public knows the commodore's ill-starred, bachelor older brother primarily for his death in a duel in which he never fired at his adversary.

Mississippi history portrays judge and attorney general Richard Stockton Jr. as an enigmatic and highly undisciplined minor player, who charmed many but for one reason or another was among the Jersey settlers who did not make his home in Natchez until near the end. He quarreled with the general assembly and became associated with the infamous practice of dueling before his own fatal fall. It is easy to second-guess the way Stockton originally handled the case of *Cochrane & Murdock v. Kitchens*. By modern lights, he likely decided the merits of the case incorrectly, though that did not impugn the practice of judicial review. Stockton's respectful manner before the house of representatives, however, ultimately resigning his judgeship, led to a sensible settlement recognizing that the Supreme Court of Mississippi could adjudge that a statute was unenforceable for its offense to the constitution. All it had to do was publish promptly and disseminate widely an opinion explaining how and why so.

In 1823, Judge Powhatan Ellis wrote a nice opinion in *Runnels*. He then moved on to a more prominent and colorful career—most of which was associated with first general and later president Andrew Jackson. *Runnels v. State* languished in *Walker's Reports* unnoticed for 160 years. Whenever the story of the birth of judicial review in Mississippi was told, it centered on *Cochrane & Murdock v. Kitchens*, Sheriff Briggs, and Judge Stockton's back-and-forth with the house of representatives in January of 1825. Without the fine imposed on Sheriff Briggs for doing what he saw as his duty, there may never have been war with the general assembly over judicial review. Had some member of the Supreme Court of Mississippi written the respectful and reasoned opinion that Stockton provided to the house committee after the fact, there may never have been a war. These are speculations. What we do know is that with Stockton's response, and then his resignation, the matter was peaceably and finally resolved. All moved on to other issues, albeit Attorney General Stockton's good judgment soon failed him again, this time fatally.

The Runnels family flourished in Lawrence County and beyond, though brother Hiram fell from governor to hot water amidst the Mississippi Union Bank debacle (see chapter 4 below).

In the 1850s the Murdock family established Canemount Plantation near Lorman, which has recently been purchased by the Mississippi Department of Wildlife, Fisheries and Parks.[68] At and after the case described above, Benjamin Kitchens was broke. In time, he decided to try his luck in the Choctaw country, which had been opened to settlers via the Treaty of Dancing Rabbit Creek of 1830. In 1841, with his fortunes apparently improved, Kitchens purchased lands in Attala County,[69] some 125 miles northeasterly, up the Natchez Trace from the Claiborne County area. The 1850 census showed Kitchens still a resident of Attala County, a sixty-nine-year-old farmer living with two daughters and two grandchildren.[70] The estate of the son of late Sheriff Briggs became involved in Claiborne County litigation shortly after the Civil War. The matter concerned Briggs's creditors and their possible remedies against Briggs's debtors.

Constitution makers in 1832, 1868, and 1890 had a shot at stripping the judicial department of the power of judicial review. None did so. It was fitting that in 1983 a native of Lawrence County would turn to the county of his roots and remind us that

[a]s long ago as 1823, [*Harmon M.*] *Runnels v. State*, Walker (1 Miss.) 146, held it the duty of the judiciary to declare void any legislative enactment which may be repugnant to the provisions of the constitution and that this duty is paramount to the authority of the legislature.[71]

Since the mid-1820s, the State of Mississippi has practiced judicial review, for the most part wisely and at times with great profit.

It would be fitting that the Supreme Court of Mississippi advise the Society of the Descendants of the Signers of the Declaration of Independence[72] and appropriate members of the Stockton family in New Jersey, that Commodore Robert Field Stockton was not the only grandson of the Signer whose accomplishments should be remembered. In January of 1825, older brother Judge Richard Stockton Jr. made a mark for the common good in Mississippi. The way he did so was sort of like the quarterback whose turnovers put his football team in a deep hole, only to rally with poise in the fourth quarter so that his team won the game of the decade.

ENDNOTES

1. *Runnels v. State*, Walker (1 Miss.) 146, 1823 WL 543 (1823).

2. *Alexander v. State by and through Allain*, 441 So.2d 1329, 1333, 1339 (1983).

3. *Marbury v. Madison*, 1 Cranch (5 U.S.) 137, 2 L.Ed. 60 (1803).

4. Miss. Const. art. 1, §§ 1–29 (1817). Of course, many important rights were only available to "all freemen."

5. Charles de Secondat, Baron de Montesquieu, *The Spirit of the Laws*, 151–154 (T. Nugent translation, 1949); and John Locke, *Second Treatise on Civil Government* (1689). See particularly Judge Leslie Southwick's explanation of the role of the French Montesquieu in his *Separation of Powers at the State Level: Interpretations and Challenges in Mississippi*, 72 Miss. L. Journ. 927, 953–955 (2003).

6. Judge Stockton had succeeded Judge Joshua G. Clarke, who held the office in and for the First District from 1818 until late 1821. Judge Clarke authored the opinion in *Harry and Others v. Decker & Hopkins*, Walker (1 Miss.) 36, 42**1, 1818 WL 1235 (1818), discussed at length in chapter 2 above.

7. David L. Cohn, *The Mississippi Delta and the World: The Memoirs of David L. Cohn* 3 (James C. Cobb ed., 1995).

8. Dunbar Rowland, *Mississippi, Heart of the South, Vol. 1*, 490, quoted in http://www.genealogy.com/forum/surnames/topics/sunnels/184/.

9. Miss. Const. art. 5, §§ 10, 11 (1817).

10. Winbourne Magruder Drake, "Mississippi's First Constitutional Convention," *Journal of Mississippi History* 79 (1956).

11. J. F. H. Claiborne, quoted in http://www.genealogy.com/forum/surnames/topics/sunnels/184/.

12. Judge Ellis's public career is outlined by James D. Lynch in his book *The Bench and Bar of Mississippi* 87–88 (1880). *See also* John Ray Skates, *A History of the Mississippi Supreme Court, 1817–1948* 5 (1973); "Ellis, Powhatan," in *Mississippi Encyclopedia* 386–387 (Ownby & Wilson eds., 2017).

13. Eulogy entitled "Hon. Powhatan Ellis of Mississippi," reproduced and online at https://archive.org/stream/honpowhatanellisooelli/honpowhatanellisooelli_djva.txt.

14. James D. Lynch, *The Bench and Bar of Mississippi* 88 (1880).

15. *State v. Moor*, Walker (1 Miss.) 134, 138, 1823 WL 542 (1823)

16. *Bradley v. State*, Walker (1 Miss.) 156, 157, 1 Morr. St. Cas. 13, 1824 WL 631 (1824). The husband's so-called right of moderate chastisement was in time repudiated in cases such as *Harris v. State*, 14 So. 266 (1894), and later *Gross v. State*, 100 So. 177, 178–179 (1924).

17. Edwin L. Cobb, "Hon. Powhatan Ellis of Mississippi: A Reappraisal," *Journal of Mississippi History* 30 (May 1968), page 98.

18. Alfred Hoyt Bill, *A House Called Morven: Its Role in American History, 1701–1954* 84 (2015).

19. On January 27, 1821, for a consideration of $750, John and Sarah Richards conveyed to Richard Stockton Jr. by deed a town lot described as 61.5 feet on Farmers' Street by 200 feet back, Southern half of Lot 3, Square 1, Suburb Ste. Mary (historic district on the National Register since 1979). Claiborne County tax rolls for 1822 show that Stockton owned 1/2 town lot valued at $600 in Port Gibson and that he owned two slaves. Similar entries appear on the Claiborne County tax rolls for 1823 and 1824, except that Stockton is listed as owning only one slave.

20. Alfred Hoyt Bill, *A House Called Morven: Its Role in American History, 1701–1954* 84–85 (2015). An after-the-fact confirmation of what Stockton told his father appears in the roster of attendees at a bar association meeting at Mr. Parker's Tavern, noted above to have taken place on December 13, 1822. *See The Mississippi Bar's Centennial: A Legacy of Service* 5 (Melanie H. Henry comp. and ed., 2006).

21. Miss. Laws, ch. 30, §2, page 30 (Nov. 26, 1821).

22. Miss. Const. art. 5, §11 (1817).

23. Miss. Laws, §3, page 86 (June 30, 1822).

24. *Runnels v. State*, Walker (1 Miss.) 146, ** 1, 1823 WL 543 (1823).

25. Meredith Lang, *Defender of the Faith: The High Court of Mississippi, 1817–1875* 9 (1977).

26. *Hackler's Heirs v. Cabel*, Walker (1 Miss.) 91, 1821 WL 440 (1821).

27. *Lee, Adm'r v. Montgomery*, Walker (1 Miss.) 109, 112, 1822 WL 913, **3 (1822).

28. *Runnels v. State*, Walker (1 Miss.) 146, 148–149 ** 2, 1823 WL 543 (1823).

29. See *Report of the Case of the Trustees of Dartmouth College against William H. Woodward, Dartmouth College, Timothy Farrar* 305–306 (1819). The words of the "distinguished statesman" are italicized.

30. Webster was more than just a lawyer for Dartmouth College. He was a graduate. The college has never forgotten his famous peroration before the Supreme Court on March 10, 1818, "Sir, as I have said, it is a small college. And yet there are those who love it." *Trustees of Dartmouth College v. Woodward*, 4 Wheat. (17 U.S.) 518, 4 Law. Ed. 629 (1819).

31. At times the family name was spelled "Cochran" without the "e" at the end. This was a not-uncommon practice two hundred years ago.

32. At times the Murdock family name was spelled "Murdoch." As with "Cochrane," the spelling used here is that which appears in the records and other papers in the litigation with Benjamin Kitchens in the early 1820s in Claiborne County, Mississippi.

33. "To Rent," *Mississippi Herald and Natchez Gazette*, Weds., Oct. 14, 1807, page 4.

34. "Notice," *Weekly Chronicle* (Natchez, Miss.), Weds., Oct. 26, 1808.

35. "La Cache Plantation & Negroes, For Sale or Rent," *Mississippi State Gazette*, Vol. VIII, No. 49 (Natchez, Miss.), Dec. 2, 1820.

36. Benjamin Kitchens is listed in the 1830 US census as residing in Claiborne County and as being at that time between forty and fifty years old, and his wife is similarly listed. His household is also shown as having five sons, one between ten and twenty years old, two between ten and fifteen years old, one between five and ten years old, and a fifth son under five years old. A nearly consistent entry for "Benj Kitchens" in Claiborne County appears in the 1820 US census.

37. Joseph Briggs in the 1820 US federal census, Claiborne County, Mississippi, page 9A, NARA Roll: M33_58; Image 27, at ancestry.com.

38. Miss. Laws, ch. 74, pages 101–106 (1824).

39. Miss. Laws, ch. 74, §§ 4–7, pages 103–104 (1824).

40. Parts of the story of *Cochrane & Murdock v. Kitchens* are told by James D. Lynch, *The Bench and Bar of Mississippi* 92–97 (1880). *See also* a paper entitled "The Power of the Courts," authored by Prof. Thomas H. Somerville (1850–1928) of the University of Mississippi, and presented to the Mississippi State Bar Association at its Annual Meeting held in Meridian on May 6, 1908. See proceedings of the meeting, at pages 69–70 (1908); *see also* Prof. Somerville's "A Sketch of the Supreme Court of Mississippi," in *The Green Bag*, Vol. 11, 505–506, ed. Horace W. Fuller (1899).). Prof. John Ray Skates's *A History of the Mississippi Supreme Court, 1817–1948* 6–9 (1973), offers a slightly different version of the facts.

41. Act of June 29, 1822, § 27, Miss. Laws, page 88 (1822).

42. US Constitution art. 1, §10, cl. 1; Miss. Const. art. 6, §10 (1817).

43. According to one projection, $100 in 1824 was the equivalent of $2,176.15 in 2015. http://www.westegg.com/inflation/infl.cgi. Another projection suggests that $100 in 1825 would have been the equivalent of $2,292.04 in 2016. http://www.in2013dollars.com/1825-dollars-in-2016?amount=100.

44. Act of June 29, 1822, § 8, Miss. Laws, page 78 (1822). The law did provide for a reporter to collect, print, and publish those written decisions that might be "deemed useful" to be delivered to the clerks of all courts "for the use of said courts." The reporter could also print and sell the reports to lawyers and others who might be interested. Act of June 29, 1822, §§ 37–39, Miss. Laws, page 85 (1822). The first reporter, R. J. Walker, was appointed in 1828 and did not produce a volume of decisions until sometime in 1834.

45. *Robert McFarland v. George Smith*, Walker (1 Miss.) 172–174, 1824 WL 1308 (1824).

46. Stella Pitts and Ernesto Caldeira, *The Plantation World of Wilkinson County, Mississippi, 1792–2012* 118 (Woodville Civic Club, 2013).

47. Mississippi House Journal, page 69 (1825); James D. Lynch, *The Bench and Bar of Mississippi* 93 (1880).

48. Mississippi. House Journal, page 73 (1825).

49. James D. Lynch, *The Bench and Bar of Mississippi* 96 (1880). At the time, Judge John P. Hampton and Judge Powhatan Ellis were senior to Judge Stockton in time of service. Judge Edward Turner, however, had not come to the court until the fall of 1824, following the death of Judge Louis Winston, some two years after Judge Stockton assumed his seat as circuit judge for District One and judge for that district on the supreme court.

50. Mississippi House Journal, page 74 (1825) (italics in original); James D. Lynch, *The Bench and Bar of Mississippi* 96 (1880).

51. Mississippi House Journal, page 74 (1825); James D. Lynch, *The Bench and Bar of Mississippi* 96–97 (1880).

52. As explained above, *Walker's Reports* was formally dated 1832 but was not disseminated until 1834. It is possible that Chairman Johnson was unaware of *Runnels*. Judge Stockton should be faulted in that regard, since he was a judge on the court in 1823.

53. James D. Lynch, *The Bench and Bar of Mississippi* 97 (1880).

54. Mississippi House Journal, page 77 (1825); Miss. Laws, § 1, page 76 (June 29, 1822). Two years later, on February 9, 1927, a memorialist offered an explanation for Stockton's resignation, that he "prefer[red] to return to the profession, in accordance with the wishes of friends and the advice of his respected father." "The Late Richard Stockton, Esq.," *Statesman and Gazette* (Natchez, Miss.), Vol. 1, No. 8, Weds., February 14, 1827, page 3, and "Domestic News, City of Natchez: The Late Richard Stockton, Esq.," in *Ariel* (Natchez, Miss.), Fri., Feb. 23, 1827, page 4.

55. Miss. Laws, page 85 (Feb. 4, 1825).

56. On February 12, 1825, the *Mississippi State Gazette* published the following announcement: "Richard Stockton, Jr., having resumed the practice of the law, offers his professional services to the public. His residence is in Natchez." *Mississippi State Gazette* (Natchez, Miss.), Vol. XIII, No. 7, Feb. 12, 1825, page 3.

57. "At Home," published in *Ariel* (Natchez, Miss.) Fri., May 26, 1826, page 7.

58. "At Home," published in *Ariel* (Natchez, Miss.), Fri., Aug. 18, 1826, page 6.

59. Mississippi House Journal, page 144 (Jan. 23, 1827).

60. In due course, Letters of Administration in chief on the estate of R. Stockton, deceased, were issued to R. M. Gaines, who on May 1, 1827, published Notice to Creditors as an advertisement in *Statesman and Gazette*, Vol. 1, No. 20 (Natchez, Miss.), Thurs., May 10, 1827, page 1. (Gaines would serve as attorney general of Mississippi from 1830 to 1834.) The issuance of letters of administration suggests that Stockton died intestate, without a will, not particularly surprising given Stockton's age, thirty-six, and the fact that he was never married and had no children. At the turn of the year 1827–1828, administrator Gaines gave notice of the public sale of an unimproved lot owned by Stockton in Gallatin, Copiah County, Mississippi, and later of "an undivided moiety of a home and lot in the town of Monticello," Lawrence County, Mississippi. Administrator's Sale, published in in *Statesman and Gazette* (Natchez, Miss.),Vol. 11, No. 4 (Thurs., Jan. 17, 1828), page 4.

61. J. W. Stockton, *A History of the Stockton Family* 38 (1881); John Ray Skates Jr., *A History of the Mississippi Supreme Court, 1817–1948* 97 (1973).

62. "Columbia Springs," https://en/wikipedia.org/wiki/Columbia_Springs.

63. http://www.nerc.com/~rfsesq/genealogy/stockton5.html (page removed). The former version is more likely correct. At a memorial service three days later, the eulogist told this version of the story, the letter in his hand, saying, "The following letter, written to an intimate friend, on the evening previous to his death, shews that such was his determination, but of which his friends were entirely ignorant— (Mr. Griffith here read parts of the letter referred to)." *See* "The Late Richard Stockton, Esq.," *Statesman and Gazette*, Vol. 1, No. 8 (Natchez, Miss.), Weds., February 14, 1827, page 3; and "Domestic News, City of Natchez: The Late Richard Stockton, Esq." in *Ariel* (Natchez, Miss.), Fri., Feb. 23, 1827, page 4.

64. Virgil A. Griffith, *Mississippi Reports and Reporters*, 22 Miss. L. Journ. 37 (1950).

65. "100 Dollars Reward," published as an advertisement in *Ariel* (Natchez, Miss.), Friday, Aug. 31, 1826, page 7.

66. *State v. McPhail*, 182 Miss. 360, 180 So. 387 (1938).

67. *See, e.g., In Re Hooker*, 87 So.3d 401 (Miss. 2012) and *Gunn v. Hughes*, 210 So.3d 969, 2017 WL 533802 (¶¶16, 17) (Miss. 2017), overruling a part of *Tuck v. Blackmon*, 798 So.2d 402, 404 (Miss. 2001). *See also* James L. Robertson, *Encyclopedia of Mississippi Law*, Vol. 3, *Constitutional Law* §§ 19:17, 19:21, 19:34 (Jeffrey Jackson et al., eds., Thomson Reuters, 2nd ed. Supp. 2018).

68. "Canemount Plantation," https://en.wikipedia.org/wiki/Canemount_Plantation.

69. Kitchens was shown as a resident of Attala County in 1840. *See* Benjamin Zephaniah Kitchens, ancestry.com.

70. US Census, 1950; ancestry.com.

71. *Alexander v. State by and through Allain*, 441 So.2d 1329, 1333 (Miss. 1983). citing and following as persuasive (though not controlling) precedent "the genesis federal case, *Marbury v. Madison*, 1 Cranch 137, 170, 2 L.Ed. 60 (1803)."

72. *The Society of the Descendants of the Signers of the Declaration of Independence*, http://www.dsdi1776.com/signers-by-state/richard-stockton/.

BIBLIOGRAPHY

Bill, Alfred Hoyt, *A House Called Morven: Its Role in American History, 1701–1954* (2015).

Claiborne, J. F. H., *Mississippi, as a Province, Territory and State* (1880; reprinted by LSU Press, 1964).

Cobb, Edwin L., "Hon. Powhatan Ellis of Mississippi: A Reappraisal," *Journal of Mississippi History* 30 (May 1968).

Cohn, David L., *The Mississippi Delta and the World: The Memoirs of David L. Cohn* (James C. Cobb ed., 1995)

Davis, William C., *A Way through the Wilderness: The Natchez Trace and the Civilization of the Southern Frontier* (1995).

Delaney, Erin F., *Judiciary Rising: Constitutional Change in the United Kingdom*, 108 Northwestern L. Rev. 543 (2014); https://www.lawteacher.net/free-law-essays/constitutional-law-essays.php.

Drake, Winbourne Magruder, "Mississippi's First Constitutional Convention," *Journal of Mississippi History* (1956).

Fortune, Porter L., Jr., "The Formative Period," in *A History of Mississippi*, Vol. 1 (Richard A. McLemore ed., 1973).

Griffith, Virgil A., *Mississippi Reports and Reporters*, 22 Miss. L. Journ. 37 (1950).

Gross, Ariela J., *Double Character: Slavery and Mastery in the Antebellum Southern Courtroom* (2000).

Haynes, Robert, *The Mississippi Territory and the Southwest Frontier, 1795–1817* (2010).

Hoffheimer, Michael H., *Mississippi Courts: 1790–1868*, 65 Miss. L. Journ. 99 (Fall 1995).

Holmes, David, in David G. Sansing, *Mississippi Governors: Soldiers, Statesmen, Scholars, Scoundrels: A Bicentennial Edition* (2016).

Holmes, David, *Mississippi Encyclopedia* (Ownby and Wilson eds., 2017).

Hopkinson, Francis, designer of the first official American flag, https://en.wikipedia.org/wiki/Francis_Hopkinson.

Lang, Meredith, *Defender of the Faith: The High Court of Mississippi, 1817–1875* (1977).

Locke, John, *Second Treatise on Civil Government* (1689).

Lynch, James Daniel, *The Bench and Bar of Mississippi* (1880).

McCain, William D., *The Story of Jackson*, Vol. 1 (1953).

Mills, Frances Preston, ed., *The History of the Descendants of the Jersey Settlers, Adams County, Mississippi*. 2 vols. (1981).

Mills, Michael P., *Slavery Law in Mississippi from 1817–1861: Constitution, Codes and Cases*, 71 Miss. L. Journ. 153 (2001).

The Plantation World of Wilkinson County, Mississippi, 1792–2012.

Powell, Susie V., supervisor, *History of Lawrence County*, quoted in http://www.genealogy.com/forum/surnames/topics/sunnels/184/.

Robertson, James L., *Encyclopedia of Mississippi Law*, Vol. 3, *Constitutional Law*. 2d ed. Supp. (Jeffrey Jackson et al. eds., 2018).

Rose, Philip F., *Mexico Redux* (2012).

Rowland, Dunbar, *Mississippi, Comprising Sketches of Counties, Towns, Events, Institutions and Persons, Arranged in Cyclopedic Form*. Vol. II (1907).

Rowland, Dunbar, *Mississippi, Heart of the South*. Vol. 1; quoted in http://www.genealogy.com/forum/surnames/topics/sunnels/184/.

"Runnels, Hiram George," in David G. Sansing, *Mississippi Governors: Soldiers, Statesmen, Scholars, Scoundrels: A Bicentennial Edition* (2016).

Runnels, Hiram G., *Mississippi Encyclopedia* (Ownby and Wilson eds., 2017).

Skates, John Ray, *A History of the Mississippi Supreme Court, 1817–1948* (1973).

Southwick, Leslie, *Separation of Powers at the State Level: Interpretations and Challenges in Mississippi*, 72 Miss. L. Journ. 927 (2003).

Stockton, J. W., *A History of the Stockton Family* (1881).

Stockton, Richard, Jr. (Nov. 8, 1791–Feb. 6, 1827), My Genealogy Home Page: Information about Richard Stockton, at genealogy.com/ftm/a/l/b/Shelley-Albertson/WEBSITE-0001 /UPH-0211.html.

Stockton Family Historical Trust; http://www.stockton-law.com/genealogy/stockton5.html.

Somerville, Thomas H., *Proceedings of Mississippi State Bar Association*, Annual Meeting (1908).

Somerville, Thomas H., "A Sketch of the Supreme Court of Mississippi," *The Green Bag, Vol. 11* (Sydney Russell Wrightington et al.).

CHAPTER 4

Mississippi Bank Wars

> Nothing was settled. Chaos had come again, or rather,
> had never gone away. Order, Heaven's first law, seemed
> unwilling to remain where there was no other law to
> keep it company.
> —JOSEPH G. BALDWIN, *THE FLUSH TIMES OF ALABAMA*
> *AND MISSISSIPPI*

It was the eighth of May, 1852. Former governor Alexander G. McNutt[1] had been dead for three and a half years. Prominent New York financier Hezron A. Johnson was suing the State in the Superior Chancery Court of Mississippi.[2] Johnson held a $2,000 Mississippi Union Bank bond that had matured two years earlier. The bond bore the signature—from more promising times—of arch "repudiator" McNutt, and of state treasurer James Phillips, for good measure. The legislature had authorized it as well, and by a cumbersome constitutional process required for no other state action.

Understand that back on August 18, 1838, the Union Bank had sold 7,500 State-guaranteed bonds to Philadelphia banker Nicholas Biddle for the aggregate sum of $5 million. Biddle had promptly sold or hypothecated these bonds in England. Each bond was in the face amount of $2,000 plus interest. For its guaranties and their attendant risks and, of course, the money Biddle provided, the State had acquired stock in the new bank. In the due course of negotiable instruments, Johnson bought one of these bonds. The purchase was an interest-bearing investment, more like a loan. Johnson expected to get his money back, and with interest. He'd been promised as much. The Union Bank itself was the primary obligor on the bond, but by its certain terms a Union Bank Bond assured its holder that, if all else failed, the State of Mississippi would pay. Johnson had been paid nothing since the February 5, 1850, due date of the bond he held. The same with fifty-dollar semiannual interest payments, which had begun coming due as much as three years earlier.

No one denied that back in August of 1838 the State of Mississippi—pledging its credit and faith as guarantor of last resort—had signed, sealed, and participated in selling the bank bonds to Biddle. The State had been up to its eyeballs in the genesis of the Mississippi Union Bank and had expected great benefits therefrom. Three governors had had their say so. Each had taken his whack at the form and substance and money-making game plan for the new bank. Legislators elected in late 1835 and 1837 had sensed the circumstances both before and after Andrew Jackson's Specie Circular[3] of July 1836 and the ensuing—ten months later—national financial Panic of 1837. "All freemen"— the people—in that idealized "social compact" that was Jacksonian Democracy, armed with their "inherent" political power, had endured these new circumstances in their fall from "flush times" of the previous few years. The people had listened to—had been harangued by—state and local candidates in the summer of 1837, and then they had voted, pro-Mississippi Union Bank.

Five million dollars had in fact been received from the sale of these bonds.[4] The money really was needed—and badly so—to get the new bank up and running in the face of hard times. Dealing primarily with Biddle and his U.S. Bank of Pennsylvania, the State was glad to see the money come rolling in. And let the Union Bank have it, in exchange for the guarantor State's purchase of its stock position, hoping the new bank would do well in getting the State beyond the financial embarrassments it had experienced so recently. But by January of 1841, McNutt was stirring up a hornet's nest, despite Mississippi's facing a relatively light public debt—$5 million on Union Bank bonds and $2 million on Planters' Bank bonds issued a few years earlier. In February of 1842, another newly elected legislature—this one dominated by antibank Democrats—repudiated the Mississippi Union Bank bonds, barely a month after its members had been seated. The new legislators invoked all sorts of pretexts, ranging from the technical to the quasi-constitutional to the purely political and—in the end—to utter nonsense: "We just don't want to!"

To be sure, a third nationwide banking crisis in less than five years had just opened its ugly sinkholes. Mississippians were broke, scared, in debt. Most folk were all three. Memories of flush times served only to push otherwise sensible people to lose perspective. But not everywhere. Neighboring Louisiana was on the hook for a lot more than Mississippi, a public debt of almost $24 million. Louisiana defaulted in February of 1843 but resumed payments on its state debts after a year. And then there was doubly deep in debt Alabama—$15.4 million by one account—that never defaulted at all, much less did it repudiate. Of course, all politics is local. More often than not, leadership is luck of the local draw, the wisdom and merit of Jacksonian Democracy to the contrary notwithstanding.

In the summer of 1841, an important lawsuit had begun on a parallel front. John Beasley Campbell (1795–1843), a veteran of the War of 1812, was a Rankin County farmer and slave owner. Together with others, Campbell held a ten-dollar post note—commonly called a bank note—that the Union Bank had issued barely a month after it opened its doors and commenced the business of banking. Today we'd call it a ten-dollar bill. Independently, the bank held a nine-month promissory note made by Campbell and the others, due to be paid in July of 1840.[5] July came and went. The makers of the promissory note did not or could not pay. Mississippi Union Bank sued Campbell and his co-obligors, filing in the Circuit Court of Rankin County what as a practical matter could be called a collection suit. Campbell had no defense on the merits. He and his co-debtors retained Volney E. Howard to defend them. A crafty lawyer, Howard was an otherwise versatile and controversial figure of the times. He counterattacked, arguing that the Union Bank had not been properly authorized, that it lacked legal capacity to enforce any rights it might otherwise hold. Campbell's counsel also invoked a new law,[6] saying it trumped all else. Howard said the new law entitled his clients to payment of the separate demand bank note they held in specie—hard coin currency, gold and silver. The bank balked. Soon it was reeling, in the swirl of liquidation. Suddenly, the constitutional legitimacy of the Mississippi Union Bank in its entirety and from the get-go was in play. The circuit court entered judgment for the bank note holders. As the appeal was winding its way up to the High Court of Errors and Appeals, Governor McNutt was leading the charge toward repudiation of the Union Bank bonds, on some of the same grounds pending in Campbell's case.

At its January 1842 term, the high court confirmed the constitutional and corporate viability of the Mississippi Union Bank.[7] The three justices were unanimous. On every front, the bank had been lawfully incorporated, chartered, organized, and capitalized and had begun banking operations. It had standing to enforce the promissory note–based claim it was making against Campbell and the others. So said the State's highest court.

Fast-forward to May of 1852.

The honor of Mississippi was at stake, though politicians were still telling a financially strapped populace something else—what it wanted to hear. At a more practical level, the creditworthiness of the State was on the block. Beneath it all was the question, How does a constitution function when it is faced with social facts and forces bigger, more powerful, and less relenting than all else? Have there not always been times when, as Joseph G. Baldwin put it (The Flush Times of Alabama and Mississippi), "society was wholly unorganized, when there was no restraining public opinion: the law well-nigh powerless—and religion . . . scarcely heard of except as furnishing the oaths and technics of profanity?" Country lawyer philosopher Baldwin was without peer with words that captured the humanity and tenor of the times.

Of course, the State had been within its rights to sit tight until the bonds it had guaranteed matured, as to both principal and interest. And until it was certain that no one with a prior legal duty would step forward, though that practical reality had been pretty clear since the very early 1840s. The day of reckoning had come—well before May of 1852. New Yorker Johnson wanted his money.

Still the State did nothing. How could the State's lawyers expect to get around the well-reasoned and controlling precedent set in the ten years earlier High Court pro-bank ruling in the *Campbell* case? How could the State expect to get around the terms of the bond,[8] the authorization of the legislature, the signatures of the governor and treasurer of the guarantor state, or a sensible reading of the legally relevant texts of the Constitution of 1832?[9]

To the surprise of no sensible person, Johnson won his case in chancery court, and the High Court affirmed.[10] Again, the justices were unanimous. The *Johnson* decision was stronger than *Campbell* had been. The enforceability of the State's pledge of its faith and credit to guarantee payment of a Union Bank bond was legally solid. The State's petitions for reargument had been finally denied. One would have thought at this point that the practical circumstances of Mississippi's bond repudiators were not unlike those of a condemned man being escorted to the gallows, having lost twice on appeal, but crying out, "The bad guys at the bank did it! What about these technicalities? And by the way, I'm innocent!" Still the State stiff-armed Hezron Johnson and all other Union Bank bondholders. Many Mississippians no doubt thought back to the—arguably apocryphal—response of their hero Andrew Jackson following an 1832 decision regarding the rights of the Cherokee Indians.[11] "John Marshall has made his decision. Now let him enforce it."

A few years later all were sidetracked by the State's cascade towards Secession, Civil War, then Reconstruction. But what came after that still stuns; at least it should, if the people of Mississippi have any sense of honor at all.

Radical Republican Reconstructionists and a more moderate variety of Republicans (including many who had been antisecession Whigs before the War), and all-white Democrats, agreed postbellum on but a single issue: the State should not pay the Union Bank bonds, or $2 million on the legally and factually unrelated Planters' Bank bonds. Period. Acting through its last Republican legislature in 1875, the State of Mississippi—guarantor, repudiator and dead beat debtor—amended its Constitution and declared that it would never honor the faith and credit it had pledged in the days following February 15, 1838.[12] As if they had not made the State's shamelessness apparent enough, constitutional draftsmen threw in for good measure a repudiation of the State's faith put behind the $2 million in Planters' Bank bonds issued a few years earlier. To this day We the People have shown no embarrassment at a constitution that still says the State will never pay "any bond or bonds, now generally known as 'Union Bank' bonds and 'Planters Bank' bonds."[13] No one had ever credibly argued that the holders of Planters' Bank bonds should not be paid, not to imply that the State ever had much of a defense to paying the Union Bank bonds either, particularly after reargument had been denied following the final judgment that was the *Johnson* decision at the High Court's April term, 1853.

Bear in mind that in 1842 a Senate committee, charged to investigate the Planters' Bank matter, had reported

> In the instance of these bonds, your committee find no violation of the constitution. In the sale no fraud appears, but an actual profit—they were sold on account of the State, this principal invested in stock, and the premium placed to the credit of the sinking fund, for the benefit of the State. Therefore, justice and good faith require that they should be paid so soon as the state of the treasury and the condition of the people will permit.

Indeed, prior to this, and again speaking of the Planters' Bank bonds, the same committee had reported its view that

> The constitution is the expressed will of the people, and your committee have all confidence that Mississippians will never repudiate a debt which has received their highest sanction—that of the constitution, which guards and protects their rights and conveys to the world an expression of their sovereign will.[14]

In 1832, there had been—if anything—a constitutional affirmance of the Planters' Bank's plan of action.[15] Sadly, this is not the way the story played out; witness the present Section 258 of the constitution and the State's and its courts' attitude regarding it.

This chapter tells a story of a people full of sanctimony and bombast. These people again and again invoked their constitution, or had it invoked on their behalf—before, on, and after February 26, 1842, the day of repudiation. But they could not or would not come to grips with the fact and law that the legislature could resolve that the bond sale had been "illegal, fraudulent and unconstitutional" until the cows come home, and that would be of no effect. No judicial power had been constitutionally vested in the legislature. All judicial power had been vested in "one high court of errors and appeals, and such other courts of law and equity as are hereafter provided for in this constitution."[16] That one high court had ruled, finally, period.

And so this is also the story of a people who never had an answer to the fact of the final judgment of the high court handed down in the *Campbell* case at its January term, 1842, much less the final judgment in the *Johnson* case at its April term, 1853. The *Johnson* judgment had been supported by an even more powerful judicial elaboration and application of the constitution as it then read. This is a story that ends with the question of whether—slavery, secession, and historical racism aside—Mississippi has ever committed an offense more morally and constitutionally bankrupt than its to-this-day refusal to honor its credit and faith pledged to redeem the Union Bank bonds and the Planters' Bank bonds.

And, in this constitutional encounter, than its refusal to respect and follow the rule of law.

Or did this all happen just too long ago? Even so, the story should be told, again and again and with as much truth and veracity and completeness as the historical record allows. We should "speak to the yet unknowing world how these things came about, . . . lest more mischance on plots and errors, happen."[17]

CAST OF CHARACTERS

Many people played important parts in the unfolding events that make up the Planters', Union, and Mississippi's other bank wars of the quarter century leading up to full Civil War. Most held some public position, including lawyers in their roles as officers of the court. Of course, governors such as Alexander G. McNutt and Tilghman M. Tucker, legislators such as Jacob Shall Yerger and Gordon Boyd, judges such as William L. Sharkey, Cotesworth Pinckney Smith, and William Yerger, and lawyers such as George S. Yerger and Volney E. Howard made extraordinary impacts. David C. Glenn was the attorney general who represented the State of Mississippi in the *Johnson* case.[18] Hiram G. Runnels[19] played lineal roles from governor to president of the Mississippi Union Bank, not to mention being a duelist at earlier points. Another Yerger brother and a brother-in-law of one—lawyers all—did their parts.

Nicholas Biddle and Hezron A. Johnson were nonresidents from up north who made their essential marks. And those were not all. There were the people whose numbers trebled during the 1830s, though unknown thousands of Native Americans had been "removed" so that public land sales to settlers could reach undreamt-of heights in mid-decade. Flush times were raucous times, when there were few limits on anything—anywhere—until 1837, when most dreams and shenanigans were flushed down dizzying drains. From governors to common men, the people had entered the Age of Jackson and been told that "when they form a social compact, [they] are equal in rights," and "that all political power is inherent in the people, and all free governments are founded on their authority, and established for their benefit."[20] Knowing a bit about the times and their people, their ideals and their foibles, may make the humanity of this complex story more apparent, its dubious details and denouement a bit less difficult to digest.

Hiram George Runnels (1796–1857) was the ninth governor of Mississippi. He hailed from Georgia. In the early 1800s, Harmon M. Runnels brought his four sons when he came southwest to Mississippi.[21] We met Harmon Sr. and Harmon Jr. in chapter 3 above. Hiram was another of those sons. He served a term as governor (1833–1835), before losing a close race while seeking reelection. In January of 1835, Governor Runnels recommended that the legislature establish a new bank along the lines of what in time became the Mississippi Union Bank.[22] His "ready to fight" reputation remained intact, as in 1838 when he caned then Governor McNutt, and in 1840 when he dueled with lawyer, court reporter, and newspaper editor Volney E. Howard.[23]

Charles Lynch[24] (1783–1853) was Mississippi's eleventh governor (1833, 1836–1838). A native of South Carolina, Lynch served six years in the state senate representing Lawrence County. Politically a Whig, Lynch defeated fellow Lawrence Countian Hiram Runnels in the latter's bid for reelection. Governor Lynch rode high during the tail end of "flush times," but his popularity plummeted with the Panic of 1837. He did not seek reelection. On January 4, 1838, as he was about to leave office, Governor Lynch urged serious thought whether the constitutionally mandated second passage[25] of the Mississippi Union Bank act might ameliorate the state's by-then ever-mounting economic woes.[26]

Alexander Gallatin McNutt[27] (1801–1848)—in time the Great Repudiator—was born in Virginia. He served two two-year terms as governor of Mississippi (January 1838 to January 1842). After studying law in what is now Washington & Lee University, McNutt came to Mississippi and set up a law office in Vicksburg. He also established a plantation partnership with Joel Cameron, some years his senior, farming flatlands north of Vicksburg and up to Deer Creek in the Mississippi Delta. In the winter of 1833, Cameron was murdered by several of his slaves, who, in short order, were tried and hanged. A few months later, McNutt married Cameron's widow—her new husband's age—acquiring not only the plantation but also a beautiful wife. All of this became of considerable interest once he became governor and signed the Married Women's Property Law in 1839.[28] Still the darker side will not die. Largely due to the reports of Henry S. Foote—himself governor for two years (1852–1854)[29] but before that a US senator, having defeated McNutt in 1847—the suggestion remains that McNutt had a hand in his partner's homicide.[30] It may or may not be going too far to suggest that anything nefarious has ever been proved.

McNutt was involved with the Mississippi Union Bank in a number of contexts. As president of the senate, McNutt signed the bill on its first passage in February 1837. In 1838, Governor McNutt's signature ostensibly sealed the State's guaranty of the Mississippi Union Bank bonds, later sued upon by Hezron Johnson and others. But McNutt did a political about-face and in the end was said to have wished that his grave be marked, "Here lies McNutt the Repudiator."[31] The obelisk that stands alone at his burial site in Greenwood Cemetery in Jackson, Mississippi, says no such thing. History accords him what at death his family and friends did not.

Tilghman Mayfield Tucker[32] (1802–1859) was born in North Carolina, lived in Alabama, and finally settled in Columbus, Mississippi, near the Tombigbee River and not far from the Alabama state line. He represented Lowndes County in the house of representatives (1831–1835) and a few years later served in the state senate (1838–1841). Tucker served an unimpressive term as governor (January 1842 to January 1844). At its January 1842 term, the High Court of Errors and Appeals upheld the constitutional viability of the Mississippi Union Bank.[33] Nonetheless, a month later, the legislature repudiated the Union Bank bonds. Governor Tucker failed utterly in his constitutional duty that he "shall take care that the laws be faithfully executed."[34] That failure was acute, given the high court's definitive pro–Union Bank ruling in the *Campbell* case. Tucker did not seek reelection as governor, but he did win and serve one term (March 1843 to March 1845) in the US House of Representatives. He retired from public life, residing at Cottonwood, a plantation home in Louisiana, until his death in April of 1859.

William Lewis Sharkey[35] (1798–1873) hailed from East Tennessee. In 1803, his family moved to an area in what is now Warren County, Mississippi, and took up farming. Sharkey was admitted to the bar in 1822. In 1828, he was elected to represent Warren County in the Mississippi legislature. A member of the convention that drafted the constitution of 1832, Sharkey strongly opposed a popularly elected judiciary. Nonetheless, an elective judiciary became a feature of the constitution that was driven by the political values of Jacksonian Democracy.[36] As fate would have it, Sharkey was elected in 1833 to the office he thought should be protected from popular political passions, justice of the High Court of Errors and Appeals, a name change for what had been and would postbellum again be known as the Supreme Court of Mississippi. Sharkey held the office of chief justice for the entirety of his service, retiring in 1851 at the age of fifty-four. As described in some detail below, Sharkey authored the 1842 opinion in the *Campbell* case upholding the constitutional and legal viability of the Mississippi Union Bank against a wide variety of challenges.[37] Sharkey spoke for the court in many other important, though less controversial, cases[38] and was widely recognized as a fine common law judge in the traditional sense. After leaving the high court, the politically Whiggish Sharkey spent the next decade of life opposing secession and disunion in every way that he could, albeit ultimately to no avail. In 1865, he served briefly as governor, once the Civil War was over. His postwar efforts to reintegrate Mississippi into the Union were equally extensive and in the end ineffective.

Cotesworth Pinckney Smith[39] (1794–1872) was a native of South Carolina. He was descended from Charles Cotesworth Pinckney (1746–1825), a veteran of the Revolutionary War and delegate from South Carolina at the 1787 constitutional convention in Philadelphia. Smith served a term on the high court that expired in 1837, and later a brief interim term. In 1849, he was elected once more to the high court, where he served as chief justice until his death in 1862. A highly regarded justice in every respect, C. Pinckney Smith is known most prominently for his 1853 opinion upholding the enforceability of his adopted state's guaranty of the Mississippi Union Bank bonds.[40]

We met Volney E. Howard (1809–1889) briefly above. He was born in Oxford County, Maine, and died in Los Angeles, California. He spent the 1840s in Mississippi, with such diverse responsibilities as representative in the legislature and official state reporter of decisions of the High Court of Errors and Appeals.[41] Less formally, he was a lawyer and a journalist. Known for his vitriolic pen, Howard steadfastly opposed the State's involvement in the Union Bank. An obituary years later recounts his duel with former governor and bank president Hiram G. Runnels.

> When the Union Bank failed Gen. Howard fearlessly criticized in his paper both the officers of the bank and their management, which led to a duel between himself and Hiram Runnels, the president of the institution, Runnels being the challenging party. The meeting took place at Columbus, and Gen. Howard was wounded, the bullet striking a rib and glancing around the breast.[42]

Howard served as counsel for Beasley Campbell and his co-plaintiffs/debtors in the first great legal attack on the Union Bank. After repudiation, Howard moved to New Orleans and established a law office there.

THREE YERGERS AND A BROTHER-IN-LAW

George Shall Yerger (1808–1860) was born in Greensburg, Pennsylvania. He was the oldest of six brothers, all but one of whom became lawyers. Politically Whigs, the Yerger family provided competent and determined legal support for legitimate banking and a sensible, pragmatic approach to Mississippi's social and economic well-being.

In 1816, the Yerger family moved to Lebanon, Tennessee. George established a law office in Nashville with his younger brother Jacob, and brother-in-law Charles Scott.[43] By 1839, the threesome had moved to Mississippi and to Vicksburg. In 1844, George moved his law office to Jackson. For the next ten years, he fought the good fight, explaining and defending the Contracts and Supremacy Clauses of the US Constitution, and the contracts clause of the Mississippi Constitution as well. He regularly represented banks in cases that were a part of the State's political "war on banks" in the 1840s and 1850s.[44] In 1841–1842, brothers-in-law George Yerger and Charles Scott appeared as bank counsel in the first of two great cases involving the validity and standing of the Mississippi Union Bank.[45] At other times, George appeared with younger brother Jacob.[46] On other occasions, George appeared with his still younger brother William.[47] More than just a bank lawyer, George served prominently as lead counsel for the defense of Daniel W. Adams in 1844 and won his client's controversial acquittal on murder charges.[48]

In 1852, Chancellor Charles Scott (1811–1861)—George's former partner and his brother-in-law, as Scott's sister, the former Miss Sally Meriwether Scott, was married to George[49]—made a trial-level ruling in favor of New York bond-holder Hezron A. Johnson. Scott told the State that its pledge of its credit and faith, guaranteeing the Union Bank bonds, really was constitutionally valid, binding, and enforceable. He ordered the State to honor its guaranty.

Jacob Shall Yerger (1810–1867) was also born in Greensburg, Pennsylvania. He was George's younger brother by two years. He studied law with George and practiced law in Nashville for a while. In 1837, this Yerger brother also established his law office in Vicksburg. Jacob was soon elected to the house of representatives and became a leader of the political forces opposing Governor McNutt, his fellow townsman, and those who sought to repudiate the Mississippi Union Bank bonds, and who had also questioned the enforceability of the State's guaranty of the Planters' Bank bonds. In January of 1841, Jacob S. Yerger, chairman of a select legislative committee, delivered a thorough and persuasive report explaining that Mississippi had a legal and moral obligation to honor its guaranty of the Union Bank bonds.[50] In 1844, Yerger appeared with his brother as appellate counsel in satellite litigation arising from the Daniel Adams murder trial.[51] Jacob later moved up to the River county of Washington, and was again elected to the legislature. In 1855, he became a circuit judge in Washington County. Along with his brothers, Jacob strongly opposed his adopted home state of Mississippi's efforts to secede from the Union.

William Yerger (1816–1872) was born in Lebanon, Tennessee, the youngest Yerger brother. He attended the University of Nashville and was reading law before he was twenty-one years old. In 1853, Justice William Yerger penned what was arguably the best legal exposition of all for enforcing the State's pledge of its credit and faith as guarantor of last resort of the Union Bank bonds, viz., his concurring opinion in the *Johnson* case.[52] Much of his story is found below.

FROM THE BEGINNING; SETTING THE STAGE

Lots of good things happened to the people of Mississippi in the first full decade of statehood, that is, for those who were white, male, and willing to work, and who had a little savvy about them and a bit of luck along the way. All in all, it was good to have become a full-fledged member of the United States of America, and of the Western world for that matter.

New technologies had become substantial enablers. Eli Whitney's cotton gin in 1793 worked wonders and in short order. Almost overnight, it became possible to separate cotton seed from lint, mechanically, easily, and quickly. Before that, cotton production had been largely limited to coastal South Carolina. The seed had to be separated from the lint by hand, a costly and time-consuming process. With the gin available, Mississippi planters found new varieties of cotton suited to their soils and climate. The sky was the limit.

More generally, the Industrial Revolution had played its part. First, water-powered textile mills, then steam-powered mills, exponentially increasing output, lowered the cost of producing fabrics. Cotton was becoming vital to the American economy as well. The textile industry had first developed in Great Britain, and in time became the Deep South and Southwest cotton producer's best customers. These were times when 75 percent of British textile mill cotton was coming from the American South. Cotton was king in Mississippi when the calendar turned to the fourth decade of the nineteenth century.

For decades, downriver keel boats and flatboats had been about the only means of transportation, for people or their products. There were stories of those in the upper South and the Midwest floating downriver to Natchez and then walking back home along the Natchez Trace. Robert Fulton's steamboat arrived in 1807. The year 1812 saw the first trial steamboat on the Mississippi River. Planters loaded cotton on steamboats and waited for profits, credit, and supplies to return.[53] Haltingly, the railroads came. The early legislative sessions show numerous small rivers in Mississippi being declared navigable and open, and thus subject to some navigational improvements. These were not enough.

Andrew Jackson had become the country's first president who came from west of the Allegheny Mountains. On May 28, 1830, Jackson signed into law the Indian Removal Act.[54] Central Mississippi lands where the Choctaw Indian Nation had lived for so many years were about to be opened to white settlers, the moment of demarcation being the so-called Treaty of Dancing Rabbit Creek, signed September 27, 1830. Two years later, the Chickasaw Nation yielded its traditional homelands in northern Mississippi. The Treaty of Pontotoc Creek. Settlement of these areas portended rapid expansions of organized existence, both public and private.

> The treaties with the Indians brought large portions . . . [of land] into market; and these portions, comprising some of the most fertile lands in the world, were settled in a hurry. . . . [These newly] public lands afforded a field for unlimited speculation, and combinations of purchasers, partnerships, land companies, agencies, and the like, gave occasion to much difficult litigation in after times. Negroes were brought into the country in large numbers and sold mostly on credit, and bills of exchange taken for the price.

Mississippi was about to join the age of internal improvements[55] that had begun to succeed nationally with the opening of the Erie Canal across northern New York. Internal improvements were a major theme of Governor Runnels's legislative address in January of 1835.[56] Steamboats were providing two-way traffic on the Mississippi River and its tributaries, including those that reached into the lands newly becoming available for white settlers. Building new roads was becoming imperative, and in time bridges and not just ferries. "An act to authorize the building and constructing of the Caledonia turnpike and bridge across the Yocknapatafa river at Dukes' ferry, in Yalobusha county"[57] or "An act to authorize the construction of a Turnpike Road from Greenwood, on the Yazoo river, to the Valley road in Carroll county,"[58] were typical of the sorts of bills regularly considered by the legislature.[59] Or to reflect another approach, there were bills like an "An act to authorize Joseph Bryant, of Lowndes County, and his associates, . . . to erect a toll bridge across the Tombigby river."[60] The state auditor urged that drawbridges and roads on piles for the passage of steamboats be constructed across the Pearl, Big Black, Tombigbee, Yazoo, Tallahatchie and Yalobusha Rivers.[61]

The quite navigable Pearl River vertically split Lawrence County, flowing through the south central part of the state before veering southeasterly to Marion County, imperceptibly growing as it divided Mississippi and Louisiana on its way to the Gulf of Mexico. Governor Lynch called Lawrence County home, and so did Governor Runnels, who saw his world evolving and emphasized the state's need for "artificial means of transportation."[62] The West Feliciana Railroad out of Woodville began operations in 1831. Over the next decade more than twenty rail lines were authorized, though most of them failed. Many of the companies would engage in banking as well as railroading, often banking first and, as it happened, banking to the exclusion of railroading. Internal improvements across Mississippi were marked by fits and starts, and by controversies among old, not so old, and newly emerging sections of the new state. Still, rail tracks were to be laid, with their iron horses affording a quantity and quality of transportation services and access theretofore unheard of.

At more local and private levels, lands were being cleared, homes built, stores and shops opened, villages and towns established. "The groceries—*vulgice* doggeries—were in full blast in those days, no village having less than a half-dozen all busy all the time." Land speculation grew,[63] extending inland particularly in the Yazoo River Basin. Life in common would never again be limited to the River counties of southwest Mississippi. Never again would Mississippi—predominantly white and male, to be sure—not need money and financial services, and services well beyond those available in New Orleans to the planter class.[64] Banks in New York, Philadelphia, and London salivated at the prospect of problematic profit opportunities among those in Mississippi and the South, and their appetites for capital and credit.

BANKING IN MISSISSIPPI

Organized economies need banks. As statehood had approached, the plantation economy in southwest Mississippi had grown to the point where banking services were not only needed. They had also become essential. In these early days, either side of December of 1817, Mississippi faced challenges not unlike those faced by the rest of the emerging country. There was not enough specie in circulation to accommodate the needs of government and commerce, provide secure credits, pay public and private debts, and provide economic stability. To meet such needs back in 1791, Alexander Hamilton had successfully proposed a national bank, owned in part by the federal government and in part by private investors. The Bank of the United States did indeed stabilize the economy, pay the national debt that had been incurred during the American Revolution, establish confidence at home and abroad in the creditworthiness of the new nation, and generally get the country off the ground and running on a sound financial basis.

In 1798, the Mississippi Territory needed a uniform currency and credit quickly converted into specie. In 1808, the territorial legislature chartered the original Bank of the State of Mississippi. Established as a private entity, this bank was still the state's only bank as the calendar reached January of 1830. After statehood, the legislature increased the bank's authorized capital from $500,000 to $3 million, with authority to establish up to three branch banks. Seven years later, the state had fourteen banks. Six of these were by their charters dedicated to promoting railroads.[65] Recall that the Second Bank of the United States had expired, not having been rechartered after 1836, thanks to the determined efforts of President Jackson. The vacuum abhorred, nine more state banks were soon chartered. Their doors opened for business in 1838.[66] Internal improvements were the primary function of five of these, with four railroad banks and one to establish a waterworks. Indeed, the banks themselves came to be viewed as internal improvements.

THE PLANTERS' BANK OF MISSISSIPPI

On February 10, 1830, Mississippi's second bank was born, with a twenty-five-year projected life. It was named Planters' Bank of the State of Mississippi, no surprise given the state's agricultural history to that time. By design or folly, a postbellum generation of Mississippians had by its state constitution assured this once-promising new bank a permanent—albeit second-level—role in state historical and financial infamy. A constitutional amendment dating to 1875 made sure that this became and would remain so.[67]

In 1830, the legislature mandated banking services with a broad coverage of areas away from the River. In addition to its central place of business in Natchez, the original state's bank had offices in Woodville, Port Gibson, and Marion County. The new Planters' Bank was also based in Natchez, but it afforded greater coverage in the River counties, adding offices in Rodney and Vicksburg.

A branch in Monticello and newly formed Lawrence County would service the Marion County area, where the original bank had an office. A Planters' Bank branch in Liberty and Amite County recognized continued development east of the River counties but west of the Pearl River. Most auspicious was the new Planters' Bank branch to the north and east over in Columbus near the Alabama state line,[68] servicing Tombigbee River area banking needs. Columbus was about to become the very busy home of the federal land office for the sale of newly opened Choctaw lands.

The new Planters' Bank had an authorized capital of $3 million, $2 million of which, according to its charter, "shall be reserved for the State of Mississippi, and may be subscribed and paid for by the State on the terms and according to the manner hereinafter prescribed." Capital from outside Mississippi would be needed for the success of this new venture. The legislature authorized the sale of bonds—loans from the public, in practical effect—to raise the $2 million to pay for the State's shares. The stock purchased by the State would be pledged to secure payment to bondholders. Of importance, given what lay ahead, the State pledged its credit and "faith," guaranteeing—up to $2 million—that no one buying bank bonds would take a loss should the Planters' Bank not respond appropriately.[69] On August 15, 1831, commissioners sold the first $500,000 in Planters' Bank bonds, making them payable at the Phoenix Bank of New York.[70]

Mississippi was still under its original constitution in 1830.[71] There were no cumbersome and time-consuming procedural obstacles to be surmounted by the legislature en route to pledging the State's credit and faith. Indeed, when such hoops were erected in 1832, it was expressly declared,

> Provided, That nothing in this section shall be so construed as to prevent the legislature from negotiating a further loan of one and a half million of dollars, and vesting the same in stock reserved to the state by the charter of the Planters' Bank of the state of Mississippi.[72]

Legislation enacted on February 5, 1833, implemented this proviso. On July 25, 1833, commissioners sold to the public the remaining $1.5 million in Planters' Bank bonds.[73]

The 1830 legislature had articulated its thinking behind "the establishment . . . [of the new Planters' Bank] for the purposes of general convenience and public revenues." While hardly enforceable and in some part mere hyperbole, it is helpful to bear in mind the countervailing expectations widely held that the new bank

> would, on the one hand by a judicious increase of the circulating medium, give impulse and vigor to agricultural labor, activity to commercial enterprise, and increased value to our lands, and on the other, by a creation of revenue, relieve

the citizens of this State from an oppressive burden of taxes, and enable them to realize the blessings of a correct system of Internal Improvements.[74]

As the State entered the latter half of the 1830s, a political subtext emerged. The newly empowered Jacksonian Democrats began coopting the business opportunities that might otherwise have led the Second Bank of the United States to establish a branch in Mississippi. The story of Andrew Jackson's blood feud with the Second Bank and his ultimate achievement or folly (depending on one's point of view) in vetoing the renewal of its charter when it expired in 1836, has been told and retold. "A page of history is worth a volume of logic"[75] is a wise insight from a collateral context.

In this second decade of statehood and beyond, corporate charters in Mississippi required the same procedures as—and took the form of—new statutes. This meant substantial state involvement in launching a new corporate venture. And more politics as well, particularly in the case of banking entities. It also meant that the State was making contracts with each new entity that it might not impair, inconsistent with either its or the US Constitution. The 1830 Planters' Bank Act chartered and regulated the banking business in which it was authorized and charged to engage.[76] For one thing, the Planters' Bank became the state's fiscal agent, serving as depository for state funds. The bank was to be governed by a thirteen-member board of directors, seven of whom would be appointed by the governor, with the advice and consent of the senate. Private shareholders would elect the other six directors.

Numerous commonsense and quite conservative safeguards were prescribed, lest the bank be tempted to take imprudent risks. For example, loans made upon the security of real property required use of a specified mortgage form worded so as to protect the bank's interests. In no event might the bank loan a customer more than one-third part of the real unencumbered value of the property so mortgaged. Such a mortgage loan could not be made upon such security for a period longer than one year, nor might the amount so loaned exceed four thousand dollars. Interest had to be paid in advance. Loan renewals required payment of one-fourth of the principal due and the regular and prompt payment of the interest. In no event could the aggregate principal amount of mortgage indebtedness exceed one-half of paid-in capital held by the bank.

The Planters' Bank's charter was originally set to expire on March 1, 1855. In time, the bank became focused on financing a new railroad from Jackson to Canton through the offices of a new and separate corporation. A legislative amendment provided "that if the said Rail Road Company should not complete a rail road from the city of Jackson to the town of Canton, in the county of Madison, by the first day of October, 1841, that said company should forfeit their banking privileges." Less legal and calendric events and circumstances would ring down the curtain long before that, save for the political prejudices that would ascend and—as though through some force of nature—prevent the State from honoring its pledge to pay the Planters' Bank bonds.[77] A hard-line, never really justified position that remains in black and white in the state constitution.[78] But we are again getting ahead of the story.

FLUSH TIMES

"Flush Times" is the label commonly used to capture the robust prosperity experienced by Mississippi and its environs over the first three-quarters of the decade of the 1830s. This "southwestern" socioeconomic phenomenon has been prominently explained as "a period constituting an episode in the commercial history of [a particular part of] the world—the reign of humbug, and wholesale insanity, just overthrown in time to save the whole country from ruin"[79] Measured by population growth, profits from cotton production and other businesses, increasing land values, easy credit—pick your criteria—life was as boisterous as it was competitive as it was optimistic as it was rascally on the new nation's southwestern frontier in the 1830s.

Jackson remained in the White House as flush times approached maturity, but there was much more to the Age of Jackson than just political office. The way people understood themselves, their neighbors, their country and its future, a way of looking at life itself, and even the ambiguity of all things human was changing everywhere. In the original Southwest,

> Money, or what passed for money, was the only cheap thing to be had. . . . Credit was a thing of course. To refuse it—if the thing was ever done—was an insult for which a bowie-knife was not too summary or exemplary a means of redress.[80]

But that was not all. "It was faith. Let the public believe that a smutted rag is money, it is money . . . it was a sort of financial biology." Since statehood and before, Natchez had provided the heart and soul of a lifestyle stretching from below the Louisiana state line up toward Vicksburg, but not far above. No longer would Charleston and Savannah on the east or the old River county culture to the west set the pace of life. Still, the foundation had been weakened. In 1832, Jackson had undermined confidence in the Second Bank by vetoing its recharter bill.

Then it happened. In January of 1836, the Second Bank of the United States' charter expired. What is more, "To get down from the clouds to level ground, the Specie Circular was issued without warning, and the splendid lie of a false credit burst into fragments." Jackson had won his war with Nicholas Biddle and Hamiltonian thinking. In short order, financial speculation was rampant, seemingly everywhere. The president, gathered into the vocabulary of the inimitable Joseph Baldwin, the Jupiter Tonans of the White House saw the monster of a free credit prowling about like a beast of apocalyptic vision, and marked him for his prey. Gathering all of his bolts in his sinewy grasp, and standing back on his heels, and waving his wiry arm, he let them all fly, hard and swift upon all the Hydra's heads.[81]

By July of 1836, Andrew Jackson had changed more than the direction of federal land policy—a sudden one-eighty in and of itself. The federal government would thenceforth accept at its busy land offices only hard currency—gold and silver— and Virginia land script. In 1837, Whig governor Charles Lynch had this take on the by-now-departing president's edict: "The unexpected call for specie payments in the land offices, has produced a shock in the money market, very sensibly felt: and if the system is persisted in, must become excessively oppressive to our citizens." Then the governor thoughtfully added,

That an accession to the metallic circulating currency would give greater solidity to that of paper, may be admitted, but it is equally certain that such a measure should be very gradual in its operations, and taken with great precaution, in order to avoid the ill effects resulting from a general derangement.[82]

A year later, Lynch reflected that, "in this posture of affairs, the specie circular made its appearance, which had the effect of disturbing the course of exchange, by making gold and silver worth more than bank bills, and causing a sudden demand and continued run for specie."[83] The panic in spring 1837 involved more than Andy Jackson out of control. Deflation settled in under the ill-fated William Henry Harrison and continued under John Tyler. Tippecanoe and Tyler Too! By February in 1842, both nationally and in Mississippi, the weak economy began to bottom out, and people started worrying about other more mortal and politically moral issues.

It was a while before anyone would think much about the Planters' Bank bonds. Six percent interest had been payable semiannually from the outset. The first series of $250,000 was payable in 1840, and similar series at five-year inter- vals after that.[84] Prior to the spring of 1837, plenty of insiders and the public perceived that the Planters' Bank was doing well. In 1836, state auditor John H. Mallory had looked at the accounts and found "the most conclusive evidence that the bank is in a prosperous condition."[85] A year later, Mallory made simi- lar findings and recommended that surplus revenues received by the State be invested in Planters' Bank stock: "The stock of that Bank stands higher than any bank in the United States."[86] An accompanying statement as of December 1836 regarding the affairs of the bank supported this glowing report.[87] There is no evidence that even in 1840, when the State first defaulted on its inter- est payments, anyone thought the Planters' Bank—much less the State that had pledged its faith—had need of a legal defense to payment.

A STRANGE AND CERTAIN BIRTH

As 1838 approached, times got tougher in Mississippi. To what extent this was a function of Andy Jackson's foibles or more generally the Panic of 1837 was neither clear nor particularly important. What was important was that the price of cotton had dropped dramatically and was remaining low. The fair market value of lands fell and continued falling. Flush times had come and were now gone. The point proved was that panics could be as local as politics. The bodacious Baldwin summarized the scene on the ground, in *Flush Times*, and with particulars.

> [M]any land titles were defective; property was brought from other states clogged with trusts, limitations and uses, to be construed according to the laws of the State from which it was brought: claims and contracts made elsewhere to be enforced here: universal indebtedness, with the hardness of times succeeding made it impossible for men to pay, and desirable for all to escape paying; hard and ruinous bargains, security ships, judicial sales; a general looseness, ignorance, carelessness in the public officers in doing business; . . . banks, the laws governing their contracts, proceedings against them for forfeiture of charter; trials of right of property; an elegant assortment of frauds constructive and actual; . . . in short all the flood-gates of litigation were opened, and the pent-up tide let loose upon the country.[88]

The idea for what became the Union Bank is traceable to the middle 1830s, this period called Mississippi's banking orgy.[89] On January 21, 1835, Governor Runnels told the legislature it should establish a new bank "placed at the control of the planters of this country [which would] insure a sound currency and at the same time, [would] enable the planters to increase their force and render more productive their lands." He noted the new constitutional procedural barriers to the State pledging its faith to support such a banking venture. No such rules—such as repetitious enactments at successive legislative sessions—had applied back in 1830 when the State pledged its faith in support of the Planters' Bank bonds. Runnels understood that the State needed outside capital to launch the new undertaking, and lots of outside capital. He urged the legislature "to determine whether such guards may not be thrown around the institution, as will render perfectly safe the lender of the capital." [90]

In January of 1837, Governor Lynch looked ahead and spoke of the public need for "certain measures of internal improvement." Auditor Mallory recommended investments for "the purpose of sustaining a general system of internal improvements."[91] Funding such efforts was another matter. Lynch was sober on the point. "The prospect of effecting a sale of the bonds to advantage in a Northern market is rather discouraging, and it may be well that an agent be appointed by your body, to negotiate a sale in Europe."[92] At that legislative session "an act to incorporate the subscribers to the Union Bank" was presented. The proposed charter created a familiar pecking order of liabilities, should all not go well. To the extent that the bank did not have funds on hand to meet its obligations, dividends from the bank stock would be appropriately rechanneled. Past that, land and other plantation assets pledged by shareholders were the assets of primary resort. In the end, Section 5 of the act/charter provided that "the faith of this State be, and it is hereby pledged, both for the security of the capital and interest in 7,500 bonds of $2,000 each payable over twenty years, with interest at five percent payable annually."[93] As a practical matter, everyone expected that the new bank would service its bonded indebtedness, both principal and interest.[94] The State's credit and faith were a pledge, a guaranty of last resort. It was such a pledge that the new two-step, two-successive-session constitutional process[95] should be invoked.

The first full legislative passage of the Union Bank bill was accomplished on January 21, 1837, consistent with constitutional commands. It bore the official and authorized signature of A. G. McNutt, at the time president of the senate. This was followed by the formal approval "so far as the action of this Legislature is recognized" by Governor Lynch.[96] The story from that point has been told again and again, its details debated and documented and denounced, again and again.[97]

Lynch did not seek reelection. In his final message to the legislature on January 4, 1838, as he was about to leave office, Lynch took somber notice of the economic difficulties that had beset the state. He had ideas of what needed to be done. The first substantive matter he mentioned was the Mississippi Union Bank Act, which was then before the legislature for its second go-round. He sought to improve on the two-successive-session rule, not to evade it. Prospective foreign investors were worthy of protection, just as much as the people who needed so badly for foreign investors to lend their money to the new State-backed bank.

Lynch prioritized his thoughts.

> First, . . . —whether the sanction of your body to the charter of the "Mississippi Union Bank," should not be immediately followed by certain amendments— whether our present difficulties do not demand your prompt action in authorizing the issue of five or six millions of dollars in state bonds.

After assessing the then-present circumstances in historical context, including the history of Planters' Bank, Lynch added, "The latest information relative to the European money market, presents the prospect of a favorable negotiation of the State bonds proposed to be issued under the charter of the Mississippi Union Bank."[98] This information proved correct, albeit augmented by the facility and financial acumen of Nicholas Biddle. It was a happy prospect in January of 1838.

Practical reality and the times cried out for a remedial measure now that the flush times party was over and the proverbial "fat lady" had well begun to wail. The idea of a new Mississippi Union Bank took on a greater urgency. Alternatives were few. Lynch's term of office would end before the legislature became primed for its second shot at the bill that proposed "[t]he establishment of a Union Bank to supply the actual or supposed deficit of banking capital, and for the relief of the general embarrassment under the pressure of the times." Many ideas and justifications were floated almost daily. "A mortgage on real estate for the payment of stock subscriptions for individuals, affords the best security, and for the payment and redemption of the interest and loan, nothing perhaps can be so safely relied upon as a well-regulated sinking fund."[99] Never mind that the values of the real estate to be mortgaged were far from stable, and the fluctuations by and large were downward, and then further downward.

On February 15, 1838, Alexander Gallatin McNutt had been governor for some thirty-seven days. The State had put in place the legal architecture within which the Mississippi Union Bank would soon organize and open its doors for business. And Governor McNutt signed a supplemental bill—the last piece in the complex legislative puzzle constituting the bank's charter, its contract—providing additional protections for the State, which was pledging its credit and faith to hold harmless the bond-buying public, should the Union Bank not make as much money as its organizers thought it should. Because it did not enlarge upon or modify the State's guaranty obligation, this supplemental bill was not submitted to a second legislative session. By then it was some nine months after May of 1837 and its financial Panic, and the warning signals it had posted for those who would see. Maybe Mississippi could not have known there would be another banking crisis in October of 1839 and still another in January of 1842. Or that plantation and other land values would tank after Union Bank bonds had in fact been bought and sold on August 18, 1838, and after the money had been received in five equal $1 million installments every two months beginning November 1, 1838, through and including July 1, 1839.[100]

The bonds were originally sold to Nicholas Biddle. As a recent commentator put it, "The United States Bank of Pennsylvania famously bought the Mississippi Union Bank bonds and used them to secure loans from European investors." According to one historical account, on August 18, 1838, the commissioners sealed the deal with Biddle.

As soon as the intelligence of the sale of the bonds reached Mississippi, the unthinking multitudes were wild with a delirium of joy. Bonfires and illuminations were the order of the day, or rather of the night, while great guns, the rattle of drums, the blare of trumpets and the shouts of the frantic multitude made night absolutely hideous.[101]

Another commentator embellished the story: "Later, in the fall of 1838, $5,000,000 in British gold and specie arrived at New Orleans, traveled up the Mississippi River to Vicksburg, and eventually reached Jackson. Enthusiastic crowds lined the route from Vicksburg to Jackson, firing guns and celebrating." It is not clear which of the five installment payments evoked this exuberant report, though presumably it was the first made on November 1, 1838. As early as 1840, Democrats were no longer thrilled that the foreign markets had been so receptive to Nicholas Biddle's approach. This was Monday-morning quarterbacking. Back in 1838, no one had come up with a viable alternative source of financing. This did not deter McNutt from throwing a politically charged monkey wrench into the mix two years later. "I have understood that the larger portion of those bonds have not been sold by the bank, but are hypothecated with European bankers, and loans obtained upon them."[97] So?!

Concerning the proposed pledge of the credit and faith of the State, Governor Lynch had set out his view that

> The State can have no motive in making such a transaction a matter of profit. In loaning its credit to carry into effect this institution, it should be influenced from higher considerations, that of the interest and prosperity of the whole community. All it can desire is an ample indemnity against the risk and any ultimate loss on the bonds.[98]

But Lynch was on the sidelines now.

Soon after the ink was dry in February of 1838, the Union Bank had been organized, grumblings by Democrats aside. One of the first orders of business was the legislature's selection of the ten managers. With each legislator voting for ten, former governor and early supporter, Hiram G. Runnels, was by far the top vote-getter. Lynch did not fare so well. On the seventh ballot for Union Bank manager, he was eliminated.[99] Politics, no doubt, given Lynch's Whig affiliation. Moreover, his popularity had waned, given the troubled times that had set in over the preceding nine months or so.

MCNUTT DECLARES WAR

A month *before* he signed the Union Bank Act and the $5 million in bonds, new governor McNutt had made his first public declaration[100] of what would become the war on banks that he would lead for the next four years. Making his own examination of the internal affairs of the state's banks was the first step. "There are now in operation twenty-eight banks and branches. The affairs of seventeen of which we have critically examined."[101] McNutt decried the "conduct of the Planters' and Agricultural Banks," which he claimed had "defied the legislative will of the people in refusing an examination of their affairs by commissioners appointed by the legislature...." In January of 1839, McNutt reminded one and all of the obligations the State had assumed regarding the Planters' Bank bonds and the Union Bank bonds. He added,

> To preserve the honor of the State unsullied, and her credit unimpaired, it is of the last importance that the interest should be promptly paid, at the places desig-nated, and ample funds provided for the redemption of the principal—it is usually much easier to borrow and spend money than to provide the means of payment.

Then McNutt began offering mea culpas for his role in the circumstances of which he had begun to complain.

> My recorded votes on the Journals of the Senate, as well as my speeches, during the canvass preceding my election to the office I now occupy, show that I never was in favor of pledging the faith of the State for banking purposes, but inasmuch as the question had been long before the people and had twice received their sanction, I signed the charter of the Mississippi Union bank, having no constitu-tional scruples.[102]

Not only had he signed the Mississippi Union Bank Act in his official capac-ity as governor, he had signed the guaranty, along with the state treasurer, acti-vating the State's pledge of its credit and faith in having guaranteed payments of principal and interest to holders of Union Bank bonds. Nor did the governor mention that there had been no other viable options for raising the capital nec-essary so that the Union Bank might open its doors for business.

Rather, Governor McNutt began laying out his case against the bonds, a case as political as it was legal, one he would embellish, expand, and elaborate for years to come. He took liberties with the facts when he argued, "The State, by her credit alone, has furnished the whole capital of the Mississippi Union Bank, and justice requires that she should have the appointment of a majority of the board of directors."[103] McNutt conveniently forgot that substantial capital con-tributions had been made by individuals in the stock subscriptions. To be sure, many pledged real property and other plantation assets, the values of which had fallen since the Union Bank opened for business in the spring of 1838, as a function of general economic conditions in the area and the country. How any of this should have impaired the legal security of the bona fide bondholders was hard to follow. Nor is it apparent that these planter stock purchasers were acting in anything other than good faith at the relevant times.

On January 5, 1841, and at beginning his third year in office, Governor McNutt included in his annual message to the legislature an important and tell-ing insight. Incompetence, inefficiency, and neglect of duty pervaded the State's revenue-raising processes, and by and large across the board. Tax collectors were not collecting taxes that were due. "Large balances were still unpaid for taxes accrued in prior years. Some assessors had failed to return their assessment rolls." "Not more than one half of the taxable property in the state is ever assessed, and large portions of the taxes collected are never paid into the state treasury." "[A] change in our whole system of assessing and collecting the revenue" will be necessary if "the expenses of government ... [are to] be sustained."[104] All points to be kept in mind as we follow the governor leading the charge toward repudiation, though there was more to come before that fateful moment.

Reports on the state's cotton crop and other issues followed, until McNutt turned to banking, finance, and currency. "I consider the whole system vicious," he declared. "It can never be so regulated, as to be useful to any community." A tirade of generalized particulars ensued regarding—with twenty-twenty hindsight—Mississippi's undisputed excess of banks, all of which the legislature had authorized with gubernatorial approval. McNutt pronounced, "Justice to their creditors, debtors and stockholders, and to the state, imperiously demand that they be placed in liquidation for the benefit of all concerned." The governor reported that the Mississippi Union Bank and the Planters' Bank were insolvent. Interest on Planters' Bank bonds was not being paid. In short order, he had issued proclamations declaring the charters of nine banks forfeited, including the Mississippi Union Bank. Eight other banks, including the Planters' Bank, were said to "have failed to comply with the injunctions of the bank laws." The governor complained that he was "not advised upon what terms the two millions of state bonds, delivered to the Planters' Bank in the year 1831 and 1833 were sold."

But the Union Bank was McNutt's principal focus. "The Mississippi Union Bank, hereafter, will be totally unable to pay the interest on the five millions of state bonds issued in 1838."[105] In addition to initiating liquidation, he advised legislators that they would be asked to consider "repudiating the sale of five millions of the bonds in the year 1838, on account of fraud and illegality." As noted above, the sale of these bonds had been documented.

[F]ive millions of bonds were disposed of on the 18th day of August, 1838, for five million dollars, payable in five equal installments, on the first day of November, 1838, and on the first days of January, March, May and July, 1839—interest accrued on the bonds from the day of the contract.

The lawyer/governor never let on that, in such circumstances and eventuality as he was suggesting, the State should return the $5 million that it had received and accepted and made available to the Union Bank. Nor did he mention whether public celebrations attended the arrival of the four installment payments made in 1839.

McNutt had a curious closing thought. "If new subjects of taxation are not resorted to, each taxpayer in the state will have to pay twenty dollars where he now pays one."[106] No mention was made of how much more each taxpayer could expect to pay if—as the governor had suggested at the outset—the deficiencies "in our whole system of assessing and collecting the revenue" were corrected.

THE SELECT COMMITTEE RESPONDS

According to custom founded on respect for the office of "his excellency," select legislative committees at each session studied the governor's various recommendations and other substantive comments. Such a select committee was appointed to study and report regarding the part of the governor's message as related to state guaranteed bonds. In due course, Jacob S. Yerger, chairman of the select committee, reported to the governor, the legislature, and the public.

Sight should not be lost of two related dimensions of the issues before the committee. First, if there had been legal problematics in the way things had been done in early 1838, should those affect bondholders who in good faith had loaned their money to the State or purchased bonds held by Nicholas Biddle or those with whom he had dealt? Put another way, if there were legal problematics, did those excuse the State from its having pledged its credit and "faith" and guaranteed to the bondholders that—if all else failed—the State would repay the loans made? Assuming, of course, that en route thereto the relevant procedures set out in the constitution had been complied with. Third, should any such concerns excuse the State from exhausting its remedies against wrongdoers, such as those allegedly responsible for corporate mismanagement within the bank? Or from satisfying its equitable duties should the remedy sought by the State include rescission? These aside, there remained the time-tested and proven Hamiltonian bedrock view that the creditworthiness of a state in the eyes of the financial community at large is a treasure the great value of which has no limits.

In the early 1830s, some $2 million had been received by the State and paid into the Planters' Bank. By contract signed on August 18, 1838, we now know that $5 million in State-guaranteed Union Bank bonds were sold to Nicholas Biddle of Philadelphia, and in five installments these funds were received by the Union Bank and the State. Were there legal concerns with either set of bonds sold, and assuming there was no fault or failure attributable to the bondholders, was there a reason why the remedy should not include return of the funds received? If the banks could not respond, was there a reason why the State should not honor its guaranty that the loans represented by the bonds would be paid in full? And should not the State then proceed against the bank officers or any others who may have been responsible?

Chairman Yerger replied, regretting that the governor had raised "questions so materially affecting the honor, character and dignity of the State." He particularly regretted that these issues "should have arisen at a time of such unusual pecuniary depression as the present." January of 1841 was barely fifteen months past the great national banking crisis of October of 1839, which had followed all too closely on the heels of the Panic of 1837. Chairman Yerger briefly explained the circumstances surrounding the Planters' Bank bonds, noting all had been fine until the spring of 1837, when "the suspension of specie payments by the banks throughout the United States, took place." These bonds had been sold back in 1831 and 1833, "bearing interest from the time of their negotiation at the rate of six percent per annum, for the payment of which the faith of the State was pledged." While records regarding the issuance and sale of the Planters' Bank bonds were less than desirable, Yerger made clear his confidence that all was legally in order. Regarding the Planters' Bank bonds, "there is not the slightest pretense for a refusal to pay, growing out of the manner in which they were negotiated."[107]

Many rose to join Governor McNutt, and others stood by Chairman Yerger's select committee report. The debates of 1841 did little more than stake out the positions for the political combatants.

Governor McNutt left office in January of 1842. In his final message, McNutt seemed to back off from any attack on the Planters' Bank bonds. He was still unhappy with that bank's opposition to his efforts at a full audit of its affairs. But McNutt confirmed that $500,000 in Planters' Bank bonds had been issued in 1831 and sold in New York by commissioners appointed by the governor and that in 1833 the remaining $1,500,000 in State-backed bonds . . . were likewise sold.[108] "With the proceeds of the bonds thus negotiated, the State took two millions of stock in the Planters' Bank."[109]

Following McNutt's departure, Rep. Gordon D. Boyd took up the fight over the Planters' Bank bonds. In 1838, the Mississippi Union Bank Act had designated then-senator Boyd as one of three managers for Attala County.[110] By 1842, Boyd was serving a term in the house. His bank politics had done a one-eighty. Representative Boyd went so far as to become an outspoken opponent of the State ever paying the Planters' Bank bonds. He denounced the notion that the State had to honor its guaranty. He argued that successive legislatures could always undo what prior legislatures had done. Any law can be repealed. Never mind that any such repeal might impair the obligations of contracts the State had made, offending both US and state constitutions. Regarding the Planters' Bank bonds, Boyd argued that "[o]ur right to repudiate is sanctioned by high heaven; and the impious assertion of man that he has the right to sell his fellow-man, born and unborn, is forbidden by those laws which come from the throne of the eternal." Dissenting to the joint select committee's view that the bonds should be honored, Boyd filled nineteen pages in the *House Journal*,[111] which were and remain a great read. A wordy Patrick Henry, if you will, his every paragraph filled with a poignant passion. The problems of such passions, of course, were many, and they were substantial. For one thing, repudiation rather blatantly impaired the obligations of contracts—the Planters' Bank bonds were contracts—that really were protected by both federal and state constitutions.[112] The equitable remedy of rescission required restoring the bondholders to their position before they had advanced the first penny. Past that, should not the State be expected to exhaust remedies against those said to have been responsible?

Returning to Governor McNutt and the Union Bank bonds, much had been made of the pass-it-twice clause of the constitution before the credit and "faith of the State" might be pledged for a debt.[113] McNutt argued disingenuously. Jacob Yerger's select committee took advantage. The State's pledge in Section 5 of the Union Bank bill had been passed at the 1837 legislature. The three-newspaper publication requirement was satisfied during the political campaigning leading to the November 1837 statewide elections. Yerger made the telling point that

> [t]he legislature which assembled in 1838, and repassed the act, was "fresh from the people" themselves and was elected after the people had full time to canvass and decide upon the propriety of the issuance of the bonds, and the pledge of the State's faith for their redemption. This [1838] sanction of the legislature . . . to the act passed in 1837, is the deliberate expression of the public will, which it is too late now to gainsay or question.[114]

McNutt had relied on this very same point, trying to explain away his having signed off on the Union Bank Act.[115] Chairman Yerger made sure that the governor was hoist with his own petard.

The twice-passed act was in practical effect the official corporate charter of the Mississippi Union Bank. Ten days later—on February 15, 1838—the legislature amended the Union Bank Act, passing a supplemental bill setting out procedural aspects of the bond issue. Ten bank directors—called "managers" in the bill—were empowered to appoint three commissioners to sell the State bonds in any market, foreign or domestic.[116] The Panic of 1837 had dealt the commissioners a tough hand. The whole idea of the Union Bank was driven by the public purpose of ameliorating the impacts of the Panic upon the long-laboring people of Mississippi. Indeed,

> contrary . . . to the expectation of everyone familiar with the distressed condition of the stock market, a negotiation of five millions of the bonds was effected by the commissioners highly advantageous to the State and to the bank, and in accordance with the injunctions of the charter, requiring them to be sold at par value. A sale reflecting the highest credit upon the commissioners themselves, and bringing timely aid to an embarrassed community.

The select committee report continued to note legislative approvals of the Union Bank bond sale. In the almost three years leading to the advent of Governor McNutt as the leading repudiator, "the Legislature have had full cognizance of the whole dealing upon the negotiation of the bonds without evincing the least disposition to avoid the state's responsibility upon them." Nonetheless, because times were tough and banks generally were in trouble in January of 1841, the legislature was being asked to "repudiate the sales of the bonds, sold on the account of the Mississippi Union and Planters' Banks, [to] withdraw the faith of the State pledged for the redemption of the bonds, and [to] refuse their payment."[117]

Chairman Yerger's select committee then considered the nuts and bolts of arguments made for repudiation, and exposed the fallacies of each. Foremost was what should have been done about the moneys that Nicholas Biddle and his successor bondholders had in fact advanced and loaned to the Union Bank on the guaranty of the faith of the State. The committee reported that "the state should pay back to the purchaser of the bonds, the sum[s] ... actually received with interest from the time of ... receipt, before she repudiates the sale of the bonds, and withdraws her faith pledged for their redemption."[118] This was a commonsense approach, equitable variety.

This was so even if one assumes that McNutt and his fellow repudiators were correct in their view of the facts. The essence of the repudiators' case was that some fraud, mistake, or illegality had put the State in a position where bond-holders were unfairly demanding payment out of the public treasury. Such circumstances gave rise to the equitable remedy of rescission, which was known in Mississippi law at least as early as 1824.[119] Such circumstances, again, if everything the repudiators argued was correct in law and in fact, meant that the bonds (treated as contracts) were unenforceable from the outset. The goal of the equitable remedy of rescission has always been returning the parties to the status quo before either party did anything under the contract to his or its detriment. Rescission has never been available except where it has been "accompanied by restitution of any actual performance, thus returning the parties to their pre-contractual position."[120]

Without reasonable doubt, the State's involvement in the Union Bank had been extensive from the inception of the idea for such a bank. Couple this with the terms of the bonds, which had been fixed by statute. Equity commanded that good-faith repudiators line up behind the view that the bondholders get their money back. To the extent that it paid what the Union Bank could not, the State would have every right to look to the malefactors on its side of the bargain for full indemnity.

Never! This was Governor McNutt's response, although he was a member of the bar, and his authorized, voluntary, and official signature was all over the documents on whose terms and validity the bondholders relied, dating back to his days as president of the senate. A year later, in 1842, McNutt would answer Union Bank bondholders Messrs. Hope & Co., Amsterdam, Holland, and reiterate his defiance, reaffirming what he had told others, of his "belief that the State is not bound for the redemption of the bonds issued in 1838. . . . [T]he State never will pay the five millions of dollars in State bonds delivered to the Mississippi Union Bank, or any part of the interest due or to become due thereon." McNutt became a bit exuberant—laying aside that which as a lawyer he was charged with knowing—as he recited the appeal others had made to the people of Mississippi that the bonds be honored.

> No power can compel them to pay a demand which they know to be unjust. This result has gloriously sustained the sacred truth, that the toiling millions never should be burdened with taxes to support the idle few. Our constituents have wisely resolved that the highest obligations of honor, faith and justice, demand of us a strict adherence to the constitution.

The governor continued. Should Mississippi succumb to the demands being made—that the State honor the pledge of credit and faith its officers had made, and "in violation of law, burthen unborn generations with onerous debts—freedom will no longer exist, and our star will be blasted forever from the constellation of republican states." In fine political fashion, and no doubt sensing that his legislative audience was with him all the way, McNutt pressed his offensive. "It is probable that all the facts in regard to the sale of the bonds delivered to the Planters' and Union Banks have not come to light." He urged the legislators to seize the moment "and send for persons and papers, and to examine witnesses on oath. I therefore earnestly recommend a searching enquiry into all the facts connected with the sale of bonds." And on and on and on.[121]

Before he was through, McNutt would place before the legislature "Letters from Fundmongers," polite if formal letters from bondholders asking that they be paid, followed by the governor's tirades in response. One such letter of inquiry bore "the official frank of Daniel Webster, Secretary of State of the United States."[122]

But the worm was about to turn. It had begun squirming as early as mid-1840.

THE MISSISSIPPI UNION BANK IN COURT

To a large extent the disputants split along party lines. Whigs argued that the State had pledged its faith in order that the Union Bank bonds could be marketed, and that the State was bound—legally, ethically, and prudentially—to stand behind that pledge, as guarantor of last resort. For a while there had been a Democratic minority that was pro-bond. By 1842, that group had dwindled so that the party became rabid repudiators. After all, the Union Bank had failed within a year of opening its doors. The arguments pro and con began to center on the question of whether the Bank had been created and organized consistent with the still relatively new constitution of 1832. Proponents and opponents were outspoken lawyers as well as politicians, many of whom have been introduced above.

McNutt had become the most rabid repudiator, his own support for the Union Bank while a state senator and in his first year as governor notwithstanding. His rhetoric was always a strong mixture of political legalisms and moralisms, viz., it would be unjust to saddle today's increasingly debt-ridden people and generations unborn with a said-to-be crushing financial burden whose source was in no way their fault. Tilghman M. Tucker assumed the role of repudiator-in-chief once he was handed the governor's gavel on January 10, 1842. Lawyer-legislator Jacob Yerger had produced a strong pro-bond argument with his select committee report in 1841. Yerger answered McNutt point by point and added moralisms as well, that the State's pledge of its credit and faith had created a moral obligation as well as a legal one. Litigation became inevitable.

The Circuit Court of Rankin County was the court of original jurisdiction, affording the venue as well. In liquidation at the time, the Union Bank brought a common law action in assumpsit[123] to establish the validity of the promissory note Beasley Campbell and others had signed on March 18, 1839. Campbell's group was well represented by Volney E. Howard. The Union Bank was represented by brothers-in-law Charles Scott and George Yerger.[124] The question was *not* whether the State had to pay a Union Bank bond that it had guaranteed. Initially, the case turned on Campbell's use of a new banking and currency statute to evade his own debt, to avoid paying his promissory note held by the bank and long overdue. On July 10, 1840, the Union Bank had refused to pay specie—hard currency, gold or silver—for its ten-dollar banknote presented by Campbell and others. Quite possibly this was a setup, or at least the beginnings of a test case. It was common knowledge at the time that financially the Union Bank was in extremis. Almost certainly the bank would not be able to comply with the new currency law. Promptly upon the bank's refusal, the matter was brought to the attention of its arch enemy, A. G. McNutt. The governor was ready and waiting. On that same day in July of 1840, he "declare[d] that all banking powers and privileges of the Mississippi Union Bank . . . are forfeited."[125]

The pleadings before the circuit court framed in legal dressing the questions that had been hotly debated in political forums over the prior two years. First, was the supplemental act passed and signed on February 15, 1838, constitutionally valid? More broadly, was the legislatively enacted charter of the Union Bank a valid act? Campbell et al. demurred to the complaint. Until modern times, a demurrer was a defendant's procedural way of saying to the plaintiff in practical effect that, if every fact you have alleged is true, you still have no case. Circuit Judge Buckner C. Harris promptly sustained the demurrer and dismissed the Union Bank's complaint.[126] A sustained demurrer afforded a procedural means for expediting adjudication in the high court of an important and controlling question of law, without the time and trouble of a trial on the facts. Judge Harris sent the case expeditiously on its way westerly and across the Pearl River.

Three justices made up the high court in 1842. By the time the Union Bank's appeal hit the docket, Chief Justice William L. Sharkey was a ten-year veteran. Justices Edward Turner and James F. Trotter filled out the threesome. Not insignificant was the fact that in the 1839 state elections, Turner had unsuccessfully challenged McNutt en route to the latter's election to a second two-year term as governor.

At its January term, 1842, the high court handed down its decision. Sharkey began his opinion with a helpful introduction. Six—maybe more—issues for decision "bring directly in question the right of the Union Bank to recover on notes discounted by the bank for the accommodation of the makers."

> On the one side it has been contended that the bank charter is unconstitutional. On the other, that the act of 1840, requiring banks to resume specie payments or forfeit their charters, is unconstitutional.

Sharkey then explained the commonsense proposition that a company or firm faced with liquidation or winding up its affairs had to have a reasonable time within which to complete the process. This was so for the benefit of creditors of the failing firm, and for shareholders as well. Banks were no different. "The power to wind up its affairs necessarily reserved to . . . [the bank] the power to collect all notes previously taken." The specie payment act of 1840 did not prevent the Union Bank from suing on contracts—promissory notes— previously made. Besides, Campbell borrowed the money and gave his note to the Union Bank well before the specie currency act was passed.

The second question had become as familiar as it had been disputed. Did the supplemental act of February 15, 1838, impair the entire Union Bank charter and constitutional viability because it had not been submitted to the legislature and the public according to the special protocols constitutionally required in order to pledge the faith of the state? The answer was easy, as it always should have been. No. The reason the answer was no was that the supplemental act did not enlarge upon the extent to which the credit and faith of the State had been pledged to guarantee payment of the Union Bank bonds. It was but an amendment to an act already finally passed twice and signed into law by the governor. "The object of the pledge is not changed; on the contrary, the supplemental act was passed in aid of the original design."[127] Sharkey's opinion was simple and to the point. "On the 5th day of February, 1838, the act, as it had originally passed, without any alteration, was passed by the succeeding legislature, and approved by the governor. It then became a law, confessedly constitutional." And so the matter remained for the next ten days.

After such uninterrupted constitutional existence and activity, on February 15, 1838, the legislature amended the Union Bank charter act with the supplemental act, which Governor McNutt had promptly signed. In Dick-and-Jane language, Sharkey explained that nothing in the specie currency statute of 1840 undid the bank's right and power to prosecute its collection suit against delinquent debtors like Beasley Campbell. For more than three full pages, Sharkey explained the point so that a grammar school student could understand it. What Sharkey said made sense. The question was whether it would suffice for those not particularly imbued with simple good sense.

Third, the court considered the authority *vel non* of the bank to issue "post notes," that is, notes payable on a date certain in the future. Post notes are understood and distinguished from demand notes or others. Then as now, the practice of issuing and trading in bills and notes was a part of the banking business. The authority was a function of the general banking powers granted the Union Bank in its legislatively created and enacted charter (which Governor McNutt had signed fully aware of the legal effect of his doing so). Again, Sharkey offered common sense, though a basic understanding of the banking business came in handy. Nothing in the charter limited the kinds of notes the bank could issue.[128] After that, two questions of corporate governance and practice were dispatched by the court with little difficulty:

Finally, Sharkey turned to the publication dimension of the "faith of the state" issue.

> The legislature had in its view to establish a bank, but it was evident that capital would be wanting to ensure their success. The bank was established . . . with a capital of fifteen million five hundred thousand dollars, to be raised by means of a loan, to be obtained by the directors of the institution. To enable them to effect this loan, the state agreed to lend its aid; . . . . The state, then, undertook to become responsible that the loan be paid, but the stockholders were . . . , required to give mortgages on real estate, for the payment of capital and interest.[129]

From all of this, and much more, Sharkey reasonably concluded that "the bank was required to pay the bonds at maturity." It had accepted "a proffer on the part of the state to become security for the stockholders, on condition of being indemnified by mortgage(s) on real estate." But even if this undertaking were void, as repudiators so passionately argued, that did not affect the bank's power and right to collect what Campbell and the others owed on the promissory note held by and payable to the bank, and which was past due and unpaid.

The constitution said that, after the legislature's first passage of the State's "faith" pledge, the proposal had to be published three times across Mississippi before the next legislative session.[130] On such an important subject, the people were entitled to know what the legislature was up to, or so the 1832 constitution makers had reasoned. But did it suffice that the legislature published only a general statement of the nature and purpose of pledging the faith of the state? If that were all that was published between the two sessions, said to have been commanded by Section 9, Article 7, of the Constitution? Or was this a letter-of-the-law issue, such that every "i" had to be dotted and every "t" crossed, with every word approved by the legislature on first passage printed and published to the people? Chief Justice Sharkey ruled that a general statement of purpose would suffice. As a matter of common sense, that was enough to inform the halfway intelligent and interested members of the public of what was afoot. It was more understandable by the average citizen than the legalese that filled the full Union Bank Act may ever have been. As a practical matter, the electoral politics in the summer and fall of 1837 that sent a new legislature to Jackson in January of 1838 removed any doubt that the people had been informed as well as could be. What had been published after the adjournment of the 1837 session was constitutionally sufficient.

And so the Union Bank Act and its charter were upheld. The bank's authority to proceed in court against Campbell and his co-obligors was valid. But no mention had been made of the eight-hundred-pound gorilla in the room. Rather, Chief Justice Sharkey had concluded his opinion, saying, "I have thus examined the several pleas, and have endeavored to confine my remarks strictly to the questions presented by the record, with a view to avoid even an intimation of an opinion on any question which is not directly raised."[131]

Like the never-directly-raised question of whether a good faith holder of one of those $2,000 Union Bank bonds could collect from the State, plus interest, if the Union Bank—so soon defunct—could not pay.

HEZRON JOHNSON WANTS HIS MONEY

Fast-forward to 1852, where this chapter began. A one-line notice appeared in an upstate New York newspaper: "Mr. H. A. Johnson, who holds a Mississippi bond, issued on account of the Union Bank, has prosecuted the State for the recovery of the amount."[132] No surprise that by now the long-defunct bank was two years in arrears in honoring the $2,000 *Five Per Cent Loan* Bond No. 91, which had been guaranteed by the State. The critical wording was and remains

> That the State of Mississippi acknowledges to be indebted to the Mississippi Union Bank, in the sum of two thousand dollars, which sum the State of Mississippi promises to pay, in current money of the United States

to the holder. The bond was signed, "A. G. McNutt, Governor," and by "James Phillips, Treasurer." By its terms that bond had been redeemable back on

February 5, 1850. Johnson also held a fifty-dollar coupon representing interest on Bond A, No. 91, unpaid though due on May 1, 1849.[133] The word "loan" also appeared in the title of this coupon, viz., *Mississippi State Loan*. This coupon had been issued by the Mississippi Union Bank, signed by "S. Gwin, Cashier," and "H. G. Runnels, Pres't." The Five Per Cent Loan instrument, Bond A, No. 91, and its additional loan for interest, had been sold to Nicholas Biddle and ultimately negotiated and transferred until it came to be owned by Hezron A. Johnson, who sued for payment.

Two practical questions would reasonably have occurred to the minds of sensible persons coming across this notice and knowing the legal facts. Why was the State not honoring the guaranty it had given? Why might Mississippi knowingly jeopardize its credit reputation within national and international financial communities?

Hezron Ayers Johnson[134] (1823–1891) may not have been as well known as Nicholas Biddle. Johnson was only a multimillionaire principal in a Wall Street brokerage house. He resided on Fifth Avenue in midtown Manhattan and had a summer villa at Newport, Rhode Island. In more rational times, the respect and trust of men like Johnson would have been important to Mississippi's political and business leaders. And in less rational times as well—times that lay less than a decade ahead, when the State had a self-inflicted need for capital as at no other time.

Johnson presented the bond—the contract—he held to Chancellor Charles Scott of the Superior Court of Chancery of the State of Mississippi, said he wanted what was owed him, and he won. As a point of interest, then-lawyer Scott had been involved a decade earlier in winding up the affairs of the Union Bank, once McNutt pulled the plug leading to liquidation.[135] Lawyer Scott had also represented the Union Bank in the *Campbell* case, where some very similar issues had been hotly litigated. Surely the attorney general knew all about this. By today's standards there may have been grounds for recusal somewhere within the prior experiences and relationships of Scott and his Yerger in-laws. Under some circumstances, one might have thought the outsider, New York bondholder Hezron Johnson, would move to recuse. Yet there appears no record of anyone having raised recusal or conflict-of-interest issues, timely or otherwise. Any such concerns were waived, as they would be even under today's more formal practice. Nonetheless, the Great Repudiator would have had something to say about the proprieties of these circumstances, were he still above ground and upright in 1852.

The matter Johnson put before the chancery court could have but one credible outcome, even without *Campbell's* precedential power and without regard to who the lawyers were. This time Chief Justice C. Pinckney Smith spoke for the court, Sharkey having stepped down a little over a year earlier. Justice William Yerger filed an even more meticulous and convincing concurring opinion, explaining the legal validity and enforceability of the State's guaranty of the

Union Bank bonds.[136] Ephraim S. Fisher (1815–1876) was another justice with a Whig political background. He did not say much in *Johnson* or about the Union Bank bonds, but what he said was enough: "FISHER, J., concurred in the foregoing opinions and decision."

Chief Justice Smith's opinion began, "The foundation of this suit was an instrument under the seal of the State, signed by the governor and countersigned by the treasurer of the State, dated 5th of June, 1838." But Smith knew the court was deciding more than just one case.

> Other claims, to the amount of many millions of dollars, exist against the State of Mississippi, of similar character, the validity of which depends upon precisely the same conditions with that which is the present subject of adjudication. So far, therefore, as the action of the judicial department is concerned, the decision which it is now our duty to pronounce, will, probably, be decisive of their fate. For that reason alone, the present contest is one of deep interest.[137]

These words could not have been more to the mark. Repudiation sentiment remained strong and widespread. The chief justice no doubt suspected that the chances of the legislature appropriating the funds with which to carry out the court's order were about the same as those of the proverbial snowball surviving long in the infernal regions. Yet Smith pressed on.

One complaint often heard from Governor McNutt and his fellow repudiators was that the Union Bank bonds had not been sold at par.[138] Jacob Yerger had confronted and refuted this same red herring in his 1841 select committee report to the legislature.[139] Nonlegal commentators still sometimes fall for this one. Chief Justice Smith explained how and why the argument was as bogus as a three-dollar bill. Preliminarily, and as a practical matter, it spoke volumes that "this objection was not urged in the argument by the attorney-general." In the first decade of repudiation politics, the State was not known for pulling punches. Rather, repudiators were well known for making every antibond argument that the mind might imagine, and throwing in the kitchen sink besides.

Smith invoked traditional equitable reasoning to explain "that it does not appear from the facts of the case that the bonds were sold for less than par value." For the details, he deferred to Justice Yerger, who walked through the practical logic and math of the matter. In sum,

> a simple mathematical calculation will show, that this accruing interest paid by the bank did not equal the premium received for the exchange, and that the bank, therefore, realized from the sale of the bonds a sum greater than the actual amount of the bonds, and the interest due on the same, when the payments were made. The sum thus received was greater than the "par value" of the bonds.

Comparing exchange rates then prevailing in Jackson and New Orleans, Yerger explained

> that every million of dollars paid to the bank in the city of New Orleans, was equivalent to a payment of one million and fifty thousand in the city of Jackson.... It will thus be seen, that the sale made by the commissioners of the bonds for $5,000,000 was equivalent to the bank to the sum of $5,250,000.[140]

This was only one example of how, page after page, point after point, Smith—and then Yerger—patiently and meticulously explained why—consistent with constitutional law, the facts dispassionately considered, and elementary rules of fair play—the case could have but one outcome: a judgment that the State must pay.[141]

Another point Smith addressed, also with an assist by Yerger, was the oft-advanced and bogus ploy that somehow the supplemental act of February 15, 1938, should have been passed at two successive sessions of the legislature with publication in three newspapers preceding the second legislative passage. Chief Justice Sharkey had considered this one in *Campbell* and effectively dispatched it. As the issue would not die, Yerger took it up again. The answer remained simple. According to the constitution—with only two exceptions—all bills enacted into law needed only to secure passage by each house of the legislature at the same term, plus the governor's signature. Amendments to bills already passed and, having gained gubernatorial approval, in full force and effect, were not one of those two exceptions. The supplemental act of February 15, 1938, was a mere amendment to a bill already passed and signed into law; hence, the supplemental act needed only the normal constitutional requisites for passage. Yerger pressed the point at length, only because the repudiators remained in denial. There are none so blind as those who will not see.

Every argument the repudiators had advanced for well over a decade was dispassionately dissected and dismantled. Throw in the persuasive concurring opinion of Justice William Yerger,[142] and the pro-bond case was about as strong as goat's milk. The political sensibilities of appropriations committee members in the legislature, however, remained in mule mode. Repudiator McNutt would have to enjoy his political victory from the grave and, as well, endure his defeat at the hands of the rule of law.

THE STATE HAD REMEDIES

It was now 1853, more than a decade since the Union Bank had failed. Arguably, that had been in substantial part the fault of bank management and practices, the political rhetoric aside. Presumably the common law of corporate governance imposed duties upon management comparable to what are today called duties of care and of good faith and fair dealing, or, more loosely, fiduciary duties. Clearly in retrospect, the Union Bank had accepted collateral mortgages from plantation-owning shareholders at values soon shown to be substantially in excess of their liquidation values. An equitable remedy like unto what is today known as a shareholders' derivative suit could and probably should have been sought. The State of Mississippi was a shareholder. It could have joined in such a suit, where it may have been suing former governor Hiram Runnels, first president of the Union Bank,[143] and no doubt other worthies with political clout. If the shareholders did not promptly head for the courthouse once management's defalcations became known, that fault was hardly chargeable to Johnson and his fellow good faith bondholders.

The State had another remedy. It was a guarantor. Justice Yerger explained that

> [t]he contract of guarantee on the part of the State was made for and on account of the [banking] corporation, and not the individual subscribers or stockholders.

$$\bullet \quad \bullet \quad \bullet$$

> The State, under both acts, as between it and the bank, always occupied the position of guarantor or surety, having the right to subject the entire assets of the bank to the payment of the bonds, or any part of them.[144]

The State had lent its credit and "faith" to the Union Bank. When the Bank failed, the State should have stepped up to the plate—stiff upper lip and all—as any honorable guarantor would, faced with the sad fact of its principal's default.

Once it repaid the bondholders—presumably close to the full $5 million plus interest—the State could have gone to court and claimed its equitable remedy of indemnity of and from both Union Bank and its directors and officers. That remedy would have included recovery of expenses, losses, and other damages even over and above the principal and interest the indemnitee State had paid on the bonds. Of course, the chances of collecting an indemnity[145] judgment against these insolvent principals were not good. We know that real property held by the bank as collateral from its individual shareholders and patrons had become reduced in value, but surely these properties were not worthless. The State's delay in doing its duty and pursuing its remedies no doubt impaired its hopes of an indemnity recovery, but, again, the consequences of that delay were hardly chargeable to Johnson. In any event, one way or another the State had solid grounds for securing a $5 million-plus indemnity judgment against the Union Bank and its problematic management,[146] with attendant enforcement remedies, such as attachment, garnishment, and execution. Collection would have been another matter, but that's the risk guarantors run. Always has been; always will be.

Repudiators and other political wags for years had argued, *inter alia*, that there were deficiencies in the legal authorization and organization of the Union Bank. In point of fact, the State had pressed some of those defenses before the courts. Beasley Campbell had done so a decade earlier. Assume *arguendo* that some of those points may not have been frivolous. After all, one who deals with the government does so at his peril that all procedural prerequisites may not have been satisfied and that the limits on an agent's authority may not have been respected.[147] Persons and entities dealing with the state must always be prepared to "turn square corners."[148] Those contracting with a government are charged to make sure of the state agent's authority and to proceed at the risk that he may have exceeded his authority.

Be that as it may, in 1842 the high court had held that the Union Bank had been legally created and organized. Eleven years later, the court had held and finally adjudged that the State was obligated to pay the principal and interest on the bond Hezron Johnson held. Once *Johnson* was decided, legally the matter should have ended. Constitutionally, the buck then passed to the executive department to enforce the *Johnson* final judgment. After all, the governor had been commanded that he "shall take care that the laws be faithfully executed."[149] On his oath of office, he could do no less. The constitution went so far as to authorize him to "call forth the militia," when that might be necessary, in order "to execute the laws of the state."[150]

Referring to the *Beasley Campbell* case as well as the *Hezron Johnson* decision, an early historian blithely reported, "These decisions, however, seem to have had but little effect on public sentiment. There could be no coercion or compulsory process against the State—the legislature never made any appropriation for their payment and the decrees were powerless."[151] Historians—and governors as well—should be made of sterner stuff.

Make no mistake about it. As the curtain rang down on the year 1853, the State of Mississippi was in fact and in law bound to Hezron A. Johnson to honor the $2,000 *"Five Per Cent Loan"* Union Bank Bond No. 91 signed by A. G. McNutt, Governor, and James Phillips, Treasurer, and with interest from date due until fully paid. The political back-and-forth that had raged since 1839 had been supplanted by an authoritative, reliable—and final—"action of the judicial department."[152] For the State's finally adjudged faith, history reports that Johnson never received a penny. Even though the State had the money, and much more, not to mention Governor McNutt's open admission in January of 1841 that no revenue at all was being received from roughly half of the property in the state subject to assessment and *ad valorem* taxation. The sad fact was that Mississippi had surrendered its honor and good name and was only a decade away from giving up treasures worth far more than these.[153]

Some historians have been kind to McNutt, perhaps unduly so. Ignoring the governor's January 1841 admission, one suggests, "Because the state treasury was depleted, Governor McNutt believed Mississippi had no alternative but to repudiate the bonds."[154] Others paint a different picture. "Mississippi had a relatively light debt burden, yet it repudiated its debt."[155] "The state's property tax revenues were enough to service the Union Bank bonds,"[156] this even though much of the assessable property was escaping taxation. The reasons the State would not levy taxes to pay the bondholders were purely political. There was similarly situated Alabama, which never defaulted or tried to repudiate, though shouldering double the public debt burden as Mississippi.

Quite arguably, the failure of the State to turn to some combination of existing tax revenue streams, enforcing tax laws on the books theretofore slipping through the cracks, and levying new taxes, was nothing less than a kind of ethical public corruption. The State had been in a far better position than the out-of-state—and out-of-country—bondholders to monitor or police bank management. Political points attributable to the fact that so many bondholders were northerners and foreigners forgets what everyone knew from the start: that Nicholas Biddle and these outsider men of means and their entities had been courted and welcomed with open arms back in 1838 as the only possible purchasers of the five million dollars' worth of Union Bank bonds that somehow had to be sold, that the State might stem the tide of troubles it faced. Legally, if not politically, it was plain enough that the repudiating State of Mississippi had impaired contracts—bank bonds were contracts—in blatant offense to federal and state constitutional bars.[157]

IMPAIRMENT OF BANK CONTRACTS

There was a lot more than repudiation to Mississippi's pre–Civil War war on banks.[158] It is not surprising that jury verdicts served as indicia of the popular pulse, as effective as the ballot box. In 1840 the *Natchez Free Trader* wrote, "We believe that few if any of our banks have been able to obtain verdicts at the late sessions of our courts." In 1841. a Senate committee found, "Juries have refused to give judgments in their [banks'] favor, without any just or sufficient plea."[159] Elected local judges were often almost as bad: "It is said to be almost impossible to collect a debt by judicial proceedings in this state." Trial courts became hypertechnical in cases brought by banks to collect just debts. Popularly chosen legislators did their share: "The whole tenor of legislation for several years has been directed against creditors."[160]

Consider two contracts clause cases that reached the state's high court almost three years after its commendable *Campbell* decision. Each case—*Payne* and *Planters' Bank*—concerned the proper understanding of other provisions of the specie bill the state legislature had passed in 1840. Politically, this pro-debtor, antibank statute said, among other things, that Mississippi banks could no longer transfer commercial paper, viz., "it shall not be lawful for any bank in this State, to transfer, by indorsement or otherwise, any note, bill receivable, or other evidence of debt."[161]

Constitutionally, the legislature had exercised the state's police power to regulate the sale of a product it thought inimical to the public welfare. More familiar and current examples include regulating the sale or transfer of alcoholic beverages, narcotic drugs, or other controlled substances. Usury laws are an ancient example. Chief Justice Sharkey pulled no punches. He explained that the new act was "intended solely and exclusively for the benefit of bank debtors. Bank paper was then generally very much depreciated, and the country was full of this depreciated currency, and it was designed to secure to debtors the right to pay banks in their own notes."[862]

Assume, for instance, that back in those days a person had owed the bank some $2,000. That person may also have held notes of that bank—twenty $100 bank demand notes, or just hundred-dollar bills, in today's language—in the aggregate face amount of $2,000. Because of the depreciation of currency circa 1840, however, in any other context those same banknotes had at that time an aggregate discounted value of only $1,000. The 1840 act had declared that, upon a debtor's tender of such notes back to the bank that issued them, the bank was required to accept them and give credit at face value, notwithstanding their depreciated practical value in all other contexts. The legislature had made the public policy value judgment that it was better for the bank than the bank's debtor to take the $1,000 loss. As with legislatures then and now, the drafting of the 1840 act was less than aptly tailored only to the perceived public evil.

By its text, the act swept broadly. Yet in 1844 the high court held that "this language is too plain to admit of more than one construction, and we cannot refuse to enforce it because the case may not seem to come fully within the mischief intended to be remedied."[163] This affected the negotiability of notes and other instruments, and much more. The question arose whether this new law impaired obligations of theretofore lawfully made contracts. Federal and state constitutions spoke prominently to the point and proscribed impairment.[164]

Bills and notes and mortgages and similar security agreements were and are contracts. So were and are corporate charters, including bank charters. No one disputed that—within the contemplation of the contracts clauses of both constitutions—such state charters issued to private entities were protected contracts. No one took exception when Sharkey said, "Legislation which impairs chartered rights is not only at war with the Constitution of the United States, but it is repugnant to a similar provision in our State constitution, and on that account would be inoperative."[165]

To be sure, neither of the bank charters at issue in *Payne* or *Planters' Bank* expressly addressed the practice of negotiating commercial paper. But no knowledgeable person doubted that trading in negotiable instruments—secured or otherwise—was an ordinary and practical part of the banking business. Nor was it reasonably open to question that, by reason of the nature and practice of their businesses, corporate entities possessed under their charters reasonably implied or incidental powers, including more than a few not expressly stated. To complete the circle, no one reasonably doubted that state-chartered private entities, banks included, were also limited in their practices to those activities expressly or implicitly authorized within the terms of their respective charters. The question became whether the instances of negotiation involved in two particular cases—*Payne* and *Planters' Bank*—were within implied banking charter powers such that the State was barred from impairing them via the commercial paper act of 1840 or otherwise. More precisely, the question was whether arguable doubt regarding an implied power should be construed as permissive or restrictive.

Speaking for the court in *Payne*, Chief Justice Sharkey followed a pattern of analysis familiar in the contexts of areas of the law with a background at common law. The negotiability of bills and notes and like instruments had no common law history.[166] Rather, in England at a time when its thirteen colonies were not even a gleam in the king's eye, it took statutes to legalize the practice of negotiating and transferring commercial paper from one person or firm to another. Conversely, to the extent that negotiation may have been practiced in Mississippi, the legislature had the constitutional prerogative of constricting that practice, had it wished to do so.[167] *Payne* arose in a context where the legislature had exercised that prerogative. The idea was analogous to the state legislatively regulating or prohibiting practices such as lotteries or other forms of gaming. With few limitations, the legislature may permit, prohibit, and regulate, as it deems in the public interest. Following the Panics of 1837 and 1839, paper money was seen in a like light.

Then the plot thickened. *Payne* and *Planters' Bank* made their way to the US Supreme Court. The two cases were consolidated and decided *sub nom. The Planters' Bank of Mississippi v. Sharp.* Lawyers before the high court in Washington included Seargent S. Prentiss, one of Mississippi's best-known courtroom lawyers and orators of the times. Prentiss had appeared for Payne, Green & Wood. A "Mr. [Daniel] Webster" appeared for the note holders. By a six-to-three vote, the US Supreme Court reversed the Mississippi decisions in both *Payne* and *Planters' Bank.* In each instance, as a matter of constitutional law, the Mississippi commercial paper act of 1840 had impaired the obligations of theretofore existing contracts, or more precisely, the implied or incidental prerogatives of banks within their charters.

Justice Levi Woodbury—the same Levi Woodbury who as Andrew Jackson's secretary of the Treasury had issued the infamous Specie Circular in 1836—spoke for the US Supreme Court. He explained carefully that receiving and selling negotiable bills, notes, instruments, and other commercial paper was a sensible and proper activity for those in the banking business, unless expressly forbidden in the bank's charter.[168] More than once, Woodbury seemingly went out of his way to suggest that Mississippi banking law and practices were sufficiently sensible (if the high court had only properly understood Mississippi's own law and banking practices) and that they supported reversal.

Timing was all-important in cases like these. When a contracts clause was invoked to challenge a new state law, the question was whether the contract said to have been impaired had already been made. "What law existed on this point when the note was actually transferred is not the inquiry, but what [law] existed when [the note] was made, and its obligations as a contract were fixed."[169] If the currency act had been on the books at the time a bank got its charter and issued the note, the new bank would have been on notice. In point of fact and law, the opposite was so. The bank's charter powers had been first established, or "fixed," as the court would put it. The new 1840 state commercial paper statute "expressly took away the right of the bank to make any transfer whatever of its notes, and virtually deprived an assignee of them of the right to sustain any suit, either in his own name or that of the bank, to recover them of the maker."[170] For context, Woodbury explained, citing a then-recent Mississippi precedent,

> One of the tests that a contract had been impaired is, that its value has by legislation been diminished. It is not, by the Constitution to be impaired at all. This is not a question of degree or manner or cause, but of encroaching in any respect on its obligation, dispensing with any part of its force.[171]

A further and laborious discussion precedes and follows, but in the end Justice Woodbury found and "assigned sufficient reasons to show that the obligation of both of these contracts [bank charters] was impaired."[172] As applied in the two, somewhat differing, contexts afforded by the *Payne* and *Planters' Bank* cases, the federal Contracts Clause had been offended. This ruling had fatal effects for persons trying to avoid paying their just debts.

The ink was hardly dry on Woodbury's opinion when George Yerger called it to the high court's attention in a new bank case he was handling, and with effect. In a brief opinion Justice Alexander M. Clayton noted his court's prior view. Like a good student slapped on the wrist by his teacher, Clayton fessed up that

> the supreme court of the United States has reversed the decision of this court upon that point, on the ground that the act of 1840 was unconstitutional. In cases of that character, that court bears the relation of an appellate tribunal to this, and we feel bound to conform to its construction of the constitution of the United States, when made upon direct appeal from this court.

Clayton accepted a second dose of the same medicine at the November 1848 term of the high court.

The views of this court were expressed on this subject in the case of *Payne et al. v. Baldwin, et al.*, 3 S. & M. 661. That opinion was reversed in the supreme court of the United States, and we have since conformed to their decision.[173]

And all was quiet for a while.

Then came 1858. The high court heard and considered *McIntyre v. Ingraham*. The bank involved was the same Grand Gulf Railroad and Banking Company that had been before the court ten years earlier.[174] In one sense, *McIntyre* was a throwback decision. On facts similar to those the US Supreme Court had before it in *Planters' Bank*, the high court resurrected its original and well-repudiated view of the commercial paper act of 1840. The *McIntyre* court pointed out that the note at issue "was made and delivered to the bank after the passage of the Act of 1840." That shouldn't have mattered. Contracts clause analysis concerned the proper understanding and application of the bank's charter—not the date of the note—coupled with reasonably implied powers found within the charter. The controlling date was 1833, the year of the charter of the Grand Gulf Bank.[175]

In *McIntyre*, the Grand Gulf Bank held a note given by McIntyre and Bridges back in November of 1841, secured by a deed of trust. In February of 1842—exercising powers reasonably implied under its 1833 charter—the bank negotiated and transferred the secured note to Ingraham and Lindsay. McIntyre and Bridges had defaulted. Ingraham and Read, successor in interest to Lindsay, deceased, sued to enforce the November 1841 secured note. McIntyre and Bridges defended on grounds that the bank's transfer was illegal under the commercial paper act of 1840, the same statute that had been at issue in all of the cases prior to the US Supreme Court's 1848 decision in *Planters' Bank*. One would have thought *Planters' Bank* had settled the proposition that, on all cases generally comparable in facts and on principle, the act of 1840 was unenforceable consistent with the federal Contracts Clause. And that the high court's two 1848 cases had accepted the point.

By the time *McIntyre* reached the high court at its April 1858 term, Justice Alexander H. Handy had replaced William Yerger and was then speaking for the court. Justice William L. Harris had just taken office, succeeding Ephraim Fisher. C. P. Smith remained in office.

The charter powers granted the Grand Gulf Bank in 1833 were worded slightly differently—though in comparable general language—than the powers enjoyed by Planters' Bank and the Mississippi Railroad Company Bank. The Grand Gulf Bank enjoyed the power to "purchase and possess personal estate of any kind and to sell and dispose of the same at pleasure" plus appropriate incidental and auxiliary powers. The Planters' Bank, by way of comparison, had enjoyed the powers "to receive, retain and enjoy effects of whatever kind and to dispose of the same." The case came down to whether the right and practice of negotiability of commercial paper might be considered within "effects of whatever kind," as in *Planters' Bank*, but not within "personal estate of any kind," as in 1848 *Grand Gulf* case and the *McIntyre* case before the court for decision. Justice Alexander Handy found enough of a difference that the US Supreme Court holding in *Planters' Bank* was not controlling, at least in his view.

Horsefeathers!

Handy's *McIntyre* opinion is in two parts. First and foremost, he presented a linguistic analysis of the respective charters of Planters' Bank and Grand Gulf Railroad and Banking Company, followed by the supposed application of so-called rules of construction of legal texts.[176] Handy's approach in part one resembles the jabberwocky of *Alice through the Looking-Glass*.

> "When I use a word," Humpty Dumpty said in a rather scornful tone, "it means just what I choose it to mean—neither more nor less."
>
> "The question is," said Alice, "whether you can make words mean so many different things."
>
> "The question is," said Humpty Dumpty, "which is to be master—that's all."

Alexander Handy thought he was master the day he authored *McIntyre*. He removed doubt of that view in the second part of his opinion.

Handy gave a nod to the then ten-year-old decision in *Planters' Bank*. True, that case held the act of 1840 unenforceable—consistent with the contracts clause—as to the two pre-1840 bank charters then before the court. "But it only declares the statute unconstitutional as to those charters, and we cannot admit its obligatory force as applicable in the present case." The master follows with

> we do not recognize the right of any other judicial tribunal, either to expound the statutes of this State, and to determine their legal construction or effect, or to prescribe the rules by which we are to be bound in their construction, with the single exception of a statute alleged to be in conflict with the Constitution of the United States.

Of course, the case to be decided lay easily within that "single exception."

Master Handy got around his court's ten-year-old decision involving the same bank and the same charter, by saying that the question for decision in *McIntyre* was not presented there,[177] and by his own prior exposition that handling negotiable instruments really wasn't necessary to banking anyway. There is only one way to make any sense at all out of Handy's *McIntyre* opinion: focus upon his claim that, if the high court doesn't have the authority he asserts,

> any matter of State policy depending upon its statutes and the expositions of its courts, would be subject to revision by the [US Supreme Court], whenever any statute subsequently passed might be alleged to affect rights acquired or claimed

under previous statutes or contracts, and under color of the power to pronounce
the statutes complained of unconstitutional, that court might proceed to reverse
all of the decisions of the State courts, . . . and thus subvert the entire policy of the
State upon the subject-matter of the controversy.[178]

Two thoughts. April of 1858 was not a time when many Mississippi leaders
were thinking straight, though Lincoln had not yet been elected, after which
things got worse. Of course, it could well be that master Handy was feeling his
oats after *Dred Scott* was decided in early March of 1857. Also recall that it was
Alexander Handy who defeated Justice William Yerger in 1853 at the ballot box
after the latter's politically unpopular opinion in *Johnson v. State.*

REFLECTIONS

This chapter has been about Mississippi's antebellum war after war on bank
after bank in one context or another. There has not been time or space to tell
the stories of all the battles in this war. All took place before the State's far more
deadly Civil War with the United States, arguably far more foolhardy. The
differences are worthy of note. "Repudiation" was the battle cry in the 1840s,[179]
"Nullification" a decade earlier, and "Secession" a decade later. Only a few clauses
of both US and state constitutions were rent in these battles with banks.[180] In
1861, the full pledge Mississippi had made to the federal Union when it accepted
statehood on December 10, 1817, was torn asunder. At least that's what the
powers that be in Mississippi thought in 1861, and certainly what they intended.

In 1875, the State of Mississippi—guarantor, repudiator, and more—declared
that it would never restore the honor and faith it had pledged in the days following February 15, 1838.[181] The state amended its first postbellum constitution
to that effect. Fifteen years later, the constitution adopted November 1, 1890,
read—and to this day reads—that the State

> shall not . . . assume, redeem, secure, or pay any indebtedness or pretended indebted-
> ness alleged to be due by the State of Mississippi to any person, association, or cor-
> poration whatsoever, claiming the same as owners, holders, or assignees of any bond
> or bonds, now generally known as "Union Bank" bonds and "Planters Bank" bonds.[182]

Over a century and a quarter, close to 120 provisions of the 1890 constitution
have been added, amended, repealed, or judicially held unenforceable. Section 258
remains in concrete, as it has always been. The evil that men do lives after them.

Clifford Thies has provided a thoughtful reflection on Mississippi's war on
banks. The "importance of institutional arrangements for the protection of debt"
is one of the lessons of this experience. One particular institutional arrangement
he and others have considered essential is an independent judiciary. Because of

popular election of judges for relatively short terms of office, Thies concludes that in antebellum Mississippi "the independence of the judiciary was merely superficial." Lifetime appointments as with the federal judiciary are a better strategy. If one focuses on Mississippi's antebellum bank wars—to the exclusion of repudiation—the case is there to be made. But Thies never mentions the judiciary's performance in the Union Bank cases. Whether that is because the *Campbell* and *Johnson* litigations embarrass Thies's arguments is beside the point. What happened in years leading up to 1842 and then up to 1853 was that a handful of state judges elected for short terms did their duty about as well as it could be done.

Circuit Judge Buckner C. Harris could have let the jury decide *Campbell*. You may have to work a bit, but trial judges know well that tactic for avoiding controversial decisions that could otherwise be pinned on them. Chancellor Scott did not have a jury to hide behind in *Johnson*. He bit the bullet and rejected the repudiationist arguments the State had advanced. It would have been hard to improve on the way Chief Justice Sharkey decided the *Beasley Campbell* case on appeal. Repudiation mania was at its most intense and least rational in 1842 when Sharkey and Edward Turner and James F. Trotter upheld the constitutional and practical viability of the Mississippi Union Bank. In 1853, C. Pinckney Smith was solid in the *Hezron Johnson* case. William Yerger could have joined Smith's opinion and otherwise kept his mouth shut. Instead, Yerger wrote a wonderful opinion, though he was open to the familiar charge that a lawyer never uses one word when two or three will do just as well, and that few lawyers shed this propensity when they become judges. Because so much was at stake, because the people had been plied by politicians with so many bogus arguments, Yerger marshalled meticulous detail and reason to explain that and why the State really did have a legal obligation to honor its 1838 guaranty. He was rewarded by a negative vote at the next election. Ephraim Fisher could have taken a repudiationist view in *Johnson*. With Smith and Yerger drawing all the fire, Fisher had a practical political path before him that many would have followed.

Leave aside the embarrassingly bad behavior of Alexander Handy in *McIntyre v. Ingraham*. And the failure of other high court justices to respect the Contracts Clauses in the bank war cases. Can we know whether in that twenty-year run-up to Secession and War a judiciary of lifetime appointees would have done much better? Clifford Thies needs only to look out the window and up the Potomac to find period after period of federal constitutional history where the appointed-for-life justices have invoked dubious, result-oriented legal reasoning and defaulted just as badly as Alexander Handy did. And the same with many appointed-for-life judges sitting on the several US courts of appeals who, as a practical matter, have the final word in the great majority of federal appeals.

In the pre–Civil War era, when repudiationists seemed to grow in political strength with every downturn in the economy, the judiciary was the only department of state government that acted with courage and correctness, consistent with the oaths and constitutional insights and industry of its officials. *Campbell* and *Johnson* were constitutionally and otherwise legally sound decisions. More important, they were courageous decisions. William Yerger, who just may have been the best of the bunch, paid the ultimate political price. It was a price that the 1832 draftsmen quite deliberately provided for when they wrote direct popular election of judges into the then-new Jacksonian constitution.

In 1996, in what was likely the last gasp in the bank wars of the 1840s and 1850s, it is sad that the Supreme Court of Mississippi would tell bona fide bondholders that they had waited too long, that their claims on the bonds they held were barred by the statute of limitations.[183] And even sadder that the court missed the twofold irony in its actions.

First, statutes of limitations proceed on the assumption that the "claim is a just one or has the sanction of moral obligation," only that the plaintiff has waited too long to sue.[184] Of course, limitations statutes are ordinarily enforced according to their tenor. Equitable estoppel is available, but "it should only be applied against the statute of limitations in the most egregious of cases."[185] The State's refusal to honor the final judgment in *Johnson*—exacerbated by the manifest wickedness of the 1875 constitutional amendment—makes this case about as egregious as one is likely to find, with the possible exception only of a known innocent man about to be hanged.

Secondly, had the shoe been on the other foot, with the heirs of Hezron Johnson or Nicholas Biddle pleading limitations in response to some likely quite viable claim Mississippi made against them, the speed of light would have been judicially approached in granting the State's motion to strike. The State is subject to no statute of limitations.[186] Not even were the State now to proceed on its otherwise viable claims against the heirs and other successors in interest of Hiram Runnels and the Union Bank officials who may have breached duties of care, loyalty, good faith, and fair dealing to the bank they ran. Or to demand title and possession of real property that Union Bank shareholders had mortgaged in favor of the bank.

Madam Mississippi, have you no shame?!

Historian J. F. H. Claiborne had another take on the bank bond business. First, he acknowledged that "[t]he bonds of the Planters' Bank were not liable to the same objection" as the Union Bank bonds, an understatement at best. Claiborne added that nonetheless the Planters' Bank bonds "were objected to on very strong grounds." Claiborne cited nothing to back up this claim. He added that "[n]o provision was ever made by the legislature for their payment. The whole [matter] dropped out of view, except for an occasional newspaper paragraph, and slept the sleep of death."

Claiborne then harkened back to the advent of the constitution of 1832. For historical purposes, a sentiment he attributed to Gen. John A. Quitman is interesting. The public policy of the State should be to keep out of debt, and have no connection with banks. The credit which so many States are craving we do not desire. Credit is a public curse on ourselves and our posterity. It is the source of debt, high taxation, litigation and war. Our own resources and the labor of our own people, are sufficient to accomplish all the public improvements we require. The true political economy is never to borrow a dollar, and to grant no exclusive or irrepealable privileges to any corporation.

A well-meant aspiration, perhaps. For practical people, Quitman and Claiborne show only that these two bank-bond debacles ended as they began, in the world of fantasy, "the eerie world of never-never land."[187]

The core lesson learned from Mississippi's bank wars—bond guaranty variety and others—is that no constitution is more of a practical reality than the people are willing to let it be. The people fall into different groupings. First are those who wrote the constitution. Then there are those in the three departments of government who exercise its powers and deal with its constraints. At the end of the day, there are We the People as a whole and the tenor of the times, deciding whether the constitution will be bent to the momentary madness of the majority. Of course, the Madisonian dilemma is ever with us, the extent to which in a majoritarian democracy the rights of individuals—be they banks, other entities, disadvantaged minorities, or other persons—will or even can be respected and enjoyed. To what extent may, can, or should the objectively bona fide interests of such individuals and entities be made safe—in practical reality, and not just on a piece of paper called a constitution?

To what extent may, can, or should the people kid themselves that they live in a viable democracy subject to the rule of law, when they aren't troubled that no one from the governor on down will lift a finger to honor and enforce a final judgment of the state's highest court in a case of great constitutional and public interest and importance? Is there a law school or any other kind of school—in Mississippi or anywhere—teaching that public repudiation of the final judgment at the end of a constitutional encounter such as *State of Mississippi v. Hezron Johnson* in 1853 is and remains a stain on the claim that We the People respect the rule of law? Or are the stains of slavery, secession, civil war, and a sesquicentennium of postbellum racism in all of its iterations so great that our other failures are just swept under the rug?

ENDNOTES

1. *See, e.g.*, "Alexander Gallatin McNutt," in David G. Sansing, *Mississippi Governors: Soldiers, Statesmen, Scholars, Scoundrels: A Bicentennial Edition* 46–50 (2016); Alexander G. McNutt, *Mississippi Encyclopedia* 802 (Ownby and Wilson eds., 2017).

2. *See, e.g, State v. Johnson*, 3 Cushm. (25 Miss.) 625, 629, 1853 WL 3667 (1853).

3. See Presidential Executive Order directing that after August 15, 1836, the federal government would accept only specie—hard currency, primarily gold or silver—in exchange for public lands. http://en.wikipedia.org/wiki/Specie_Circular.

4. On July 14, 1841, Gov. A. G. McNutt did argue to a bondholder in Amsterdam, Holland, "The money paid for those bonds did not come into the State treasury. The officers of this Government had no control over its disbursement!" Letter addressed to Messrs. Hope & Co., Amsterdam, Holland, reproduced at Senate Journal, page 70 (1842). But see Select Committee Report, Senate Journal, page 234–247(1841) for a detailed view answering Governor McNutt. The validity and enforceability of the terms and conditions of the State's guaranty did not turn on who was right on this point of formality.

5. *Campbell v. Mississippi Union Bank*, 6 Howard (7 Miss.) 625, 626, 671, 1842 WL 3050 (1842).

6. An Act Requiring the Several Banks in this State to Pay Specie, and for other purposes, enacted February 21, 1840, ch. 15, § 7; Hutchinson's Code 325 (1848).

7. *Campbell v. Mississippi Union Bank*, 6 Howard (7 Miss.) 625, 1842 WL 3050 (1842).

8. The terms of the bond had been enacted by the legislature, *State v. Johnson*, 3 Cushm. (25 Miss.) 625, 642–643, 1853 WL 3667 (1853), all in Section 5 of the Union Bank Bond Act approved February 5 and 15, 1838.

9. There were several constitutional texts in play. Most often debated was the special process mandated before the State could pledge its credit and faith—and guarantee—the debt of another. Miss. Const. art. 7, § 9 (1832). As the bond was a contract, there were questions how the State might get around the federal Contracts Clause, U.S. Const. art. 1, § 10, cl. 1, or the nearly identical Mississippi contracts clause, Miss. Const. art. 1, § 19 (1832). Then there was the governor's duty, viz., "He shall take care that the laws be faithfully executed." Miss. Const. art. 5, § 9 (1832), and the governor's oath of office, viz., Miss. Const. art. 7, § 1 (1832).

10. *State v. Johnson*, 3 Cushm. (25 Miss.) 625, 796, 1853 WL 3667 (1853).

11. *Worcester v. Georgia*, 6 Pet. (31 U.S.) 515 (1832).

12. Miss. Const. art. 12, § 5, amend. 1 (as amended in 1875).

13. Miss. Const. art. 14, § 258 (1890).

14. *See* Senate Committee Report, per J. W. Mathews, chairman, Senate Journal, pages 725–726 (1842).

15. *See* the "provided" clause in Miss. Const. art. 7, § 9 (1832).

16. Miss. Const. art. 4, § 1 (1832); *see also* Miss. Const. art. 2 (1832).

17. William Shakespeare, *Hamlet*, act 5, scene 2, lines 390–405.

18. *See State v. Johnson*, 3 Cushm. (25 Miss.) 625, 664, 1853 WL 3667 (1853).

19. *See* "Hiram George Runnels," in David G. Sansing, *Mississippi Governors: Soldiers, Statesmen, Scholars, Scoundrels: A Bicentennial Edition* 36–40 (2016); Hiram G. Runnels, *Mississippi Encyclopedia* 1102–1103 (Ownby and Wilson eds., 2017).

20. Miss. Const. art. 1, §§ 1, 2 (1832).

21. See chapter 3 above for a more complete discussion of the Runnels family. Hiram's brother, Harmon M. Runnels Jr., was the clerk who fought and won the right of judicial review in *Runnels v. State*, Walker (1 Miss.) 146, 1823 WL 543 (1823).

22. Senate Journal, page 21 (1835).

23. "Hiram Runnels," https://en.wikipedia.org/wiki/Hiram_Runnels; *see also* "Gen. Volney E. Howard," *Los Angeles Times* (Los Angeles, California), Weds., May 15, 1885, page 2, Newspapers. com, https://www.newspapers.com/image/155667054.

24. *See* "Charles Lynch," in David G. Sansing, *Mississippi Governors: Soldiers, Statesmen, Scholars, Scoundrels: A Bicentennial Edition* 42–44 (2016); "Charles Lynch," *Mississippi Encyclopedia* 755–756 (Ownby and Wilson eds., 2017).

25. Because the Union Bank Act included the State's pledge of its faith, guaranteeing $5 million in Union Bank bonds, it had to be enacted twice, at successive legislative sessions. *See* Miss. Const. art. 7, § 9 (1832).

26. Senate Journal, page 26 (January 4, 1838).

27. *See* "Alexander G. McNutt," in David G. Sansing, *Mississippi Governors: Soldiers, Statesmen, Scholars, Scoundrels: A Bicentennial Edition* 46–50 (2016); "Alexander G. McNutt," *Mississippi Encyclopedia* 802 (Ownby and Wilson eds., 2017);

28. The story of the Married Women's Property Law, and not just its 1839 chapter, is told in full in chapter 8.

29. *See* "Henry Stuart Foote," in David G. Sansing, *Mississippi Governors: Soldiers, Statesmen, Scholars, Scoundrels: A Bicentennial Edition* 74–79 (2016); Henry Stuart Foote, *Mississippi Encyclopedia* 447 (Ownby and Wilson eds., 2017).

30. *See* Stanley Nelson, "The Murder of Joel Cameron," *Concordia Sentinel* (June 1, 2016), http://www.hannapub.com/concordiasentinel/the-murder-of-joel-cameron/article _ed567oc2-2823-11e6-ab9b-13bcd9563660.html.

31. "Alexander Gallatin McNutt," *Find A Grave*, Memorial #10342943. http://www.findagrave .com/cgi-bin/fg-cgi?page=gr&GRid=10342943.

32. See "Tilghman Mayfield Tucker," in David G. Sansing, *Mississippi Governors: Soldiers, Statesmen, Scholars, Scoundrels: A Bicentennial Edition* 52–54 (2016); Tilghman M. Tucker, *Mississippi Encyclopedia* 1249–1250 (Ownby and Wilson eds., 2017).

33. *Campbell v. Mississippi Union Bank*, 6 Howard (7 Miss.) 625, 1842 WL 3050 (1842).

34. Miss. Const. art. 5, § 9 (1832).

35. Dunbar Rowland, "William Lewis Sharkey," in *Courts, Judges, and Lawyers of Mississippi, 1785–1935*, 87–92 (1935), reproduced in "Mississippi Biographies, Mississippi Genealogy Trails," http://genealogytrails.com/miss/bios_s.htm. *See* "William Lewis Sharkey," in David G. Sansing, *Mississippi Governors: Soldiers, Statesmen, Scholars, Scoundrels: A Bicentennial Edition* 96–98 (2016); William Lewis Sharkey, *Mississippi Encyclopedia* 1127 (Ownby and Wilson eds., 2017).

36. Miss. Const. art. 4, §§ 2, 8, 11, 16, 18, 23 (1832).

37. *Campbell v. Mississippi Union Bank*, 6 Howard (7 Miss.) 625, 1842 WL 3050 (1842).

38. *See, e.g., Morgan v. Reading*, 3 Smedes & M. (11 Miss.) 366, 1844 WL 3217 (1842), discussed in chapter 8 below, regarding the common law of riparian rights.

39. https://www.geni.com/people/Justice-Cotesworth-P-Smith/6000000042604211111.

40. *State v. Johnson*, 3 Cushm. (25 Miss.) 625, 724–769, 1853 WL 3667 (1853).

41. *See Reports of Cases Argued and Determined in the High Court of Errors and Appeals of the State of Mississippi*, Vols. 2–39 (1834–1860/63).

42. See "Gen. Volney E. Howard," *Los Angeles Times* (Los Angeles, California), Weds., May 15, 1885, page 2, Newspapers.com, https://www.newspapers.com/image/155667054.

43. *See, e.g.,* "Law Partnership," *Tennessean* (Nashville, Tenn.), Tues. Sept. 16, 1834, page 1, Newspapers.com, https://www.newspapers.com/image/118731025; "Law Notice," *Tennessean* (Nashville, Tenn.), Tues., Feb. 5, 1834, page 4, Newspapers.com, https://www.newspapers.com /image/118731339.

44. *See, e.g., Commercial and Railroad Bank of Vicksburg v. Atherton*, 1 Smedes & M. (9 Miss.) 641, 642, 1844 WL 3201 (1844); *Commercial Bank of Rodney v. State*, 4 Smedes & M. (12 Miss.) 439, 474, 1845 WL 1992 (1845); *Nevitt v. Bank of Port Gibson*, 6 Smedes & M. (14 Miss.) 513, 517, 1846 WL 1658 (1846); *Commercial Bank of Natchez v. State*, 6 Smedes & M. (14 Miss.) 599, 611, 1846 WL 1659 (1846); *Commercial Bank of Natchez v. Chambers*, 8 Smedes & M. (16 Miss.) 9, 38, 1847 WL 1741 (1847); *Grand Gulf Railroad and Banking Co. v. State*, 10 Smedes & M. (18 Miss.) 428, 432, 1848 WL 1997 (1848); *State v. Dickerson*, 12 Smedes & M. (20 Miss.) 579, 582, 1849 WL 3330 (1849); *Ingraham v. Gregg*, 13 Smedes & M. (21 Miss.) 22, 26, 1849 WL 2300

(1849); *State v. Commercial Bank of Manchester*, 13 Smedes & M. (21 Miss.) 569, 574, 1850 WL 3394 (1850).

45. *Campbell v. Mississippi Union Bank*, 6 Howard (7 Miss.) 625, 652 (Charles Scott), 671 (G. S. Yerger), 1842 WL 3050 (1842).

46. *See, e.g., Commercial and Railroad Bank of Vicksburg v. Atherton*, 1 Smedes & M. (9 Miss.) 641, 642, 1844 WL 3201 (1844) (appearing with J. S. Yerger).

47. *See, e.g., Campbell v. Brown*, 6 Howard (7 Miss.) 106, 112, 1842, WL 2044 (1842).

48. "D. W. Adams—Acquitted." *Tennessean* (Nashville, Tenn.), Weds., July 17, 1844, Newspapers.com, htpps://www.newspapers.com/image/118866546. See chapter 8 below.

49. *See* Sarah Meriwether (Sally) Scott Yerger, www.wikitree.com/wiki/Scott-16288.

50. *See* Report of J. S. Yerger, Select Committee Chairman, House Journal, page 239 (1841).

51. *Ex Parte Hickey*, 4 Smedes & M. (12 Miss.) 751, 768, 769, 770, 772, 773, 775, 778, 782, 1845 WL 1999 (1845). See chapter 8 below.

52. *State v. Johnson*, 3 Cushm. (25 Miss.) 625, 769–796, 1853 WL 3667 (1853) (Yerger, J., concurring).

53. David Withers's plantation in Wilkinson County is an exemplar. *See Commissioner of Homochitto River v. Withers*, 7 Cushm. (29 Miss.) 21, 1855 WL 107 (1855), discussed at the outset of chapter 8.

54. Indian Removal Act, 4 U.S. Statutes at Large 411 (1830).

55. The phrase "internal improvements" came into increasing public use. For example, in 1830 the legislature authorized the Planters' Bank, *inter alia*, to enable persons "to realize the blessings of a correct system of Internal Improvements." Miss. Laws, ch. 74, "Whereas paragraph," page 92 (1830). *See generally*, David G. Sansing, *Mississippi: Its People and Culture* 113–115 (1981).

56. Governor H. G. Runnels address, Senate Journal, pages 19–20 (1835).

57. Senate Journal, page 61 (1839).

58. Senate Journal, page 412 (1841).

59. *See, e.g.*, a comprehensive bill to provide for internal improvements, Senate Journal, pages 183–187 (1839).

60. Senate Journal, page 412 (1841).

61. Senate Journal, page 107 (1837).

62. Governor H. G Runnels address, Senate Journal, page 19 (1835).

63. Charles S. Sydnor has summarized the financial speculation in this period, set in Mississippi in the context of the Indian lands becoming available and the emergence of banks.

64. William C. Davis has well told the story of settlers coming into what was then the Southwest in his *A Way through the Wilderness: The Natchez Trace and the Civilization of the Southern Frontier* 208–211 (1995).

65. John Edmond Gonzales lists the new railroad and banking ventures of the flush times, including those that never got to first base.

66. William Davis's take on the rise of banking in Mississippi leading up to the Panic of 1837 is a useful backdrop for understanding the bank bond wars that are the primary focus of this chapter. Porter Fortune's overview bears different emphases and is equally valuable.

67. Miss. Const. art. 14, § 258 (1890).

68. Miss. Laws, ch. 74, §§ 3, 5, page 94, 96 (1830).

69. Miss. Laws, ch. 74, §§ 1, 2, 7, 8, 11 (1830); *see also* Senate Committee Report, per J. W. Mathews, chairman, Senate Journal, pages 717, 718, 719, 725–726 (1842).

70. *See* Senate Committee Report, per J. W. Mathews, chairman, Senate Journal, page 718 (1842).

71. Miss. Const. (1817).

72. Miss. Const. art. 7, § 9 (1832).

73. *See* Senate Committee Report, per J. W. Mathews, chairman, Senate Journal, page 720 (1842).

74. Miss. Laws, ch. 74, "Whereas paragraph," page 92 (1830).

75. *New York Trust Co. v. Eisner*, 256 U.S. 345, 349 (1921) (Holmes, J.).

76. *Planters' Bank v. Sharp*, 4 Smedes & M. (12 Miss.) 17, 1844 WL 67 (1844), reversed *sub nom. The Planters' Bank of Mississippi v. Sharp*, 6 Howard (47 U.S.) 301 (1848).

77. A full and detailed story of the trials and tribulations of the Planters' Bank is found in Senate Committee Report, per J. W. Mathews, chairman, Senate Journal, pages 716–726 (1842).

78. Miss. Const. art. 14, § 258 (1890).

79. Governor Charles Lynch, Annual Message to Legislature, January, 1837, Senate Journal, page 46 (1837).

80. Senate Journal, page 29 (1838).

81. Miss. Laws, ch. 74, § 7, page 97 (1830).

82. Senate Journal, page 30 (1835).

83. House Journal, pages 20, 105 (1837).

84. House Journal, pages 25–26 (1837); Senate Journal, pages 26–27 (1837).

85. Clifford Thies, *Repudiation in Antebellum Mississippi*, 19 *Independent Review* 193–196 (Fall 2014). *See also* the chronological listing of banks being chartered in John Edmond Gonzales, "Flush Times, Depression, War and Compromise," in *A History of Mississippi, Vol. 1*, pages 289–292 (Richard A. McLemore ed., 1973).

86. Senate Journal, page 21 (1835).

87. House Journal, pages 105–108 (1837).

88. Senate Journal, page 48 (1837).

89. Senate Journal, act § 5, page 88 (1837); House Journal, act § 5, pages 141–142 (1837).

90. For a helpful summary of this business model and order of liability, *see, e.g.,* J. J. Wallis, *Sovereign Default and Repudiation: The Emerging-Market Debt Crisis in the U.S. States, 1839–1843*, National Bureau of Economic Research, page 7 (2004), www.nber.org/papers/w10753.

91. Miss. Const. art. 7, § 9 (1832).

92. Senate Journal, page 111 ((1837).

93. One important version of these events was provided by Chief Justice William L. Sharkey in his opinion upholding the constitutional and legal viability of the Union Bank. *See Campbell v. Mississippi Union Bank*, 6 Howard (7 Miss.) 625, 674–679, 1842 WL 3050 (1842). William L. Coker's *Repudiation and Reaction: Tilghman M. Tucker and the Mississippi Bond Question* (1969) is a useful read, though the author pays little attention to the legal analyses in the *Campbell* and *Johnson* cases, much less to the meaning of the final judgments in those cases for a state that considered itself constitutionally bound by the rule of law.

94. Senate Journal, pages 26–30 (January 4, 1838).

95. Senate Journal, page 47–48 (1837); see Miss. Const. art. 7, § 9 (1832).

96. *See, e.g., State v. Johnson*, 3 Cushm. (25 Miss.) 625, 637, 728, 767, 1853 WL 3667 (1853). See Report of J. S. Yerger, Select Committee Chairman, House Journal, page 239 (1841).

97. Senate Journal, page 24 (1840).

98. Senate Journal, pages 30–31 (Jan. 4, 1838).

99. House Journal, page 352–356 (1838).

100. Senate Journal, pages 129–138 (1838).

101. Report of Board of Bank Commissioners, Jan. 12, 1838, Senate Journal, page 138 (1838).

102. Senate Journal, page 131 (1838).

103. Senate Journal, pages 20–28 (1839).

104. Senate Journal, page 15 (1841).

105. Senate Journal, pages 15–23 (1841).

106. Senate Journal, pages 23–26 (1841).

107. Select Committee Report, Senate Journal, pages 234–235 (1841).

108. Senate Committee Report, per J. W. Mathews, chairman, Senate Journal, pages 718–720 (1842).

109. Governor A. G. McNutt annual message, January 4, 1842, Senate Journal, page 18 (1842).

110. House Journal, pages 97, 139 (1837).

111. House Journal, pages 937–956 (1842).

112. U.S. Const. art. 1, § 10, cl. 1; Miss. Const. art. 1, § 19 (1832).

113. Miss. Const. art. 7, § 9 (1832).114. Select Committee Report, Senate Journal, page 237 (1841).

115. A. G. McNutt, Senate Journal, page 20 (1839).

116. Select Committee Report, Senate Journal, page 238 (1841).

117. Select Committee Report, Senate Journal, pages 240–242 (1841). Compare Governor McNutt's remarks at Senate Journal, page 23 (1841).

118. Select Committee Report, Senate Journal, pages 242–244 (1841).

119. *Harrison v. Stowers*, Walker (1 Miss.) 165, 169, 1824 WL 638 (1824); *Markham v. Merrett*, 7 Howard (8 Miss.) 437, 444, 1843 WL 2031 (1843) (if a party wishes to rescind, he must pay back what he has received); *Lewis v. Starke*, 10 Smedes & M. (18 Miss.) 120, 130, 1848 WL 1969 (1848) (suggesting no grounds for rescission absent fraud, with which the Union Bank bond-holders were never charged, foreigners though some of them were); *Johnson v. Jones*, 13 Smedes & M. (21 Miss.) 580, 583–584, 1850 WL 2219 (1850) (where innocent party cannot be restored to position occupied before transaction, court will deny other party the equitable remedy of rescission); *Shipp v. Wheeless*, 4 George (33 Miss.) 646, 652–653, 1857 WL 2669 (1857) (where suit by party seeking to rescind "contains no offer to surrender possession and to account justly for the use and occupation of the land . . . ; [f]or this reason he is not entitled to relief."] See Gregory, Moody & Gregory, *Contracts, Encyclopedia of Mississippi Law*, §21:72 *Rescission*, pages 540–541(Jeffrey Jackson, Mary Miller, and Donald Campbell eds., 2016)

120. *Harrison v. Stowers*, Walker (1 Miss.) 165 (1824); *see* Gregory, Moody & Gregory, *Contracts, Encyclopedia of Mississippi Law*, §21:72 *Rescission*, pages 540–541(Jeffrey Jackson, Mary Miller, and Donald Campbell eds., 2016); Black's Law Dictionary, *Rescission* 1174 (5th 1979) (return to status quo).

121. Senate Journal, pages 21–22 (1842).

122. Senate Journal, pages 57–71 (1842).

123. See the explanation of the common law action for assumpsit in Justice Virgil A. Griffith's, *Outlines of the Law: A Comprehensive Summary of the Major Subjects of American Law* at pages 57–578 (Mississippi edition, 1940); *see also* "Legal definition of assumpsit," https://legal-dictionary.thefreedictionary.com/assumpsit; "Assumpsit," https://en.wikipedia.org/wiki/Assumpsit.

124. *Campbell v. Mississippi Union Bank*, 6 Howard (7 Miss.) 625, 629 (Howard), 652 (Charles Scott), 672 (G. S. Yerger), 1842 WL 3050 (1842).

125. An Act Requiring the Several Banks in this State to Pay Specie, and for other purposes, enacted February 21, 1840, ch. 15, § 7; Hutchinson's Code 325 (1848). This nine-page, seventeen-section act is described more fully in *Campbell v. Mississippi Union Bank*, 6 Howard (7 Miss.) 625, 626, 673, 1842 WL 3050 (1842). The "other purposes" included a ban on banks transferring negotiable instruments, which led to almost fifteen years of litigation, from *Payne v. Baldwin*, 3 Smedes & M. (11 Miss.) 661, 675, 1844 WL 66 (1844) to *McIntyre v. Ingraham*, 6 George (35 Miss.) 25, 1858 WL 4580 (1858).

126. *Campbell v. Mississippi Union Bank*, 6 Howard (7 Miss.) 625, 628, 671, 674–679, 682–683, 1842 WL 3050 (1842).

127. *Campbell v. Mississippi Union Bank*, 6 Howard (7 Miss.) 625, 676, 1842 WL 3050 (1842).

128. Any question whether corporate charters were contracts had been resolved a generation earlier in the well-known *Dartmouth College v. Woodward*, 17 U.S. 518 (1819).

129. *Campbell v. Mississippi Union Bank*, 6 Howard (7 Miss.) 625, 680–682, 1842 WL 3050 (1842).

130. *See* Miss. Const. art. 7, § 9 (1832).

131. *Campbell v. Mississippi Union Bank*, 6 Howard (7 Miss.) 625, 682–683, 1842 WL 3050 (1842).

132. *Albany Evening Journal* (Albany, N.Y.), Sat., June 12, 1852, Newspapers.com, https://www/newspapers.com/image/82639452.

133. The facts, terms, and circumstances of the Union Bank bond held by Hezron Johnson are set out in *State v. Johnson*, 3 Cushm. (25 Miss.) 625, 630–631, 1853 WL 3667 (1853).

134. The court found that "the testator [Johnson] died in September, 1891." *In Re Johnson's Estate*, 47 N.Y.S. 963, 964 (Surrogate's Court, New York County, New York, 1892).

135. Copy of Assignment of the Mississippi Union Bank to James Elliot, Charles W. Clifton, and Charles Scott appears in Senate Journal, pages 90–99 (1842); *see also* Extract from the Minutes of the Mississippi Union Bank in relation to the Deed of Assignment, signed by C. W. Clifton, cashier. Senate Journal, pages 100–101 (1842).

136. *See, e.g., State v. Johnson*, 3 Cushm. (25 Miss.) 625, 770–796, 1853 WL 3667 (1853). The courage behind and power within Justice William Yerger's opinion has been noted. *See, e.g.,* James D. Lynch, *The Bench and Bar of Mississippi* 326–341 (1880); John Ray Skates Jr., *A History of the Supreme Court of Mississippi, 1817–1948*, 105–106 (1973); Clayton Rand, "William Yerger," in *Men of Spine in Mississippi* 222–225 (1940).

137. *State v. Johnson*, 3 Cushm. (25 Miss.) 625, 725, 1853 WL 3667 (1853).

138. *See, e.g.,* Hanson Alsbury, Select Committee Report, Feb. 1840, Senate Journal, page 497 (1840); A. G. McNutt, Senate Journal, page 20 (1841); Senate Journal, pages 496–500 (1841).

139. Jacob S. Yerger, Select Committee Report, Senate Journal, page 241 (1841).

140. *State v. Johnson*, 3 Cushm. (25 Miss.) 625, 794, 1853 WL 3667 (1853) (Yerger, J., concurring).

141. Chief Justice Smith's entire opinion may be found in *State v. Johnson*, 3 Cushm. (25 Miss.) 625, 724–769, 1853 WL 3667 (1853). It may be the longest opinion in what is collectively the longest reported decision in Mississippi history.

142. *State v. Johnson*, 3 Cushm. (25 Miss.) 625, 769–796, 1853 WL 3667 (1853).

143. On January 27, 1841, H. G. Runnels resigned as a director of Mississippi Union Bank. House Journal, page 336 (1841); Senate Journal, pages 298–299 (1841). At that time he began another brief stint in the legislature, representing Hinds County. In 1842, Runnels joined the G. T. T. crowd—Gone To Texas—where he established himself as a planter on the Brazos River and with a new political career in what became the Lone Star State. https://en.wikipedia.org/wiki/Hiram_Runnels.

144. *State v. Johnson*, 3 Cushm. (25 Miss.) 625, 792, 1853 WL 3667 (1853) (Yerger, J., concurring). Both Chief Justice Smith and Justice Fisher signaled their joinder in Justice Yerger's opinion.

145. *See, e.g., State v. Johnson*, 3 Cushm. (25 Miss.) 625, 637, 728, 1853 WL 3667 (1853).

146. *See, e.g., Bush v. City of Laurel*, 215 So.2d 256, 259–260 (Miss. 1968); and *Keys v. Rehabilitation Centers, Inc.*, 574 So.2d 579, 584–586 (Miss. 1990) for discussions of traditional principles of indemnity law.

147. *Butte A & P Ry Co. v. United States*, 290 U.S. 127, 135 (1932) (Brandeis, J.).

148. *Rock Island, A. & L. R. Co.*, 254 U.S. 141, 143 (1920) (Holmes, J.); *Pickering v. Hood*, 95 So.3d 611, 620 (¶37) fn. 23 (Miss. 2012) (quoting cases).

149. Miss. Const. art. 5, § 9 (1832); *see also* the constitutional oath of office then applicable, Miss. Const. art. 7, § 1 (1832).

150. Miss. Const. art. 5, Militia, § 3 (1832). *See State v. McPhail*, 182 Miss. 360, 182 So. 387 (1938), construing and applying almost identical clauses of the constitution of 1890.

151. J. F. H. Claiborne, *Mississippi, as a Province, Territory and State* 479 (1880; reprinted by LSU Press, 1964).

152. *State v. Johnson*, 3 Cushm. (25 Miss.) 625, 725, 1853 WL 3667 (1853) (C. P. Smith, C. J.).

153. This story is told rather colorfully and quite incisively in "The New Nation of Mississippi," *New York Times*, January 29, 1861, http://www.nytimes.com/1861/01/29/the-new-nation -of-mississippi.html?pagewanted=all&pagewanted=print.

154. David G. Sansing, "Alexander G. McNutt, Twelfth Governor of Mississippi: 1838–1842," *History Now*, December 2003, http://mshistorynow/mdah.state.ms.us/index.php?s=extraid=117.

155. Clifford Thies, "Repudiation in Antebellum Mississippi," *Independent Review* 19 (Fall 2014), 191, 192.

156. *Sovereign Default and Repudiation: The Emerging-Market Crisis in U.S. States, 1839–1843*, Panel A, Table 7 for Mississippi Property Tax Revenues. "Interest payments on the Union Bank bonds were $250 thousand per year."

157. U.S. Const. art. 1, § 10, cl. 1; Miss. Const. art. 1., § 19 (1832).

158. Meredith Lang tells this story well in chapter 2 of her *Defender of the Faith: The High Court of Mississippi 1817–1875* 31–47 (1977). *See also* Clifford Thies, "Repudiation in Antebellum Mississippi," *Independent Review* 191, 201–206 (Fall 2014).

159. Report of Senator John Kerr, chairman of Select Committee re Governor's Message on Banks and Currency, Jan. 30, 1841, Senate Journal, page 327 (1841).

160. Clifford Thies, "Repudiation in Antebellum Mississippi," *Independent Review* 19 (Fall 2014), 201.

161. An Act Requiring the Several Banks in this State to Pay Specie, and for other purposes, enacted February 21, 1840, ch. 15, § 7; Hutchinson's Code 325 (1848); Mississippi Acts of 1840, page 15.

162. *Planters' Bank v. Sharp*, 4 Smedes & M. (12 Miss.) 17, 28–29, 1844 WL 67 (1844) (Sharkey, C. J., dissenting).

163. *Planters' Bank v. Sharp*, 4 Smedes & M. (12 Miss.) 17, 27, 1844 WL 67 (1844) (Clayton, J., for the court).

164. U.S. Const. art. 1, § 10, cl. 1; Miss. Const. art.1, § 19 (1832).

165. *Payne v. Baldwin*, 3 Smedes & M. (11 Miss.) 661, 675, 1844 WL 66 (1844).

166. See chapter 8, below.

167. *Payne v. Baldwin*, 3 Smedes & M. (11 Miss.) 661, 676–680, 1844 WL 66 (1844).

168. *The Planters' Bank of Mississippi v. Sharp*, 6 Howard (47 U.S.) 301, 322–323 (1848).

169. *The Planters' Bank of Mississippi v. Sharp*, 6 Howard (47 U.S.) 301, 322–323 (1848).

170. *The Planters' Bank of Mississippi v. Sharp*, 6 Howard (47 U.S.) 301, 322–323 (1848).

171. *The Planters' Bank of Mississippi v. Sharp*, 6 Howard (47 U.S.) 301, 322–323 (1848).

172. *The Planters' Bank of Mississippi v. Sharp*, 6 Howard (47 U.S.) 301, 324–334 (1848).

173. *Montgomery v. Galbraith*, 11 Smedes & M. (19 Miss.) 555, 574, 1848 WL 2055 (Nov. Term, 1848).

174. *Grand Gulf Railroad and Banking Co. v. State*, 10 Smedes & M. (18 Miss.) 428, 434, 1848 WL 1997 (1848).

175. *McIntyre v. Ingraham*, 6 George (35 Miss.) 25, 50, 1858 WL 4580 (1858).

176. *McIntyre v. Ingraham*, 6 George (35 Miss.) 25, 51–55, 1858 WL 4580 (1858).

177. *McIntyre v. Ingraham*, 6 George (35 Miss.) 25, 62, 1858 WL 4580 (1858), ostensibly distinguishing *Grand Gulf Railroad and Banking Co. v. State*, 10 Smedes & M. (18 Miss.) 428, 434, 1848 WL 1997 (1848).

178. *McIntyre v. Ingraham*, 6 George (35 Miss.) 25, 58–59, 1858 WL 4580 (1858).

179. *See* Miss. Laws, ch. 127 (1842).

180. Most prominently, see the dual constitutional injunctions that the state might never take any government action that impaired the obligation of contracts. U.S. Const. art. 1, § 10, cl. 1. The Mississippi Bill of Rights at the time protected one and all from any "law impairing the obligation of contracts." Miss. Const. art. 1, § 19 (1832).

181. Miss. Const. art. 12, § 5, amend. 1 (as amended 1875).

182. Miss. Const. art. 14, § 258 (1890).

183. *Grant v. State*, 686 So.2d 1078 (Miss. 1996), *cert. den. sub nom., Grant v. Mississippi*, 520 U.S. 1240 (1997). Of course, there is a sense in which it is hard to argue with *Grant's* straight-forward statute of limitations ruling. On the other hand, the bondholders did plead equitable estoppel. *See, e.g.,* cases such as *Christian Methodist Episcopal Church v. S & S Constr. Co.*, 615 So.2d 568 (1993); *PMZ Oil Co. v. Lucroy*, 449 So.2d 201 (Miss. 1984); *Covington County v. Page*, 456 So.2d 739 (Miss. 1984). *Grant* looks at Section 258 of the Constitution and says it only bars payment on the bonds, not lawsuits. True. But do not the *Campbell* and *Johnson* cases make it pretty clear that even getting a final judgment that the bonds are valid will get a bondholder nowhere? The Contracts Clause argument [U.S. Const. art. I, § 10, cl. 1] was available at the time of *Campbell* and *Johnson* and would have been precluded by *res judicata* in the *Grant* case. Moreover, in the 1850s, the High Court of Errors and Appeals established a notorious practice of ignoring the Contracts Clause, and the Supremacy Clause as well, even after *Planters' Bank v. Sharp*, 47 U.S. 301, wherein the US Supreme Court reversed earlier decisions. Surely all of this is enough to change the equitable analysis in *Grant*. One might argue that it's for the legislature to address this issue, not the courts, but that one surely fails in the face of the fact that Section 258 is in the constitution, not a mere statute that can be amended or repealed.

184. *Parker v. Livingston*, 817 So.2d 554, 565 (¶41) (Miss. 2002); *Lee v. Thompson*, 859 So.2d 981, 992 (¶26) (Miss. 2003).

185. *Southern Win-Dor, Inc. v. RLI Insurance Company*, 925 So.2d 884, 888 (¶13) (Miss. Ct. App. 2006).

186. Miss. Const. art. 4, § 104 (1890).

187. The quote comes from *Meredith v. Fair*, 298 F. 2d 696, 701 (5th Cir. 1962), and refers to the arguments advanced by the State of Mississippi and its institutions of higher learning as to why James Meredith, an African American, should not be a admitted as a student at the University of Mississippi.

BIBLIOGRAPHY

Baldwin, Joseph G., *The Flush Times of Alabama and Mississippi* (1853, 1974).

Brough, Charles, "The History of Banking in Mississippi," Publications of Mississippi Historical Society.

Campbell v. Mississippi Union Bank, 6 Howard (7 Miss.) 625, 1842 WL 3050 (1842).

Claiborne, J. F. H., *Mississippi, as a Province, Territory and State* (1880).

Coker, William L., *Repudiation and Reaction: Tilghman M. Tucker and the Mississippi Bond Question* (1969).

Davis, William C., *A Way through the Wilderness: The Natchez Trace and the Civilization of the Southern Frontier* 214 (1995).

Foote, Henry S., *Casket of Reminiscences* (1874).

Fortune, Porter L., Jr., "The Formative Period," in *A History of Mississippi, Vol. 1* (Richard A. McLemore ed., 1973).

Gonzales, John Edmond, *Flush Times, Depression, War and Compromise*, in *A History of Mississippi, Vol. 1* (Richard A. McLemore ed., 1973).

Harris, William C., *The Day of the Carpetbagger* (1979).

James, Marquis, *The Life of Andrew Jackson* (1938).

Lang, Meredith, *Defender of the Faith: The High Court of Mississippi 1817–1875* (1977).

Lowry, Robert, and William H. McCardle, *A History of Mississippi* (1891).

Lynch, James D., *The Bench and Bar of Mississippi* (1880).

McCraw, Thomas K., *The Founders and Finance* (2012).

Meacham, Jon, American Lion: *Andrew Jackson in the White House* (2008, 2009).

Mississippi Encyclopedia (Ownby and Wilson eds., 2017).

Mississippi House Journals (1838–1842)

Mississippi Senate Journals (1838–1842)

"The New Nation of Mississippi," *New York Times*, January 29, 1861.

Owen, Harry P., *Steamboats and the Cotton Economy: River Trade in the Yazoo-Mississippi Delta* (1990).

Rand, Clayton, *Men of Spine in Mississippi* (1940).

Robertson, James L., *Constitutional Law* in *Encyclopedia of Mississippi Law* 2nd (Jeffrey Jackson, Mary Miller, Donald Campbell, Editors, Thomson Reuters), Vol. 3 (2018).

Robertson, James L., *The Law of Corporate Governance: Coming of Age in Mississippi?*, 65 Miss. L. Journ. 477 (1996).

Rowland, Dunbar, *Courts, Judges, and Lawyers of Mississippi, 1785–1935* (1935), reproduced in "Mississippi Biographies," *Mississippi Genealogy Trails*, http://genealogytrails.com/miss/bios_s.htm.

Sansing, David G., *Mississippi Governors: Soldiers, Statesmen, Scholars, Scoundrels: A Bicentennial Edition* (2016).

Sansing, David G., *Mississippi: Its People and Culture* (1981).

Schlesinger, Arthur M., Jr., *The Age of Jackson* (1945, 1953).

Skates, John Ray, Jr., *A History of the Supreme Court of Mississippi, 1817–1948* (1973).

State of Mississippi v. Hezron A. Johnson, 3 Cushm. (25 Miss.) 625, 1853 WL 3667 (1853).

Sydnor, Charles S., *The Development of Southern Sectionalism, 1819–1848* (1948).

Thies, Clifford, "Repudiation in Antebellum Mississippi," *Independent Review* (Fall 2014).

Wallis, J. J., *Sovereign Default and Repudiation: The Emerging-Market Debt Crisis in the U. S. States, 1839–1843* (2004), National Bureau of Economic Research, www.nber.org/papers/w10753.

Weber, "Early State Banks in the United States," *Journal of Economic History* 66 (June 2006).

CHAPTER 5

Agricultural Liens and Related Policy Products of Police Power

The [crop lien] system had its vices, but it also had one
overriding virtue: it lent money.
—DAVID L. COHN, *THE LIFE AND TIMES OF KING COTTON*

The Civil War was over. Dixie had been defeated. Devastation and despair
were everywhere, more so in Mississippi than in other southern states, though
Georgia and Virginia may have disagreed. In 1866 one-fifth of the state's budget
had been spent providing artificial limbs, a stark and oft-cited datum.[1] The
cleared lands lay desolate. Only a few years earlier, they had been so productive
and annually reliable as a source of food and fiber and wealth and pride and
hope for all, except, of course, African American slaves—those over whom the
War had been fought. Fire, floods, droughts, soil depletion, no crop rotation,
lack of cultivation because there had been no one to till the soils—all of these
surpassed perceived Union meanness among the causes of calamity. Livestock
and farmwork animals like mules had been killed or maimed or just died from
lack of nourishment. Survivors exhibited their skeletons, their unkempt skins
tight around their bones. One observer reported, "Plows and wagons were as
scarce as mules, with no means to buy new ones. The cavalryman fortunate
enough to have been paroled with his horse . . . was the envy of his neighbor."[2]
William L. Nugent, in time a successful Jackson lawyer, described the scene as
the War wore down: "The largest plantations are . . . grown up in weeds . . .;
fences pulled down and destroyed; houses burned."[3]

Postbellum southern humanity suffered a darker side. Without surprise,
newly emancipated slaves sought tastes of freedom however they could. But
they were up against a wall of harsh realities—no land, no capital, no farm
equipment or working stock, illiteracy, not even basic math skills, plus a white
population convinced that their foremost character traits were mental sloth,
immorality, ineptness, undependability, and dishonesty. Still, there was talk in
the air of "fawty acres an' a mule." "Over my dead body" was the response of

resolved whites, who opposed any semblance of black independence and education, and who collectively held on to the land as well.[4] Dreams of the Day of
Jubilee faded as the freedmen lapsed back into the all-too-familiar drudgery
of farming the white man's fields, only now as tenants or sharecroppers or field
hands. A change of status de jure, though barely noticeable de facto. A generation later, only 6.7 per cent of all farm land in the Cotton South belonged to
African Americans.

"Debt was one of the two economic realities that helped determine the perspective African Americans developed towards goods in the years after emancipation. The other was the hope of owning land."[5] Less ambitious but still
important was the wish of most freedmen to grow their own foodstuffs. That
was not to be either. For the few lucky enough to have a patch of ground they
could farm, when they sought credit—next to none really had a choice on that
score—the creditor's first condition was that they plant cash crops. In the mind,
if not the market reality, cotton was *the* cash crop, almost the only salable product of southern soil. African American tenants or croppers were stuck, accepting a course that was hardly removed from the slavery they had been told they
had been freed from.

But not all tenants and croppers were black, not by a long shot. Once away
from the Mississippi River counties and the prairie soils, and in many other
parts of the South, there were the white tenant and the white cropper, "head
and front of the poor-white class . . . ; a mighty and always multiplying horde
of the landless, who, in order to eat, must turn to laboring for their more fortunate neighbors on whatever terms the latter offered."[6] Savvy southern journalist
W. J. Cash (1900–1941) made sure we knew of "[t]he jungle growth of poverty
and ruin . . . closing in on the southern white man's clearings faster than he can
make them," and of the South's "yeoman farmers and, to a large extent, of poor
whites."[7]

David L. Cohn (1894–1960), native and astute observer of the Mississippi
Delta, looked back and found that in the postbellum world "[m]en no longer
believed, or affected to believe, that Negroes alone could bear the heat and toil
of cotton culture. In time, whites outnumbered Negroes in the cotton fields." A
local historian in Washington County, Mississippi, reported more contemporaneously that

> In those days there was quite an influx of white families into this country, men of
> small means, with a pair of mules, or a yoke of oxen, a few cows, and a wagon load
> of household effects, and usually, a large family of children, all hunting a home or
> a place to better a bad condition in a former environment.[8]

Now it was the summer of 1865, and then the fall, and too late to do much
for the first full crop year after Appomattox Court House. The issue front and

center as the South contemplated rebuilding was getting the agricultural engine going again. Somehow! But how? Folks in Mississippi were broke—and in the entire Deep South for that matter—including those who never dreamed they would have to do without. For the white planter class—so many now reduced to mere farmers—the loss of slaves and not loss of land had brought their financial ruin. In Mississippi it was debatable who was the more bankrupt, the State or its people. "Just strapped" may have been a fair descriptive, though when it came to the State's banking system, never very strong, and certainly not since the late 1830s, "shambles" captured its essence in the years after the War. The only alternative was money and credit from outside sources, loans on terms—but what sort of terms? Who in Mississippi had any assets to offer as collateral to secure the needed credits? Never had the ox been so stuck in the ditch. Never had southern legislatures faced such a challenge in just how to enable and provide incentives for an agricultural comeback, and in devising stratagems that could offer any practical hope at all.

Understand that searching for solutions and addressing such broad socioeconomic concerns are what a state's legislative power is for. This is why constitutions recognize a legislative power, authorize its use, commit that power to a discrete department of government, and give it a primacy, augmented by a judiciary charged with adjudications and en route fair and reliable applications of the law. The executive is charged to see that the law is faithfully executed, a charge that centers on enforcing the final judgments of the courts. We focus here upon a passive power, dormant except when a legislature decides otherwise. The facts and circumstances may more or less be assembled and understood. Alternative stratagems for hopefully helpful action may be identified, their effects projected and assessed. Then there are the passions and politics of the matter, in this instance seldom more emotionally charged, contentious and challenging than in the wake of the greatest disaster the state had known, before or since. As the calendar turned to 1866, there sat the passive power, the sine qua non for We The People doing something with effect about the great mess they were in.

Of course, executive leadership can help, even when it is not wholly enlightened. In October of 1866, Governor Benjamin G. Humphreys[9] (1808–1882) surveyed Mississippi's post-war predicament and told the legislature that "capital and labor . . . within the limits of the state are insufficient, and the supply must come from abroad. Capital should be invited, and emigration of free white labor should be encouraged." The governor was right as to the need for outside capital, and also as to the need for immigrant white labor. If only he could have seen the contribution that nonwhite labor could have made, if properly respected and encouraged, or maybe just allowed.

In early 1867 the Mississippi legislature was holdovers from antebellum days but hardly a stable political institution. The national elections of November of 1866 portended the demise of President Andrew Johnson's ineffectual efforts to treat the South in some respects as he thought Lincoln would have, had Lincoln lived. A state legislature with a different makeup was easy to foresee, and sooner rather than later. Still, a Whig majority legislature convened in Jackson at the beginning of January. It had the prerogative, nay the duty, to do something about farm credit as a crucial need of (alas, mostly only) white people trying to crawl back on to their feet. A new species of credit vendor, in time called supply merchants—or sometimes "furnish merchants"—had begun to appear. These immediate postbellum, well-focused loan sharks made it possible for cash-strapped landowners, on the one hand, and landless freedmen and poor whites, on the other, to make a crop. The system was informal. It was also full of risks. Uncontrollable external forces were everywhere, or so it seemed, and more so with each passing year. Adequate and practicably accessible agricultural collateral was as hard to come by as it was critically needed.

Savvy and skillful players were needed at every position, on offense and in the field and particular on the pitcher's mound. Rep. A. P. Barry (1814–1892) was a very valuable player. He added an important ingredient to the early postbellum legislative process. Farming knowhow. More commonly known as Major Barry, this gentleman presided over the Copiah County Agricultural Association. He had improved and perfected farm implements, such as his widely admired manure distributor and his horse hoe or scraper.[10] And so Rep. Barry had credibility when he proposed an "Act for the encouragement of agriculture." Add to that ideas borrowed from other southern states struggling similarly. On February 18, 1867, Mississippi formally legislated a pragmatic approach to farm credit. Not only did the new law recognize and declare legally effective a lien upon a crop that had not even been planted; the seeds were not even in the barn. The legislature created that novel and desperately needed lien upon inchoate crops—a property right that was vested and perfected though no judge or court clerk or sheriff had signed the first paper, had lifted the first finger. And it gave that crop lien a priority—a first priority—to the end that those among the emerging class of credit merchants with a certain bent of mind and fortitude would be attracted and would come and make their capital available, for a price and a profit. A favored few might even think of a small fortune.

By 1870, Jonathan Tarbell (1820–1888) had become a player of note. This native New Yorker, then a Mississippi plantation owner, had been an antebellum Whig, now turned moderate Republican. Tarbell was practical and sympathetic to blended Reconstruction and emancipation, much more so than many defeated Confederate sympathizers could see or would let on. Speaking for the state supreme court in an early case under the new lien law, Tarbell saw that it had been

> passed at a time when our people were prostrated and impoverished, without
> means, and without credit. To supply these; to aid the people in undertaking the
> cultivation of their farms; for the support of their families; to enable them to

contribute to the support of the government; and to increase the wealth of the state; these were among the worthy objects of this law.

Such practical realities and understandings had to be brought to bear whenever the judiciary was called upon to apply and enforce a new law. Certainly, this was so for the many new laws—legislated and judge-made—that are the core of this chapter.

Mississippi's early postbellum legislators may or may not have been aware of the gallows humor in the insight of Louis XIV (1638–1715) that "credit supports agriculture, as the cord supports the hanged!" But they plunged ahead. A legislatively designed, first priority crop secured credit program was seen so imperative that the State should have it. Mississippi should run the risk that three quarters of a century later a Southern sage would come along and condemn it as "one of the worst systems ever developed; that of the supply merchants,"[11] though he would immediately justify it. Some evils must be borne.

The core idea was simple, grounded in practical reality. People who would plant, cultivate, and hopefully harvest and market the crop had to have a variety of farm equipment—mules, plows, hoes, and wagons, not to mention barns and sheds, and a roof over the family's head. Starting with seeds, supplies were essential to producing a crop. The farmer needed labor, too. Emancipation had come, and the slave system was gone with the wind. The farmer had to pay the hired help who would go to the fields and do backbreaking work in the hot summer suns. He found he could pay cash or in kind, and in one or more of several ways—creating a tenancy by renting the land to the farmer, granting the worker a share of the crop produced, providing tangibles such as food, clothing, and housing, by paying him or her small amounts of cash or extending credit at the commissary or company store. Often farm laborers received what little they could command through two or more of these means.

Then there was the issue of timing. The farmer needed the supplies, equipment, and other necessaries in the spring and through the growing season. He needed workers at planting and for cultivation until lay-by time, and at harvest to beat the bad weather that could come along with barely a moment's notice and ruin everything. And he needed cash, working capital, if you will. The farmer's asset of value—the harvested crop—would have no marketable existence until the cotton had been picked, ginned and baled. But it was all he had, could hope for.

The common law had never recognized a property right or interest in a thing ephemeral, not yet in being. Enter Justice Horatio F. Simrall (1818–1901), a colleague of Jonathan Tarbell and similarly dispositioned. A native of Kentucky, Simrall in time became lawyer and planter in Wilkinson County, Mississippi. Like many who prior to the War had engaged in Whig politics, Simrall became an active postbellum Republican, opposing black codes and other similarly harsh policies but at the same time seeking to moderate the Reconstruction policies emanating from Washington, DC. Judge Simrall understood that "whether such security could be created at common law was of no matter, it was certainly within the [constitutional] power of the legislature to authorize it."[12] If the legislature did its part, Simrall would do his to assure that the courts would uphold and enforce any such lien in a crop as it came into being.

There were more legislative facts that faced legislators like Maj. A. P. Barry and jurists like Jonathan Tarbell and Horatio Simrall. Remember, postbellum the farms were significantly smaller than they had been antebellum. What land a man had was already mortgaged to the hilt, and he was debt-ridden besides. The few that had some equity in their lands faced the fact that its fair market value was at an all-time low, as no potential buyer had money or credit to make a decent offer. Less than a handful of farmers—landowners, tenants, or croppers—could produce a crop without substantial advances along the course of the growing season. Without substantial unencumbered assets to provide as collateral, what was the farmer to do? No one would furnish the farmer without some financially adequate and accessible security—legally and practicably enforceable security. The crop to be grown was not just the obvious choice of collateral; it was the only real choice, though it would have no redeemable value until harvest time. This took creativity, and of the most practical variety.

In short order, the shape of the playing field and rules of the game would change. Versatile and at times colorful players would be needed.

MORE POLICY-MAKING CHARACTERS

The complex and controversial life story of the crop liens, post–Civil War variety, involves categories of characters that challenge the memory as we proceed. Legislative players like A. P. Barry deserve to be remembered. So many were interesting characters, flaws and all, though not nearly so much is known—or even knowable—about them. Still, legislators were those whose steps and missteps provided incentives and deterrents to which most everyone else responded. Then came the judges with not quite an everyday job—in agricultural economics and its jurisprudence, that is—but one that required insight and wisdom often enough. Judges were the ones who worked through and decided the contests and conflicts between and among the supply merchants, cotton factors whose role was evolving downward, the croppers, many of whom were newly freedmen, the landlords and many more.

The challenge before the judges was not only learning the practical realities of the business of farming. About every four or five years, the legislature would enact new ground rules, not exactly turning the worlds they worked in upside down but coming close. A quarter of a century after Lee surrendered, Justice Tim E. Cooper (1843–1928) provided a useful bit of hindsight. His well-written opinion in *Newman v. Bank of Greenville*[13] was released on April 15, 1889. It's a history lesson and more. The 1867 crop lien law. Then the 1872 laborer's wage lien. Finally, in 1876, the landlord was back on top with his new lien act. This, of course, undid much of the good done over the past decade, reinstating impediments to a bit better world, albeit a favored few would benefit in the short run. Appellate judges, imbued with an overdose of classical legal formalism because that's the way they'd learned the law, invariably generated mischief, then as now. It's a shame so many not only shunned pragmatic agricultural economics but were unable to see that freedmen really did have the capacity and deserve the opportunity for a higher quality of life without the shackles of the stereotypes and prejudices in which so many whites were determined to keep them.[14]

We've begun our note of Rep. A. P. Barry and the part he played in passing the first crop lien law, the one in early 1867. At the 1870 Copiah County Fair, Barry unveiled his "universal planter." By the spring of 1871, an astute observer reported that Barry had "developed his thinking into the simplest, cheapest, lightest, most easily managed and most effective corn planter I have ever seen."[15] Perhaps no surprise that Barry's bill listed corn in addition to cotton as the inchoate crops named, the production to be encouraged by enticing supply merchants to furnish Mississippi's farms.

Five years later, Albert T. Morgan (1842–1922), said to have been a lawyer, was legislatively active in affording farm laborers a new first lien that would protect their supplies as well as unpaid wages. This was the second stage set out in Justice Cooper's history lesson.[16] Having served in the Union Army, Wisconsin-native Morgan brothers Albert and Charles became conventional carpetbaggers moving to the Delta part of Yazoo County as soon as the War was over. They tried their hand at growing cotton but failed. Then Albert got into politics, Mississippi Reconstruction variety. Running as a Radical Republican, Morgan was elected to the state senate from the Thirteenth District, foremost including Yazoo County. Without apologies, Morgan sought a new social order. He went so far as to acquire a beautiful mulatto wife, Carrie Highgate, a school teacher from Syracuse, New York.[17] He was reelected to the senate in November of 1870. Those whose displeasure Albert had incurred were by and large unable to vote, while freedmen for the most part had been enfranchised. Albert was particularly proud of his subsequent service as sheriff and tax collector in Yazoo County. It was no surprise that when the worm began to turn in 1876, the Morgan brothers were ridden out of town on a rail.[18] But Senator Morgan had been a strong voice supporting the laborer's wage lien law enacted April 5, 1872.

Less colorful in those turbulent and trying postbellum days, B. T. Kimbrough (1846–1906) represented Benton County—Tennessee supplying its northern boundary—in the legislature. Kimbrough's politics were evidenced by his active support in 1872 of the Horace Greeley Liberal Republican ticket, ultimately unsuccessful in its challenge to sitting president Ulysses S. Grant.[19] Earlier in that same year, Representative Kimbrough steered the wage lien bill to passage in the house of representatives. In 1884, Kimbrough moved southwesterly to Oxford, whence he would become a highly regarded chancellor.[20]

A well-known summary of Kimbrough and Morgan's new bill noted the alarm that some landowners were expressing in 1872 at the priority granted laborers.[21]

Within a few years, the political worm began to turn again. Rep. Mayre Dabney (1846–1911) of Raymond and Hinds County appears to have been a primary proponent of the landlord's lien act of 1876. In August of 1875, preliminary to the state elections, Dabney was announced as a legislative candidate on the Conservative-Democratic ticket. In his campaign for re-election two years later, Representative Dabney found praise before a western Hinds County precinct for his "arduous and then apparently forlorn struggle for honest government." Dabney's career was posthumously summarized as including Civil War service on behalf of the Confederacy, clerk, lawyer, judge, public official, Democratic Republican legislative representative, and state constitutional convention of 1890.

Several other judges, briefly discussed below, play substantial roles in the stories arising from the judicial encounters that are our focus below, the judges from Tennessee being excepted. The efforts of postbellum appellate judges should be judged on their merits, and not their political past or route to office.

Hamilton H. Chalmers[22] (1835–1885) was a native of North Carolina, whose parents moved the family to Holly Springs, Mississippi, in 1839. His legal career began in 1853 but was interrupted by his service in the Confederate Army. At the close of Reconstruction in 1876, Gov. John Marshall Stone appointed Chalmers to the Supreme Court of Mississippi, where he served until his death on January 3, 1885.

James Zachariah George[23] (1826–1897) served on the Supreme Court of Mississippi for three years, 1878–1881. Prior to that, he had been counsel for the supply merchants in an early crop lien case.[24] As a lawyer, George represented the appellees John T. Dyche and Gates, Gillespie & Co., in the 1869 case discussed below and focusing on statutory changes to the common law distress for rent. George's judicial service ended with the beginning of his sixteen-year service as US senator from Mississippi. Senator George has been generally regarded as a dominant and influential figure at the convention leading to the Mississippi Constitution of 1890, and its restrictions on African American citizens' right to vote.

Ephraim Geoffrey Peyton[25] (1802–1876) served on the Supreme Court of Mississippi during Reconstruction, 1867–1876. His service and approach substantially paralleled those of Justices Horatio Simrall and Jonathan Tarbell. Before the War, Peyton mentored Albert Gallatin Brown (1813–1880), who in time became governor of Mississippi and a US senator. Politically a Whig in antebellum days, Peyton became enough of a Republican after the War that he was appointed to the state supreme court by Gov. James L. Alcorn (1816–1894), another ex–Mississippi Whig returned to public service postbellum. Peyton authored the opinion of the court in the 1869 case of Mary P. Marye vs. John T. Dyche and Gates, Gillespie & Co., discussed below.

THE ACT FOR ENCOURAGEMENT OF AGRICULTURE

The stage summarily set, some of the players given a short introduction, this part of Mississippi's story began formally when the legislature passed a planned design "for the encouragement of agriculture."[26] It was the beginning of a series of constitutional encounters that lasted close to fifteen years, well beyond April 14, 1876, and passage of the last of such laws, one called "An act to provide for agricultural liens, and for other purposes," though this one had shifts in emphases and effects. There were assorted fits and starts, tugs toward one interest group and then another, not always regarding the original endgame or the truths of practical agricultural economics. Not much could have been done had not the state legislature possessed passive political power that could be activated to make new laws. At least since statehood that power has been publicly anchored in written constitutions.

The first formal legislative step, taken February 18, 1867, "was . . . authorizing the creation of liens not known before, and making them valid in all courts." The second, separate and arguably more crucial step was affording those liens a first priority over competing interests. By filing the written lien contract in the courthouse and enrolling an abstract of it, "the lien springs up. *Cooper v. Frierson*, 48 Miss. 300, 310. It is denominated a 'first lien.' The intendment is that it shall have preference over other encumbrances on the products of the soil."[27] Mississippi was not alone in affording merchants such a special lien priority. Five other states from the defunct Confederacy had passed like laws before Mississippi's more comprehensive effort.[28] Shortly afterward, North Carolina[29] and Louisiana[30] would follow suit.

Still it was important that, in February of 1867, the legislature had enacted that a crop lien—whether memorialized in the form of a chattel mortgage or other writing contractual in nature—

> shall have priority, from its date, whether the crop be planted or not. The pro-
> spective crop, before the seed is sown, is such a potential interest or expectancy
> in property that it may be thus conveyed. And when the crop grows, the *subject*
> has come into *esse*, and the mortgage or trust deed at once takes effect upon it.[31]

The legislature's first stab at a fix was to afford the supply merchant a lien on "cotton, corn or other produce, of such farm or plantation" which would prime any competing lien or other right. Of course, many of the merchants who flocked to the scene demanded and were afforded greater collateral, such as a prior lien on equipment from mules to plows without which no crop could be produced.

Historian C. Vann Woodward (1908–1999) opined that such a lien law, ostensibly "for the encouragement of agriculture," "represented one of the strangest contractual relationships in the history of finance."[32] But that was not so at all. Years earlier the general maritime law had recognized a "last-in-time, first-in-right" approach to liens for vessel repairs, for taking on supplies and other necessaries that the voyage might be completed. The "whole object"—the policy premise—was

> to furnish wings and legs to the . . . hull, to get back for the benefit of all concerned, that is, to complete her voyage. . . . The vessel must get on; this is the consideration that controls every other; and not only the vessel, but even the cargo, is *sub modo* subjected to this necessity.[33]

In time the Supreme Court of Mississippi would put forth a similar rationale for the crop lien priority rule in favor of supply merchants, and later farm workers.

> The charges are for work done for the common good of all parties, which was absolutely essential in order that the crop might be made available to those interested. No matter when done, if by a party in interest, they must be paid, since they accrued to the common benefit of all.[34]

Writing about a decade before Woodward, the less academically proficient Mr. Cash observed, "From one standpoint this system may be said to have been most admirably contrived, for it brought the available resources of the South to focus on the purpose and with great effectiveness."[35] So said Mississippi Deltan David Cohn as well, albeit in retrospect.

Sadly, and without much surprise, the 1867 lien priority law soon had tacked on to it one exception after another, much the same as the maritime lien priority rule that made so much sense in its pristine form became riddled with exceptions. On land as earlier at sea, various interest groups put on blinders to all except immediate concerns with their own pocketbooks and asserted their quasi-legislative political power. A few years after the first lien law, federal Reconstruction policy meant more representation of the interests of freedmen.

And so the wage lien priority was enacted in 1872, "extending the lien to the cropper on shares, and the landlord."[36] The landlord's lien priority was enhanced in 1876, by which time the federal forces were becoming fewer and fewer. The purpose embedded in this conglomerate lien legislation was becoming—albeit *sub silentio*—one of an equitable division of the crops raised and subject to the various liens. Each interest group, of course, fervently believed and argued that equitable division of necessity meant a fair advantage for itself. All of this made perfectly good sense from a political point of view, as long as you didn't care about choking off the incentives that in 1867 you had aimed at the outsider—indeed the infamous carpetbagger, no way around it—so that he would come to Mississippi, bring his money, and extend credits for the encouragement of agriculture. The question in hindsight is whether more merchants would have extended more credit—with more aggregate socioeconomic public benefit—if their collateral had not been watered down by rights and priorities given the wage, cropper, and landlord liens? And with what effect on the size of the overall socio-agri-economic pie and the fairness of its division at any given time? Equity and efficiency and self-centeredness engaged in a constant tug-of-war—not just annually but seemingly almost daily—for this part or that of the ever-evolving or devolving pie.

Cash reflected that "by the 1880s almost every crossroads was provided with at least one such banker merchant, and every village had from two to half a score." Fifteen years later, Cohn announced the same historical finding. "By the 1880s nearly every crossroads village, every hamlet lost in malarial swamps or deep woods, had one or more banker-merchants, and towns had them by the dozen."[37] All such insights were subject to whether the observer was at the ten-thousand-foot level taking annual snapshots, or down on the hard, cruel earth wondering what tomorrow would bring, and how the next day would be met.

The normally perceptive Mr. Cohn missed it when he denied that the lien system that underlay merchant credit was of planned design. To be sure, furnish merchants had begun setting up shop or coming to Mississippi and neighboring states at least since word of Lee's surrender filtered southerly. These merchants began making possible modest agricultural pursuits that might otherwise have been for more difficult, if not impossible. In this sense, the crop lien system wasn't just dreamt up in the abstract by desperate legislators who had to do something, even if it was wrong. The first priority crop lien laws were the product of purposeful human legislative intervention. Without these, the postbellum story in the Deep South may have been different, arguably bleaker than the all-too-familiar version we know so well.

THE CHALLENGING AND MORE COMPLEX LANDSCAPE

There was a broader backdrop, lest we paint an incomplete picture in our focus on the legislative empowerment of crop lien practice. In these same times—maybe a year before—and in the minds of many of these same legislators, so-called black codes were being enacted, a most enduring feature of which was the vagrancy law.[38] Enough has been written about these instances of legislative power run amuck. Yet a reminder is in order that in these early postbellum years, the people—freed by emancipation—awoke few mornings without knowing that very day that they would have to deal with the practical incidents of all of these new laws.

Ten years and several legislative amendments later, Chief Justice Josiah A. P. Campbell[39] (1830–1917) would have a lot to say about Mississippi's crop lien legal practice. In this business, the risks taken by the supply merchant were "considered to be so great as to justify a profit which in other circumstances might be regarded as shockingly exorbitant." Campbell added that making a financially successful cotton crop "is dependent on so many contingencies as to make the hazard great."[40] One of those contingencies was the price that cotton was bringing on the commodities market, a price more or less declining soon after the War.

Cotton sold at $1.02 a pound in 1864 but was down to $.32 a pound by 1867. In a case dating back to 1866, the court noted that the "course of the market was downward" and that the insolvency of a farmer before the bar was "referable to the decline in the value of cotton."[41] Of course, times got worse, so that it wasn't much longer before folk thought wistfully of the price of fiber and "the high levels prevailing in the first decade after the war."[42] Outside economic influences were as omnipresent as they were beyond the power of much of anyone in the South to affect, much less control.

History tells of the Panic of 1873.[43] The cotton crop of 1873 brought fourteen cents a pound. Between 1872 and 1877, cotton prices fell by 50 percent, according to James C. Cobb, who has reported that the Delta was so severely affected "by early 1874 [that] even big-time planter and former governor Charles Clark was scrambling to secure supplies and credit."[44] Such swirls and downward spirals invariably inflicted the greatest harm on those within their wakes most economically vulnerable. In time, it would be celebrated that over 1878 "average prices continued their steady upward climb, from 10.8 cents to 12 cents a pound,"[45] only confirming in practical reality just how bad times had been. That boomlet did not last. And in the next twenty years, the general trend was fatally downward, until in 1898 it plunged below five cents—the lowest level in history.[46] One cause of this overall decline in price was overproduction, and one cause of overproduction was the one-crop economy built in substantial part on another of the white South's great prejudices—that cotton was the only crop. The Panic of 1893 was the icing crushing the collapsing cake.

Supply merchants faced more localized risks. More than a few were left holding the bag when they had failed to ascertain accurately the respective rights and interests of husbands and wives in plantations that the merchants had supplied.[47] It is easy enough to say now that such merchants should have secured the advice of counsel prior to extending such credits. It is not easy to gauge how practical that was back in the 1870s. Then there was the risk that prospective farmer-borrowers would withhold important information needed to assess a credit risk. To be sure, the R. G. Dun Company traced its origins to 1841, and its rival, the John M. Bradstreet Company, was founded in 1849. By the 1870s credible credit information was far more available than one might have thought[48] and was accessed by savvy merchants. Yet risks remained.

We know that in August of 1876, B. H. Smith "was a man of small means, engaged in farming on a limited scale." By 1877 he had been adjudged a crook.[49] Smith had applied for credit with merchants in Brandon in Rankin County. He was questioned at length regarding his creditworthiness. Smith neglected to disclose that only four days earlier, he had opened accounts with three separate supply merchants in Morton and Scott County, though he did fess up that he owed twenty dollars to a man in the town of Trenton, one county away. Through the remainder of the growing season, Smith bilked the merchants in Rankin and Scott Counties for considerable sums. Come harvest time, and Smith had only two bales of cotton to show for his efforts, though at the outset he had assured his creditors that he ordinarily produced six or seven bales. The only thing a bit atypical about Smith's case was that he would spend three years as an involuntary guest of the State, following his conviction of fraud by false pretenses.[50] These were times when full and credible credit information was hardly as easy to come by as it would become, and when the human heart was as crafty and nefarious as ever, with strong incentives to hone its natural propensities. Lots of supply merchants were stung by the likes of B. H. Smith.

In 1880, Campbell emphasized that "the only hope" that the farmer would ultimately pay the merchant for the supplies furnished was "the success of the operations of the year."[51] That hope was measured against such realities as "that cotton had long ago begun to exhaust even those plantation lands that had once seemed so eternally fecund."[52] Even before he factored in the ever-evaporating prices that a bale of cotton would bring on the open market, Cash saw that "the growing of cotton in the South was saddled with a crushing burden, with such a burden as no agricultural product could be expected to bear and still afford a decent return for the producer."[53]

In a burst of candor, Campbell stated publicly that he regarded Mississippi's legislatively authorized and regulated crop lien practice "as a most pernicious system, which has produced wide-spread evil." He added quickly and correctly that the system had been fostered by legislation and, as such, it "must be dealt with as it is, and not as I wish it was."[54] Of course, neither Campbell nor any other critic of the system offered a viable alternative, much less did they deny that something had to be done in the wake of economic collapse following the War. Nor did much of anyone seem to understand the well-after-the-fact and altogether correct insight of latter-day sage Gene Dattel—Mississippi Delta and Sunflower County–born and bred—that "[f]inance is amoral. It will respond to the theoretical opportunity to make money within an existing legal and cultural framework."[55]

AN EARLY CASE IN POINT

One of the first cases under the new law for encouragement of agriculture recognized the legislative nature of what Mississippi had done. "The whole policy of the law respecting distresses for rent has been changed by our statute," said Justice Ephraim G. Peyton, speaking for the soon-to-be-renamed Supreme Court of Mississippi at its April term, 1869. A distress was one of those legal notions of ancient origins that confused even lawyers at times. It was essentially a way that a person claiming a debt due and unpaid might have the high sheriff seize the debtor's property as a means of compelling payment, without first getting a by-your-leave from any court.[56] But as Peyton explained, by reason of the new legislation, "[t]he common-law process of distress [for unpaid debts] does not exist in this State." The law in those early postbellum years recognized "the general right of the tenant to dispose of his property, which is no more embarrassed on account of rent in arrears than it is by any other description of outstanding debts." "Rent is not *per se* a lien on goods found on the [lands that had been leased and with respect to which the rent was due but unpaid]," Peyton continued. "It binds as a lien only when the goods are seized under an attachment for rent."[57] Until 1872, that is.

What had led to this judicial recognition of a then brand-new and proper exercise of legislative power? It takes a little math, and keeping up with a few people, but bear with me. For the crop year 1867, James M. Wadlington and Isaac R. Dyche leased lands in Sunflower County from landowner Mary P. Marye and set about to plant their crops. The then forty-seven-year-old Mary had lost her husband earlier in 1867 and was in no position to farm in her own right. Wadlington and Dyche "employed on said plantation a considerable number of laborers, and being without sufficient means to carry on said plantation, they had to borrow the same on the credit of the crop to be raised by them."[58] Summer passed. Cotton factors called Gates, Gillespie & Co. of New Orleans had advanced money and supplies to Wadlington and Isaac Dyche in the amount of about $4,300, which in time had been paid down to about $1,200. Wadlington and Isaac in turn gave Gates, Gillespie a crop mortgage filed for record on September 30, 1867. John T. Dyche furnished supplies to the amount of about $4,900. He has also loaned mules and a wagon to the partnership to use in making its 1867 crop. Wadlington and Isaac Dyche gave John a $5,000 note. The proper filings were made in the Sunflower County courthouse.

But the crop fell short. Wadlington and Isaac Dyche were struggling financially. On December 16, 1867, landowner Mary P. Marye sought a distress for unpaid rent of $3,600. The sheriff seized 1,800 bushels of corn, sixteen bales of cotton, five mules, and a wagon. By reason of the act for encouragement of agriculture, however, Gates, Gillespie & Co. and John T. Dyche held liens, newly recognized in law and made prior in right to all other rights in the crops.

Specifically, the Gates, Gillespie and John Dyche crop liens primed all claims of landlord Mary P. Marye for what farmers Wadlington and Isaac Dyche owed her. If there was not enough left to pay what was owed to recently widowed landlord Marye, well, that was just too bad. The legislature had established the public policy of the state.

We the People had made a value judgment of what should be done in terrible circumstances, where everyone knew going in that there would be no way to make everyone—or maybe even much of anyone—happy in the end. To get Mississippi's farming economy cranked up again and break out of the depression that followed the War, new financial knowhow and resources somehow had to be brought to bear. To that end, the legislature had enacted that parties such as Gates, Gillespie & Co. and John T. Dyche—and those lesser lowlifes depicted by Cash and Cohn—should be encouraged to extend credit to farmers. The legislatively selected carrots took the form of perfected liens, which if properly and timely filed for record, were made prior in right to all others. In *Marye v. Dyche*, the 1867 crop lien law was applied and yielded the precise results the legislature had planned. According to more natural fates, and on October 1, 1868—before the April 1869 final judgment of the state supreme court—poor Mary P. Marye had followed her husband and passed from this life.

Of course, no self-respecting landlord could accept the state of lien priorities recognized in the *Marye* case. After all, owning land meant prestige in the community, pride in oneself. These worthies were offended that the law would put supply merchants—always of a social and economic class below—at the head of the pack in any contest for the pickings from the tenant's short crop. Landowners looked inward, unable to see or even sense the broader purpose embedded in the legislative text—or Governor Humphreys's exhortation before that—of bringing badly needed financial and human wherewithal to the state and its agricultural economy, wherewithal that had a new form and substance, and that had to come from outside.

Fast-forward and by 1879 the landlords were riding high—relatively speaking—no doubt in substantial part because of the shifting of political winds by 1876, when the Democratic South traded a Samuel Tilden presidency for the practical ending of the federal occupation phase of Reconstruction. A list of the landlord's remedies had come to include a crop lien, and "the security of the terror of punishment threatened against the tenant or anyone who disposes of, or removes, the crop before he is satisfied." In 1879, the court added that the landlord "may recover from the tenant, and his aiders and abetters who join with him in getting the crops off the premises to evade the rent."[59] Lost in the shuffle was that, however flawed its original plan, the 1867 legislature had been trying collectively to think a bit bigger than landowner landlords who—many living from day to day themselves—believed in their souls that they were the ones who should be preferred.

ENOUGH TO DRIVE A MAN TO DRINK

Back to the furnish merchant. What, then, were the outer limits on articles legitimately furnished the farmer or bought with advances as to which the new (but gradually being watered down) crop lien priority applied? The legislature listed "farming implements, work stock." Rather than trying to enumerate all, the draftsmen concluded with a catchall "or other things necessary for the cultivation of a farm or plantation." Inevitably a question arose: How about a gallon or two of whiskey? The point was presented in *H. Herman & Co. v. Perkins*, decided in 1876. By that time, the court had some experience to draw on, such that it could say with fair confidence that

> [a]ll would agree that work animals, plows, hoes, wagons, provender for beasts, food and clothing for laborers, and medicines were necessary things in the production of a crop. . . . [Still w]hat might be necessary on a large plantation would be extravagant for the cultivation of a few acres.[60]

Construing the Code of 1880, § 1301, the court added that "[c]hiefest among those means and supplies the mule is fairly entitled to be ranked." As for food, the outer limit of the reasonable seemed a blur: "[T]he query is, does it include luxuries, and what are luxuries? Shall sugar and coffee be excluded? Shall the meat be ham or pickled pork? Shall the bread be flour or meal?"[61]

After concluding that "approximate right" was the best one could hope for as an approach to the outer limits of the statute's catchall clause, the court acknowledged, "There is a large range of debts for which this lien cannot be created—those which have no relation to agriculture, and do not arise out of assistance in production of crops." In between we find Chief Justice Simrall's penultimate paragraph.

> Nor should the articles furnished be scanned too closely when the merchant is enforcing his lien. Herman & Co. let Spivy have one or two gallons of whisky. Ought that to be rejected? It may be used medicinally, both for man and beast. Most generally it is drunk as a beverage; but how, if the farmer buys but a gallon or two of liquor, can the merchant know whether he is going to drug sick horses with it, make tonics, or consume it as a beverage?[62]

THE ARRIVAL OF SNOPESES, BEFORE AB AND FLEM

In short order, the merchant became "the most important economic power" in postbellum Mississippi and in the southern countryside in general. He often ran a general store that sold everything from food to clothing to whiskey and tobacco—and credit. Understand that the banks, such as they were, refused financing to any except the most reliable borrowers. Crop lien priority laws opened the door for merchants who thrived on credit sales. Illustrating the practical reality was the country store that in June of 1874 had cash sales of $21.35 and credit advances of $1,191.46.[63] The country store began to rival the courthouse as the hub of the community. The key to the merchant's power was his virtual monopoly over credit extensions within his local universe.[64]

W. J. Cash assessed the circumstances and the mindset of the merchant.

> But the opportunity on the land was as nothing to that afforded by the career of supply merchant. There was little room here for those not made of the sternest stuff.... But let a man have an eye for the till ... —and his prospects of growing rich were very bright.

Their numbers increased steadily and substantially. "The Natchez district counted 130 merchants in 1860, 218 in 1870, and 283 in 1880."[65] But the stage should be better set.

Foremost, the antebellum plantation system was dead. Before the War, cotton factors had facilitated that system. Factors were go-between agents, commissioned by a plantation owner or other persons to arrange financing in the spring and then to market the baled cotton at the best price and receive the proceeds. "The factor has a special property or lien on the cotton for his indemnity."[66] Even postbellum, the law reports in Mississippi exhibited the names of firms like Gates, Gillespie & Co. of New Orleans, and Messrs. Howard, Preston & Barrett, also doing business in New Orleans. The cotton factors and commission merchants in New Orleans—and to a lesser extent on Front Street in Memphis—remained active.

But the world of cotton finance had grown more complex. Indeed, the rise of sharecropping, tenant farming, and the rural merchant after the War marked the virtual cessation of economic growth in the South. As the number of large plantations declined, factors found it more and more difficult to remain sufficiently knowledgeable of both the cotton grower debtors and the cotton commodities market. The size of cotton belt farms declined from an average of 401 acres in 1860 to 229 acres in 1870[67] and then smaller as the years rolled by. More and more for information and credit, the supply merchant became an essential link in the chain, between the cotton factor and the farmer.

The examples abound and are readily identified in the litigations of the new era. *Hilliard v. Cagle* arose from the postbellum circumstance where W. P. Badgett, a merchant and cotton dealer in Brookhaven, Mississippi, had an established business relationship with Summers & Brannin, cotton factors in New Orleans. Similarly, *Cotton & Co. v. Hiller & Co.* concerned a litigation between a supply merchant in Amite County and Hiller & Co., also cotton factors in New Orleans. Lehman Abraham & Co., cotton factors and commission merchants in New Orleans, provided substantial financing for J. W. Bissell, who was a country supply merchant in Vicksburg.[68] Such relationships and practices remained prevalent in 1887. In that year, H. & C. Newman, cotton factors and commission merchants with offices on Gravier Street in New Orleans, handled 50,000 bales of cotton and also a large quantity of sugar.[69] Newman provided financial resources and other customary services to supply merchant Moyses & Co. as far upriver as Greenville, Mississippi. Moyses leased lands and produced crops in addition to "conducting a mercantile business [in the course of which it] had secured from various customers mortgages upon crops to be grown to secure advances made during the year."[70]

E. Merton Coulter, an accomplished historian of the South, explained crop lien financing's effects on pricing, given the near-universal scarcity of money. For the farm supplies that the farm tenant and landlord received,

> they paid . . . a credit price twice as high as the cash price. The merchant who sold nine-cent bacon for eighteen cents had little profit left after he had paid the money lenders 25 per cent interest, or particularly if through crop failures or other misfortunes he was unable to collect from those he had credited.[71]

After several decades of legislative actions and reactions, W. J. Cash—in his classic argument explaining the South to a nationwide jury—reflected on the landscape, these well-intentioned if not desperate legislative tinkerings, and the plight the farmer faced.

> Specifically, what he had to submit to in order to get credit from this source was the following: first, he gave a mortgage on the projected crop; . . . —and finally he undertook to pay charges, what with "time prices," interest rates, and so on, commonly averaged in most districts from 40 per cent to 80 percent.[72]

The supply merchant was making his mark, and the question was whether he was more cause or effect or just going with the flow. A familiar and not altogether humorous epitaph of the time read

> Here lies Thirty-six per cent,
> The more he got, the more he lent;
> The more he got, the more he craved—
> Good God! Can such a soul be saved.

David Cohn agreed that little cash was involved in these transactions and added that the farmer would "take it out" in supplies delivered by the merchant-lender: sowbelly, corn-meal, clothing, molasses, plow points, harness, sometimes coffins, and so forth. These goods were often evaluated at 30 to 70 per cent more than their cash prices. On top of this was piled an interest rate that might be 40 per cent or higher.[73]

So seldom was cash paid that as a practical matter a cash price was little more than an arbitrary number on some sort of tag arbitrarily associated on tangible goods almost certain to be sold on time.

In a case that arose in the heart of the Mississippi Delta in 1877, the court observed that the price charged by merchants allowed him "a profit of about ninety to one hundred per cent, besides the two and one-half per cent commissions," plus interest at "ten per cent per annum from date" some nine months before harvest. "As a condition of the loan the planter was required to grant a 2½ per cent commission on each and every purchase or sale from or to the factor. This commission charge was not extravagant, but it added up because of the frequency of sales and purchases."[74] And later, "the inflated price charged by merchants in the vicinity to insolvent purchasers was accidental and abnormal, and resulted from a perversion of the laws of trade."[75]

Once he took advantage of the Act for encouragement of agriculture, the farmer became caught for life within a web that came to be called debt peonage.

> When one of these mortgages has been recorded against the Southern farmer, he has usually passed into a state of helpless peonage. . . . With the surrender of this evidence of indebtedness he also surrenders his freedom of action and his individual autonomy. . . . Until he has paid the last dollar of his indebtedness, he is subject to the constant . . . direction of the merchant. Every mouthful of food that he purchases, every implement . . . his mules, his cattle, clothing for himself and his family, the fertilizers for his land, must be bought of the merchant who holds the crop lien, and in such amount as the latter is willing to allow.[76]

Joseph M. Jayne II (1851–1906) was a prominent Greenville-based lawyer involved in a number of crop lien cases. As a brash twenty-eight-year-old, this son-in-law of future governor Robert Lowry was the landlord's lawyer in the Mississippi Delta case noted above. Jayne could not have been more focused on the practical point. He made sure the appellate court knew that the transcript of the proceedings in the trial court

> show[ed] that the kind of credit business as carried on by Langsford [supply merchant] was to get all that the mortgagors [Paxton's seventeen tenant farmers] made, irrespective of the amount of supplies furnished to them. The charges are admitted to be such as to allow the mortgagee [Langsford] to clear one hundred per cent. The kind of credit business seems to be the same as is engaged in all over the country.[77]

The men who worked this perversion were of Snopsean genre, though they moved among us several decades before Ab[78] and Flem[79] and the other Snopeses began to crawl from around and beneath the rocks in and around Yoknapatawpha County, Mississippi.

John Storm (1812–1882) was a proto-typical supply merchant in Lincoln County, doing business under the name of Storm & Co. He was miffed that prior to the 1873 crop year, the legislature had granted landlords a lien for their rent. Peter Harrison farmed lands owned by John J. Green and for the year 1873 agreed on a rental of eight bales of cotton. Merchant Storm furnished supplies to Harrison. The farming fates were not kind to Harrison that year. He delivered only three bales to Green, his landlord. Green took the bales to Brookhaven to sell, when he was accosted by Storm and henchmen who forcibly took the cotton. It turned out that—on November 1—Storm had somehow pressured Harrison into signing a $1,000 note, payable the next day, and secured by a chattel deed of trust on "three or four work animals, a wagon and all the agricultural crops, which Harrison might produce that year." [80] At trial, farmer Harrison said "he did not think he had obtained more than $400 worth of goods and supplies." He "repeatedly tried to get his account from Storm & Co., but they had never given it to him." The court found the testimony "direct that ... [Storm] took the security for the very purpose of defeating Green in getting his rent." Storm & Co. never overcame Harrison's testimony "by production of the accounts and credits." In the end, Green recovered a judgment against Storm for $442, his due as landlord. Tenant Harrison was left with nothing for his year of hard work. A quarter of a century later, if Storm & Co. had moved to Yoknapatawpha County, many might have mistaken it for a Snopesean enterprise.

Of course, the supply merchants had no monopoly on sharp dealings. After all, as we have seen above, farmers were as prone to lies, concealments and connivances as the rest of the human species.[81] To the contrary, the merchant was always at risk that the farmer applying for a furnish loan was far deeper in debt than he would let on, as noted above in the case of B. H. Smith, in the pokey for three years because he lied when he told the merchant that he had a good crop, that he had traded with no one else during the crop year, and that he had no other debts save a small one.

There was another dimension to the legislatively enabled, postbellum credit experience for those without tangible assets. Freedmen for the most part continued as farm laborers. Their access to foodstuffs and consumer goods were largely at the plantation commissaries or the general store nearby. By 1880, there were some 8,000 general stores in the "Cotton South"—the Carolinas west through East Texas. But they were paid annually, when the crops were in the barn. Invariably this occurred at the advent of the Christmas season, when the newly freed farm laborers had the greatest need and desire for consumer goods related to the season.[82] The landed farmers found this system agreeable, as so many of them were low on cash until the crops were harvested. In the first year or two after the war, landed farmers provided clothing for their laborers. By 1867, all except just over a quarter of Mississippi farmers still provided clothing for their workers. All of this meant that the former slaves had to resort to credit and debt for the goods and stuff they needed at all other times of the year. These credit purchases consisted of subsistence goods and foodstuffs such as meat, corn, flour, sugar, beans, meal, tobacco, seed, and bagging.[83]

Those sympathetic to the plight of the freedmen saw sharecropping as another form of debt peonage from which there was no escape. White farm landowners insisted it was a practical system for both themselves and the newly freed farm laborers. The ostensible benefit for the laborer was a function of his perceived inability to manage money. Periodic wages would invariably be spent and promptly so, leaving the non-sharecropping laborers broke come Christmas time. Or as David Cohn put it,

> At the end of a year of toil and worry, the farmer was fortunate enough to find himself holding a "clear receipt," showing that his indebtedness to the merchant had been discharged, and able to buy a bottle of "Chrismus whiskey" and a few shells for rabbit hunting. But his troubles were not over. He not only needed credit for the next season, but his contract bound him to renew the lien to the same merchant for the next crop.[84]

A LONG-RUNNING NON-DELTA CASE

Foremost, 1872 is marked as the year of the first freedmen's labor lien law. Senator Morgan and Representative Kimbrough saw to that. But in 1872 and again in 1873—though not nearly so fully as in 1876—the legislature also exercised its constitutional powers to address the landowners' concerns. After all, they had no lien to secure payment of rentals which, of course, ordinarily could be made only after the crop had been harvested and sold. In 1874, Andrew Jackson Wooten (1827–1907) leased lands he owned in Marshall County to Mark and James Smith. The parties agreed upon an in-kind rental. The Smiths promised on or before November 1, 1874, that they would deliver to their landlord four bales of cotton. As fate would have it, the Smiths made a short crop. They took two bales to the railroad station in Marshall County and sold them to J. G. Westmoreland. Wanting money instead of the cotton, Wooten went to his local justice of the peace and demanded a judgment against Westmoreland "for $150, the alleged value of said two bales."[85]

Wooten prevailed at first. On appeal, however, Justice Josiah A. P. Campbell spoke for the Supreme Court of Mississippi in holding that landlord Wooten's lien extended only to the cotton itself. "A lien is a right to resort to the thing on which it operates, and cotton subject to such a lien may be followed and seized, ...; but the purchaser of such cotton is not liable for its value." Wooten's rights in the cotton were as much a function of his lease agreement with the Smiths as of the legislative enactments of 1872 and 1873. No lien priority question arose, since there was no competing lien being claimed.

The case returned to the Supreme Court of Mississippi at its January term, 1879. Chief Justice Horatio Simrall and Justice Hamilton H. Chalmers provided an articulate debate regarding the rights the law afforded the landlord whose rent had not been paid by his cotton-farming tenant. The critical facts were that, at the time he bought the bales at the railroad station, Westmoreland did not know the Smiths had not paid the rent due Wooten, nor was Westmoreland "cognizant of any facts that would suggest inquiry."[86] Though he had bought and paid for the two bales—his purchase was complete—Westmoreland was confronted by Wooten before the train pulled out of the station. Wooten demanded the cotton. Cotton buyer Westmoreland "declined to surrender it, or to point it out, so that it might be taken into possession by an officer who had a writ authorizing its seizure." In short order and at Westmoreland's insistence, the baled, sold, and paid-for cotton was shipped to New Orleans.

Simrall rightly recognized "the great practical importance to the agricultural and mercantile interests, especially, of any construction which may be placed upon the acts of 1872 and 1873." Fundamentally, the legislative policy judgment had shifted from providing incentives that outside credit sources come to Mississippi to securing an equitable division of the crop, subject to the multiple liens recognized by 1873. Collectively, the laws impressed liens on the cotton in mass. No lien creditor—laborer, cropper on the shares, tenant, landlord, or supply merchant—was permitted to "make such disposition or removal [of the cotton] as would defeat or impair the lien in behalf of another." The problem came where someone did something that would defeat or impair the lien, and where that someone was an innocent purchaser for value like Westmoreland "who buys in the open market where cotton is the common subject of trade, and is in nowise connected with the removal or disposition of the cotton from the place where grown." Simrall reasoned that, for the legislature to be held to have allowed the liened bales to be taken from the innocent purchaser "would so embarrass the marketing of almost the only salable product of our soil, as to be exceedingly detrimental to both the agricultural and mercantile classes."[87]

When Chalmers's turn came, he did not oppose the general premises his chief justice had articulated, only he did not think those fit the facts of the case. He correctly began that "we all[88] agree that the product [two bales of cotton] still remained subject to the [landlord's] lien and would remain so as long as it could be found in this State." The reason Chalmers would have held that Wooten had a tort remedy for conversion of the baled cotton was that "[t]he shipment to New

Orleans took place after he [Westmoreland] had full knowledge of the landlord's claim, and the shipment beyond the State was the only act by which it was possible to defeat the lien." In other words, the law should set aside Westmoreland's innocent purchase for value of the cotton because, before he had disposed of it, he had lost his innocence. Wooten had stepped forward to assert his lien. Chalmers pressed his points with elegance and passion. The Smiths' wrongful sale of baled cotton was an act that the legislature had made criminal. Notwithstanding Westmoreland's original innocent purchase, Chalmers would have held that he "committed a penal act in sending the cotton out of the State after he knew of the landlord's unsatisfied lien."[89] In the end, this view failed, as Campbell concurred on technical grounds in the judgment announced by Simrall.[90]

WARRING LIEN PRIORITY CLAIMANTS AND MUCH MORE

There is hardly an aspect of our experiences chronicled in this chapter that did not arise in the story leading to the April 1872 decision in *Hunt v. Wing*,[91] including a judicial performance ranging from the wooden to infection with the biases of the times. There was also the unfortunate circumstance of judges just not up to the task nonetheless serving on the Supreme Court of Tennessee. The core of the case was the problem of priorities among three competing lien claims made against the same crop. The case began on Driver Plantation in the northwest Delta county of Tunica along the Mississippi River. Eli Moore Driver (1796–1851) had lived in Memphis, less than forty miles north of his cultivatible lands. The last antebellum census had Driver Plantation owning between 133 and 146 slaves, third-largest among thirty-five "large slaveholders" in Tunica County. By the end of the War, the plantation was still being managed by William R. Hunt and Giles L. Driver, among the coexecutors of the estate of Eli M. Driver, by that time long deceased.

For the crop year 1867, the executors/landowners had leased Driver Plantation to Wing, Cox & Co. for $4,000. Wing in turn gave a note in that amount payable to the landowners on October 1, 1867, presumably about the time of the expected harvest and sale of the crops of cotton and corn to be produced. For an additional $675, the landowners had leased to tenant Wing certain mules, horses, farm implements, and equipment. To secure these two rental obligations, Wing granted to the landowners a lien on the crops to be produced, together with a separate lien on farm equipment and work animals that tenant Wing anticipated using over the 1867 growing season. Landowners timely made the proper filings in the courthouse in Tunica County, Mississippi.

Wing, Cox & Co. hired Sylvia Brooks, Jesse Christian, and about thirty-eight other farm workers—freedmen all—to work the land and harvest the crops. Presumably all forty had been among Driver Plantation's slaves prior to 1863.

Wing had agreed to pay these workers partly in cash and, in addition, with shares of the cotton and corn to be grown and harvested. Needing additional farm equipment and supplies, Wing turned to the Memphis office of commission merchant White & Billingsley, who made advances to Wing, secured by a chattel mortgage lien on all crops to be grown and all tangible farm equipment. White & Billingsley filed in the Tunica County courthouse, perfecting its lien and the priority of that lien. No such filings, however, were made by the forty farm workers. It is doubtful that they held written employment contracts. Farm workers' wage liens were a legal work-in-process at the time.[92]

At this point and as the growing season began, Wing—lessee, farmer, tenant, whatever—had granted three liens ("security interests" in today's terminology) in the anticipated but still inchoate crops of cotton and corn. The supposedly secured parties were (1) the executors/landowners for their two agreed-upon rentals, and (2) commission merchant, White & Billingsley.[93] After the fact, farm workers would claim a third crop lien and priority for their labor over and above their cash wages, which presumably remained unpaid. Only a Front Street cotton factor was missing, though in time one would be brought into the fray along with its successor in interest. Insofar as it appears, no term in any of the agreements suggested the priorities among the liens, who should get what in the event that Wing produced a short crop. October 1, 1867, came and passed. Wing had paid no one a penny.

Landowners made the first move. Down in Tunica County, they sued out a distress warrant for the rent, under which the Tunica County sheriff seized the cotton and corn, together with the mules, horses, and farming implements. In November of 1867, said high sheriff "sold all of the property so seized except for twenty-four bales of cotton."[94] Landowners were paid $4,000. Their rental note was discharged. Landowners' separate $675 equipment note could not be paid. Nothing was paid any of the others who claimed to be lien creditors secured by Wing's crops.

Things got sticky when a Freedmen's Bureau federal agent seized the cotton held by the sheriff and shipped it to an "agent, consigned to Farrington & Howell,[95] cotton factors, in the City of Memphis." Farrington & Howell "turned [the cotton] over to J. N. Pettit & Co., who soon thereafter sold it for about $1,200." On April 17, 1868, "Sylvia Brooks and some thirty-eight or nine others, free persons of color, all of Tunica county, Mississippi," filed suit in the Chancery Court of Memphis. From this point forward we have tangible evidence supporting the northern aspect of David Cohn's sociological insight that "[t]he Mississippi Delta begins in the lobby of the Peabody Hotel in Memphis and ends on Catfish Row in Vicksburg." Put otherwise, Driver Plantation and Tunica County were a part of the apocryphal state of "North Mississippi," the capital of which has always been Memphis. Eli Driver certainly operated on that practical premise during his lifetime. Co-Executor Hunt lived in Panola County,

Mississippi, and another co-executor was from Pontotoc County, Mississippi. Each was well within North Mississippi.

Before the cotton reached the Front Street factors, commission merchant White & Billingsley—quick on the draw—had it seized under the authority of a writ of replevin issued by a Memphis court. In short order the Memphis authorities delivered the twenty-four bales to J. N. Pruitt, who sold them, but for still not enough money to go around. Before the Memphis court, the landowners had not been paid the $600 they were owed. White & Billingsley had been paid nothing, and the freedmen laborers were in the same empty boat. In a fully flawed opinion, the Supreme Court of Tennessee held that the landowner lessors came first, and they got their additional $600. Supply merchants White & Billingsley got the remaining $600, presumably better than nothing, which is what the freedmen farm laborers got.

In divvying up the inadequate pie, the court first had to decide who had enforceable liens on the crop. Lots of subquestions there, but the second big step, once the liens had been identified, was ranking them, deciding who got first dibs, who came next, and so forth. And after a few years of trial and error and many substantial losses by ostensibly deserving creditors, the question would become, Was there a better way of encouraging agriculture? Of accommodating legislatively created and other legitimate and conflicting creditor interests? And of making sure that the judiciary was properly schooled regarding its interstitial but all important law-making job?[96] And, of course, its law application job.

In April of 1872, the *Hunt* court had Memphis, Mississippi, and the River as three separate sources of law to draw from. The *Hunt* judge chose dubious fourth and fifth sources, relying ostensibly on the common law and the court's own notion of good public policy. It decided that the landowners came first: "The right of the owner of soil to obtain compensation for the use of his land has always been favored both in this country and in England." At the time, however, Mississippi law was crystal clear that landlords had no lien to secure their timely receipt of agreed-upon rentals. At its October 1874 term, the Supreme Court of Mississippi would report that "neither at common law, nor under our statute [of February 18, 1867], does the landlord have a lien upon agricultural products, or the chattels on the premises for his rent."[97] The *Hunt* court took note but rather problematically said it did not matter. Why not? Because executors/landlords had fixed property rights in the crop under their Tunica County distraint. The *Hunt* judges took no note of Justice Peyton's assurance three years earlier in the *Marye* case that the common-law distress process no longer existed in Mississippi.

The land lay in Mississippi. Landowners and their lessee, Wing, Cox & Co., were Mississippi parties. They made their agreement in Mississippi, and it had been filed in the Tunica County courthouse. The freedmen wage laborers did their hard work under the hot Mississippi summer sun. Under conventional choice of law rules, now and then, the Tennessee court deciding *Hunt* should have applied and enforced Mississippi law. Of course, the parties could have agreed on choice of law. They could have provided that the landlord's right to its rental was secured by a consensual lien on the crops to be grown or the supplies and equipment the lessee tenant farmer brought to bear in producing the crop, or both. Such a private law agreement should have been enforceable between the parties. But some rule of positive law—legislated or judge-made— was needed before placing the agreement in the public records gave enough notice, and before this alone perfected the landlord's lien to the point where it would prime the liens held by third persons, such as the supply merchant or the freedmen wage laborers.

The next question was whether White & Billingsly, the supply merchant, had a lien on the crops of cotton and corn. Here the act of 1867 should have come into play, viz.,

> [A]ll debts hereafter contracted for advances of money, purchase of supplies, farming utensils, working stock, or other things necessary for the cultivation of a farm or plantation, shall constitute a prior lien upon the crop of cotton, corn or other produce, of such farm or plantation, . . . , and also on the animals and implements employed or used in cultivating the same, which shall have been purchased with the money so advanced.[98]

Such a statutory lien held by a would-be secured creditor took effect from the date of its enrollment in the courthouse records, so that public notice was given to others who might consider doing business with the farmer. It is not clear from the *Hunt* opinion whether the supply merchant made its deal with Wing before or after February 18, 1867. After that date, a written agreement to the effect set out in the statute should have created a crop lien, which should have become a perfected lien, prior in right from the date it was filed in the courthouse. Not just any filing for record would do. All of the "i's" in the recording process should be dotted, and the "t's" crossed, before the lien would enjoy priority vis-à-vis competing liens.[99]

Hunt never considered the particulars of the supply merchants' lien claim, except to say—quite erroneously—that it had a lower priority than the would-be landlord's crop lien. Rather, the court focused on the wage lien claims that the farm workers made against the twenty-four bales of cotton they had labored to produce. The court denied those claims. The priority aspect of those claims was said to fail because the agreements on which landowners and the merchants claimed were made "prior to their employment as laborers." In fact, the *Hunt* court denied that there was any such legal creature as a wage lien. The court said such a "doctrine is entirely new and unknown to a court of chancery, and if it has any foundation whatever we have failed to discover it." It may well be that the judges knew of no such premise, and that the freedmen's lawyers had not helped. But the legal raw materials from which a farm worker's first priority wage lien may have been judicially found, fashioned, and enforced were readily available.

For one thing, on April 5, 1872, Mississippi had enacted the laborer's wage lien law that Rep. B. T. Kimbrough, Sen. Albert T. Morgan and others had sponsored, and it was already drawing attention and fire from landlords and farmer employers.[100] For the moment and the foreseeable future, it had become the statute law of Mississippi that there

> be a first lien in law upon all agricultural products raised in this State, to receive payment of any wages that may be due for labor done, in the raising, handling, saving or transportation of such agricultural products, and the person or persons to whom such wages shall be due, shall have the security of such lien, as against all landlords, sub-lessors, and all other persons interested in such agricultural products.

In practical effect the 1867 supply merchants' lien law had been significantly amended in April of 1872. The next several sections set out the procedure for enforcing the new farm laborer's first priority lien. All contracts made under the law of February 1867 were reaffirmed as valid, although their priority had been supplanted, viz., "The lien hereby created shall take precedence and priority over rent, and every other species of lien." The legislature had also decreed that

> this Act shall be construed in the most liberal manner for the protection and encouragement of labor; and that all Acts or parts of Acts in conflict with this Act be, and the same are hereby repealed, and that this Act take effect and be in force from and after its passage.[101]

It is not known on what day the Supreme Court of Tennessee decided *Hunt*. The opinion simply reads at its outset "April Term 1872." If the decision had been formally made after April 5, 1872, the laborer's wage lien law may have affected the outcome. Of course, a point against the workers could have been made—and with legal force—that *Hunt* should be governed by the law in existence at the time of the transactions involved—the beginning of the crop year 1867. Arguably, any vested right that a supply merchant held was protected by the (then almost brand new) Due Process clause of the Fourteenth Amendment, or the federal and state contracts clauses.[102] More clearly, we have practical evidence of the long-standing existence of a separate state of "North Mississippi," the capital of which is Memphis.

The unpaid farm workers were broken down into two categories. Sylvia Brooks and most of the others had worked for wages, which were not paid. Little is known about Brooks except that she was about forty-eight years old at the time and had been born in Maryland.[103] "Jesse Christian and some four or five others" were sharecroppers who claimed they were entitled to one-third of the crop,[104] presumably pro rata with their fellow farm laborers. The court, however, held that the laborers had no crop lien. At best, these laborers could file an independent action against the bankrupt Wing, Cox & Co., and have an attachment upon any Wing assets they might be able to locate.

For whatever reason, the Tennessee judges ignored a long-standing legal analogy staring them in the face, had they only opened their eyes. Crew members of the steamboat or other vessel that may have carried the cotton to its final destination had a lien of the highest priority on the vessel, its tackle, equipment, and appurtenances securing any unpaid wages. In Mississippi and elsewhere, analogies drawn from the maritime law were a legitimate source of law in courts at common law and sitting in equity.[105] For one thing, several decades had passed since the US Supreme Court made it clear that the maritime law applied to the inland waterways, easily including the Mississippi River. The vessel involved in that early case was the "steamer Memphis."[106] Crew members' wage liens were "sacred liens, and so long as a plank of the ship remains, the sailor [and merchant seamen are] entitled, against all other persons, to the proceeds as a security for [their] wages."[107] The legislative facts and policy premises underlying the claim made by the freedmen farm laborers were substantially the same as those that had given rise to the first priority lien of crew members for their wages earned aboard a river steamboat. The traditional maritime solicitude for the seaman was easily within the equitable premises that traditionally moved the conscience of a court of equity, such as the Chancery Court at Memphis should have been.

If the *Hunt* court had considered the analogous seaman's or crew member's wage lien, that should have carried with it the general maritime law's priority rule. In point of fact, the freedmen farm laborers argued a version of last-in-time, first-in-right. Without their labor, the crop may have been lost altogether. The court missed the commonsense underpinning of this unique priority rule. What was the last point in time when, if a party had not stepped up to the plate, all would have been lost? Of course, Wing and its landlord provided the land, and the land was necessary. But late in the crop year, labor was essential. It became a sine qua non to the harvest of a cotton crop at all, without which the fertility of Driver soil would have gone for naught. That is the point where practical incentives are the most critical. Workers know the ox is in the ditch. Their bargaining position is the greatest it will ever be. They can withhold their labor until they are assured they will be paid in full. It was the only point in time when Sylvia Brooks and Jesse Christian and the others had any leverage at all, and that leverage remained only for so long as no competing workers could be found and put to work. In fact, the workers stepped up to the plate. Their labor was provided not just to make a living wage for themselves (never paid, however). Harvesting the crop inured "to the common benefit of all."[108] If the Supreme Court of Tennessee had seen this "appeal with great potency to a court of chancery to relax its rules,"[109] a remedy would have been fashioned for Brooks and Christian and their co-workers. Their fate—and the fate of their claim for a first priority wage lien—before the court was in substantial part a function of the color of their American skin and previous condition of servitude.

The legal bottom line here is important. If White & Billingsly had made their deal with Wing after the effective date of the act of 1867, and if they had followed faithfully the public filing process, their statutory lien would have primed all else. Such a statutory lien would have even primed the priority of a wage lien, which could and should have been borrowed from the law governing the inland waterways. Providing such a priority lien was the Mississippi legislature's—and thus the law's—preferred strategy "for the encouragement of agriculture," until the policy reasons for enacting wage lien and landlord lien laws gave way to new priority rules and led to amended statutes. Under the law as it stood and should have been understood in *Hunt*, the merchant's crop lien should have primed the landlord's lien, if any. Even if the original distress for rent may have had some legal effect, perhaps because objections had been waived, that should not have affected the priorities question. Because the wage lien priority was not then in statutory form, the merchant's crop lien for its advances—made after February 18, 1867—should have primed the freedmen farm workers' wage lien, if any. By analogy to the seaman's wage lien, the farm workers should have recovered any crumbs that may have been left after the merchant's debt was paid in full. The landlord, via a longed-for distress for rent or otherwise, brought up the rear!

FURTHER CONSTITUTIONAL ENCOUNTERS FROM 1867 TO 1876

The efficacy of Mississippi's legislative efforts to encourage agriculture can be assessed in many ways. One is by taking a look at the litigation that followed. Bear in mind that in any era the cases that make their way to the state supreme court are the tip of the iceberg. And there are always many claims and disputes that never make it to the courthouse at all, and for a wider variety of practical reasons. Understanding the tip is not unimportant, but it does not always paint a clear picture of what lies below.

The Mississippi law reports after 1867 reveal many crop lien cases that made their way to the top. Of course, there were competing interests. The farmer. The landowner. The supply merchant in the store or on the street corner, and the cotton factor who may have been functioning upstream. The tenant. The "cropper."[110] The farm laborer or just plain field hand. This cast of characters varied from the Mississippi Delta area and the River counties below, to the prairie lands in central Mississippi, and to the hill country to the northeast, then to the Tombigbee River basin along the eastern boundary of the state. The Pearl River flowed down the middle of the north–south state until it reached the old Spanish West Florida area and for some forty miles or so separated Mississippi from Louisiana to the west.

It is hard to imagine many of these players having the resources for extended litigation. Equally difficult to see are lawyers willing to pursue such complex and difficult litigation without being reasonably well paid. But there the cases are, in the law reports, and the top of what has to have been hundreds of trips by hundreds if not thousands of people—parties, witnesses, lawyers, judges and other court functionaries, and just folk taking in the entertainment of the trial—to and into the Faulknerian courthouses that lie at the hub, the heart of practically every county in Mississippi and beyond.[111]

We have seen a few of these cases, beginning with the *Marye* case in 1869. There are lessons in each of the decisions that follow. With one big case still to be visited below, it is eye-opening to survey a cross section of fifty-three appellate cases found,[112] giving a context before diving into the weeds and to particular cases above and below for particular lessons.

For better or worse, the prevailing white man's stereotypical view of freedmen was hard to shake. In 1868, Jesse Christian, "Sylvia Brooks and some thirty-eight or nine others, free persons of color" were before the court in Memphis. In considering the lien claims made by these freedmen for their unpaid farm wages, the judge said that

> Sylvia Brooks, and others, belong to a race which have but recently been emancipated from slavery; that as a race they are far below the white man in intelligence, but we also know that by law they are under no disability to sue, and have all the rights, before the courts of the country, possessed by any other class of citizens. Yet their want of intelligence, and their ignorance of the complicated relations of business life, appeal with great potency to a court of chancery to relax its rules;. . . .[113]

After this special pleading, the *Hunt* court—perhaps from its ignorance or ineptness or the biases of the times—never mentioned quite respectable and persuasive legal sources that favored the freedmen's lien claims and their priority. The landlord plantation owner got the lion's share of the value of the crop for its rentals, though its claim was full of holes. What little was left after that went to the supply merchant. The freedmen who had done all the work and provided all the sweat equity got nothing.

THE PAXTON CASE

How judges saw freedmen and their humanity was at the core of a case that arose about ten years after *Hunt v. Wing* and a hundred miles down the River from Tunica County. The case also laid bare some of the practical realities of the crop lien system after a decade of legislative interventions, particularly regarding the profit-making practices of furnish merchants.

For the crop year 1877, Bohlen Lucas, Drew Whitley, and fifteen other African Americans were tenant farmers on a plantation in Washington County, Mississippi, owned by Andrew Jackson (A. J.) Paxton (1816–1900), lawyer, nephew, and, in years long past, private secretary of Gov. A. G. McNutt, whom we met in chapter 4. Not much is known of sixteen of the tenant farmers, but Lucas had a notable past. In antebellum times, he had been a slave and had worked as a driver. A local historian said he was a man "of rare mental calibre and good sense." Though illiterate, after the War he had been sufficiently savvy to earn and save money, enough to make a down payment on 200 acres of his own. One who knew Lucas commented that he "was no less the thoughtful, considerate man. Freedom never turned his head."[114] In time, Lucas would face financial reverses, due to the death of a white partner. He was hardly deserving of the experience that lay ahead.

These seventeen freedmen tenants needed farm supplies in order to grow cotton on lands they leased from Paxton for an agreed-upon rental. For the 1877 growing season, a supply merchant named Langsford agreed to furnish the tenant farmers as needed, up to $1,700 worth of farm supplies. These would be credit sales. No clause in papers provided by the merchant mentioned how the supplies would be valued or their prices fixed. To secure payment of their anticipated production debt, the seventeen granted Langsford a lien on the crops they hoped to harvest. With each sale and delivery of supplies, however, Langsford entered on account exorbitant prices, which the tenants had no choice but to accept. These paper prices were believed to afford the merchant a net profit of about 90 to 100 percent, on top of which there was a 2.5 percent commission on each such sale and 10 percent per annum interest on sums that remained unpaid after January 1, 1878.

In midstream and well before harvest, Langsford stopped providing supplies. Though the supply contract did not specify prices, Langsford said he knew when the $1,700 limit had been reached, and so declared. Or at least it so appeared. It was by this time apparent that the tenants were dealing with the sort of Snopsean merchant that Cash and Cohn—and Faulkner—wrote about. Paxton became apprised of the problem. The rental the seventeen would owe him in the fall of 1877 was at risk. Paxton assumed his rent was secure under the landlord's lien law the legislature had passed the year before. Still, there had to be a profitable crop in order for the tenants to pay rent, secured or otherwise.

And so without request from or notice to merchant Langsford, Paxton stepped in and made advances he thought necessary that the crops might be completed. The hardworking tenants were at Paxton's mercy, and Langsford's as well.

Come fall, and the crop was short. Paxton took charge. He harvested the cotton and sold it to third parties, for sums below what he had advanced. Notwithstanding his knowledge of the crop lien agreements that Lucas, Whitley, and the others had made with Langsford, landlord Paxton kept for himself all proceeds from the sale of the crop. Remember, Paxton was a lawyer.

In the meanwhile, the said Langsford seemed to have faded from the scene, having assigned all of his rights in the crop lien agreements to Meyer, Weis & Co., cotton factors and commission merchants with principal offices in New Orleans and New York, but doing business in Mississippi and nearby states.[115] Paxton declined to pay Meyer Weis any of the cotton crop sales proceeds. At that point Meyer Weis sued. It named as defendants Paxton, along with Lucas and Whitley and the fifteen other tenant farmers who had made crop lien agreements with Langsford. The plight of the tenants was dire and becoming more so by the day. Interest was running on the exorbitantly priced supplies they had been furnished.

The central question in the litigation became how the law would value the farm supplies Langsford furnished for Lucas and his fellow tenants toward producing the crop, and those supplies he was supposed to have furnished but didn't. Conversely, how would the court decide what, if anything, should be paid to Meyer Weis? Deciding these mixed questions of law and fact would determine the dollar values to be assigned to the supplies, the crop lien for which had priority under Mississippi law as it then read. After, of course, Paxton deducted the rent secured by his landlord's lien. Did Paxton get to pocket all the money that sale of the crops had brought, or, for that matter should, he get to keep any at all? And if so, what? How would the court compute what should be left over for Meyer Weis? And what about the seventeen tenant farmers who had done the hard work of planting, cultivating and harvesting the crop?

Court records reflect that Meyer Weis was represented by Percy & Yerger, prominent Washington County lawyers. William L. Nugent of Jackson argued for Meyer Weis before the state supreme court. That same lawyer Nugent whose letter home from the front in the spring of 1864 helped open this chapter. Joseph M. Jayne II of Greenville appeared for Paxton, who, not surprisingly, argued orally for himself on appeal. No record suggests Lucas or Whitley or their fellow tenants had a lawyer, or even that they made a *pro se* filing. His reputed character and acumen notwithstanding, history reports that Lucas was and remained illiterate.

As down to earth as the questions became on the Meyer Weis appeal, underneath lay constitutional concerns about the relative roles of the legislature and the judiciary in making public policy calls. How should the court construe and apply the law where the legislative text fell short of a clear answer? Embedded within the debate between three state supreme court justices was the appropriate constitutional view of the humanity of the seventeen tenant farmers and, more generally, of all freedmen. But the matter wasn't that simple. To what extent, if at all, could the court consider the known creditworthiness of the seventeen in determining the value of farm supplies? To what extent, if at all, could the court consider Langsford's failure to make written provision for prices to the seventeen, and to have done so from the get-go? Should the judge-made law hold that the seventeen should have so insisted before they made their deal with Paxton, much less before they began accepting farm supplies from Langsford? That thereafter the tenants proceeded with their agribusiness cotton production venture at their risk?

We know today that the fair market value of property is a function of what some call the willing buyer/willing seller test. At what price would the property—land or personal property—most likely sell following a hypothetical negotiation? The conditions of that negotiation have always been to assume that each party is a competent and reasonable adult with the financial wherewithal to pay or accept as he might wish, that each is reasonably informed of the relevant facts and circumstances, including alternatives, and that neither is under any compulsion or duress to sell or buy.[116] In other words, each party was assumed to have been a rational self-interested wealth maximizer. To be sure, behavioral economists of late have called some of these premises into question, but the law has not changed, at least not yet.

In *Paxton*, the trial judge had applied a very different valuation rule. He did so in a context where the legislature had enacted no approach to valuation, nor had the parties fixed a standard by contract. The *Paxton* trial judge said the supplies whose value would control all other practical questions in the case were to be considered at such prices "as shall appear to have been customary, fair, and reasonable in the kind of credit business and with the class of people with which and by whom said accounts were contracted in 1877."[117] A subsidiary question was whether—absent legislation or contract—the law would recognize one value for a sale and purchase of farm supplies where the buyer paid cash and then a separate and much higher value for a credit or time sale. The supply merchant "kind of credit business" was a separate element of that test. But the lightning rod was the trial judge's ruling that the proper valuation should take into account "the class of people" involved. David Cohn preserved insights in this regard of cotton commentator M. B. Hammond that might otherwise have been lost. "Hammond tartly observed that

> honesty is a virtue which is little regarded by many people . . . of the South, especially by freedmen, who are nearly all recorded on the books of the merchants as credit purchasers. The danger of losses involved in doing business with this class of purchasers has been that the prime cause of the great difference between cash and

"time" prices, while the frequent failures of advancing merchants ... do not furnish proof of the statement that, "the road to wealth in the South ... is merchandising."[118]

When the time came for Chief Justice Chalmers to speak, he pulled no punches. "We cannot think that the [trial judge] meant colored in contradistinction to white customers." A page later, he added, "I repudiate the idea that any universality of custom can ever sanction charging poor men more than rich ones," or that the value of the goods at issue could be "determined by whether the buyer is white or black, or rich or poor, or lives in the country or resides in town."[119]

Justice Campbell put the issue in sharp relief. The controversy central to the suit arose in the context of a business regulated by law which involved "the mortgaging of a crop to be grown, as the basis of credit for the means to secure its production, ..., but which must be dealt with as it is, and not as I wish it was."[120] Fair enough, but that did not excuse the court from the hard job of construing a difficult and incomplete text provided by the legislature as best could be, augmenting that construction interstitially as necessary, and then with optimal reliability applying that aggregated construction of the law to the facts of the case.

A third justice, James Z. George, authored the opinion of the court. The core context was the failure—at some point in the course of the crop's emergence from the soils—on the part of Langsford to continue to furnish the necessary supplies. Looking to the past, the court had to decide what supplies and in what quantities and values it took to make up $1,700 worth. Again, the contracts had not said how this question was to be answered, though it certainly could have. In this contractual vacuum, George said the court should look to "what the goods were worth at the time and place of sale." He was correct that actual sales price does not equate with value. Actual price was and remains an indicium of value, but nothing more. In 1880 and before the advent of the willing buyer/willing seller test, Justice George saw the judge-made law of the market value of the goods at the time and place of sale to have been a function of "transactions between regular dealers," which was "fixed by competition among buyers and sellers." The trial judge had suggested that the rule should also consider the solvency of the tenant farmers and the risks assumed by Langsford, the supply merchant. George rejected that view. "The inflated price charged by merchants in the vicinity to insolvent purchasers was accidental and abnormal, and resulted from a perversion of trade."

> The evidence in the trial court showed that the prices charged and assented to by the customers [tenant farmers] were exorbitant, largely more than the reasonable value of the goods, and having for their justification only the alleged insecurity of the debt.[121]

George recognized that Lucas, Whitley, and the other fifteen tenants had acted under compulsion, that they "had encumbered all, or the principal or essential part of [their] means of obtaining credit, and therefore [were] not free to decline the purchase of the supplies because the price charged was unreasonable." The tenants "acquiesced" and accepted the prices charged "from an overruling necessity." Conversely, Langsford had failed to honor his contract "to furnish the goods at a reasonable price" and then used that as part of his excuse to stop furnishing further supplies needed to complete the crop. This "was an act of bad faith, and the extorted assent of the [tenants] to the price fixed by [Langsford] was without consideration and void." Langsford's contract—construed and applied as above—was valid and enforceable by Meyer Weis under the assignment it held.

George then turned to the landlord Paxton's claim. He held that Paxton had no right to furnish the supplies "in derogation of Langsford's right" and priority "after he had notice of it. Langsford was not requested by Paxton to furnish the supplies necessary to raise and gather the crop, nor notified that Paxton would furnish them in case he failed to do so."[122] There is a problem here. It seems clear that the crop would have failed, or at least been even more substantially short, had Paxton not stepped in. Absent a clear expression otherwise in the statutes, it could not be sound policy, judge-made variety, that in the face of such a looming crop disaster, landlords should be given incentives to do nothing. How, then, does this stack up with *Hunt v. Wing*, where the landlord got everything and the hard-working freedmen got shut out entirely? Was this not the situation noted above, where Paxton did as much as was reasonably practicable, and this "accrued to the common benefit of all?"[123] True, that did not necessarily mean that Paxton got to keep all of the money, but was he not entitled to some consideration?

A further concern was that, as decided both in the trial court and on appeal, the judgment of the court left Bohlen Lucas, Drew Whitley, and fifteen other freedmen tenant farmers with nothing to show for an entire crop year's back-breaking efforts. Justice George left these important questions aside and unanswered. The other two justices would then have their say.

Chief Justice Chalmers authored a separate concurring opinion, given "the great practical importance of the questions involved, and the fact that this court is not unanimous." He agreed with the trial judge that the exorbitant prices for the farm supplies that merchant Langsford had recorded unilaterally were not controlling. Chalmers then noted and considered consequential the "shocking injustice" of Langsford charging the tenants prices "in some instances nearly double those at which the same goods were sold on the same credit to more favored buyers." Because extortionate, those prices should be disregarded in favor of the "reasonable worth" of those supplies. Three times Chalmers used the strong word "repudiate" in describing his view of—and action regarding—the trial judge's having considered "the class of people" Langsford was dealing with. These seventeen tenant farmers "were entitled to the prices charged for the same quality of goods when sold upon the same period of credit to persons whose solvency was undoubted."[124] In the end, Chalmers joined the judgment that Justice George had announced.

Justice Campbell dissented. First, he argued that the legal legitimacy of the price charged the tenant farmers "on each delivery of goods is not before us, because the seller of the goods . . . did not appeal." Chalmers had agreed with this technical—and quite debatable—point. But Langsford's assignee certainly did appeal. Past that, Lucas and Whitley and their fellow tenants were parties to the case. There is no known reason why right and fairness for them was not a concern of the three justices. There was certainly a sense in which a constitutional question of the contours of the judicial power was presented. For reasons grounded more in history than in practical reason, judges have traditionally shrunk from deciding questions not assigned and argued. Only in this weak sense could it be said that the two-justice majority in *Paxton* may have been out of bounds.

The trial judge had not only erred in stating the rule controlling the value calculations. He had also offended humanity. Soberly, we know that the thinking of the trial judge—that the law really should consider "the class of people . . . by whom the accounts were contracted"—was likely shared by most white persons in 1877. After all, merchant Langsford was gone, having sold his rights to the cotton factor from New Orleans.

Paxton arose from circumstances a decade after the legislature had declared the public policy for the state or the encouragement of agriculture. That much happened. It was clear enough. But other effects became exposed and interests were advanced with political effect to the point where "secur[ing] an equitable division" of the crop subject to multiple liens was forced to the foreground as a public policy to be balanced with and against the forward-looking idea of the encouragement of agriculture. The seeds of Gene Dattel's idea that "[f]inance is amoral" and that it would "respond to the theoretical opportunity to make money within an existing legal and cultural framework"[125] had been afoot since the days of David Hume and Adam Smith. Still, *Paxton* leaves us with as many questions as answers.

REFLECTIONS

The legislative power found in Mississippi's constitutions is not nearly so flashy as some of the individual rights traceable back to the Declaration of Independence and in a few instances even to Magna Carta.[126] The judicial power held and exercised by officials making interstitial and subordinate law is less understood (though we will try hard in chapter 8 below). After all, the state judiciary as a whole has no authority not to decide a matter presented by a flesh-and-blood or juridical person. When it discharges this duty, making law is inevitable. The governor is more in the public eye simply because it's so much easier to follow and cover and critique the acts or omissions of one person than a cumbersome bicameral legislature with so many instances of internecine strife among diffused political interests and views of what should be done. Still, coupled with universal adult suffrage, the legislative power is at the core of any constitutional democracy.

In chapter after chapter of this work, legislative activity has been in the fore-front, though often the clumsy exercise of political power in response to some perceived public need. We have seen the Act for Relief of Debtors in chapter 3, the legislative creation of the Mississippi Union Bank and then repudiation of Union Bank bonds in chapter 4. Still to come are the Railroad Regulation Act of 1884 in chapter 6, a ten-hour workday law in chapter 7 for employers engaged in "manufacturing and repairing," the repeal of the disabilities of coverture in chapter 8, the innovative and costly you'd-better-not-do-it-again bonds author-ized for those held to have practiced a common nuisance explained in chapter 9, the Balance Agriculture with Industry Act in chapter 10, and much more.

Arguably the most important dimension of the exercise of legislative power, albeit the least understood, is the quest for and the utility of legislative facts[127] and circumstances, the conditions, activities and practices—economic and other behavioral forces at work—of organized society that suggest the need for improvement, or just reasonable regulation of one sort or another in the public interest. The Civil War left in its wake devastation as never before. The state's economy had been destroyed, and that was just the beginning. The people of Mississippi turned to their legislature to pull a rabbit or two out of the hat. Many schools of thought needed to be brought to bear and understood as a predicate to coherent and productive legislation, giving proper and measured incentives for socioeconomic behavior. It is hard to argue against economics as more important and useful—and challenging—than the others.

Agricultural economics has always had its own discrete set of principles and practices and legislative facts. Foremost or close, it must contend with the weather. Crop-eating pests have come and caused disasters at times. Economic forces are almost as unpredictable and beyond the control of man. There is only a finite amount of accessible, cultivatable land, though the amount has var-ied with the times and the capabilities and good sense of men thinking more should be cleared. Without land, a farmer's chances are slim and none, unless he or she is willing to slave long hours in the hot summer sun for meager wages—but only at particular seasons not always approaching the worker's convenience. Then there is that mystifying force called inelastic economics—both on the sup-ply side and the commodities. The farmer has next to no practical control of his economic fate on half-a-dozen scores.

This chapter has explored parameters of one constitutional encounter after another stretching from February of 1867 through April of 1876 and well beyond. For one thing, Mississippi's legislative tenor changed several times and considerably over that time frame. There were successes and failures—more partial than complete—and unintended consequences and complications. Hundreds if not thousands of disputes arose under these legislative enactments that taxed the judiciary's abilities to perform with justice, reliability and fairness its role in a constitutional democracy. Legislators and judges were challenged to learn basic and then more complex principles of agricultural economics, and the evidence shows that some took their duties very seriously. Justice George, for example, cited the work of the British economist and preeminent Utilitarian John Stuart Mill (1806–1873) in the *Paxton* case discussed above.

The present chapter, as with a number of others, has presented the several species of law in their hierarchical rankings—from the privately made law of contracts utilized and invoked under so many labels, always subject to the statutory law made by the legislature, with both elaborated and applied through the process of adjudication, albeit with varying levels of reliability. The legislative and judicial constitutional powers have made it all possible. But there has been more. We have focused upon law *and* economics, and the emerging parameters of each. We are well past the point where it is defensible to study one without the other.[128] The most important insight offered here just may be Gene Dattel's reminder that "finance is amoral," quoted and elaborated in this chapter.

Hunt v. Wing litigated from Tunica County to Memphis exposed a very different problem of constitutional dimensions. How are claims made, defended, and adjudged in a (recently restored) federal union where there are parties involved and interests affected derived from two or more states? Mississippi is one of those states where substantially populated areas lie just across state lines and where people have always interacted with one another on a dozen fronts with the state political boundaries at best a fortuity and at worst an outright nuisance. Memphis is just across the northwest Mississippi state line. Arkansas is westerly across the River. Mobile is just across the southeast state line that separates Mississippi from Alabama extending well into the Gulf of Mexico. Then there are New Orleans and Baton Rouge in Louisiana, and the River towns, parishes and, counties westerly from Natchez, Vicksburg, Greenville, and smaller communities farther north. Few of the matters discussed above, as well as those simply cited, were without parties or effects on more than one state. Sometimes it was the cotton factor in New Orleans or on Front Street in Memphis, the St. Louis commission merchant with an office in Memphis, or the absentee landlord like Eli Driver and in time his executors acting under the authority of a Tennessee probate court. Of course, this did not enhance the yield or value of the crop that was the ultimate collateral.

The shortcomings of Mississippi's lien law of 1867, as amended, constricted, and expanded again and again through 1876 and thereafter, were in part a function of the fact that the legislative texts and underlying assumptions did not quite fit the practical agricultural, economic, and social realities being regulated, much less the complex humanity of the people affected. In a crude sort of way, the legislature may have been on target in February of 1867 when it enacted the crop lien priority to entice outsiders—supply merchants aka carpetbaggers, by and large—to come to Mississippi and extend credit. And the same for men already here—the scalawags—made of sterner stuff who got into the hardscrabble, high-risk, small-farm credit business. Still, the task was too big. War devastation and defeat added to natural forces that in some years standing alone had been too much. In the cotton capital that was the Mississippi Delta, folk feared God and the Mississippi River long before David Cohn coined his pithy phrase.

The particular economics policy that drove the new crop lien law was undermined as the makeup of the postbellum legislature changed, and then changed again. Landowners did not have the luxury of foregoing receipt of rentals when the crops were bad. However shortsighted the landlord's lien priority may have been, it was as necessary for his immediate pocketbook as for his self-esteem. Conditions were conducive to the ill-considered and excessive use of fertilizers by Cotton South farmers, who had no practical choice but to focus on immediate results. Other practices such as crop diversity or rotation would have provided better long-term results, but the farmer's cash flow and limited access to credit could not tolerate lowered year-to-year profits from such stratagems.

Past the somewhat overwhelming natural realities and risks, at least four broad sets of participants in the agricultural economy found themselves on one side or the other of inherently risky credit transactions, where seldom did anyone have enough wherewithal and savvy to moderate those risks. Or maybe there is a better way to put it. The post-1867 laws for the encouragement of agriculture provided incentives, that at least four categories of agri-economic participants with competing interests stick their necks out a bit further than otherwise they might. Plantation and lesser landowners rented or leased lands in the late winter with no practical expectation that the rent would be paid by those who would farm the land until they harvested and sold crops in the following fall. Landlords extended credit as well, through the commissary, the company store and otherwise. Those who actually planted crops and harvested crops had to buy or have credit to acquire the resources they needed to do so, from farm equipment and animals to supplies such as seeds, and to farm labor to work the land. The incentives intentionally built into the 1867 version of the new priority lien law attracted new players to the scene, supply or furnish merchants—small, localized agricultural store owners and lenders, if you will. The cotton factors' diminished role has been noted. The more one reads the reports of actual cases, what was happening to people on the ground in these times, and in the Cotton South, the functional division between cotton factors/commission merchants, on the one hand, and supply or furnish merchants, on the other, seems more shades of gray than the sharp divisions that Cash, Cohn, and others describe. This was so temporally as well as latitudinally as, over time, some merchants moved up the ladder while some factors slipped down a notch or two or ten. Finally, there were the people who toiled in the hot sun, did the work—some tenants, some croppers, and others just field hands—many of whom were African American freedmen who had been slaves prior to war and emancipation. These were due a break. They seldom got one.

The results might have been a bit better if—say in February or early March of each year—there could have been some sort of coordinated negotiations among representatives of the loosely configured interest groups where each would talk to the others, each with some bargaining power and bargaining skills vis-à-vis the others, as each set of participants really did need the others to be there and contribute, and to do well enough in each crop year that most all could and would be enduring players. Results might have been different had legislators—in the course of activating and exercising their constitutionally passive power—been able to conjure and talk through a hypothetical negotiation between these participants. Socioeconomic and political realities permitted no such dream world. In fact, the politics of 1867 brought the steadily increasing numbers of supply merchants to Mississippi with their lending power. Radical Reconstruction politics soon led to the laborer's lien legislation in 1872. Four years later, white Democrats were reascending politically, and the act of April 14, 1876, put the landlords back on top—of a bed of agri-economic quicksand. With the benefit of hindsight, few could fail to be amused at reconstruction and reenactment of those days through the lenses of today's behavioral economists, who have so cleverly identified many circumstances in which ordinarily sensible folk engage in utterly irrational behavior.

A pragmatic jurisprudence may have had an ameliorating effect. The economic incentives of 1867 had provided a promising start. Legal formalism fought back until you read *Newman v. Bank of Greenville*, decided in 1889, and realize that judges and the bar from which they came could not help but think in terms of "the character of the right" and "privity of estate" to the exclusion of practical incentives that just might have had a beneficial effect on the lives of people. "Fair market value" had found legislative recognition in 1876 and then in J. A. P. Campbell's Code of 1880. By 1889, Justice Tim E. Cooper held forth that "the history of this legislation demonstrates that the lien secured to the landlord by section 1301 is of a much higher right"[129] before floating off into the never-never land of legislative intent. From the perspective of publicly beneficial lawmaking, it is hard to deny that 1867 was the high-water mark, though in candor that mark was not particularly high, nor was it much more supportive than water itself.

One perennial problem was that few entered the new crop year with a clean slate. Most remained encumbered on a variety of fronts from commitments, carry-over debts, and other circumstances, often dating back more than a few years. It was a sort of common denominator that no one had much cash when the calendar turned to January each winter. Debt peonage. Matters were complicated by the sociological tug-of-war with planters and farmers shorn of their slaves, struggling to maintain a stable and dependable labor force. On the other hand, the last thing the freedmen wanted were working conditions that were hard to distinguish from the conditions they had lived in and worked in prior to 1863.

It would have been nice if the commodities market primarily for cotton had remained strong, or at least stable. But, of course, it didn't, on either front. Lien laws with all of their amorality across the cotton-producing South led to more and more cotton being produced. True, prices were not backbreakers for several years after the War, in substantial part a function of pent-up demand from almost a decade of low production. For the rest of the nineteenth century, cotton prices gradually and inexorably tanked.

Then there was the economic fallacy of the static pie. In theory, legislators have the constitutional prerogative and duty of enacting so that the pie will enlarge and at once assure a more or less currently fair division. The problem with this economic goal, however, is that the pie is dynamic, a continuous process of becoming, and might as likely contract as expand, at times for reasons beyond the legislature's ken or control. Both of these seem exactly what happened in the postbellum Cotton South. Deciding in theory or even on paper what is a currently fair division is difficult enough. Achieving that end in fact is little short of impossible.

Mississippi's landlord's lien law was tinkered with for several years and matured in 1876 just about the time the price of cotton was slightly recovering from the Panic of 1873, after which it would begin its slow but steady descent to the bottom in 1898. Demanding that these landowners either waive or subordinate their landlord's lien was among the more civilized business stratagems of the supply merchants, but that put the landowner right back in the same boat he had struggled for a decade to get out of. A Hobson's choice where the only option off the table was doing nothing.

A postscript, following a reference above. Economic theory, thought, and practice are critical to understanding the issues discussed in this chapter. Gene Dattel offered one such insight. In recent years, there has been considerable rethinking of the role of behavioral economics, a process that could well lead to refining some of the premises and reflections presented in this chapter. The seriousness of this postscript is made clear in that the twenty-first century has seen three Nobel Prizes in Economics awarded for work in the field. In 2002, Daniel Kahneman was awarded the prize, Robert J. Shiller in 2013, and Richard H. Thaler in 2017. Attention should be paid.

ENDNOTES

1. *See, e.g.*, Hodding Carter, *Lower Mississippi* 289–291 (1942); David L. Cohn, *The Life and Times of King Cotton* 152 (1956); David M. Oslinsky, *Worse than Slavery: Parchman Farm and the Ordeal of Jim Crow Justice* 12, n. 3 and accompanying text (1996).

2. Frank E. Smith, *The Yazoo River* 169–170 (1954), quoted in David M. Oslinsky, *Worse than Slavery: Parchman Farm and the Ordeal of Jim Crow Justice* 12–13, n. 5 (1996).

3. William L. Nugent to his wife, March 13, 1864, in John K. Bettersworth, *Mississippi in the Confederacy: As They Saw It*, 63 (Baton Rouge, 1961).

4. Roger L. Ransom and Richard Sutch, *One Kind of Freedom; The Economic Consequences of Emancipation* 13–24 (1977). For a number of references regarding the importance of land ownership to newly emancipated slaves, see Charles Lewis Nier III, "Emancipation, Reconstruction and the Failure of Land Reform, Part III," and "Sharecropping and Credit in the Post-Bellum Era," Part IV. B., in *The Shadow of Credit: The Historical Origins of Racial Predatory Lending and Its Impact on African American Wealth Accumulation*, 11 U. Pa. Journ. Law and Social Change (2007–2008).

5. Ted Ownby, *American Dreams in Mississippi; Consumers, Poverty & Culture, 1830–1998*, 76 (1999).

6. W. J. Cash, *The Mind of the South* 157–158 (1941, 1991).

7. The plight of poor white southerners in the antebellum decades has been well presented in a variety of sources. *See, e.g.*, W. J. Cash, *The Mind of the South* 145–175 (1941, 1991); Charles C. Bolton, *Poor Whites of the Antebellum South: Tenants and Laborers in Central North Carolina and Northeast Mississippi* (1994).

8. "Memoirs of Henry Tillinghast Ireys," *Papers of the Washington County Historical Society, 1910–1915* (McCain and Capers eds., 1954).

9. See "Benjamin Grubbs Humphreys," in David G. Sansing, *Mississippi Governors: Soldiers, Statesmen, Scholars, Scoundrels: A Bicentennial Edition* 100–103 (2016); Benjamin Grubbs Humphreys, *Mississippi Encyclopedia* 603–604 (Ownby and Wilson eds., 2017).

10. "Interesting to Planters—Valuable Inventions," *Clarion-Ledger* (Jackson, Miss.), Thurs., April 20, 1871, page 1, Newspapers.com, https://newspapers.com/image/253140428.

11. W. J. Cash, *The Mind of the South* 148 (1941, 1991).

12. *Betts v. Ratliff*, 50 Miss. 561, 567 (1874).

13. *Newman v. Bank of Greenville*, 66 Miss. 323, 5 So. 753 (1889).

14. This is a good time to add to one's bucket list a careful reading of Oliver Wendell Holmes's contemporaneously written first chapter of *The Common Law* (1881) together with the principal constitutional encounters discussed below and Justice Cooper's *Newman* opinion. Reading these now would enhance understanding of what follows in this chapter.

15. "Interesting to Planters—Valuable Inventions," *Clarion-Ledger* (Jackson, Miss.), Thurs. April 20, 1871, page 1, Newspapers.com, https://newspapers.com/image/253140428.

16. *Newman v. Bank of Greenville*, 66 Miss. 323, 5 So. 753, 755 (1889).

17. "Morgan on His Rounds," *Semi-Weekly Clarion*, Fri., Aug. 19, 1870, page 2, Newspapers. com, https://newspapers.com/image/242021788; also, *Semi-Weekly Clarion*, Fri., Aug. 12, 1870, page 2, Newspapers.com, https://newspapers.com/image/242021681.

18. In 1884, Morgan authored a colorful account of his life in Mississippi *sub nom.*, *Yazoo; Or On the Picket Line of Freedom in the South* (1884), recently rereleased by the University of South Carolina Press, https://www.sc.edu/uscpress/books/2000/3359.html.

19. The *Semi-Weekly Clarion* (Jackson, Miss.), Fri., Oct. 25, 1872, page 2, Newspapers.com, https://www.newspapers.com/image/24203094; *Clarion-Ledger* (Jackson, Miss.), Thurs., Feb. 1, 1894, page 4, Newspapers.com, https://www.newspapers.com/image/235266675; "Judge B. T.

Kimbrough," *Democratic-Herald* (Charleston, Miss.); Thurs., Jan. 20, 1898, page 1, Newspapers
.com, https://www.newspapers.com/image/316111792.

20. *Clarion-Ledger* (Jackson, Miss.), Weds., Aug. 20, 1884.

21. "The New Laborers' Lien Law," *Natchez Democrat*, Sat., July 13, 1872, page 1, Newspapers
.com, https://www.newspapers.com/image/235133398.

22. John Ray Skates Jr., *A History of the Mississippi Supreme Court, 1817–1948*, 67 (1973); *see
also* James D. Lynch, *The Bench and Bar of Mississippi*, 177–181 (1880) for a brief biography of
Justice Chalmers's father.

23. John Ray Skates Jr., *A History of the Mississippi Supreme Court, 1817–1948*, 76–78 (1973).
George has been enshrined in the Mississippi Hall of Fame, administered by the Mississippi
Department of Archives and History. http://www.mdah.ms.gov/oldcap/hall-of-fame.php.

24. *Marye v. Dyche*, 42 Miss. 347, 360, 1869 WL 3763 (1869).

25. John Ray Skates Jr., *A History of the Mississippi Supreme Court, 1817–1948*, 85–86 (1973);
James D. Lynch, *The Bench and Bar of Mississippi*, 359–365 (1880); Peyton has been enshrined
in the Mississippi Hall of Fame, administered by the Mississippi Department of Archives and
History. http://www.mdah.ms.gov/oldcap/hall-of-fame.php.

26. Miss. Laws, 1866–67, pages 569–572 (February 18, 1867).

27. *Cloud v. State for Use of McAlexander*, 53 Miss. 662, 664, 1876 WL 7409 (1876).

28. See Florida Acts of 1866, pages 61–62 (January 13, 1866); Alabama Acts of 1865–66, page
44 (January 15, 1866); South Carolina Acts of 1866, pages 380–381 (September 20, 1866); Texas
Acts of 1866, page 64 (October 27, 1866); Georgia Acts of 1866, page 141 (December 15, 1866).

29. North Carolina Public Laws of 1867, pages 3–4 (March 1, 1867).

30. Louisiana Acts of 1867, page 351 (March 28, 1867).

31. *Betts v. Ratliff*, 50 Miss. 561, 567, 1874 WL 4617 (1874).

32. C. Vann Woodward, "The Unredeemed Farmer," in *Origins of the New South, 1877–1913*,
180 (1951), quoted in Harold D. Woodman, *New South—New Law: The Legal Foundations of
Credit and Labor Relations in the Postbellum Agricultural South* 5 (1995), and quoted without
attribution by Gene Dattel in *Cotton and Race in the Making of America: The Human Costs of
Economic Power*s 306, 312 (2009).

33. *The St. Jago De Cuba*, 9 Wheat. (22 U.S.) 409, 416 (1824).

34. *Strauss v. Bailey*, 58 Miss. 131, 138, 1880 WL 4848 (1880).

35. W. J. Cash, *The Mind of the South* 148 (1941, 1991).

36. *Wooten v. Gwin*, 56 Miss. 422, 441–442, 1879 WL 6408 (1879) (Simrall, C. J.).

37. David L. Cohn, *The Life and Times of King Cotton* 163 (1956).

38. Miss. Laws, pages 82–93, 165–167 (October, November, and December 1865 and 1866).
Article 2 of the "black code" was entitled Vagrancy Law. *See generally* E. Merton Coulter, *The
South during Reconstruction, 1856–1877* 38–40 (1947); W. J. Cash, *The Mind of the South* 105, 322,
409 (1941, 1991); Gene Dattel, *Cotton and Race in the Making of America: The Human Costs of
Economic Power* 248–252, 262, 354 (2009); David M. Oshinsky, *Worse than Slavery: Parchman
Farm and the Ordeal of Jim Crow Justice* 20–23 (1996); Dennis J. Mitchell, *A New History of
Mississippi* 188–189, 193–194 (2014); "Black Codes (United States)," en.wikipdia.org/wiki/Black
-Codes-United-States.

39. Chief Justice Campbell's storied career in public service is featured more prominently
in chapter 6 below, which tells the story of Mississippi's first legislative effort to regulate the
railroads and is centered on *Stone v. Yazoo and Mississippi Valley Railroad Company*, 62 Miss. 607,
1885 WL 3015 (April Term, 1885) and other railroad regulatory decisions that Campbell authored.

40. *Paxton v. Meyer, Weis & Co.*, 58 Miss. 445, 464, 1880 WL 4865 (1880) (Campbell, J.,
dissenting).

41. *Hilliard v. Cagle*, 46 Miss. 309, 337, 1872 WL 4282 (1872).

42. W. J. Cash, *The Mind of the South* 149 (1941, 1991).

43. The story of the Panic of 1873 is told by Jennifer S. Lee in "New York and the Panic of 1873," *New York Times*, October 14, 2008, http://cityroom.blogs.nytimes.com/2008/10/14 /learning-lessons-from-the-panic-of-1873/?_r=0; *see also The Panic of 1873, U. S. Grant: Warrior*, WGBH, *American Experience*, PBS, http://www.pbs.org/wgbh/americanexperience/features /general/article/grant-panic/; David Blanke, *Panic of 1873*, http://teachinghistory.org/history -content/beyond-the-textbook/24579; *Panic of 1873*, https://en.wikipedia.org/wiki/Panic_of _1873; *Crisis Chronicles: The Long Depression and the Panic of 1873*, http://libertystreeteconomics .newyork.fed.org/2016/02/crisis-chronicles-the-long-depression.

44. James C. Cobb, *The Most Southern Place on Earth: The Mississippi Delta and the Roots of Regional Identity* 63 (1992).

45. Robert L. Brandfon, *Cotton Kingdom of the New South* 4 (1967).

46. *See, e.g.*, W. J. Cash, *The Mind of the South*, 149 (1941, 1991); David L. Cohn, *The Life and Times of King Cotton* 168 (1956); Robert L. Brandfon, *Cotton Kingdom of the New South* 112 (1967).

47. *See, e.g.*, *Lucy E. Wright and Husband v. Sarah J. Walton and Husband*, 56 Miss. 1, 1878 WL 4518 (1878); *Caldwell v. Hart*, 57 Miss. 123, 1879 WL 4036 (1879).

48. *See, e.g.*, Roger L. Ransom and Richard Sutch, *One Kind of Freedom: The Economic Consequences of Emancipation* 116–123 (1977). From the beginnings noted above, beginning with the rating agency founded by dedicated abolitionist Lewis Tappan, the firm known today as Dun & Bradstreet ultimately emerged.

49. "Obtaining Goods under False Pretenses," *Brandon Republican/ Vicksburg Herald*, Sat., Sept. 1, 1877, page 1, Newspapers.com, https://www.newspapers.com/image/264402161.

50. *Smith v. State*, 55 Miss. 513, 519, 1878 WL 4495 (1878).

51. *Paxton v. Meyer, Weis & Co.*, 58 Miss. 445, 464, 1880 WL 4865 (1880) (Campbell, J., dissenting).

52. W. J. Cash, *The Mind of the South* 147 (1941, 1991).

53. W. J. Cash, *The Mind of the South* 149 (1941, 1991).

54. *Paxton v. Meyer, Weis & Co.*, 58 Miss. 445, 464, 1880 WL 4865 (1880) (Campbell, J., dissenting).

55. Gene Dattel, *Cotton and Race in the Making of America: The Human Costs of Economic Power* 307 (2009).

56. *Black's Law Dictionary*, "Distress," at page 426 (5th ed., 1979). *See Stamps v. Gilman & Co.*, 43 Miss. 456, 1870 WL 6676 (1870).

57. *Mayre v. Dyche*, 42 Miss. 347, 377–379, 1869 WL 3761 (1869).

58. *Marye v. Dyche*, 42 Miss. 347, 378, 1869 WL 3761 (1869).

59. *Wooten v. Gwin*, 56 Miss. 422, 443, 1879 WL 6408 (1879) (Simrall, C. J.).

60. *H. Herman & Co. v. Perkins*, 52 Miss. 813, 816, 1876 WL 4734 (1876).

61. *Trimble v. Durham*, 70 Miss. 295, 12 So. 207 (1892).

62. *H. Herman & Co. v. Perkins*, 52 Miss. 813, 816–817, 1876 WL 4734 (1876).

63. Glenn N. Sisk, "Rural Merchandising in the Alabama Black Belt, 1875–1917," *Journal of Farm Economics* 46 (1995), 706, 710.

64. *See, e.g.*, Roger L. Ransom and Richard Sutch, *One Kind of Freedom: The Economic Consequences of Emancipation* 126–127 (1977); Charles Lewis Nier III, "The Merchant and the Origins of Predatory Lending," Part IV. C., nn. 128–133 in *The Shadow of Credit: The Historical Origins of Racial Predatory Lending and Its Impact on African American Wealth Accumulation*, 11 U. Pa. Journ. Law and Social Change 131 (2007–2008), and accompanying text.

65. Gene Dattel, *Cotton and Race in the Making of America; The Human Costs of Economic Power* 305 (2009).

66. *Cotton & Co. v. Hiller & Co.*, 52 Miss. 7, 14, 1876 WL 5155 (1876).

67. David L. Cohn, *The Life and Times of King Cotton* 161 (New York 1956).

68. *Wolfe v. Crawford*, 54 Miss. 514, 1877 WL 7391 (1877).

69. Andrew Morrison, *New Orleans and the New South* 114 (1888).

70. *Newman v. Bank of Greenville*, 66 Miss. 323, 5 So. 753 (1889).

71. E. Merton Coulter, *The South during Reconstruction, 1856–1877* 194–195 (1947). *See also* Gene Dattel, *Cotton and Race in the Making of America: The Human Costs of Economic Power* 305 (2009).

72. W. J. Cash, *The Mind of the South* 148–149 (1941, 1991).

73. David L. Cohn, *The Life and Times of King Cotton* 164 (1956).

74. Robert L. Brandfon, *Cotton Kingdom of the New South* 109 (1967).

75. *Paxton v. Meyer, Weis & Co.*, 58 Miss. 445, 453, 457, 1880 WL 4865 (1880). *See, e.g.*, Roger L. Ransom and Richard Sutch, *One Kind of Freedom: The Economic Consequences of Emancipation* 147–148 (1977) (exorbitant prices for supplies).

76. David L. Cohn, *The Life and Times of King Cotton* 164 (1956), quoting M. B. Hammond writing in *Cotton Industry*.

77. *Paxton v. Meyer, Weis & Co.*, 58 Miss. 445, 447, 1880 WL 4865 (1880) (J. M. Jayne, for the appellant Paxton).

78. William Faulkner's fictional Ab Snopes first appears in the mid-1890s in his short story "Barn Burning" in *Collected Stories* 20 (1977). *See also* Faulkner, *The Hamlet* 9–18 (1940).

79. Flem Snopes is the protagonist in William Faulkner's *The Hamlet* (1940). *See, e.g.*, John Pilkington, "Materialism in the Country," *The Heart of Yoknapatawpha* 217–242 (1981).

80. *Storm v. Green*, 51 Miss. 103, 106, 110, 1875 WL 4680 (1875).

81. *Evans v. Forstall & Jumonville*, 58 Miss. 30, 1880 WL 6883 (1880) (purchaser not bound to search records for a crop lien when lienee represents he has no interest in the land or crop).

82. Ted Ownby, *American Dreams in Mississippi; Consumers, Poverty & Culture, 1830–1998* 72, 79–18 (1999).

83. Ted Ownby, *American Dreams in Mississippi; Consumers, Poverty & Culture, 1830–1998* 61–71 (1999).

84. David L. Cohn, *The Life and Times of King Cotton* 164 (1956).

85. *Westmoreland v. Wooten*, 51 Miss. 825, 827, 1876 WL 7297 (1876).

86. *Wooten v. Gwin*, 56 Miss. 422, 425, 1879 WL 6408 (1879).

87. *Wooten v. Gwin*, 56 Miss. 422, 441–443, 1879 WL 6408 (1879).

88. Justice Josiah A. P. Campbell had joined in the result announced by Chief Justice Simrall on the rather wooden and questionable ground that "the remedy given by the statute is exclusive of all others." *Wooten v. Gwin*, 56 Miss. 422, 431, 1879 WL 6408 (1879). The legislature certainly could have precluded a tort remedy being available to the disappointed lien holder, but it had not done so. Campbell fundamentally misunderstood the way the judge-made common law interacts with and supplements the statutory law made in the legislature and with the approval of the governor. See chapter 8, below.

89. *Wooten v. Gwin*, 56 Miss. 422, 432–435, 1879 WL 6408 (1879).

90. *Wooten v. Gwin*, 56 Miss. 422, 431, 1879 WL 6408 (1879) (Campbell, J., concurring).

91. *Hunt v. Wing*, 57 Tenn. 139, 1872 WL 3955 (Tenn. 1872). The discussion that follows differs in part from that offered a generation ago by Harold D. Woodman in his little book *New South—New Law: The Legal Foundation of Credit and Labor Relations in the Postbellum Agricultural South* 16–27 (1995). Nonetheless, Woodman's valuable discussion is well worth a reading and reflection.

92. The first Mississippi wage lien law was enacted several years later, on April 5, 1872. AN ACT to receive the payment of wages for labor and liabilities for supplies," Miss. Laws, ch, CVII [108], § 1 (April 5, 1872).

93. White, Billingsley & Co. appears to have been a St. Louis–based firm that did business up and down the River and inland westward as well. After the war and in the latter 1860s, the firm advertised itself as "Wholesale Grocers and Commission Merchants, No. 106 N. Second St., St. Louis, Mo." *See* advertisement in *Howard Union* (Glasgow, Mo), Thurs., Aug. 3, 1865, page 2, Newspapers.com, https://www.newspapers.com/image/61384107; and in *Osage County Chronicle* (Burlingame, Ks., Sat., July 28, 1866, page 2, Newspapers.com, https://www.newspapers.com /image/58973125. At some point the firm dissolved, and Billingsley established a new firm with J. S. Nanson and J. C. Garth, under the name of Billingsley & Nanson, General Commission Merchants, No. 527 North Second Street, St. Louis, Missouri. *St. Louis Post-Dispatch*, Tues., Jan. 18, 1881, Newspapers.com, https://www.newspapers.com/image/138971647.

94. *Hunt v. Wing*, 57 Tenn. 139, 141, 1872 WL 3955 (Tenn. 1872).

95. In 1869, William M. Farrington and Henry R. Howell d/b/a Farrington & Howell advertised as cotton factors, grocers, and commission merchants, 266 Front Street, Corner of Court, in Memphis. Farrington and Howell were partners for twenty years. They were financial intermediaries in the area's agricultural economy and, along with several others, for a considerable time dominated the commercial life of Memphis. Farrington & Howell were active litigants in the courts in those days, including *Field v. Farrington*, 77 U.S. 141 (1869). *See Commercial Appeal*, June 18, 1911, part 2, page 10. David Cohn tells the story of Cotton Row on Front Street in *The Life and Times of King Cotton* 185–194 (1956). So does Robert A. Sigafoos in his *Cotton Row to Beale Street: A Business History of Memphis* (1979).

96. This premise is explained more fully below in chapter 8 regarding the common law in Mississippi.

97. *Arbuckle v. Nelms*, 50 Miss. 556, 558, 1874 WL 6523 (1874). *Stewart v. Rollins*, 47 Miss. 708, 1873 WL 6002 (1873); and *Marye v. Dyche*, 42 Miss. 347, 377–379, 1869 WL 3763 (1869) are two such cases.

98. The statute is by and large set forth in *Howard, Preston & Barrett v. Simmons*, 43 Miss. 75, 82–84, 1870 WL 2845 (1870).

99. *Cooper v. Frierson*, 48 Miss. 300, 1873 WL 4123 (1873).

100. *See, e.g.*, "The New Laborers' Lien Law," *Natchez Democrat* (Natchez, Miss.), Sat., July 13, 1872, page 1, Newspapers.com, https://newspapers.com/image/235133398.

101. "AN ACT to receive the payment of wages for labor and liabilities for supplies," Miss. Laws, ch. CVII [108] (April 5, 1872), and particularly §§ 1, 13, 14. The legislature continued to exercise its constitutional power to tinker in 1873, and this should be noted, though of no particular impact on the present story. See brief descriptions in *Betts v. Ratliff*, 50 Miss. 561, 570–571, 1874 WL 4617 (1874); *Cayce v. Stovall*, 50 Miss. 396, 402, 1874 WL 4605 (1874).

102. The new Mississippi Constitution of December 1, 1869, also provided that "[n]o . . . laws impairing the obligations of contracts shall ever be passed," and that "[p]rivate property [presumably including vested property interests and contract rights] shall not be taken for public use, except upon due compensation." Miss. Const. art. 1, §§ 9, 10 (1869).

103. The 1880 census reflects that a Silva Brooks, born about 1820 in Maryland, was living in Searcy in Phillips County, Arkansas, just across the Mississippi River and slightly southwest of Tunica County, Mississippi. "Silva Brooks in the 1880 United States Federal Census," ancestry.com.

104. *Hunt v. Wing*, 57 Tenn. 139, 149–150, 1872 WL 3955 (Tenn. 1872).

105. *See, e.g.*, *Cayce v. Stovall*, 50 Miss. 396, 400, 1874 WL 4605 (1874) (the law regarding "the earnings of a vessel, as freight, on a voyage, or the produce of oil or fish, got in a whaling expedition" was considered by analogy in a case involving the enforcement of liens against after acquired property).

106. *Fretz v. Bull*, 12 Howard (53 U.S.) 466, 468, 469 (1851).

107. *The John Stevens*, 170 U.S. 113, 119 (1898).

108. *See Strauss v. Bailey*, 58 Miss. 131, 138, 1880 WL 4848 (1880).

109. *Hunt v. Wing*, 57 Tenn. 139, 146, 1872 WL 3955 (Tenn. 1872).

110. This is not the time or the place to get into the often remarked about "crucial distinction on the agricultural ladder between renters [tenants] and croppers." Charles Lewis Nier III, "The Merchant and the Origins of Predatory Lending," Part IV. A., fn. 112 in *The Shadow of Credit: The Historical Origins of Racial Predatory Lending and its Impact on African American Wealth Accumulation*, 11 U. Pa. Journ. Law and Social Change 131 (2007–2008), and accompanying text; *see also* Harold D. Woodman, *New South—New Law; The Legal Foundations of Credit and Labor Relations in the Postbellum Agricultural South*, page 68 (LSU Press 1995).

111. William Faulkner, *Requiem for a Nun* 35, 37 (1950); see chapter 1, page 1, above.

112. *See, e.g., Marye v. Dyche*, 42 Miss. 347, 1869 WL 3763 (1869) (common law respecting distress for rent changed by statute; supply liens entitled to preference and priority over claim for rent); *Howard, Preston & Barrett v. Simmons*, 43 Miss. 73, 1870 WL 2845 (1870) (whether previously enrolled judgment lien has priority over crop lien, though supplies used in raising crop were furnished by crop lien holder); *Stamps v. Gilman & Co.*, 43 Miss. 456, 1870 WL 6676 (1870–71) (whether landlord has a lien on tenant's effects); *Hilliard v. Cagle*, 46 Miss. 309, 1872 WL 4282 (1872) (on Dec. 19, 1866, supply merchant gave deed of trust for substantial assets to cotton factors in New Orleans who did not record deed of trust; inference of fraud where merchant continued to do business until Jan. 30, 1867, as though assets had remained unencumbered); *Hunt v. Wing*, 57 Tenn. 139, 1872 WL 3955 (1872) (three competing lien claimants—supply merchant, landlord, farm laborers; case incorrectly decided; see above); *Bain v. Brooks*, 46 Miss. 537, 1872 WL 6144 (1872) (whether act of 1867 required deed of trust, mortgage or other lien creating writing before priority arose from properly filed writing; failure not cured by verbal agreement); *Stewart v. Hollins*, 47 Miss. 708, 1873 WL 6002 (1873) (whether priority granted by act of 1867 extended to rent for leased farmlands); *Allen & Co. v. Montgomery*, 48 Miss. 101, 1873 WL 4113 (1873) (ordinary business between commission merchant and planter, former supplying money in aid of crop; whether lien arose from advances where no agreement of compliance with act of 1867; fraudulent conveyance claim; bankruptcy); *Cooper v. Frierson*, 48 Miss. 300, 310–311, 1873 WL 4123 (1873) (whether merchant's lien creating contract properly filed; "defect goes to foundation of his suit"); *French v. Picard*, 49 Miss. 320, 1873 WL 6048 (1873) (must filed contract give notice of amount to be advanced; lien and priority limited to amount actually advanced); *Cayce v. Stovall*, 50 Miss. 396, 1874 WL 4605 (1874) (supplier's crop line perfected by filing on July 26, 1873; judgment enrolled on April 11, 1873; as to crops supplier's crop lien has priority; judgment lien attached to cotton only once harvested and does not relate back); *Arbuckle v. Nelms*, 50 Miss. 556, 1874 WL 6523 (1874) (act of April 17, 1873 protected landlord's lien on crop; landlord leased to tenant in January of 1873, with agreed rental of three bales of cotton; merchant filed crop lien contract filed June 2, 1873; *held*, landlord prevailed; new statute could not impair landlord's right under lease); *Betts v. Ratliff*, 50 Miss. 561, 1874 WL 4617 (1874) (supplier of farm laborer working for shares had lien priority over lien granted to landowner/employer who also furnished supplies; construing Acts of April 5, 1872 and of April 17, 1873); *Storm v. Green*, 51 Miss. 103, 1875 WL 4680 (1875) (landowner recovered three bales of cotton produced by laborer for share, defeating competing claim of supply merchant relying on note and deed of trust belatedly signed by laborer; construes landlord's lien under Act of April 17, 1873; see above); *Cotton & Co. v. Hiller & Co.*, 52 Miss. 7, 1876 WL 5155 (1876) (relationship between cotton factor and local supply merchant; recognizes factor's lien); *White v. Thomas*, 52 Miss. 49, 52, 1876 WL 5159 (1876) (two-year lease of cotton plantation; lease granted landlord lien on crops, mules and implements to secure payment of rent; *held* enforceable between parties, where no third person or firm involved); *Harris v. Frank & Reinach*, 52 Miss. 155, 1876 WL 7312

(1876) (Landlord leased to tenant for 1873 crop year, rent secured by crop to be grown; tenant made partial sublease to sublessee for four bales of cotton; supply merchant furnished sublessee; entire premises subject to burden of tenant's original rental obligation to land-owner; sublessee responsible *pro tanto* for burdens imposed on sublessor); *Hester v. Allen*, 52 Miss. 162, 1876 WL 7313 (1876) (overseer is not among persons granted lien on crop by acts of 1872 and 1873); *Doty v. Heth*, 52 Miss. 530, 1876 WL 7338 (1876) (lessee entered "cropping on shares" contracts with laborers; merchant furnished supplies to laborers; lessee failed to pay rent to his lessor; lien on crops; litigation arose prior to then recent statutes regarding landlord's claim of lien for rent); *H. Herman & Co. v. Perkins*, 52 Miss. 813, 1875 WL 4734 (1875) (for purposes of lien priority under act of 1867, "other things necessary for cultivation" takes into account nature of farming system); *Phillips v. Douglas*, 53 Miss. 175, 1876 WL 7371 (1876) (under act of April 17, 1873, landlord who reserves rent payable in money and not in part of the crop had no lien on the crop); *Cloud v. State for use of McAlexander*, 53 Miss. 662, 1876 WL 7409 (1876) (under act of 1867, lien holder's right is against the cotton; lien holder has no claim against sheriff who seized and sold cotton at instance of another); *Taylor v. Nelson*, 54 Miss. 524, 1877 WL 7392 (1877) (landlord's lien under act of 1873 is assignable); *Evans v. Robertson*, 54 Miss. 683, 1877 WL 4975 (1877) (supply merchant's crop lien enforceable against estate farming land with court authority); *Shackelford v. Hooker*, 54 Miss. 716, 1877 WL 7412 (1877) (supply merchant's lien on crops); *Smith v. State*, 55 Miss. 513, 1878 WL 4495 (1878); *Wright v. Walton*, 56 Miss. 1, 1878 WL 4518 (1878) (wife liable for supplies contracted for her plantation by her husband); *Caldwell v, Hart*, 57 Miss. 123, 1879 WL 4036 (1879) (husband farmer secured supplies and loan; wife owned plantation; husband made misrepresentations); *Hartsell v. Myers*, 57 Miss. 135, 1879 WL 6458 (1879) (no deficiency judgment allowed under Act of 1876 in excess of value of crop seized under lien; statute allows only *in rem* proceedings); *Love v. Law*, 57 Miss. 596, 1879 WL 4046 (1880) (same as *Hartsell v. Myers*); *Strauss v. Bailey*, 58 Miss. 131, 136–138, 1880 WL 4848 (1880) (statute law gave landlord priority of lien for rent and for mules furnished to tenants and for money paid for handling, ginning and packing the cotton); *Tucker v. Whitehead*, 58 Miss. 762, 1881 WL 7689 (1888) (procedure re lien for rent in year of death of landowner); *Baldwin v. Flash*, 59 Miss. 61, 1881 WL 4551 (1881) (application of proceeds of cotton sold among commission merchants holding factor's lien and other creditors); *Jones v. Porter*, 59 Miss. 628, 1881 WL 4274 (1882) (deed of trust signed by married woman in 1887 to merchant for advancing supplies void unless husband joins); *Chaffe v. Mississippi and Tennessee Railroad*, 59 Miss. 182, 1881 WL 7708 (1881) (debtor ships cotton to factor and creditor for sale and application to debt and sends bill of lading may change shipment to another person); *Henry v. Davis*, 60 Miss. 212, 1882 WL 7580 (1882) (landlord's right against crop broader than remedy by statutory attachment for rent); *Paine v. Aberdeen Hotel Co.*, 60 Miss. 360, 1882 WL 4310 (1882) (landlord's claim under lien good against everyone not a good faith purchaser for value); *Mortimer v. McKay*, 1 Miss. Dec. 585, 1883 WL 6834 (1883) (advance secured by crop lien; appropriation of payments; when note and deed of trust extinguished); *Roberts v. Sims*, 64 Miss. 597, 2 So. 72 (1887) (landlord had right to three bales of cotton paramount to claim of supply merchant); *Cohn v. Smith*, 64 Miss. 816, 2 So. 244 (1887) (landlord may recover value of crops grown on leased lands from purchaser with notice of landlord's lien); *Lumbley v. Thomas*, 65 Miss, 97, 5 So. 823 (1887) (wage hand and general laborer had statutory lien on crop he helped prepare for market); *Newman v. Bank of Greenville*, 66 Miss. 323, 5 So. 753, 757 (1889) (landlord's lien exists without writing or record and must prevail even against *bona fide* purchaser for value); *Watts v. Bonner*, 66 Miss. 629, 6 So. 187 (1889) (supply merchant who fails to supply all of advances agrees upon has crop lien for so much as he advanced, subject to any loss caused by his breach of contract); *Hollingsworth v. Hill*, 69 Miss. 73, 10 So. 450 (1891) (landlord has prior lien on all crops grown for rent and supplies he furnished; supply merchant takes anything left); *Sanford v. Starling & Smith Co.*, 69 Miss. 204, 10 So. 449 (1891) (supply merchant provided cotton farmer supplies amounting to $1,340; that two or three bottles of spirituous liquors were included did not impair crop lien); *Ellis v. Jones*, 70 Miss. 60, 11 So. 566 (1892) (whether landlord had lien where he merely guaranteed supplies furnished by third party); *Trimble v. Durham*, 70 Miss. 295, 12 So. 207 (1892) (mules are supplies but not advances); *Coleman v. Low*, 13 So. 227 (1893) (replevin action for possession of jack claimed under crop lien); *Weise v. Rutland*, 71 Miss. 933, 15 So. 38 (1894) (whether overseer entitled to lien on crop he helped produce; Code 1880, § 1360, extended lien right to "every employee, laborer, cropper, part owner or other person"); *Mask v. Allen*, 17 So. 82 (1894) (rights to two mules contested by and between conditional seller and furnish merchant); *Cocke v. Maynard*, 16 So. 908 (1895) (contest over cotton raised by tenant and Memphis supply merchant claiming crop lien); *Millsaps v. Tate*, 75 Miss. 150, 21 So. 863 (1897) (landlord's statutory lien and priority shorn from crop—absent fraud—when it crossed state line to Memphis, where commission merchants took possession and enforced their crop lien); and so, so many, many more.

113. *Hunt v. Wing*, 57 Tenn. 139, 146, 1872 WL 3955 (Tenn. 1872).

114. "Memoirs of Henry Tillinghast Ireys," *Papers of the Washington County Historical Society, 1910–1915* (McCain and Capers eds., 1954), 268.

115. See *Succession of Patrick Condon*, 1 McGl. 351, 363, 1881 WL 8894 (La. App. 1881) ("Meyer, Weis & Co. were not bankers, . . . but were cotton factors and commission merchants in this city and New York"). Other reasonably contemporaneous Mississippi litigation in which Meyer, Weis & Co. was involved included *Meyer, Weis & Co. v. Baldwin*, 52 Miss. 263, 1876 WL 7322 (1876); *Smiley v. Meyer, Weis & Co.*, 55 Miss. 555, 1878 WL 4501(1878); and *Meyer v. Casey*, 57 Miss. 615, 1880 WL 4808 (1880). Other cases in Louisiana are easily found, *e.g.*, *Meyer, Weis & Co. v. Atkins*, 29 La. Ann. 586, 1877 WL 8133 (La. 1877); and *Helm v. Meyer, Weis & Co.*, 30 La. Ann. 943, 1878 WL 8709 (La. 1878). Arkansas litigations included *Meyer, Weis & Co. v. Portis*, 45 Ark. 420, 1885 WL 705 (Ark. 1885).

116. See, *e.g.*, *Hartman v. McInnis*, 996 So.2d 704, 711 (¶23) (2007); *Cotton v. McConnell*, 435 So.2d 683, 686 (1983). In the hypothetical negotiation, each party is assumed to be a rational, informed, self-interested wealth maximizer, in addition to the other general criteria noted above.

117. *Paxton v. Meyer, Weis & Co.*, 58 Miss. 445, 453, 1880 WL 4865 (1880).

118. David L. Cohn, *The Life and Times of King Cotton* 168 (New York 1956), quoting M. B. Hammond writing in *Cotton Industry*.

119. *Paxton v. Meyer, Weis & Co.*, 58 Miss. 445, 461–462, 1880 WL 4865 (1880).

120. *Paxton v. Meyer, Weis & Co.*, 58 Miss. 445, 464, 1880 WL 4865 (1880) (Campbell, J., dissenting).

121. *Paxton v. Meyer, Weis & Co.*, 58 Miss. 445, 452–458, 1880 WL 4865 (1880).

122. *Paxton v. Meyer, Weis & Co.*, 58 Miss. 445, 459, 1880 WL 4865 (1880).

123. *Strauss v. Bailey*, 58 Miss. 131, 138, 1880 WL 4848 (1880).

124. *Paxton v. Meyer, Weis & Co.*, 58 Miss. 445, 459–462, 1880 WL 4865 (1880) (Chalmers, C. J., concurring).

125. Gene Dattel, *Cotton and Race in the Making of America: The Human Costs of Economic Power* 307 (2009).

126. The rights secured by Article I, §§ 2, 3, and 28, Miss. Const. (1869), and today by Article 3, §§ 14, 21, and 24, Miss. Const. (1890), are generally accepted as having their origin at Runnymede, England, in Magna Carta, June 15, 1215. See *State v. McPhail*, 182 Miss. 360, 180 So. 387, 392 (1938), presented in chapter 9 below concerning these same three constitutional sections and their derivation from Magna Carta. See also *Ex Parte Hickey*, 4 Smedes & M. 751, 769 (1844) considered in chapter 8.

127. Legislative facts are tools of important judicial utility as explained in my *Variations on a Theme by Posner: Facing the Factual Component of the Reliability Imperative in the Process of Adjudication*, 84 Miss. L. Journ. 471–683 (2015); see particularly pages 527–533.

128. The obligatory citation here is Richard A. Posner's majestic one-thousand-page survey, *Economic Analysis of Law* (9th ed. 2014).

129. *Newman v. Bank of Greenville*, 66 Miss. 323, 5 So. 753, 756 (1889).

BIBLIOGRAPHY

Appelbaum, Binyamin, "Nobel in Economics Is Awarded to Richard Thaler," *New York Times*, October 9, 2017.

Blanke, David, *Panic of 1873*, http://teachinghistory.org/history-content/beyond-the-textbook /24579.

Bolton, Charles C., *Poor Whites of the Antebellum South; Tenants and Laborers in Central North Carolina and Northeast Mississippi* (1994).

Brandfon, Robert L., *Cotton Kingdom of the New South* (1967).

Carter, Hodding, *Lower Mississippi* (1942).

Cash, W. J., *The Mind of the South* (1941, 1991).

Cobb, James C., *The Most Southern Place on Earth: The Mississippi Delta and the Roots of Regional Identity* (1992).

Cohn, David L., *The Life and Times of King Cotton* (1956).

Cohn, David L., *Where I Was Born and Raised* (1948).

Coulter, E. Merton, *The South during Reconstruction, 1856–1877* (1947).

Crisis Chronicles: The Long Depression and the Panic of 1873, htt://libertystreeteconomics .newyork.fed.org/2016/02/crisis-chronicles-the-long-depression.

"Crop Lien System (Sharecropping) Entrenches Itself in Former Plantation Areas," https:// historyengine.richmond.edu/episodes/view/324.

Crop-Lien System, https://en.wikipedia.org/wiki/Crop-lien_system.

"Crop Liens" and "Sharecropping," in *Mississippi Encyclopedia* 305, 1125–1127 (ed. Ownby and Wilson, 2017).

Dattel, Gene, *Cotton and Race in the Making of America; The Human Costs of Economic Power* (2009).

Faulkner, William, "Barn Burning," in *Collected Stories* (1977).

Faulkner, William, *Requiem for a Nun* (1950).

Faulkner, William, *The Hamlet* (1940).

Gilmore, Grant, and Charles Black, *The Law of Admiralty* (2d. ed., 1975).

Johnson, K. Todd, "Crop Lien System," 2006, http://ncpedia.org/print/2292.

Lee, Jennifer S., "New York and the Panic of 1873," *New York Times*, October 14, 2008, http:// city room.blogs.nytimes.com/2008/10/14/learning-lessons-from-the-panic-of-1873/?_r=0.

"Lesson Transcript—The Crop-Lien System," https://study.com/academy/lesson/crop-lien-system-definition.html.

Mitchell, Dennis J., *A New History of Mississippi* (2014).

Morrison, Andrew, *New Orleans and the New South* (1888).

Nier III, Charles Lewis, "The Credit System in the Post-Bellum Era," Part IV. B., in *The Shadow of Credit: The Historical Origins of Racial Predatory Lending and Its Impact on African American Wealth Accumulation*, 11 U. Pa. Journ. Law and Social Change (2007–2008).

Oshinsky, David M., *"Worse than Slavery: Parchman Farm and the Ordeal of Jim Crow Justice* (1996).

Ownby, Ted, *American Dreams in Mississippi: Consumers, Poverty & Culture, 1830–1998* (1999).

Panic of 1873, https://en.wikipedia.org/wiki/Panic_of_1873.

"The Panic of 1873, U. S. Grant: Warrior," WGBH *American Experience*, PBS, http://www.pbs.org /wgbh/americanexperience/features/general/article/grant-panic/.

Pilkington, John, "Materialism in the Country," *The Heart of Yoknapatawpha* (1981).

Ransom, Roger L., and Richard Sutch, *One Kind of Freedom; The Economic Consequences of Emancipation* (1977).

Sansing, David, "Benjamin Grubb Humphreys," in *Mississippi Governors: Soldiers, Statesmen, Scholars, Scoundrels, A Bicentennial Edition* 100–103 (2016).

Sisk, Glenn N., "Rural Merchandising in the Alabama Black Belt, 1875–1917," *Journal of Farm Economics* 46 (1995), 706.

Skates, John Ray, Jr., *A History of the Mississippi Supreme Court* (1973).

Smith, Frank E., *The Yazoo River* (1954).

Tunica County, Mississippi, Largest Slaveholders from 1860 Slave Census Schedules, transcribed by Tom Blake, February, 2002, http://freepages.genealogy.rootsweb.ancestry. com/-ajac/mstunica.htm.

"What Was the Crop Lien System?" https://www.reference.com/business-finance/crop-lien -system-5021f0982a23f1cf.

Woodman, Harold D., *King Cotton & His Retainers: Financing and Marketing the Cotton Crop of the South, 1800–1925* (1968).

Woodman, Harold D., *New South—New Law: The Legal Foundations of Credit and Labor Relations in the Postbellum Agricultural South* (1995).

Woodman, Harold D., *The Political Economy of the New South: Retrospects and Prospects*, *Journal of Southern History* 67 (2001).

Woodward, C. Vann, *Origins of the New South, 1877–1913* (1951).

CHAPTER 6

Advent of the Regulatory State in Mississippi

The creation of a public agency to stand between the railroad companies and those dealing with them, to see that the obligation of the former to be reasonable in their charges is duly observed, is not an infraction of any right.

—CHIEF JUSTICE JOSIAH A. P. CAMPBELL, IN *STONE V. NJ&C RAILROAD CO*, 62 MISS. 646, 653 (1885)

It was February 17, 1882, when the Yazoo and Mississippi Valley Railroad Company sprang forth—like Athena from the head of Zeus, but from a less godlike legislature.[1] Such was the nature of firm incorporations in Mississippi, in the early days dating back to statehood. In time the "Y&MV" would become essentially a Memphis-to-New Orleans railroad, by way of Vicksburg, with spurs and auxiliary lines throughout the Mississippi Delta. Trains and their tracks added color, grit, and awe to a storied era. Most of those north–south lines and spurs are still captured on old Y&MV grid maps.[2]

The main lines more or less shadow what became US Highway 61 and State Highway 1, "the River Road," US Highway 49 West from Clarksdale to Itta Bena, and filled the lands within.[3] Except, of course, that the automobile was not even a gleam in the eye in the years we're talking about. It would be more accurate to say that the railroads shadowed what in time would become US and state highways. Texture and humanity remain in longtime Speaker "Buddie" Newman's[4] great turn-of-the-century photo, featuring a Y&MV section foreman and crew that serviced the rails and tracks in the South Delta to and through the likes of Egremont, Kelso, Midnight and his hometown of Valley Park.[5]

If you're going "where the Southern Cross the Dog," you're headed for a railroad crossing in Moorhead and Sunflower County, Mississippi, near the eastern edge of the Y&MV's Delta. Turn south off US Highway 82 on to State Highway 3, and you can't miss the Yellow Dog Café. There someone can lead you to the crossing about a hundred yards away. At that point, you are a little over forty miles south of Tutwiler on what used to be the Y&MV and today is US Highway 49W, where W. C. Handy got stuck in the station waiting on the train long enough to discover "the Blues."[6] The scene and its ambiance have drawn judicial notice.[7]

The great eastern wall of the Delta is marked by near-alpine ascents such as Highway 82 easterly past the cotton city of Greenwood, State Highway 12 before one reaches Lexington—though being in and around Lexington has always seemed like you're still in the Delta—and that unforgettable up and up and up—and then up further—main drag in Yazoo City, the southern link of Highway 49W where many a young boy has suffered broken bones or worse while trying to set a new downhill speed record on his bicycle. Fortress Vicksburg on Highway 61—the southern boundary of the Yazoo River Valley— is the Delta's southeastern wall except for that sliver of land along the River that leads to Catfish Row. In the times we are talking about, the parent company, the Illinois Central Railroad—"ICRR" or sometimes just the "IC"—had lines that with not quite surveyor's precision, but close, skirted the Delta's eastern boundary from Holcomb in Grenada County southerly to Yazoo City but would then veer easterly, cutting through the hills and prairies to Jackson, and on down to Brookhaven, McComb, and ultimately New Orleans.

There was hardly a time when the Y&MV wasn't under the thumb of the ICRR.[8] In 1901, IC president Stuyvesant Fish (1851–1923) would reflect less than bashfully, "The Illinois Central Railroad and the Yazoo and Mississippi Valley Railroad Company are, and have been for very many years, probably ever since they began operating railroads in the State, the largest payers of taxes in Mississippi."[9] In 1888, the Mississippi Railroad Commission's records reflect that the IC had 637 miles of track in the state, while the Y&MV had 623 miles.[10] Today the IC's historical society recalls that "in the 1870s railroads began to penetrate the fertile Yazoo Delta along the western edge of Mississippi. IC's entry was the Y&MV Railroad."[11]

But other tracks were laid by laborers whose paymasters bore still differing railroad names. The Louisville, New Orleans and Texas Railroad was completed in January 1885, providing a main line of 456 miles, with several lines to Lake Washington branch, Bolivar branch, Bayou Sara branch, Clinton, and Port Hudson.[12] Before that it had absorbed the Memphis and Vicksburg Railroad and a couple of other area lines. People worried about rates and routes and fairness among shippers—and the constitutional consequences of trying to do something—before the Y&MV reached the full configuration in law so familiar on the ground, in the towns, and on those folding maps, and not just for kids who loved to run down to the station when the train was coming in or a little too close to the tracks out in the country when it was just roaring by.

On October 24, 1892, the Y&MV purchased and assimilated the lines of the Louisville, New Orleans and Texas Railroad. In 1899, the Y&MV owned 105 locomotives, 76 passenger cars, and 3,286 freight and work cars.[13] After operating separately for some fifty-eight years, the Y&MV became formally merged and absorbed into the Illinois Central Railroad. But the story that now needs telling, and the contentious constitutional encounters that it generated, had approached *finis* by that time.

R. T. WILSON

Richard Thornton Wilson (1831–1910) was born in Georgia and raised in the South. He spent many of his growing-up days in Tennessee and Kentucky. During the Civil War, Wilson served as commissary general in the Confederate Army. The Confederate government sent him to Europe to help sell its cotton crop, and he may or may not have had other less overt missions.[14] After the War, he founded and led the banking house of R. T. Wilson & Co. of New York City.

From 1880, Wilson lived at 511 Fifth Avenue. He had a summer home on Narragansett Avenue in Newport, Rhode Island, one of the earliest to be built at that iconic site by the financial and social elite of New York. Wilson was long connected with railroads and the people and firms they served in his postbellum years.[15] In May of 1882, a brief report in the Atlanta Constitution caught the eye.

> In conversation Colonel R. T. Wilson of New York, (a former president of the East Tennessee road) said that he was on his way south "to build a railroad of his own," as he was "tired of partnership business." Colonel Wilson is a Dalton [Georgia] boy who commenced his career at eight dollars per month.[16]

In that year Wilson began building and assembling a railroad paralleling the River, from Memphis to New Orleans.[17] Vicksburg reacted to the news with excitement.

> No event in the history of this city ever foreshadowed greater possibilities for future growth and prosperity. The early completion of these roads, as now assured, will be the dawning of a new era in the commercial growth of Vicksburg and bring new life to every department of trade.[18]

Wilson made an extensive inspection tour of the probable route of his proposed new railroad, and talked to reporters along the way. He was acting on his belief that a "railroad through [the Yazoo River Valley] will open up to producers fields the equal of which can hardly be found on the globe. The Yazoo Valley is capable of producing as much cotton as the present crop of the entire world, such is its fertility."[19] His plan bore the promise of many benefits. "It will enable planters to get their laborers cheaper," but more important, the overall facilities will allow them "to prevent destructive overflows so disastrous to their places. Of course, it will give the population living along the river rapid transportation for freight and travel, and will open up the Yazoo Valley for settlers and increase the production of cotton."

When asked about the legitimacy of the grants he had received from the states and whether he feared federal constitutional problems, Wilson answered that

> the wants of a great and growing community forced such an interpretation of the Constitution as was necessary in order to permit the development and growth of the nation; and it may safely be assumed that anything that will promote the general welfare of the nation comes within the scope of proper consideration unless there is some express or absolute prohibition against it in the fundamental law.

This native of Georgia, then Tennessee and Kentucky, and former Confederate commissary general, concluded

> From a national standpoint this may be most appropriately compared with the great questions that grew out of the [Civil W]ar—and where would this nation have been today if it had waited to find within the limits of its constitutional powers the authority to wage war on the States, as the late civil war was called in this section of the Union. No such authority as that could therein be found. . . . [Yet that] cannot be unconstitutional which has for its object the universal good of the entire country.

Local communities anticipated good things as well. Discernible progress was often the occasion for civic socials. The IC's Durant-Lexington Line was built in 1882–1883. The forty-three-mile Yazoo City–Jackson line was completed in the same period.[20] It was publicly announced on August 17, 1883, that the IC tracks had

> been completed to Pocahontas Station, located on the place of Mr. Joe Lane, about 16 miles from Jackson. A telegraph line is also completed to the same point. It is confidently expected that Flora, six miles further, will be reached next Monday. Track laying to the latter place will be finished by Saturday night. A grand barbecue is on the tapis to celebrate the occasion at Flora.

To show what it all meant, this Jackson-oriented report emphasized that the work is going "right along, and in a few months our Yazoo friends can come over, take breakfast with us, take a look at Jackson and eat supper at home."[21]

The Y&MV from New Orleans north via Baton Rouge, Natchez, and Vicksburg was completed in 1884. That was the year the ICRR bought the Grenada-to-Memphis line,[22] adding a line to Tchula, Mississippi, in 1885. In relevant part, the corporate genealogy of the Y&MV by the end of 1884 appears to have been set out and summarized in a US Supreme Court decision made in 1901.

[T]he Yazoo & Mississippi Valley Railroad Company, as now constituted, was the result of a consolidation made October 24, 1892, between a company of the same name, chartered as above stated, February 17, 1882, and the Louisville, New Orleans & Texas Railway Company, which latter company was itself formed by a consolidation made August 12, 1884, of the Tennessee Southern Railroad Company, the Memphis & Vicksburg Railroad Company[23], the New Orleans, Baton Rouge, Vicksburg & Memphis Railroad Company, and the New Orleans & Mississippi Valley Railroad Company.[24]

Little evidence remains that R. T. Wilson came to the greatest basin in North America, but what a difference he once made. Ask the people in the little town of Wilson, Louisiana, just a few miles across the state line below Centreville, Mississippi. Its importance as a railroad town was borne out by a report during the yellow fever epidemic of 1898.

Fever at Wilson, La.

A bulletin from Superintendent Grerf's office, reports yellow fever at Wilson, Louisiana. Wilson is a very small place on the Y. &. M. V. Railroad, and is 113 miles south of Vicksburg. The only importance that is attached to the little place is the fact that it is the end of a division or [sic] the road—a point where crews are changed. This circumstance makes it very important that our health authorities exercise every possible precaution to prevent further communication with Wilson, and to see to it that all persons who have been exposed to the disease there not be permitted to endanger this community.

As usual the Railroad authorities are willing to co-operate in every way with the health officials, for the preservation of the public health.[25]

EDWARD H. HARRIMAN

At his death in 1910, R. T. Wilson was said to have "left a fortune of over $20,000,000 to the members of his family."[26] A year earlier another up-from-nothing New York banker who took an interest in railroading had died and left his wife maybe ten times that much.[27] Edward Henry Harriman (1848–1909) took scant notice of Mississippi in his sixty-one years on this good earth. The Illinois Central Railroad was hardly the largest such company that Harriman came to control, but in the 1880s the IC said he was the man.[28]

By 1883, Harriman sat on the IC's board of directors, this through the influence of Stuyvesant Fish, who was vice-president at the time.[29] In 1887, Harriman moved up to vice-president.[30] In time, he would come to control the Union Pacific Railroad, the Southern Pacific Railroad, and several others, in addition to the ICRR. It is a safe bet that in the mid-1880s Harriman was an active architect of company policy at the time that the IC, the Y&MV, one other IC affiliate, and at least five other railroads headed for the courthouses and challenged Mississippi's plans to "supervise" their profitable common carriage activities.

ALFRED H. DAVIS

Alfred H. Davis[31] (1865–1949) had his own special memories of the beginnings of what became the Y&MV. He grew up in the old River town of Warrenton about eight miles south of Vicksburg. The youngster was pretty sure it was in the year 1872 that the steamboat *Mollie E. Moore* docked not far from Ben Walthen's Store and began unloading equipment that, in time, would give the steamers more than just a competitive run for their money. People from all over came down "to witness the novel sight, as many of them had never seen a locomotive (the writer being among the number)."[32] The steel gangs began laying rail until "the line had been built from the Walthen to the Leach store, a distance of about five hundred yards, and by morning the line was complete from the river front to the main line, which gave Warrenton a mile of fully equipped railroad, and the 'Old Mississippi' (locomotive) fired up ready to make the first run."

Such were the humble beginnings of what ten years later became R. T. Wilson's railroad that "grew into one of the magnificent trunk lines that traverse the country" and "one of the most important railroad lines in the South." There were many fits and starts, debts not paid, and people wondering if the line would ever really go anywhere. Yet Davis recalled that in the "summer of 1882 a party of gentlemen came down from Vicksburg on the little train and walked down to the river front, to where the original line had run out from the landing through the railroad cut, ten years before." These gentlemen were representing the R. T. Wilson & Company of New York.

Not too many moons crossed the nighttime sky before Davis would remember and write,

> The time consumed in the days of river travel between Vicksburg and adjacent landings, was six days for the round trip to New Orleans, while the same trip can now be made in one day, and still give the traveler a few hours in which to transact business when making the trip by rail.

And the rest, as they say, is history.

THE PRE-REGULATION LANDSCAPE

Remember, railroads in Mississippi dated back at least to 1831 and the West Feliciana Railroad, which first headquartered in Woodville.[33] Lots of railroads came and went over the next three decades, and most failed before the Civil War, and for a variety of reasons, a common one being that management never got past the notion that they were in the banking business first and foremost.

Coming out of the War, the technology and utility of railroading began to improve and grow and to be understood and appreciated. Common carriers by their nature, each railroad became a sort of man-made natural monopoly. Passengers and particularly shippers seldom had real alternatives. The practical realities of their transportation needs meant railroads were the only option. Steamboats on the inland waterways were being more and more outdistanced. Railroads began to flex their monopoly-power muscles. Rates rose. Rate discriminations did, too, as short haulers—particularly farmers with little bargaining power vis-à-vis the larger carriers—found themselves saddled with tariffs a lot steeper than those for long-haul shippers. These twin concerns—monopoly rates and rate discrimination—pinched enough people that politicians took notice. Of course, this led to a new form of rate discrimination, as railroads began granting perks to legislators and public officials and to influential citizens, all of whose political support the railroad might need.

Few failed to notice what was afoot. The IC and the Y&MV were becoming "a great interstate highway for the transportation of persons and property from one state to another, and from one commercial mart to another. . . . This wonderful and immense mode of transportation" was to serve a "common purpose which was to constitute one corporate body for . . . transportation from New Orleans to Cairo" and far from either of those, to the rest of the country, and to the world at large.[34] And the same for the Mobile & Ohio Railroad system,[35] providing another "great national highway," this one "extending from Mobile in Alabama [near the Gulf of Mexico through Mississippi, Tennessee and Kentucky] to a point opposite Cairo . . . at the junction of the Mississippi and Ohio Rivers," and to the world.[36] And lest modern man forget, all of this was at a time when Mississippi and the South were still smarting from the sting of Reconstruction, such that "it was this Yankee's fate to have made [the Southern mind] one of the most solidly established, one of the least *reconstructable* ever developed." Even among the more informed and worldly wise, "the great banking interests of New York" were held "guilty of having exploited the South . . . on their own private account."[37]

RAILROAD REGULATION ARRIVES

The Y&MV was still in its infancy when Mississippi first moved to regulate the railroads. On March 11, 1884, Gov. Robert Lowry[38] (1829–1910) signed into law a bill entitled "An act to provide for the regulation of freight and passenger rates on railroads in this State, and to create a commission to supervise the same, and for other purposes."[39] "Regulation" is the term used by most people today to describe the public administrative activity that had just been authorized. Leading up to and for a time after 1884, many latched on to the term "supervise." Those who favored such a bill were supervisionists or pro-supervision, while others were anti-supervision. The new law was said to be about setting up a commission to supervise intrastate commerce.

Massachusetts had enacted the first railroad regulation law of note. Charles Francis Adams (yes, *that* Adams family) inspired and successfully lobbied for what became known as the Sunshine Commission, a railroad regulatory statute passed in 1869. A board of three commissioners, including Adams, had no authority other than to make public reports and recommendations. Over a ten-year-period, the commission made important investigations and appeals to the public regarding railroad rates, safety, and a lone labor dispute.[40] Under Adams's leadership, the commission preferred policy making and persuasion over legal processes. Though hardly enough to satisfy some, history regards the Sunshine Commission as a success.

In the 1870s, the Granger movement[41] had swept through the northwestern farm states. Eschewing the "Sunshine Commission" approach, Grangers pressed for relief from railroad rates farmers thought harmfully high. Illinois, Iowa, Minnesota, and Wisconsin were the first to enact laws setting maximum rates that railroads could charge and establishing state agencies to regulate the railroads. In 1877, the US Supreme Court decided *Munn v. Illinois*[42] and recognized the practical and national constitutional principle of public regulation of private enterprises devoted to public use, including state regulation of rates. This was an important inroad into the practical political power and prerogatives the railroads had been acquiring and enjoying. States now saw opportunities and incentives to enact their own regulatory schemes. Mississippi was not alone. The overall result was a mixed bag.

Coming out of Reconstruction and through the 1880s, all of the states of the old Confederacy initiated some sort of railroad regulatory commission. These ranged in type from the Virginia commission of 1877, which resembled the Massachusetts experience and "only had advisory capacity and narrowly restricted jurisdiction, to the powerful Georgia commission of 1879, which had authority to fix and enforce uniform rates, prevent discrimination, and establish freight classifications."[43] Mississippi had templates—and a few legislative false starts of its own—to reflect upon before 1884.

In the latter part of the 1878 legislative session, state senator Frederick George Barry (1845–1909) had introduced a bill to declare "all railroads to be public highways and the companies common carriers, prohibiting discrimination and setting maximum rates for cotton."[44] Barry's bill died when Gov. John

Marshall Stone (1830–1900) exercised a pocket veto. At the next session, Stone sent a veto message, explaining that the new act was an impairment of the obligation of contracts contrary to the US Constitution.[45] The idea was simple. At least since 1819 charters granted to corporate and other legal entities had been taken as contracts between the issuing sovereign and the entity.[46] The constitution forbade the states from making laws that impaired the obligations of then existing and otherwise legally valid and enforceable contracts.[47] Some thought bills like Senator Barry's would impose terms, conditions, and restrictions on the railroads over and above the terms found in the charters the legislature had approved and granted. Such bills would take away business freedoms the railroads thought their birthrights.

In 1880, Senator W. W. Humphreys of Lowndes County introduced a bill that would put an end to railroads charging what were thought to be excessive and discriminatory rates.[48] Under Humphreys's bill, the legislature would have chosen a railroad commissioner to oversee enforcement of the proposed new law. The senate approved Humphreys's bill. The house debated it at length, but the bill died on the last day of the session. The legislature adopted a memorial to Congress appealing to that body to regulate freight rates on interstate railroads.[49]

ICRR president Stuyvesant Fish would later recall that "liberal charters were granted in 1882 and 1884" and that these "resulted in there being within the State in 1890, more than double the mileage which had been built in all the years preceding 1880, to wit, 2,471 miles."[50] Only 1,127 miles of track had been in use in 1880.[51]

During these times, the IC's line from Yazoo City to Jackson was completed. The first train arrived in Jackson with its locomotive proudly bearing the golden letters "Robert Lowry," no doubt to curry favor with the incumbent governor.[52] In 1884, the governor talked about railroad regulation in his annual message to the legislature.

> I do not doubt the jurisdiction of the State to protect her citizens from abuses committed by railroads, with reference to domestic or internal commerce, but whether it is competent for the State to regulate interstate commerce or such parts thereof as may directly affect her people, I regard as unsettled and doubtful.... I apprehend that evils might be so great as to justify the enactment of laws of doubtful constitutionality, in order to have them tested by the proper tribunals, for the purpose of obtaining relief by this means, if possible, where there is no other remedy, but when this course is adopted, there should be no doubt of or uncertainty as to the existence or gravity of the evils.[53]

The debate that followed was carried on in the press as well as the legislative chambers, and among the public at large. A Jackson newspaper wrote,

We assert without fear of contradiction that a majority of the people as well as the press of Mississippi are opposed to a railroad commission. If the politician would close his mouth on the subject the proposition would not be mentioned once in a month, except to be ridiculed.[54]

The *Vicksburg Evening Post* sarcastically commented,

A nice little supervision bill will no doubt soon be passed by the Legislature, and approved by the Governor, and then all hands connected with the business can go before the "dear people" and with satisfaction as to what "we" supervisionists have done. Speaker Inge will be at the head of the supervision procession.

The day before the railroad regulation bill received final passage, the *Post* added, "If the money that will be spent in maintaining the railroad commission was devoted to the building of school-houses and the improvement of public roads, the State would reap ten times more practical benefit."[55] The next day, Lowry signed the bill into law, but only after it had been amended to permit the governor to appoint the commissioners.[56]

THE NEW RAILROAD REGULATION LAW

The new Mississippi law had two main dimensions. One was substantive. State law would thenceforth and in practical effect regulate "freight and passenger rates on railroads in this state."[57] It spoke to two problem areas. Unilaterally, rates should be reasonable and just, both to the railroad and to the public whence came its customers. The legal effect of this was to codify the common law rule of reasonable rates. Bilaterally there should be no unjust discrimination in rates charged to different customers who were in relevant respects similarly situated, except, of course, for their bargaining power vis-à-vis the railroads. The practical problem was that there was no mathematical precision to be had on either front. Past that were the economic realities ranging from monopolies to competition that force-fed rate making, the best-laid strategies of regulators to the contrary notwithstanding.

This led to the second dimension of the act, which was administrative. The legislature created a three-person commission "to exercise a watchful and careful supervision over" the railroads in the assorted particulars otherwise set forth in the act.[58]

Sections 4 and 5 of the act made other customary provisions for the commissioners' qualifications and service.[59]

The new railroad supervision law[60] began with a general declaration of the public policy of the state: "the track of every railroad in this state is a public highway." As such "all persons have equal rights of transportation for passengers and freights on the payment of just compensation to the owner of the railroad for such transportation." The act then turned to the points of perceived abuse and set out general rules. Excessive rates *per se* included "more than the rate specified in any bill of lading." *Per quod* violations included the circumstance where any railroad "for his or its advantage, or for the advantage of any connecting line, or for any person or locality, shall make any discrimination, in transportation, against any individual, locality, or corporation." Any railroad that "shall exact, receive or demand" either form of unjust rate "shall be guilty of extortion."[61]

Civil and criminal penalties would be levied against any railroad engaged in such extortion. If an offended party sued within a short ninety-day time frame, he could recover double damages, viz., "twice the amount of damages sustained by the overcharge or discrimination."[62] In addition, the said-to-be-extorting railroad could be prosecuted for a misdemeanor and, upon conviction, fined "not less than ten nor more than five hundred dollars."[63]

But a railroad could easily avoid these civil or criminal hazards. All it had to do was submit "its passenger rates and schedule of freight charges to the railroad commission," have those rates and charges "approved by said commission," and then honor the rates and charges so approved.[64]

Section 6 provided the practical meat in the coconut. Each railroad had "to furnish the commission with its tariff of charges of transportation of every kind." The commission then had the job of determining "[1] whether or not, and in what particular, if any, said charges are more than just compensation for the services to be rendered, and [2] whether or not unjust discrimination is made in such tariff of charges."[65] The commission was enabled in its job by a later section that said the railroads had to "furnish the said commission with all information required relative to the management of their respective lines."[66] Of course, the commission did not have to take the railroad's word for anything. It had full power of independent inquiry.

Railroads should have been happy with what came next, in theory at least, assuming, of course, that they could learn to live with any regulation at all. To be just, a railroad's base rates would take into account "the character and nature of the service to be performed, and the entire business of such railroad, together with its earnings from passenger and other traffic." Past that, the railroad was to be allowed "a fair and just return on the value of such railroad, its appurtenances and equipment." The commission was told to watch "over every such tariff of charges, . . . as justice to the public and each of said railroad companies may require." All of this was stated at the highest level of practical generality, with neither the commission nor the railroad having a clue of what might be found "a fair and just return" beyond its own wits. Once the commission approved a tariff, the railroad had to submit to sunshine inspection. Quite sensibly, each railroad was told "to post at each of its depots all rates, schedules, and tariffs for the transportation of passengers and freights made or approved by ... [the] railroad commission, with ... [the] certificate of approval [that the commission had issued]."[67] Here sunshine inspection could and almost certainly would become a potent regulatory strategy. Aware that competitors would be making their tariffs public, no railroad would knowingly get too far out of line. Certain knowledge that the commissioners would be aware of rates approved for other railroads would have a constraining effect as well.

The legislative draftsmen expected commission-approved reasonable and nondiscriminatory rates to be the general practice. The legislature found as a matter of public policy, however, that several categories of rail service—for the transportation of persons or freight—should be eligible for preferred rates or, at the discretion of the railroad, service with no charge at all. These included rail transportation "free of charge, or at reduced rates, [1] for any religious, charitable or benevolent purpose, or [2] for any industrial exposition, fair, or association of a public nature, or [3] for transporting immigrants into this State, or persons prospecting with a view of locating or bringing immigrants into this State, or [4] for pleasure excursions."[68]

When a railroad had its tariff approved, it opted into a regulatory hearing process where customers or others might complain of unjust or discriminatory rates. The act called for adjudicative hearings "conforming to the mode of proceedings, as nearly as may be convenient, to that required of arbitrators."[69] Railroads no doubt thought this preferable to defending charges of unjust or discriminatory rates before a local jury.[70] Other parts of the act told the railroad to report all serious personal injuries resulting from railroad accidents, so that the commission might investigate.[71] Each railroad was required to have a comfortable and suitable reception room at each depot. If a passenger train were running late, the railroad had to post notice on the bulletin board in the depot, "stating as nearly as can be ascertained, the extent of the delay and probable time of arrival."[72] Assuming that regulation was inevitable, the act of March 11, 1884, all in all, was sensible enough. Of course, there remained the matter of how competently and fairly the commission would do its part.

As soon as the new law took effect,[73] Governor Lowry appointed the three commissioners. One was none other than John Marshall Stone, who had been governor from 1876 until 1882. Stone had a background in railroading, serving as a station agent for the Memphis and Charleston [South Carolina] Railroad at Iuka both before and after the Civil War.[74] W. B. Augustus of Noxubee County and William McWillie, son of Governor McWillie and a Madison County native, were the other two commissioners appointed for two-year terms. In 1886, McWillie, J. F. Sessions of Franklin County, and John C. Kyle of Panola County were named commissioners.

Historian C. Vann Woodward offered an insightful perspective to the effect that from 1876 to 1896 the governor's office in Mississippi was occupied

> by only two men—John M. Stone [1876–1882, 1890–1896] and Robert Lowry [1882–1890]. [A conservative businessman and a lawyer], both men resisted regulatory legislation and conformed to the Lamar[75]-Walthall[76] approach towards Northern capital and corporate interests in the seventies and eighties. Stone . . . was to prove more adaptable to the ground swell of agrarian sentiment. Governor Lowry, a former Whig, proved a consistent friend of factories, railroads, and textile mills in quest of tax exemptions and freedom from regulation.[77]

EIGHT LAWSUITS, NOT JUST ONE!

In short order, the state was off and running headlong into a new constitutional encounter. The enforceability of the new railroad supervision law was attacked immediately, on not just one front but eight. The Y&MV sued the commissioners in the Chancery Court of Madison County, Mississippi.[78] This was no surprise. The Natchez, Jackson and Columbus Railroad Company—commonly known as "Little J"[79]—brought a similar suit in Hinds County.[80] Chancellor E. G. Peyton[81] (1846–1889) presided in each of these neighboring counties. In June of 1884, the Canton, Aberdeen & Nashville Railroad[82] sued in Aberdeen in a courthouse closer to Yoknapatawpha County[83] and housing the Chancery Court of Monroe County, with Chancellor Baxter McFarland[84] presiding. But before that, five more railroads had sued in federal court in Jackson to stop the new commissioners from regulating the trains and tracks and tariffs.

The Farmers' Loan & Trust Company of New York sued on behalf of the Mobile & Ohio Railroad Company.[85] The ICRR struck separately, filing its own federal test case.[86] By April 4, 1884, the New Orleans & Northeastern Railroad Company[87] had moved against the new commissioners.[88] And so had the Vicksburg and Meridian Railroad Company.[89] On May 13, 1884, the Louisville & Nashville Railroad Co.[90] joined the federal fray.

JAMES FENTRESS, RAILROAD LAWYER

James Fentress (1837–1903) was a leading American railroad lawyer of the last quarter of the nineteenth century. He hailed from Rutherford County, Tennessee, and for most of his life made his home in Bolivar in the western part of the state, though he was said to have made New Orleans his winter headquarters.[91] In the end, he was buried near his home in Hardeman County, Tennessee.[92]

After the War and beginning in 1869, as a young and talented thirty-two-year-old lawyer, Fentress represented his county at the convention to draft a new Tennessee state constitution.[93] From 1870 to 1872, Fentress served his state as chancellor, presiding in the Tenth Chancery Court District that included Hardeman County. Thenceforth, he was "Judge Fentress" to many, though he returned to the private practice of law in late 1872. He had been on the bench long enough to earn the title for life, but not long enough to make many enemies. Chancellor was and remains that quintessential judicial office where one gets a 50 percent approval rating no matter what one does, there being no jury to blame for an unpopular decision.

In 1876, Fentress was appointed general solicitor for the Illinois Central Railroad, with extensive lobbying duties.[94] Judge Fentress's responsibilities and service extended to those IC-affiliated railroads, the Y&MV, the Canton, Aberdeen & Nashville Railroad, the Mississippi & Tennessee Railroad, the West & East Railroad, and the New Orleans Belt Line.[95] Indicative of his range of duties is a note that appeared in 1884 in a Vicksburg newspaper.

MEMPHIS, Nov. 8—James Fentress [and five others] to-day applied for a charter for the Memphis and New Orleans Railroad Company, for the purpose of constructing a railway from within the city of Memphis to a junction with the Yazoo and Mississippi Railroad [Y&MV] in the State of Mississippi, at the dividing line between the States of Mississippi and Tennessee, in a southerly direction from Memphis, and thus to form with the said Yazoo and Mississippi Railroad [Y&MV] and the Chicago, St. Louis and New Orleans Railroad a continuous line of Railway from the city of Memphis to New Orleans.[96]

More on this one below.

Over the years, Fentress became known for an above-board approach to lobbying, a reputation by no means shared by others engaged in the same field of endeavor. "Fentress drew a distinction between improper influence—bribery and illegal electioneering—which he labeled 'lobbying,' and proper efforts to prevent adverse legislation, namely, committee appearances and arguments before public officials." He was evidently one of the few railroad lawyers who "voiced some discomfort over any lobbying that did not take place in public view."[97] In 1882, he was responsible for governmental relations efforts in four states—Kentucky, Louisiana, Mississippi, and Tennessee—when the IC took over the New Orleans, Jackson & Great Northern Railroad and the Mississippi Central Railroad. An experienced Southern lawyer, Fentress understood that "the real work of lobbying took place before any legislative session ever convened, before the issues were hammered out in committee, in the summer, out of season, before making their way to the floor for a vote."

In one report to IC management in 1882, Fentress touched the tenor of his endeavors. He wrote, "I made another deal set at Jackson, Miss., with the Governor and Legislature as to the two new bills of adverse legislation that are pending ... unless the Governor violates his faith with me, he will veto any bill that is passed of that character."[98]

J. W. C. WATSON, FOR THE COMMISSION

John William Clark Watson (1808–1890) defended the Mississippi Railroad Commission in all challenges to its constitutionality in the middle 1880s. And he perfected and argued—and ultimately won—the appeals discussed below. Professionally known as Jno. W. C. or, often, just J. W. C., Watson was born in Albermarle County, Virginia. For many years he made his home in Holly Springs, Mississippi, where he also maintained his law office.[99] In 1857, Watson drew political encouragement that he seek the office of attorney general of Mississippi. According to a Hinds County newspaper, "everyone will recognise [Watson as] one of the ablest lawyers, purest minded gentlemen, and true hearted Americans in the State."[100] Despite such high praise, Watson declined the nomination,"[101] though he did serve as a Confederate States senator, 1864–1865.[102] After the War, he sought to limit the right to vote along racial and class lines, as did most other prominent whites at the time.

> No republic has ever existed in which there were not some disenfranchised classes. The most thorough Radical among us would not give the ballot to idiots, or to felons, or to minors, or to women—and the exclusion of any one of these classes is sufficient to prove my position.[103]

No fair turning to twenty-first-century values to judge whether Watson really was "one of the ... purest minded gentlemen, and true hearted Americans in the State."[104] In 1874, however, Watson drew fire for his outspoken opposition to the formation of a white man's political party.[105] He was a state circuit judge based in Marshall County from 1876 to 1882.[106] He is remembered as a venerated citizen in Holly Springs history, a Presbyterian elder of great probity.

In the Y&MV case in state court, and in the IC case in federal court, John Fentress was lead counsel for the railroad,[107] assisted by W. P. Harris.[108] And so they were when the Canton, Aberdeen & Nashville Railroad—also a part of the IC system—sued in state court up in Aberdeen to block the commissioners. In those days, Fentress appeared often before the US Supreme Court on behalf of the ICRR and its affiliated companies.[109] J. W. C. Watson appeared often as well in the high court in Washington in railroad cases and others.[110]

While the suits the Y&MV and others filed were hardly friendly, everyone knew at least one or two needed to happen. All saw the federal Commerce Clause as a potential obstacle. No one tried to pretend that the Y&MV did not provide interstate rail service from Memphis to New Orleans. The IC was already engaged in much longer routes. By their very names, the Mobile & Ohio, the Louisville & Nashville, the New Orleans & Northeastern, and the Canton, Aberdeen & Nashville contemplated and engaged in interstate rail service. The Vicksburg & Meridian Railroad planned east–west service to and from Alabama and in time would become the Alabama & Vicksburg Railroad. It would be hard to argue that interstate railroading was not at the root and core of each of the eight cases.

Which leads to another practical aspect of the lawsuits, a plus for the state and its commissioners in making their defense. In the spring of 1884, the railroad commission had not done anything to the Y&MV for which it might complain, at least not yet. And the same for the other seven railroads that had filed suit. In more modern phrasing, the railroads were attacking the constitutional enforceability of Mississippi's new law "on its face," and not "as applied." That gave the suing railroads a tougher row to hoe. To suggest that under the new law the commissioners might at some point in the future do something that might offend the railroad's rights—that the commission should then be enjoined—was not enough. Some judges today might say the cases failed for lack of ripeness.

The constitutional practice of judicial review had been around for a long time.[111] Leading up to 1884, the courts had shown no propensity even where there might be some problem to throw out the baby with the bathwater. Success on the Commerce Clause preemption argument would still leave the commission free to regulate intrastate railroading. The railroads needed to prevail on their impairment-of-contracts arguments, or one of their Fourteenth Amendment arguments, to show that the act was flawed altogether. The railroads needed to show that—if they continued their ordinary course of business—the day after the new law took effect, they were arguably at risk of substantial penalties.

TRIAL COURT INJUNCTIONS

We know that the three state cases all began in chancery court. Chancellor Peyton would hear the Y&MV and Little J cases. Chancellor McFarland would hear the suit brought by the Canton, Aberdeen & Nashville Railroad. We know it wasn't long after Governor Lowry signed the railroad regulation bill on March 11, 1884, that the five other railroads with lines in Mississippi had turned their quarrels into federal cases.[112] Six weeks after its effective date, the new railroad regulation law and its commissioners would begin taking a series of body blows from trial-level judges.

On April 24, 1884, Judge Hill[113] preliminarily enjoined the commissioners in the *Farmers' Loan* case—really about the M&O—citing the federal Contracts Clause and Commerce Clause.[114] In short order, Hill made a similar ruling in the ICRR suit.[115] In federal cases brought by the New Orleans & Northeastern Rail Company[116] and the Vicksburg & Meridian Railroad, Hill signed orders "at chambers in Aberdeen [Mississippi]" enjoining the commissioners from enforcing the new law. In the L&N's case, an injunction preliminarily restraining the commission from enforcing the new law was entered by US Circuit Judge Don A. Pardee.[117] In at least some of the federal cases, it appears that Judges Pardee and Hill heard the arguments together. A Vicksburg newspaper told its readers that "Judge Pardee is reported as saying that the arguments on the railroad injunction suits was [sic] the greatest feast of law and reason he ever enjoyed."[118] But all of this is getting ahead of the story.

Robert Andrews Hill[119] (1811–1900) had been a federal trial court judge in Mississippi for eighteen years when he found himself with five separate railroad litigants knocking on his door, asking for federal help. While the state had a northern district and a southern district for trial-level federal courts, one judge served the whole state in those days. Presumably, there wasn't enough business to justify a separate judge for each district. Hill hailed from North Carolina, had practiced law in Tennessee for many years, but had moved to northeast Mississippi before the Civil War. He had been a probate judge and a chancellor before President Andrew Johnson nominated him to become a federal district judge, being confirmed on May 1, 1866. Hill would serve as a federal trial court judge in Mississippi until 1891. He lived his later years in Oxford and was buried there.

We have noted above the filing formalities of the five federal cases. Farmers' Loan's interest was that the M&O

> being in need of money, had given a trust deed to ... [Farmers' Loan], as trustee therein, to secure certain bonds, upon which it had raised the needed funds for the purpose of discharging its other indebtedness, and for the better equipping and operating said railroad.[120]

M&O Annual Reports listed Farmers' Loan & Trust Co., N. Y., as Register of Stocks and Debentures. Historically, Farmers' Loan's status as a plaintiff may have put the case in federal court as one between parties from different states. That was no longer necessary, as in 1875 the Congress had created what is commonly called "federal question subject matter jurisdiction."[121] Based in New York, the Farmers' Loan & Trust Co. was often involved in litigation, most famously in 1895 when it was front and center in the case that struck down the federal income tax as unconstitutional,[122] leading ultimately to the Sixteenth Amendment. It was no surprise that in the railroad regulation case, Farmers' Loan was represented by John A. Campbell,[123] former US Supreme Court justice from the antebellum days, E. L. Russell, vice-president, director, and general solicitor of the M&O Railroad, and Peter Hamilton, a director of the M&O and a lawyer practicing in Mobile.[124]

Judge Hill treated the suit on behalf of the M&O Railroad as the lead case among the five filed in federal court. The first paragraph of his decision set the tone. The case presented "questions of grave importance to the people and the commercial interests of the country generally," and not just the particular parties to the case and those whose interests might "be affected by the result." Hill then struck the new Mississippi railroad regulation act at its core and declared the law "null and void." Hill said the new law impaired the charter, that is, the contract, between the state and the M&O. He also found that the new state law purported to regulate interstate commerce, though that authority had been granted exclusively to the US Congress. It is not clear how many at the time sensed the imminence of the exercise of this regulatory power, the Interstate Commerce Act being enacted in February of 1887 after the US Supreme Court had given the green light with the *Wabash* case decided in October of 1886.

Historically, the route from the Great Lakes and the Midwest south to New Orleans and the Gulf of Mexico was of great commercial importance, albeit theretofore shipping on the inland waterways had been the only practical avenue for such commerce. In the context of this history, Hill found that four states—Alabama, Mississippi, Tennessee, and Kentucky—had passed laws

> with a common purpose ... to construct, equip, and operate a railroad to extend from Mobile, in Alabama, to a point opposite Cairo, in the state of Illinois, at the junction of the Mississippi and Ohio Rivers, so as to connect the channels of commerce at each end of this line with all of those at intermediate points, thus creating a great national highway for the transportation of persons and property ... with other states and the markets of the world.[125]

Of course, Hill was right about this. He understood that the quite legitimate purpose of this railroading venture was to render a common carriage service that would prove acceptable to or at least tolerable by the rate-paying public, so that the M&O could earn profits and pay dividends to its shareholders, after, of course, staying current with its foremost creditor, the Farmers' Loan & Trust Company. Hill then turned to the question whether, given this a priori assumption,

> the charter would have been accepted, with the understanding that the legislature of any one of the states [Alabama, Mississippi, Tennessee, and Kentucky] could at pleasure place any restrictions or limitations upon the rights and powers conferred, and which were not reserved in the act of incorporation.

Maybe not, but was this really what had happened? Was the State really claiming that much of a blank check? Hill said it was, and that it was "clear that the legislature intended to give such power to the commission, and impose severe penalties upon the corporation and its officers for demanding or receiving different rates than those fixed by the commission, and for other violations of the act."[126] We saw above that the new Mississippi law was not so broad, particularly in section 6. And the railroad always had the fallback that "it may be shown in defense that such tariff so fixed was unjust."[127]

There was a greater flaw in Hill's Contracts Clause analysis, one he seemed utterly unable to see, though the opinion he authored makes it fairly clear. The State might well make a *Dartmouth College*–variety contract with a railroading entity. In doing this, however, the State did not thereby surrender its police power. The State was "not at liberty to part ... [with its authority or responsibility in] such matters as affect the public peace, public health, public morals, public convenience, and the like."[128] Entities such as the M&O Railroad "accepting corporate rights take them subject to this power on the part of the legislature." Reasonable and nondiscriminatory rates and charges for common carriage service—assuming such might be mathematically divined or at least approached—seem easily within the "public convenience" component of the police power. Yet Hill rejected the argument of the commissioners and ruled that the "right to fix the charges for compensation certainly does not fall within any police power of the states."

Judge Hill then turned to what, in time, some would call the dormant or negative Commerce Clause. The idea had been that, because the Congress had been given the authority to regulate commerce "among the several states," it followed that the states had no role. The states had been ousted from the field, or so some thought. In this setting, Hill said

> it is difficult to see how the right to fix and regulate charges for the transportation
> of persons and freight can be considered in any other light than a regulation of
> commerce, and that when a railroad passes through more states than one, and the
> transportation passes from one state to another, or through more than one state,
> it does constitute commerce among the states.

Fine, well, and good, but why did that oust the states, except where interstate commerce might be burdened significantly? Hill repeated his open-ended "one common purpose" and "great commercial highway of communication and transportation" theses.[129] He was right about these, only the practical and constitutional question before him was more subtle. Could not a competent and informed state railroad commission provide valuable regulatory or supervisory services without unreasonably burdening interstate commerce or the railroads that practiced such commerce? A supremacy clause is not necessarily an exclusivity clause, unless it says so in no uncertain terms. Remember, the Interstate Commerce Act was not yet on the books.

Nonetheless, sitting "In Equity," Judge Hill declared the new law null and void and enjoined former governor Stone and his two fellow railroad commissioners from enforcing it. He made the same ruling in the Illinois Central Railroad case, and on the same grounds.[130] The only noticeable difference in the two cases was that *ICRR* concerned a line from New Orleans, thence northerly to a point in Kentucky across the Ohio River from Cairo, Illinois, while in *Farmers' Loan*, concerning the M&O Railroad, the southerly end or beginning of the line was Mobile. Presumably, he also made the same ruling in favor of the New Orleans & Northeastern Railroad Company, though no opinion to that effect has been identified. At which point, in all three cases, J. W. C. Watson and Mississippi's railroad commissioners booked prompt passage to the US Supreme Court.

The *Clarion*, published in Jackson and calling itself the "Official Journal of the State of Mississippi," generally favored the railroad regulation law. Noting that Judge Hill's opinion in the *Illinois Central* case "has been published in many newspapers at home or abroad," on May 14, 1884, the *Clarion* published the *Farmers' Loan* opinion in its entirety.[131] The *Clarion* then set out a lengthy column, explaining why it thought the decision unfortunate, though speaking well of Judge Hill and making clear that "not one word of what we may utter shall be taken in any sense as a reflection upon his ability or his integrity."

Other judges were not treated so courteously. Before he had even ruled in the injunction suit brought by the Little J railroad, Chancellor Peyton was being second-guessed. Noting such criticisms, the *Brandon Republican* editorialized, "This thing of charging every man on the bench with being influenced by personal considerations in making his decision is unjust, and ought to be stopped. Chancellor Peyton is a Christian gentleman, and will decide the question according to his understanding of the law."[132] The *Clarion* followed with its own strong defense of the character, integrity, and ability of Chancellor Peyton. Noting that Judge Hill's decision had already been handed down, the writer concluded, "Whether Chancellor Peyton will be bound by the old time doctrines of the courts concerning corporations or whether he will put himself alongside of Chief Justice [Morrison] Waite [who authored *Munn v. Illinois* for the US Supreme Court] remains to be seen."[133]

Chancellor Peyton's Y&MV opinion enjoining the commission from implementing the new law was given wide publicity. The *Vicksburg Evening Post* declared that the chancellor's opinion was "a thoughtful and able document, with a clear, pure metallic ring, denoting a high order of legal talent coupled with a thorough knowledge of the subject matter under discussion."[134] The *Post* had published the opinion in its entirety the day before.[135] By May 23, 1884—a little over ten weeks after Mississippi's new supervisory law took effect—all demurrers filed by the commission had been overruled, and all injunctions against it had been made final. The Railroad Commission has lost all eight cases at the trial-court level.

In the wake of these rulings, a Vicksburg newspaper generally opposed to regulation—or supervision, as it was more often called at the time—offered its perspective: "State politics are becoming extremely dull and uninteresting. The unanimity and regularity with which the Courts are disinheriting the Railroad Commission is becoming monotonous."[136]

Again, J. W. C. Watson and his commissioner clients would live to fight another day—and turn the tables on appeal.

THE COMMISSION APPEALS

Three appeals were taken to the Supreme Court of Mississippi. The parties— the new state railroad commissioners proceeding affirmatively as the appellants and with the Y&MV, the CAN[137] and the Little J railroads responding as the appellees—argued about federal and state constitutions and what each said that mattered.[138] The commissioners grounded their arguments in the do's and don'ts of the state's legislative power. The state constitution had put the legislative power in a senate and a house of representatives.[139] A more particular dimension of that power—though still quite broad and general—was the so-called police power. The executive department necessarily played a big role in the State's exercise of its police power.

To begin with, the governor picked the three railroad commissioners. An even bigger role lay ahead once the commission might begin finding that this railroad or that was charging unjust or discriminatory rates, or in some other way was not playing by the new rules. There was no way around the fact that enforcing a penalty that the commission might impose, or a cease and desist order, would be an exercise of executive power. It was the governor's "duty to see that the laws are faithfully executed,"[140] but to what extent could he get help from others such as a railroad commission in doing so? As an agency charged to enforce the Act of March 11, 1884, the railroad commission was charged to exercise executive powers.[141]

From the standpoint of the Y&MV—and, as well, the Little J—three distinct constitutional premises were crucial. In no particular order, one was the by now familiar Commerce Clause preemption argument. The question became, to what extent—if any—the Congress had regulatory powers, say, if a freight ship-ment northbound from Vicksburg were delivered in northern DeSoto County, Mississippi, rather than being carried across the state line and on to Memphis? Had the states—in ratifying the US Constitution—ceded to the federal govern-ment whatever authority the states may have had to regulate commerce? *Munn v. Illinois,*[142] decided in 1877, seemed to have left the states with good-sized regulatory balls in their respective courts.

Second, the Y&MV and Little J had available to them the Contracts Clauses of the US Constitution[143] and of the Mississippi Constitution.[144] These have been noted.[145] Corporate charters legislatively granted to the Y&MV and to the Little J were regarded as contracts between the state and the entity, though in form these charters looked a lot like legislation. Beyond this, well prior to March 11, 1884, the railroads had many ongoing and recurring contracts with their customers, regarding rates and terms of service.

Conceptually, the Contracts Clauses trumped both the Commerce Clause and the state's legislative power. The state supreme court put forth its view that "The power to contract is an essential attribute of sovereignty.... The power to contract implies the power to make a valid contract."[146] When you think about it, the no-impairment injunction in the Contracts Clauses makes no sense unless people and firms are free to make contracts in the first place, contracts that are presumptively valid and enforceable. Governments cannot mess with such contracts, except to enforce them. So the question was, how did the Act of March 11, 1884, stack up against these notions?

This led to the third constitutional premise important to the railroads, that they might not be deprived of liberty or property, except by due process of law. Keep in mind that the liberty interests of a person or firm secured by textually identical clauses of the federal Fourteenth Amendment and the state constitution[147] included at some level a liberty to contract.[148] "Property" in each due process clause was broad enough to include rights under valid contracts. The railroads thought the new law—and the railroad commission's authority thereunder—would take from them liberty and property interests for public purposes—at least in part—without due process of law and without "due compensation."[149]

JOSIAH ADAMS PATTERSON CAMPBELL

Josiah A. P. Campbell[150] (1830–1917) was born in the Lancaster District of South Carolina. His father was a Princeton-educated Presbyterian minister. His equally learned mother was the daughter of a wealthy planter with lands along the Savannah River in the Abbeville District of South Carolina. In 1845, the Campbell family moved to Madison County, Mississippi. Josiah would become one of the state's dominant figures of the last quarter of the Nineteenth Century.

Campbell had already attended Davidson College in North Carolina before he was fifteen years old. By the time he was seventeen, he had been admitted to the bar. He first opened an office for the private practice of law in Kosciusko, Mississippi. At his first opportunity after turning twenty-one, Campbell sought and was elected to the state house of representatives. By age twenty-nine, he had become Speaker of the House. Two years later, Campbell represented Attala County at Mississippi's secession convention. In short order, he became the youngest delegate to the Confederate constitutional convention in Montgomery, Alabama. Then the War came. Campbell served in the Confederate cavalry, rising to the rank of colonel. He saw action at Iuka, Corinth, Grenada, and Vicksburg.

After the War, Campbell counseled a course of moderation and caution regarding the role of the former slaves, by then newly freedmen. He was critical of the "black codes" passed by the legislature in 1865, labeling them "foolish" and going "entirely too far" in the severe restrictions that they placed on the freedmen.[151] Campbell became a circuit judge in 1865 but soon had to relinquish the office as he would not take the oath required by the federal reconstruction acts. Off and on for the remainder of his life, Campbell made regular appearances on occasions where those who had fought for the Confederacy were honored, and when those who had fallen were remembered.

In 1871 and again in 1880, Campbell rendered invaluable state service of a less visible nature—outside the world of the legal professionals, that is—with two codifications of Mississippi law. First, he served as one of three commissioners who produced the Code of 1871. This code proved inadequate, and, besides, it was tainted by the post-1876 view of the Reconstruction times in which it was prepared. By early 1877, the federal forces had departed, and white Democrats had returned to political power in the southern states. In short order, the legislature engaged Campbell to produce a new and improved codification of state statutory law to be considered at the 1880 legislative session. This time he produced a formal structure with chapters and sections numbers, coupled with valuable notes and references to relevant case law under each particular section, and an index at the end.

Somewhat controversially, Campbell added a number of new provisions that went beyond merely organizing and regurgitating all legislative enactments to date. These enhancements were by and large in keeping with newly emerging views of legal scholars and public policy across the country. For example, he completed the emancipation of married women from what was left of the common law disabilities of coverture.[152] His new code abolished the rules of dower and curtesy which had provided life estates for spouses upon the death of the other. Formal estates by the entirety and joint tenancy were curtailed, with tenancy in common becoming the default rule of land titles without express provision otherwise. The law of fraudulent conveyances was clarified, elaborated and codified. The formalities of documents under seal were abolished, along with all distinctions between sealed and unsealed instruments, giving rise to an exchange with a former chief justice, evidence of Campbell's wry sense of humor.

Ephraim G. Peyton—the father of soon-to-be-chancellor E. G. Peyton—served on the Supreme Court from 1867 until 1876.[153] When he saw Campbell's proposed new code, he remonstrated vigorously that "you have ruthlessly destroyed all of the learning of a century on the subject of seals. I have spent many years of my life endeavoring to master the subject and now, Sir, you have thrown the fat in the fire." Campbell is said to have replied, "Judge, there is nothing in the world to prevent you from continuing your studies of the law of seals to the end of your life, and I trust your study of the subject will be interesting."[154]

According to one observer, the Code of 1880 "contains nearly two hundred sections written solely by Judge Campbell."[155] The code Campbell produced was enacted by the legislature with only a few minor revisions.[156]

Following the November 1876 elections, the term of carpetbagger Jonathan Tarbell on the Supreme Court of Mississippi expired, and Governor Stone appointed Josiah A. P. Campbell to fill the vacant seat.[157] Campbell would remain on the court for the next eighteen years, serving two stints as chief justice. In that capacity, he left lasting marks on Mississippi jurisprudence, authoring many important opinions, and participating in the decisions of many more. As we will see shortly, come the April term, 1885, Chief Justice Campbell would sit in judgment of the man who had appointed him. Stone had become the first chairman of the then newly created Mississippi Railroad Commission.

Before turning the page to the appellate chapter of this constitutional encounter, and all that it involved, note should be taken of one further Campbell extracurricular excursion. By the mid-1880s, and as the Mississippi Democrats settled into political power, ferment began for a new constitution, one primarily focused upon restricting the right of African Americans to vote. In 1888, Benjamin Harrison was elected President and the Republicans also took control of both houses of the Congress. Uncertain as to whether there might be a risk of restored federal protections on the franchise for African Americans, the state's political leaders decided it was time to do something, to take preventive action. Under the leadership of US Senator James Z. George, briefly a justice on the state supreme court,[158] a constitutional convention was called. Campbell wanted to be a part of the action. He offered creative ideas for assuring white supremacy at the ballot box, such as proposing a weighted voting scheme with landowners being entitled to an extra vote for each forty acres of land they owned.[159] As fate would have it, the sitting justice was defeated in his bid to become an at-large delegate. A split within the Democratic state committee caught Campbell with his politics not quite right and kept him on the sidelines. The new constitution replaced blatant intimidation of black voters with the in-time-infamous poll tax, plus a verbal test in state constitutional law. No person could be registered as a qualified elector until he was "able to read any section of the constitution of this state, or . . . be able to understand the same when read to him, or give a reasonable interpretation thereof."[160]

THE STATE SUPREME COURT UPHOLDS THE ACT

The three state trial court injunctions against the railroad regulatory act reached appellate ripeness before any of the five federal cases got to the US Supreme Court. On Monday, April 20, 1885, the Supreme Court of Mississippi and Chief Justice Campbell handed down their decisions in the three state cases. The Y&MV case[161] came first. It was the biggie. But Campbell's *Y&MV* opinion was in many ways a bafflement.

The chief justice began with the Commerce Clause. He looked at its simple text. The Congress has the power "to regulate commerce . . . among the several states."[162] From this Campbell asked, "How far is the State disabled . . . from governing railroads within its limits as to rates and freights?" But before answering that one, Campbell thought he first should take up a subsidiary question— "[W]hat is it to regulate commerce?"—a question to which he promptly and strangely answered, "Prescribing rates of compensation for service rendered by a railway company does not appear to us to be regulating commerce." As a matter of economic and practical reality, that can't be right. Should it not have been apparent—in 1885 as well as now—that state approval of prices and rates others must pay for a service would be a pretty good way of regulating the rendering of rail transportation service to the public, for good or ill? Federal Judge Hill had figured that one out a year earlier.

Mississippi could prospectively set rates that railroads could charge, so long as—and to the extent that—the state-issued charter did not say otherwise. This power then and now "belong[ed] to the sovereignty of the State and is essential to the regulation of its internal police." This is the point that Judge Hill had articulated twice, albeit apparently without sensing its implications. Campbell answered and insisted, "It is the sovereign power to govern the institutions of the State, and [that] is not regulating commerce."[163] This seems a non sequitur.[164] And on and on Campbell went, extolling with some grace and style that states have power to control what they have created,[165] in this instance, a company authorized to run a railroad. But was not the question at issue a bit more complex?

Remember, Campbell was considering the Commerce Clause argument that the Y&MV had advanced. Campbell agreed "[t]hat the State cannot, in regulating rates, or in any other manner, discriminate against persons or products of other States or countries." But what about effects that state regulation might have in other states? "It might be admitted that Congress could lawfully legislate on this matter to the extent necessary in its judgment to smooth the way of commerce carried on over railroads from State to State." At the time, however, "Congress has not attempted to regulate the charges to be made by railroad companies."[166] After much fluid prose, Campbell approached the core idea that "commerce among the different States must be free—not free from the cost of service, not to go without paying its way, but free from impositions on it the necessary effect of which is to hinder it."

The chief justice then rambled all over the countryside, following many a rabbit trail with little profit. There was an exception: "The railroad commission is not a restriction or hindrance of the freedom of commerce, but is intended to facilitate it and smooth its way by removing hindrances." A sage sentiment in a facial challenge to the act of March 11, 1884, and at a time when the commission had done nothing to hinder or help anyone. In the end, what Campbell said made sense. The state supreme court "held that the railroad commission cannot interfere with the rates fixed by the board of directors of . . . [Y&MV] from time to time for transporting persons and property over its railroad, if those rates are within the limits prescribed by the charter."[167] Fine, so far, and so long as we remember that the charter was the Y&MV's contract with the state. "[T]he commission cannot adopt any rule or regulation as to rates violative of the clearly expressed or necessarily implied charter rights of the . . . [Y&MV]." No problem there either.

On the other hand, the court held that "the commission may investigate the control and operation of the . . . [Y&MV] in order to ascertain that it is conforming to its authorization by the charter." The commission

> may do many things contemplated by the act creating it without any violation of the inviolable rights of the company. No reason is perceived why the company may not be required to submit its tariff of charges to the commission in order that it may see that it conforms to the limits fixed in the charter. So it may be said that the company has no right to make unjust discrimination or show partiality not authorized by its charter in transporting persons and things,. . . .

Other administrative jobs given the commission equally passed constitutional muster, such as investigating serious railroad accidents, making sure that the railroad publicly posted its rates, and that it had a suitable reception room at each depot.[168]

At the end of the day, the injunctions entered by the Chancery Courts of Madison County and of Monroe County were reversed. The Y&MV/CAN decision rejected the Commerce Clause attack on the act of March 11, 1884 and the "no impairment of contracts" argument advanced by the railroad, though the Contracts Clauses were never mentioned per se. And with sweeping generality, the court found no Fourteenth Amendment violation.

> We hold that the State had the right to create an agency of the State to exercise such supervision as it may lawfully employ over railroads within its limits and have declared the immunity from interferences secured to the . . . [Y&MV] by its charter, and this is all that is necessary to dispose of this case.[169]

"Within its limits" suggests Campbell understood that Mississippi could regulate only intrastate commerce, though he seemed a bit confused as to how that understanding should be applied.

The *Y&MV/CAN* case dealt with, Chief Justice Campbell turned his attention to the commissioners' similar appeal against the Little J railroad,[170] and with the same result. The Chancery Court of Hinds County—again acting through Chancellor Peyton—had also erred when it struck the new law. The legislature had used somewhat different wording in granting the Little J the power to set rates, tolls, and charges as compared with those granted the Y&MV. No maximums or minimums. In the context of the charter granted the Little J, Campbell said, "Annexed to every such grant [of the power to set rates] is the implied condition that the charges shall be reasonable." After all, "that is the limit of the right imposed by the common law."[171] He then added that "it is competent for the legislature to establish an agency to secure conformity by its creatures to the standard of reasonableness." All of this was within the police power as Judge Hill had articulated it back in 1884.

Campbell took note that railroad counsel had conceded "the right of judicial control to prevent extortion and unjust discrimination [in rates, tolls, and charges]." From this he reasoned that "if the State can control or supervise at all, it may select the agency through which to exert its right." "Power" may have been a better word than "right." To a large extent, no doubt so, but surely subject to the constitutional command for the interactive separation of the three great powers of all governments.[172] But Campbell then added a less-than-complete thought: "The final test of reasonableness of rates is not with the railroad commission, but . . . with the government through its judiciary."[173] What he left out were the implications of the rule of reasonableness, and proscribing unjust discrimination, both of which were common law rules. As such, the legislature—or even the courts for that matter—might alter or amend such rules, each acting within its lawmaking authority.[174]

In time, of course, the regulatory authority would be given considerable power to prescribe reasonable and just rates, subject to great deference on judicial review.

For the moment, what was important was the legislature's point in section 23 of the new law that in all rate cases "it may be shown [by the railroad] in defense that such tariff so fixed was unjust."[175] Chief Justice Campbell failed to see that the legislature might have the superior authority when it came to establishing rules regarding the rates that may be charged. The job of the judiciary was the same as in any other case, that of determining reliably what the law requires or permits, given the facts. But where an agency or commission had the primary jurisdiction, it followed that the judges' role required some deference, its focus being on whether it could be said that the agency or commission had failed to apply the law reliably to the facts it had found.

The press took note of these state supreme court decisions handed down in the spring of 1885. The *Raymond Gazette* offered a confusing analysis. Still, it realized that the final word had not been said. Federal appeals to the US Supreme Court remained pending.[176] "Let's all keep cool and wait for the final determination. Till then we can indulge in as much good natured speculation as to the result as we choose."[177]

A citizen from Tippah County made the practical case in a letter to the *Clarion*.

> The advocates of supervision simply want a committee to stand between the railroads and the people, to see that the interests of the latter are protected, while no injustice is done to the former. A poor man may have his stock injured or killed, and the railroad may refuse to pay for same, and he must either bear the loss or employ an attorney, and the fee of the latter may be more than the stock is worth.

The commission could investigate and adjust the matter, the writer continued,

> on the principles of equity, and thus maintain that good will that should subsist between the people and the railroads—each being dependent upon the other for patronage and prosperity.[178]

Six weeks later the discussion continued.

> Who believes for a moment that the railroads will remain silent and passive if the rates proposed by the commission do not suit them? They will fight the case from one court to another until the last tribunal has settled the law, and we can see no advantage gained by the people until a decision is reached which would settle what constituted reasonable rates.[179]

THE US SUPREME COURT HAS ITS SAY

The US Supreme Court followed Judge Hill's approach, treating *Farmers' Loan* brought on behalf of the Mobile & Ohio RR as the lead case. On January 4, 1886, Morrison Remick Waite (1816–1888), a Yale graduate who had practiced law in Toledo, Ohio, and was in his eleventh year as Chief Justice of the United States, opened with a "now settled" general premise

> that a state has the power to limit the amount of charges by railroad companies for the transportation of person or property within its own jurisdiction, unless restrained by some contract in the charter, or unless what is done amounts to a regulation of foreign or interstate commerce.

Then Waite spoke in the context of an even more general premise.

> The power of regulation is a power of government, continuing in its nature; and if it can be bargained away at all, it can only be by words of positive grant, or something which is in law equivalent. If there is reasonable doubt, it must be resolved in favor of the existence of the power.[180]

Still another premise seemed relevant to the chief justice. It was that a corporation's "rights and privileges in its business of transportation are just what those of a natural person would be under like circumstances; no more, no less. The natural person would be subject to legislative control as to the amount of his charges. So must the corporation be."

And so the question became whether the State had made a contract, surrendering its "power of control over fares and freights." By the words of the legislatively granted charter qua contract, the State had not so surrendered. "The argument concede[d] that the power of the company ... [remained] limited by the rule of the common law which requires all charges to be reasonable." What this amounted to was that

> all the power which the state had in the matter before the charter it retained afterwards. The power to charge being coupled with the condition that the charge shall be reasonable, the state is left free to act on the subject of reasonableness, within the limits of its general authority, as circumstances may require. The right to fix reasonable charges has been granted, but the power of declaring what shall be reasonable has not been surrendered.[181]

Eight and a half months earlier, the Supreme Court of Mississippi had decided *Y&MV*. Waite took note and explained that it presented no conflict with what he was saying in *Farmers' Loan* regarding the M&O Railroad. The reason was simple. In the charter qua contract at issue in *Y&MV*, "the power had been surrendered in favor of that company because in that charter a maximum of rates was fixed." This was still a general grant of corporate authority to fix rates that "is not a renunciation of the right of legislative control so as to secure reasonable rates. Such a grant evinces merely a purpose to confer power to exact compensation which shall be just and reasonable."

Still in the lofty and comfortable world of general and unquantifiable propositions—which are never enough to decide concrete cases reliably—Waite reassured one and all that "[t]his power to regulate is not a power to destroy, and limitation is not the equivalent of confiscation." Under the pretense of regulation or supervision, the state cannot "do that which in law amounts to a taking of private property for public use without just compensation, or without the due process of law."

Chief Justice Waite emphasized that the US Supreme Court had before it a facial attack on the constitutionality of Mississippi's new railroad regulation act, not an "as applied" challenge. He concluded, "What would have this [unconstitutional] effect we need not now say, because no tariff has yet been filed with the commission, and the statute of Mississippi expressly provides 'that in all trials of cases brought for a violation of any tariff of charges, as fixed by the commission, it may be shown in defense that such tariff so fixed is unjust.'"[182]

Waite then turned to Judge Hill's "one common purpose" and "great commercial highway of communication and transportation" theses. However valid these may be, they did not preclude the state's interests and authority regarding intrastate activities. The State

> may certainly require the company to fence so much of its road as lies within the state, to stop its trains at railroad crossings; to slacken speed while running in a crowded thoroughfare; to post its tariffs and time-tables at proper places; and other things of a kindred character affecting the comfort, the convenience or the safety of those who are entitled to look to the state for protection against the wrongful or negligent conduct of others.

Wisely, Waite added in this part of his opinion,

> Precisely all that may be done, or all that may not be done, is not easy to say in advance. The line between the exclusive power of congress and the general powers of the state in this particular is not everywhere distinctly marked, and it is always easier to determine when a case arises whether it falls on one side or the other, than to settle in advance the boundary, so that it may be in all respects strictly accurate. As yet the commissioners have done nothing.

Past this, the chief justice brushed off the remaining points that had been briefed and argued on grounds they could not be decided on a facial challenge to the new Mississippi railroad regulatory law.[183]

When the sun set on January 4, 1886, all federal suits filed challenging the act of March 1884, and the Mississippi Railroad Commission, had been dismissed.[184] The railroads' strident attacks had been rebuffed, at least until the state or the commission did something that provided a more concrete concern. On that day, Morrison Waite had spoken for six—sometimes seven—of the justices.[185] John Marshall Harlan filed the lone written dissenting opinion.[186] In short order, *Stone v. Illinois Central RR Co.*[187] and *Stone v. New Orleans & Northeastern RR Co.*[188] also upheld the state statute, reversing Judge Hill's decisions at the trial-court level. And with that, Judge Hill's decree was "reversed, and the cause remanded, with instructions to dismiss the bill."[189] In these cases, Justice Stephen J. Field joined Harlan in dissent.[190] Justice Samuel Blatchford took no part.

Two days later, the *Vicksburg Evening Post* added two cents worth of perspective.

> We do not think the Railroad Supervisionists will find much encouragement or comfort in the decision. The Railroad Commissioners of this state have done nothing as yet, except draw their salaries, and the Supreme Court says, "when the Commission has acted and proceedings are had to enforce what they have done, questions may arise as to the validity of some of the various provisions which will be worthy of consideration."[191]

Then and now, though a facial challenge to a statute may fail, this in no way precluded an "as applied" challenge when the regulators really did something that arguably infringed a particular right that a person or firm might enjoy under the constitution.

A *WABASH* CANNONBALL

A little over nine months later, the US Supreme Court announced a broader perspective. The case was *Wabash, St. Louis & Pacific RR Co. v. Illinois.*[192] It had been argued at the same term as the Mississippi federal cases discussed above. *Wabash* was an unjust-discrimination case. The railroad charged one shipper fifteen cents per hundred pounds of cargo for carriage from New York City to Peoria, Illinois, while another shipper had been charged twenty-five cents per hundred pounds for shipping goods from New York to Gilman, Illinois. An Illinois statute imposed a heavy penalty for such discriminatory pricing. Fine, well, and good, so long as the shipment was from one point to another always in Illinois. But this discriminatory rate making arose in the context of commerce among several states between New York and Illinois. The facts in *Wabash* fell within Chief Justice Waite's earlier exception, viz., "unless what is done amounts to a regulation of foreign or interstate commerce."[193]

In *Wabash*, the court split six to three and spoke through Justice Samuel F. Miller, who had served since Abraham Lincoln appointed him in 1862. Five other justices joined the view Harlan had taken back on January 4, 1886. Not only did *Wabash* hold the facts to present a case within the Commerce Clause, such circumstances "show[ed] the value of the constitutional provision which confide[d] the power of regulating interstate commerce to the congress of the United States, whose enlarged view of the interests of all states, and of the railroads concerned, better fit[] it to establish just and equitable rules.[194] Thenceforth, hauling freight over railroad lines from points in one state to other points in another state was interstate commerce. No more artificial dissections into one after another intrastate segment of what in practical reality and as a whole was a multistate long haul. Regulating the rates of those shipments was a regulation of commerce among the several states, an authority reserved for the US Congress. Justices Field, Harlan, Blatchford, William B. Woods, and Stanley Matthews joined Miller's majority opinion, finding regulatory teeth in the Commerce Clause. Justice Joseph P. Bradley filed a dissenting opinion. Chief Justice Waite, who had spoken for the court in *Farmers' Loan, Illinois Central,* and *New Orleans & Northeastern,* joined in the dissent, as did Horace Gray. Because Miller, Woods, and Matthews took a different view from that they joined on January 4, 1886, plus the fact that Justice Blatchford participated, joining the majority, the railroad regulatory world was enriched and enlightened. Congress took the cue and promptly passed the Interstate Commerce Act, which President Grover Cleveland signed into law on February 4, 1887.[195]

Of interest, two of the justices who in the end stood in favor of the Commerce Clause preemption argument were from states immediately affected by the Mississippi cases decided a few months earlier. Harlan from Kentucky had been of this view all along. Woods from Alabama switched from the view he had taken back in January of 1886. We may never know whether both or one was thinking of railroad regulation in his home state when he helped cast the die in October of 1886. At the end of the day, the view that Judge Robert A. Hill had accepted back in April of 1884 had been vindicated, his somewhat exaggerated suggestions of what the states were up to notwithstanding. One might even go so far as to say that Mississippi's lone federal trial court judge had been more articulate to the point—in *Farmers' Loan* and in *Illinois Central*—than the seventy-year-old and twenty-four-year judicial veteran Justice Samuel Miller had been in *Wabash.* The lesson for railroad lawyers who had pleaded so arduously for federal preemption under the Commerce Clause was the eternal "be ever so careful for what you ask, lest in the end your client be hoist with his own petard."

In short order, the new regime had become settled. By November of 1887, Attorney General T. Marshall Miller could advise the Mississippi Railroad Commission as to intrastate railroading,

> I would say that the decision of the Supreme Court in *Stone v. Y&MV* may be considered as fully settling the principle in Mississippi that where in the charter of incorporation of any railroad company the right is given to the company to fix rates for transportation of persons or property within *stated* or *maximum* limits, a contra rule which may not be impaired by subsequent legislation. In other words, the tariffs adopted in the pursuance of such a charter are not subject to alteration by the Legislature or the Railroad Commission under its authority.[197]

Miller followed with quotes from the opinion: "When the commission has acted, and proceedings are had to enforce what it has done, questions may arise as to the validity of some of the various provisions worthy of consideration, but we are unable to say that, as a whole, the statute is invalid."[198]

RAILROAD SAFETY IN PERSPECTIVE

The nature, mechanics, and practical utility of the iron horse have always suggested a wide variety of safety concerns. There was the "Revere disaster" in the summer or 1871 near a popular beach resort not far from Boston. Twenty-seven died, fifty-seven were seriously injured, in what proved a defining moment for Charles Francis Adams's Sunshine Commission.[199] We have seen matters involving the danger to livestock along the tracks.[200] The Canton, Aberdeen & Nashville Railroad was defending just such a case before the state supreme court only a few months after the Y&MV and Little J cases were decided.[201] Crossing accidents involving travelers were common, though the automobile was of no concernin the mid-1880s. Steam combustion carried its own inherent risks.

The eight-case assault on Mississippi's first regulatory act of March 11, 1884, at its core was the railroads' across-the-board plea to be left alone. The war was mainly about rates. In time, the parties went to war over taxes.[202] Safety issues were at best a third-order concern, and even those often focused upon damage to freight or cargo,[203] or damage to property adjoining a railroad track.[204] The common law was regulation enough. The law of torts addressed harms suffered by people, their livestock, and less animate personal property in their assorted encounters with the locomotives and their trains. The common law of employer and employee extended a wide variety of protections to the railroads vis-à-vis their hired hands.

The Mississippi act of 1884 had but a single section that said anything about safety, and it did not say much. Coverage was triggered by "the occur-rence of any accident to a train attended with serious personal injury." Presumably "personal injury" included injuries to persons, be they passengers on the train, railroad workers, or third persons seriously injured by a force much more powerful than themselves. Given the tenor of the times, it would have been easy to see cynically the legislature's foremost concern as "any acci-dent to a train," the "serious personal injury" being an attendant or second-order consideration. But that's not necessary, since that part of the new state law had no teeth anyway. All that was required was that the railroad notify the commission within twenty-four hours. The commission would "dispatch one or more of their number to the scene of said accident, [who would then] inquire into facts and circumstances thereof."[205] Upon such inquiry, the only step the commissioners were told to take was to record what they learned "in their annual report." This was tantamount to Charles Francis Adams's sun-shine approach dating back to 1871.

Accidents and carnage increased as the railroads ascended as fixtures on the American landscape. In 1890, Mississippi convened a constitutional convention to address and restrict the voting rights of African Americans. It could not ignore the railroads and their regulation. Foremost, the new constitution said what the public already knew, that "[a]ll railroads which carry persons or property for hire shall be public highways, and all railroad companies so engaged shall be common carriers."[206] This was a time when railroad lobbyists were among the most powerful in the country. The constitutional draftsmen applied brakes: "No railroad or other transportation company shall grant free passes or tickets, or passes or tickets at a discount, to members of the Legislature, or any State, district, county, or municipal officers, except railroad commissioners."[207] In other words, railroad lobbyists could not bribe state officials except the ones who most directly regulated them, the railroad commissioners themselves. Presumably, this was justified by the commissioners' need to ride the trains in the discharge of their regulatory duties, or something of the sort. Even so, putting this clause in the new 1890 constitution was a move toward a better regard for the public vis-à-vis the all-powerful railroads. Regarding the safety of railroad workers, the new constitution took the extraordinary step of eliminating the common law "fellow servant rule," which had allowed employers to escape liability for workplace injuries where blame for the accident could be pinned on a co-worker.[208]

James J. Hill may have been the greatest railroad man of the North, unless it was Ned Harriman. R. T. Wilson remembered his southern roots and played his part in Mississippi. To learn of these and other railroad tycoons, you had to go to books or, more recently, the Internet. None of these worthies had their tales told in a ragtime ballad sung by an admiring African American who had no formal musical training, only a banjo. Wallace Saunders, an engine wiper for the Illinois Central Railroad, made Casey Jones[209] the mightiest locomotive engineer for a century of Americans. The modest Casey Jones Railroad Museum State Park at Vaughan, Mississippi,[210] stood as testament to bravery and daring and heroism and legend until 2004, when the state and its younger generation lost interest in favor of more pedestrian priorities. In early 2018, a Casey Jones Railroad Museum remained in Water Valley, Mississippi, open three afternoons a week.[211] The tragic and yet heroic saga of Casey Jones remains a part of this constitutional encounter. Railroads have always posed dangers, and in so many ways and contexts. Crossing accidents are likely with us for the duration. If anything, safety regulation is more complex than ever, given the federal–state constitutional interactions via a plethora of federal statutes and regulations and federal preemption jurisprudence.[212] Constitutionally, the states may "regulate railroad safety" only "when there is, as yet, no federal standard, or when the state is seeking to eliminate an essentially local hazard."[213]

Casey wasn't even John Luther Jones's (1864–1900) real name. His growing-up hometown was Cayce, Kentucky, which people pronounced "Casey." The only other facts everyone agrees on were his trademark whistle[214]—a long, drawn-out note that rose and rose as his locomotive-drawn train approached but then faded away slowly, "a sort of whippoorwill call"—and that he died when the "Cannonball Express," a passenger train en route from Memphis headed to Canton, Mississippi, plowed into a stalled caboose and freight cars at Vaughan on April 30, 1900, at 3:52 a.m.[215] Most—including Sim Webb, his African American fireman that Jones forced to jump from the engine moments before the crash—said his quick thinking and engineering savvy saved lots of lives and limbs. Some even said his body was found with one hand holding the warning whistle cord and the other tightly holding the brake lever.

When it came to his job and his boss, the ICRR, John Luther Jones was loyal to a fault. He was proud of his reputation as an engineer that would "get her there on the advertised"—the time the written schedule said the train would arrive—and that he would never "fall down"—bring his train in late. While he was said to have had these compulsions as a man, and was a known risk taker, Jones well understood that there was no job performance criterion more important to the ICRR than for its trains to run on time. On that fateful April night, Jones was a substitute engineer. That his train, the Cannonball Express, was seventy-five minutes late leaving Memphis headed for Canton, Mississippi, was no fault of his, nor a deterrent. At speeds up to 100 miles per hour, Jones had caught up to the point where the Express was only two minutes behind schedule. As fate would have it, Jones then hit Vaughan, eternity, and a reputation ranging between the heroic and a mere legendary role model for young American boys.

We know that Jones and the Cannonball descended on a long curve approaching the station. He knew that there were other trains in the area, but they were supposed to get out of the way. Jones and the Cannonball Express had the right-of-way. Those on the ground in Vaughan knew Jones was coming. The story goes that "an air hose broke on [train] No. 72, locking its brakes and leaving the last four cars of No. 83 on the main line." Jones reversed the throttle and slammed the airbrakes into emergency stop, but his engine still plowed through a wooden caboose, a carload of hay, another of corn, and halfway through a car of timber before leaving the track.

None of this, of course, stopped the ICRR from throwing Jones under the train. The railroad never deviated from its report filed five hours after the accident that "Engineer on No. 1 failed to answer flagman who was out proper distance. It is supposed he did not see the flag." If it complied with Section 13 of the act of 1884, presumably the ICRR reported possibly serious personal injuries as including

- Simon T. Webb, Fireman Train No. 1, body bruises jumping off Engine 382
- Mrs. W. E. Breaux, passenger, 1472 Rocheblave Street, New Orleans, slight bruises
- Mrs. Wm. Deto, passenger, 25 E. 33rd St., Chicago, slight bruises left knee/left hand
- Wm. Miller, Express Messenger, injuries to back and left side, apparently slight
- W. L. Whiteside, Postal Clerk, jarred
- R. A. Ford, Postal Clerk, jarred
- John Luther Jones, engineer, deceased.[216]

The headline the next day was "HEROIC ENGINEER, STICKS TO HIS POST AT COST OF LIFE. Railroad Wreck at Vaughan, on Illinois Central Railroad— Terrible Fatality Prevented by Engineer's Loyalty to Duty—A Passenger's Story."[217] A decade later a nation was singing "Come all you rounders, if you want to hear / A story about a brave engineer." The *St. Louis Post-Dispatch* had discovered and published the story of "The Ballad of Casey Jones" with a carica-ture of banjo-playing Wallace Saunders, who idolized him, and a lengthy bold-face headline reading "*His Nickname was 'Cay-ce,' His Home Was Jackson, Tenn., and the Admiration of an Old Darky Locomotive Oiler was the Foundation of the Song which Has Made Him Known Everywhere.*"[218] In time this song would be recorded by Mississippi John Hurt, Pete Seeger, Johnny Cash, Billy Murray, and Furry Lewis, and played live by The Grateful Dead.[219]

More recently, the Illinois Central Historical Society posted a list of mile-stones in the company's history. Among these is found a rather wooden entry.

> In 1900 a minor train wreck at Vaughn [*sic*], Mississippi, achieved world wide fame because an engine-wiper Wallace Sanders [*sic*] wrote [it is doubtful Saun-ders could write much of anything, music or otherwise] a song about the incident. The only person killed was one John Luther Jones, nicknamed "Casey."[220]

No mention is made that Jones was the engineer, much less The Heroic Engineer. Nor, for that matter, is mention made of Arlo Guthrie's still-performed version of Steve Goodman's chords and lyrics inspired by the ICRR's personified *City of New Orleans*: "Good morning, America, how are you? Don't you know me? I'm your native son."[221]

REFLECTIONS

We have seen that on March 11, 1884, Mississippi joined the growing list of states moving to regulate and supervise railroads, regarding the reasonableness of their rates, nondiscrimination in rates, and other aspects of the services they offered to the public. Not only that, rate fairness toward largely captive customers—similarly situated—seemed like a good idea, crucial, given the practical monopoly powers possessed by the railroads. And so Governor Lowry had signed into law an act to regulate railroading and create a state-level supervisory commission. In short order, eight railroad companies took exception. They sued in federal and state courts. They were fighting for what they saw as their fundamental economic liberties. That twenty-two-month-long constitutional encounter is worthy of study and reflection for what its history may teach us. Its comparative precedents in other states, and postmortems for the future of the regulatory state going forward, are instructive as well.

These eight railroads argued that the new law impaired contracts in the forms of their corporate charters and contracts with their shipping customers, contrary to the contracts clauses of both federal and state constitutions. Charges were also made that the State was taking the property of the railroads without due process of law and, in any event, without due compensation. Ephemeral equal protection claims were made by some. To the extent that the railroads provided common carriage services across state lines, the State of Mississippi faced—and largely lost—the charge that it had invaded the prerogatives of the federal Congress to regulate commerce among the several states.

At its April term, 1885, the Supreme Court of Mississippi rebuffed three facial challenges to constitutional enforceability of the state's first regulatory law and agency. On January 4, 1886, the US Supreme Court decided three federal cases that confirmed the state court view, vacating injunctions that a trial-level federal court back in Mississippi had entered, restraining the commissioners. The honeymoon was a short one. Of course, the territorial and political scope of that new state law and commission was swiftly limited to railroading activity beginning and ending within Mississippi, or regarding essentially local hazards.[222] The US Supreme Court saw to that with its October 1886 decision in the *Wabash* case. Still the State's police power had gained traction.

In the wake of all of this, the Constitution of 1890 provided that

> [t]he Legislature shall pass laws to prevent abuses, unjust discrimination, and extortion, in all charges of . . . sleeping-car . . . and railroad companies, and shall enact laws for the supervision of railroads, . . . sleeping-car companies, and other common carriers in this State, by commission or otherwise, and shall provide adequate penalties, to the extent, if necessary, for that purpose, of forfeiture of their franchises.[223]

A further section decreed that "the exercise of the police powers of the State shall never be abridged."[224]

For reasons known mostly to unrecorded history, none of the early courts addressed the constitutional authority of the legislature to create regulatory agencies, boards, and commissions in the first place. Or the authority to empower these regulatory entities to exercise some or all of the three great political powers—legislative power through rule-making, judicial power through administrative adjudications, and executive power through licensing, requiring periodic reports and enforcing penalties. In its *Farmers' Loan* decision in early 1886, the US Supreme Court said one of the questions presented was whether Mississippi's new railroad law of March 1884 "confer[red] both legislative and judicial powers on the commission, and is thus repugnant to the constitution of Mississippi."[225] No further mention of this state constitutional law point was made. In time, delegation issues became quite controversial and vexing, at both state and federal levels, but that matter was for another and later day.

One teaching is clear. The seeds of state administrative and regulatory law in Mississippi were planted in 1884. These seeds germinated and generated roots and stems that broke dirt and grew branches that have spread outward and upward and have survived and still grow. Most of the massive Mississippi Code today provides statutory regulatory law of one form or another. The fullest extent of this emergence is set out in Judge Leslie Southwick's periodically updated exposition on state administrative law.[226] The railroad commission itself can be seen as a forerunner of what is now the Mississippi Public Service Commission.[227]

Over the years, regulation itself became controversial on grounds economic and practical, as well as on grounds that have seemed ideological and political and legal. Laissez-faire economics still had many adherents in the latter part of the nineteenth century and the early decades of the twentieth century. Fast-forward, and in 1936, Chief Justice Sydney Smith would report that laissez-faire had become "an anachronism in a state that exists to make life good, and which the American states have already partially abandoned."[228] Yet we have never seen the time when there were not some who found eternal truths in laissez-faire and thought regulation as a damnable evil, and a time-tested and proven failure as well. Other more sober observers, however, have come to sense that important markets are often less than perfect, some less so than others, and that many have built-in and quite problematic imperfections. Arguably, some markets would experience outright failure without regulatory support. Corporations and other businesses fail because of poor management, bad business judgments, bad luck, or sometimes just "on account of the economy," as Bruce Springsteen understood and once articulated.[229] One need look no further than the assorted Mississippi forays made into the business of railroading prior to the Civil War—a case study no less in market failure and, in particular, exposing inadequacies in a laissez-faire approach as the engine of economic complexity fostered by the Industrial Revolution.

In response to cries in some quarters, political forces moved to require that the economic impact of regulation be studied and exposed.[230] This came a century after Holmes warned of the "futility of arguments on economics questions by anyone whose memory is not stored with economic facts."[231] Not surprisingly, it has come to be seen that an economic impact statement has its own costs, risks, imperfections, and other impacts, not to mention the practical problem of generating useful data and stratagems that approach being worth as much as they cost.[232] The notion of transaction costs is easy enough to grasp. Bringing that understanding to bear in real-world circumstances—and with net bene-fit—has confounded the best of us.

As Mississippi—and, indeed, the nation—entered the last decade of the nine-teenth century, there could be no *reasonable* doubt but that some regulation was imperative for common carriers such as railroads, and for banks and other financial institutions as well, in time, for the protection of natural resources and other national treasures, and in many other contexts. The politics of the day, though, leading to the dawn of the twentieth century had not evolved to the point where some of the problems holding over from the foibles of the Age of Jackson could be effectively redressed. Step back for a broader view. Creative destruction over the history of common carriage in this country is apparent to those with eyes to see and brains with which to think. Regulators need these big-picture understandings. The rest of us need to be force-fed them, particu-larly when we are about to enter the voting booth.

Practical concerns with regulation emerged as Mississippi eased into the regu-latory state, well behind the federal government and most of the states as well. Competent and intelligent regulation was one thing, incompetent and misguided regulation quite another. One major goal of the Interstate Commerce Act of 1887 was removing politics from the regulation of railroads. Easier said than done, and at all levels. And besides, regulation impacts people's lives. Should they not have a say-so? Yes, but can there be any doubt that mastering the socioeconomics of the surface transportation business was and remains beyond the ken of the aver-age citizen, and beyond the ken of most all of those who might come to office in our representative democracy? Not to mention that the rail traveler's only real concerns have long been and remain reasonable rates and that the trains run on time. Casey Jones! Finding, recruiting, and retaining experts for regulatory responsibilities has been hard enough. Whether the actions of those regulatory experts should receive any special deference became a chicken-and-egg proposi-tion, ultimately to be resolved in favor of deference—at least in theory.

There is another takeaway so simple that you might miss it. It is founded on the familiar truism that information is power. Chief Justice Campbell saw noth-ing wrong with having a commission to keep tabs on how the railroads were doing, whether they were staying in line with what their charters authorized and what they did not authorize, and the applicable rules of the common law. And later what the constitution, statutes, and regulations did or did not autho-rize or require. Of course, there were—and still are—times when proprietary information received from regulated firms should be kept under wraps. Yet it is hard to imagine an organized society functioning without the information the regulatory agencies gather and make available to people as well as policy makers. As we plunge well into the twenty-first century, few insights are more imperative than that in regulation information and informed ideas simply must be allowed to trump ideology and politics. Science and technology must be allowed to trump the isms of the times, and religion as well, except at the level of personal free exercise. Yet we must not live in the moment. Efforts to maximize the size of the socioeconomic pie, while at once providing for an optimally fair division in the current moment, must never be allowed to trump the needs and interests of generations unborn.

Mississippi-born, Ole Miss–bred business historian Thomas K. McCraw found his pulpit at Harvard. In the mid-1980s, amidst fervent belief in the failure of regulation, McCraw saw that "regulators should always exploit the natural incentives of regulated interests to serve particular goals that the regulators themselves have carefully defined in advance." Labeling this the theory of public use of private interest, McGraw cautioned that "the historical record suggests that regulation in America has succeeded best when it has respected these incentives instead of ignoring them; when it has based its strategies less on some idealized vision of that the economy should do and more on a clear understanding of what the economy is actually doing."[233]

"Bureaucracy is not an obstacle to democracy but an inevitable complement to it," is not the only lesson Joseph Schumpeter taught us that we would do well to keep in mind.[234] Yet there is a sense in which nostalgia for another time should be valued, cherished. No nostalgic reflections about the railroads and Mississippi are more real—and more reflective about our humanity—than the oral and recorded memories and stories told by those who lived in a time when the largest and mightiest man-made object many had ever seen was a locomotive, truly a gigantic iron horse. For more than a century the railroad was not just a common carrier of freight of every imaginable species. Nor just as a provider of an elegant and efficient means of travel. It was about people and their energetic and awe-struck views of their country. And in time about the generation of youngsters who headed each annual letter to Santa Claus with a fervent plea for an electric train—Lionel, not Gilbert—then additional tracks, more cars, augmenting appurtenances, year after year, until reaching the age when another form of romance became interesting.

There was a time when practically everyone down here had ridden on the railroad, had waited at the station to meet a friend or loved one coming in from St. Louis or maybe just Clarksdale. How many thousands of parents have taken their children to Chicago for that one last ride on the train before passenger service (outside the Northeast corridor) shuts down completely, and experienced the awe of that increasingly lonely cathedral called Union Station? Of course, we enjoy the bike paths along beds from which the rails have been so unceremoniously ripped. Many a train station is now a restaurant still holding a touch of the ambiance of the past. The museums are nice, though they seem to attract fewer visitors each year. As time goes by.

Many have written nostalgia pieces about the trains and their heyday. Noel Workman's reminiscence in *Delta Magazine* a few years back may not be the best, but maybe it is.[235] It's good enough to make old timers remember the romance and humanity and wonder of very special moments that so many thousands experienced, a time they thought would never end.

ENDNOTES

1. See Miss. Laws, ch. DXLI [541] (Feb. 17, 1882), "AN ACT incorporating the Yazoo and Mississippi Valley Railroad Company, and declaring its powers."

2. See *Map of the Yazoo-Mississippi Valley*, in Robert L. Brandfon, *Cotton Kingdom of the New South* 84 (1967).

3. See *Railroad Commissioners Map of Mississippi*, 1888, www.history-map.com; also http://www.railroads.com/images/Y&MV_Map-1.jpg.

4. C. B. (Buddie) Newman, in *Mississippi Encyclopedia* 932–933 (Ownby and Wilson, eds., 2017). Newman was Speaker of the Mississippi House of Representatives from 1976 to 1988. He lived in Valley Park in Issaquena County.

5. "The Yazoo & Mississippi Valley Railroad, The Issaquena Genealogy & History Project," http://www.rootsweb.ancestry.com/~msissaq2/railroad/

6. "Where the Southern Cross the Dog," http://www.mrjumbo.com/contents/delta99/3delta/moorhead.hmtl; "Where the Southern Crosses the Dog," http://www.msbluestrail.org/blues-trail-markers/where-the-southern-crosses-the-dog; *see also Mississippi Railroad Heritage: Men & Iron—Steam & Diesel* 138, 352 (Sharron Daniel Cauthen comp., 2006). See "Blues" in *Mississippi Encyclopedia* 112 (Ownby and Wilson eds., 2017); "Southern Cross the Dog," in *Mississippi Encyclopedia*, 979, 1056, 1180, 1205 (Ownby and Wilson eds., 2017).

7. *See, e.g., Pearson v. Columbus and Greenville Railway Company*, 737 So.2d 390, 392 (¶5) (Miss. App. 1998).

8. The story of the Illinois Central is told in full by Carlton J. Corliss in *Main Line of Mid-America: The Story of the Illinois Central* (1950) and more recently by John F. Stover, *History of the Illinois Central Railroad* 227–229 (1975).

9. Letter authored by Stuyvesant Fish on May 28, 1901, reproduced in *Mississippi Railroad Heritage: Men & Iron—Steam & Diesel* 82 (Sharron Daniel Cauthen comp., 2006).

10. *See Mississippi Railroad Heritage: Men & Iron—Steam & Diesel* 279–297, 322–323 (Sharron Daniel Cauthen comp., 2006).

11. Illinois Central Historical Society, "A Brief Historical Sketch of the Illinois Central Railroad," icrrhistorical.org/history.html. Other aspects of the story of the Y&MV and the ICRR have been told by Robert L. Brandfon in his *Cotton Kingdom of the New South* (1967), particularly in the chapter "A Marriage of Interests," at pages 65–90.

12. Dunbar Rowland, "Railroad Commission," in *Mississippi: Comprising Statistics of Towns, Events, Institutions and Persons, Arranged in Cyclopedic Form, Vol. 2*, 510 (1907).

13. "Yazoo & Mississippi Valley," in *Mississippi Rails*, http://www.msrailroads.com/Y&MV.htm, citing Poors.

14. "Richard T. Wilson Dead, Aged Head of Banking House Had Long Suffered from Heart Disease," *New York Times* (New York, N.Y.), Sat., Nov. 26, 1910, Newspapers.com, https://www.newspapers.com/image/25989461; "Richard T. Wilson Dead, Famous in Wall Street and Father

-in-Law of Cornelius Vanderbilt," *Brooklyn Daily Eagle* (Brooklyn, N.Y.), Sat., Nov. 26, 1910, Newspapers.com, https://www.newspapers.com/image/53947401.

15. For a further history of R. T. Wilson's railroading history in the South, see John F. Stover, *The Railroads of the South* 103, 113–120, 128–129, 137, 184, 198 (1955), and Carlton J. Corliss, *Main Line of Mid-America: The Story of the Illinois Central* 237–238 (1950).

16. *Atlanta Constitution* (Atlanta, Ga.), Tues., May 23, 1882, page 4, Newspapers.com, http://www.newspapers.com/image/26942974.

17. Dunbar Rowland, "Railroad Commission," in *Mississippi: Comprising Statistics of Towns, Events, Institutions and Persons, Arranged in Cyclopedic Form, Vol. 2*, 510 (1907).; John F. Stover, *History of the Illinois Central Railroad* 227 (1975); Robert L. Brandon, *Cotton Kingdom of the New South* 70–72 (1967).

18. "A Big Sale," *Vicksburg Commercial*, reprinted in *Public Ledger* (Memphis, Tenn.), Fri., April 7, 1882, page 1, Newspapers.com, http://www.newspapers.com/image/171512441.

19. Wilson interview, *Times-Democrat* (New Orleans, La.), Thurs., May 11, 1882, page 2, Newspapers.com, https://www.newspapers.com/image/130926636.

20. Dunbar Rowland, "Railroad Commission," in *Mississippi: Comprising Statistics of Towns, Events, Institutions and Persons, Arranged in Cyclopedic Form, Vol. 2*, 510 (1907)..

21. "Sixteen Miles Nearer to Yazoo City," *Clarion*, page 15, reprinted in *Vicksburg Evening Post* (Vicksburg, Miss.), Fri., Aug. 17, 1883, page 1, Newspapers.com, http://www.newspapers .com/image/201500801.

22. *See Mississippi Railroad Heritage: Men & Iron—Steam & Diesel* 113 (Sharron Daniel Cauthen comp., 2006), which in turn cites John F. Stover's *History of the Illinois Central Railroad* (1979).

23. Miss. Laws, ch. XII [112] (August 8, 1870).

24. *See Yazoo & Mississippi Valley Railroad Company v. Adams*, 180 U.S. 1, 2 (1901).

25. "Fever at Wilson, La.," *Vicksburg Evening Post* (Vicksburg, Miss.), Mon., Sept. 26, 1898, page 1; Newspapers.com, https://www.newspapers.com/image/212201256. On more than one visit, the yellow fever took its tragic tolls along the railroads. *See Mississippi Railroad Heritage: Men & Iron—Steam & Diesel* 324–326 (Sharron Daniel Cauthen comp., 2006).

26. "Wilson Leaves Big Fortune," *Atlanta Constitution* (Atlanta, Ga.), Sun., Dec, 11, 1910, page 5, Newspapers.com, https://www.newspapers.com/image/26940181.

27. "Estimates of his estate ranged from $150 million to $200 million. It was left entirely to his wife." "E. H. Harriman," https://en.wikipedia.org/wiki/E._H._Harriman.

28. Illinois Central Historical Society, "A Brief Historical Sketch of the Illinois Central Railroad," icrrhistorical.org/history.html.

29. *See Mississippi Railroad Heritage: Men & Iron—Steam & Diesel* 290 (Sharron Daniel Cauthen comp., 2006); John F. Stover, *History of the Illinois Central Railroad* 178–179, 206–242 (1975).

30. Among the many sources consulted regarding the life and career of Edward H. Harriman are Carlton J. Corliss, *Main Line of Mid-America; The Story of the Illinois Central* 138, 210, 216–227, 240–241, 261, 270–272, 320–322 (1950); *Mississippi Railroad Heritage: Men & Iron—Steam & Diesel* 113, 297 (Sharron Daniel Cauthen comp., 2006); "Railroad Magnate, Edward H. Harriman," https://www.american-rails.com/edward-harriman.html; "Edward Henry Harriman, American Financier," https://www.britannica.com/biography/Edward-Henry-Harriman; "Edward Henry Harriman," https://www.encyclopedia.com/people/social-sciences-and-law/business-leaders /edward-h . . . ; "E. H. Harriman," https://en.wikipedia.org/wiki/E._H._Harriman.

31. "Alfred Hankinson Davis," *Find A Grave*, Memorial #53449906, https://www.findagrave .com/memorial/53449906/alfred-hankinson-davis .

32. Alfred H. Davis grew up to become an official of the Illinois Central Railroad. On September 23, 1910, Davis published "Memories of the Y&MV" in the *Greenville, Miss., Times*. Davis's "Memories" was reprinted in Gordon Cotton's "Courthouse Comments" in the

Vicksburg Sunday Post. In late October of 2016, a typed copy of Davis's "Memories" was found among the papers at the Meridian, Mississippi, Railroad Museum.

33. For a brief history of the railroads in Mississippi, see chapter 4 above; also Dunbar Rowland, "Railroad Commission," in *Mississippi: Comprising Statistics of Towns, Events, Institutions and Persons, Arranged in Cyclopedic Form, Vol. 2*, 502–516 (1907).; *see* "Railroads" in *Mississippi Encyclopedia*, 1055–1056 (Ownby and Wilson eds., 2017).

34. US District Judge Robert A. Hill, speaking in *Illinois Central R. Co. v. Stone*, 20 Fed. 468, 474 (S. D. Miss. 1884).

35. The Mobile and Ohio Rail-road Company was incorporated in Alabama on February 4, 1848. In short order thereafter, the Mississippi legislature, "desirous to aid in accomplishing the objects of said act," enacted that the M&O might lay tracks through Mississippi, "from the Alabama line to the State of Tennessee, in such direction and on such a route as shall be deemed most expedient." Miss. Laws, ch. 10, pages 83–95 (Approved February 17, 1848). For a summary history of the M&O RR, *see Mississippi Railroad Heritage: Men & Iron—Steam & Diesel* 294–296 (Sharron Daniel Cauthen comp., 2006)

36. US District Judge Robert A. Hill, speaking in *Farmers' Loan & Trust Co. v. Stone*, 20 Fed. 270, 271 (S. D. Miss. 1884).

37. W. J. Cash, *The Mind of the South* 107, 160 (1941, 1991).

38. "Robert Lowry," in David G. Sansing *Mississippi Governors: Soldiers, Statesmen, Scholars, Scoundrels: A Bicentennial Edition* 122–124 (2016); and "Robert Lowry," in *Mississippi Encyclopedia* 751 (Ownby and Wilson, eds., 2017).

39. Miss. Laws, ch. 23 (1884); *see also* Supplemental Act of March 15, 1884, Miss. Laws, ch. 24 (1884).

40. Thomas K. McCraw, *Prophets of Regulation* 17–44 (1984).

41. *See, e.g.,* "Granger Movement," Encyclopedia.com; http://www.encyclopedia.com/history/united-states-and-canada/us-history/granger-move . . . ; "The Granger Revolution," http://cs.stanford.edu/people/eroberts/cs201/projects/corporate-monopolies/dangers_gran . . .

42. *Munn v. Illinois*, 94 U.S. 113 (1877).

43. C. Vann Woodward, *Origins of the New South, 1877–1913*, 379 (1951).

44. Dunbar Rowland, "Railroad Commission," in *Mississippi: Comprising Statistics of Towns, Events, Institutions and Persons, Arranged in Cyclopedic Form, Vol. 2*, 499 (1907).

45. Dunbar Rowland, "Railroad Commission," in *Mississippi: Comprising Statistics of Towns, Events, Institutions and Persons, Arranged in Cyclopedic Form, Vol. 2*, 499 (1907).

46. *Trustees of Dartmouth College v. Woodward*, 17 U.S. 518 (1819).

47. U.S. Const. art. 1, § 8, cl. 1. The state constitution included a textually identical prohibition. Miss. Const. art. 1, § 8 (1869).

48. Senate Bill No. 59, Senate Journal 407 (February 24, 1880); *see also* full Majority and Minority Reports, Senate Journal 544–549, 552, 570–574, 584, 588, 595 (1880); House Journal 162, 245, 267, 269–270, 333–334, 350, 353, 358, 366, 562, 567 (1880).

49. Dunbar Rowland, "Railroad Commission," in *Mississippi: Comprising Statistics of Towns, Events, Institutions and Persons, Arranged in Cyclopedic Form, Vol. 2*, 499 (1907)..

50. Act of March 11, 1884, §§ 4, 5.

51. Letter authored by Stuyvesant Fish on May 28, 1901, reproduced in *Mississippi Railroad Heritage; Men & Iron—Steam & Diesel* (Sharron Daniel Cauthen, comp.) 81 (2006). Interactions between Fish and R. T. Wilson are described in Robert L. Brandfon, *Cotton Kingdom of the New South* 79–81 (1967).

52. "Railroads," in *Mississippi Encyclopedia* 1055 (Ownby and Wilson eds., 2017).

53. *See Mississippi Railroad Heritage: Men & Iron—Steam & Diesel* 323 (Sharron Daniel Cauthen comp., 2006).

54. Dunbar Rowland, "Railroad Commission," in *Mississippi: Comprising Statistics of Towns, Events, Institutions and Persons, Arranged in Cyclopedic Form, Vol. 2*, 499 (1907); House Journal, pages 33–34 (Jan. 9, 1884).

55. *New Mississippian* (Jackson), reprinted in *Vicksburg Evening Post* (Vicksburg, Miss.), Thurs., Feb. 21, 1884, page 2, Newspapers.com, https://www.newspapers.com/image/201515415.

56. *Vicksburg Evening Post* (Vicksburg, Miss.), Mon., March 10, 1884, page 2, Newspapers. com, https://www.newspapers.com/image/201516691.

57. James G. Revels, "Redeemers, Rednecks and Racial Integrity," in *A History of Mississippi, Vol. 1*, 597 (Richard A. McLemore ed., 1973); Dunbar Rowland, "Railroad Commission," in *Mississippi: Comprising Statistics of Towns, Events, Institutions and Persons, Arranged in Cyclopedic Form, Vol. 2*, 499–500 (1907).

58. Act of March 11, 1884.

59. Act of March 11, 1884, § 6.

60. Act of March 11, 1884, Miss. Laws, ch. 23, §§ 1–28 (1884).

61. Act of March 11, 1884, § 1.

62. Act of March 11, 1884, § 2.

63. Act of March 11, 1884, § 3.

64. Act of March 11, 1884, § 3.

65. Act of March 11, 1884, § 6.

66. Act of March 11, 1884, § 12.

67. Act of March 11, 1884, § 6.

68. Act of March 11, 1884, § 8.

69. Act of March 11, 1884, § 9.

70. See Miss. Const. art. 1, § 12 (1869) ("The right of trial by jury shall remain inviolate").

71. Act of March 11, 1884, § 13.

72. Act of March 11, 1884, § 18.

73. Act of March 11, 1884, § 28.

74. Ben Earl Kitchens, "John Marshall Stone" (2014); "John Marshall Stone," in David G. Sansing, *Mississippi Governors: Soldiers, Statesmen, Scholars, Scoundrels: A Bicentennial Edition*, 118–121 (2016); David G. Sansing, "John Marshall Stone: Thirty-First and Thirty-Third Governor of Mississippi, 1876–1882, 1890–1896," http://mshistorynow.mdah.state.ms.us/index .php?s=extra&id=133.

75. Woodward's take on Lucius Quintus Cincinnatus Lamar is scattered throughout his *Origins of the New South, 1877–1913* (1951). Regarding Lamar generally, *see* William Rogers, "Lucius Quintus Cincinnatus Lamar," mshistorynow.mdah.state.ms.us/articles/173/lucius-quintus -cincinnatus-lamar; and https://en.wikipedia.org/wiki/Lucius_Quintus_Cincinnatus_Lamar_II.

76. Woodward makes only a few references to Edward C. Walthall in *Origins of the New South, 1877–1913* 18, 282 (1951). *See also* "Edward Cary Walthall, U.S. Senator (1885–1898)," https://en.wikipedia.org/wiki/Edward_C._Walthall; and "Edward Cary Walthall (1831–1898), Memorial #11104," findagrave.com/cgi-bin/fg.cgi?page=gr&GRid=11104.

77. C. Vann Woodward, *Origins of the New South, 1877–1913*, page 18 (1951).

78. This case became *Stone v. Yazoo and Mississippi Valley Railroad Company*, 62 Miss. 607, 1885 WL 3015 (April Term, 1885).

79. The nickname "Little J" was a contrast with the "Big J," the New Orleans, Jackson & Great Northern Railroad. *See Mississippi Railroad Heritage: Men & Iron—Steam & Diesel* 126, 322 (Sharron Daniel Cauthen comp., 2006); also John F. Stover, *History of the Illinois Central Railroad* 228 (1975).

80. This case became *Stone v. Natchez, Jackson and Columbus Railroad Company*, 62 Miss. 646, 1885 WL 3016 (April Term, 1885).

81. "Ephraim G. Peyton, *Find A Grave*, Memorial #29115046," findagrave.com/cgi-bin /fg.cgi?page=gr&GRid=29115046. A notice of his death reminded the public: "As a citizen and a jurist he was held in deservedly high esteem. In the community where he so long resided he was beloved by all classes, identified, as he was, with every movement for the welfare of the people." *Clarion Ledger* (Jackson, Miss.) Thurs., June 27, 1889, page 4. Chancellor Peyton's father, also Ephraim G. Peyton (1802–1876), served on the Supreme Court of Mississippi from 1867 until his death. John Ray Skates Jr., *A History of the Mississippi Supreme Court, 1817–1948* (1973).

82. The Canton, Aberdeen & Nashville Railroad was chartered by the Mississippi legislature on February 17, 1882, the same day as the Y&MV.

83. William Faulkner, *Requiem for a Nun* 35, 37 (1950); see chapter 1, above.

84. For a biography of Chancellor McFarland, *see Mississippi: Contemporary Biography, Baxter McFarland*, pages 545–549 (Dunbar Rowland ed., 1907); *see also* http://www.clanmacfarlane .org/public_html/Genealogical-Histories/baxter-mcfarland-bio . . .

85. This case became *Stone v. Farmers' Loan & Trust Co.*, 116 U.S. 307 (Jan. 4, 1886), reversing *Farmers' Loan & Trust Co. v. Stone*, 20 Fed. 270 (S. D. Miss. Apr. 24, 1884). The Mobile & Ohio Railroad had been chartered in Mississippi in 1850, according to *Mississippi Railroad Heritage: Men & Iron—Steam & Diesel* 125 (Sharron Daniel Cauthen comp., 2006).

86. This case became *Stone v. Illinois Central Railroad Co.*, 116 U.S. 347 (Jan. 4, 1886), reversing *Illinois Central Railroad Co. v. Stone*, 20 Fed. 468 (S. D. Miss. 1884).

87. In 1881, the New Orleans & North Eastern Railroad had been acquired by the Alabama, Texas & Pacific Jct. *See Mississippi Railroad Heritage: Men & Iron—Steam & Diesel* 127 (Sharron Daniel Cauthen comp., 2006).

88. This case became *Stone v. New Orleans & Northeastern Railroad Co.*, 116 U.S. 352 (Jan. 4, 1886).

89. In 1881, the Vicksburg & Meridian Railroad had emerged from a reorganization of the Southern Railroad of Mississippi orchestrated by New York financiers. "Not too long thereafter the V. & M. came to fall on hard times and was eventually bought at foreclosure by some English companies led by one baron Emile Beauford d'Erlanger of London in 1889." It was reorganized as the Alabama & Vicksburg Railroad. *See Mississippi Railroad Heritage: Men & Iron—Steam & Diesel* 123, 126, 127 (Sharron Daniel Cauthen comp., 2006).

90. A brief history of the L&N is found in *Mississippi Railroad Heritage: Men & Iron—Steam & Diesel* 133–134 (Sharron Daniel Cauthen comp., 2006).

91. For a good once-over-lightly biographical sketch, focusing on the Civil War, see "Judge James Fentress—Hardeman County Tennessee Civil War History," https://sites.google.com/site /civilwarhardemancotn/family-biographies/judge-james-fentress.

92. "Judge James Fentress," *Find A Grave*, Memorial #83154766, findagrave.com/cgi-bin /fg.cgi?page=gr&id+83154766.

93. "For Representative from Hardeman to the Constitutional Convention, James Fentress," *Bolivar Bulletin* (Bolivar, Tenn.), Sat., Dec. 11, 1869, page 2, Newspapers.com, https://www .newspapers.com/image/70824776; *see also Bolivar Bulletin*, Sat., Dec. 18, 1869, page 1, Newspapers.com, https://www.newspapers.com/image/70824891; *Nashville Union and American* (Nashville, Tenn.), Tues., Feb. 8, 1870, page 4, Newspapers.com, https://www.newspapers.com /image/80682623. *See also* "Personal—James Fentress, Member of the Late Convention, from Hardeman County, Returned Home Yesterday, Looking Well and Hearty," *Bolivar Bulletin* (Bolivar, Tenn.), Sat., Feb. 26, 1870, page 3, Newspapers.com, https://www.newspapers.com /image/70783262.

94. William G. Thomas III, *Lawyering for the Railroad: Business, Law, and Power in the New South* 86 (1999); Robert L. Brandfon, *Cotton Kingdom of the New South* 176–177 (1967). In a news article in 1888, Fentress was referred to as "general solicitor, southern lines [ICRR],

Bolivar, Tenn.," in "Big Officials—Little Depot," *Decatur Herald* (Decatur, Ill.), Wed., Jan. 20, 1888, page 3, Newspapers.com, https://www.newspapers.com/image/ 87737936.

95. These and other biographical details are set out in "Judge James Fentress—Hardeman County Tennessee Civil War History," https://sites.google.com/site/civilwarhardemancotn /family-biographies/judge-james-fentress, and readily confirmable elsewhere; *see also* John F. Stover, *History of the Illinois Central Railroad* 202, 204 (1975).

96. "New Line Chartered," *Vicksburg Evening Post* (Vicksburg, Miss.), Weds., Nov. 10, 1884, page 1, Newspapers.com, https://www.newspapers.com/image/209776024.

97. William G. Thomas III, *Lawyering for the Railroad: Business, Law, and Power in the New South*, page 86 (1999); *see also* Robert L. Brandfon, *Cotton Kingdom of the New South* 177 (1967).

98. William G. Thomas III, *Lawyering for the Railroad: Business, Law, and Power in the New South* 86–87 (1999).

99. *See, e.g.*, "Watson & Craft," *Memphis Daily Appeal* (Memphis, Tenn.), Weds., May 26, 1858, page 2; Newspapers.com, https://www.newspapers.com/image/39793574; "Watson & Watson," *Memphis Daily Appeal* (Memphis, Tenn.), Sat., Feb. 10, 1872, page 2; Newspapers.com, https://www.newspapers.com/image/163955916; "Watson & Watson," *Memphis Daily Appeal* (Memphis, Tenn.), Sat., May 13, 1882, page 1; Newspapers.com, https://www.newspapers.com /image/168350167.

100. *Hinds County Gazette* (Raymond, Miss.), Weds., Sept. 9, 1857, page 3; Newspapers.com, https://www.newspapers.com/image/214733009.

101. "Another Plank Gone," *Memphis Daily Appeal* (Memphis, Tenn.), Tues., Sept. 15, 1857, page 2, Newspapers.com, https://www.newspapers.com/image/39789337.

102. For further particulars regarding J. W. C. Watson's activities and service of the Confederate cause, *see* "J. W. C. Watson," http://nlp.perseus.tufts.edu/hopper /nebrowser?id=watson%2Cj.%2Cw.%2Cc.

103. "Mr. Watson's Speech," *Public Ledger* (Memphis, Tenn.), Sat., Mar. 28, 1868, page 1, Newspapers.com, https://www.newspapers.com/image/215148602.

104. *Hinds County Gazette* (Raymond, Miss.), Weds., Sept. 9, 1857, page 3, Newspapers.com, https://www.newspapers.com/image/214733009.

105. "A Natural Consequence," *Newton Weekly Ledger* (Newton, Miss.), Thurs., Aug. 13, 1874, page 2, Newspapers.com, https://www.newspapers.com/image/199679405.

106. *See, e.g.*, *Hines v. Potts*, 56 Miss. 346, 347, 1879 WL 6405 (1879); *Duke v. Shackleford*, 56 Miss. 552, 1879 WL 3993 (1879); *Ex Parte Gore*, 57 Miss. 251, 1879 WL 4056 (1879).

107. *Stone v. Yazoo and Mississippi Valley Railroad Company*, 62 Miss. 607, 625, 626, 1885 WL 3015 (1885); *Stone v. Illinois Central Railroad Co.*, 116 U.S. 347, 348 (Jan. 4, 1886).

108. *Stone v. Yazoo and Mississippi Valley Railroad Company*, 62 Miss. 607, 626, 633, 1885 WL 3015 (1885); *Stone v. Illinois Central Railroad Co.*, 116 U.S. 347, 348 (1886). Prior to the Civil War, Wiley Pope Harris was a circuit judge for six years and served a term in the US House of Representatives. During the years of the railroad litigation, Harris was engaged in the private practice of law with his office based in Jackson. *See* "Wiley P. Harris," en.wikipedia.org/wiki/ Wiley P. Harris, and *Mississippi Railroad Heritage: Men & Iron—Steam & Diesel* 80–81, 113, 297, 322(Sharron Daniel Cauthen comp., 2006).

109. *See, e.g.*, *Yazoo & M. V. R. Co. v. Thomas, Sheriff*, 132 U.S. 174, 183 (1889); *Illinois Cent. R. Co. v. Walker*, 163 U.S. 691 (1896); and *Yazoo & Mississippi Valley Railroad v. Adams*, 180 U.S. 41, 43 (1901).

110. *See, e.g.*, *Best v. Polk*, 85 U.S. 112, 115 (1873); *Stone v. New Orleans & Northeastern R. Co.*, 116 U.S. 352, 353 (1886); and *Leonard v. Ozark Land Co.*, 131 U.S. 439 (1889); and *Leonard v. Chatfield*, 131 U.S. 439 (1889).

111. *See Runnels v. State,* Walker (1 Miss.) 146, 1823 WL 543 (1823), and chapter 3 above. *See also Marbury v. Madison,* 1 Cranch (5 U.S.) 137, 170, 2 L. Ed. 60 (1803).

112. *Farmers' Loan & Trust Co.* 20 Fed. 270 (S. D. Miss., April 24, 1884), reversed in *Stone v. Farmers' Loan & Trust Co.,* 116 U.S. 307 (1886).

113. "Robert Andrews Hill," in *Mississippi Encyclopedia* 573–574 (Ownby and Wilson, eds., 2017).

114. *Farmers' Loan & Trust Co. v. Stone,* 20 Fed. 270 (S. D. Miss. 1884).

115. *Illinois Central Railroad Co. v. Stone,* 20 Fed. 468 (S. D. Miss. 1884); *see also* Dunbar Rowland, "Railroad Commission," in *Mississippi: Comprising Statistics of Towns, Events, Institutions and Persons, Arranged in Cyclopedic Form, Vol.* 2 500 (1907).

116. This case would become *Stone v. New Orleans & Northeastern R. Co.,* 116 U.S. 352 (1886), a 7–2 reversal of Judge Hill. Regarding the New Orleans & Northeastern Railroad, *see Mississippi Railroad Heritage: Men & Iron—Steam & Diesel* 113, 126–127, 297 (Sharron Daniel Cauthen comp., 2006).

117. "Don Albert Pardee (1837–1919)," en.wikipdia.org/wiki/Don_Albert_Pardee.

118. *Vicksburg Evening Post,* Tuesday, May 20, 1884.

119. *See* Clara Hamlett Robertson Flanagan, "Hill, Robert Andrews," encyclopedia.org /biography/hill-robert-andrews (1980); "Robert Andrews Hill," en.wikipedia.org/wiki/robert _andrews_hill.

120. *Farmers Loan & Trust Co. v. Stone,* 20 Fed. 270, 271 (S. D. Miss. 1884), reversed *Stone v. Farmers Loan & Trust Co.,* 116 U.S. 307 (1886).

121. Federal Judiciary Act of 1875, now 28 U. S. C., § 1331.

122. *Pollock v. Farmers Loan & Trust Co.,* 157 U.S. 429 (1895).

123. "John Archibald Campbell," en.wikipedia.org/wiki/John Archibald Campbell.

124. *See Farmers' Loan & Trust Co. v. Stone,* 20 Fed. 270 (S. D. Miss. 1884), reversed *Stone v. Farmers' Loan & Trust Co.,* 116 U.S. 307, 6 S. Ct. 334, 335 (1886).

125. *Farmers' Loan & Trust Co. v. Stone,* 20 Fed. 270, 271 (S. D. Miss. 1884).

126. *Farmers' Loan & Trust Co. v. Stone,* 20 Fed. 270, 274, 275 (S. D. Miss. 1884).

127. Act of March 11, 1884, § 23.

128. *Farmers' Loan & Trust Co. v. Stone,* 20 Fed. 270, 274 (S. D. Miss. 1884). A nearly identical statement appears in Judge Hill's opinion in *Illinois Cent. R. Co. v. Stone,* 20 Fed. 468, 472 (S. D. Miss. 1884).

129. *Farmers' Loan & Trust Co. v. Stone,* 20 Fed. 270, 274–275 (S. D. Miss. 1884).

130. *See Stone v. Illinois Cent. R. Co.,* 116 U.S. 347, 349 (1886) ("Relief is also asked on the same grounds. The court below granted the injunction prayed for, and this appeal was taken for a review of a decree to that effect.").

131. *Clarion* (Jackson, Miss.), Weds., May 14, 1884.

132. *Brandon Republican,* reprinted in *Vicksburg Evening Post,* Thurs., May 16, 1884.

133. *Clarion,* Wednesday, May 21, 1884.

134. *Vicksburg Evening Post,* Thurs., May 23, 1884.

135. *Vicksburg Evening Post,* Thurs., May 22, 1884.

136. *Vicksburg Evening Post,* Thurs., May 22, 1884.

137. It appears that the appeals by the Y&MV and the Canton, Aberdeen & Nashville RR were consolidated for hearing before the Supreme Court of Mississippi. On November 29, 1884, James Fentress filed a consolidated Brief of Appellees on behalf of these two railroads, each a part of the Illinois Central system. "Y&MV" should be seen as including the CANRR for this discussion of the state court appeals.

138. On April 24, 1884, while appeals to the Supreme Court of Mississippi taken by the Railroad Commissioners in the Y&MV and NJ&C cases were pending, the U. S. Cir. Ct., S. D.

Miss., three times held that the act was unconstitutional. *Farmers' Loan & Trust Co. v. Stone*, 20 Fed. 270 (S. D. Miss. 1884); *Illinois Central Railroad Co. v. Stone*, 20 Fed. 468 (S. D. Miss. 1884). The US Supreme Court would later—on January 4, 1886—reverse these district court rulings in *Stone v. Farmers' Loan & Trust Co.*, 116 U.S. 307 (1886); in *Stone v. Illinois Central RR Co.*, 116 U.S. 347 (1886); and in *Stone v New Orleans & Northeastern RR Co.*, 116 U.S. 352 (1886).

139. Miss. Const. art. 4, § 1 (1869); *see also* Miss Const. art. 3, § 1 (1869).

140. Miss. Const. art. 5, §§ 1, 9 (1869).

141. See Miss. Const. art. 5, §§ 1, 9 (1869); *see also* Miss Const. art. 3, §§ 1, 2 (1869).

142. *Munn v. Illinois*, 94 U.S. 113 (1877).

143. U.S. Const. art. 1, § 10, cl. 1.

144. Miss Const. art. 1, § 9 (1869).

145. See chapter 4 above. There were contracts clause issues concerning the Union Bank bonds and legislative interference with bank charters.

146. *Stone v. Yazoo and Mississippi Valley Railroad Company*, 62 Miss. 607, 642 (1885).

147. U.S. Const. amend. XIV, § 1; Miss. Const. art. 1, § 2 (1869). Railroads also argued that their equal protection rights were being offended. They said they were being treated unequally when compared with other means of transportation of persons and goods, such as the public waterways—the coastal zones, rivers, streams, and, more recently, canals—and over-the-road transportation such as wagons, stagecoaches, and the like. Though argued fervently, these arguments never found much traction.

148. See chapter 7 below.

149. Miss. Const. art. 1, §§ 2, 10 (1869).

150. *See, e.g.*, "Josiah A. P. Campbell," in Dunbar Rowland, *Courts, Judges, and Lawyers of Mississippi, 1798–1935* 103–110 (1935); also pages 6–13 at http://genealogytrails.com/miss/bios_c.htm; John Ray Skates Jr., *A History of the Mississippi Supreme Court* 65–67 (1973); "J. A. P. Campbell," in *Mississippi Encyclopedia* 167–168 (Ownby and Wilson eds., 2017). *See also* Judge Leslie H. Southwick's unpublished and undated paper "Chief Justices Josiah A. P. Campbell, Tim E. Cooper, and Albert H. Whitfield: The Court from the 1876 Revolution to the First Decade of a New Century," pages 4–6, used in years past in a course in Mississippi Supreme Court history that Judge Southwick taught at the Mississippi College School of Law.

151. John Ray Skates Jr., *A History of the Mississippi Supreme Court* 66 (1973).

152. See chapter 8 below.

153. John Ray Skates Jr., *A History of the Mississippi Supreme Court* 85–86 (1973).

154. Robert H. Thompson, address entitled *Mississippi Codes*, Proceedings of the 21st Annual Meeting of the Mississippi State Bar 37–75 (1926).

155. "Josiah A. P. Campbell," in Dunbar Rowland, *Courts, Judges, and Lawyers of Mississippi, 1798–1935* (1935); also page 8 at http://genealogytrails.com/miss/bios_c.htm.

156. Judge Leslie H. Southwick's unpublished and undated paper "Chief Justices Josiah A. P. Campbell, Tim E. Cooper, and Albert H. Whitfield; *The Court from the 1876 Revolution to the First Decade of a New Century*, page 5. Judge Southwick once used these materials in teaching a course at the Mississippi College School of Law.

157. John Ray Skates Jr., *A History of the Mississippi Supreme Court* 66, 98 (1973).

158. "James Z. George," in *Mississippi Encyclopedia* 495–496 (Ownby and Wilson eds., 2017); John Ray Skates Jr., *A History of the Mississippi Supreme Court* 76–78 (1973).

159. Albert D. Kirwan, *Revolt of the Rednecks: Mississippi Politics, 1876–1925*, at 67–68 (1951).

160. Miss. Const. art. 12, §§ 243, 244 (1890).

161. Again, the appeal that the commissioners took against the Canton Aberdeen & Nashville Railroad (CAN) had as a practical matter been consolidated with the Y&MV's appeal. The same lawyers represented the two railroads and had filed a joint brief.

162. U.S. Const. art. 1, § 8, cl. 3.

163. *Stone v. Yazoo and Mississippi Valley Railroad Company*, 62 Miss. 607, 633, 1885 WL 3015 (1885).

164. The paragraph above has been written subject to the perennial dilemma and risk of mis-applying contemporary standards and ways of thinking to important events and circumstances of more than 130 years before. Prescience may be worthy of reward, but remaining within some of the patterns of the times is not always deserving of condemnation. See Preface. We have no insight into Campbell's unexpressed thinking in 1885. Defending this new state-created entity and its functions articulated by the Legislature may at the time have been so appropriate in its own right that there was no occasion for hard thinking about what it meant to regulate commerce.

165. *Stone v. Yazoo and Mississippi Valley Railroad Company*, 62 Miss. 607, 634–638, 1885 WL 3015 (1885).

166. *Stone v. Yazoo and Mississippi Valley Railroad Company*, 62 Miss. 607, 638, 641, 1885 WL 3015 (1885). This was so in 1885. A couple of years later, the Congress passed the Interstate Commerce Act of 1887.

167. *Stone v. Yazoo and Mississippi Valley Railroad Company*, 62 Miss. 607, 639, 640, 644, 1885 WL 3015 (1885).

168. *Stone v. Yazoo and Mississippi Valley Railroad Company*, 62 Miss. 607, 644–645, 1885 WL 3015 (1885).

169. *Stone v. Yazoo and Mississippi Valley Railroad Company*, 62 Miss. 607, 645, 1885 WL 3015 (1885).

170. In *Mississippi Reports*, Vol. 62, *Stone v. NJ&C RR*, 62 Miss. 646, 1885 WL 3016 (April Term, 1885), is the very next case following *Stone v. Y&MV RR*, 62 Miss. 607, 1885 WL 3015 (April Term, 1885).

171. *Stone v. NJ&C RR*, 62 Miss. 646, 653, 1885 WL 3016 (April Term, 1885). See chapter 8 below for a fuller discussion of common law.

172. Miss. Const. art. 3, § 1 (1869).

173. *Stone v. NJ&C RR*, 62 Miss. 646, 653, 1885 WL 3016 (April Term, 1885).

174. See chapter 8, below.

175. Act of March 11, 1884, § 23.

176. On August 6, 1885, the Little J railroad took an appeal to the US Supreme Court with supersedeas. Apparently, that appeal was never prosecuted to final decision, perhaps given that the arguments the Little J was making against the Mississippi Supreme Court's decision were controlled and disposed of by the series of decisions that Chief Justice Waite would announce on January 4, 1886.

177. "Not Exactly," *Raymond Gazette*, April 1885 (apparently reprinted in the *Clarion*).

178. "Another Letter from Tippah," *Clarion*, April 1885.

179. "Once More," *Clarion*, Weds., June 10, 1885.

180. *Stone v. Farmers' Loan & Trust Co.*, 116 U.S. 307, 325–326 (1886).

181. *Stone v. Farmers' Loan & Trust Co.*, 116 U.S. 307, 329–330 (1886).

182. *Stone v. Farmers' Loan & Trust Co.*, 116 U.S. 307, 330–331 (1886).

183. *Stone v. Farmers' Loan & Trust Co.*, 116 U.S. 307, 334–336 (1886).

184. Apparently, counsel for the Vicksburg & Meridian Railroad and the Louisville & Nash-ville Railroad, on the one hand, and J. W. C. Watson for the commissioners left their fate to the outcome of the three federal cases that were appealed further.

185. *Stone v. Farmers' Loan & Trust Co.*, 116 U.S. 307 (1886).

186. *Stone v. Farmers' Loan & Trust Co.*, 116 U.S. 307, 388 (1886).

187. *Stone v. Illinois Central RR Co.*, 116 U.S. 347 (1886). In an otherwise massive his-tory of the Illinois Central Railroad, the story of government regulation focuses on the

post-*Wabash* era beginning with the Interstate Commerce Act, with no mention of the Mississippi regulatory litigation. See John F. Stover, *History of the Illinois Central Railroad* 257–262 (1975).

188. *Stone v. New Orleans & Northeastern RR Co.*, 116 U.S. 352 (1886).

189. *Stone v. Farmers' Loan & Trust Co.*, 116 U.S. 307, 337 (1886).

190. *Stone v. New Orleans & Northeastern RR Co.*, 116 U.S. 352, 355, 356 (1886).

191. "Railroad Supervision," *Vicksburg Evening Post* (Vicksburg, Miss.), Weds., June 6, 1886, page 2, Newspapers.com, https://www.newspapers.com/image/212121437.

192. *Wabash, St. Louis & Pacific RR Co. v. Illinois*, 118 U.S. 557 (1886). For a perceptive discussion of *Wabash* in historical context, *see* Thomas K. McCraw, *Prophets of Regulation*, 57–62 (1984).

193. *Stone v. Farmers' Loan & Trust Co.*, 116 U.S. 307, 325 (1886).

194. *Wabash, St. Louis & Pacific RR Co. v. Illinois*, 118 U.S. 557, 577 (1886).

195. Ch. 104, U.S. Statutes at Large 379. The original ICC Act was amended from time to time. Then came the era of deregulation, beginning with the Railroad Revitalization and Regulatory Reform Act of 1976, and subsequent legislation. The Congress closed out the year 1995 by passing the Interstate Commerce Commission Termination Act, Pub. L. 104–88, 109 U.S. Statutes at Large 803.

196. William Shakespeare, Hamlet, act 3, scene 4, line 207.

197. Reply of Attorney General, Jackson, Miss., Nov. 27, 1887, to the Railroad Commission.

198. *Stone v. Farmers' Loan & Trust Co.*, 116 U.S. 307, 336–337 (1886).

199. Thomas K. McCraw, "Prophets of Regulation" 25–31 (1984).

200. *See, e.g., Vicksburg and Jackson Railroad Company v. Patton*, 2 George (31 Miss.) 156 (1856), discussed in chapter 8 below.

201. *Canton, Aberdeen & Nashville Railroad Co. v. McCoy & Clark*, 1 Miss. Dec. 47, 1885 WL 3085 (1885) (affirming $150 award made by a justice of the peace "for the value of a horse alleged to have been killed by one of defendant's trains").

202. *See, e.g., Yazoo & Mississippi Valley Railroad Company v. Adams*, 180 U.S. 1 (1901); *Yazoo & Mississippi Valley Railroad Company v. Adams*, 180 U.S. 41 (1901), rehearing denied 181 U.S. 580 (1901); *Gulf & Ship Island Railroad Company v. Adams*, 90 Miss. 559, 45 So. 91 (1907).

203. *See, e.g., Yazoo & Mississippi Valley Railroad Company v. Jackson Vinegar Company*, 226 U.S. 217 (1912) (damage to shipment of vinegar carried over railroad's lines).

204. *See, e.g., Tribbette v. Illinois Central Railroad Company*, 71 Miss. 212, 13 So. 899 (1893) (building said to have caught fire from sparks from train); *Vicksburg and Jackson Railroad Company v. Patton*, 2 George (31 Miss.) 156, 176 (1856) (livestock).

205. Miss. Laws, ch. 23, § 13 (1884).

206. Miss. Const. art. 7, § 184 (1890).

207. Miss. Const. art. 7, § 188 (1890).

208. Miss. Const. art. 7, § 193 (1890).

209. "Casey Jones," in *Mississippi Encyclopedia* 664–665 (Ownby and Wilson eds., 2017).

210. *See Mississippi Railroad Heritage: Men & Iron—Steam & Diesel* 177–178 (Sharron Daniel Cauthen comp., 2006).

211. *See* www.caseyjonesmuseum.com; *Mississippi Railroad Heritage: Men & Iron—Steam & Diesel* 180 (Sharron Daniel Cauthen comp., 2006). John F. Stover's comprehensive *History of the Illinois Central Railroad* (1975) includes a depiction of a cotton platform at the Water Valley station from the 1880s.

212. *See, e.g., Richardson v. Norfolk Southern Railway Company*, 923 So.2d 1002, 1007–1009 (¶¶ 10–15) (Miss. 2006).

213. *Pearson v. Columbus and Greenville Railway Company*, 737 So.2d 390, 399 (¶32) (Miss. App. 1998).

214. *See* "The Saga of Casey Jones," in Carlton J. Corliss, *Main Line of Mid-America; The Story of the Illinois Central* 304–305 (1950).

215. The account presented here of the famous fatal events of railroad history on the evening and early morning of April 29–30, 1900, are taken from a combined reading of "Casey's Last Ride," by Bruce Gurner, published in *Mississippi Railroad Heritage: Men & Iron—Steam & Diesel* 312–316, 350 (Sharron Daniel Cauthen comp., 2006); "Heroic Engineer," *Times-Democrat* (New Orleans, La.), Tues., May 1, 1900, page 3; Newspapers.com, https://www.newspapers.com/image/140333369; "Wreck Described by Passenger; Engineer Jones Died a Heroic Death," *Times-Democrat* (New Orleans, La.), Tues., May 1, 1900, page 3, Newspapers.com, https://www.newspapers.com/image/140333369; Passenger Train, Hit a Freight, and an Engineer Was Crushed to Death," *Cincinnati Enquirer* (Cincinnati, Ohio), Tues., May 1, 1900, page 2; Newspapers.com, https://www.newspapers.com/image/32588578; John Luther "Casey" Jones, *Find A Grave*, Memorial # 10214, https://www.findagrave.com/memorial/10214?search=true; "Casey Jones, Folk Hero (1864–1900)," http://www.biography.com/people/casey-jones-9357038; Danger Ahead! Vaughan Mississippi (1900), http://danger-ahead-railfan.net/accidents/vaughan.htm; *Roots of the Grateful Dead*, "The True Story of Casey Jones," http://taco.com/roots/caseyjones.html; "The Saga of Casey Jones," in Carlton J. Corliss, *Main Line of Mid-America; The Story of the Illinois Central* 301–311 (1950); John F. Stover, *History of the Illinois Central Railroad* 224–225 (1975); and "Casey Jones," https://en.wikipedia.org/wiki/Casey_Jones.

216. *See* "Casey Jones; Injuries/losses from wreck," https://en.wikipedia.org/wiki/Casey_Jones.

217. "Heroic Engineer," *Times-Democrat* (New Orleans, La.), Tues. May 1, 1900, page 3, Newspapers.com, https://www.newspapers.com/image/140333369.

218. *See* three related stories published by the *St. Louis Post-Dispatch* on Sunday, Sept. 10, 1911, page 53, Newspapers.com, https://www/newspapers.com/image/138159209.

219. *See* "Casey Jones; Casey Jones References in Music," https://en.wikipedia.org/wiki/Casey_Jones.

220. Illinois Central Historical Society, "A Brief Historical Sketch of the Illinois Central Railroad," icrrhistorical.org/history.html.

221. Arlo Guthrie, "City of New Orleans" (1972), https://www.youtube.com/watch?v=TvMS_ykiLiQ .

222. *Pearson v. Columbus and Greenville Railway Company*, 737 So.2d 390, 399 (¶32) (Miss. App. 1998).

223. Miss. Const. art. 7, § 186 (1890).

224. Miss. Const. art. 7, § 190 (1890).

225. *Stone v. Farmers' Loan & Trust Co.*, 116 U.S. 307, 319 (1886).

226. Leslie Southwick, *Administrative Law*, chapter 2 in *Encyclopedia of Mississippi Law*, Vol. 1 (Jeffrey Jackson, Mary Miller, and Donald Campbell eds., 2017).

227. Miss. Code Ann. §§ 77-1-1, et seq. *See* Miss. Code, ch. 134, §§ 4273–4336 (1892); Miss. Code, ch. 139, §§ 4826–4899 (1906); Miss. Code, ch. 170, §§ 7023–7138 (1930). Railroads were removed from MPSC jurisdiction in 1997. *See* Miss. Laws, ch. 460, § 1 (1997), repealing Miss. Code Ann. § 77-9-1. For railroad regulation in Mississippi more recently, *see* Miss. Code Ann. 77-9-1, et seq., and 77-9-119.

228. Sydney McCain Smith, *The State and the Social Process*, 9 Miss. L. Journ. 147, 149 (December 1936).

229. Bruce Springsteen, "The River."

230. *See, e.g.*, Miss. Code Ann. §§ 25-43-3.105, -4.104, 49-2-11.

231. Holmes, *Law in Science and Science in Law*, 12 Harv. L Rev. 443 (1899), reprinted in *The Essential Holmes* 198 (Richard Posner ed., 1992).

232. *See, e.g.*, the Mississippi Major Economic Impact Act, §§ 57-75-1, et seq. For recent adjustments in the requirements for and use of economic impact statements, see particularly Leslie Southwick, *Administrative Law*, § 2:24 in chapter 2 in *Encyclopedia of Mississippi Law*, Vol. 1 (Jeffrey Jackson, Mary Miller, and Donald Campbell eds., 2016).

233. Thomas K. McCraw, *Prophets of Regulation* 308–309 (1984).

234. It is sad that our colleges and universities allow young men and women to go forth and call themselves college graduates without having had a quality course in economics with a required reading of Joseph Schumpeter's classic *Capitalism, Socialism and Democracy* (1942), or without at least had an exposure to "Epilogue, The Legacy" at the end of Mississippian Thomas K. McCraw's *Prophet of Innovation* 495–506 (2007), team-taught by caring professors of economics and constitutional law. Most would profit as well from a follow-up class based on the late Professor McCraw's Pulitzer Prize–winning *Prophets of Regulation* (1984).

235. Noel Workman, "Stopped in Its Tracks," *Delta Magazine* (May 12, 2012), http://deltamagazine.com/features/stopped-in-its-tracks/.

BIBLIOGRAPHY

Brandfon, Robert L., *Cotton Kingdom of the New South* (1967).

Cash, W. J., *The Mind of the South* (1941, 1991).

Corliss, Carlton J., *Main Line of Mid-America: The Story of the Illinois Central* (New York, 1950).

Holmes, Oliver Wendell, *Law in Science and Science in Law*, 12 Harv. L Rev. 443 (1899), reprinted in *The Essential Holmes* (Richard Posner ed., 1992).

Illinois Central Historical Society, "A Brief Historical Sketch of the Illinois Central Railroad," icrrhistorical.org/history.html.

Kirwan, Albert D., *Revolt of the Rednecks: Mississippi Politics, 1876–1925* (1951).

Kitchens, Ben Earl, *John Marshall Stone; Mississippi's Honorable and Longest Serving Governor* (2014).

McCraw, Thomas K., *Prophet of Innovation* (2007).

McCraw, Thomas K., *Prophets of Regulation* (1984).

Mississippi: Contemporary Biography, Baxter McFarland (Dunbar Rowland ed., 1907).

Mississippi Encyclopedia (Ownby and Wilson eds., 2017)

Mississippi Railroad Heritage: Men & Iron—Steam & Diesel (Sharron Daniel Cauthen ed., 2006).

Revels, James G., "Redeemers, Rednecks and Racial Integrity," in *A History of Mississippi, Vol. 1* (Richard A. McLemore ed., 1973).

Rowland, Dunbar, *Courts, Judges, and Lawyers of Mississippi, 1798–1935* (1935)

Rowland, Dunbar, "Railroad Commission," in *Mississippi: Comprising Statistics of Towns, Events, Institutions and Persons, Arranged in Cyclopedic Form, Vol. 2* (1907).

Sansing, David G., *Mississippi Governors: Soldiers, Statesmen, Scholars, Scoundrels: A Bicentennial Edition* (2016).

Schumpeter, Joseph, *Capitalism, Socialism and Democracy* (1942).

Skates, John Ray, Jr., *A History of the Mississippi Supreme Court* (1973).

Smith, Sydney McCain, *The State and the Social Process*, 9 Miss. L. Journ. 147 (December 1936).

Southwick, Leslie H., "Administrative Law," § 2:24, in chapter 2 in *Encyclopedia of Mississippi Law*, Vol. 1 (Jeffrey Jackson, Mary Miller, and Donald Campbell eds., 2016).

Stover, John F., *History of the Illinois Central Railroad* (1975).

Thomas, William G. III, *Lawyering for the Railroad: Business, Law, and Power in the New South* (1999).

Woodward, C. Vann, *Origins of the New South, 1877–1913* (1951).

Workman, Noel, "Stopped in Its Tracks," *Delta Magazine* (May 12, 2012), http://deltamagazine.com/features/stopped-in-its-tracks/.

"The Yazoo & Mississippi Valley Railroad, The Issaquena Genealogy & History Project," http://www.rootsweb.ancestry.com/~msissaq2/railroad/.

CHAPTER 7

The Police Power of the State Moves to the Piney Woods

> There were pine forests here a long time ago but they are gone. The bastards got in here and set up mills and laid the narrow-gauge tracks and knocked together the company commissaries and paid a dollar a day and folks swarmed out of the brush for the dollar. . . . The saws sang soprano and the clerk in the commissary passed out the blackstrap molasses and the sowbelly and wrote in his big book, and the Yankee dollar and Confederate dumbness collaborated to heal the wounds of four years of fratricidal strife, and all was merry as a marriage bell. Till, all of a sudden, there weren't any more pine trees.
>
> —ROBERT PENN WARREN, *ALL THE KING'S MEN*

A seismic shift occurred in Mississippi's history of constitutional encounters beginning less than two months after the *Titanic* sank. It changed the way people working here and their bosses would get along and accept each other and at times struggle with each other. Economic variables and health and social effects on working folk were put forth in legislative and constitutional calculations as never before. Interest group politics inserted its skewed views, with short-term self-interests front and center. Powerful businessmen fell back on a formulaic view of the constitution and classical economic theory, augmenting their sense of entitlement. To these people, objective and empirically verifiable social facts were secondary considerations, if indeed they were known or considered at all. Still, the empirical-evidence-based Brandeis Brief had been birthed in *Muller v. Oregon*,[1] decided by the US Supreme Court four years earlier. The constitutional practice of judicial review had matured since *Runnels v. State*[2] and *Cochrane & Murdock v. Kitchens* and the early days of statehood.[3] A potentially problematic precedent was set for the state's future responses to unpopular Supreme Court decisions made in Washington, DC, though the last sawmill would close—and another half century would pass—before the seeds of that precedent would grow and ripen into bitter fruit.

In March of 1912, the legislature passed a bill[4] expecting that it would affect many of the future citizens of Mississippi. It was a ten-hour workday law. Employers engaged in businesses that substantially involved "manufacturing or repairing" could not "work their employees longer than ten hours per day, except in cases of emergency" or "public necessity."[5] Many states had passed similar laws regulating a variety of workplace activities.[6] In 1898, the high court in the nation's capital had upheld a Utah statute limiting the hours of work in underground mines.[7]

The perceived need for such laws came to Mississippi a few years later than in many states. Most folk here were still farmers of one kind or another approaching the end of the first century of the state's formal existence. But the state had experienced a "rapid increase in manufacturing enterprises."[8] Before the subject began to arouse legislative interest in Mississippi, the US Supreme Court had struck down—on federal constitutional grounds—a ten-hour workday law ostensibly protecting bakery workers in New York.[9] Conversely, in 1908, *Muller* had upheld a ten-hours-per-day law limiting the labor of women engaged in laundry work. By the first week in January of 1913, the Supreme Court of Mississippi had relied heavily on its own constitution—not to mention the state's Tenth Amendment prerogatives under the federal Constitution—and had denied two challenges to the new six-months-old workday law.[10] Two months later, the state supreme court affirmed the conviction of a corporate offender.[11]

J. J. NEWMAN LUMBER COMPANY

It was the dawn of the twentieth century. The Civil War and Reconstruction were receding further. The new 1890 constitution had been a watershed. The great World War was not foreseen. The day had passed when people thought "carpetbaggers" at the mention of northerners coming to Mississippi to reap profits. Well-heeled Yankee entrepreneurs brought jobs. Men could escape the vagaries of farm life where families barely eked out a living. "People who had grown up on farms preferred jobs in the lumber industry and became loggers or sawmill workers."[12] A modest though dependable wage became an option. Never mind that the outsider employer might make all the money in Mississippi that it could, exhaust all accessible natural resources that could be converted into profits, and disappear—as would the jobs families had come to depend on. One such entrepreneurial enterprise—the biggest of the times—was the J. J. Newman Lumber Company.

Judson Jones Newman (1847–1900) was born in Buffalo, New York. He, his wife, Flora, who hailed from McKean County, Pennsylvania, and their son, Edmund—along with four more Pennsylvanians—came to Hattiesburg, Mississippi, in early 1894. On December 6, 1894, the state chartered the J. J. Newman Lumber Company. There is little evidence that the Newmans ever assimilated among the people of the Piney Woods area of south Mississippi.[13] By 1900, Flora Newman had died, and the Newman men were boarding with other sawmill workers from the North. At death, the remains of each Newman were returned to Buffalo, where they were buried in the Forest Lawn Cemetery.

As fate would have it, Newman and his co-investors were not able to raise the capital they needed to sustain their company's lumber business. In early 1896, Newman approached Fenwick Lyman Peck (1854–1943), whom he had known in Pennsylvania. Peck visited Hattiesburg, "drove a hundred miles in a buggy through the surrounding virgin timber," and quickly acquired a controlling interest in J. J. Newman Lumber Company. In short order, the Peck-controlled company opened two large sawmills in Sumrall in adjacent Lamar County. Railroads were vital to the lumber business.[14] Newman Lumber built its own railroad. Ultimately, the Mississippi Central Railroad stretched some eighty-five miles from the southeast and a point named Pines near Brooklyn[15] westward to Natchez and the Mississippi River. By the early 1900s, Newman had become the largest lumber company in Mississippi, and one of the largest in the entire South.

Long before the south Mississippi Pine Belt was within its sights, the Peck family had a history in the lumber business. The 1880 census listed Jonathan W. Peck as a lumber manufacturer. His son Fenwick, who never went past the eighth grade in school, resided in Blakely, now known as Peckville, near Scranton in Lackawanna County, Pennsylvania. In his day, Fenwick owned one of the largest lumber mills in his home state. He infused Newman Lumber with capital and entrepreneurship, with a constant eye toward expansion, though he maintained his business interests in Pennsylvania, foremost being the Lackawanna Lumber Company back in Scranton. In 1899, Peck organized the Cherry River Boom & Lumber Company in West Virginia but soon sold his interest to others. In 1901, Peck and his business partners consolidated Lackawanna Lumber with the J. J. Newman Lumber Company and interests they held in New Mexico, all under the umbrella of United States Lumber Company.[16] In 1911, U.S. Lumber expanded its Mississippi presence when it organized the Homochitto Lumber Company, based in Brookhaven.[17]

On the surface Peck sought to show an interest in Hattiesburg beyond the lumber business per se. He became a director of the National Bank of Commerce in Hattiesburg and a director of the State Bank of Sumrall in Lamar County. Evidence abounds, however, that Peck's base of operations remained in Pennsylvania and the Northeast.[18] Like the Newmans, those who had been born and raised and lived in the Piney Woods were never able to say that Fenwick L. Peck had become "one of us."

By 1910, Newman Lumber was producing 150,000 board feet of yellow pine lumber a year at Hattiesburg and another 175,000 board feet in Sumrall.[19] At its height, the company owned 400,000 acres of timberlands and annually produced 200,000,000 board feet of lumber or more.[20] Newman Lumber ultimately had as many as 1,200 employees. The company operated a substantial naval stores business and sold turpentine and resin domestically and to markets throughout the Western World, and in Africa as well.

Its growth and success aside, the lumber industry in south Mississippi was sensitive to political and social forces that might inhibit its liberties and interfere with the ambitions of its entrepreneurs. To be sure, sawmill companies would in time choose to waive some of those liberties, in the interest of greater opportunities for profit. They "formulated price lists, established a uniform lumber grade, and compiled statistics, but their chief activities were directed toward the establishment of a uniform price profitable to the manufacturers."[21] As a result, the southern pine industry was frequently charged with monopolistic practices and price-fixing, partially as a result of the activities—real or perceived—of its trade associations. Newman Lumber and its fellow yellow-pine lumber producers were collectively active on many fronts. But how they did business was their business, and not the government's. Most saw Mississippi's 1912 ten-hour workday law as an interference with their exercise and enjoyment of fundamental rights.

James E. Fickle reports, "The law was passed with the support of some Mississippi lumbermen, who believed that it was humane and that workers would produce as much in ten hours as in twelve. In fact, Philip S. Gardner's company voluntarily reduced the workday to ten hours as early as 1906."[22] Nollie W. Hickman adds that Gardner "called upon the manufacturers to assume responsibility for the welfare of their workers, pointing out that a betterment of social conditions improved the efficiency of labor."[23] Newman Lumber, on the other hand, was more than willing to wage war when the State moved aggressively to enforce its meddlesome new law.

THE GATHERING CLOUDS

Numbers may be marshalled to show that the lumber industry in south Mississippi reached its peak in the decade straddling the year 1910. At the time, the state was third highest in the country in lumber production, behind only Washington and Louisiana.[24] But all was not well. The underbelly of the economy was in turmoil and flux. The Panic of 1907 had given rise to as many fears as actual problems in the industry, particularly among those from the Northeast so heavily invested in larger, more mechanized and productive sawmills. According to one historical observer, the panic began a period of depression in the overexpanded lumber industry. The lumber entrepreneurs who so fervently touted laissez-faire economics had found that their self-interests required something quite different. Control of production became concentrated. And so lumber trade associations worked toward price fixing and uniform terms of sale. Still, industry spokesmen complained that, except for short periods in 1912 and 1913, prices had been unsatisfactory since 1907, and ruinous since 1914. At the same time, to men like Fenwick Peck, the anti-big-business political ideas emerging in the Progressive Era were ominous clouds. A plan to merge the largest lumber producers into a single corporation modeled on United States Steel was scuttled by progressive-minded state attorneys general.[25]

There was political ferment across Mississippi at the time. No story is more telling than the political rise and fall of the gentleman planter LeRoy Percy[26] (1860–1929) of Washington County in the Mississippi Delta. Sen. Anselm J. McLaurin[27] had died in office on December 22, 1909. The legislature was charged to select his successor. Frenzied politicking ensued around the candidacy of the ignoble James K. Vardaman[28] (1861–1930), "the Great White Chief," the race-baiting patron of the "rednecks" and "white trash" of Mississippi. The legislature elected Percy by a close vote to serve out the unexpired term. That election was hardly over before nasty politicking began in earnest for the full term to begin in March of 1913. This time, the (white male) electorate at large voted in the Democratic primary, which at the time in this one-party state was tantamount to election, and Vardaman won. The rednecks had revolted.[29] LeRoy Percy's son, Will, reported, "An old man wet with tobacco juice and furtive-eyed summed up the result: 'Wal, the bottom rail's on top and it's gwiner stay thar.'"[30]

Fenwick Peck and his Newman Lumber Company, and most others in the lumber business in south Mississippi, took note, but they were not about to let such political winds thwart their pursuit of profits.

THE TEN-HOUR WORKDAY LAW

In 1912, Rep. Clitus Bordeaux Walker, a farmer and merchant from Meridian, introduced the ten-hour workday bill. In legislative language, it became known as House Bill No. 628,[31] or simply H.B. 628. The bill was handled on the floor by Rep. Guy Jack Rencher.[32] H.B. 628 passed in the house with seventy-three yeas and sixty-four nays, absent, or not voting.[33] In the senate, Sen. Lee Maurice Russell,[34] a lawyer from Oxford, proposed "except in case of emergency" and "public necessity" amendments to H.B. 628.[35] Russell would be elected lieutenant governor in 1915, and then governor in 1919.[36] H.B. 628 as amended passed the Senate with twenty-five yeas, one nay, and nineteen absent or not voting.[37]

Representative Oscar Goodbar Johnston, a lawyer from Friars Point, handled the amended version of H.B. 628 on the floor.[38] Johnston moved that the house non-concur with Russell's amendments. In response, Representative Rencher moved to table Johnston's motion. Ultimately, the house concurred in Senator Russell's amendments, with sixty-nine yeas, eight nays, and sixty absent or not voting.[39]

On July 12, 1912, with the approval of Gov. Earl Leroy Brewer,[40] the ten-hour workday became law.[41] At the time, the standard working day at most sawmills in Mississippi was eleven hours, and in the woods usually more. The law was intensely disliked by most mill owners, though many grudgingly complied with it. Newman Lumber Company was not among those. It decided immediately to test the constitutionality of the new law. Newman Lumber made sure it was the first company in the state to be charged with violating it. Nothing suggests Newman had anything concrete to fear from the new law.[42] Despite some ups and downs and the troubles of others in the business, several subsequent decades of profitable operations lay ahead for Newman Lumber. Still, circa 1912, entrepreneurs like Fenwick Peck saw incrementally increasing workplace reform "class legislation" as a threat far greater than the Hun to their view of America.

On July 18—six days after the new law took effect—a Lamar County grand jury indicted Newman Lumber. Nine misdemeanor offenses were charged, said to have been committed on July 15, 1912. The counts were similar, each naming a different Newman Lumber employee in a separate department of the company's Sumrall sawmill operations. With each of the nine, Newman Lumber was said "to contract . . . for work, to permit to work, and then and there to work . . . more than ten hours per day." The nine said to have worked eleven hours on July 15 were:

1. L. W. Bowman, foreman of yard number three, saw and planing mill plant;
2. H. E. Thompson, sawyer, sawmill plant;
3. R. E. McKaskey, millwright or machinist, sawmill plant;
4. Lee Moore, tail sawyer or slab tripper, sawmill plant;
5. T. C. Gibson, planing machine feeder, sawmill plant;
6. Hicks Dewitt, engineer in charge of engines, sawmill plant;
7. John Chance, checker in lumber shed, sawmill plant;
8. S. Newman, night watchman, sawmill plant; and
9. Will Loggins, conductor on logging train, logging railroad.

W. J. Haynen, the assistant general manager, was said to have been "in the control and operation of said saw and planing mill plant and logging railroad" and to have been responsible for overworking these men that day.[43] In each count, the indictment charged that the excessive hour of work was "not a case or work of emergency or a case of work where the public necessity required it," thus not fitting within an exception in the new statute. The indictment was signed by Toxey Hall, District Attorney, who filed it in the Lamar County courthouse.

On Monday, July 22, 1912, Newman Lumber struck back. It formally denied all charges. The company filed what lawyers then called general and special demurrers to the indictment, signed by W. J. Haynen, for the company, and by S. E. Travis, its lawyer with his office in Hattiesburg.[44] Lawyers know that demurrers are procedural acts of defiance. Newman Lumber was saying to the court that, even if everything charged in the indictment were true, the State still had no case. As a matter of practice, every factual allegation made in the indictment was taken as true for purposes of testing whether the defendant should have to stand trial at all.

The case moved quickly. The next day Circuit Judge A. E. Weathersby sustained the demurrers and dismissed the indictment. Later that day, District Attorney Hall filed a bill of exceptions requesting an appeal, and the next day he filed a formal notice of appeal. Twelve days after the effective date of the new law, Newman Lumber's challenge to its constitutional enforceability was on its way to the Supreme Court of Mississippi.

THE SUPREME COURT OF MISSISSIPPI IN 1912

In 1912, three justices constituted the state supreme court, all appointed by the governor and each representing a geographical district. It was a relatively inexperienced court. Justice Sydney McCain Smith[45] (1869–1948) of Holmes County had served from the central district since May 10, 1909, when Gov. Edmund F. Noel[46] elevated him from the office of circuit judge. Smith became chief justice in August of 1912, when he became the senior member of the court.[47]

In May of 1912, Justice Sam C. Cook (1855–1924) joined the court from the northern district. After receiving his law degree from the University of Mississippi in 1878, Cook lived and worked in his native Oxford under the tutelage of Judge James Stone,[48] father of Phil Stone, farmer, lawyer, and mentor to a young fellow who later made a name for himself, William Faulkner.

Cook practiced briefly in Holmes County, and then in Panola County, before settling in Clarksdale in the northwestern part of the Mississippi Delta. He served three two-year terms in the legislature, from 1886 to 1894. In 1902, Gov. Andrew H. Longino[49] appointed Cook a circuit judge for the Eleventh District, which included Clarksdale and Coahoma County. A decade later, Gov. Earl L. Brewer appointed Cook to the supreme court, where at times he showed himself a well-read man. For example, the core substantive issue in *State ex rel. Collins v. Jones*[50] was whether Mississippi should make a Progressive Era return to an elective judiciary. The war was waged on grounds of constitutional *stare decisis*, the amendment process having been before the supreme court in 1900, fourteen years earlier.[51] Justice Sam C. Cook closed his dissent with Shakespeare:

In the celebrated case of Shylock v. Antonio, Bassanio makes a powerful appeal to the judge to depart from the fixed rules and find a rule to fit the special case. I quote the appeal and the reply of the wise and just judge, viz:

Bassanio: And I beseech you / Wrest once the law to your authority: To do a great right, do a little wrong / And curb this cruel devil of his will.

Portia: It must not be; there is no power in Venice / Can after a decree established: 'Twill be recorded for a precedent, / And many an error, by the same example, Will rush into the state: It cannot be.[52]

Shakespeare's use of the King's English was as powerful as ever. Justice Cook's selection of the passage to make his point was also on the mark. The *Jones* majority no doubt sensed its sting and stood firm.

Shortly thereafter, so-called Progressive reform had restored popular election of the state's judiciary. Cook had sympathized with the Percy faction in the political wars with Vardaman. With the "bottom rail on top," Cook was defeated in 1921 when he sought election for another term. Cook's biographer said of him, "Few men in the State of Mississippi have borne themselves in high public office with more dignity and ability than Judge Sam C. Cook."[53] Cook's facsimile signature graces the ceiling of the old Stone Law Office on West Jackson Avenue, off the Oxford Town Square. James Stone of Oxford was an honorary pallbearer at Cook's funeral in Clarksdale in February of 1924.[54]

In the late summer of 1912, Governor Brewer appointed Richard Forman Reed (1861–1926) of Natchez to fill an unexpired southern district term, assuming the seat vacated by retiring Chief Justice R. B. Mayes. Two days later, the circuit clerk of Lamar County certified the appellate record in *State of Mississippi v. J. J. Newman Lumber Company*. Justice Reed and his court, and Newman Lumber plus another, were on course toward a constitutional encounter that peaked three months later.

A WISE AND GENTLE MAN

Richard Forman Reed would prove himself a judicial statesman in November of 1912. Born into one of the first families of antebellum Natchez,[55] he was educated at the University of Mississippi and studied law at Vanderbilt in 1884–1885. Reed then returned home, was admitted to the bar, and began the practice of law.

In 1911, fellow townsmen persuaded Reed to run for the office of state senator. He agreed but did not campaign. Instead, he slipped out of town shortly before the election. He was reported being abroad, soaking up the humanity of "'Shakespeare Country' when the cablegram came telling [him] of [his] election."[56] The following year Reed was an active candidate for a seat in the US

House of Representatives, when Chief Justice Mayes resigned from the supreme court. In short order, Governor Brewer offered the vacant court seat to Reed, who took the oath of office on August 12, 1912.[57]

For two years and nine months, Reed served with Chief Justice Smith and Justice Cook. When his term expired, on May 10, 1915, Reed returned to the private practice of law in Natchez. His local newspaper said of his service that his opinions "are masterpieces of English composition, and sometimes scintillate with that keen yet delicate sense of humor for which he was distinguished."[58] Before and after his time on the bench, Reed's love for his hometown was evident in his service as unofficial local historian.[59] He wrote a little book, *The Natchez Country*, detailing the history of lands where he was born and raised, from the arrival of Pierre le Moyne d'Iberville and the French about 1700. Years later, a local commentator noted that Reed "held the citation as the most eloquent and persuasive man who ever sat on the bench."[60] He died on May 31, 1926.

What we know of Richard Forman Reed, the man, the lawyer and the judge, aids understanding of what he did before, on, and shortly after November 18, 1912. His stature as a lawyer is evidenced by his successful litigation before the US Supreme Court in a complicated construction-law dispute in connection with the then-new post office building in Natchez.[61] In his postjudicial career, Reed appeared in another case in the US Supreme Court. In his law practice, Reed rarely took part in criminal cases. He was considered by some to be too kind, gentle, sympathetic to be a prosecutor. He was an officer in the American Humane Association,[62] a man who cared for God's creatures, great and small.

Two weeks before Justice Reed stood up to the powerful J. J. Newman Lumber Company, he stood up for "a negro boy 14 years of age" falsely accused by the white lady he worked for of stealing a diamond pin, which she valued at about $350. Mrs. Heath had young John Matthews whipped until he confessed, and then she had him prosecuted and convicted for larceny. Emphatically, Reed ruled that "such confessions were surely not free and voluntary."[63] It is not unfair to say that, at the time, more than a few state judges would have sided with Mrs. Heath.

A year and a half later, and with like humanity, he told the story of "Lou Garner's monkey biting Sarah Phillips on her leg." "He was a great big old monkey," according to Sarah. "Yes, sir; I drug him all the way up the steps and into the house. He had me by the leg, by the teeth." "The monkey also attacked a girl and a dog while out of his cage on this occasion." After explaining for the court that the law holds the owner of a wild animal strictly liable for personal injuries it might inflict, Justice Reed concluded, "Lou Garner should not have permitted her monkey to run at large. She should have kept it confined and secure, so that it would do no harm. It was at large and did harm. She is answerable in damages for the hurt it has done."[64]

CROCODILE TEARS AND RABBIT TRAILS

On November 8, 1912, lawyer S. E. Travis filed with the clerk of the Supreme Court of Mississippi the brief of appellee Newman Lumber Company. His written argument of why the ten-hour workday law should fall began with the rhetorical question "Is sawing logs into lumber manufacturing?"[65] In fairness, Newman Lumber never seriously argued that its sawmill and railroad operations were not enough to establish that the company was "engaged in manufacturing or repairing" within the new act. Still, as we approach the argument that Newman Lumber did make, it is important to have well in mind that "labor in the sawmills was extremely demanding and, depending on the job, required intelligence, quick-thinking, agility, strength, and the ability to withstand brutal heat and humidity amid the deafening screams of high-speed saws. The noise level was so high that sawyers communicated with block setters through hand signals. Some of the work was extremely dangerous."[66]

Newman Lumber made a problematic admission at the outset. It conceded that states do have the police power "by appropriate legislation, to prescribe hours of labor in so far as may be reasonably necessary to protect the public health, safety, morals and general welfare."[67] Perhaps counsel advised that such a concession had to be made. After all, the Mississippi Constitution said that "the exercise of the police powers of the State shall never be abridged."[68] Still, the lumber company argued that the new ten-hour workday law was not within the state's police powers. One reason was that—by its terms—the new law could apply to some work activities where there might be minimal, if any, risk of harm from an employee's working more than ten hours a day. In other words, Newman Lumber's lawyer was insisting upon a legislative scalpel that could include with precision all activities where there is harm to the public health, safety, morals, and general welfare of the workers—as the employer might measure that harm—but would at once exclude every other work activity.

The Newman Lumber brief never questioned the commonsense premise that—by reason of the work environment it provided in its logging, sawmill, and railroad operations—at a certain point in a long day, the men became more susceptible to injury if they continued working. A quick thumb-through of the photographs that lumber industry historian Gilbert Hoffman has provided in his classic work removes any doubt that Newman's premises and equipment qualified as a dangerous place to work.[69] Verbal descriptions by others are equally impressive.

> The log carriage, which moved the logs to the head of the saw at great speed, sometimes split into sharp, pointed pieces, endangering the workers who operated the carriage blocks. The band saw blades sometimes fractured, sending sharp steel projectiles throughout the space in the vicinity of the head rig. Carriage gears

broke, and the carriage would run out of control and crash, throwing its operators into the air and into great danger. One longtime industry observer remembered that a "man with five fingers had trouble getting a job in some planing mills. The foreman figured that unless he had lost a finger or two he lacked experience."[70]

And so "accidents around a sawmill and in the log woods were a frequent occurrence because of the dangerous nature of both operations."[71]

Serious workplace accidents on Newman Lumber's premises were documented. On August 6, 1910, Thomas Mayott, a twenty-five-year-old lumber handler, was killed on the job.[72] On September 30, 1911, W. W. Quinn, a night sawyer, was severely injured when a log struck Quinn over his heart, causing injuries with doubtful recovery.[73] On September 23, 1912, John Walters, a minor, suffered a crushed, bruised, and broken ankle on a logging car on a Newman train.[74] On November 14, 1912, John Boyd, age thirty-seven, a Newman employee, was killed while riding a Newman log train.[75] On March 6, 1913, John Russell, age twenty-four, a brakeman, was killed when he was caught and crushed between a Newman boxcar and a projecting log from a log car.[76] That the work in Newman Lumber's sawmills presented occupational hazards was further evidenced by the fact that in 1913 "a negro boy about 16 or 17 years of age" was injured on the job "which resulted in the amputation of . . . [his] leg above the knee."[77] A skidder foreman, just twenty-two years old, suffered a similar accident at Newman Lumber's Sumrall mill a few years later. "I had a drum man who was not good and he got his line tangled up in the skidder. I got up on there to help him untangle that and got in the gear wheel and cut my foot off."[78]

Newman Lumber's lawyer never mentioned a number of other points one would have thought quite relevant, had they in fact been so. Newman never argued

- that its business would suffer if it were forced to comply with the new law;
- that there was any occupational necessity that the nine workers named in the indictment—and no doubt many others—work eleven hours on July 15;
- what the normal workday theretofore had been for employees like the nine, though the eleven-hour workday seemed to have been the known norm;[79]
- that a single employee had ever asked to be allowed to work more hours a day, that he needed more work because he needed more income to support his family;
- that its workers were paid by the hour, that working extra hours would mean extra income for its employees; or
- that laborers as a group would not benefit from the new law, except to say that a laborer had a right to work as many hours as his boss would let him work.

What Newman Lumber Company never said, as well as what it did say, was consistent with the views of industrialists and businessmen prevailing before

World War I. Widely accepted theories of Social Darwinism argued that, in the struggle for survival in the industrial world, the strongest succeeded. Classical laissez-faire economic theory enjoyed near-biblical authority among American captains of industry[80] within whose ranks Fenwick Peck sought to be included. The land-of-opportunity view of the United States meant that every entrepreneur was of right entitled to produce and market such products or services as he had the capacity to produce or provide and as he believed the public would buy, and without state interference. To assist in his production and marketing, each employer was of right entitled to hire whomever he pleased and whoever would agree to work for him. En route he could use whatever operational strategy he chose and could provide for his workers such conditions, practices, workday hours, equipment—and pay—as he thought best, and as the workers would accept. Unhappy workers were always legally free to seek a livable income elsewhere or otherwise.

Never mind that "liberty" in the constitutional due process sense had conventionally been thought of in terms of jails and prisons and other forms of incarceration by the state. For businessmen, no liberty was cherished more than liberty of contract, accepting, of course, the fiction that employer and employee had even a semblance of equal bargaining power when it came to contracting for wages and hours and other terms and conditions of employment. This called to mind the tongue-in-cheek insight of French writer and Nobel Prize laureate Anatole France, viz., "The law, in its majestic equality, forbids the rich as well as the poor to sleep under bridges, to beg in the streets, and to steal bread,"[81] words well known in the early twentieth century. Still, Newman Lumber argued, "Legislation has usually proceeded on the theory that men are 'free and equal' and the courts have always required substantial and valid reasons to uphold class legislation of any kind."[82] Nationwide, these views had been under increasing attack for more than a decade. In the courts, the "men who made America" were not winning as often as they thought they should. By 1912, the fight had reached Mississippi.

Lochner[83] in 1904—striking down the New York ten-hour workday for bakery workers—had been a setback for the reformers. Eight years later it was Newman Lumber's big gun in its brief on appeal—a block quote taking up almost four full pages of single-spaced, legal-size paper.[84] Notably, Newman Lumber's lawyer said the State's "counsel seems to lose sight of the fact that our own Constitution is perhaps more sweeping and exacting as regards the questions involved than the Federal Constitution."[85] With some justification, the argument cited and quoted from the State's due process clause,[86] the State's no-impairment-of-contracts clause,[87] and from the "remedy by due course of law" prong of the state open-courts clause.[88] After all, federally guaranteed rights provide only a floor, a minimum potpourri of rights of persons and firms that the states must respect. States have always been free to assure their individual and corporate citizens of greater freedoms from governmental interference.[89]

Then Newman Lumber's lawyer turned up the heat. The written argument moved to rhetoric, exaggeration, and hyperbole: if this law were to be upheld, "we can no longer boast of 'the land of the free.'" If employers and workers cannot decide for themselves the length of the working day, "they cease to be free."[90] If this law is upheld, "no man and no business is free from this limitless police power." A decision against Newman Lumber "would transform [the police power] into an agency for oppression and tyranny which would shackle every business and calling and deprive every man of that liberty, freedom of vocation and pursuit of happiness guaranteed by the federal and state constitutions." "The act in question is so arbitrary, extravagant, discriminatory and oppressive as to strike at the very foundation of free government, and we feel and earnestly submit must be held unconstitutional if we are to remain a free people."[91]

This sort of rhetorical bombast was common among industry lawyers of the time. The men who argued so genuinely convinced themselves that they were speaking eternal verities. Their fervor had increased, as in the years leading to 1912. Top management in big business had been under attack, at least since the Sherman Anti-Trust Act in 1890.[92] They pressed to extremes the breadth of economic liberty within the protections of federal and state due process clauses. *Lochner* had given traction to the idea that some, if not most, employment reform statutes impermissibly interfered with the employer's liberty. The State was thought to have no way around the entrepreneur's article of faith that such laws deprived him of cherished liberty of contract without due process of law.

JUSTICE REED'S REASONABLE RESPONSE

Ten days after the Newman Lumber brief was filed, the Supreme Court of Mississippi ruled. The order sustaining the demurrers was reversed. The case was remanded to the Circuit Court of Lamar County, where the J. J. Newman Lumber Company would have to stand trial on the indictment. Justice Richard Reed had spoken for the court.

After a labored introduction, telling in lawyer language what the case was about, Reed penned a civics lesson.[93] "No society can continue without its members being required to give up some of what they deem are their personal rights and liberties." He spoke of the personal imperative for self-discipline. Though Newman Lumber argued federal and states' rights, Justice Reed took particular note of the Tenth Amendment prerogatives of the states. "The powers not delegated to the United States by this Constitution, nor prohibited to it by the States, are reserved to the States respectively, or to the people." The parties and the public were reminded that state government "is instituted solely for the good of the whole," and that this included employees as well as—and as much as—entrepreneurs. And that "the legislative power of this state shall be vested in the Legislature."[94]

Reed's cogent walk through the practice of judicial review followed, as he explained the judicial duty to defer to the enacting legislature.[95] Courts should be "very careful before holding [unconstitutional and thus unenforceable] any law passed touching the welfare of the citizens." "But it is not for the court to decide whether a law is needed or advisable in the general government of the people." A pithy Holmes supporting paragraph of then recent vintage followed.[96] Finally, "the controlling question in this case is whether the law before us is for the welfare of the people, and whether it will promote the health, morals and good order of the people affected." The opinion soon refined the "controlling question" to mean whether the legislature rationally may have found that "the law before us is for the welfare of the people," and that it may credibly be thought to "promote the health, morals and good order of the people affected."

Next Reed turned to *Holden v. Hardy*, a ruling from fourteen years earlier upholding an eight-hour workday statute, albeit for employment in Utah's underground mines. He described the law's flexibility and capacity for growth, only to show "the probability that other changes of no less importance may be made in the future."[97] Mississippi's ten-hour workday law "may not have been needed half a century ago, but may be needed at the present time. In fact, the department of the government of this state, known as the Legislature, has decided that the law is needed." Justice Reed then slid into the sensible notion that rights in contracts and property are "subject to such reasonable limitations in their enjoyment as will prevent them from being injurious," quoting the widely respected Chief Justice Lemuel Shaw from Massachusetts. Such limitations are imposed "as the Legislature, under the governing power vested in them by the Constitution may think necessary and expedient."[98]

Few knowledgeable persons would have criticized Justice Reed if he had held, notwithstanding all else, that the court was bound by *Lochner*, a sweeping exposition though only the hours worked by bakery workers in New York were formally at issue. It would have been easy enough to distinguish *Holden v. Hardy*. Everyone knows that subsurface mine workers face great dangers. Besides, *Lochner* was then the most recent utterance from the US Supreme Court. Justice Brewer had carefully limited *Muller v. Oregon*, so that it applied only to women workers, ostensibly leaving *Lochner* undisturbed.[99]

Reed recognized that the *Lochner* majority's rhetoric needed to be deflected. He used a twofold approach. First, he noted that the Mississippi ten-hour workday law had an exception for emergencies and cases of public necessity. The New York bakery worker statute had none. The *Lochner* majority had cited the point in avoiding the holding of *Holden v. Hardy*. Reed seized upon that *Lochner* quote to show that the *Newman Lumber* case was not controlled by *Lochner* but by *Holden v. Hardy*.[100]

Second, Reed noted that *Lochner* was a five-to-four decision, and then quoted from dissents by Justices John Marshall Harlan and Oliver Wendell

Holmes[101] to the point that the *Lochner* dissenters had the better of the argument.[102] Not only was *Lochner* probably wrong, and would likely be distinguished when the US Supreme Court next had the chance. President Taft had reconstituted the court, appointing five new justices. Three of the *Lochner* dissenters—Holmes, White, and Day—remained on the bench in 1912. Arguably, *Muller* had weakened the *Lochner* precedent. Through the "Brandeis Brief," empirical evidence had triumphed over arid legal logic as grounds for decision. These developments portended a change in the way such social and economic reform cases would be presented to the courts.[103] Mississippi might ultimately have to fall in line with *Lochner*. The State could wait, however, until the signals from Washington became clearer, and came from the newly constituted court. The Tenth Amendment and the open-textured wording of the Mississippi constitutional clauses called to the court's attention in the arguments of the parties to give Reed the needed wiggle room, at least in the short run.

Newman Lumber's Fourteenth Amendment federal due process argument dispatched, Reed moved to clean-up mode, adding a number of congenial quotes from Mississippi cases. He concluded this part of his opinion with the most persuasive authority of all, given the venue and the times, the "statutes governing Jehovah's ancient people, Israel" as handed down by "the greatest lawmaker." When men might work and when they were forbidden to work had long been matters regulated by law from the highest source.

Overblown rhetoric from Newman Lumber's lawyer set up Reed's summation. "It is well known that, in the work connected with the running of machinery, the operation is subject to a mental as well as physical strain." The point seemed sensible enough. "In many cases the nearness to machinery makes the work dangerous in case of an overtaxing of the strength of the worker, or any lessening of his alertness." A simple observation simply made, referencing only "many cases." The Legislature might "readily" so "understand" the matter.[104]

Justice Reed followed with a legalistic articulation of the police power worded for the lay reader. No dogmatic "ten hours a day are enough"—only that the Mississippi legislature could rationally have thought this so, in its sense of "the good of the whole" people of the state.[105] No over-the-top invocation of the Mississippi Constitution.[106] He then gave a nod to "the present manner of laboring, the use of machinery, the appliances requiring intelligence and skill." The then-modern sawmill required skilled workers to operate the machines that were central to production.[107] Reed added, "It seems to us quite reasonable, and in no way improper, to pass such a law so limiting a day's labor."

And what did Newman Lumber's lawyer say about all of this? He propounded a shrill charge that the new law was "an unreasonable, unnecessary, and arbitrary interference with the property, liberty, rights, privileges and immunities of those engaged in manufacturing or repairing, and their employees." The last phrase would make a high school student pause. Just how and when had "their employees" so complained? Reed let this one pass, ending with deference: "The Legislature of Mississippi has decided that this is not so, and we abide by their decision."[108]

Reed had addressed and answered the arguable points Newman Lumber put forward, but he had not followed the rabbit trails. The Newman Lumber brief had argued everything but the case at hand. Its crocodile tears were seen as such. Reed had kept his eye on the ball. He had respected and practiced judicial review and with reasonable restraint. Ninety years after *Runnels v. State* and the brouhaha that followed *Cochrane & Murdock v. Kitchens*, judicial review had become accepted practice.[109] With a deference not unlike that articulated by Judge Powhatan Ellis in *Runnels*,[110] Reed had found the legislature within its prerogatives this time, when it passed the ten-hour workday bill. He had seized the constitutional moment and eased us through it.

A SECOND WILD SHOT

What happened next suggests that Fenwick Peck and Newman Lumber Company's top management were stunned by the court's decision. The company added more legal firepower for the next round. The law firms of Green & Green and Whitfield, McNeil and Whitfield, both of Jackson, were retained. Through these lawyers, Newman Lumber filed a suggestion of error on December 2, 1912.[111] Forty-two pages of angry arguments: "This crudest imaginable piece of legislation is an Act in one section."[112]

Justice Sam C. Cook—in his eighth month as a member of the court—had primary responsibility for Newman Lumber's suggestion of error. Common sense suggests it is an appropriate institutional practice that, in the event of such a request, the court reconsider its decision, primary responsibility for handling the request should be assigned to a justice not so invested in outcome as the author of the original opinion. On January 6, 1913, the court released Cook's opinion, overruling the suggestion of error. The opinion is worth a read, although it does not hold up as well as Reed's original opinion. Cook responded directly to the strident tone that Newman Lumber's new Jackson lawyers put forth, letting them set the agenda.

He began with a pointed barb, as he "paused here to remark the notable fact that it is rare for the seller of labor to appeal to the courts for the preservation of his inalienable rights to labor. This inestimable privilege is generally the object of the buyer's disinterested solicitude."[113] In its original written argument, Newman Lumber had been careful to profess great caring and concern for the freedom and liberty of its workers. In its new counsel's forty-two-page suggestion of error, Newman Lumber sets out the various ways in which the freedom and liberty of entrepreneurs were being destroyed, planting as many ploys as counsel could think of. New counsel argued that the statute might be applied in ways that would seem absurd, without ever saying it was being so applied in the case before the court. Ironically, Newman Lumber had stripped any credibility from such arguments by its strategic decision to test the statute and the indictment with demurrers, rather than going to trial and trying to prove the points of legislative and industrial fact argued with testimony, empirical analyses, and other evidence.

Tellingly, at a last-minute proofreading of the suggestion of error, new counsel realized they had forgotten to argue the rights of employees too! Near the end, we find counsel's handwritten corrections and inserts. After arguing that the statute's "classification of persons, firms and corporations engaged in manufacturing ... is ... arbitrary and unreasonable," counsel inserted in cursive script a new sentence, "Think of the injury to the rights of the employees!"[114] Careful comparison of the handwriting on pages 36 and 37 with the lawyer's handwritten certificate of service on page 42 suggests the same person scripted all.

Cook took note of the "many illustrations of the far-reaching effects of the [new] law and the calamitous consequences which will inevitably follow its enforcement," as suggested by Newman Lumber's new lawyers. This parade-of-horribles argument strategy was no more persuasive then than it has ever been. In January of 1913, it did, however, put Cook into a defensive mode. He responded that "when we now speak of manufacturing we *usually* have in mind an organized force of laborers, working with machinery, to produce from raw materials the finished product. The broader language in our former opinion is qualified to harmonize with this definition."[115] But with what effect? The enforceability of the ten-hour workday statute had been upheld. The text of that statute remained as the legislature enacted it. Fenwick Peck couldn't have cared less that the reading and application of the state's police powers may have been narrowed somewhat from the opinion of November 18, 1912. His company had still been ordered to trial on the indictment.

Cook was correct that "the English language is elastic." And he was correct when he quoted the wise insight of an earlier case that "human language is not a perfect vehicle for conveying thoughts," including those of legislators and judges. But Cook was off the mark when he began musing about the unexpressed subjective intentions of legislators, which may hardly be known with any level of confidence.[116] The question before the justices in a case like *Newman Lumber* was not "what the legislature *meant* ... [but] what the statute *means*."[117] To be sure, "legislators must be presumed to be reasonable and sane men,"[118] rhetorical expositions to the contrary notwithstanding.[119] But this did not mean the court might expound upon unexpressed intent and—without substantial documentation through reference to underlying legislative facts— rely on its views of what the legislature ought to have meant when it enacted the ten-hour workday law.

Read as a whole, Cook's opinion was talking about the traditional assumed difference between agricultural labor and manufacturing. This dichotomous mind-set was manifest a century later, as farm labor remains excluded from coverage under the Mississippi Workers' Compensation Act.[120] But it was not a distinction the legislature enacted as a part of the ten-hour workday law. And so the question is, how we should read—and to what extent we should credit— what Cook said when he said, "It would be absurd, we think, to construe this statute to apply to the work of laborers engaged in felling timber in the open air in the equable climate of this state, because he is employed by an employer engaged in manufacturing. It would be fully as reasonable to suggest that the plowman, working in company with a band of agricultural laborers, was covered by the terms of the law."[121]

In a nod to the era, and perhaps disclosing a prejudice, Cook added that "we believe the most radical Progressive would hesitate to give the law an application so broad."[122] His words suggested he may not have fully appreciated what sort of work was involved in felling trees and hauling logs, or how much of the work in a sawmill was not done "in the open air in the equable climate of this state." He showed no awareness of the industrial dangers that logging and timber production presented the worker, much less of the actual loss of life and limb attendant on the Newman Lumber operations, as evidenced by the records of other cases before the court on which he served. Cook seemed to have spent a lot more time in a law office and in the courthouse (albeit in the days before air conditioning) than in the open air in the flat, treeless fields of rural Coahoma County under a hot, burning summer sun. His words did not suggest an objective reading of an enacted text, applied to facts admitted by the demurrers.

More fundamentally, Cook stepped out of the judicial role du jour when he said that whether Newman Lumber was engaged in manufacturing or repairing was a question of fact. That was a core question for the jury at the trial on remand. It may well have been a question of evidentiary fact whether "a particular laborer . . . is required to work in manufacturing within the meaning of the law," but that was of no concern to the court, given the procedural posture in which Newman Lumber had chosen to stand and fight. That was not a question within the court's role in its judicial review of the ten-hour workday statute. The court then said terms of the new law were "intended to be reasonable in their application," which means the court must stay tethered to those terms. But Cook became more than a quasi-legislator when—in a direct response to the wild charges argued by Newman Lumber's new lawyers—he argued that "to interpret the words used . . . in their broadest and most comprehensive sense would, to our way of thinking, destroy the law, as well as the intention of its makers." He should have reread Holmes's *Lochner* dissent before writing his opinion denying Newman Lumber's suggestion of error.

In the end, Justice Cook returned to the mark. Newman Lumber "was indicted for a violation of the statute and filed demurrers to the indictment, which demurrers were sustained. The demurrers should have been overruled."[123]

All the while, there had been a similar case from the Circuit Court of Lincoln County involving the Butterfield Lumber Company.[124] The appeal in that case was perfected in September of 1912, on a track only slightly behind that of *Newman Lumber*.[125] Lawyers T. Brady Jr.[126] and Jones & Tyler, all of Brookhaven, had appeared for Butterfield Lumber on appeal.[127] On January 6, 1913, the court reversed the *Butterfield Lumber* judgment for the company on the authority of the *Newman Lumber* decision and remanded the case for trial. On January 20, 2013, the suggestion of error in *Butterfield Lumber* was denied.[128]

The ten-hour workday law emerged formally unscathed. It remained in full force and effect according to its terms, the rhetoric of Newman Lumber's new lawyers—and some emanating from the pen of Sam C. Cook as well—to the contrary notwithstanding.

J. J. Newman Lumber Company survived its appellate defeat of January 6, 1913. The company grudgingly paid its fine without trial. In the end, Newman Lumber "had to reduce the working hours of its employees to comply with the state law." Then again, Newman Lumber never really said it had any concrete concerns about the ten-hour workday law. At one point, Newman Lumber vowed to take the case all the way to the US Supreme Court, but it never did so. Other lumber companies in Mississippi knuckled under, complying with the new law without any adverse effect on their business.[129]

Not all of Newman Lumber's employees fared so well, though for reasons beyond the hours they worked. In a case noted above, Adolph Dantzler was injured while at work, "which resulted in the amputation of plaintiff's leg above the knee." Justice Cook spoke for the court in reversing a $3,000 damage award in the circuit court. In an opinion less thoughtful than the one he wrote in *Newman Lumber*, but arguably consistent with the law at the time, Cook invoked the fellow servant rule and assumption of risk to deny "a negro boy about 16 or 17 years of age" the $3,000 judgment he had won at trial.[130]

The boy did not get his leg back either.

WHITTLING AWAY AT *NEWMAN LUMBER*

Six weeks after *Newman Lumber*, the third member of the court, Chief Justice Sydney Smith, spoke to the meaning and effect of the ten-hour workday law. Buckeye Cotton Oil Company, doing business in Hinds County, had been charged with working five employees for more than ten hours on a day named. *Buckeye Cotton Oil Co. v. State*[131] upheld a company's conviction for violating the new law. Four dimensions of the decision merit mention.

First, the court reaffirmed the constitutionality of the statute: "We have again, at the request of counsel, taken up the constitutionality of this statute for consideration, and see no reason for receding from the views expressed by us in State v. Newman Lumber Co." The court next considered and rejected the arguments that "the statute was not intended to apply to cotton seed oil mills" and that "the employees worked by it for more than 10 hours are not of the class of employees contemplated by the statute."[132] The court recited the details of the operation of the cotton oil mill, as per an agreed statement of facts, then applied the *Newman Lumber* holding on the point: "From this it clearly appears that appellant is engaged in manufacturing."

Smith then went beyond the words of the statute. He considered—one by one—the work done by each of the five employees. Three of the workers were held to be "within the protection of the statute, and appellant violated it in working them more than 10 hours in one day." On the agreed statement of facts, a fourth worker may have been "on duty only for one hour at a time and then off for an hour, and not then . . . charged with some responsibility for the operation of the machinery." If "he was . . . at work . . . for more than 10 hours . . . , it is immaterial that he may have had at times practically nothing to do."[133] A fifth worker was a supervisor and thus may not have fallen within the statute.[134] No such worker-by-worker analysis was authorized by the text of the statute.[135] What Smith did was a function of Cook's dubious musings of six weeks earlier.[136]

Fourth, and finally, *Buckeye Cotton Oil* construed the statute and held that but a single offense had been committed. The statute read that "each day's violation shall constitute a separate offense."[137] The text did not add that each person who worked more than ten hours on each day represented a separate offense. "Had the Legislature desired the working of each employee to constitute a separate offense, it could easily have used language so indicating."[138] Perhaps so, but it might seem unlikely that the legislative plan had been to impose the same penalty per day for working each of five men—or maybe twenty-five—more than ten hours a day, as for a single laborer. In the end, *Buckeye Cotton Oil* concluded what *Newman Lumber* had begun. A misdemeanor conviction of a company violating the ten-hour workday statute had been upheld.

The statute next came under legislative attack. An amendment was passed in 1914 to exclude employers or workers "engaged in handling or converting perishable agricultural products in season."[139] A more extensive amendment came two years later. Railroads and public service corporations were removed from the coverage of the law.[140] Flexibility was added to the permissible hours of work per day, provided that in the end "sixty hours shall constitute a full week's work under the provisions of this act."[141]

Two regressive child labor cases followed.[142] In each, the injured youth worker had filed a tort action against his employer, a lumber company. In each, Justice Eugene O. Sykes[143] (1876–1945) authored an opinion affirming a judgment below for the employer. In *Hardy v. Mercantile Lumber Co.*, the court quoted from Sam Cook's opinion in *Newman Lumber*, then from Sydney Smith's opinion in *Buckeye Cotton Oil*.[144] By 1920, the ten-hour workday law had survived constitutional assault. Legislative amendments followed by restrictive judicial applications had confirmed the familiar adage that there is more than one way to skin a cat. The mere fact that a legislative initiative is constitutionally permissible does not mean it is politically sustainable.

LIBERTY OF CONTRACT

There really is a liberty of contract that each of us—person or firm—may enjoy. The common law of contracts affords the historical and conceptual context. This page of legal history and practice is as important as it has been often ignored when *Lochner*-type issues were being argued. In 1908, the Butterfield Lumber Company had been reassured that "[t]here is no law restricting the right of all persons to make contracts to suit themselves, when the contract violates no law. The safety of commercial transactions depends on this."[145] The qualifier—"when the contract violates no law"—was one way of putting a point that dates to decades past. There has always been a common law exception—a public policy exception to the practice of liberty of contract. As far back as the reign of the Mississippi Constitution of 1832, it has been the law that contracts contrary to public policy were unenforceable.[146] The exception has persisted in cases after the constitution of 1890 took effect, with no mention made of any constitutional connotations.[147]

For the most part, judges have made and fleshed out this exception to contract enforceability. Courts have asked whether a contract was "violative of public policy, or of a positive rule of law, or against good morals."[148] Such judicial lawmaking was supposed to have been grounded in the facts of organized society and how people have lived with each other, though in years past reliable assessments of those facts may have been problematic. At least it so appears, given twenty-twenty hindsight. Such judge-made law could always be overruled by a higher order of law, such as a statute or administrative regulation or a later common law court case. Whatever the species of law employed, such exceptions were but particular instances of public policy offenses that could vitiate an otherwise enforceable contract.

All of Mississippi's constitutions have said that the legislature is the foremost expositor of public policy, save only for the constitution itself. But no sensible person suggests the courts in their inherent lawmaking role should hesitate to fill gaps until the legislature gets around to exercising its lawmaking powers. This, of course, assumes a proper case has arisen, that the legislative facts have been fairly identified and assessed, the court taking care not to disappoint reasonable reliance expectations.[149] The rule of precedent would take it from there. The ten-hour workday law in 1912 was nothing more than a legislative public policy exception to the enforceability of common law contracts of employment that in other times would have raised no eyebrows.

There are respectable constitutional groundings for the prerogatives of persons and firms practicing their liberty of contract. These start with the political freedoms secured and historically enjoyed in the Western World. They include the judicial power to hold people to their promises.[150] Past that, the State has been told that it might not deprive a person or firm of liberty or property except by due process of law. This injunction is a function of the Fourteenth Amendment to the US Constitution[151] and Section 14 of the Mississippi Constitution.[152] Federal and state constitutions also remind the State that it may not impair the obligations of valid and enforceable contracts.[153] To be sure, these provide principles, not commands that may be read or enforced with geometric precision. The men of James Madison's time understood constitutions as providing principles the meaning and application of which would evolve through the ages. Each of Mississippi's four constitutions—as with all good constitutions—has been presumed capable of ordering human affairs decades after its making, "under circumstances beyond the prescience of the draftsmen."[154] Sensible men so see the state's present constitution. Only recently have willful and short-sighted men returned and sought once again to enshrine in particular constitutional texts the majority's meanness of the moment.[155]

It does not matter that neither the word "contract" nor the phrase "liberty of contract" appears. Nor does it matter that the same constitutional texts protect other liberties, such as freedom from imprisonment or other forms of incarceration, except where due process of law prior thereto yields a decision otherwise. In any organized society the practice of "liberty" includes making arrangements with others that each may expect the other will honor. That this value—and its public policy exceptions—were first and more often expressed as common law does not mean that it is not a constitutional value that cannot be removed without amending the text. "Property" is broad enough to include rights held under enforceable contracts.

Making and performing new contracts are familiar enough that those useful practices should enjoy a measure of protection, to the extent that the constitutional text will permit. And the same for exceptions in cases where clauses are "violative of public policy, or of a positive rule of law, or against good morals."[156] At this level of generality, no constitution inquires as to the relative bargaining power of the parties. It may be that a person who borrows money from a bank—and signs a contract in that regard—has no more bargaining power vis-à-vis the bank than H. E. Thompson or R. E. McKaskey had back in 1912 vis-à-vis the Newman Lumber Company. Our constitutions honor liberty of contract, albeit that liberty—like all liberties—is not without constraints. All rights in one way or another are subject to reasonable regulation as to time, place, and manner of enjoyment or enforcement.

PETTY AND NOT-SO-PETTY LARCENY

The other side of the coin is equally a lesson from constitutional encounters straddling both sides of the new year 1913. Justice Richard Reed put it well when he reminded us, "No society can continue without its members being required to give up some of what they deem are their personal rights and liberties."[157] And so a person's or a firm's liberty of contract, freedom of contract, right to contract, common law prerogative—whatever the label chosen—may be constrained or even lost by due process of law.[158]

The phrase "due process of law" invites an insight often missed. Newman Lumber Company suffered its rather minimal deprivation at the hands of the legislature. The legislature has a process for making law. The constitution vests the substantive and the procedural dimensions of "the legislative power of this state" in a bicameral legislature.[159] The legislature enacted and the governor signed into law the ten-hour workday bill. That was the process constitutionally due before such a law might become enforceable. Such a bill was within the political power constitutionally so vested in the legislature, a particular kind of legislative power, commonly called the "police power." And so we reflect upon the familiar, the petty larceny of the police power.[160] Hardly a law may be imagined that does not impose some cost on someone. It is the job of the court—when properly called upon—to exercise its judicial power and determine whether the act exceeded the legislature's prerogatives. And to determine whether considering all else the legislative process was within that which the constitution said it was due to exercise. Of course, in the end, the court must reliably engage and exercise the process of adjudication, applying particular law to the facts of the particular case.

Persons and firms are protected from partial deprivations of their property, though those should be substantial. In the summer of 1912, Newman Lumber Company was not deprived of all freedom to contract with its workers, only of its apparent habit and preference that its workers labor more than ten hours a day. The new law's practical impact on employers engaged in "manufacturing and repairing" was *de minimis*. Neither Newman Lumber nor any other company that litigated the point ever even tried to prove it would experience any quantifiable harm from the ten-hour workday law. Today we might think of the familiar eight-hour workday, or eight-hour shift in many manufacturing contexts. No constitutional problem there either, though there is a limit. The state may not constrict the standard workday so greatly that its utility becomes substantially impaired. Enforceability turns on the question of practical consequences, though the greatest of reasonable deference must be afforded those in whom the constitution vests the legislative power, and particularly the police power.

Justice Sam Cook spoke to these matters in 1913. But he added confusion when he argued, "The liberty to contract is not a fundamental constitutional right."[161] The idea that some rights are conceptually more fundamental than others is a will-o'-the -wisp, elusive to the grasp and to the practical mind. One's right to exercise religious freedom is protected because and to that extent the constitution says so, and that is all. Of course, constitutional rights or powers trump—to the extent of a conflict—other lower-order rights, powers, or interests protected or regulated by statutes or common law. We have the constitutional practice of judicial review to address these conflicts. But "fundamental constitutional right" has no practical meaning beyond what may be found in the phrase "constitutional right."

A constitutional power may butt heads with a constitutional right. Police power versus liberty of contract as per *Newman Lumber* is such a case. Another is the police power to require vaccination of schoolchildren against some dreaded and contagious disease, trumping a parent's insistence that such a vaccination is contrary to his or her sincerely held religious beliefs.[162] In each instance, the police power is being legislatively exercised in enacting public policy. Each recognizes a public policy exception to an otherwise quite genuine and enforceable right. Without more, it is never an answer to the question that yields, that the right is "fundamental." Against the backdrop of these constitutional tensions, *Newman Lumber* leaves little doubt that questions such as whether the people should have wage and hour laws are for their democratically elected legislature. This is certainly so in the first instance.

LEGISLATIVE FACTS AND ECONOMIC ANALYSES

Newman Lumber leaves us with the serious question of how citizens in a representative democracy—confronted with whether a limited-workday law should be enacted—should want their legislators to go about deciding what to do. And secondarily, on judicial review, how people should want their judges to go about deciding the enforceability of such a law, where the stakes are higher and the considerations more complex than in *Runnels* or in *Cochrane & Murdock*.[163] These are questions upon which reasonable citizens disagree and may be confounded when confronted with a reminder of the constitutional exhortation "All government of right ... is instituted solely for the good of the whole."[164]

For one thing, the arguable applications of the constitution to a ten-hour workday law and other like laws should be subjected to practical economic analyses.[165] By the time of *Newman Lumber*, it had been fifteen years since another state supreme court justice in another part of the country had famously proclaimed, "For the rational study of the law the black-letter man may be the man of the present, but the man of the future is the man of statistics and the master of economics."[166] Moreover, it had long been accepted practice that on judicial review in such cases courts go "outside the record" to consider such legislative facts and learn from the ideas and works of scholars. In January of 1913, there was nothing improper in Justice Cook's citing, quoting, and applying the work of Prof. Ernst Freund, a respected American academician of the times.[167] A century earlier, Judge Joshua G. Clarke had drawn on the insights of the French political philosopher Jean-Jacques Rousseau.[168] A generation later, (still) Chief Justice Sydney Smith would rely heavily on the thought of Dean Roscoe Pound, albeit without direct attribution. We are in college now.

We have learned that, in searching for "the good of the whole,"[169] legislators and governors and judges and lawyers, political interest groups, and just plain folk should do their best to understand enough economics to assess reliably how people might be affected if employers were forced to reduce the length of their workday. At what point does such a law generate incentives that employers reduce daily wages paid each worker?[170] Stop hiring altogether? Should the court consider employers in the aggregate, or some informed selection of employers as in a particular industry or type of service, or merely the employer whose case is before the court? And the same for workers? How should legislatures and governors—and later courts—factor in what a worker gains from intangibles such as additional time for leisure, or more tangible access to healthcare and safety? And what those gains cost employers—and consumers—and how those gains and costs should be weighed and balanced? Again, regarding social reform legislation, an insight from Holmes, the wise, viz.,

> To know what you want and why you think that such a measure will help it is the first but by no means the last step towards intelligent legal reform. The other and more difficult one is to realize what you must give up to get it, and to consider whether you are ready to pay the price.[171]

Common sense suggests a worker's productivity for hours worked beyond ten hours per day is likely below his level of productivity for hours worked earlier in the day, though that general premise is no doubt riddled with variables. Younger workers may have greater alertness, attention spans, work stamina. Older experienced workers may be more valuable to the employer, in the short run. Like as not, workplace injuries increase with longer hours of work. It is the ultimate irony of this story of workday limitations that most hospital nurses, whose work literally involves matters of life and death, still work twelve-hour shifts. We must learn to assess the kind of work done and how it should inform workday limits.

Newman Lumber thrusts not just the judges but all of us into the realm of social science and empirical investigations regarding the fact and circumstances that may explain and justify legislation. A ten-hour workday imposes social costs. Implementing it and administering it imposes transaction costs.[172] We duck these lessons at our peril, and at a risk of harm to the state and its people. Though hardly as insightfully and meticulously as is expected in the second decade of the twenty-first century, Justice Cook struck a responsive chord with this passage:

> To "stick to the bark" often destroys the purpose of the law; but when we take into consideration the history of the law, the birth and growth of the theories embodied in the statute, and then think in the language of the masses, we have a better understanding of the evils the representatives of the common morality were endeavoring to regulate. Thinkers, working to conserve the mental and physical health of toilers in the modern manufactories, have discovered, or think they have discovered, that the concentration of the human mind and muscle, for many consecutive hours, upon the watching and manipulation of rapidly moving machinery, tends to weary the body of the worker, and to weaken his reasoning facilities, and ultimately, to permanently impair his physical and mental efficiency.[173]

From this Cook said the act should be construed toward that elusive end of "promoting the general welfare and protecting the workers in that class of manufacture using machinery of a character which requires in its operation constant tension of mind and body."[174]

But we can't stop there. *Newman Lumber* insists we study a further lesson, likely a harder one. If a manufacturer experiences greater labor costs, and lowered productivity from its workers, it will likely (depending on its profit margin) increase the price the consuming public is asked to pay for its goods and services if it can. And if higher prices lead to fewer sales and dwindling profits, what then? There may come a point where increased labor costs become such that the employer will no longer bear them, and just go out of business. Or, as in more recent times, move to another jurisdiction or another country. Were not these economic assumptions a major part of the thinking of Gov. Hugh L. White and those who designed and implemented Mississippi's Balance Agriculture with Industry program, first authorized in the last week of the summer of 1936?[175] Is it not among our continuing takeaways from *Newman Lumber* that, in like cases going forward, employer and workers need counsel who know enough about statistics and economics that they help the legislature and governor and, ultimately, the judges to understand and approach an optimal equilibrium among the respective interests of all affected persons or firms? And, of course, we need legislators and governors and judges willing and able to listen and learn. What the judges should do with this information—which they must have in some minimally adequate quality and quantity—turns on the posture of the case. In a judicial review posture as in *Newman Lumber*, the court had far less discretion to draw on economic analysis to inform its decision than on remand, where the court is charged to produce a reliable adjudication on the merits of the case.

No bigger mistake can be made—in considering the effect of an incentive (such as a ten-hour workday law) on an economy—than to look only at the present slice in time. Herein of the "fallacy of the static pie."[176] We must factor in that organized society is an ongoing enterprise with a past to learn from, and a present followed by both short- and long-range futures. Assuming that each person is a rationally self-interested wealth maximizer, are not, then, our goals that we should maximize the wealth of the economy and at once approach a currently fair distribution of that wealth—with fairness a function of equality of reasonable practical opportunity, not equality in fact at the end of the day? How is this new law or that going to affect the people's collective pursuit of both of these goals over time?[177] Most of us accept that the state must afford some not insignificant social safety net, though we may argue in good faith how high that net should be placed, how it should be administered, and who should bear what part of its costs and other burdens.

Many judges will have a knee-jerk response to all of this: It's not our job. Horsefeathers! If a man takes a whack, he is likely to affect some one or more persons. Even if he strikes no one, he may be charged with assault or at least negligence, because public policy commands that each of us take care of the effects of our actions. When legislators enact a workday law, we expect them to learn all they can of the aggregate past, present, and future effects of that law. When judges judicially review such a law, they too are charged to know what can be known, for their decision is likely to be pretty near final as to the fate of that law, and its effects on "the good of the whole." Judicial immunity does not exclude judicial responsibility within constitutionally assigned roles, however daunting the sound exercise of that responsibility may be.

And in all of these considerations, what should be done about people at the margins—manufacturers, service providers, workers, consumers, the aged, the infirm, the member of the less-than-loved minority—who will always be harmed, at least in the short run? The legislature may well deem it for "the good of the whole"[178] that employers profit a little less and that consumers pay a little more, that some of those workers at the margin be able to earn a livable wage, but this only moves the margin. In 1912, careful and deliberate lawmakers could see but a generation ahead, and only partially at that. A century later, perhaps not even that far. What new technologies, their time come around, are about to be born and change everything?

THE MAJORITY'S RIGHT TO BE WRONG

Once Newman Lumber Company's suggestion of error was denied, it was easy to say it had always been for the legislature to decide whether employers engaged in manufacturing or repairing could require of their laborers more than ten hours of work a day, "except in cases of emergency" or "public necessity."[179] But how likely is it that any democratically elected legislature will maximize practical wisdom in exercising its police powers? This was and remains our least impracticable way of proceeding. Dissenting in *Lochner*, Holmes recognized in 1904 "the right of a majority to embody their opinions in law" and then added:

> It is settled by various decisions of this Court that state constitutions and state laws may regulate life in many ways which we as legislators might think as injudicious or if you like as tyrannical as this, and which equally with this interfere with the liberty to contract. Sunday laws and usury laws are ancient examples. . . . The liberty of the citizen to do as he likes so long as he does not interfere with the liberty of others to do the same, which has been a shibboleth for some well-known writers, is interfered with by school laws, by the Post Office, by every state and municipal institution which takes his money for purposes thought desirable, whether he likes it or not. . . . Some of these laws embody convictions and prejudices which judges are likely to share. Some may not. But a constitution is not intended to embody a particular economic theory, whether of paternalism and the organic relation of the citizen to the state or of laissez faire. It is made for people of fundamentally differing views, and the accident of our finding certain opinions natural and familiar or novel and even shocking ought not to conclude our judgment upon the question whether statutes embodying them conflict with the Constitution of the United States.[180]

Or, for that matter, the constitution of a particular state.

The legislature is just as capable of passing laws that honor laissez-faire economics as it is capable of acts of paternalism, and at times, a potpourri of the two and less coherent approaches. No matter. On judicial review, what the court of last resort does is going to have social and economic impacts on many people, often great impacts. And so the question becomes, How are legislators and governors and then judges and lawyers to acquire the insights and understandings in the realm of socioeconomics that they may stand a reasonable chance of doing more aggregate good than harm? In the immediate aftermath of 1912? Today? And, keeping Holmes in *Lochner* ever in mind, how do public officials respect both the "is" and the "ought" of the limited role of the court on judicial review?

Then there is the reflection that some, if not many, may be motivated by matters beyond the art of economics. In 1912, in Mississippi and elsewhere, Social Darwinism was more readily received and admired and accepted than natural

Darwinism. The political potency of a Vardaman or the Progressive Movement in general notwithstanding, many who lived in south Mississippi were grateful that men like J. J. Newman and then Fenwick Peck came among them and gave them jobs. As a middle class has emerged, individually and in the aggregate, still short-sighted and fearful Mississippians have established a very long track record of voting against their economic self-interests, but is this not their right? Few who cheered secession, went to war, and fought and died between 1861 and 1865 were slave owners.

Neither Holmes in *Lochner* nor Section 5 or 6 of the Mississippi Constitution[181] resolves the Madisonian dilemma: the tensions inherent in respecting the right of the individual in a majoritarian democracy. "The whole" cannot mean every person at any one time or over the years, because it is known and inevitable that organized society is made up of "people of fundamentally different views" who do and always will disagree on "the good."[182]

VIEWS THE LEGISLATURE NEVER ENACTED

Newman Lumber teaches a drafting lesson of constitutional dimensions. Recall that by its nature legislation is forward looking. It is difficult to foresee all of the circumstances in which a bill like the ten-hour workday law might be applied. Even skilled draftsmen find it hard to make law that sensibly cuts the corners that may emerge with experience and over time. Drafting the statute narrowly might exclude circumstances where in retrospect the law may be needed. The present practice of defining legislatively key terms can go only so far in eliminating uncertainties in drafting. Given these practical realities, the legislative draftsman reasonably relies on the other two departments of government. And so sensibly does the citizenry.

In 1912, the legislature did not define "manufacturing or repairing." These are general activities reasonably understood by people of common sense and experience. Justice Cook consulted the dictionary and encyclopedia, though without much profit.[183] And the same with Justice Reed.[184] Still, the legislature faced the practical problem of setting criteria for identifying—within a particular workplace—which workers are actually engaged in manufacturing or repairing. Are these enough that a particular employer ought reasonably to be covered? Legislators may sensibly see that there are times when they should enact a general rule that covers all employees, including some that at times might not be within "manufacturing" or "repairing" work. Textually, this is what the legislature did in 1912. The problem of overinclusion versus underinclusion is complicated by the probability that there are times when the transaction costs of implementing and complying with a particularized rule may exceed those of tolerating a level of arbitrariness in practice. We have to hope the executive may reasonably withhold prosecution where reasonably it may seem grossly unfair or absurd. And, when a zealous prosecutor demands compliance with the letter of the law, that the judiciary should soften the edges.

We have seen, however, that at least three justices would have engrafted upon the ten-hour workday law terms and conditions that the legislature never enacted. Cook did this when he suggested constricting the application of the law because he thought, "[i]t would be absurd . . . to construe this statute to apply to the work of laborers engaged in felling timber in the open air in the equable climate of this state, because he is employed by an employer engaged in manufacturing."[185] This dictum did not change the text or best reading the text of the new law might be given. Smith, however, went beyond the legislative text and performed a worker-by-worker analysis.[186] Justice Eugene O. Sykes was shameless in squeezing from the law much of the meaning the legislature put there.[187]

Only Richard Forman Reed played it straight. He was the only one to accept the new law as the legislature had made it. And the only one to constrain his practice of judicial review to its proper practical and constitutional limits.

THE SUPREMACY CLAUSE APPLIED

Or did he? Under the Supremacy Clause,[188] each state and its people are always subject to the paramount authority of the Constitution and laws of the United States.[189] The Mississippi Constitution enjoins that the state may make no law "in derogation of the paramount allegiance of the citizens of this state to the government of the United States."[190] In this vein, *Newman Lumber's* failure to follow *Lochner's* lead is a separate subject for reflection. Granted that there may be a difference between miner's work before the US Supreme Court in *Holden v. Hardy*,[191] on the one hand, and general "manufacturing or repairing," on the other. But was the difference enough, given the level of danger inherent in logging, sawmill, and attendant railroad labor? *Lochner* had marginalized *Holden*. But had not *Muller* marginalized *Lochner*, the former's dicta notwithstanding? What did the exception for "cases of emergency" or "public necessity" do for Newman Lumber Company and other employers? The World War may well have presented a "case of emergency" or "public necessity," but were these lumber companies any the less deprived of their "'liberty of contract by such exceptions? Barely, if at all.

In reflecting on *Newman Lumber*, we cannot escape the question whether there was any excuse at all for Justice Reed's quoting and relying on the *Lochner* dissenting opinions in avoiding the otherwise likely controlling effect of a five-to-four decision. Perhaps. As 1912 was drawing to a close, there was good reason to see a US Supreme Court open to whittling away at *Lochner*, if not overruling it, especially with the election of President Woodrow Wilson.

A century later, two justices of the Supreme Court of Mississippi relied heavily on quotations from four dissenting justices in a politically charged case in arguing that the opinion of another five-justice majority just might be so dubious that state judges were not bound to enforce it.[192] How did that differ from what Justice Reed did in *Newman Lumber*?

Did not *Newman Lumber* send a signal for future (unreconstructed white) Mississippians that an offensive US Supreme Court decision may always be susceptible of being distinguished—and ignored, if not defied—by this state's manipulation of the meaning, scope, and tenor of its police powers? In his constitutional moment in 1912, Justice Reed gave a hefty citation to the Tenth Amendment, quoting it in full.[193] Was the mischief he was making foreseeable? That, several generations later, racial segregation in this country would begin crumbling on moral grounds, and that those not yet "reconstructed" could argue "states' rights" citing the Tenth Amendment. With this strategy and more, these willful men would retard—and for almost a generation block—dismantling "our (racially perverted) way of life" in Mississippi. Of course, the court should always strive to see a bit past the case of the moment. These reflections having the benefit of a century of hindsight may suggest that the court not stray too far into fields dimly seen, leaving those to the more informed insights of a later day.

REFLECTIONS

In late 1916, Newman Lumber Company had serious labor troubles that resulted in a strike for much of December, including violence between strikers and non-strikers on December 15. Hattiesburg and Sumrall mills shut down for nearly three weeks before Christmas. Reports of those weeks leading to a settlement on December 21 have wages as the sole issue in dispute.[194] Hours of work and working conditions appear to have played a lesser role in the workers' grievances, or no role at all.

In the years that followed, Newman Lumber became a regular appellate litigant.[195] A 1923 case may be revealing. Leseray Norris, a minor, was injured on the job. A jury found Newman Lumber liable and assessed damages at $17,500. In final argument to the jury, plaintiff counsel argued, "Who is the J. J. Newman Lumber Company? It is a corporation. It has taken your land. It has taken your timber. It has taken your homes."[196] The Supreme Court of Mississippi held this was improper argument, though the trial judge had sustained a defense objection. The legal points aside, it is telling that the injured worker's lawyer thought such an argument would resonate with a Lamar County jury. And that it apparently did.

"Encouraged by local tax laws, sawmill operators tried to cut as much timber in as short a period of time as possible. Many small mills had cut all the timber available to them within a few years, while the larger mills lasted more than forty years. Dwindling timber supplies, coupled with the effects of the Great Depression to shut down.... For the most part, the timber boom that started in the 1890s was over by the 1930s."[197] "Unfortunately, most Mississippi lumbermen of this period, including the Newman Lumber Company, were not interested in good forest management or reforestation."[198]

The Sumrall mill closed in 1931. The Hattiesburg mill cut its last log in November of 1935.[199] The last reported case of an injured worker suing Newman Lumber reached the Supreme Court of Mississippi in 1937. Sydney M. Smith, who had served on the court in 1912 and 1913, began his opinion stating matter-of-factly that Newman Lumber was "engaged, among other things, in the manufacture and sale of lumber, and owned a number of railroad cars."[200] A Forrest County jury found for the injured worker and assessed his damages at $30,000. The Supreme Court of Mississippi affirmed.

With a deft and caring touch, south Mississippi lumber industry biographer Gilbert Hoffman tells the story of the last years of Piney Woods sawmills and the parts people played. You even feel you've gotten to know Fenwick Peck, the Yankee entrepreneur and capitalist who more than anyone else made it all happen, the good and the not so good. In January of 1930, Peck came south from Scranton, Pennsylvania, for his annual inspection of Newman facilities and operations. The atmospheric angst was omnipresent. The supplies of virgin timber to be cut were dwindling. The end was in sight. The stock market had crashed on Wall Street in October of 1929. Mr. Peck was Mr. Peck, and he put the people of south Mississippi in their place as only he could do.

"We have a great deal of sentimental interest in Hattiesburg. We consider South Mississippi as an ideal location for industrial development.... The labor is comparatively cheap [—everyone knew what that meant—] and efficient and the weather conditions are ideal.... Down here [we have no] labor troubles ... due to radical elements in labor unions.... I do see a fine combination of industrial and agricultural development for South Mississippi, *if its own people will get down to work*."[201] Peck was hardly original in his views. Nor were they limited to the Piney Woods of Mississippi. Less than a decade later, W. J. Cash, in his classic and yet affectionate narrative, explained again and again that "cheapness of labor ... was the South's main advantage,"[202] and in cotton mills and other emerging industries, not just sawmills.

In December of 1933, Peck's company started selling the lands it had raped— in George, Greene, and Perry Counties—to the US government. By September of 1935, the government had some 100,700 acres of former Newman Lumber lands. In time, as nature would have it, pine trees returned to this special land, which is now a part of the DeSoto National Forest. Peck went back to Scranton for good after the Hattiesburg mill closed. Promises for further economic development in south Mississippi never materialized. In early April of 1943, Hoffman reports, "Peck died penniless, as a result of losing millions of dollars from poor investments made in the 1920s and 1930s."[203]

If the J. J. Newman Lumber Company ever lost a penny because of the ten-hour workday law the Mississippi legislature enacted in July of 1912, it has not been recorded. Similarly, there is no evidence that Fenwick Peck or any other management official within Newman Lumber Company lost a minute's sleep over the ten-hour workday law after the fight they started and fought and lost in January of 1913. If the law was a problem, it was of the midget variety. And so we wonder why Peck and Newman Lumber felt they should fight so, and with such hyperbole and bombast. The reason can be found only in the same condescending arrogance that Fenwick Peck summoned in those latter years when he told the Piney Woods folk that they'd be just fine if they would just get down to work. Peck can only be turning over in his grave at the thought that he—no doubt unwittingly—generated a constitutional encounter that demonstrably and at least for a while made Mississippi a bit better place to live than it might have been.

J. J. Newman Lumber Company—and the people whose self-interests and dreams and fears and humanity were a part of this socio-legal struggle—added more than a few lines to the story of Mississippi. What happened between July of 1912 and January of 1913 came at the dawn of a new era of constitutional contests for the state and the country. Greater learning and vision would be demanded of lawyers and judges. Greater citizenship would be needed from the people they served. Section 6 of the Mississippi Constitution declares, "The people of this state have the inherent, sole, and exclusive right to regulate the internal government and police thereof."[204] And Section 190 added, "The exercise of the police powers of the State shall never be abridged."[205] In the early years of the twentieth century, the practice and defense of the police power became a new ballgame. Its intelligent understanding and practice in the public interest presented new challenges, empirical, sociological—and ideological as well.

Over the last decade of the twentieth century, Gilbert Hoffman made life in the lumber mills of South Mississippi—and the rails and trains that served them—seem still alive.[206] Even when you knew those days were past and those men were dead, Hoffman reminded us of the humanity of a very real time and place, begging that it be still seen through many and differing eyes, and telling enough of the stories that its lessons and its pleas are hard to resist.

For one thing, and while he had featured Newman Lumber, Hoffman has made sure we know that there were many others in the lumber business in south Mississippi. In practical and human terms, we have the stories of the Tatum Lumber Company, the Camp and Hinton Brothers mills and others at Lumberton, including the Edward Hines Yellow Pine Trustees.[207] And of Butterfield Lumber Company, its successor Denkmann Lumber Company, and others in the southwest part of the state centered around Lincoln County.[208] And still more. Each of these enterprises had its ups and downs, its trials and tribulations, but Hoffman tells their story with no waffling from his view that—regarding the ten-hour workday law—each and every sawmill operator took it in stride "without any adverse effect on their business." Hoffman's humanity is a wonderful part of Mississippi's takeaway from *Newman Lumber*'s constitutional encounter.

Consider the final chapter in the story of Tatum Lumber Company. A home-grown, family-partnership, Hattiesburg mill, in its time Tatum Lumber was second in size only to Newman Lumber. It had begun lumber operations in the early 1890s. Tatum Lumber "cut its last log about 3:00 p.m." on Saturday, October 22, 1938. It wasn't the 1912 ten-hour workday law that brought down Tatum Lumber. But Frank Tatum truly hated the New Deal. He focused particular wrath on the forty-four-hour workweek limit in the Federal Wage and Hour Bill set to take effect on October 24, 1938.[209] "Having run the Tatum Lumber Company successfully from 1893 with no forced shutdowns, the very idea that some New Deal bureaucrat in Washington should dictate how they were to operate was absolutely unthinkable."[210] When things go bad, forget the facts. Blame the government.

A pragmatic and prolific judge who bestrode the millennium has reminded us, "Certitude is not the test of certainty. A wise person realizes that even his unshakeable convictions may be wrong—but not all of us are wise."[211] As we study *Newman Lumber* and prepare for the lessons to be learned over the hundred years of constitutional encounters in Mississippi that followed—and particularly the present and the foreseeable future—it is good to recall that "time has upset so [so] many fighting faiths!"[212]

And, as well, to reflect with Faulkner on the humanity of the sawmill town facing its fate: "All the men in the village worked in the mill or for it. It was cutting pine. It had been there seven years and in seven years more it would destroy all the timber within its reach. Then some of the machinery and most of the men who ran it and existed because of and for it would be loaded onto freight cars and moved away."[213] And upon the land left behind, "baffled and bemused upon a stumppocked scene of profound and peaceful desolation, unplowed, untilled, gutting slowly into red and choked ravines beneath the long quiet rains of autumn and the galloping fury of vernal equinoxes."[214]

ENDNOTES

1. *Muller v. Oregon*, 208 U.S. 412 (1908).

2. *Runnels v. State*, Walker (1 Miss.) 146, 1823 WL 543 (1823).

3. See chapter 3 above.

4. Miss. Laws, ch. 157 (1912), approved March 16, 1912.

5. Miss. Laws, ch. 157, § 1, page 165 (1912), effective July 12, 1912.

6. *See* Labor Laws and Regulations, Legislation in the United States Limiting Hours of Labor for Men, Monthly Labor Review 1076–1083 (1918).

7. *Holden v. Hardy*, 169 U.S. 366 (1898).

8. *State vs. J. J. Newman Lumber Co.*, 102 Miss. 802, 59 So. 923, 926 (1912). Despite this assertion in the court's opinion, perceptive observers were still saying "Mississippi's manufacturing
enterprises were limited ... almost entirely to cotton gins and lumber mills." Thomas D. Davis,
"Mississippi: Its Opportunities and Resources," *Journal of Mississippi History* 8 (Oct. 1946), page
237. *See also* Connie L. Lester, "Balancing Agriculture with Industry: Capital, Labor, and the
Public Good in Mississippi's Home-Grown New Deal," *Journal of Mississippi History* 70 (Fall
2008), page 239 ("few industrial jobs beyond timbering").

9. *Lochner v. New York*, 198 U.S. 46 (1904).

10. *State vs. J. J. Newman Lumber Co.*, 103 Miss. 263, 60 So. 215, 217 (1913); *State v. Butterfield
Lumber Co.*, 60 So. 217 (Miss. 1913); suggestion of error overruled, 103 Miss. 286, 60 So. 286 (Jan.
20, 1913).

11. *Buckeye Cotton Oil Co. v. State*, 103 Miss. 767, 60 So. 775 (1913).

12. *Mississippi History Now*, "Growth of the Lumber Industry (1840–1930),"(2001); http://
mshistorynow.mdah.state.ms.us/articles/171/growth-of-the-lumber-industry-1840-to-1930
posted May 2001. For the full story of sawmills come and gone from south Mississippi, and
the humanity of that by-gone time and place and way of life, see Gilbert H. Hoffman, *Dummy
Lines through the Longleaf: A History of the Sawmills and Logging Railroads of Southwest Mississippi* (2d ed., 1999); Gilbert H. Hoffman, *Steam Whistles in the Piney Woods*, Vol. 1, pages 3–7
(1998), and Vol. 2 (2002); James E. Fickle, *Mississippi Forests and Forestry* 65–119 (2001); Nollie
W. Hickman, *Mississippi Harvest: Lumbering in the Longleaf Pine Belt, 1840–1915* (1962).

13. See "Pine Forests and Piney Woods," in *Mississippi Encyclopedia* 999–1003 (Ownby and
Wilson eds., 2017).

14. *See* Gilbert H. Hoffman, *Dummy Lines through the Longleaf: A History of the Sawmills
and Logging Railroads of Southwest Mississippi* (2d ed., 1999); Gilbert H. Hoffman, *Steam
Whistles in the Piney Woods*, Vol. 1, pages 3–7 (1998) and Vol. 2 (2002), devoted particularly to
railroads serving the lumber industry; and Nollie W. Hickman, "The Lumber Industry in South
Mississippi, 1890–1915," *Journal of Mississippi History* 20 (1958), pages 211, 212–213, 220, for an
overview of the role and importance of railroads in the emergence of the lumber industry in
south Mississippi. *See also* Tony Howe, "Growth of the Lumber Industry (1840 to 1930)," *Mississippi History Now*, pages 3–4 (May 2001), http://mshistorynow.mdah.state.ms.us/articles/171
/growth-of-the-lumber-industry-1840-to-1930; *Mississippi Rails*, http:/ww.msrailroads.com
/NC&M.htm.

15. *Mississippi Rails*, http://www.msrailroads.com/Newman_JJ_Lbr.htm.

16. Fenwick L. Peck, *American Lumbermen: The Personal History and Public and Business
Achievements of Eminent Lumbermen of the United States*, Vol. 2, 261–265 (1906); Nollie W.
Hickman, *Mississippi Harvest: Lumbering in the Longleaf Pine Belt, 1840–1915*, pages 181–182
(1962).

17. http://www.lib.usm.edu/legacy/archives/m286text.htm.

18. In 1907 and 1908, Newman Lumber's insurance needs for its Hattiesburg and Sumrall
plants were being managed through "Fulton & Bradley, insurance brokers, of Scranton, Pa." *See
Northern Assur. Co. v. J. J. Newman Lumber Co.*, 105 Miss. 688, 63 So. 209, 210, 211 (1913). A late-
summer of 1911 amendment to the Charter of Incorporation of J. J. Newman Lumber Company
established and ensured that corporate headquarters would remained in Lackawanna County.
Fenwick Peck, his son E. S. Peck, and another family member, George L. Peck (1869–1935) all
signed the charter amendment in Lackawanna County.

19. *Mississippi Rails*, http://www.msrailroads.com/Newman_JJ_Lbr.htm.

20. James E. Fickle, *Mississippi Forests and Forestry* 90 (2001); Nollie W. Hickman, "The
Lumber Industry in South Mississippi, 1890–1915, *Journal of Mississippi History* 20 (1958), pages
211, 217.

21. Nollie W. Hickman, "The Lumber Industry in South Mississippi, 1890–1915," *Journal of Mississippi History* 20 (1958), 211, 218, fn. 34 and accompanying text.

22. James E. Fickle, *Mississippi Forests and Forestry* 105 (2001), fn. 43, citing numerous sources in Notes, page 279.

23. Nollie W. Hickman, *Mississippi Harvest: Lumbering in the Longleaf Pine Belt, 1840–1915*, at 248 (1962).

24. Tony Howe, "Growth of the Lumber Industry (1840 to 1930)," *Mississippi History Now* 2 (May 2001), http://mshistorynow.mdah.state.ms.us/articles/171/growth-of-the-lumber-industry-1840-to-1930.

25. Nollie W. Hickman, "The Lumber Industry in South Mississippi, 1890–1915," *Journal of Mississippi History* 20 (1958), 211, 216, 218, 219, fn. 39.

26. "LeRoy Percy" in *Mississippi Encyclopedia*, 984–985 (Ownby and Wilson eds., 2017).

27. *See* "Anselm Joseph McLaurin," in David G. Sansing, *Mississippi Governors: Soldiers, Statesmen, Scholars, Scoundrels* 126–129 (2016); "Anselm Joseph McLauren," in *Mississippi Encyclopedia* 794 (Ownby and Wilson eds., 2017).

28. *See* "James Kimble Vardaman," in David G. Sansing, *Mississippi Governors: Soldiers, Statesmen, Scholars, Scoundrels* 134–138 (2016); "James K. Vardaman," in *Mississippi Encyclopedia* 1281–1282 (Ownby and Wilson eds., 2017).

29. *See* Albert D. Kirwan, *Revolt of the Rednecks, Mississippi Politics 1875–1925* (1951).

30. William Alexander Percy, *Lanterns on the Levee: Recollections of a Planter's Son* 153 (1941), the centerpiece of a chapter Percy titled "The Bottom Rail on Top."

31. Representative Walker's father was a soldier in the Confederate Fifth Mississippi Infantry and Second Mississippi Calvary during the Civil War. He was also elected to the Mississippi legislature in 1880 and was a special agent of the Interior Department. Dunbar Rowland, L.L.D., *The Official and Statistical Register of the State of Mississippi* (1912).

32. Representative Rencher's great-great-grandfather Captain James Jack was chosen to carry the Mecklenburg Declaration of Independence of May 1775, to the Continental Congress in Philadelphia. Captain Jack's son, Representative Rencher's great-grandfather, was a soldier in the War of 1812. Representative Rencher's father fought during the Civil War with a Confederate Alabama regiment and surrendered at last with part of General John Bell Hood's men at Meridian, Mississippi.

33. Mississippi House Journal, p. 1227 (1912).

34. *See* "Lee Maurice Russell," in David G. Sansing, *Mississippi Governors: Soldiers, Statesmen, Scholars, Scoundrels* 158–161 (2016); "Lee Maurice Russell," in *Mississippi Encyclopedia* 1105 (Ownby and Wilson eds., 2017).

35. Mississippi Senate Journal, pages 1030–31 (1912). Senator Russell was born in Lafayette County and later attended the University of Mississippi. He successfully passed a bill prohibiting secret and exclusive societies at public institutions for higher learning, which remained in effect for twelve years. *See* David Sansing, *The University of Mississippi: A Sesquicentennial History* 177 (1999) (The traditional story is that Russell "was a poor country boy from Lafayette County who was blackballed by the Greek societies and he vowed to get even."), https://en.wikipedia.org/wiki/Lee_M._Russell (last visited Feb. 29, 2016)

36. In 1923, as governor, Russell was sued for seduction and breach of promise by his former secretary Frances Birkhead, of which he was ultimately acquitted. Ms. Birkhead alleged that Governor Russell had impregnated her. She further alleged that she had an abortion that left her unable to have children.

37. Mississippi Senate Journal, page 1048 (1912).

38. Representative Johnston received his literary education at Kentucky Military Institute, where he graduated salutatorian of his class. In addition, Representative Johnston was a

Methodist, a Mason, and member of the Delta Kappa Epsilon fraternity (which, ironically, had blackballed Senator Russell years earlier, leading to his antifraternity bill). Dunbar Rowland, L.L.D., *The Official and Statistical Register of the State of Mississippi* (1912).

39. Mississippi House Journal, pages 1603–1604 (1912).

40. *See* "Earl Leroy Brewer," in David G. Sansing, *Mississippi Governors: Soldiers, Statesmen, Scholars, Scoundrels* 144–148 (2016); "Earl Leroy Brewer," in *Mississippi Encyclopedia* 134–135 (Ownby and Wilson eds., 2017).

41. Miss. Laws, ch. 157 (House Bill No. 628), § 3 (1912).

42. Section 2 of ch. 157 provided a penalty of "not less than ten dollars nor more than fifty dollars for each offense, and each day's violation shall constitute a separate offense." This may or may not have been "pocket change" for Newman Lumber.

43. Gilbert Hoffman has told the central role of W. J. Haynen in Newman Lumber operations for the decade beginning in 1906. Gilbert H. Hoffman, *Steam Whistles in the Piney Woods, Vol. 1* 30–52 (1998).

44. S. E. Travis has been recognized for his service as president of the Mississippi Bar Association, 1918–1919, in *The Mississippi Bar's Centennial: A Legacy of Service* at 49 (Melanie H. Henry comp. and ed., 2006).

45. *See* "Sydney McCain Smith," in *Mississippi Encyclopedia* 1167–1168 (Ownby and Wilson eds., 2017). Smith's service as president of the Mississippi Bar Association is recognized in *The Mississippi Bar's Centennial: A Legacy of Service*, at page 43 (Melanie H. Henry comp. and ed., 2006). Smith is featured far more prominently in chapter 10 below.

46. *See* "Edmund Favor Noel," in David G. Sansing, *Mississippi Governors: Soldiers, Statesmen, Scholars, Scoundrels* 140–143 (2016); "Edmund Favor Noel," in *Mississippi Encyclopedia* 935–936 (Ownby and Wilson eds., 2017).

47. By law, the justice whose continuous service has been the longest becomes chief justice of the Supreme Court of Mississippi. Miss. Code § 9-3-11, formerly Miss. Code § 4917 (Code of 1906).

48. Susan Snell, *Phil Stone of Oxford: A Vicarious Life* 30 (2008).

49. *See* "Andrew Houston Longino," in David G. Sansing, *Mississippi Governors: Soldiers, Statesmen, Scholars, Scoundrels* 130–133 (2016); "Andrew Houston Longino," in *Mississippi Encyclopedia* 742–743 (Ownby and Wilson eds., 2017).

50. *State ex rel. Collins v. Jones*, 64 So. 241, 256 (Miss. 1914).

51. *State ex rel. McClurg v. Powell*, 27 So. 927 (Miss. 1900).

52. *State ex rel. Collins*, 64 So. at 261 (Cook, J., dissenting) (quoting from William Shakespeare, *The Merchant of Venice*, act 4, scene 1, lines 214–222).

53. Anna Pittman, "Cook, Sam C.," on file at the State Law Library, Supreme Court Building, Jackson, Mississippi. Another document in Justice Cook's file at the State Law Library includes this quotation, though neither identifies Cook's biographer. *See* Dunbar Rowland, *The Official and Statistical Register of Mississippi*, Vol. 4, page 535 (1917).

54. *See* "Sam C. Cook, Former Supreme Court Justice and Prominent in Political Circles," obituary published in *Clarion Ledger* (Jackson, Miss.), Feb. 16, 1924.

55. On September 22, 1911, Richard F. Reed completed a biographical memorandum in his own hand. "Our Reed immigrant was from Scotland. His name Joseph. He came about 1700 to New England." Re Thomas Reed, father of Richard Forman Reed, *see also The History of the Descendants of the Jersey Settlers, Adams County, Mississippi*, Vol. II, page 74 (Frances Preston Mills ed., 1981). "The Formans and Howells were early settlers of New Jersey and very prominent in that state. Both families I understand are English [Welsh]. My mother's great grandfather was Colonel Richard Howell (from whom I get my name), the famous Governor of New Jersey and Colonel in the Revolutionary War." *See also The History of the Descendants of the Jersey Settlers, Adams County, Mississippi*, Vol. II, page 398 (Frances Preston Mills ed., 1981).

56. Biographical memorandum completed by Richard Forman Reed on September 22, 1911, on file in the Thomas Reed papers in Archives at Louisiana State University.

57. Anna Pittman, "Reed, Richard F.," on file at the State Law Library, Supreme Court Building, Jackson, Mississippi.

58. "Judge Richard Forman Reed," *Natchez Democrat*, March 3, 1926.

59. *See, e.g.*, "Old Historic Natchez," a lengthy article Judge Reed authored for the *Natchez Democrat*, published November 15, 1921.

60. Earl Drane, "Jersey Settlers Ready for Reunion," *Natchez Democrat*.

61. *Mankin v. United States for the Use and Benefit of Ludowici-Celadon Company*, 215 U.S. 533 (1910).

62. "Judge Richard Forman Reed," *Natchez Democrat*, March 3, 1926.

63. *Matthews v. State*, 102 Miss. 549, 59 So. 842 (1912).

64. *Phillips v. Garner*, 106 Miss. 828, 64 So. 735–736 (1914).

65. Brief of Appellee, J. J. Newman Lumber Company, page 26, filed Nov. 8, 1912.

66. James E. Fickle, *Mississippi Forests and Forestry* 109 (2001).

67. Brief of Appellee, J. J. Newman Lumber Company, page 2, filed Nov. 8, 1912.

68. Miss. Const. art. 7, §190 (1890).

69. Gilbert H. Hoffman in *Steam Whistles in the Piney Woods*, Vol. 1, pages 20, 21, 23–26, 33, 36, 40–41, 46, 55–57, 64, 79, 84, 88–89 (1998).

70. James E. Fickle, *Mississippi Forests and Forestry*, page 109–110 (2001).

71. Gilbert H. Hoffman, *Steam Whistles in the Piney Woods*, Vol. 1, page 135 (1998).

72. "A Fatal Accident at Newman's Saw Mill. Young Man Sustained Injuries Which Resulted in His Death Early Today. Fell through a Hold and Fractured Skull," *Hattiesburg News*, Aug. 6, 1910.

73. "W. W. Quinn Is Severely Injured," *Hattiesburg News*, Sept. 30, 1911.

74. "Suit against M. C. and Newman," *Hattiesburg News*, March 1, 1913.

75. "Negro Man Fell between Cars; Was Killed," *Hattiesburg News*, Nov. 14, 1912.

76. "Brakeman Met Instant Death. John Russell, Employee of Newman Lumber Company, Killed While Coupling Cars," *Hattiesburg News*, March 7, 1913. Workers employed by Newman Lumber, of course, were not the only lumber company workers suffering injuries. A brakeman for Butterfield Lumber had his hand crushed between two railcars while making a coupling. *Hope v. Natchez, C. & M. R. Co.*, 98 Miss. 822, 54 So. 369 (1911). Harsh tort rules such as contributory negligence and the fellow servant rule left workers particularly vulnerable, and without a practical remedy for workplace injuries.

77. *See J. J. Newman Lumber Co. v. Dantzler*, 107 Miss. 31, 64 So. 931 (1914).

78. James E. Fickle, *Mississippi Forests and Forestry* 110–111 (2001).

79. James E. Fickle reports a sawmill worker of the times remembering that "[m]ost mills . . . operated on an eleven-hour day from six in the morning to six in the evening, with an hour off at noon." James E. Fickle, *Mississippi Forests and Forestry* 104 (2001). *See also* Nollie W. Hickman, *Mississippi Harvest: Lumbering in the Longleaf Pine Belt, 1840–1915*, at 248 (1962); and Gilbert H. Hoffman, *Steam Whistles in the Piney Woods*, Vol. 1, page 39 (1998). Hoffman tells the story of Hulon Brister, a fifteen-year-old, who in 1899 worked for Norwood & Butterfield Company on the southwest side of the state. "For 10 to 12 hours of labor a day he was paid $1.25." Gilbert H. Hoffman, *Dummy Lines through the Longleaf* 190 (1992). In February of 1908, Butterfield Lumber Company was "operating six days a week and cutting 100,000 feet of lumber in a 10-hour working day." Gilbert H. Hoffman, *Dummy Lines through the Longleaf* 217 (1992). Butterfield Lumber was pursuing parallel litigation in Lincoln County and then in the supreme court. *See State v. Butterfield Lumber Co.*, 60 So. 217 (Miss. 1913); suggestion of error overruled, 103 Miss. 286, 60 So. 286 (Jan. 20, 1913).

80. *See, e.g.,* Richard A. Posner, *Economic Analysis of Law* § 26.1 (9th ed., 2014).

81. Anatole France, "Le Lys Rouge" (1894), reproduced in 5 *Works of Anatole France* 91 (W. Stephens transl., 1924).

82. Brief of Appellee, J. J. Newman Lumber Company, page 23, filed Nov. 8, 1912.

83. *Lochner v. New York,* 198 U.S. 46 (1904).

84. Brief of Appellee, J. J. Newman Lumber Company, pages 7–11, filed Nov. 8, 1912.

85. Brief of Appellee, J. J. Newman Lumber Company, page 19, filed Nov. 8, 1912.

86. Miss. Const. art. 3, § 14 (1890).

87. Miss. Const. art. 3, § 16 (1890).

88. Miss. Const. art. 3, § 24 (1890).

89. *See, e.g., Michigan v. Long,* 463 U.S. 1032, 1037, 1040 (1983); *Pruneyard Shopping Ctr. v. Robins,* 447 U.S. 74, 81 (1980). Though more prominent in recent decades, this constitutional premise was never doubted in the days of the *J. J. Newman Lumber Company* case.

90. Brief of Appellee, J. J. Newman Lumber Company, page 4, filed Nov. 8, 1912.

91. Brief of Appellee, J. J. Newman Lumber Company, page 27, filed Nov. 8, 1912.

92. See Vol. 15, United States Code, § 1.

93. See Parts [1], [2], and [3] of Justice Reed's opinion in *State vs. J. J. Newman Lumber Co.,* 102 Miss. 802, 59 So. 923, 925–926 (1912), which will repay a reading in its entirety.

94. *State vs. J. J. Newman Lumber Co.,* 102 Miss. 802, 59 So. 923, 925–926 (1912).

95. See chapter 3, "Judicial Review," above.

96. *State vs. J. J. Newman Lumber Co.,* 102 Miss. 802, 59 So. 923, 926 (1912), quoting *Noble State Bank v. Haskell,* 219 U.S. 104, 110 (1911).

97. *State vs. J. J. Newman Lumber Co.,* 102 Miss. 802, 59 So. 923, 925–927 (1912), quoting *Holden v. Hardy,* 169 U.S. 366 (1898).

98. *State vs. J. J. Newman Lumber Co.,* 102 Miss. 802, 59 So. 923, 926–927 (1912), quoting *Commonwealth v. Alger,* 7 Cush. (61 Mass.) 53, 84 (1851).

99. *Muller v. Oregon,* 208 U.S. 412, 418–419 (1908).

100. *State vs. J. J. Newman Lumber Co.,* 102 Miss. 802, 59 So. 923, 927–928 (1912), discussing and quoting *Lochner v. New York,* 198 U.S. 46, 55 (1904).

101. Justice Holmes's *Lochner* dissent would in time be dubbed "possibly the most famous and influential of all of his opinions." Richard A. Posner, *The Essential Holmes* xvii (Posner ed., 1992). Holmes had two decades of service ahead. Judge Posner later provided an extended analysis and critique of Holmes' dissent, concluding "It is merely the greatest judicial opinion of the last hundred years." Richard A. Posner, *Law and Literature* 346 (3d ed., 2009).

102. *State vs. J. J. Newman Lumber Co.,* 102 Miss. 802, 59 So. 923, 928 (1912), quoting at length from *Lochner v. New York,* 198 U.S. 46, 68–73, 75–76 (1904) (Harlan, J., and Holmes, J., dissenting).

103. The reference is to the brief filed by then lawyer Louis D. Brandeis in *Muller v. Oregon,* 208 U.S. 412 (1908). The story is sketched in *Samuels v. Mladineo,* 608 So. 2d 1170, 1185–86 (Miss. 1992). The Brandeis brief was enough of a landmark event that the Supreme Court Historical Society staged a reenactment of the oral argument in *Muller v. Oregon* on its hundredth anniversary. Justice Ruth Bader Ginsburg, *Muller v. Oregon: One Hundred Years Later,* 45 Willamette L. Rev. 359 (2009); *see also First Frank C. Jones Reenactment Revisits the Case of Muller v. Oregon,* 31 Sup. Ct. Hist. Soc'y Q., no. 2, 2009 at 1; Tony Mauro, "Re-Envisioning *Muller v. Oregon,*" *Blog Legal Times* (Dec. 16, 2008, 10:14 AM), http://legaltimes.typepad.com/blt/2008/12/reenvisioning-muller-v-oregon.html.

104. *State vs. J. J. Newman Lumber Co.,* 102 Miss. 802, 59 So. 923, 929 (1912).

105. Miss. Const. art. 3, § 5 (1890, as amended).

106. Miss. Const. art. 7, §190 (1890).

107. Nollie W. Hickman, "The Lumber Industry in South Mississippi, 1890–1915," *Journal of Mississippi History* 20 (1958), 211, 214, 222.

108. *State vs. J. J. Newman Lumber Co.*, 102 Miss. 802, 59 So. 923, 929 (1912).

109. See chapter 3 above.

110. *See Runnels v. State*, Walker (1 Miss.) 146, ** 1, 1823 WL 543 (1823) discussed in chapter 3 above.

111. The case was called for trial in circuit court in early December 1912. Apparently, no stay had been entered by the supreme court, pending rehearing on suggestion of error. "On account of the illness of Mr. Travis, attorney for the Newman Company, the case was continued. The judge stated that inasmuch as the lumber company was now obeying the law as near as possible, there was no hurry to bring the case to trial." *St. Louis Lumberman*, Dec. 15, 1912, page 69.

112. J. J. Newman Lumber Company's Suggestion of Error, page 17 (Dec. 2, 1912).

113. *State vs. J. J. Newman Lumber Co.*, 103 Miss. 263, 60 So. 215, 217 (1913).

114. J. J. Newman Lumber Company's Suggestion of Error, page 37, lines 19–20 (Dec. 2, 1912).

115. *State vs. J. J. Newman Lumber Co.*, 103 Miss. 263, 60 So. 215, 216 (1913).

116. I have often explained the fallacies in the problematic penchant of so many judges to try to find legislative intent. *See, e.g.*, "The Circumstanced External Approach to Legal Interpretation," in *The Law of Business Torts in Mississippi*, 15 Miss. College L. Rev. 13, 31–33 (1994). The thesis I advance there is drawn from expositions known well before *Newman Lumber* was decided.

117. Oliver Wendell Holmes, *Collected Legal Papers* 207 (1921); Holmes, *The Theory of Legal Interpretation*, 12 Harv. L. Rev. 417, 419 (1899).

118. *State vs. J. J. Newman Lumber Co.*, 103 Miss. 263, 60 So. 215, 216 (1913), quoting *Kennington v. Hemingway*, 101 Miss. 259, 57 So. 809, 811 (1912).

119. *See, e.g.*, Justice George Ethridge's less-than-reverent depiction of the legislature, dissenting in *Crippen v. Mint Sales Co.*, 103 So. 503, 505–506 (Miss. 1925) (Ethridge, J., dissenting).

120. Miss. Code Ann. § 71-3-5; see Miss. Laws, ch. 412 (1948). This exemption does not extend to sawmill workers. *See Eaton v. Joe N. Miles & Sons*, 238 Miss. 605, 119 So.2d 359 (1960) (workers compensation insurance policy for sawmill excluded exempt farm labor); *see also Lopanic v. Berkeley Co-op Gin Co.*, 191 So.2d 108 (Miss. 1966) (cotton gin is manufacturing, not agricultural employment).

121. *State vs. J. J. Newman Lumber Co.*, 103 Miss. 263, 60 So. 215, 216–217 (1913).

122. *State vs. J. J. Newman Lumber Co.*, 103 Miss. 263, 60 So. 215, 217 [3] (1912).

123. *State vs. J. J. Newman Lumber Co.*, 103 Miss. 263, 60 So. 215, 217 (1913).

124. The story of the Butterfield Lumber Company is told by Gilbert H. Hoffman, *Dummy Lines through the Longleaf* 192–233 (1992).

125. In early November of 1912, the lawyers for Butterfield Lumber entered a stipulation with the attorney general to the effect that it was "the desire of all parties interested in the two cases may be considered in the light of all of the argument and authorities in both."

126. Tom Brady Jr. was Butterfield Lumber Company's lawyer in a number of other contexts as well, *see* Gilbert H. Hoffman, *Dummy Lines through the Longleaf* 232–233 (1992).

127. *State v. Butterfield Lumber Co.*, 60 So. 217 (Miss. 1913). T. Brady Jr. was the father of Justice Thomas P. Brady, who would serve on the Supreme Court of Mississippi from 1964 until 1973. The Brief of the Appellee signed and filed by T. Brady Jr. and Jones & Tyler in November of 1912 is more skillfully written and argued than the briefs filed on behalf of Newman Lumber. The ultimate decision regarding the constitutionality of the ten-hour workday law would almost certainly have been the same if the Butterfield Lumber case had been the lead case.

128. *State v. Butterfield Lumber Co.*, 103 Miss. 286, 60 So. 322 (1913).

129. Gilbert H. Hoffman, *Steam Whistles in the Piney Woods*, Vol. 1, page 39 (1998).

130. *J. J. Newman Lumber Co. v. Dantzler*, 107 Miss. 31, 64 So. 931, 932 (1914).

131. *Buckeye Cotton Oil Co: v. State*, 103 Miss. 767, 60 So. 775 (1913).

132. *Buckeye Cotton Oil Co. v. State*, 103 Miss. 767, 60 So. 775, 776 (1913).

133. *Buckeye Cotton Oil Co. v. State*, 103 Miss. 767, 60 So. 775, 777 (1913).

134. This worker-by-worker analysis is more consistent with the argument that had been made on appeal by the lawyers for Butterfield Lumber. It is inconsistent with the text of the act the legislature passed.

135. Miss. Laws, ch. 157, page 165 (1912), effective July 12, 1912.

136. See discussion above of *State vs. J. J. Newman Lumber Co.*, 103 Miss. 263, 60 So. 215, 217 (1913), denying suggestion of error.

137. Miss. Laws, ch. 157, § 2, page 165 (1912), effective July 12, 1912.

138. *Buckeye Cotton Oil Co. v. State*, 103 Miss. 767, 60 So. 775, 777 (1913). Chief Justice Sydney Smith would have a much better day some twenty-five years later. See chapter 10 below.

139. Miss. Laws, ch. 168, § 1, page 217 (1914), effective March 28, 1914.

140. Miss. Laws, ch. 239, § 2, page 349 (1916), effective April 7, 1916.

141. Miss. Laws, ch. 239, § 1, page 349 (1916), effective April 7, 1916.

142. *Bledsoe v. Bostic Lumber & Mfg. Co.*, 113 Miss. 118, 73 So. 881 (1917); *Handy v. Mercantile Lumber Co.*, 121 Miss. 489, 83 So. 674 (1920).

143. In 1916, the Supreme Court of Mississippi was expanded to six justices. Miss. Const. art. 6, § 145-A, Miss. Laws, ch. 154 (1916). Justice Sykes was appointed to one of the new positions to serve from the northern district by Gov. Theodore G. Bilbo, whom Sykes had supported in the 1915 gubernatorial election. John Ray Skates Jr., *A History of the Mississippi Supreme Court, 1817–1948*, page 97 (1973).

144. *Handy v. Mercantile Lumber Co.*, 121 Miss. 489, 83 So. 674, 675 (1920).

145. *Butterfield Lumber Co. v. Guy*, 92 Miss. 361, 46 So. 78, 80 (1908).

146. *See, e.g., Doughty v. Owen*, 2 Cushm. (24 Miss.) 404, 1852 WL 2032 (1852); *Deans v. McLendon*, 1 George (30 Miss.) 343, 357, 1855 WL 2570 (1855).

147. *See, e.g., Montjoy v. Delta Bank*, 76 Miss. 402, 24 So. 870 (1899); *Woodson v. Hopkins*, 85 Miss. 171, 37 So. 1000, 1001, 1002, 1003, 1005 (1905); *Rodge v. Kelly, Tax Collector*, 88 Miss. 209, 40 So. 552, 553, 554 (1906); and *Gray Robinson*, 95 Miss. 1, 48 So. 226 (1909).

148. *Montjoy v. Delta Bank*, 76 Miss. 402, 24 So. 870 (1899); *Gray Robinson*, 95 Miss. 1, 48 So. 226 (1909).

149. This important encounter with the judicial power is considered in chapter 8.

150. Miss. Const. art. 1, §1; art. 6. §144 (1890).

151. U.S. Const. amend. XIV, § 1.

152. Miss. Const. art. 3, § 16 (1890).

153. U.S. Const. art. 1, § 14; Miss. Const. art. 3, § 16 (1890).

154. *Myers v. City of McComb*, 943 So.2d 1, 7 (¶22) (Miss. 2006); *Van Slyke v. Board of Trustees of State Insts. of Higher Learning*, 613 So. 2d 872, 876 (Miss. 1993); *State ex rel. Mississippi Bureau of Narcotics v. Lincoln County*, 605 So.2d 802, 803 (1992); *Alexander v. State ex rel. Allain*, 441 So. 2d 1329, 1334 (Miss. 1983); *Albritton v. City of Winona*, 181 Miss. 75, 102 to 103, 178 So. 799, 806 (1938).

155. *See, e.g.*, Miss. Const. art. 3, § 12-A, elaborating and regulating the right to hunt and fish; art. 3, § 17-A, placing precise limits on the power of eminent domain; art. 14, §263-A, declaring, "Marriage may take place and may be valid under the laws of this State only between a man and a woman." This mandate was held unenforceable in *Campaign for Southern Equality v. Bryant*, 791 F.3d 625 (5th Cir. 2015). An earlier instance in Mississippi is its constitutional "right to work" law. Miss. Const. art. 7, § 198-A, ratified in 1960.

156. *Montjoy v. Delta Bank*, 76 Miss. 402, 24 So. 870 (1899); *Gray Robinson*, 95 Miss. 1, 48 So. 226 (1909).

157. *State vs. J. J. Newman Lumber Co.*, 102 Miss. 802, 59 So. 923, 925 (1912).

158. Miss. Const. art. 3, § 14; U.S. Const. amend. V ("nor be deprived of . . . without due process of law"); amend. XIV, § 1 ("nor shall any state deprive . . . without due process of law").

159. Miss. Const. art. 4, §§33, 54–77; *State v. Wood*, 187 So. 2d 820, 827 (Miss. 1966).

160. *See, e.g., Thrash v. Mayor and Commissioners of City of Jackson*, 498 So.2d 801, 806 (Miss. 1986) ("petty larceny of . . . police power is one of the inevitabilities of organized society"); *Mississippi Soc'y v. Musgrove*, 44 Miss. 820 (1870); *Ryals v. Pigott*, 580 So. 2d 1140, 1154 (Miss. 1991); *City of Gulfport v. Anderson*, 554 So. 2d 873, 874 (Miss. 1989); and, of course, *State v. J.J. Newman Lumber Co.*, 102 Miss. 802, 59 So. 923, 928 (1912), suggestion of error overruled, 103 Miss. 263, 60 So. 215 (1913).

161. *State vs. J. J. Newman Lumber Co.*, 103 Miss. 263, 60 So. 215, 217 (1913).

162. *See Prince v. Massachusetts*, 321 U.S. 158 (1944), building on *Jacobson v. Massachusetts*, 197 U.S. 11 (1905).

163. See chapter 3 above.

164. Miss. Const. art. 3, § 5 (1890, as amended).

165. *See, e.g.*, Richard A. Posner, *Economic Analysis of Law* (9th ed., 2014).

166. Oliver Wendell Holmes, *The Path of the Law*, 10 Harv. L. Rev. 457, 469 (1897).

167. *State vs. J. J. Newman Lumber Co.*, 103 Miss. 263, 60 So. 215, 217 (1913).

168. *Harry and Others v. Decker & Hopkins*, Walker (1 Miss.) 36, **1, 1818 WL 1235 (1818). See chapter 2 above, page 38, note 50 and accompanying text.

169. Miss. Const. art. 3, § 5 (1890, as amended).

170. *See, e.g.*, Richard A. Posner, *Economic Analysis of Law* § 26.1, page 907 (9th ed., 2014).

171. Oliver Wendell Holmes, *Ideals and Doubts*, 10 Illinois Law Review 1 (1915), in *The Essential Holmes*, at 119.

172. The obligatory citation here is the seminal work of Nobel Prize laureate Ronald Coase, *The Problem of Social Cost*, 3 Journ. Law & Economics 1 (1960); *see further* Richard A. Posner, *Economic Analysis of Law* §§ 1.1, 1.5, 3.5, pages 8–9, 25–25, 52 (9th ed., 2014).

173. *State vs. J. J. Newman Lumber Co.*, 103 Miss. 263, 60 So. 215, 217 (1913).

174. *State vs. J. J. Newman Lumber Co.*, 103 Miss. 263, 60 So. 215, 217 (1913).

175. See chapter 10 below.

176. See chapter 6 above. *See, generally*, Henry M. Hart Jr. and Albert Sacks, *The Legal Process: Basic Problems in the Making and Application of Law* 111–112 (Tentative. ed. 1958).

177. Our most thoughtful and credible lawyer economist in recent years had often said that, by decisions like *Lochner* and others, "the Supreme Court may have made the United States marginally more prosperous than it would otherwise have been." *See, e.g.*, Richard A. Posner, *Law and Literature* 347 (9th ed., 2009).

178. Miss. Const. art. 3, § 5 (1890, as amended).

179. Miss. Laws, ch. 157, § 1, page 165 (1912), effective July 12, 1912.

180. *Lochner v. New York*, 198 U.S. 46, 75–76 (1904) (Holmes, J., dissenting).

181. Miss. Const. art. 3, § 5 provides: "All political power is vested in, and derived from, the people; all government of right originates with the people, is founded upon their will only, and is instituted solely for the good of the whole." Art. 3, § 6 provides: "The people of this state have the inherent, sole, and exclusive right to regulate the internal government and police thereof, and to alter and abolish their constitution and form of government whenever they deem it necessary to their safety and happiness; Provided, Such change be not repugnant to the constitution of the United States."

182. *See, e.g.*, Robertson, *Judge William C. Keady and the Bill of Rights*, 68 Miss. L. Journ. 1, 5 to 6 (1998).

183. *State vs. J. J. Newman Lumber Co.*, 103 Miss. 263, 60 So. 215, 216–217 (1913).

184. *State vs. J. J. Newman Lumber Co.*, 102 Miss. 802, 59 So. 923, 926 (1912) (citing *Century Dictionary*).

185. *State vs. J. J. Newman Lumber Co.*, 103 Miss. 263, 60 So. 215, 216–217 (1913).

186. *Buckeye Cotton Oil Co. v. State*, 103 Miss. 767, 60 So. 775, 777 (1913).

187. *Bledsoe v. Bostic Lumber & Mfg. Co.*, 113 Miss. 118, 73 So. 881 (1917); *Handy v. Mercantile Lumber Co.*, 121 Miss. 489, 83 So. 674 (1920).

188. U.S. Const. art. 6, §2.

189. *See, e.g., Bolton v. City of Greenville*, 178 So. 2d 667, 672 (Miss. 1965).

190. Miss. Const. art. 3, §7.

191. *Holden v. Hardy*, 169 U.S. 366 (1898).

192. *Czekala-Chatham v. State*, 195 So.3d 187, 189–193, 198–204 (Miss. 2015); *see* Robertson, "The Confession of Justice Thomas Pickens Brady," www.caba.ms/articles/features/confessions -justice-thomas-pickens-brady.html.

193. *State v. J. J. Newman Lumber Co.*, 102 Miss. 802, 59 So. 923, 925 (1912).

194. Gilbert H. Hoffman, *Steam Whistles in the Piney Woods*, Vol. 1, pages 50–52 (1998).

195. *See Northern Assur. Co. v. J. J. Newman Lumber Co.*, 105 Miss. 688. 63 So. 209 (1913); *J. J. Newman Lumber Co. v. Dantzler*, 107 Miss. 31, 64 So. 931 (2014); *J. J. Newman Lumber Co. v. Lucas*, 108 Miss. 784, 67 So. 216 (1915); *London Guarantee & Accident Co. v. J. J. Newman Lumber Co.*, 116 Miss. 534, 77 So. 522 (1918).

196. *J. J. Newman Lumber Co. v. Norris*, 130 Miss. 751, 94 So. 881 [2] (1923).

197. *Mississippi History Now*, "Growth of the Lumber Industry (1840–1930)," page 5 (2001); http://mshistorynow.mdah.state.ms.us/articles/171/growth-of-the-lumber-industry-1840 -to-1930, posted May 2001.

198. Gilbert H. Hoffman, *Steam Whistles in the Piney Woods*, Vol. 1, page 54 (1998).

199. Gilbert H. Hoffman, *Steam Whistles in the Piney Woods*, Vol. 1, pages 96, 102, 104 (1998).

200. *J. J. Newman Lumber Co. v. Cameron*, 179 Miss. 217, 174 So. 571 (1937).

201. Gilbert H. Hoffman, quoting Fenwick L. Peck, in *Steam Whistles in the Piney Woods*, Vol. 1, page 99 (1998) (emphasis supplied).

202. W. J. Cash, *The Mind of the South* 176, 197, 198, 201, 203, 346, 348 (1941, 1991).

203. Gilbert H. Hoffman, *Steam Whistles in the Piney Woods*, Vol. 1, page 104 (1998).

204. Miss. Const. art. 3, §6 (1890).

205. Miss. Const. art. 7, §190 (1890).

206. See Gilbert H. Hoffman, *Dummy Lines through the Longleaf: A History of the Saw-mills and Logging Railroads of Southwest Mississippi* (2d ed., 1999); Gilbert H. Hoffman, *Steam Whistles in the Piney Woods*, Vol. 1 (1998) and Vol. 2 (2002).

207. Gilbert H. Hoffman, *Steam Whistles in the Piney Woods*, Vol. 1, pages 106–254 (1998).

208. See Gilbert H. Hoffman, *Dummy Lines through the Longleaf: A History of the Sawmills and Logging Railroads of Southwest Mississippi* (2d ed., 1999).

209. Gilbert H. Hoffman, *Steam Whistles in the Piney Woods*, Vol. 1, pages 39, 106, 175–176 (1998).

210. Gilbert H. Hoffman, *Steam Whistles in the Piney Woods*, Vol. 1, page 176 (1998).

211. Richard A. Posner, *The Problematics of Moral and Legal Theory*, 259 (1999).

212. *Abrams v. United States*, 250 U.S. 616, 630 (1919) (Holmes, J., dissenting), quoted in *The Essential Holmes*, at 320 (Posner ed., 1992).

213. William Faulkner, *Light in August*, page 4 (1932).

214. William Faulkner, *Light in August*, page 5 (1932). I am indebted to James E. Fickle for reminding me of these passages, no doubt included in my copy of the allegorical tale of Joe Christmas and Lena Grove and Lucas Burch and Gail Hightower and Joanna Burden that I last

read some fifteen or more years before Fickle quoted those passages in his thoughtful volume *Mississippi Forests and Forestry*, at 118 (2001).

BIBLIOGRAPHY

Cash, W. J., *The Mind of the South* (1941, 1991).

Coase, Ronald, *The Problem of Social Cost*, 3 Journ. Law & Economics 1 (1960).

Davis, Thomas D., "Mississippi: Its Opportunities and Resources," *Journal of Mississippi History* 8 (Oct. 1946), page 237.

Faulkner, William, *Light in August* (1932).

Fickle, James E., *Mississippi Forests and Forestry* (2001).

Ginsburg, Ruth Bader, *Muller v. Oregon: One Hundred Years Later*, 45 Willamette L. Rev. 359 (2009).

Hart, Henry M., Jr., and Albert Sacks, *The Legal Process: Basic Problems in the Making and Application of Law* (Tentative ed. 1958).

Hickman, Nollie W., "The Lumber Industry in South Mississippi, 1890–1915," *Journal of Mississippi History* 20 (1958).

Hickman, Nollie W., *Mississippi Harvest: Lumbering in the Longleaf Pine Belt, 1840–1915* (1962).

Hoffman, Gilbert H., *Dummy Lines through The Longleaf: A History of the Sawmills and Logging Railroads of Southwest Mississippi* (2d ed., 1999).

Hoffman, Gilbert H., *Steam Whistles in the Piney Woods*, Vols. 1 (1998) and 2 (2002).

Holmes, Oliver Wendell, *The Essential Holmes* (Richard A. Posner ed., 1992).

Holmes, Oliver Wendell, *The Path of the Law*, 10 Harv. L. Rev. 457 (1897).

"Labor Laws and Regulations, Legislation in the United States Limiting Hours of Labor for Men," *Monthly Labor Review* (1918).

Lester, Connie L., "Balancing Agriculture with Industry: Capital, Labor, and the Public Good in Mississippi's Home-Grown New Deal," *Journal of Mississippi History* 70 (Fall 2008), page 239.

Posner, Richard A., *Economic Analysis of Law* (9th ed., 2014).

Posner, Richard A., *Law and Literature* (3d ed. 2009).

Posner, Richard A., *The Problematics of Moral and Legal Theory* (1999).

Skates, John Ray, Jr., *A History of the Mississippi Supreme Court, 1817–1948* (1973).

Warren, Robert Penn, *All the King's Men* (1946).

CHAPTER 8

The Coming of the
Common Law in Mississippi

The common law is not a brooding omnipresence in
the sky but the articulate voice of some sovereign or
quasi-sovereign that can be identified.... It is always the
law of some state.

—*SOUTHERN PACIFIC CO. V. JENSEN*, 244 U.S. 205, 222
(1917) (HOLMES, J., DISSENTING)

A YANKEE LANDOWNER IN MISSISSIPPI ENCOUNTERS COMMON LAW

The days when New York native David D. Withers (1822–1892) would be known
as "the Sage of Brookdale" lay ahead.[1] It was a quarter of a century before
Withers and his partners acquired Monmouth Race Track near Red Bank, New
Jersey. In his sunset years, Withers was thought the "foremost racing man of the
world," without peer "in influence, in authority, and in reputation in turf affairs,
... [with] no rival in America, in England, upon the Continent of Europe or in
Australia."[2] The annual Withers Stakes at Aqueduct Racetrack in Queens, New
York, honors his memory and service.

Our story begins with a Mississippi constitutional encounter that arose
from an earlier and quite different Withers venture—his large cotton plantation in Wilkinson County, Mississippi.[3] Louisiana lies below a land line to the
south, and across the Mississippi River to the west. In the mid-1850s, Withers's
"large and valuable estate in lands, slaves, &c, was worth about $200,000,[4] on
Old River,"[5] once the main channel of the mighty Mississippi. The River had
changed its course in 1796.

The Homochitto River has long fed the Mississippi from sources as far
northeasterly as Copiah County. It forms the westernmost part of the boundary between Franklin and Amite Counties, and the entire boundary separating Adams County to the north and Wilkinson County to the south.[6] In the

1850s, the Homochitto emptied its waters into Old River a bit above Withers's lands. During low-water months, its current scoured mud from the bottom of Old River. Each summer's channel clearing was of considerable advantage to Withers and others with lands on Old River, as it kept open an outlet to the Mississippi, to New Orleans, to the Gulf of Mexico, and to the Western World. Access to the waters was crucial in those days, and for Withers's plantation in particular, "for agricultural purposes, and for navigation in transporting crops to market, and receiving supplies."[7]

In 1850, the Mississippi legislature passed a bill to improve navigation on the Homochitto and its outlets, "for removing obstructions in said streams, and excavating and digging a canal." Withers was unimpressed with this purported public benefit. The proposed canal would divert the waters he had been using for years and "cause the outlet of Old River to fill up."[8] The river commissioners were about to impede the operation of his plantation and devalue his property. No one proposed to compensate him for this loss of value. Nor did the commissioners offer to reimburse costs he might incur, if he could find a feasible alternative way to keep open his outlet to the Mississippi. And so David Withers went to the courthouse. Because he needed relief in the nature of an equitable remedy, he sued in the chancery court.

Withers asked the chancery court to enjoin the commissioners that they cease and desist from their plans. When he did this, he entered into what became for him a bewildering maze of different kinds of primary rules of law, and from different sources as well. Some rules Withers found on their face might be helpful; others, not so helpful. Some were sufficiently unwritten, intangible, that they hardly seemed like laws at all. Constitutional premises that might affect his case were found nowhere in the constitution itself,[9] at least not where he could see and understand them. Withers was asking a court to exercise its constitutional "judicial power" and adjudge his case. This was his only option. Once in court, he found that the legal conundrum he faced went well beyond the act of 1850 and the commissioners' plans. The only thing he was sure of was that these public plans would upset the way he ran his plantation. This would cause him trouble and cost him money.

For starters, Section 14 of the constitution told Withers that "for an injury done him in his lands . . . [he] shall have a remedy by due course of law."[10] Fine, that's all he was asking. Section 13 said the legislature could take a man's property but not "without just compensation being first made therefor."[11] The legislature certainly was taking property, but it wasn't any that Withers held title to, at least not according to the official county land records. Besides, he did not so much care that the state pay him money—how would he show with any level of certainty what he was about to lose, unless, of course, he figured out a way to keep the outlet to the river open on his own? Withers wished the state and its local officials would just leave him alone. Of course, the act of 1850 was a law. The legislature had passed it. It was within the legislative power.[12] The governor

had signed it. In time, the court that heard his case would sweep it under the
label of "eminent domain."[13] But since he didn't own the lands or parts of the
river where the work was to be done, did he still have a case?

Withers was invoking a particular "judicial power," one granted to the chancery court as a court of equity.[14] He was trying to thwart the exercise of a "legislative power." Another part of the constitution recognized and governed the
legislative power,[15] which was to be kept separate from the judicial power.[16] But
how did that work? At some point Withers would learn of a process called judicial review, dating in Mississippi back to 1823.[17] He could ask the court to look
at what the legislature had done and see if that squared with its powers. Not
being a lawyer, he may have wondered how some idea never put in writing in
the constitution could authorize this oversight, which as a practical matter just
might be the most important constitutional process of all.

There was federal law going back to statehood that might help. The 1817
Mississippi Constitution accepted that the state was being admitted "into the
Union on an equal footing with the original States."[18] Under that quasi-constitutional premise, the United States conveyed to Mississippi in trust all navigable
waters within the state's boundaries, the same as similar waters were enjoyed by
the original thirteen states and all new states since Independence.[19] The act of
Congress that authorized forming the state had provided the particulars, which
included, "That the River Mississippi, and the navigable rivers and waters leading into the same, or into the Gulf of Mexico, . . . , shall be common highways,
and forever free."[20]

That ought to help. After all, the federal constitution near its end included
a rule called the Supremacy Clause. It said federal law trumped state law, and
specifically that "the Judges in every State shall be bound thereby, any Thing in
the Constitution or Law of any State to the Contrary notwithstanding."[21] But did
this include the Homochitto River? And Old River? It certainly should. These
waters flowed into the River Mississippi and into the Gulf of Mexico.

Withers's next question was in what sense "waters" had to be "navigable."
Navigable for how much of the year? By whom or what? Steamboats? Flatboats?
Logs? If none of these, how were courts to know whether the Homochitto and
Old River were "navigable rivers" or just "waters"? Did not "forever free" mean
Withers should win his case in any event? If the state would leave these waters
"forever free," natural low-water channel clearing would do the rest.

Ultimately, Withers would learn that all of these questions could only be
answered under something called the common law.[22] And that this so-called
common law initially came from England, where it had been made by judges,
not the Crown and not the Parliament. And also that particular rules of this
common law might mean something very different in this country than what
everyone understood them to have meant a century earlier and an ocean to
the east. It was easy enough for Withers to find out *that* this common law controlled, to the extent that it addressed the points at issue. The inhabitants of all

new states coming into the Union were entitled to "the benefit of . . . judicial proceedings according to the common law," as guaranteed by Article the Second in the Northwest Territory Ordinance of July 13, 1787.[23] The Georgia Compact of 1798 had established the Mississippi Territory and extended to it the benefits of the first five articles of the Northwest Ordinance,[24] and to any states that may be made from the territory. Another part of the Equal Footings Doctrine. Not just Mississippi, but all new states would be admitted "into the Union on an equal footing with the original States."[25] But what *was* this common law, often presented with a capital "C" and a capital "L" as though it really were a discrete and ascertainable body of rules of law?[26] How would one learn with confidence what it might have to say about what the commissioners were planning, about the claims Withers was making, and the defenses others might invoke?

Withers would come to see in time that there was indeed a series of common law rules regarding natural waters. Those rules had been held accepted into Mississippi law in 1844 by a very wise man, Chief Justice William Lewis Sharkey,[27] and in a matter out of Vicksburg called *Morgan v. Reading.*[28] Withers may have pressed the point, asking assurance what this Article the Second of the Northwest Ordinance was all about. How did Sharkey know he had the right common law regarding natural waters, much less exactly what that law said, or what it meant? Or whether and how it may apply in his case?

At some point Withers's lawyer[29] likely just handed his persistent Yankee client a copy of the *Morgan* opinion: "Read it yourself." After a few pages, there it is. All persons living in territories becoming new states "shall always be entitled to the benefits of . . . judicial proceedings according to the course of the Common Law."[30] To be sure, *Morgan* was a matter about a somewhat different aspect of the law of waters, the nature and extent of owners' rights when a river or stream bounded their lands. These are called riparian rights. They involve such questions as whether riparian owners can charge boatmen for the use of the landowner's riverbanks and wharfage areas. Even the befuddled Mr. Withers could see that his rights of access to the waters of the Homochitto and Old River suggested this same body of law, this so-called common law. But he may not have sensed that his case was against public officials working for the State, and that this might make his case different than the *Morgan* case, which was a dispute between two private persons.

Reading *Morgan* further, Withers no doubt saw Sharkey relying on English cases, beginning with "*Ball v. Herbert,* 3 Durn. & East, 253, . . . a leading case," and concluding half a page later, viz., "The case of *Blundell v. Cantrell,* 5 Barn. & Ald. 91, must put this question to rest, so far as the English decisions can do so." And he likely was thinking that this country fought a pretty tough war about three-quarters of a century earlier, the whole point of which was to get out from under the king's view of what English law meant in this country. An extended discussion in *Morgan* down through the next page compounded the felony. Sharkey was relying on law set out by English courts that no legislature ever enacted, much less a Mississippi or other American legislature.[31] The English judges who decided the *Ball* and *Blundell* cases did not get their law from the British Parliament. They got it from Lord Matthew Hale's treatise *De Jure Maris*. Sharkey took the point further, also drawing legal premises from Lord Hale's *De Portibus Maris*. Only after that did Sharkey turn the page and find that "the American decisions have generally conformed to the Common Law doctrine."[32]

In England, the common law considered as navigable only those waters within the ebb and flow of the tide. There wasn't any tidal effect on the waters near Withers's plantation, though he may have found out that in 1847 the US Supreme Court had struggled with this same legal oxymoron and had imagined an "occult tide" as far inland and upriver as ninety-five miles above New Orleans.[33] The Homochitto River and Old River experienced no ebb and flow of any tide as that phenomenon had ever been known. Withers was sure of that. So that meant these could not possibly be "navigable rivers and waters leading into the [Mississippi River], or into the Gulf of Mexico."[34] Right?

So this common law was no help after all.

But wait! Just a few years earlier, the US Supreme Court had ruled that this ebb-and-flow-of-the-tide business was so much English gibberish that made no sense in this country. Federal authority here "was not limited by tide-water, but was extended to the lakes and navigable rivers of the United States."[35] Did that mean that Withers would win under the federal Equal Footings Doctrine after all? Never mind that this would leave a well-defined and accepted judge-made common law rule meaning in England something quite different from what it meant here. All Withers had to do was convince the judge that the Homochitto River and Old River were navigable in fact, and he was home free. The common law difference between navigable waters and non-navigable waters that *Morgan* had accepted from England would not be a problem. In time this view prevailed. Practical reality suggested that "this common law rule should have but little or no force when applied to the great fresh water rivers and lakes of this country, which have not been inaptly characterized as 'inland seas.'"[36]

There was another difference between Withers's case and the *Morgan* matter decided back in 1844. He recalled that the court there was concerned with the rights of riparian owners. At the end of the day, the court had held that riparian owners whose titles and boundaries extend to the Mississippi River "own at least to low water mark." To be sure, riparian lands were subject to others' access to the riverbank as an incident of their right of navigation. But that did not include an adverse party taking possession of the riverbank and occupying it for four months without paying a wharfage fee. Withers had no quarrel with neighbors or third persons wanting to moor their craft temporarily along the riverbanks that Withers now realized he owned. Other riparian landowners in the area were equally amenable, and equally opposed to the commissioners' plans to monkey with the channel of Old River and the Homochitto.

Another surprise was just around the corner.

Before the state supreme court, Withers found that his claim against the Commissioners of the Homochitto River would be decided according to still further rules that no constitution or legislative body had ever enacted. He was brought face-to-face with constitutional powers called "eminent domain,"[37] mentioned before. And, as he was learning, he had little hope of thwarting the commissioners' plans, Withers was told he did not even have property rights with enough oomph behind them that he could claim compensation for the loss of value his lands would suffer.[38] Justice Alexander H. Handy, whom we met near the end of chapter 4, instructed him that "it is not easy to understand how a man can be said to have a property in water, light or air of so fixed and positive a character as to deprive the sovereign power of the right to control it for the public good and the general convenience."[39] Ouch! He was claiming property rights in waters that his property did not surround.

And so the court sent Withers packing, leaving no doubt but that

> the rule of the common law is not applicable to our large public rivers used for navigation,—that the rights of the owners of lands bounded by such streams are subordinate to the right and power of the State to use and appropriate them to the public good in the promotion of navigation.

And as to his argument that supreme federal law guaranteed that the rivers would remain "forever free," that meant only that citizens could navigate the rivers of the state without charge. It had no effect on the power of the state to improve or change the condition of those waters, or alter their course, as the legislature saw the public interest.

If David Withers couldn't live with that, he needed to go see his senator or representative. "If the private injury be great, it is not to be presumed that the legislature will turn a deaf ear to the application. But if it were to be so, it would furnish no reason against the power of the legislature to carry out the improvement."[40]

For the moment, we have introduced the role of the common law—or is it the Common Law?—in Mississippi. We have made this introduction in the context of the trials and tribulations of David Withers vis-à-vis the Commissioners of the Homochitto River and then the chancery court and ultimately the High Court of Errors and Appeals of Mississippi.[41] Withers took a shot at an appeal to the US Supreme Court, only to be told there was no federal offense. Past that, this was a state matter.[42]

The common law may "always be the law of some state."[43] It is always of interest in the context of some state's exercise of its constitutionally grounded police power and power of eminent domain, and most often in contexts where there is other competing or auxiliary law, and not infrequently other outcome-determinative law. A common law rule may be as solid as a rock from the standpoint of accepted criteria for legal validity,[44] but for any number of reasons it may not carry the day. The facts need to be marshaled. Then the general must be linked up with the particular. The law must be applied reliably to the relevant facts.[45] This happens in each case that comes to one of the Faulknerian courthouses[46] across the state. *Withers* is but one of dozens—hundreds—of practical contexts where this is so. These thoughts should be kept in mind as the story turns to the common law in its most misunderstood dimension, its validity as judge-made law that governs and regulates the hopes and fears and behavior of thousands at the level of primary private activity.

THE LEGITIMACY AND PRACTICAL DESIRABILITY
OF JUDGE-MADE COMMON LAW

The practical uses of constitutionally authorized common law—and their limits—are what this chapter is about. Stories of more people like David Withers follow below, and of their particular encounters with this particular dimension of judicial power. Construing the behavior and motives of most is fraught with ambiguity. People who are judges and—more so than in other chapters—others who are legal writers play their respective roles.

Formally, common law has been a substantial part of the law of Mississippi because the Georgia Compact of 1798 said so. The United States has always called the shots on the ground rules for new states entering the Union. Practicably, it is a safe bet that Mississippi and the other states would have accepted and practiced common law had the federal sovereign remained silent. Cases had to be decided. The moment you add that cases needed to be decided justly and fairly and reliably,[47] you have incorporated "judicial proceedings according to the course of the common law" into the state's constitutional judicial power and practice. Bear in mind that in the antebellum era, common law was just about all there was. Statutes were relatively few. Before we get to the more particular stories of particular people who have been caught up in the way Mississippians have encountered and dealt with the judge-made common law, a few more basics should be helpful.

By high school, if not sooner, most youngsters in Mississippi have been taught a simplistic truism—the legislature makes the law, the judiciary interprets the law, and the executive enforces the law. This is not unlike what students are exposed to in most of the rest of the country.[48] Many—hopefully most—gain a richer appreciation of the judicial power as they mature, whether in history and political science courses in college or by following current events, so many of which involve some aspect of government, federal and state, or otherwise.

The stories told below center in large part upon what happens in the court-house. Trials are held there, as well as a variety of different kinds of hearings leading up to trial or concerning matters to be addressed after trial. Then there are appeals. Appellate judges in Mississippi hold court in Jackson. The Court of Appeals of Mississippi also sits in other locations in different parts of the state. David Withers's case against the Commissioners of the Homochitto River unfolded in the courthouse in Natchez. A. B. Dawson, vice-chancellor, heard the case without a jury in what was formally known as the southern district of the Chancery Court of Mississippi. On appeal, Justice Handy and his two fellow justices of the High Court of Errors and Appeals of Mississippi[49] sat in the northern courtroom on the top floor of the Old Capitol State House, now a museum in Jackson at the foot of East Capitol Street and State Street.[50]

At each stage in a case, there comes a point where the judge identifies the relevant law and then reliably applies it, or at least he or she is supposed to do that. Often the judge uses shorthand. Today a judge may rule that the admissibility of certain evidence is controlled by Rule 404(b)[51] or some other rule of evidence. She or he may invoke the common law *res gestae* rule.[52] Whether a case should be dismissed because of a statute of limitations, for example, may turn on whether a discovery rule applies. Did the limitations period begin to run when the said-to-be actionable event occurred, or only when the plaintiff should reasonably have discovered that he had suffered an injury he could sue for? Law identification necessarily occurs at pretrial hearings, at the trial itself, in post-trial hearings in the court where the case was tried, and on appeal.

But what counts as law? Judge Handy struggled with that one in *Withers*. Outside the courthouse, few think of that question, except when they hear of a court ruling that is not to their liking. A person may be charged with a crime, tried, and convicted, and all most people hear about are highlights of the facts, and the sentence of the court. Of course, there has to be something pretty serious or unusual about a case for the public to learn that much. People are even more in the dark regarding civil cases—enforcing contracts, condemnations, car wreck injuries, divorces, boundary line disputes, civil frauds, products liability, and so many others. Still, that question—what counts as law?—arises in every case, every single one. Some judge at the trial level decides what counts as the law of a particular case. On appeal that call is made by a panel of justices or judges, or on rare occasions *en banc*, with all members of the appellate court participating. Judge-made common law has been and remains a great big part of what counts as law in particular cases.

Every use of common law is a constitutional encounter, and for several reasons. Each such use includes the practical exercise of the constitutional "judicial power." This exercise involves a judge, a constitutional officer. Every case involves persons or entities in the practical exercise of a constitutional right to petition the court and be heard. Every such matter involves a judge with two options: decide the matter or transfer it to another judge more properly empowered. All authority that there is to decide cases is vested in some trial-level court, with the circuit judges having been told they get all matters not placed before some other type of judge.[53] No judge may decline to decide a case within his or her jurisdiction.[54] It "would be treason to the constitution to so decline."[55] There are no cases—"matters" is the more inclusive word used in the constitution[56]—not assigned to some court. None. No jurisdiction has been left undelegated.[57] More practicably, it cannot be said too often that judges get paid to decide cases, not to think up reasons not to decide cases. And so every person claiming under the common law, or asserting some common law defense, is experiencing a constitutionally authorized and protected process that is said to be his due. The constitution has always said, "Every person for a [legal] injury done him in his lands, goods, or reputation, shall have a remedy by due course of law, and right and justice administered without sale, denial, or delay."[58] This is more than just state constitutional law. Its historical anchor lies in Magna Carta.[59]

There is a sense in which this constitutional experience is just one encounter after another and another, and so forth. Some such experiences are harder to isolate than others. Common law as a discrete series of practical happenings is presented here because it matters in every chapter of this work. The stories told vary greatly. Hopefully, those above, here, and below give a flavor of the massive and diverse whole. We noted at the outset that, despite the plethora of statutes found in the Mississippi Code in the twenty-first century, the greater quantity of what counts as law that regulates the organized society in which we live is still judge-made (including privately made law like contracts, the authority for which comes from the judicial power and thence to the enabling or secondary rules found in the judge-made common law of contracts). Even lawyers can be numbed by the everydayness of goings-on in the courthouse. But these adjudications have practical effects upon the parties, and often on many others. They set precedents, formal and sometimes not so formal; they will be looked to in cases down the line, learned from and followed more or less. They determine whether a man can pay his bills, plant his crops, see his children, or be euthanized with the same effect as hanging a hundred years ago. And so much more.

We saw common law questions enmeshed in chapter 2. In the spring of 1818, Judge Joshua G. Clarke's weapons were those of the common law tradition, brought to bear as best he could, given his own not inconsiderable powers of reason and expression. "Reason is the life of the law," Sir Edward Coke famously declared of that tradition, "nay, the common law is nothing else but reason."[60] Justice Horatio F. Simrall quoted Coke en route to reasoning, "A contract made in 1860, by a citizen of this state, to deliver cotton to a citizen of New York, on the 1st day of October, 1861, at Vicksburg, is not necessarily annulled by the war."[61] Judge Clarke understood that the common law was as much a process as it was a not-altogether-written body of law. In 1821, he found it and enforced it in deciding whether a man would die on the gallows.[62] In 1824, in *Bradley v. State*,[63] Judge Powhatan Ellis gave a tongue-in-cheek answer to the question whether Mississippi law would recognize a husband's common law "right of chastisement of his wife."[64] But such answers may be changed, as men's mode of thinking has evolved. On the one hundredth anniversary of its original answer, the court declared, "The common law on the subject stands as if the *Bradley Case* had never been decided or decided the converse of what it was."[65]

These are but a few.

Whatever the origin of a common law rule, all that need be shown for its application and enforcement is "the fact of its existence . . . entirely beyond question or dispute."

> Were it otherwise, the rules of law would be fluctuating and unsettled as the opinions of the different judges administering them might happen to differ in relation to the existence of sufficient and valid reasons for maintaining and upholding them.[66]

On the other hand, not every law in England booked passage on the *Mayflower*, Article the Second of the Northwest Ordinance of 1787 and its sweeping statements to the contrary notwithstanding. For one, this legal inheritance has always been understood "to exclude all English statutes."[67] For another, it was said early on that "*all* the rules of the common law were not in force in this state, but *only such* as were adapted to our institutions and circumstances and not repealed by the legislature or varied by the usages which superseded them."[68] The *Withers* case presented an instance of this limited acceptance. The common law rule limiting public waters to those within the ebb and flow of the tide was originally held to "have but little or no force when applied to the great fresh waters and lakes of this country."[69]

In 1842, Chief Justice Sharkey declared that Mississippi would recognize and enforce only those "common law remedies which are not repugnant to the spirit and form of our government."[70] This limitation on common law has been carried forward long since Sharkey's day. In 1924, the court would declare that "the principles of the common law unsuited to our condition or repugnant to the spirit of our government are not in force in this state."[71] Through the years, important effects were felt from this insistence. After all, "slavery as it exists in this country, was unknown to the common law of England."[72] Both constitutional and statutory regulations regarding slavery declared, and courts secured and enforced, this darker difference between "our conditions" and the common law.

Understanding the institution and practice of slavery is important in other contexts in which the common law was overridden by legislation, at times with defenders of the common law kicking and screaming all the way. Two such instances are presented below. Legislation limited and then replaced the *Rule in Shelley's Case* and its common law regulation of donative transfers of property within families. The common law disabilities of coverture suffered by married women were similarly legislatively limited, although it took some forty years for these disabilities to be abrogated altogether. The practice of slavery was smoldering beneath the stories of these legislative/judicial constitutional encounters. In

more recent times, common law rights would clash with the constitutional eminent domain and police powers, the *Withers* case being an early chapter there.
Tort reform has reminded Mississippi[73] and the other states that the common
law always has been subject to modification or outright repeal by the legislature.

COMMON LAW, KILLINGS, AND MAGNA CARTA, TOO!

In the late spring of 1843, a young Daniel Weisiger Adams (1821–1872), took
offense to newspaper editor James Hagan's (1805–1843) public criticisms of
Adams's father, George, a lawyer and briefly a US district judge.[74] On June 7,
the younger Adams hurried from Jackson and confronted Hagan, editor of
the *Vicksburg Sentinel*, on a public street in mid-afternoon.[75] An altercation
ensued, the details of which are disputed to this day, except that in the end
Hagan lay dead from a shot to the head, and Adams had a pistol in his hand.[76]
Daniel Adams, also a lawyer, was indicted by a Warren County grand jury and
charged with murder. Circuit Judge George Coulter[77] ordered Adams released
after posting a $6,000 bond.[78] Successor *Sentinel* editor, Walter Hickey (?–1849),
undeterred by the fate of his predecessor, proceeded to publish a journalistic
and quite public indictment of Judge Coulter. For his intemperance, Hickey
found himself in contempt of court. Coulter ordered Hickey committed to the
Warren County jail for five months. For good measure, Hickey was also ordered
to pay a $500 fine—likely the cost of his room and board in county facilities—
plus court costs.

Editor Hickey sought a pardon, which Governor A. G. Brown promptly
granted. Judge Coulter questioned whether the governor's pardon power
extended to relief from contempt of court. Finding that Hickey had "by some
means escaped from said jail, and is now going at large in contempt of said
order of said court,"[79] Coulter had a bench warrant issued for his arrest. Two
days later, Hickey was back in jail. Later that day, Justice Joseph S. B. Thacher
granted Hickey's application that he be heard whether of right he should be
released again. The stage was set for a remarkable moment, with Thacher not
only exploring important premises of the common law having to do with the
Adams-Hagan-Hickey affair, but also a number of constitutional grounds traceable back to England and June of 1215.

Joseph Stevens Buckminster Thacher (1812–1867) had been born in Boston.
He graduated from Harvard College in 1832 but soon moved to Mississippi,
where he was admitted to the bar.[80] In 1843, Thacher was sworn in as a justice on
the Supreme Court of Mississippi. He began his response to Hickey's application, summarizing the prerogative, jurisdiction, and procedure for habeas corpus. As familiar as the point may be to lawyers, it is important to bear in mind
that a "writ" is in the nature of an order and that the Latin phrase "habeas corpus" means "have the body."[81] The officer on whom the writ of habeas corpus is

served is being told to produce before the court the person in custody and show that this detention is consistent with due process of law.

The constitution provided that "the privilege of the *writ of habeas corpus* shall not be suspended, unless, when in the case or rebellion or invasion, the public safety may require it,"[82] but that was a limitation. The right itself was a function of the common law accepted in Mississippi. The *ab initio* question in *Hickey* was whether a single judge had authority to issue and act under this writ. Answering this question was a two-step process. "What was the writ at common law in England?" After that, "[W]hat is . . . the writ under the constitution, statutes and common law of this state of Mississippi?"[83] Thacher left no doubt but that the answer to the first question informed the answer to the second.

Hickey begins at Runnymede. "Magna charta[84] declares that no freeman shall be taken or imprisoned, but by the lawful judgment of his equals, or by the law of the land (Mag. Chart. C. 29)."[85] This all-important clause—one of the few remaining in effect in England to this day—is a function of the core premise that "personal liberty, by the laws of England, was considered a strictly natural right, and not to be abridged without sufficient cause." Any person restrained of his liberty by anyone, from the king down to his lowest functionary, "was entitled, on demand, to have judgment upon the justice of his commitment." Thacher added that "the glory of the English law consists in clearly defining the times, the causes, and the extent, when, wherefore and in what degree, the imprisonment of the subject may be lawful."[86] From this followed one of the unique features of habeas corpus practice. A person held in custody was entitled to have the legality of his detention examined without regard to what process may have taken place in the past, or when that prior process was had.

To the question of whether a single justice might entertain the application, Thacher found that in England, this "high prerogative writ is issuable" by any court or any judge at any time. He quoted Sir William Blackstone, who had explained that

> this writ is founded on the common law, and gradually improved and extended in England by statutes to carry into actual and practical utility the free privileges of the subjects secured to them by *magna charta* and the constitution. It creates a jurisdiction, distinct, separate and independent, and though courts, and judges of those courts, are nominated by law to exercise it, they do so, not by virtue of their otherwise judicial character, authority or jurisdiction, but by the actual grant of power to act in this particular.

Some years later, Justice Oliver Wendell Holmes put the point nicely.

> But habeas corpus cuts through all forms and goes to the very tissue of the structure. It comes in from the outside, not in subordination to the proceedings, and

although every form may have been preserved opens the inquiry whether they may have been more than an empty shell.[87]

Thacher then turned to Mississippi law, the second stage of considering whether a single judge could act alone. He answered yes, adding,

> Through the force of the constitution, the statutes and the common law, the judges ... possess a full jurisdiction, and one greatly enlarged by the statutes beyond that of the writ at common law, over this writ, but in their individual capacity alone....[88]

With his authority to proceed explained, Thacher next took up the law of contempt. Editor Hickey was languishing in the Warren County Jail for going too far in showing his personal and public contempt for Judge Coulter. Without surprise, Thacher began, "The power of courts to imprison for contempts is declared by English writers and so quoted by writers on this side of the Atlantic."[89] Hickey's said-to-have-been-offensive editorial exhortation was considered a consequential contempt,[90] as it was not committed in open court in the presence of Judge Coulter. Thacher concluded "that the doctrine of consequential contempts, in its present broad understanding, was unknown to and not confirmed by the earliest constitutional law of England—*magna charta.*"[91]

Thacher carefully considered the law and practice of contempts in England and concluded that not all of those had been adopted in Mississippi. Rather, "each independent state may have its own common law which may not be considered in effect in another."[92] And so Thacher focused upon the constitution and laws of Mississippi as "the only proper, legal and safe criterion by which [this case] can be judged and decided upon."

> Immediately upon the adoption of our constitution, and before the enactment of any statutory law, so much of that which is generally termed "the common law" *and which is also strictly in accordance with that constitution*, was likewise necessarily adopted.

Contempt being in the nature of an interference with the operation of the courts, the question was whether "the act for which the petitioner [Hickey] is now imprisoned [had put] a clog upon the wheels of courts of justice."[93]

Focusing on Mississippi foundations, the *Hickey* opinion condemned the judicial discretion seemingly at the core of the law of contempt. Whether one such as the intemperate Hickey might be incarcerated "is a *quasi* political question, as all such are, which involve the liberty of the citizen, restrained upon grounds not palpably and clearly established and defined by law."

> It is a maxim of law that where a discretion is allowed courts in the punishment
> of defined offenses, that discretion must be regulated by law. . . . It is certainly bet-
> ter that the freedom of the citizen should be controlled by fixed and plain laws,
> than to be left dependent upon the uncertain moderation of those in power.[94]

Regarding the legislative role in authorizing and regulating contempt
proceedings, Thacher found the process "not to be governed, to quote the
words of Lord Coke, 'by the crooked cord of the discretion of judges,' but to be
'measured by the golden metewand of the law.'"

Thacher added to his reflections the "shield which our constitution throws
around the press."[95] "Every citizen *may freely speak, write and publish* his sentiments *on all subjects*, being responsible for the abuse of that liberty."

> When passed through the crucible of our state constitution, instead of a contempt
> of court ['the reflections of the petitioner (Hickey) upon the circuit judge of War-
> ren county'] become a mere libel on the functionary, and subject only to the pun-
> ishment prescribed by law for the latter offense.[96]

In the end, *Hickey* recognized the Governor's pardon power, found that the
editor was "held in custody by unlawful authority, and that he is clearly entitled
to discharge therefrom."[97]

At this late date, it is hard to know—with any level of reliability—what to
make of the underlying altercation between Daniel Adams and James Hagan
that June afternoon on the streets of Vicksburg.[98] One historian who has studied Adams's later career as a Confederate officer lays out a strong case each way.
Overall, Adams was "a very violent gentleman." This same historian also reports
that Hagan was "a noted hothead who had already fought a duel with another
newspaper editor."[99] Successor editor Hickey, apparently a daredevil Irishman
like Hagan, was himself to die in a duel a few years later.

By the end of 1839, Gov. A. G. McNutt had cast a jaundiced eye at all in the
banking business.[100] He had appointed James Hagan as commissioner to examine the affairs of the Agricultural Bank. But Hagan soon came under attack
by pro-bank forces. The governor replied that Hagan's "duties were ministe-
rial, not judicial. I am not aware that his avocation as an Editor, or his having
expressed an opinion on certain points, produced such a 'disqualifying bias' as
to preclude him from a faithful discharge of the duties he was sworn to perform."[101] It seems that in the course of his duties as commissioner, Hagan had
asked that the bank produce to him "a list of the debtors and securities" of the
bank. The bank's board of directors refused, resolving, "That in the opinion of
this board, the furnishing of such a list would be a violation of the 11th section
of the charter of this institution."[102] The only certainties from this exchange are
that Commissioner/Editor Hagan and the board of the Agricultural Bank each

thought the other might be up to no good, and that political banking critic Governor McNutt stood behind Hagan.

In mid-February of 1840, interspersed between reports regarding the affairs of various banks, including the Planters' Bank and the Mississippi Union Bank, the following item appeared in the *Senate Journal*:

> Be it resolved by the Senate of Mississippi, That the Sergeant-at-arms be directed to bring, forthwith, before this body, James Hagan, the Editor of the *Vicksburg Sentinel*, and that he be required to establish the criminal charges he has preferred against the honorable members of the Senate.

After some procedural motions, the resolve was tabled.[103] Again, three years before his fatal altercation with young Daniel Adams, editor Hagan had become publicly known for his wicked pen.

We know that venue of the trial of Daniel Adams was transferred from Vicksburg to Raymond. A Hinds County jury found Adams not guilty.[104] That may or may not mean only that the facts of the fatal encounter were so muddled that fair-minded jurors could not find beyond a reasonable doubt that Adams was the aggressor.[105] After all, James Hagan was not around to give his version of what happened on the fateful afternoon. On what is known, it is hard to see a fair verdict less than manslaughter at its most lenient. Then there is the insight of that sage of the mind of the South, W. J. Cash,

> The common murderer who had slain a man in a personal quarrel and with some appearance of a fair fight, some regard for a few amenities, need not fear the indignity of hanging. If the jury was not certain to call it self-defense, the worst verdict he had to expect was manslaughter.[106]

Of course, it could have been that a Hinds County jury practiced a little "home cooking" in favor of their fellow county resident Adams. Reports suggest a "turn around" verdict. That jury may have seen the hot-headed Yankee from Ireland who had engaged in such divisive journalism—once he gave up the healing arts and moved south[107]—as having been the victim of what has been colloquially called a "civic improvement homicide." The partisan *Vicksburg Sentinel* under the editorship of Walter Hickey[108] reported "the cold blooded assassination of the proprietor of this journal."[109] A Louisiana newspaper praised Hagan as "this Ajax of Democracy—this Apostle of Liberty" and as "this fearless champion of Human Rights."[110]

The remains of James Hagan lie in Cedar Hill Cemetery in Vicksburg, marked by an obelisk. On one side Hagan is called "a martyr to his devotion to the rights and interests of people, and his uncompromising vigilance and zeal, in detecting and exposing the usurpations and corruption of place and power."

The reverse side reads "In testimony of the many noble virtues and command-ing talents of the deceased, whom but to know was to Love and admire, His numerous friends have erected this Monument above his lifeless remains."[111]

Daniel Adams was only twenty-two years old when he is said to have avenged a defamation of his father. In time he became Brigadier General Adams, who fought many bloody battles with the Confederate forces, from Shiloh to Chickamauga.[112] Adams was thrice seriously wounded, was held for a time by Union forces as a prisoner of war, but after the war practiced law in New Orleans. He died there in June of 1872.[113] His remains are believed to lie in an unmarked grave in Greenwood Cemetery in Jackson, Mississippi, next to his older brother William Wirt Adams.

Walter Hickey had several subsequent duels and other altercations, surviving all. In time Hickey moved on to Texas, where he died violently in 1849.[114]

For present purposes, what happened in Vicksburg on June 13, 1843, cou-pled with successor editor Walter Hickey's published response, afforded Justice Joseph S. B. Thacher a time to soar, which he accepted with zest and moments of eloquence. More broadly, intemperance among Vicksburg journalists set within the penchant of the times toward violence enabled this milestone constitutional encounter in antebellum Mississippi,[115] and any number of ancillary interac-tions of humanity. Thacher's adjudication that Hickey should suffer no greater sanction than a charge of libel was probably sound for the times. In the more modern era of the public figure doctrine in First Amendment jurisprudence, Hickey would almost certainly have survived even a libel action.[116]

AN ALWAYS SUBORDINATE—THOUGH OFTEN QUITE STUBBORN—SPECIES OF LAW

Magna Carta and collateral clauses of the Constitution have not always been available to augment a common law practice. Then as now, judge-made law has been a subordinate form of law, always subject to legislative revision (directly and—more recently—indirectly through the rule-making authority of regulatory agencies in the executive branch). But where there has been a long-standing common law rule and no explicit statutory change, there have been times when that judge-made law could be as stubborn as a mule. Wills, deeds, and other advantageous means of distributing interests in land and personal property among familial heirs came under judicial scrutiny in England before the Crown ever dreamt of colonies in Jamestown and other New World venues. Men often left their property to their children with legal strings tightly attached. They faced the sad practical reality of the times, that one or more of one's children often predeceased their parents. Most often, these property owners were trying—come what may—to keep the property within the family even when the children passed away.[117] Instruments of donative transfer would often designate a class of recipients such as "heirs of my body" or simply "my heirs."

One feudal era problem seemed to have been that donative transfers—practicably worded given the uncertainties the donor faced—had the effect of giving rise to what today would be thought an estate tax avoidance scheme. In merry old England, the lord of the manor where a fee simple landowner lived was—at the landowner's death—entitled to "incidents of tenure"[118] or "the fruits of his seignory,"[119] a sort of estate tax. Words and phrases like "heirs" and "heirs of my body" generated contingencies that precluded the "vesting" of property interests being transferred and postponed payment of the "tax." The king and his lords did not like this. Judges began to declare such donative transfers to vest full fee simple title in the first-named heir, notwithstanding the clear language otherwise found in the donative document. Some date this practice to at least 1366,[120] though its origins are murky. In 1581, this Crown remedy gained fame or notoriety—depending on one's point of view—with what was called *Shelley's Case*.[121] Such contingency-laden donative schemes were declared unenforceable. The first-named donee or devisee took outright. The Crown and its lord got their tax as timely as they could.

In legal jargon, the *Rule in Shelley's Case* was a rule of law, not a rule of construction. It made sure that property passed down within the family was taken "by descent," in which event the "tax" was owing, rather than "by purchase," wherein no tax would be due. Where it applied, the *Rule* defeated the unmistakable intent of the person conveying property, or disposing of it by will or gift.[122] The law was saying to the donor, we know what you are trying to do, but we won't let you do it. The Crown had revenues at stake, and the Crown ran the courts. In the common context, that of a will or other donative document, the *Rule* required that the first-named heir take outright, notwithstanding the donor's well-expressed intent to limit or further constrain the title.[123]

To many, the *Rule* was long thought bad law, certainly bad policy. The power of a person to transfer title to whomever one pleased and as one pleased has been seen a fundamental incident of the institution of private property.[124] Mississippi's early experience with *Shelley's Case* shows how the courts of this state within their constitutional judicial power dealt with the *Rule*, its policy objectives and its effects. Remember, at statehood the federal sovereign had assured inhabitants of Mississippi that they would enjoy the "benefits" of judicial proceedings according to common law. The *Rule in Shelley's Case* was well settled at common law long before December 1817.

That the *Rule* may have dated back only to the reign of Elizabeth I (1558–1603) does not exempt it from at least a rebuttable presumption that it falls under Holmes's famous dictum, viz.,

It is revolting to have no better reason for a rule of law than that so it was laid down in the time of Henry IV [1399–1413]. It is still more revolting if the grounds upon which it was laid down have vanished long since, and the rule simply persists from blind imitation of the past.[125]

As noted, some serious antiquarians point back to the reign of Edward III (1327–1377) as the point of beginning. Feudal justifications for the *Rule* began fading well before the American Revolution. More than a century before Holmes's time, a new policy ground for the *Rule* emerged, said to be attributable to Blackstone. The *Rule* should be retained "in order to facilitate the alienation of estates, by giving the power and control of the inheritance to the ancestor one generation sooner that it would otherwise have been alienable."[126]

We know that in 1822 the legislature took a stab at ridding Mississippi of the *Rule in Shelley's Case*.[127] An 1852 Mississippi case "threw upon the court the necessity of deciding whether or not the celebrated rule in Shelley's case is in force in this State." After an extended discussion, Justice William Yerger got to the core judicial circumstance. The courts in

> every State in the Union, where the common law constitutes a part of their judicial system, . . . have declared the existence of the rule in Shelley's case, have enforced it as rigorously as any other well settled principle of that law; and we are of opinion, that in common with other principles of the common law, that rule constitutes a part of the judicial system of this State and must be enforced, unless it has been repealed by some statutory provision.[128]

To be sure, the legislature had addressed the point early on, but its enactment covered real property only,[129] or so the court said. As the plantation-based economy grew in the 1830s and beyond, the merchantability of slaves became increasingly important. A powerful public purpose emerged, justifying the *Rule in Shelley's Case* in Mississippi and the rest of the Deep South, a purpose unknown in England in 1581. One of the hallmarks of common law has always been that from time to time a rule arose for one purpose only to have time and changing circumstances eviscerate the original supporting policy. Still the rule would be sustained where new insights into the public interest and convenience so justified.[130]

Powell v. Brandon concerned a father's bequest so familiar in the Deep South at the time. In 1823, Gerald Brandon of Wilkinson County left lands and slaves to each of his children. The practical question before the court was whether a son had acquired enough of a title to the slaves that his creditors might seize them as a means of satisfying debts owed by the son. Opponents of the *Rule* believed fervently that fathers should be empowered to protect their sons—and the family's real and personal estate—from hands outside the family. Brandon had gone a bit overboard in his will. He bequeathed his lands and slaves "to the lineal descendants of [his son] the said Matthew N., to the latest posterity." The court found that might not be

> for a hundred or a thousand years; and during the whole of that period of time, the property would have been tied up and inalienable, if the manifest and clear intentions of the testator should be carried out.... Such being the case, is the limitation valid? Most surely not. It is against the principles of the common law, at war with the settled policy of the State, and, in our opinion, in violation of the spirit, if not the letter, of the 26th section of the act of 1822. Hutch. Code, ch. 42, p. 610.[131]

Powell also held that enough of the *Rule* remained in effect as to personalty that included slaves. The son had inherited full fee simple title to the slaves. They could be seized by creditors to satisfy the son's debts.

Leading to war and emancipation, other cases affirmed that the *Rule in Shelley's Case* was in full force and effect regarding conveyances or bequests of personal property, the testator's clear purpose and prose to the contrary notwithstanding.[132] After the War, the state supreme court still applied the common law rule to real property. A testator's son "was [held] vested, with absolute ownership of the property, though such was manifestly not the intention of the testator."[133] In time, the legislature did away with the *Rule* once and for all.[134]

After all, there was no contracts clause bar, nor would repeal disappoint any reasonable reliance interest. In 1980, *All Persons v. Buie* served as a reminder that judicial affection for common law rules is sometimes hard to shake. After noting that the *Rule in Shelley's Case* had been abolished by statute,[135] the court added, "Obviously, it is the intent of the legislature for the *Doctrine of Worthier Title* to remain active as a rule of construction."[136] Nothing in the case or any collateral sources suggested any such legislative text or intent or the desirability of any such effect. No one doubted that the legislature could modify or repeal a common law rule, but it had better do so in very clear and unequivocal language.

OTHER CASES WHERE THE LEGISLATURE CHANGED
THE COMMON LAW—A REPRESENTATIVE SAMPLING

An early instance where a Mississippi statute was understood as overriding a common law rule arose in 1822. The heirs of a man named Cole sued to eject George Winn from lands in Adams County the heirs claimed to have been given to them. It appears Cole had made a gift of the lands during his lifetime, retaining possession until his death. In defense, Winn invoked an arcane common law rule that, no matter how strong his title, a man without a right of immediate possession could not have another ejected. The court rejected the defense, citing "our statute of jeofails," a term as quaint as it was practical. Exercising its constitutional judicial power, the court held that Cole's heirs had enough title to sue for ejectment "and the only defect is in the manner of setting it out, and are protected by the statute just recited."[137] Arcana and quaintness aside, the point is simple, and it is important. No matter how venerable a rule of the common law might be, the legislature has always had the power to enact a qualifying law or one that replaces the common law rule altogether.

An 1823 decision handed down by Judge Powhatan Ellis illustrates another and historically different dimension of judge-made law accepted in Mississippi. Equity jurisprudence arose in England under the auspices of the Lord Chancellor long before American Independence. In December of 1817, Mississippians had been assured that they would enjoy "the benefits of . . . judicial proceedings according to the common law." But this did not stop the new state from importing equity jurisprudence from across the Atlantic as well. We saw in chapter 2 that in late 1821, but after his *Jones* decision, Joshua G. Clarke resigned his dual office as supreme court and circuit court judge and became the first chancellor of Mississippi. In *Kerr v. Baker*,[138] Ellis sent his former colleague some business.

Baker sued Kerr and a man named McClelland on a promissory note. McClelland said he was only a surety. Baker was having trouble collecting the debt due on the note. When that became apparent, McClelland had given creditor Baker formal notice that he should proceed first against Kerr. McClelland argued that he had been harmed because Baker failed to act timely against Kerr, the principal debtor. As fate and history would have it, this was an equitable defense, not recognized at common law. The mule in another form. Judge Ellis affirmed the ruling of the circuit court that both who signed the note had to pay, leaving McClelland to his own devices to secure in the chancery court what relief, if any, he may in equity be entitled to.

The law of equitable remedies grew up under a separate system in England, a major feature of which was that there were no jury trials. Equity arrived in Mississippi before *Kerr* and grew gradually over the years.[139] As noted, *Withers* was a matter in equity because the equitable remedy of a cease and desist injunction was sought. Except for a legislatively created interregnum shortly before and during the Civil War, an increasingly modernized and practical equity practice has flourished in the constitutionally authorized and created chancery courts.[140] Rather than try to make sense of such a development,[141] one might with profit recall Holmes's insight that in the law "[a] page of history is worth a volume of logic."[142] Still, a well-crafted statute is enough to thwart dozens of cases—at common law or in equity jurisprudence—and centuries of history, as well.

A suit to recover one's personal property illegally held by another goes by the strange name of replevin. No one doubts that the notion comes from

England. It is said to date back to the time of Henry II (1154–1189). Later, several English statutes regulated the replevin remedy.[143] An 1842 case considered the extent to which this civil remedy was available in Mississippi. Slaves were the personal property sought to be replevied. Wheelock claimed that Cozzens wrongfully detained a slave rightfully the property of Wheelock. Of importance, replevin is a prejudgment remedy. The property in dispute is taken from the defendant in possession and restored to him only if the trial results in a judgment against the plaintiff.

Above are only a few of the many settings where judge-made law did cross with the *Mayflower*. More follow, and in more detail. Over time, some judge-made rules of law were modified by statute, or replaced altogether. Others were modified or overruled by common law decisions, Mississippi variety. Through these processes and practices, the law is not something that is but rather has always been a continuous process of becoming. And so it is certain to remain, and as well a function of the constitutional judicial power and its proper practice.

UNDISGUISED JUDICIAL LEGISLATION *SUB NOM.* COMMON LAW, VINTAGE 1856

The year after his decision in *Withers*, Justice Alexander Handy[144] was charged to practice the process of adjudication in another case that involved a landowner at war with an instrumentality of transportation. This time the owner of grazing livestock locked horns with a company that provided passenger service by rail between Brandon and Jackson in central Mississippi. The railroad was as young as the bed of Old River was old.

The fourteen-mile Brandon-to-Jackson line began service in 1849. It had taken the old Jackson and Brandon Railroad and Bridge Company some six years to get its affairs in order, including arrangements for state financing of the new line. In time, the company owned two hundred to three hundred slaves. The fourteen miles of track were laid entirely by slave labor.[145] By 1850, the new railroad had merged—legally and along the tracks—with the Vicksburg and Jackson Railroad Company. A few years later, all became a part of the Southern Railroad Company.

Go back to July of 1851. Vicksburg Railroad's train consisting of a locomotive and eight cars (five for freight only) was making its "usual morning trip from Brandon to Jackson."[146] The train was fated to have a run-in with landowner William Lee Patton (1822–1913), who had been born in Danville City, Virginia. In time he moved to Mississippi. In 1851 he lived in rural Rankin County out from Brandon. Patton was a slave owner and thought of himself as a planter. He called his place Lee Chase.[147]

On a July morning in 1851, several of Patton's slaves had ridden his horses to a wooded area for the day's work. The horses were turned loose, "their owner being in the habit of pasturing them upon unenclosed and uncultivated lands adjoining the railroad track, owned by other persons." At least since 1829 many in the neighborhood had used these open lands for pasturage. Domestic animals had become accustomed to roaming and grazing at large without interference or objection by anyone. On the summer morning in question, Patton's free-roaming horses were on and near the railroad tracks. As the morning train approached, the horses "turned and ran down the track until . . . they were overtaken by the locomotive and mangled or killed; and the locomotive thrown from the track down the embankment, a distance of some thirty or forty feet."[148] Patton sued for his losses, charging Vicksburg Railroad with negligence. A Rankin County jury returned a generous verdict in his favor.

Much was in dispute at the trial. That there were no fences in the area, to keep livestock or persons in or out, was never disputed. Before the court, the parties debated whether it was Patton's duty to have kept his horses fenced in. Or was it the railroad's duty to have kept its tracks fenced so as to keep livestock out and off the tracks? Either way, arguments based on common law rules were front and center. The court considered whether the day-to-day lives of these Mississippians differed from circumstances and customs of the people whence those common law rules had grown up. An old Mississippi free-range statute was also a part of the field.

Alexander Hamilton Handy made no bones about it. The court was charged to decide what in time would come to be called a case of first impression. But not just any matter of first impression here. "Several questions of great importance and of the gravest public interest, are here presented for the first time for the determination of the court." Handy—and the court deciding the case—looked out the window and took account of general facts regarding popular practices and customs, evidence of which was nowhere found in the trial or appellate record. These would be called "legislative facts"[149] today. This is only one interesting feature of the *Vicksburg RR* case.

In a case like *Vicksburg RR*, what was the role of this common law, the benefits of which had been secured to Mississippians at statehood?[150] And how did the justices go about learning that role and making the promised enjoyment a reality in the lives of the people affected? The lessons from these aspects of the case are not so concrete as how the case was finally decided, who won and who lost, and with what consequences. These more elusive lessons, however, are important for understanding just how the constitutional "judicial power" functions, sometimes more precisely called the process of adjudication. Of course, the work product of different judges practicing judicial power and processes in different cases and times is all over the lot—the ambiguity of all things human.

For starters, at least three times the *Vicksburg RR* opinion said that whatever rights and responsibilities the parties may have enjoyed, all were "to be exercised in subordination to the general laws and policy of the State."[151] Most prominent of those general laws was the common law. Those general laws, once identified, left lots of wiggle room to decide a case either way. The first specific question was "fence or no fence." Once that one was answered, what were the nuances of the rights and duties of landowner vis-à-vis livestock owner? Public policy—not legal doctrine—lay at the foundation of the *Vicksburg RR* adjudication, as at the foundation of most other cases, when you think about it.[152]

Justice Handy began with the *prima facie* premise that the common law controlled, the same as he had in *Withers* the year before. He expanded and elaborated the customary caveats.

He then set about identifying the customs and circumstances and conditions of the people that might inform the answer to the theretofore unanswered— in Mississippi, at least—legal questions of "the gravest public interest."[153] "Considerations of what is expedient for the community concerned,"[154] as Holmes would put the point a quarter of a century later.

The experience of others was available to Handy. He was not starting from scratch. That experience included the work "of the most learned courts in this country and in England." As it turned out, the common law rule in England and in four American states—Michigan, New York, Pennsylvania, and Vermont— said one thing about fencing, while a different common law rule was found in Alabama, Connecticut, Indiana, Ohio, and South Carolina. But what were the legislative facts in those other jurisdictions?

> In a densely populated country like England, with small farms and but few cattle, the reason of the rule that every man shall prevent his cattle from going at large is apparent; and the rule prevails, because it is suited to the condition of that country. The policy of the common law, therefore, was, that it was more convenient that a man should be bound to *fence his cattle in*, than that he shall *fence his neighbors' out*.[155]

Handy then observed that similar circumstances must have existed in Michigan, New York, Pennsylvania, and Vermont, as the rule there was the same as the common law rule from England. Careful attention to wording suggests he was guessing on those four states, though he likely had a clue since he grew up in Maryland, Pennsylvania's neighbor to the south.

Turning to Mississippi (and, presumably, rural Rankin County and its environs), Handy found that "the circumstances of our people are widely different from those of such communities" and explains how so. Most important are the "large numbers of cattle, hogs, and other animals" here, and how in rural central Mississippi there arose the local custom of common pastures without fences. "By the universal understanding and usage of the people," unfenced rural lands "are regarded as commons of pasture, for the range of cattle and other stock of the neighborhood." "This policy is sanctioned by strong reasons of public convenience, growing out of the condition of the people [of Mississippi]."[156] Handy then elaborated for another page, explaining why as a practical matter a rule requiring fences would not work in Mississippi.

Next the *Vicksburg RR* opinion took note of the free-range statute that had apparently been on the books in Mississippi since territorial days. The text of the law "recognize[s] the right of any owner of horses, cattle or other stock to put them in *range*, which means unfenced wood lands, or other pasture lands in the neighborhood." "It was the object of this statute to change the rule of the common law."[157] Handy was right to take seriously a statute in the field. The legislature's policy-making prerogative in a popular democracy—or as a republic[158]—should always be respected as far as it goes, generously and ungrudgingly. More modern and politically sensitive illustrations are the state supreme court's construction of the well-known comparative negligence statute to subsume the common law defense of contributory negligence and the oft-amended wrongful death statute replacing the common law vacuum.[159]

Handy's opinion was commendable for its focus on the legislative facts—the facts and circumstances a good legislator would reasonably need to access reliably and consider objectively before making laws of general application that would govern all cases going forward. But how could we know he had identified those facts reliably? Nothing in *Vicksburg RR* suggested any knowledgeable witnesses testified as to these matters. Nothing suggests he read any books or other published research regarding the customs and practices of the people, or even that there were any such works available had he had a mind to study them. Or that he talked to people informally, something judges are not supposed to do anyway.

Likely, Handy was relying on his general knowledge from having grown up in Maryland, moving to Mississippi when he was twenty-seven years old. At the end of the day, he said the law should not require either party to have built a fence that might have prevented the accident. Past that, he opted for what was traditionally known as the contributory negligence rule. The owner of the livestock killed or maimed cannot recover from the railroad where "both parties were mutually in fault, and both the immediate cause of the injury."[160] Handy then added a nuance. Patton's negligence in not taking better care to protect his horses was a remote cause, while the railroad's negligence was the more immediate and proximate cause of what happened that summer morning. As later put by others, the Vicksburg Railroad's locomotive engineer had the last clear chance to avoid the accident.[161]

Before getting to the final holding and decision in the case, Handy took two steps that might have raised eyebrows. First, having surveyed the field for what might be learned from jurisdictions that had addressed the sort of legal questions before the Mississippi court for the first time, Handy picked Ohio. He cited *Kerwhaker v. Cleveland Railroad Company*,[162] and said it provided "so much clearness and force . . . as to justify our adoption of the views of the subject there taken."[163] It might come as a surprise to many that Ohio's circumstances were so like unto Mississippi's, to the exclusion of the circumstances in Michigan and Pennsylvania, with each of which Ohio has always shared a substantial state line. At least some explanation grounded in the legislative facts would seem to have been called for.

Second, Handy accepted the rule that a party may not recover "where the party committing the injury might have avoided it by the use of common and ordinary caution." As support, he then cites a large number of English cases, plus one from Connecticut and another from the US Supreme Court.[164] Upon receiving the opinion, Vicksburg Railroad's lawyers could not be blamed had they thought that Justice Handy had simply decided that Mr. Patton should win, and then cited whatever he could find that might support that view. Not unlikely the justices were looking for the rule that (as they understood the matter) would best promote the practical public interests of the people going forward. Whether those purported precedents fit the facially attractive rationale the opinion articulated was beside the point, if Handy had noticed it at all. Were not the English cases cited nothing more than iterations of the same common law that earlier the *Vicksburg RR* opinion had said did not apply?

AN HISTORICAL IRONY AND THE AMBIGUITY OF ALL THINGS HUMAN

It is good to recall the cluster of rights that the United States assured to the people of each new state. "Judicial proceedings according to the course of the common law" was embedded among those that history traces to Magna Carta, and are the core of Article the Second of the Northwest Ordinance. The substantive component of "the course of the common law" included rules regulating property rights that were proving a mixed bag as the state's calendar cascaded toward the middle of the nineteenth century.

Legal thefts of tribal lands in 1820, 1830, 1832, and 1837 made a mockery of the protections supposedly afforded Native Americans in Article the Third, the heavy hand and hardened heart of Andrew Jackson the driving force after he became president in March of 1829. What had long been American practice and policy—seizing Indian lands for white uses—quickened apace. The moral stain of slavery deepened and darkened as one justification after another emboldened southerners. With each passing year, the defenders dug their heels in deeper.

In the 1820s, the Chickasaw nation occupied all of western Tennessee, extreme western Kentucky, a small sliver of land in northwest Alabama, and a solid tier—twice as deep on the east as on the west—across northern Mississippi. In northeastern Mississippi, the Chickasaw domain extended down the Alabama state line as far south as Monroe County, as it was known in the latter half of the twentieth century. On a date not known but during the era of the American Revolution, Elizabeth Love was born into the culturally mixed Chickasaw family of Thomas Love and Sally Colbert.[165] James[166] Allen came from North Carolina. He was white. In 1797 or 1798, Elizabeth—better known as "Betsy"—married James in a Chickasaw ceremony. There seems no dispute that "the relation of husband and wife, existing between them, arose under the tribal customs of the Chickasaws." At the time of the marriage, Betsy owned many slaves.[167] James and Betsy made their home on Love family lands in the Chickasaw territory in what became modern Monroe County. Betsy was James's second wife. She bore him eleven children.[168]

Years later, a lawyer named John Fisher did some legal work for James Allen. For reasons unknown, Allen never paid Fisher. No earlier than August of 1830, Fisher sued for his fee and recovered a $200 judgment.[169] When Allen still did not pay, Fisher asked for and, in March 1831, was granted a writ of execution. The sheriff of Monroe County was charged to seize property belonging to Allen and having a value believed to be sufficient to pay the judgment.[170] Before all of this, however, Betsy Love Allen had signed a deed of gift in which she "gave separate property to ten of her children."[171] On November 2, 1830, this deed of gift was placed in the public records of Monroe County. In due course, the sheriff, acting under the authority of the writ of execution, seized Toney, a slave believed to be Allen's property. In fact, Betsy had given Toney to her daughter, Susan, still a minor, and the question before the court was, With what effect? Did the common law rule of coverture apply to legitimate the seizure of Toney, and, if not, why not?

In January of 1830, the legislature had enacted that Indians living in Mississippi became full citizens of the state, enjoying all of the benefits but subject to all of the burdens of state citizenship. Among other things, this act provided "that all marriages and matrimonial connections entered into by virtue of any custom or usage of the said Indians, and by them deemed valid, should be held as valid and obligatory as if the same had been solemnized according to the laws of the state."[172] The question, however, was whether so much of the act of 1830 as abolished tribal laws and customs, and began treating Indians as other citizens of the state, resulted in James Allen—via the common law of coverture—holding an ownership interest in the slave Toney. The High Court of Errors and Appeals brushed that one off, viz., the new statute could "not be construed to extend so far as to interfere with the rights to property previously acquired." The point is nonetheless important and worth a pause.

Historically, the Chickasaw tribe enjoyed and practiced a custom that made latter-day observers face the question of whose was the more enlightened civilization for its time.

By the customs of the Chickasaws, the husband acquired no right to the property of the wife which she possessed at the time of marriage. It remained to her
separate use and subject alone to her disposition and constraint. She was, so far
as it regards the obligation of contracts, the acquisition and rights of property,
perfectly independent of the husband."[173]

By way of contrast, the original 1817 state constitution had guaranteed to all
"persons" a number of rights derived and descended from Magna Carta.[174]
By accepting admission into the Union under the Equal Footings doctrine,
all "inhabitants" of this state were assured of "judicial proceedings according
to the common law."[175] The substantive dimension of proceedings according
to the common law included enjoying "the benefits" of the common law, one
component of which was the law of coverture.

The custom and practice in England prior to American independence,
however, was that, "upon marriage, a woman's legal rights and obligations
were subsumed by those of her husband, in accordance with the wife's [new]
legal status of *feme covert*." On the other hand, "[a]n unmarried woman,
a *feme sole*, had the right to own property and make contracts in her own
name."[176] There can be no doubt that circa 1830 the disabilities of coverture
were among those common law rules in full force and effect in Mississippi. In
time, lawyer plaintiff John Fisher would argue that the rule of coverture was
effective in Mississippi back to "1799, immediately upon the organization of
the territorial government."

It was not until 1837 that the state's highest court considered Fisher's claim
that the slave Toney "could be subject to the claims of Allen's creditors" in general—and to the writ of execution issued and served at his instance in particular. There the case met Chief Justice William L. Sharkey and Justice C. Pinckney
Smith, each of whose service dated back to 1832, and whom we met in chapter
4 above. Each wrote an opinion in *Fisher v. Allen*, and each affirmed that Betsy's
gift of Toney to her minor daughter had been valid and enforceable.

Fisher had argued that the gift amounted to a fraudulent conveyance by
Betsy. Sharkey rejected the argument.

There does not seem to have been any claim existing against Betsy [Love] Allen
at the time of making the gift nor at any time afterwards, and it is shown that the
creditors of James Allen could have no claim on it, even if these debts had existed
at the time of making the gift, but it does not appear that any such debts existed
at the time.[177]

Smith added that, even if by its terms the act of January 1830 operated to vest
title to Toney in James Allen,

such a construction would bring the case in conflict with the constitution; for Allen, by the marriage, acquired no interest in the property of his wife. . . . It was not the intention of the legislature, nor could they, if they had so intended, violate the sanctity of private property.[178]

On its merits, the final decision in *Fisher* is attractive. An unfortunate treble irony remains, offensive to the contemporary conscience. First, the act to make full citizenship available to Chickasaw and Choctaw tribe members would, going forward, destroy the established custom of the Chickasaws that a woman's marriage had no effect on her right to property she owned prior thereto. Second, of course, the otherwise sensible opinions of Sharkey and Smith treat "a negro boy" named Toney as though he had no humanity and really was just property. Third, it was not just irony but hypocrisy for the Chickasaws, who would suffer so under the heel of Andrew Jackson's boot, to practice the enslavement of human beings, who in turn suffered the fortuity of being born with black American skin.

THE BATTLE AGAINST COMMON LAW DISABILITIES
OF COVERTURE MOVES TO THE LEGISLATURE

Faced with the act of January 1830, and augmented by the careful wording in *Fisher v. Allen* that it might have been decided differently had Betsy Love and James Allen married after 1831, the opponents of coverture had still not made it to first base. Article 7, Section 18 of the new constitution—the one that ostensibly would enshrine Jacksonian Democracy in Mississippi forever—had empowered the legislature

> to admit to all the rights and privileges of free white citizens of this state, all such persons of the Choctaw and Chickasaw tribes of Indians, as shall choose to remain in this state, upon such terms as the legislature may from time to time deem proper.[179]

Besides that, passions were strong that the traditional common law rule of coverture was sound public policy, given the paternalistic view of natural relationship of man and wife prevalent at the time, and the more practical— some might say cynical—view that abolishing coverture would aid unscrupulous husbands in defrauding their creditors. To be sure, then as now courts could set aside fraudulent conveyances.[180] Running down the rascal, haling him into court, proving the case, and then collecting were not always easy. Retroactive application of any act modifying coverture was constitutionally proscribed as with other vested property rights, not to mention the proscriptions at both the federal and state levels against laws that would impair the obligations of contracts.[181]

The proponents of married women's property rights moved to the legislature.[182] To be more precise, the scene of action may have moved to a boardinghouse in Jackson run by Mrs. Piety Smith Hadley. In 1831, Piety Smith had married Thomas B. J. Hadley. The story goes that Piety's father had little confidence in his new son-in-law's business and political discretion. He added a codicil to his will, leaving two young female slaves "to and for the use and benefit of his said daughter, Piety Smith Hadley and her heirs forever."[183] Father-in-law Smith's interests and connections were far broader than affording his seventh child a measure of protection from a spendthrift husband.[184]

Thomas Benjamin Jefferson Hadley (1801–1870) served in the state senate in 1838 and 1839. He had served as state auditor of public accounts from 1830 to 1833.[185] The boardinghouse that Thomas and Piety owned was not far from the capitol. They housed and fed three meals a day to many a senator and representative during the legislative sessions. The reputed congenial atmosphere at the Hadley boardinghouse was said to have been not so subtly modified by short rations for legislators whose support or opposition went awry on issues that Piety cared about.[186] Piety favored getting rid of all notions of coverture. She wanted to protect women's rights in any property they brought to or acquired during their marriages. Senator Hadley introduced a bill to do just that.

On January 21, 1839, the bill "for the protection and preservation of the rights and property of married woman" was formally filed. In this, Senator Hadley invoked the legislative power and process, as laid out in Article 3 of the state constitution.[187] What was about to unfold was as much of a constitutional encounter as any exercise of the judicial power described above and in other chapters. Piety's subtle and not-so-subtle support was needed, as her husband's financial circumstances laid him open to the charge of pushing the bill in order to protect his own interests. Hadley had gone so far as to introduce and secure passage of a separate bill to protect himself from certain creditors.[188]

The arguments pro and con over the next several weeks have been recorded and are familiar. Senator Hadley and others supporting the bill argued human dignity and fair play. Before marrying, a woman could own property and had every right to her earnings therefrom. All of that changed if and when she married. What sense did that make? The original logic of restricting ownership to males was long a part of the past, that is, the obligation to perform the incidents of fealty, but in the nineteenth century there remained a firm social consensus that a married woman's place was in the home. Besides, the legal vesting in her husband of title to her property placed a woman and her children at an unfair risk. Even where the husband in good faith sought to discharge his marital duties as breadwinner, he might fail through no fault of his own. Circumstances in the state's economy made this risk a reality over and over, and not always as a result of what had come to be known as the Panic of 1837 and its financially disastrous aftermaths.[189] Then, of course, there were men who were genuine rascals, who not only failed in their duties to support their wives but took advantage of what coverture gave them and squandered it.

The argument against the bill ranged from the fanciful to the cynical. It reflected the heyday of the Cult of True Womanhood. By their upbringing and acumen, women, it was said, were not very good at business matters. The better nature of women and mothers was enhanced, not despoiled, by relieving them of duties regarding any money and property. The view of marriage as a state where the husband and wife became one—and the husband was the one—was well entrenched. So many of the arguments were precursors of the ones trotted out in later years as to why women should not be allowed to vote, and should not serve on juries,[190] and the like. In 1839, there was an additional practical reality. Often slaves were the most valuable property the woman brought to the marriage. On the other hand, women were said by nature not disposed to being good stewards and managers of black-skinned human property. The cynical argument contra, of course, was that abolishing coverture would create unlimited opportunities for husbands to defraud their creditors.

Many of the legislators who made these arguments pro and con are known to history. Their particular arguments are reproduced in one or many of the published works telling some aspect of the story.[191] One major player, however, seems to have remained under the radar. It is time for the story of Sen. Gordon D. Boyd (1802–1850) to be told. Much of the story is likely true, at least in its broad strokes. A Kentucky native, Boyd had come to Mississippi as a young man, read law, and was admitted to the bar. He occasionally bought newspapers to publish his political opinions, and he was an early supporter of Andrew Jackson's campaign for the presidency. We know for sure that Boyd was elected to and held a state constitutional office, was exercising a constitutional authority, and—more than most—helped an important Mississippi constitutional encounter to become a practical reality. We also know that shortly prior thereto, Boyd had held a federal appointive office[192] with reasonably well-documented evidence of self-dealing and other shenanigans.

Then there are stories like the one published in early 1840, viz.,

> The Natchez Courier says: —"Our Jackson correspondent writes us that it is rumored that Gordon D. Boyd, the celebrated U.S. Defaulter, killed the Marshal of Northern Mississippi with a bowie knife, about a fortnight since, after the Marshal had discharged a pistol at him.[193]

A like story appeared in the *Nashville Tennessean* about the same time.[194] In early February, however, the following item was published in Philadelphia.

> CONTRADICTION.—A paragraph is going the rounds, stating that A. G. Weir [*sic*], Marshal for the Northern District of Mississippi, had been killed in a rencontre with Gordon D. Boyd, Esq. The National Intelligencer, on the authority of a

member of Congress, contradicts the report and says that Mr. Weir is in perfectly good health, and has not even had a quarrel with Mr. Boyd.[195]

This allegation–contradiction, allegation–contradiction sequence was evidence of the notoriety Senator Boyd had been steadily acquiring and may or may not reflect on the credibility of reports of his doings in his more official capacities.

His extracurricular activities aside, Senator Boyd from Kosciusko supported married women's property rights. In 1837, he had been elected from a three-county district—Attala, Leake, and Neshoba Counties—and served from 1837 to 1840 and again in 1844.[196] Recall that still in the early days of the Age of Jackson, the United States had employed duress, undue influence, and tactics less com-mendable in procuring the Choctaw Cession. The Treaty of Dancing Rabbit Creek in 1830 memorialized that venture.[197] The Treaty of Pontotoc Creek and the Chickasaw Cession followed two years later.[198] In 1833, the government established a land office in Columbus, Mississippi, to be manned by a receiver of public moneys. Effective December 27, 1836, President Jackson—only a few months before he was to turn over the White House to Martin Van Buren—appointed Gordon D. Boyd to run the Columbus land office for the next four years. But Boyd resigned in the fall of 1837, in time to run for and gain election to the state senate.

As fate would have it, leading up to late 1837, persons ostensibly purchasing public lands and receiving patents out of the US government at its Columbus office often gave bad checks, and for a variety of reasons. The Panic began in May of 1837 and provided the economic milieu that made financial shenanigans possible, if not imperative. None of these circumstances can excuse the fact that the said Gordon D. Boyd from time to time sold former Choctaw lands to him-self and to others for his benefit "and gave the usual certificates for that purpose, without paying for same."

All the while Boyd was showing in the accounts of his office the receipt of so much money. The fact that credit sales of public lands were strictly prohibited[199] was only one of the reasons Boyd's actions came under scrutiny. On June 15, 1838, the US Government obtained a judgment against Boyd for $53,722.50[200] in public moneys for which he was responsible but which were said to be unac-counted for. According to one report, the publication of this fact

> did not at all abash him. He [Boyd] immediately betook himself to the stump for the vindication of his character. "I did appropriate the money to my own use," exclaimed he, "and I expected to be able to repay it, but my speculations turned out unfavorably. 'Tis my misfortune and not my fault. I hope, gentlemen, you are satisfied.' "O yes" replied his loco-foco[201] hearers, "we are perfectly satisfied."[202]

In June of 1838, Boyd and two others advertised that anyone wishing to sub-scribe to stock in the Mississippi Union Bank might apply to them.[203] In short order, the Union Bank and the Planters' Bank were only the most prominently known state banks that failed during this era.[204] Suffice it to say that as the calendar approached the year 1839, being financially strapped was the least of the contretemps in which Senator Boyd was embroiled.[205] At this time, moreover, Boyd was seeking the hand in marriage of the daughter of Judge J. P. Williams of Kosciusko.[206]

To the point, Boyd rose on the senate floor in early February of 1839 to support Senator Hadley's Married Women's Property bill.[207] He covered the waterfront, answering all of the points made by others why the law should be left as it had always been. He said he could see no "good reason why, by marital rights, a man should acquire absolute ownership and control over his wife and all her property, while she acquires none from her husband, except such as are promised by the marriage vow." Boyd argued that

> our English laws, which are nothing more than the relics of barbarians and the ancient feudal system of government, so far as they recognize and regard the rights of women, are not consonant with the spirit and genius of our free institutions, and our republican government.

By way of contrast, he reminded his fellow senators that "[w]herever the civil law predominates, and in all those countries which have derived their law from civilized Greece and Rome, the rights of females are recognized and respected." The implied irony that in the United States native "inhabitants" had been assured that they would enjoy the benefits of the common law was hard to miss. In point of fact, the civil law was in full force and effect just across the River to the southwest, in Louisiana, which had become a state five years before Mississippi. Senator Boyd and his brother, James H. Boyd, had lived in the St. Francisville area of Louisiana for a while. Likely they were familiar with the civil law insofar as the rights of married women were concerned.

Boyd then offered his fellow senators a practical point, that the proposed new law would only make lawful what people were already and regularly achieving by subterfuge and device. The then-present laws were

> so repugnant to our common sense judgment, and unjust in their character, that it has become an everyday business to endeavor to evade them by marriage contracts, and by making wills and deeds of conveyance in a manner that shall secure the patrimony of a daughter or the property of a female friend or relative in such a manner that it cannot be squandered by an improvident husband,[208] or taken from her and her children by his creditors for debts from which his family have derived no benefits.[209]

As for the argument that the proposed law would be used to defraud creditors, "if the law were a general one creditors would be better advised and more upon their guard, and these debts, which so often prove the ruin of the family, would not be contracted."[210] It was hard to argue with that one.

On the afternoon of February 11, 1839, the senate passed the bill. Four days later, the house of representatives followed suit.[211] Governor A. G. McNutt timely signed into law the Married Women's Property Act.[212] Proponents who thought the war was won, however, were wrong. Opponents who had objected to any amelioration of the so-called benefits of the common law disabilities of coverture had lots of fight left in them. And by the time the calendar turned to the new year 1840, Thomas B. J. Hadley and Piety Smith Hadley were G. T. T. (Gone to Texas). The Hadleys made a mark or two in their new home, died, and are buried in Glenwood Cemetery in Houston.[213]

Whether his fingers were crossed or not, Sen. Gordon Boyd's speech on the floor had been a stem-winder. Of particular note were his words in reply to two legislative opponents who were fellow lawyers.

> Lawyers, taken as a body of men, are usually most hostile to anything like innovations, or changes from that which from their early reading they have learned to be the law, and which they usually regard as good law . . .
>
> Precedent is the lawyer's tyrant, and one who views any subject or proposed change in the laws merely as a lawyer, will always pronounce it bad, unless he can find something of the kind in the musty old volumes which he had been plodding over.
>
> Sir, had our forefathers looked at the policy of the Declaration of Independence in no more enlarged a view and feeling than as mere lawyers, they never would have declared that these colonies were of right and ought to be free.[214]

In point of fact, on this and other fronts, lawyers had already swung into action. They were preparing for the onslaught that Jacksonian Democracy seemed so certain to mount against the stale benefits of the common law they were supposed to enjoy by reason of the Equal Footings doctrine. *Powell v. Brandon*[215] would leave unscathed so much of the common law *Rule in Shelley's Case* as had not been expressly abrogated by statute. After the Civil War, *Hemingway v. Scales*[216] reinforced this principle of construction in favor of common law rules vis-à-vis any meddlesome statute passed in the legislature. *Hollman v. Bennett* is to like effect: "The common law of England brought over by the colonists, as a part of their heritage as British subjects, so far as applicable to the new circumstances and conditions, and so far as not changed by statute, is the law of this state."[217]

In time this pro–common law bias took the form of the so-called canon of construction that "statutes in derogation of the common law are to be strictly construed."[218] In its heyday, the canon was the ultimate instance of antidemocratic judicial arrogance, grounded in jurisprudential misunderstanding and the thought that judges make better laws than legislatures. Maybe on balance they do—maybe even probably—but that view cannot be sustained in a democratic society.[219] These notions were in the air as the future of coverture was being debated and litigated and otherwise fought over. Strong winds remained to be faced by any who favored progressive legislation.

But back to the Married Women's Act of 1839. Understand that it was "evidently an enabling statute. It was passed . . . for the purpose and with the intent of giving to married women rights, which, by the strict rules of the common law, they did not possess."[220] It became easy pickings for its opponents, those whose way of viewing the world was such that they found the idea of coverture congenial, or others of baser political motivations. Notwithstanding a married woman's newly recognized title and protection from her husband's debts, the new law provided that "the control and management of all such slaves, the direction of their labor, and the receipt of the productions thereof, shall remain to the husband, agreeably to the law heretofore in force."[221] And so in its first significant opportunity to construe and apply the new act, the court, speaking through Justice Alexander M. Clayton, ruled that a cotton crop produced with slave labor could be seized to satisfy a husband's debts, even though the wife held title to the slaves: "The proceeds of the wife's property, as regulated by that law, during the coverture, belong to the husband."[222] Two years later Clayton struck another blow, holding that the new law did not extend her power of contracting, or of binding "herself or her property. Its effect rather is to take away all power of subjecting her property to her contracts, except in the particular mode specified in the statute."[223]

In 1846, the legislature took a hard look at the adequacy of the 1839 act[224] and found it wanting. Notwithstanding judicial defense of the common law tradition, the legislature advanced the ball, enacting that a married woman was entitled to the "rents, issues and profits" of real estate she owned.[225] Married women were also empowered to do all things necessary to own and operate a plantation with slaves. In particular, the 1846 amended law provided that "the products and proceeds of the labor of all slaves owned by a married woman, in her sole and separate right, shall inure to her sole and separate use and benefit."[226] Her legal power to contract, however, was exercisable only with the joinder of her husband.[227] Overall, the 1846 amendment was more progressive and practical from the point of view of married women than the original 1839 act had been. Another amendment followed in 1857,[228] though it was more clarifying in nature and effect. After the War, the principles of the married women's law became enshrined in the state constitution.[229]

Still, the common law and its disability of coverture had a bit of fight left in them. In 1873, the court grudgingly summarized the state of the law. If a woman "owns property at the time of the marriage, or acquires it afterwards, in any of the modes known to the law, for many purposes, she deals with it as a *feme sole*; and, as to all others she is subject to the disability of coverture."[230] At issue was whether a married woman could "purchase real estate, in part upon credit." The all-male court's answer was predictable.

> She could buy with ready money, but she could not make an obligation to be dis-charged at a future day. As to that, she was still under the disability of coverture. The statutes did not enfranchise her so as to confer capacity to engage in such risky bargains.[231]

In 1880, the legislature removed the last vestiges of coverture.[232] Or did it? The extent to which married persons could sue each other continued to vex the courts for more than another century,[233] and even the case abolishing interspousal tort immunity was not unanimous.[234]

But back to Gordon Boyd. Newspaper stories about his financial dealings as receiver in the Land Office continued apace, long after Boyd's praiseworthy and effective support for the first Married Women's Property Act. Many reporters played fast and loose with the numbers, but no doubt there was a substantial basis in fact for what was reported.[235] For example, in 1840, a Salisbury, North Carolina, newspaper published,

RICHLY PAID

> It is stated in the Ohio State Journal, that Gordon D. Boyd, a defaulter to the General Government in the sum of $59,939.29, is now engaged in editing a Van Buren paper at Kosciusko in Mississippi. He may well afford to scribble for his master when he has been so well paid for his services.

> *Raleigh Star.*[236]

In 1838, the Mississippi Union Bank Act had designated Sen. Gordon D. Boyd as one of three managers for Attala County.[237] He sold Union Bank stock to his younger brother, James H. Boyd, and no doubt to others. But it was through a big-brother-induced Union Bank investment that by 1846 the younger James H. Boyd had lost his home, its contents, and his shirt besides.

On April 8, 1850, while on a trip to Louisiana, the elder Boyd died of cholera at a site about forty miles below New Orleans. A eulogist back in Mississippi paid his respects.

> The energy and industry he constantly displayed in endeavoring to repair his fallen fortunes could but inspire all with respect for the unfortunate man, whose prospects and usefulness had been so greatly destroyed by his connection with the Land Office. Peace to his remains.[238]

But Gordon Boyd's reputation enjoyed no peace. Well over two years after his death, a Tennessee newspaper had this to say of "the great defaulter of Mississippi."

> INDEBTED TO THE PEOPLE.—It appears that Gordon D. Boyd, the great defaulter of Mississippi, was a stump orator. In a public harangue, sometime since, he exclaimed at the top of his lungs.—"No man in the nation is more indebted to the people than I am." "Except Swartwout," retorted a bystander, "he owes a million and a Quarter, while you owe only seventy thousand."[239]

Shakespeare qua Marc Antony was probably right, viz., "The evil that men do lives after them. The good is oft interred with their bones."[240] Antony used Caesar's will to great effect before the people.

Perhaps some Attala County orator could have caused pause among Boyd's critics with a passage from Gordon Boyd's holographic will made and signed January 8, 1849, in Galveston, Texas, viz., "it is my wish that . . . [my executor] pay all my just debts other than the pretended claims of the government of the United States or its officers by several of whom I have been much injured and wronged."[241] Boyd had begun his will by noting "the uncertainty of life." Regarding his wife, Rebecca Frances Boyd (1821–1900), he took note that "most of the property that we have is owned by her or held in her name as trustee for our children and as I owe but little . . ."[242] This could only be a reference to Boyd's continuing awareness of his legislative success of ten years earlier, augmented by the 1846 amendment to the Mississippi Married Woman's Property Act.

On June 1, 1853, the younger brother, James H. Boyd (1809–1877), completed arrangements for a new homestead in what was then northeast Jackson. A nice lot two city blocks east of where the Hadleys had operated their boarding-house.[243] Courthouse records show that title to the lands was taken exclusively in the name of wife, Eliza Ellis Boyd[244] (1823–1902). James H. Boyd served four one-year terms as mayor of Jackson, and at least six terms as alderman.

The names of Betsy Love Allen and Piety Smith Hadley are a part of Mississippi history. Sandra Moncrief summed up their roles nicely.

> The drive of two strong-willed women—one the daughter of an Indian Chief, the other the daughter of an Indian fighter—coalesced with the practical concerns of men to secure the passage of the first law in the nation regarding women's property rights.[245]

The name of Gordon D. Boyd is also known to Mississippi history. May the good that he did in support of married women's property rights become better known in the years ahead. His eloquence and learning in opposing the very idea of pledging the state's faith deserve as well a resurrection from the musty pages of *House Journal* of 1842, as does the rest of the story of the Planters' Bank bonds.[246]

SO JUST WHAT IS THIS COMMON LAW?

From David Withers's war with the Commissioners of the Homochitto River through the legislature's struggle for supremacy against judicial reluctance to part with the disabilities of coverture, we have seen a thing or two. Very different contexts where common law was a central circumstance. It is time to circle back. What about this common law that Mississippi and other states inherited from England, the "benefits" of which—by quasi-constitutional law— were promised to the state's inhabitants for their enjoyment? Where was this common law reliably to be found? Who made it, and under what authority? What did it mean? How was it to be practiced? "Enjoyed"? Enforced? Changed? And dozens of other questions.[247]

Textually, the Northwest Ordinance is quite like the US Constitution, the meanings of many clauses of which have proved so vexing from time to time. This is no surprise, as both had their birth in 1787. One good place to start answering these questions is a careful look at what the early—and then not so early—Mississippi courts did in fact. Official reporters reflect that the courts looked to England and to the most eminent jurists and legal scholars there. Again, there wasn't much home-grown law here at the time. Most prominent among these Brits were Edward Coke[248] (1552–1634), Matthew Hale[249] (1609– 1676), and William Blackstone (1723–1780).[250] One reason the early state judges looked to these worthies for the content of the common law was that the lawyers cited them. Conversely, lawyers cited these sources as they could be pretty sure the judges would credit them and use them in deciding particular cases. These and other lesser-known British jurists had articulated rules and principles and their rationales, histories, applications, and justifications, value-laden bursts of wisdom. Formalistic straitjackets were found on other occasions, in the interests of regularity and legitimacy and, of course, habit. Though they are cited, quoted, and discussed constantly, it is hard to find evidence that these honored scholarly sources—standing alone—were outcome determinative in particular cases.

In 1822, the state supreme court cited Coke for a common law point of procedure as to whether a litigant had what today we might call "standing" to question a party's performance of conditions in a deed.[251] A year later in a case noted above, Judge Powhatan Ellis cited Coke and Blackstone, and other English jurists as well, and what they had to say about the discharge of a jury without a verdict having been reached and returned.[252] Later, in 1823, Ellis cited Coke for a point of law concerning a surety's common law duties.[253] In 1831, the lawyers cited Coke and Blackstone on whether a man was qualified to serve as a juror. Justice J. R. Nicholson cited Coke in deciding a similar case.[254] *Shaffer v. State* in 1835 was another juror case. Counsel for the parties—and Chief Justice Sharkey for the court—relied upon Hale and another English jurist for the common law of jury practice.[255] In an 1843 case concerning the rights of a child born out of wedlock, the appellant's lawyer cited Coke. The attorney for appellee cited Blackstone. Justice Clayton for the court relied on both Coke and Blackstone, reversing the judgment below.[256] We have seen the extent to which Chief Justice Sharkey cited and quoted Hale in 1844 in an all-important riparian rights case.[257] A decade later, Justice Handy relied on Hale in *Withers* concerning the common law of navigable waters.[258] In 1908, the court reaffirmed that "the business of a common carrier is one which is 'clothed with a public interest,' [as] was pithily remarked by Sir Matthew Hale nearly 400 years ago."[259] In 1931, Justice George Ethridge relied on Blackstone and Coke in a powerful exposition of the approach at common law to prosecuting an insane person for a capital offense.[260] As recently as 2003, Judge Leslie Southwick traced an accused's right to have a jury polled after its verdict all the way back to Hale in 1672.[261]

Trial by jury was a right and practice and point of particular interest at common law. Blackstone was prominent. "The trial by jury has always been, and always will be, the pride of our system of law. *See* 3 William Blackstone, *Commentaries on the Laws of England* 379," cited by Justice James Graves in affirming a capital murder conviction.[262] Blackstone was once cited to show that at common law women were excluded from jury service under the doctrine of *propter defectum sexus* (literally, the defect of sex).[263]

Jury practice has been revered in Mississippi history as well. A case that makes the point arose in 1839. A man was charged, tried, and found guilty of perjury by a jury of only eleven men. The court observed that, while trial by jury was constitutionally protected at both the federal and state levels, in neither constitution had "the number necessary to constitute 'a jury,' been fixed." At common law, the number "could never be less than twelve."[264] The court held controlling the numerical requirement that existed at common law at the time the Constitution was adopted. Juries had to have at least twelve members, though the people always had the prerogative of amending the Constitution to adopt a different number.[265] *Byrd v. State* was another juror case. On appeal by a free black man from a murder conviction and death sentence,[266] the court reversed because one of the jurors "declared that he was neither a freeholder nor a householder." Explaining his decision, Chief Justice Sharkey traced the history of the "freehold" requisite for jury service back to England, citing Coke and Blackstone.[267]

These big three British jurists and scholars were so well regarded that Mississippi judges referred to them more colloquially. In 1821, Judge Joshua G. Clarke observed that "even in Coke's time, the killing of any rational being was murder."[268] In 1881, Chief Justice H. H. Chalmers decided a case, relying on a "doctrine . . . no less recognized and maintained now than in the days of Coke and Sir Matthew Hale." He also cited Blackstone twice.[269] In 1952, Justice James G. Holmes applied the premise, quoting Chalmers's opinion.[270] In 1968, struggling with the perennially problematic legal standard for the insanity defense to a criminal charge, Justice Henry Lee Rogers wrote, "Many of the great English judges and English law writers wrote on this subject. Coke, Hale, Blackstone and others have written upon the subject."[271]

Beyond the namedropping, though more often in combination with it, the court would regularly cite and rely on English cases. In 1852, the High Court of Errors and Appeals, considering questions concerning the dissolution of a banking corporation, interchangeably cited English and American scholars and precedents, and said

> All the personal estate of the corporation vests in the crown, with us, in the people of the State, as succeeding, in this respect, to the rights and prerogatives of the king. Co. Lit. 13 *b*.; 1 Black, Comm. 484; Angell & Ames on Corp. 513; 3 Burr. Rep. 1868, *Commercial Bank of Lockwood*, 2 Harr. 8; 1 Blackf. Rep. 283; *Fox v. Horah*, 1 N.C. Rep. 353; 2 Kent, Comm. 309.[272]

The court ended with an abbreviated citation to Chancellor James Kent (1763–1847) of New York, an early American legal scholar, and an early North Carolina case for good measure.

Almost a century after statehood, Chief Justice Sydney McCain Smith, at the outset of his three decades of service, addressed the question, "What is the common law?"[273] He well knew the point was not always understood, even by many lawyers. Smith would have done well to recall a passage from Justice William L. Harris penned in 1860.

> Independent of written constitutions, as early as the seventeenth century it was said by Lord Coke, when Chief Justice of the King's Bench, in Dr. Bonham's case, "that the *common law* doth control acts of Parliament, and adjudges them void when against common right and reason." Lord Chief Justice Hobart, a few years after, in *Day v. Savage*, declared that an act of Parliament made against natural equity (as to make a man judge in his own case[274]) was void; and Lord Chief Justice Holt is reported to have said, in relation to the declaration of Lord Coke cited above, that it "was not extravagant, but was a very reasonable and true saying." *City of London v. Wood*, 12 Mod. 687, and 10 Mod. 118.[275]

Talk such as this is a bit "over the top." It reflected the thought of many in the early years of the United States. And it had descendants here such as the silly notion noted above that "statutes in derogation of common law should be strictly construed."[276]

Eschewing the natural law milieu in which Harris was mired, Chief Justice Smith answered the question—what is common law?—with a series of insights and quotations from others, at times drawing upon American scholars and jurists as his predecessors had earlier drawn on English scholars and jurists. He began with a quote from Kent.[277]

> The common law includes those principles, usages and rules of action applicable to the government and security of persons and property, which do not rest for their authority upon any express and positive declaration of the will of the Legislature.[278]

Smith then turned to US Supreme Court Justice David Josiah Brewer, who added

> As it does not rest on any statute or other written declaration of the sovereign, there must, *as to each principle thereof, be a first statement. Those statements are found in the decisions of courts,* and the first statement presents the principles as certainly as the last. Multiplication of declarations merely adds certainty. For, after all, *the common law is but the accumulated expressions of the various judicial tribunals* in their efforts to ascertain what is right and just between individuals in respect to private disputes.[279]

Brewer's important perspective overlooks the legal and social fact that "decisions of courts" and "expressions of . . . tribunals" are "other written declaration[s] of the sovereign."

Smith then borrowed a valuable insight from the US Court of Appeals for the Eighth Circuit.

> If a case is presented [within the court's jurisdiction] not covered by any law, written or unwritten, . . . [the judges'] powers are adequate, and it is their duty to adopt such rule of decision as right and justice in the particular case seem to demand. *It is true that in such a case, the decision makes the law, and not the law the decision, but this is the way the common law itself was made, and the process is still going on.*[280]

Again, a judge's exercise of his adequate powers in such a case of first impression is "[an]other written declaration of the sovereign" and thus a form of law with meaning and effect in the next and future similar cases.

Sydney Smith then turned to American legal scholars, much as his predecessors had so readily relied on English legal scholars. He quoted Dean Roscoe Pound (1870–1964) for the insight that "the fundamental idea of law is that of a rule or principle underlying a series of judicial decisions."[281] He drew attention to and quoted from Holmes, *The Common Law* (1881), arguably the "best book on law ever written by an American."[282] A third of the way through the second century since its publication, many of the insights in Holmes's classic work seem as fresh as ever.

A decade after Smith's peroration, Justice Virgil A. Griffith summarized the principle of common law growth, as well as the policy justifications that underlie that principle.

> The common law . . . , both in its substantive and in its adjective features, is not now, never has been, and never will be, static or stagnant. It has been one of the proudest boasts of the common law that it has within itself the potency of steady improvement, and this by judicial action, so long as that action is in accord with existing fundamental principles. It is the duty of courts, as attested by numerous decisions in this court, and in all courts throughout the nation, not only to keep the common law and its processes of enforcement abreast, or nearly so, with the substantial innovations of time, with the higher moral and material attainments in the general progress of enlightened civilization, proceeding always, however, upon established fundamental legal principles [citations omitted], but it also is equally the duty of courts to see that the state of the law shall continually profit from experiences and observations of the past and that, when such experiences have definitely disclosed a mischievous imperfection in previous precedents, the mischief shall be removed by recourse to another and fitter, legal principle.[283]

A half century later, the justices who had followed continued to honor and practice the insights from Griffith's summation, coupled with Smith's 1915 insights from the *Scott* case. In 1992, Justice Fred Banks took note that over time the court had expanded tort remedies by abolishing common law immunities that had outworn their welcome,[284] and then added, "The common law is not static. What the court gives, it can take away. This Court faces no constitutional impediment to ceasing to recognize criminal conversation as a viable tort."[285] And in 2016, Justice Evelyn Keyes of Texas faced the question, does a common law judge reason legally in a particular case? She concludes that, though guided by precedent and rules of construction, the living common law is "always subject to legal and equitable empirical adjustment to accommodate novel facts, new case law, and new legislation."[286]

Still, the courts have traditionally been hesitant—slower than some would prefer—to abandon that which has been accepted and practiced through the years. Chief Justice Sharkey recognized the common law principle that a party out of possession of land held adversely by another, under a title, though it be imperfect, cannot sell so as to pass a good title to his vendor: "We cannot say that the policy on which this principle is founded, is so far changed [in 1848] as to justify us in declaring it obsolete. On the contrary, there may still be good policy in holding on to this [common law] principle."[287]

As usual, no one said it better than Holmes. Recall his insight as far back as 1881, in an era of few statutes and when the common law reigned.

[I]n substance the growth of the law is legislative. And this in a deeper sense than that what the courts declare to have always been the law is in fact new. It is legislative in its grounds. The very considerations which judges most rarely mention, and always with an apology, are the secret root from which the law draws all the juices of life. I mean, of course, considerations of what is expedient for the community concerned.[288]

Such insights raised few eyebrows in Holmes's day, before so many less informed persons began to question the propriety of judges making law where the need was apparent. As far back as 1844 in Mississippi, Justice Joseph S. B. Thacher well explained with the pointed insight that "[t]he common law was the product of the experience of time, and the necessities of men living under a form of government."[289] And this was thirty-seven years and a Civil War before—and 1,500 miles to the south of—Holmes's famous introduction in his opening lecture in 1881.

The life of the law has not been logic; it has been experience. The felt necessities of the time, the prevalent moral and political theories, intuitions of public policy, avowed or unconscious, even the prejudices which judges share with their fellow-men, have had a good deal more to do than the syllogism in determining the rules by which men should be governed.[290]

Thirty-six years later, he added that the judge-made positive law long called common law "is not a brooding omnipresence in the sky but the articulate voice of some sovereign or quasi-sovereign that can be identified, ... It is always the law of some state."[291] And so

[i]t cannot be denied that the common law of England is the law of this State [but] only so far as it is adapted to our institutions and the circumstances of the people, and is not repealed by statutes, or varied by usages which, by long custom, have superseded it; and that where the reason of it ceases, the rule itself is inapplicable.[292]

Justice Handy's strong discussion of choice of law back in 1856 turned on policy, grounded in the relevant legislative facts as they appeared in Mississippi at the time, as distinguished from facts in England and other states that may have a different rule.

THE JUDICIAL AUTHORITY TO DECLARE THE COMMON LAW

One of the most important (and most often misunderstood) dimensions of the judicial power is not so much its de facto power to make law as its legitimacy.

We have seen that Mississippi's courts make law—commonly called common law—in a wide variety of contexts, and how they have long gone about it. It always starts with some person or entity—public or private—going to the courthouse and filing some sort of formal petition or complaint. But what gives the courts the authority to make law that has legal validity and is then obligatory and enforceable as to persons and firms? An early instance of a judge making law and in the gravest of contexts is presented in chapter 2 above. In late July of 1821, a man named Isaac Jones was hanged in Natchez for murder according to a law no legislature had enacted. Judge Joshua G. Clarke borrowed and applied the English common law of murder to decide that Jones's killing of a slave—one with whom he had no prior relationship—was murder when done with malice aforethought.[293] As recently as 1924, the crimes of assault and battery in this state were still common law crimes and not statutory offenses.[294]

Cases still arise where there are no rules that are up to the job of adjudication, and to repeat, because it cannot be said too often "If a case is presented not covered by any law, written or unwritten, the powers [of the court] are adequate, and it is their duty to adopt such rule of decision as right and justice in the particular case seem to demand."[295] It will not do for the court to say simply that there is no law and send a plaintiff packing, because in the next case the court will find a precedent has been set. Not to decide is to decide. A rule of decision will be deemed to have been established that on facts like those the defendant should prevail.[296] This is so because judges on their oaths are supposed to produce such adjudications according to reason and principle, the law reliably applied to the facts but taking a peek out the window at the legislative facts, reliance interests, and consequences that may lie ahead, all at least to the extent reasonably practicable. The rule so made—pro or con, yea or nay—will be seen a common law rule. Like as not it will have been made in a courthouse, "protector of the weak, judiciate and curb of the passions and lusts, repository and guardian of the aspirations and the hopes."[297]

In early 1929, Justice William D. Anderson penned the sentence "The Supreme Court has the authority to declare for itself what the common law of this state is."[298] Two months later, Justice Sam C. Cook, again speaking for a unanimous court, made that same dogmatic claim.[299] Almost half a century later, Justice Lenore Prather resurrected and reaffirmed this arrogant sentiment.[300] Four years later, Justice Armis E. Hawkins followed suit.[301] In 1998, Justice Michael D. Sullivan said, yes, we really mean it when we say that the court can "declare for itself what the common law of this state is."[302] Of course, each of these justices and others say more, and with practical reason. For the moment, this bald claim of lawmaking authority in the state supreme court is important. It is far more blatant than anything Justice Handy ever said in *Withers* or *Vicksburg RR*, though otherwise some might say Handy was the least bashful man ever to sit on the court.[303] Seventy years of such assertions smack us between the eyes and slow to a near stall those who might hope that judicial legislation will someday be inhibited.

But where and how is this authority constitutionally conferred on the state supreme court? Or are the exhortations from Justice Anderson in 1929 to Justice Sullivan in 1998 nothing more than almost three-quarters of a century's worth of judicial hubris? The answer lies in an understanding of the constitutionally conferred "judicial power." Not just the label but the activity. And an understanding of the judge's oath to "administer justice."[304] Every time an official applies some rule to facts and from that decides what is to be done, he has—by positive definition—practiced adjudication and exercised judicial power. On his oath, he should adjudge reliably according to the three-step process of adjudication.[305] Every time another official in another case looks to a prior exercise of judicial power as a precedent, she recognizes that something we call law has been made at some level. People may debate the legitimacy of practical judicial excursion at the penumbra of its authority—language, for example, that some call dicta. No one questions that adjudication is the core activity that the judiciary is charged to perform reliably,[306] every time one or more parties enter the courthouse. Any adjudication—by an administrative law judge, by legislative officials deciding whether legislative rules have been offended, or by an Article 6[307] state judge—is both a legitimate and obligatory exercise of judicial power in both the Article 1[308] sense and in the Article 6 sense.

Over the same span of seventy years, this Anderson-down-to-Sullivan claim of authority was followed by a very different assertion. "The common law is the perfection of reason, and when a rule of the common law ceases to be reasonable and just, it is no longer the common law."[309] Chief Justice Lemuel Shaw of Massachusetts combined experience with reason and explained how, as a practical matter, the common-law-making process works.

> When new practices spring up, new combinations of facts arise, and cases are presented for which there is no precedent in judicial decision, they must be governed by the general principle, applicable to cases most nearly analogous, but modified and adapted to the new circumstances by considerations of fitness and propriety, of reason and justice, which grow out of those circumstances.[310]

A generation later, Holmes provided an apt description of Shaw's contribution. "The strength of that great judge lay in an accurate appreciation of the requirements of the community whose officer he was. . . . Few have lived who were his equals in their understanding of the grounds of public policy to which all laws must ultimately be referred."[311]

The advent of the railroad brought a necessary and further constitutional lawmaking development. The common law of railroads as common carriers grew from Shaw's insight in the *Norway Plains* case. It became a basis for "making reasonable and suitable regulations as regards passengers."

Under the acts of congress and the common law with reference to which they were enacted, the licensed carrier might adopt its own reasonable regulations for the accommodation of passengers.[312]

And in a companion case concerning rates and tolls that a railroad might charge its customers, the court said,

Annexed to every such grant is the implied condition that the charges shall be reasonable, because that is the limit of the right imposed by the common law, and . . . the power of the corporation is to be exercised in subordination to this tacit condition.[313]

More than a century later, a similar view was penned in *Blackledge v. Omega Ins. Co.*

Courts are often charged with interpreting enigmatic areas within the law. This is the primary function of the judicial branch. Though clearly written statutes are preferred, in the absence of such, we, as judges, must apply consistent legal principles bound by common sense.[314]

A familiar and simplistic—and erroneous—view of many has long been that in such instances the state supreme court "did not make law, but accepted the law from the Legislature and the common law."[315] A 2015 instance—a constitutional encounter *sub silentio*—gives the lie to that one. In *Parker v. Benoist*, the state supreme court faced what it called "a case of first impression in Mississippi." A man's will contained a forfeiture *in terrorem* clause. The clause provided that any beneficiary taking anything under the terms of the will would forfeit such benefits if he or she contested the will and if the contest failed. Pursuing a legal will contest would trigger the forfeiture clause, "regardless of whether or not such proceedings are instituted in good faith and with probable cause." Ordinarily, whatever a person provides in his or her will is deemed as sacred, and it is enforceable as a matter of law. An ordinary forfeiture *in terrorem* clause is no exception.

In *Parker*, the said-to-be-offending beneficiary argued that she had acted in good faith and with probable cause in charging that her brother had been up to no good in convincing their father to prefer the brother in his will. Mississippi had no law on the point, other than the general rule that whatever a person's will says goes. The legislature had never enacted whether there was or should be a good faith or a probable cause exception to the enforceability of a forfeiture clause. No other lawmaking authority in Mississippi had spoken to the point. So what did the Supreme Court of Mississippi do? It declared a new rule of law: "In Mississippi, forfeiture provisions in wills are enforceable unless a contest is brought in good faith and based on probable cause."[316] The court then applied that new rule to the case before it, although in doing so the court kidded itself a bit, viz., in such cases "the decision makes the law, and not the law the decision"—a centuries-old insight noted above.[317] "We find that there is sufficient evidence before us to determine whether Bronwyn's challenge to the 2010 will was undertaken in good faith and founded upon probable cause."[318]

To be sure, the legislature has the authority to override or alter this new rule of law. For example, the legislature might well delete the free-standing "good faith" requirement. Many have come to see those words—"good faith"—as importing a subjective test that becomes meaningless (if not mischievous).[319] If the facts show that the contesting beneficiary had probable cause to suspect that the testator had been subjected to undue influence that led to his making the will, what's the point of requiring a separate and additional "good faith" showing? For the moment, no one doubts that in its *Parker* decision the state supreme court has made a rule of law that enjoys all of the indicia or other trappings of legal validity and is wholly enforceable in all cases where the statute of limitations has not run.[320]

Not only does the Supreme Court of Mississippi have and practice the authority to make new law, but it may also change law that it has made. In the example just given, somewhere down the line the court itself can modify *Parker* and jettison the potentially mischievous "good faith" requirement. An objective probable cause standard is quite adequate without more. The field of products liability affords a familiar instance of the lawmaking court belatedly accepting its responsibility to look out the window and from what it sees make more and better law. For many years it was thought that ordinarily liability in tort should follow only where the defendant was at fault. Negligence was the most common form of fault that a plaintiff had to prove if he wished to recover damages for personal injuries caused by another person.[321]

Then came the consumer age. People purchased products that from time to time would prove defective. Every now and then those product defects would cause personal injuries. For example, at times the brakes in a motor vehicle would fail. Because the driver could not stop his car, as rules of the road required, wrecks would occur and people would be injured through no fault of their own. Proving that the vehicle manufacturer was negligent, however, presented practical difficulties. Gathering evidence of the manufacturer's negligence was a daunting and expensive task. Yet without such evidence, the injured person had no hope of recovering damages for his losses. And so in time the supreme court changed the law. Proof of negligence or some other level of fault would no longer be required of the injured person.[322] In time, the so-called consumer-expectations test of liability was judicially replaced by a more nuanced "risk-utility" test.[323] As the court said a century ago, "this is the way the common law itself was made, and the process is still going on."[324] Then, and more in response to political interests than any particular deficiency in the state's juris-prudence, the legislature enacted Tort Reform.[325] Wrongful death acts had been an early statutory correction of a long-standing view in the common law that any tort action died with the potential plaintiff.[326]

REFLECTIONS

Identifying the ground rules for judicial revisions to judge-made law is serious business. This is particularly so given one major difference between judge-made law and new laws made by a legislature. Ordinarily, legislatures take a forward-looking approach. New statutes are almost always prospective only. The simple idea is that people should have fair notice before a new law takes effect. Laws not likely to disappoint reasonable reliance interests are often made effective "from and after passage" (which means from and after the governor signs it several weeks after final passage in the legislature). An effective date somewhere in the future—such as July 1 or sometimes January 1—is often specified where in fairness people need time to learn of the new law, and make plans to conform or otherwise modify their behavior. On the other hand, judge-made law is normally thought retroactive. For one thing, the new rule is applied in the case before the court where it is made. *Parker* was such a case. But any case pending at the time in which a probable cause defense was being asserted against violating an *in terrorem* forfeiture clause would also apply that rule, though the new rule did not exist at the time of the said-to-be offending conduct by the disappointed heir.

Giving retroactive effect to a new judge-made common law precedent is thought important to deter courts from changing judge-made law without some very good reason coupled with deliberate reflection. Ordinarily, courts considering new judge-made law think of whether there are likely persons who have reasonably relied on the current state of the law and who will unfairly have the rug pulled out from under them by an unanticipated change in the law. Such thoughts are of legislative facts not a part of any trial or appellate record but nonetheless essential to quality, reliable, and just judging. That there are persons whose good-faith compliance with present law would be put at risk is a strong argument for leaving the matter for possible action by the legislature. On the other hand, where there is no likelihood of disappointed reliance or independent basis for fearing unfair harm to persons or the public interest, the court is freer to act.

There will always be a penchant in some quarters for statutory law-making, which, to be sure, is the constitutionally superior species of law, if not always the most carefully crafted. Historically, codification began to be discussed seriously leading up to the turn of the nineteenth century.[327] Leaving aside politically driven legislation discussed in the public media, the work of the National Conference of Commissioners on Uniform State Laws has been exemplary. Mississippi has enacted NCCUSL statutes by the dozens.[328] Recently, the state enacted the Uniform Statutory Rule against Perpetuities. After years of tortured common law decisions,[329] of interest at most to a small handful of antiquarian legal scholars, in 2015 the legislature passed the simple ninety-year uniform rule, effective prospectively.[330] This is a textbook exemplar, a clearly superior form for the legal articulation of the underlying public policy that no common law court would dream of adopting!

Still, many common-law-making challenges lie ahead. Common law is the once and future king of lawmaking.[331] Empirically based common law judging is the engine that will drive this inevitable force, so essential that the state may more effectively pursue the social ends set out in Sections 5 through 8 of the Mississippi Constitution,[332] adding a bit of pragmatic substance with each adjudication. The Restatements of the Law have been an important resource to which Mississippi and other courts have resorted for their common law lawmaking. In *Parker v. Benoist*,[333] noted above, the court cited the *Restatement of Property: Wills and Donative Transfers* (2003).[334] Similar citations abound through the appellate opinions of the courts of Mississippi.[335]

One particular challenge is worth a note. In 1881, Oliver Wendell Holmes wrote, "I do not say that the criminal law does more good than harm."[336] The substantive law of crimes, the criminal procedural process, and dispositions have historically been equally important parts of "the criminal law." In 1897, Holmes put the matter slightly differently: "What have we better than a blind guess to show that the criminal law in its present form does more good than harm?"[337] A decade later, he embellished, "Who has any reason for believing that half our criminal law does more good than harm, better than tradition, vague sentiment, and the fact that we never thought of another way of doing things?"[338] The looming crisis in eye-witness identification evidence adds a sense of urgency to Holmes's perennial doubts. Study after study suggests a serious reliability concern with at least 10 percent of all in court identifications made in criminal prosecutions.[339] This can only mean that there are hundreds of innocent persons incarcerated in Mississippi's prisons today, and thousands of innocents in jails nationwide. And yet reviewing courts cling to the traditional judge-made common law abuse of discretion standards of review of evidentiary rulings at trial, and substantial evidence standards for reviewing jury verdicts. And in dozens of other ways, judge-made finality considerations are held to trump reopening cases of probable errors in convictions.

In this context, consider one value judgment grounded in practical reality that many have learned by high school, if not before, attributable to one of the greats of the common law inherited in this state and this country. Sir William Blackstone once said, "For the law holds, that it is better that ten guilty persons should escape, than that one innocent suffer."[340] Benjamin Franklin added another zero to Blackstone's dictum: "That it is better 100 guilty persons should escape than that one innocent person should suffer, is a maxim that has been long and generally approved."[341] Claiborne showed that this one was known in Mississippi back in the nineteenth century, reporting, "The criminal law of this State has always been administered with due regard to the benign inculcation of the common law, 'that it is better that ninety-nine men should escape, than that one innocent man should suffer.'"[342] There can be little doubt that this justification for the presumption of innocence is traceable back long before Blackstone and to Abraham's parting shot in his debate with Jehovah over the fate of Sodom and Gomorrah. "Oh let not the Lord be angry, and I will speak yet but this once: Per adventure ten [righteous men] shall be found there. And he said I will not destroy *it* for ten's sake."[343]

Another Holmesism provided a broader perspective. Approaching seventy-two years old, and after twenty years as a state supreme court justice and more than ten on the US Supreme Court, the Yankee from Olympus reflected

> that fear . . . translated into doctrines . . . [has] no proper place in. . . the common law. Judges are apt to be naif, simple-minded men, and they need something of Mephistopheles. We too need education in the obvious—to learn to transcend our own convictions and to leave room for much that we hold dear to be done away with short of revolution by the orderly change of law.[344]

ENDNOTES

1. "David D. Withers," http://en.wikipedia.org/wiki/David_D._Withers.

2. See the *New York Times* article on the funeral of David Dunham Withers, February 21, 1892, http://query.nytimes.com/gst/abstract.html?res=9A07E7D91631E033A25752CA9649C94639ED7CF.

3. Many of the facts that follow are taken from the record of proceedings in *Commissioners of Homochitto River v. Withers*, 7 Cushm. (29 Miss.) 21, 1855 WL 107 (1855), affirmed *sub nom. Withers v. Buckley*, 20 Howard (61 U.S.) 84 (1857).

4. In today's US dollars, this would be approximately $5,750,000. At the time of his death in 1892, Withers left an estate "valued at between $3,000,000 and $4,000,000 and bequeathed to the family," or in today's US dollars between approximately $80 million and $107 million. See "David D. Withers' Will," *New York Herald*, no. 53, Feb. 22, 1892, page 11. It appears that Withers still owned property in Mississippi, including a parcel of land said to have a value of $6,000, in today's US dollars, approximately $160,000. The inflation estimates are a function of a table found at http://www/westegg.com/inflation/. *See also Lewis v. Monson*, 151 U.S. 545 (1894). Withers also appears to have left a nephew, "William B. Withers, of Lockleven, Adams County, Miss." *New York Tribune*, Feb. 24, 1892, page 11.

5. *Commissioners of Homochitto River v. Withers*, 7 Cushm. (29 Miss.) 21, 30, 1855 WL 107 (1855).

6. *See* county line statutes, Miss. Code Ann. § 19-1-1 (Adams County), § 19-1-5 (Amite County), § 19-1-37 (Franklin County), § 19-1-157 (Wilkinson County); for a current summary

narrative description of the Homochitto River, *see* "Homochitto River," https://en.wikipedia. org/wiki/Homochitto_River.

7. *Commissioners of Homochitto River v. Withers*, 7 Cushm. (29 Miss.) 21, 31, 1855 WL 107 (1855).

8. *Commissioners of Homochitto River v. Withers*, 7 Cushm. (29 Miss.) 21, 31, 1855 WL 107 (1855).

9. The reference is to the Mississippi Constitution of 1832.

10. Miss. Const. art. 1, § 14 (1832).

11. Miss. Const. art. 1, § 13 (1832).

12. Miss. Const. art. 2, § 1; art. 3, § 4 (1832).

13. *Commissioners of Homochitto River v. Withers*, 7 Cushm. (29 Miss.) 21, 32, 1855 WL 107 (1855).

14. Miss. Const. art. 5, §§ 1, 16 (1832).

15. Miss. Const. art. 3, § 4 (1832).

16. Miss. Const. art. 2, §§ 1, 2 (1832).

17. *Runnels v. State*, Walker (1 Miss.) 146, 1823 WL 543 (1823). *Marbury v. Madison*, 1 Cranch 137, 170, 2 L.Ed. 60 (1803), decided by the US Supreme Court, did not bind the states to practice judicial review of acts of the state legislature or executive that might contravene the state constitution. See chapter 3, above.

18. Miss. Const. Preamble (1817).

19. *See, e.g.*, *Ryals v. Pigott*, 580 So.2d 1140, 1146–1147 (Miss. 1990) (regarding the Bogue Chitto River and citing cases); *see also Commissioners of Homochitto River v. Withers*, 7 Cushm. (29 Miss.) 21, 38–39, 1855 WL 107 (1855).

20. 3 U.S. Statutes at Large 348, 349 (1817).

21. U.S. Const. art. 6, cl. 2.

22. *Commissioners of Homochitto River v. Withers*, 7 Cushm. (29 Miss.) 21, 32–38, 1855 WL 107 (1855).

23. See Michael H. Hoffheimer, *Mississippi Courts: 1790–1868*, 65 Miss. L. Journ. 99, 103 fn. 12 and accompanying text (Fall 1995).

24. Act of April 7, 1798, ch. 28, § 3, 1 Stat. 549, 550 (authorizing establishment of Mississippi Territory consisting of the present states of Alabama and Mississippi). The Georgia Compact of 1798 established the Mississippi Territory and declared applicable the first five articles of the Northwest Ordinance. Article 6, however, was omitted. The Georgia Compact limited slavery only in the sense that the foreign slave trade was declared illegal in the Mississippi Territory.

25. See Act of March 1, 1817, 3 Stat. 348 (1817); Act of December 10, 1817, formally admitting Mississippi to the Union, 3 Stat. 472, 473 (1817).

26. For those impatient, take a look at the opinion of Chief Justice Sydney McCain Smith in *Yazoo & M. V. R. Co. vs. Scott*, 108 Miss. 871, 67 So. 491, 492–493 (1915).

27. We met Chief Justice Sharkey in chapter 4 above.

28. *Morgan v. Reading*, 3 Smedes & M. (11 Miss.) 366, 1844 WL 3217 (1844).

29. George S. Yerger, one of Withers's lawyers on appeal, was introduced in chapter 4 concerning the Union Bank bonds. Justice Alexander H. Handy had run against Yerger's youngest brother, Justice William Yerger, and was elected after the younger Yerger authored a very unpopular opinion supporting the validity of the Union Bank bonds.

30. *Morgan v. Reading*, 3 Smedes & M. (11 Miss.) 366, 398–399, 1844 WL 3217 (1844); *Boarman v. Catlett*, 13 Smedes & M. (21 Miss.) 149, 152, 1849 WL 2315 (1849).

31. Statutes were excluded from the common law accepted from England. *Boarman v. Catlett*, 13 Smedes & M. (21 Miss.) 149, 152, 1849 WL 2315 (1849); *Yazoo & M. V. R. Co. v. Scott*, 108 Miss. 871, 67 So. 491, 493 (1915); *Martin v. State*, 190 Miss. 32, 199 So. 98, 100 (1940).

32. *Morgan v. Reading*, 3 Smedes & M. (11 Miss.) 366, 402, 1844 WL 3217 (1844).

33. *Jackson v. The Magnolia*, 20 Howard (61 U.S.) 296, 302 (1857), referring to *Waring v. Clarke*, 46 U.S. 441, 442 (1847).

34. 3 U.S. Statutes at Large 348, 349 (1817).

35. *Fretz v. Bull*, 12 Howard (53 U.S.) 466, 468 (1851), citing *Genesee Chief v. Fitzhugh*, 12 Howard (53 U.S.) 443 (1851), which had on its facts concerned only with matters related to the Great Lakes, and applying that view of the law to the whole of the Mississippi River, tide or no tide. There is a conceptual distinction between federal authority to regulate public waters under Article 1's legislative power and Article 2's executive power, as distinguished from the admiralty and maritime jurisdiction included within the judicial power under Article 3, but no practical difference of concern here.

36. *Commissioners of Homochitto River v. Withers*, 7 Cushm. (29 Miss.) 21, 35, 1855 WL 107 (1855).

37. Miss. Const. art. 1, § 13 (1832) provides, in relevant part, that no "person's property" "shall ... be taken or applied to public use without the consent of the legislature, and without just compensation being first made therefor."

38. Miss. Const. art. 1, §§ 13, 14 (1832).

39. *Commissioners of Homochitto River v. Withers*, 7 Cushm. (29 Miss.) 21, 32, 1855 WL 107 (1855).

40. *Commissioners of Homochitto River v. Withers*, 7 Cushm. (29 Miss.) 21, 38, 1855 WL 107 (1855).

41. For a full understanding of the judge-made and accepted law of public waters and riparian rights leading up to the Civil War, *Steamboat Magnolia v. Marshall*, 10 George (39 Miss.) 109 (1860), should be studied along with the earlier *Morgan* cases decided in 1844 and *Withers* in 1855. The story is carried forward in *Dycus v. Sillers*, 557 So.2d 486 (Miss. 1990), which concerned a small lake created following the Mississippi River Flood of 1912. *Black v. Williams*, 417 So.2d 911 (Miss. 1982) concerned the small water body wholly upon and within a landowner's real property, and which was susceptible of private ownership in its entirety. *Ryals v. Pigott*, 580 So.2d 1140 (Miss. 1990) concerned the Bogue Chitto River, one quite similar to the Homochitto only a bit to its east. The Bogue Chitto flows into the Pearl River and thence into the Gulf of Mexico. By *Ryals*' time, statutes and regulations had become a part of the legal landscape, supplanting much of the judge-made law from the *Morgan-Withers-Magnolia* era. Navigable waters enjoy constitutional protection today. See Miss. Const. art. 4, § 81 (1890), as amended in 1968.

42. *Withers v. Buckley*, 20 Howard (61 U.S.) 84 (1857).

43. *Southern Pacific Co. v. Jensen*, 244 U.S. 205, 222 (1917) (Holmes, J., dissenting).

44. I refer here to the concept of legal validity (CLV) as I have explained it in James L. Robertson and David W. Clark, "An Interpretive Stratagem," in *The Law of Business Torts in Mississippi*, 15 Miss. C. L. Rev. 13, 27–28 (1994).

45. This is called the process of adjudication, which I have explained in Robertson, *Variations on a Theme by Posner: Facing the Factual Component of the Reliability Imperative in the Process of Adjudication*, 84 Miss. L. Journ. 471, 489–497 (2015), augmented in my *Practical Benefits of Literature in Law, and Their Limits*, 35 Miss. Coll. L. Rev. 266, 282 (2016).

46. William Faulkner, *Requiem for a Nun* 35, 37 (1950). See chapter 1 above.

47. A state may not be said to function according to the rule of law unless to a substantial extent it addresses the eight components of what Lon L. Fuller called "the morality that makes law possible." Fuller, *The Morality of Law* 33–94 (1964).

48. Justice Evelyn Keyes of the Texas Court of Appeals (and a native of Mississippi) has put the point well at the fundamentally different federal level. "The Constitution ... empowers Congress to make general laws. It empowers the executive to enforce the laws. And it empowers

judges to construe and apply the laws fairly and impartially [and I would add "reliably"] to do justice in particular cases and to maintain the integrity and justice of the law in furtherance of the common good as the people themselves have defined it. It empowers judges to preserve, protect and defend the rule of law." Keyes, *Hedgehogs and Foxes: The Case for the Common Law Judge*, 67 Hastings Law Journal 749, 774 (2016). The difference, of course, is that common law plays a much more limited role at the federal level, where all courts are courts of limited jurisdiction, while most states have at least one trial court of general jurisdiction and an appellate prerogative of making new common law and to amend and extend the common law they were formally granted going back to Article the Second of the original Northwest Ordinance of 1787.

49. In the constitution of 1832, the highest court of the state of Mississippi was referred to as a "high court of errors and appeals." Miss. Const. Art. 4, §§ 1, 2, 7 (1832). At all other times, the highest court has been called a supreme court.

50. Armed with reflections on Faulkner's courthouse, *see* William Faulkner, *Requiem for a Nun* 35, 37 (1950), see chapter 1 above, a leisurely visit to the courtroom in the Old Capitol Museum is well worth one's while.

51. Rule 404(b), Miss. R. Evid.

52. *See, e.g., Wade v. State*, 583 So.2d 965, 967 (Miss. 1991).

53. Miss. Const. art. 6, § 156 (1890).

54. *Shewbrooks v. A. C. & S., Inc.*, 529 So.2d 557, 560 (Miss. 1988).

55. *Cohens v. State of Virginia*, 19 U.S. 264, 404 (1821) (per Chief Justice John Marshall, expressing a view later embedded in the Mississippi Constitution of 1890).

56. Miss. Const. art. 6, §§ 156, 159 (1890), and prior thereto Miss. Const. art. 6, § 14 (1869), and Miss. Const. art. 4, § 14 (1832).

57. *See Farrar v. State*, 191 Miss. 1, 5–6, 2 So.2d 146, 147 (1941); *State v. Speakes*, 144 Miss. 125, 109 So. 129, 133 (1926). This goes back to the Constitution of 1832, Art. 4, §§ 1, 14, 23, and the case known as *Houston v. Royston*, 8 Miss. 543, 548–549, 1843 WL 2035 (1843). *See* Robertson, Subject Matter Jurisdiction, § 1:23, in *Mississippi Civil Procedure* (Jackson, Campbell, and Matheney eds., 2018).

58. Miss. Const. art. 1, § 14 (1817); Miss. Const. art. 1, § 14 (1832); Miss. Const. art.1, § 28 (1869); Miss. Const. art. 3, § 24 (1890). *See State v. McPhail*, 182 Miss. 360, 180 So. 387, 392 (1938) per Justice Virgil A. Griffith. Regrettably, more than a few try to read too much into this constitutional text, while others fail to see what is really there. *See* Robertson, Constitutional Law, §§ 19:119–19:121, Vol. 3, *Encyclopedia of Mississippi Law* (2d ed., 2018).

59. Magna Carta, cls. 39, 40 (1215), as edited by Sir William Blackstone. In *State v. McPhail*, 182 Miss. 360, 180 So. 387, 392 (1938), Justice Virgil A. Griffith outlines and explains in the aggregate the clauses of the Mississippi Constitution of 1890 that derive from Magna Carta, though he never mentions Runnymede. Just substitute "governor" for "king," and start with the "but whenever" clause halfway down the third paragraph from the end of the *McPhail* opinion.

60. Edward Coke, *The First Part of the Institutes of the Laws of England, or, A Commentary on Littleton* (1628).

61. *Statham v. New York Life Ins. Co.*, 45 Miss. 581, 598–599, 1871 WL 4009 (1871).

62. *Jones v. State*, Walker (1 Miss.) 83, 85–86, 1820 WL 1413 (1821).

63. See chapter 3 above.

64. *Bradley v. State*, Walker (1 Miss.) 156, 157, 1 Morr. St. Cas. 13, 1824 WL 631 (1824).

65. *Gross v. State*, 100 So. 177, 178–179 (1924). Other cases in which the so-called common law right of moderate chastisement was repudiated include *Harris v. State*, 14 So. 266 (1894).

66. *Powell v. Brandon*, 2 Cushm. (24 Miss.) 343, 363–364 (1852).

67. *Boarman v. Catlett*, 13 Smedes & M. (21 Miss.) 149, 152, 1849 WL 2315 (1849); *Yazoo & M. V. R. Co. v. Scott*, 108 Miss. 871, 67 So. 491, 493 (1915).

68. *Gross v. State*, 135 Miss. 634, 100 So. 177, 178 (1924) (emphasis supplied). This same conditional, limited, and qualified acceptance in Mississippi of the rules of the common law was declared in cases such as *Noonan v. State*, 9 Miss. 562, 573 (1844); *Vicksburg & J. R. Co. v. Patton*, 31 Miss. 156, 185 (1856); *Green v. Weller*, 32 Miss. 650 (21); *Crane v. French*, 38 Miss. 503, 528 (1860); *Kansas City, M. & B. R. Co. v. Smith*, 72 Miss. 677, 17 So. 78, 80 (1895); *Planters Oil Mill v. Yazoo & M. V. R. Co.*, 153 Miss. 712, 717, 121 So. 139, 140 (1929); *Interstate Co. v. Garnett*, 154 Miss. 325, 347, 122 So. 373, 378 (1929); *Burns v. Burns*, 518 So.2d 1205, 1298 (Miss. 1988); *Clark v. Luvel Dairy Products, Inc.*, 731 So.2d 1098, 1105 (¶¶ 20, 21) (Miss. 1998).

69. *Commissioners of Homochitto River v. Withers*, 7 Cushm. (29 Miss.) 21, 35, 36, 1855 WL 107 (1855).

70. *Wheelock v. Cozzens*, 6 Howard (7 Miss.) 279, 282, 1842 WL 2045 (1842).

71. *Gross v. State*, 100 So. 177, 178 (Miss. 1924) and cases cited therein. *Gross v. State*, 100 So. 177, 178 (1924) and cases cited therein. Other states took a similar approach. Among the original states, the Supreme Court of Pennsylvania explained, "It required time and experience to ascertain how much of the English law would be unsuitable to this country. By degrees, as circumstances demanded, we adopted the English usages, or substituted others better suited to our wants, until at length, before the time of the Revolution, we had formed a system of our own, founded in general on the English constitution, but not without considerable variations." *Commonwealth v. Lehigh Valley R. Co.*, 165 Pa. 162, 171–172, 30 A. 836, 839 (1895). In Rhode Island, "the common law of England, with reference to the nature of the estates in which land might be held . . . was adopted at the time of the Revolution and became a part of the common law of this state." *Bloomfield v. Brown*, 67 R.I. 452, 25 A.2d 354, 356 (1942). "[A]n estate by the entirety as known to the English common law was recognized and allowed by the common law of Rhode Island." *Bloomfield v. Brown*, 67 R.I. 452, 25 A.2d 354, 356 (1942). Dubiously, the court concluded that "whether an estate by the entirety should be abolished or modified in the future, in view of the change in conditions from those existing at common law, is a question of policy to be decided by the legislature rather than by the court." *Bloomfield v. Brown*, 67 R.I. 452, 25 A.2d 360 (1942). There is no sensible reason why the court might think it lacks power to decide that policy question, subject, of course, to being overridden by the legislature. Our border state to the North, Tennessee, borrowed its law from its "mother state, North Carolina," which in turn had a statute that declared "that all such parts of the common law, as were heretofore in force and use within this territory,* as are not destructive of, or repugnant to, or inconsistent with, the freedom and independence of this state, and the form of government therein established, * * * and not abrogated, repealed or expired, * * * are hereby declared to be in full force and effect within this state." *Moss v. State*, 131 Tenn. 94, 173 S.W. 859, 861 (1915) (recognizing common law rule that court sessions should not be held on Sunday). The North Carolina view is found in *Crump v. Morgan*, 38 N.C. 91, 98–99 (1843), with citations to the teachings of Hale and Blackstone, and to Chancellor Kent. *Crump v. Morgan*, 38 N.C. 96–99 (1843). Our sister state of Alabama recognized before the Civil War that "[t]he common law of England, however, . . . is not to be taken, in all respects, to be that of America. Our ancestors brought with them its general principles, and claimed it as their birth-right, but they brought with them, and adopted, only that portion which was applicable to their condition." *Harkness v. Sears & Walker*, 26 Ala. 493, 497 (1855) (recognizing the common law rules (1) of vendor and vendee and (2) of fixtures). Similar views of the level of acceptance the common law received in particular states are found in *Clark v. Allaman*, 71 Kan. 206, 80 P. 571, 574–580 (1905) (rights of riparian owners); *Reno Smelting, Milling & Reduction Works v. Stevenson*, 20 Nev. 269, 21 P. 317 (1889), holding that "the common-law doctrine of riparian rights is unsuited to the conditions of our state." *Reno Smelting, Milling & Reduction Works v. Stevenson*, 20 Nev. 269, 21 P. at 322; *McKennon v. Winn*, 1 Okla. 327, 33 P. 582, 584 (1893) (common law rule recognizing oral contracts for sale of interests in land enforceable, unless overridden by

legislatively enacted statute of frauds); *Hageman v. Vanderdoes*, 15 Ariz. 312, 319–321, 138 P. 1053, 1056–1057 (1914) (husband's common law liability for torts of wife under rule of coverture).

72. *George v. State*, 8 George (37 Miss.) 316, 320, 1859 WL 3637 (1859).

73. Mississippi Tort Reform Act of 2004, H. B. 13, 2004 Miss. Laws 1st Ex. Sess; http://bill-status.ls.state.ms.us/20041e/pdf/history/HB/HB0013.htm; H. B. 2, 2002 Miss. Laws 3d Ex. Sess.; http://billstatus.ls.state.ms.us/20023E/pdf/history/HB/HB0002.htm.; Mississippi Tort Claims Act, Miss. Code Ann. §§ 11-46-7, et seq.

74. "George Adams," en.wikipedia.org/wiki/George Adams_(judge).

75. A substantial public scandal emerged regarding proprieties in the state treasurer's office in late 1842 and on into 1843. The primary disputants were Treasurer Richard S. Graves and Gov. Tilghman M. Tucker. George Adams supported Governor Tucker in the matter. Editor Hagan made public and less-than-complimentary comments about Adams's role in the matter, to which the younger Adams took great offense. A longer and more colorful account of this sordid mess may be found in "The Defalcation of Richard S. Graves," in William D. McCain, *The Story of Jackson*, Vol. 1, 165–167 (1953). See also *The Papers of Jefferson Davis, June 1841–July 1846*, 319 fn. 17, Vol. 2 (James T. McIntosh ed., 1974).

76. A news report of the coroner's inquest provides considerable detail as well as a summary of the testimony of witnesses. "A Coroner's Inquest," *Evening Post* (New York, N.Y.) Mon., June 26, 1843, page 2, Newspapers.com, https://www.newspapers.com/image/31963928. A shorter version of the facts with suggested motives appears as "Dr. Hagan," *Brooklyn Daily Eagle* (Brooklyn, N.Y.) Thurs., June 22, 1843, Newspapers.com, https://www.newspapers.com /image/50331736.

77. For a short biography of Judge Coulter, including a summary of the Hickey episode, *see The Papers of Jefferson Davis, June 1841–July 1846*, 154 fn. 6, Vol. 2 (James T. McIntosh ed., 1974).

78. The story of the Hagan-Adams altercation has been widely reported. *See, e.g.*, Terry L. Jones, "A Very Violent Gentleman," *New York Times*, Sept. 20, 2013, http://opinionator.blogs. nytimes.com/2013/09/20/a-very-violent-gentleman/?_r=0.

79. *Ex Parte Hickey*, 4 Smedes & M. (12 Miss.) 751, 755 (1844).

80. Joseph Stevens Buckminster Thacher, *Find A Grave*, Memorial #100143376, findagrave. com/memorial/100143376/joseph-stevens_buckminster-thacher.

81. *Black's Law Dictionary*, "Habeas corpus," page 638 (5th ed., 1979).

82. Miss. Const. art. 1, § 17 (1832) (emphasis in original). The current constitution provides that "[t]he privilege of the writ of habeas corpus shall not be suspended, unless when in the case of rebellion or invasion, the public safety may require it, nor ever without the authority of the legislature." Miss. Const. art. 3, § 21 (1890).

83. *Ex Parte Hickey*, 4 Smedes & M. (12 Miss.) 751, 769 (1844); *see also State v. McPhail*, 180 So. 387, 392 (Miss. 1938).

84. At times, "Carta" is spelled with an "h," so that it reads "Charta."

85. *Ex Parte Hickey*, 4 Smedes & M. (12 Miss.) 751, 769 (1844). The original Magna Carta was one long paragraph. Sir William Blackstone is credited with improving the form so that Magna Carta would be more easily read and understood. The clause cited above is Clause 39 in all reliable versions today. A more apt text of Clause 39 appears at the beginning of the discussion of the law of contempts in *Hickey* at page 773.

86. *Ex Parte Hickey*, 4 Smedes & M. (12 Miss.) 751, 769–770 (1844).

87. *Frank v. Mangum*, 237 U.S. 309, 346–347 (1915) (Holmes and Hughes, JJ., dissenting).

88. *Ex Parte Hickey*, 4 Smedes & M. (12 Miss.) 751, 770–771 (1844).

89. *Ex Parte Hickey*, 4 Smedes & M. (12 Miss.) 751, 772 (1844).

90. In time, such contempts came to be known as constructive contempts. *See* Jackson and Miller, Contempt of Court, § 20:9 *Criminal contempt—Constructive contempt*, Vol. 3, *Encyclopedia of Mississippi Law* (2d ed., 2018).

91. *Ex Parte Hickey*, 4 Smedes & M. (12 Miss.) 751, 773 (1844). Justice Thacher appears not to have known of the several iterations of Magna Charta and that the version that contained Clause 39 and other clauses in effect in 1844 was not issued and sealed by King Edward I until 1297. See Magna Carta (1297), statutelaw.gov.uk.

92. *Ex Parte Hickey*, 4 Smedes & M. (12 Miss.) 751, 777 (1844).

93. *Ex Parte Hickey*, 4 Smedes & M. (12 Miss.) 751, 774 (1844).

94. *Ex Parte Hickey*, 4 Smedes & M. (12 Miss.) 751, 778 (1844).

95. *Ex Parte Hickey*, 4 Smedes & M. (12 Miss.) 751, 781 (1844).

96. *Ex Parte Hickey*, 4 Smedes & M. (12 Miss.) 751, 782 (1844).

97. *Ex Parte Hickey*, 4 Smedes & M. (12 Miss.) 751, 783, 784 (1844).

98. For several accounts, *see* "The Hagan Family of Bourbon County, Kentucky," compiled by James G. Faulconer (Jan. 20, 2000), Bourbon County, KY, Family Histories, http://bourboncoky.info/HaganandJones.html. Dr. Hagan is reported to have been a native of County Derry, Ireland, though he had become a US citizen.

99. *See, e.g.*, Terry L. Jones, "A Very Violent Gentleman," *New York Times*, Sept. 20, 2013, http://opinionator.blogs.nytimes.com/2013/09/20/a-very-violent-gentleman/?_r=0. The suggestion that Dr. James Hagan was a hothead seems confirmed by the account of his altercations in and around Jackson prior to June of 1843. *See The Papers of Jefferson Davis, June 1841–July 1846*, Vol. 2, 318 fn. 17 (James T. McIntosh ed., 1974); and William D. McCain, *The Story of Jackson*, Vol. 1, pages 167–169 (1953). *See also* "The Hagan Family of Bourbon County, Kentucky," compiled by James G. Faulconer, *Bourbon County, KY, Family Histories*, www.bourboncoky.info/HaganandJones.html.

100. *See* discussion of Governor McNutt's role in the "repudiation" constitutional experience set out in chapter 4 above.

101. Senate Journal, Mississippi State Senate, page 134 (Jan. 14, 1840) (Special Message of His Excellency, A. G. McNutt, Governor of Mississippi).

102. Senate Journal, Mississippi State Senate, page 147 (Jan. 14, 1840) (Response of A. P. Merrill, Cashier, Agricultural Bank, Jan. 3, 1840).

103. Senate Journal, Mississippi State Senate, pages 480–481 (Feb. 9, 1840).

104. "D. W. Adams—Acquitted," *Tennessean* (Nashville, Tenn.), Weds., July 17, 1844, page 2, Newspapers.com, https://www.newspapers.com/image/118866546. Although the fatal altercation took place on the streets of Vicksburg, the trial appears to have been held in Hinds County and in the courthouse at Raymond. See William D. McCain, *The Story of Jackson*, Vol. 1, page 167 (1953). According to one account, when the word spread that Adams had been acquitted, editor Hammet of the *Vicksburg Whig* rejoiced. In February of 1844, new *Sentinel* editor James Ryan challenged Hammet and met the same fate as Hagan. See Mark G. Schmeller, *Invisible Sovereigns: Imagining Public Opinion from the Revolution to Reconstruction* (2016).

105. See Jane Johansson, "A Crime Scene: Vicksburg, Mississippi," *Trans-Mississippian*, Sun., June 3, 2012, http://transmississippian.blogspot.com/2012/06/crime-scene-vicksburg-mississippi.html. Two photographs of the spot where Adams shot Hagan are shown, depicting the scene as of early June of 2012.

106. W. J. Cash, *The Mind of the South* 74 (1941, 1991).

107. See Jack K. Williams, *Dueling in the Old South: Vignettes of Social History* 32 (1980).

108. In time, according to one account, Hickey shot and killed local doctor C. F. Martin, was charged with manslaughter, but was acquitted. In 1848, Hickey himself was killed in a duel. See Mark G. Schmeller, *Invisible Sovereigns: Imagining Public Opinion from the Revolution to Reconstruction* (2016).

109. "Death of Dr. Hagan," *Marksville (La.) Expositer*, June 17, 1843, page 2. *See* findagrave. com. In ten years, the *Vicksburg Sentinel* lost five editors in formal or jackleg duels. *See* Lindsey Williams, "Journalism Once a Dangerous Business," May 14, 1969, http://www.lindseywilliams

.org/LAL_Archives/Journalism_Once_a_Dangerous_Business.html; Mark G. Schmeller, *Invisible Sovereigns, Imagining Public Opinion from the Revolution to Reconstruction* (2016).

110. Several months after Hagan's death, two admirers, John Lavins and Richard Elward of Natchez, proposed that a biography of Hagan's life and public career be prepared and published. They published a proposed table of contents and outline, including an explanation that Dr. Hagan had originally come to Mississippi as a representative of the Washington Monument Association. *See* "Life and Writings of Dr. Jas. Hagan," dated August 1, 1843, but published in the *Attala Register* (Kosciusko, Miss.), Oct. 7, 1843, http://chroniclingamerica.loc.gov/lccn /sn87065294/1843-10-07/ed-1/seq-4/.

111. The monument shares a site with a similar monument over the remains of John Jenkins, another *Vicksburg Sentinel* editor who lost his life violently "because of political disagreements.... The Sentinel, founded by James Hagan and Willis Green, lasted from 1836–1860, leaving a legacy of tragedy." Monument, Cedar Hill Cemetery, Vicksburg, Mississippi.

112. "Daniel Weisiger Adams," *Find A Grave*, Memorial #9850, findagrave.com/memorial/9850/daniel-weisiger-adams. Shelby Foote has reported that "Daniel W. Adams, an accident-prone or perhaps merely unlucky Kentucky-born Louisianan who had lost an eye at Shiloh and been severely wounded again at Murfreesboro, was shot from his horse and captured." Foote, *The Civil War: A Narrative*, Vol. 2, *Fredericksburg to Meridian*, 734 (1963).

113. "Daniel Weisiger Adams," *Find A Grave*, Memorial #9850, findagrave.com/memorial /9850/daniel-weisiger-adams; *see* "Sudden Death of Gen. D. W. Adams, Organ of the Republican Party of the State of Louisiana, New Orleans, Friday morning, June 14, 1872.

114. Si Sheppard, *The Partisan Press: A History of Media Bias in the United States* 117 (2007).

115. For a fuller flavor of the times centering on journalism and violence in Vicksburg, including the deaths of James Hagan and several other journalists, see "The Vicksburg Press," *Warren County Mississippi MSGENWEB Project*, http://www.msgw.org/warren/vicksburgpress.htm.

116. *See* Robertson, Constitutional Law, § 19:62 *Freedom of the press*, in *Encyclopedia of Mississippi Law*, Vol. 3 (2d ed., 2018).

117. The idea was not unlike a major underlying storyline in such popular BBC programs as *Downton Abbey* and *Monarch of the Glen*.

118. Cornelius Moynihan, *Introduction to the Law of Real Property* (West Group, 3d ed., 2002), cited and quoted in https://en.wikipedia.org/wiki/Rule_in_Shelley%s_Case.

119. *Powell v. Brandon*, 2 Cushm. (24 Miss.) 343, 363 (1852).

120. The reference is to *The Provost of Beverly's Case*, Y.B. 40 Edw. IV, Hill No. 18 (1366).

121. *Wolfe v. Shelley*, 1 Co. Rep. 93b, 76 Eng. Rep. 206 (K.B. 1581).

122. *See, e.g.*, *Pressgrove v. Comfort*, 58 Miss. 644, 647, 1881 WL 7681 (1881) ("It was held that Edward Turner Garth was vested by the rule in Shelley's case, with absolute ownership of the property, though such was manifestly not the intention of the testator").

123. Rule in Shelley's Case, https://en.wikipedia.org/wiki/Rule_in_Shelley%27s_Case. The Rule in Shelley's case has been widely repudiated throughout the United States. 3 Restatement (Third) of Property: Wills and Donative Transfers § 16.2, 185–188 (2011).

124. See my exposition in *Myth and Reality—Or, Is It "Perception and Taste"?—In the Reading of Donative Documents*, 61 Fordham L. Rev. 1045, 1050–1051 (1993).

125. Oliver Wendell Holmes, *The Path of the Law*, 10 Harv. L. Rev. 457, 469 (1897).

126. *Powell v. Brandon*, 2 Cushm. (24 Miss.) 343, 363 (1852).

127. Act of 1822, §§ 24, 26, Hutch. Code, 609, 610, cited in *Hampton v. Rather*, 1 George (30 Miss.) 193, 201 (1855); and *Carradine v. Carradine*, 4 George (33 Miss.) 698, 732, 1857 WL 2674 (1857). The impact of the Rule was of enough importance to draw the attention of an early general historian of the state. J. F. H. Claiborne, *Mississippi, as Province, Territory, and State*, 480–482 (1880, reproduced by Louisiana State University Press 1964).

128. *Powell v. Brandon*, 2 Cushm. (24 Miss.) 343, 364 (1852).

129. Act of 1822, Hutch. Code, ch. 42, pp. 609, 610.

130. *See* Oliver Wendell Holmes, *The Common Law*, 5–30 (1881).

131. *Powell v. Brandon*, 2 Cushm. (24 Miss.) 343, 367–368 (1852).

132. *Hampton v. Rather*, 1 George (30 Miss.) 193, 206 (1855); *Carradine v. Carradine*, 4 George (33 Miss.) 698, 732 (1857).

133. *Pressgrove v. Comfort*, 58 Miss. 644, 647 (1881).

134. *See Stigler v. Shurlds*, 131 Miss. 648, 95 So. 635, 636 (1923); Miss. Code Ann. §§ 89-1-9, -15 (1972).

135. *All Persons v. Buie*, 386 So.2d 1109, 1112 fn. 2 (Miss. 1980). Miss. Code Ann., §§ 89-1-9, -15 (1972); Miss. Code, ch. 44, § 1201 (1880) (section entitled "The Rule in Shelley's Case Abolished).

136. The Doctrine of Worthier Title is another common law rule. https://en.wikipedia.org /wiki/Doctrine_of_worthier_title. It also has been repudiated in the overwhelming majority of American states. 3 Restatement (Third) of Property: Wills and Donative Transfers § 16.3, 188–194 (2011).

137. *Winn v. Cole's Heirs*, Walker 119 (1 Miss.) 119, 130, 1822 WL 407 (1822). "Jeofails" refers to an error or oversight in pleadings. *Black's Law Dictionary* 749 (5th ed., 1979). The principle is traceable back to England, though its substance and history have little to do with the point above that common law may be modified by statute. For those nonetheless interested in this quaint statute, note that it last appeared in an opinion of the Supreme Court of Mississippi in 1978, with little profit for the party invoking it. *Burns v. Delta Loans, Inv.*, 354 So. 2d 268, 270 (Miss. 1978), citing Miss. Code Ann. § 11-7-167. Alas, jeofails met its demise at the hands of the legislature in 1991, as the statute was inconsistent with and was superseded by the Mississippi Rules of Civil Procedure and Mississippi Rules of Evidence. Miss. Laws, ch. 573, § 141 (effective July 1, 1991).

138. *Kerr v. Baker*, Walker (1 Miss.) 140, 1823 WL 1097 (1823).

139. Regarding the early history of equity practice in Mississippi, see Kate Margolis, *A Brief History of Mississippi's Chancery Court*, www.caba.ms, posted May 2012). Regarding historical equity practice borrowed from England by other states, *see Crump v. Morgan*, 3 Ired. Eq. (38 N. C.) 91, 96–103 (1843) (domestic relations law applied to mentally deficient persons); *Quinn v. Phipps*, 93 Fla. 805, 113 So. 419 (1927) (equitable remedy of constructive trust).

140. In time, the courts developed the doctrine of pendent jurisdiction, so that in a case with both common law and equity issues, whichever court first acquired jurisdiction would hear the entire case. *See* Robertson, "Subject Matter Jurisdiction," § 1:20. Pendent Jurisdiction, in 1 Mississippi Civil Procedure, chapter 1 (Jackson, Campbell, and Matheny eds., 2018).

141. Arkansas, Delaware, New Jersey, and Tennessee are the only other states with any sort of separate chancery court of equity. *Crump v. Morgan*, 31 Fed. 9 (38 N.C.) 91, 96–103 (1843) (domestic relations are applied to insane, lunatic, mentally defective); *Quinn v. Phipps*, 93 Fla. 805, 113 So. 419 (1927) (equitable remedy of constitutional trust).

142. *New York Trust Co. v. Eisner*, 256 U.S. 345, 349 (1921) (Holmes, J.).

143. *Wheelock v. Cozzens*, 6 Howard (7 Miss.) 279, 282, 1842 WL 2045 (1842).

144. *See, e.g.,* "Alexander H. Handy," An AHGP Transcription Project, http://msmadison. genealogyvillage.com/Biography/Handy/AlexanderH.html; "Alexander H. Handy (1809–1871), http://msa.maryland.gov/megafile/msa/speccol/sc3500/sc3520/0013400/013499/html/13499b . . . See also chapter 4 above and pages 306, 308, 321–325, 342 in this chapter.

145. These facts found and documented in George M. Crowson, *History of Alabama and Vicksburg R. R.*, http://www.nchgs.org/html/history_of_a-v_r-r.html.

146. *Vicksburg and Jackson Railroad Company v. Patton*, 2 George (31 Miss.) 156, 176 (1856).

147. A decade later, Patton would serve in the Confederate Army and see action first at Bull Run and later at Vicksburg. These and other facts about Patton are shown on his tombstone in

Greenwood Cemetery in Jackson, Mississippi. https://s3-us-west-2.amazonaws.com/find-a
-grave-prod/photos/2005/301/12200055_11306 ...

148. *Vicksburg and Jackson Railroad Company v. Patton*, 2 George (31 Miss.) 156, 177 (1856).

149. *See* the familiar Advisory Committee Note to Fed. R. Evid. 201(a), relying on the
insightful work of Prof. Kenneth Culp Davis, explaining the difference between legislative facts
and adjudicative facts. See also Robertson, *Variations on a Theme by Posner: Facing the Factual
Component of the Reliability Imperative in the Process of Adjudication*, 84 Miss. L. Journ. 471,
516–537 (2015).

150. Act of April 7, 1798, ch. 28, § 3, 1 Stat. 549, 550 (authorizing establishment of Mississippi
Territory consisting of the present states of Alabama and Mississippi). The Georgia Compact
of 1798 established the Mississippi Territory and declared applicable the first five articles of the
Northwest Ordinance of 1787, including particularly Article the Second regarding the common
law, but excluding English statutory law. *Boarman v. Catlett*, 13 Smedes & M. (21 Miss.) 149, 152,
1849 WL 2315 (1849); *Yazoo & M. V. R. Co. v. Scott*, 108 Miss. 871, 67 So. 491, 493 (1915).

151. *Vicksburg and Jackson Railroad Company v. Patton*, 2 George (31 Miss.) 156, 181 (1856);
also at 183 ("subject to the laws and general policy of the State"), at 183 ("by our laws and˙
policy"). In this context, judicial reliance on public policy is entirely appropriate. Oliver Wendell Holmes, *The Common Law* 35, 68 (1881).

152. More recent cases revising or abolishing long-settled common law premises similarly
(and, I dare say, without exception) are the product of judges legislating in the public interest
See, e.g., Carter v. Berry, 140 So. 2d 843 (Miss. 1962), noted in Recent Case, *Perpetuities—In
General—A Class Gift Is Not Invalid Merely Because the Interest of One Member Might Vest Too
Remotely.*—Carter v. Berry *(Miss. 1962)*, 76 Harv. L. Rev. 1308 (1963) (judicially legislating the
abolition of the all-or-nothing rule for class gifts); *State Stove Mfg. Co. v. Hodges*, 189 So. 2d 113,
118 (Miss. 1966) (abolishing privity requirement in products liability in tort); *Mitchell v. Craft*,
211 So. 2d 509, 510, 512–13 (Miss. 1968); *Craig v. Columbus Compress & Warehouse Co.*, 210 So.
2d 645, 649–650 (Miss. 1968) (adopting most significant relationship test for choice of law);
Pruett v. City of Rosedale, 421 So. 2d 1046, 1052 (Miss. 1982); *Presley v. Mississippi State Highway
Commission*, 608 So.2d 1288 (Miss. 1992) (judicially legislating the abolition of sovereign
immunity defense to tort actions); *Burns v. Burns*, 518 So. 2d 1205, 1211 (Miss. 1988) (abolishing
interspousal tort immunity); *In re Estate of Anderson*, 541 So. 2d 423, 430 (Miss. 1989) (empowering courts to imply a savings clause where devise would violate rule against perpetuities);
Saunders v. Alford, 607 So. 2d 1214, 1219 (Miss. 1992) (abolishing tort of criminal conversation);
Sperry-New Holland v. Prestage, 617 So. 2d 248, 253 (Miss. 1993) (judicially legislating the risk-
utility test in products liability actions, rejecting the consumer expectations test).

153. *Vicksburg and Jackson Railroad Company v. Patton*, 2 George (31 Miss.) 156, 180 (1856).

154. Holmes, *The Common Law* 35 (1881). This Holmes passage, give or take a few lines
above or below, enjoys biblical authority. Richard Posner, *Divergent Paths: The Academy and the
Judiciary* 41 n. 3 (2016).

155. *Vicksburg and Jackson Railroad Company v. Patton*, 2 George (31 Miss.) 156, 185 (1856).

156. *Vicksburg and Jackson Railroad Company v. Patton*, 2 George (31 Miss.) 156, 185 (1856).

157. *Vicksburg and Jackson Railroad Company v. Patton*, 2 George (31 Miss.) 156, 187 (1856).

158. The US Constitution art. 4, § 4, cl. 1, provides that "[t]he United States shall guarantee
to every State in this Union a Republican Form of Government." For a useful discussion of the
core idea of a republic, see https://en.wikipedia.org/wiki/Republic.

159. *Churchill v. Pearl River Basin Development District*, 757 So.2d 940, 943–945 (¶¶10, 12, 21)
(Miss. 1999); *Horton v. American Tobacco Co.*, 667 So.2d 1289, 1292, 1306 (Miss. 1995). See Miss.
Code Ann. §11-7-15, which formally abolished the common law contributory negligence rule,
and the Mississippi Wrongful Death Act, Miss. § 11-7-13.

160. *Vicksburg and Jackson Railroad Company v. Patton*, 2 George (31 Miss.) 156, 192 (1856).

161. *See, e.g., Mitchell v. USAA*, 831 So.2d 1144, 1148, 1156 (¶¶20, 52) (Miss. 2002); *Missouri Pac. RR v. Hanna*, 168 Miss. 867, 152 So. 282, 283, 284 (1934).

162. *Kerwhaker v. Cleveland Columbus and Cincinnati Railroad Company*, 3 Ohio St. 172, 1854 WL 2 (1854).

163. *Vicksburg and Jackson Railroad Company v. Patton*, 2 George (31 Miss.) 156, 189–190 (1856).

164. *Vicksburg and Jackson Railroad Company v. Patton*, 2 George (31 Miss.) 156, 192–193 (1856).

165. LeAnne Howe, "Betsy Love and the Married Women's Property Act of 1839," *Mississippi History Now* (September 2005), http://www.mshistorynow.mdah.ms.gov/articles/6/betsy-love -and-the-married-womens-property-act-of-1839.

166. In his opinion, Justice Smith refers to Allen as "John Allen." *Fisher v. Allen*, 2 Howard (3 Miss.) 611, 612, 1837 WL 1080 (1837). LeAnne Howe has explained that this is a mistake, that the man's name was "James Allen." LeAnne Howe, "Betsy Love and the Married Women's Property Act of 1839," *Mississippi History Now* (Sept. 2005), http://www.mshistorynow.mdah.ms.gov/articles/6 /betsy-love-and-the-married-womens-property-act-of-1839. Chief Justice Sharkey refers to him as "James Allen." *Fisher v. Allen*, 2 Howard (3 Miss.) 611, 614, 615, 616, 1837 WL 1080 (1837).

167. *Fisher v. Allen*, 2 Howard (3 Miss.) 611, 612, 1837 WL 1080 (1837); LeAnne Howe, "Betsy Love and the Married Women's Property Act of 1839," *Mississippi History Now* (Sept. 2005), http://www .mshistorynow.mdah.ms.gov/articles/6/betsy-love-and-the-married-womens-property-act-of-1839.

168. LeAnne Howe, "Betsy Love and the Married Women's Property Act of 1839," *Mississippi History Now* (Sept. 2005), http://www.mshistorynow.mdah.ms.gov/articles/6/betsy-love-and -the-married-womens-property-act-of-1839.

169. *Fisher v. Allen*, 2 Howard (3 Miss.) 611, 612, 1837 WL 1080 (1837); LeAnne Howe, "Betsy Love and the Married Women's Property Act of 1839," *Mississippi History Now* (Sept. 2005), http:// www.mshistorynow.mdah.ms.gov/articles/6/betsy-love-and-the-married-womens-property-act -of-1839. The story of Betsy Love Allen and her successful thwarting of the common law rule of coverture is also well told by Sandra Moncrief, "The Mississippi Married Women's Property Act of 1839," *Hancock County Historical Society*, http://www.hancockcountyhistoricalsociety.com /vignettes/the-mississippi-married-womens-property-act-of-1839.

170. This execution sale process was the same as that employed in *Cochrane & Murdock v. Kitchens*, discussed in chapter 3 above.

171. *Fisher v. Allen*, 2 Howard (3 Miss.) 611, 615, 1837 WL 1080 (1837).

172. Act of January 1830, §4, quoted in *Fisher v. Allen*, 2 Howard (3 Miss.) 611, 613–614, 1837 WL 1080 (1837). Such an enactment was within the "legislative power" vested in the bicameral general assembly created in the original constitution. Miss. Const. art. 3, §4 (1817). The constitution of 1832 expressly authorized such a legislative enactment regarding "all such persons of the Choctaw and Chickasaw tribes of Indians." Miss. Const. art. 7, §18 (1832).

173. *Fisher v. Allen*, 2 Howard (3 Miss.) 611, 612, 1837 WL 1080 (1837).

174. *See* Miss. Const. art. 1, §§ 10, 11, 14, 17, 28 (1817).

175. See Michael H. Hoffheimer, *Mississippi Courts: 1790–1868*, 65 Miss. L. Journ. 99, 103 fn. 12 and accompanying text (Fall 1995).

176. "Coverture," https://en.wikipedia.org/wiki/Coverture.

177. *Fisher v. Allen*, 2 Howard (3 Miss.) 611, 616, 1837 WL 1080 (1837) (per Sharkey, C. J.).

178. *Fisher v. Allen*, 2 Howard (3 Miss.) 611, 614, 1837 WL 1080 (1837) (per Smith, J.).

179. Miss. Const. art. 7, §18 (1832). For context, the Treaty of Dancing Rabbit Creek of September 27, 1830, had effectively removed the Choctaw Indian Tribe from its traditional lands in central Mississippi. U.S. Statutes At Large 333 (1830). The Treaty of Pontotoc Creek of October

20, 1832, had effectively removed the Chickasaw Indian Tribe from its traditional lands in northern Mississippi. 7 U.S. Statutes at Large 381 (1832).

180. *See, e.g., Allen v. Montgomery,* 48 Miss. 101, 109, 1873 WL 4113 (1873).

181. Miss. Const. art. 1, §19 (1832); US Constitution art. 1, § 10, cl. 1, which was enforceable against states.

182. The story of events leading to the Married Women's Property Act of 1839, Miss. Laws, ch. 46 (1839) has been told any number of times. *See, e.g.,* Elizabeth Gaspar Brown, *Husband and Wife—Memorandum of the Mississippi Woman's Law of 1839,* 42 Michigan L. Rev. 1110 (1944); Judith T. Younger, *Marital Regimes: A Story of Compromise and Demoralization, Together w/Criticism and Suggestions for Reform,* 67 Cornell L. Rev. 45–102 (1981); Sandra Moncrief, *The Mississippi Married Women's Property Act of 1839,* 47 Journal of Mississippi History 110–125 (1985); Megan Benson, "*Fisher v. Allen:*The Southern Origins of the Married Women's Property Acts," *Journal of Southern Legal History* 97–122 (1997–1998); Robert Gilmer, *Chickasaws, Tribal Laws, and the Mississippi Married Women's Property Act of 1839* (History 452, Dr. Tracy Rizzo, 11/21/03). By far the most extensive "on the ground" study and analysis is Amanda K. Sims's dissertation, *Patriarchy and Property: The Nineteenth-Century Mississippi Married Women's Property Acts,* Brigham Young University Scholars Archive (2007), Paper 1433. Not everyone tells the story as others. Most draw on the work of their predecessors but advance the ball with less carefully mined facts. For illustration, the story leading to 1839 and the Married Women's Property Act draws from the work of others but includes the significant role played by Sen. Gordon D. Boyd of Attala County, who, insofar as the author has been able to determine, has not been mentioned before.

183. Sandra Moncrief, "The Mississippi Married Women's Property Act of 1839," Hancock County Historical Society, http://www.hancockcountyhistoricalsociety.com/vignettes/the -mississippi-married-womens-property-act-of-1839.

184. Smith had organized a military unit largely among his own kin and fought with Gen. Andrew Jackson at Horseshoe Bend in the War of 1812. His older daughter, Obedience, married Hiram G. Runnels, governor of Mississippi from 1833 to 1835. Hiram G. Runnels was the brother of Harmon M. Runnels Jr., a central figure in chapter 3 and in *Runnels v. State,* Walker (1 Miss.) 146, 1823 WL 543 (1823). Runnels served as president of the ill-fated Union Bank, and was known to fight a duel or two. See chapter 4, above. Smith County in central Mississippi is named for Maj. David Smith.

185. "State Auditor of Mississippi," en.wikipedia.org/wiki/State Auditor of Mississippi.

186. The story of the Hadleys' boardinghouse is told by Sandra Moncrief in "The Mississippi Married Women's Property Act of 1839," *Hancock County Historical Society,* http://www .hancockcountyhistoricalsociety.com/vignettes/the-mississippi-married-womens-property -act-of-1839. That story was told as early as 1880 by J. F. H. Claiborne, *Mississippi, as a Province, Territory and State* 475–476 (1880; reprinted by Louisiana State University Press in 1964).

187. The legislative power vested by Section 4 was procedurally regulated by Sections 15 through 24 and no doubt additional internal rules. Miss. Const. art. 3, § 4 (1832); *see also* Miss. Const. art. 1, § 2 (1832), and Miss. Const. art. 3, § 15–24 (1832).

188. *See* "An act for the benefit of T. B. J. Hadley, and Samuel M. Puckett, his security," Senate Journal, pages 290–291, 298 (Feb. 13, 1839); Miss. Laws, ch. 129, pages 280–281 (1839). Again, these stories are told well and in full by Sandra Moncrief in "The Mississippi Married Women's Property Act of 1839," *Hancock County Historical Society,* http://www.hancockcountyhistoricalsociety .com/vignettes/the-mississippi-married-womens-property-act-of-1839.

189. Charles S. Sydnor has provided the familiar historical report that the Panic of 1837 was caused by "inflation of credit, speculation in land and slaves, multiplication of banks, overproduction of cotton, and unsound practices in public and private finance." Sydnor, *The*

Development of Southern Sectionalism, 1819–1848 at 262 (1948). For a more complete discussion of this period, see chapter 4 above.

190. At common law, women were excluded from jury service. *See, e.g., Simon v. State*, 633 So.2d 407, 415 (Miss. 1993) (Banks J., dissenting, citing Blackstone's *Commentaries on the Laws of England*).

191. *See, e.g.,* Elizabeth Gaspar Brown, *Husband and Wife—Memorandum of the Mississippi Woman's Law of 1839,* 42 Michigan L. Rev. 1110 (1944); Judith T. Younger, *Marital Regimes: A Story of Compromise and Demoralization, Together w/Criticism and Suggestions for Reform,* 67 Cornell L. Rev. 45–102 (1981); Sandra Moncrief, "The Mississippi Married Women's Property Act of 1839," *Journal of Mississippi History* 47 (1985), 110–125; Megan Benson, "Fisher v. Allen: The Southern Origins of the Married Women's Property Acts," *Journal of Southern Legal History* (1997–1998), 97–122; Robert Gilmer, *Chickasaws, Tribal Laws, and the Mississippi Married Women's Property Act of 1839* (History 452, Dr. Tracy Rizzo, 11/21/03); Amanda K. Sims, *Patriarchy and Property: The Nineteenth-Century Mississippi Married Women's Property Acts,* Brigham Young University Scholars Archive (2007), Paper 1433.

192. Boyd resigned his position in the Federal Land Office on Sept. 30, 1837. *See U.S. v. Boyd,* 40 U.S. 187, 192 (1841). He was elected to the Mississippi Senate in the fall of 1837 and formally entered that office in the first week of January 1838. It does not appear that Boyd ever simultaneously held federal and state offices. See Miss. Const. art. 7, §13 (1832).

193. *St. Johnsbury Caledonian* (St. Johnsbury, Vt.), Tues., Jan. 28, 1840, page 2, Newspapers. com, https://www.newspapers.com/image/76503922.

194. "Outrageous," *Tennessean* (Nashville, Tenn.), Mon., Jan. 13, 1840, page 2, Newspapers. com, https://www.newspapers.com/image/118794349.

195. "Contradiction," *Public Ledger* (Philadelphia, Penna.), Tues., Feb. 4, 1840, page 2, Newspapers.com, https://www.newspapers.com/image/40140526. To like effect is "Wrong" in *the Baltimore Sun* (Baltimore, Md.) Weds., Jan. 15, 1840, page 2, Newspapers.com, https://www .newspapers.com/image/35022676.

196. Gordon Boyd was elected in 1841 to serve a term in the house of representatives.

197. U.S. Statutes at Large 333 (1830).

198. *See Papasan v. Allain,* 478 U.S. 265 (1986), decided by the US Supreme Court, for a more modern chapter in the story of the Chickasaw Cession.

199. Act of April 24, 1820, 3 U.S. Statutes at Large 566 (1820).

200. In today's US dollars, the judgment would have been in an amount approximating $1,206,000. *See* http://www/westegg.com/inflation/.

201. "Locofocos," http://en.wikipedia.org/wiki/Locofocos. The Loco Focos were a wing of the Democratic Party that existed from the middle 1830s until the late 1840s.

202. *Star and Banner* (Gettysburg, Pa.), Tues. Oct. 23, 1838, page 3, Newspapers.com, https:// www.newspapers.com/image/36676181.

203. *See, e.g., The Spirit of Kosciusko,* July 7, 1838.

204. *See* Charles S. Sydnor, *The Development of Southern Sectionalism, 1819–1848* 260–264 (1948). See chapter 4 above for a more complete telling of the tale of one of Mississippi's most unfortunate constitutional experiences.

205. See, particularly, *United States v. Gordon D. Boyd,* 40 U.S. 187 (1841), and *United States v. Gordon D. Boyd,* 46 U.S. 29 (1847).

206. On April 1, 1841, Gordon D. Boyd married Rebecca Frances Williams. Betty Couch Wiltshire, *Marriages and Deaths from Mississippi Newspapers,* Vol. 1, page 177 (1989).

207. Boyd's address was published in *Tri-Weekly Mississippian* (Jackson, Miss.), Sat., Feb. 16, 1839, five days after it was given.

208. Boyd was correct. Equity practice was being used to evade the common law disabilities of coverture. Cameron Fields has provided a useful survey of this practice in his article "Equity Law

Consequences upon the Mississippi Married Women's Property Act of 1839," *Journal of Mississippi History* 77 (2015), 69–85. Fields provides the flesh of then-recent historical vintage that supports and justifies the practical argument Boyd was making on the floor of the senate. But there was a fly in the ointment. One of the influential Maxims of Equity, by which the Chancery Court of Mississippi was bound, was "Equity follows the law." This is the same court whose existence dates back to the early 1820s and Joshua Giles Clarke's service as the state's first chancellor, set forth more fully in chapter 2 above. Fields acknowledges the problem he has noted and adds that the maxim means "that if the common law explicitly offered a solution to a case, the equity court must follow that solution" (*Journal of Mississippi History* 77 (2015), 74. As explained below, the verdict of history is that legislation and ultimately a constitutional amendment were the needed and effective antidote for the stubborn common law disability under which married women suffered.

209. *Tri-Weekly Mississippian* (Jackson, Miss.), Sat., Feb. 16, 1839.

210. *Tri-Weekly Mississippian* (Jackson, Miss.), Sat., Feb. 16, 1839.

211. Senate Journal, page 325 (Feb. 15, 1839).

212. Senate Journal, page 351, 356 (Feb. 15, 16, 1839); Miss. Laws, ch. 46, pages 72–73 (1839). *See* Elizabeth Gaspar Brown, *Husband and Wife—Memorandum of the Mississippi Woman's Law of 1839*, 42 Michigan L. Rev. 1110, 1116 (1944).

213. "Thomas Hadley," *Glenwood Cemetery*, Glenwoodcemetery.org/search? /name=Thomas&lastname=Hadley&date_from=&date_to=

214. *Tri-Weekly Mississippian* (Jackson, Miss.), Sat., Feb. 16, 1839.

215. *Powell v. Brandon*, 2 Cushm. (24 Miss.) 343 (1852).

216. *Hemingway v. Scales*, 42 Miss. 1, 18, 1868 WL 2219 (1868).

217. *Hollman v. Bennett*, 44 Miss. 322, 326, 1870 WL 2892 (1870).

218. Antonin Scalia and Bryan Garner, *Reading Law* 318 (2012).

219. In any event, back in 1978, Justice Robert Sugg devastated this derogation myth in Mississippi, *McCluskey v. Thompson*, 363 So. 2d 256, 262–64 (Miss. 1978), after which one would have thought a judge there would be embarrassed to let on that he takes it seriously, at least not in public. Otherwise sensible judges still cite the canon. *See, e.g., Howard v. Estate of Harper ex rel. Harper*, 947 So. 2d 854, 859 (Miss. 2006*); Warren ex rel. Warren v. Glascoe*, 880 So. 2d 1034, 1037 (Miss. 2004). Even the late justice Antonin Scalia and his colleague Prof. Bryan A. Garner supported a milder version of the canon in their useful resource *Reading Law*, at 318–319.

220. *Ratcliffe v. Dougherty*, 2 Cushm. (24 Miss.) 181, 184 (1852). Later, reading the 1839 and 1846 acts together, the court explained that "[t]hey enlarge their [married women's] capacity to acquire and hold property, real and personal, and are to be regarded strictly in the character of enabling statutes." *Lee v. Bennett*, 2 George (31 Miss.) 119, 125 (1856).

221. Miss. Laws, ch. 46, § 4 (1839).

222. *Beatty v. Smith*, 2 Smedes & M. (10 Miss.) 567, 570, 1844 WL 2058 (1844). There was a point of equity jurisdiction in the case that is not relevant to the present discussion.

223. *Davis v. Foy*, 7 Smedes & M. (15 Miss.) 64, 67, 1846 WL 1670 (1846). A decade later, the court said that "the rule has been uniform, that, under the Act of 1839, the '*property*' in the slaves, is severed from the right to the '*proceeds*' of their labor; that the possession of the slaves is *joint* in the husband and wife; and that such 'property,' or possession of the wife in her slaves, cannot be taken from her, for the debts, contracts, or liabilities of the husband." *Smith v. Williams*, 7 George (36 Miss.) 545, 547–548 (1858) (italics in original).

224. In addition to *Beatty* and *Davis*, decisions of the High Court of Errors and Appeals that were likely available to the legislature at its 1846 session include *Moore v. McKie*, 5 Smedes & M. (13 Miss.) 238, 1845 WL 3159 (1845); *McGee v. Ford*, 5 Smedes & M. (13 Miss.) 769, 1846 WL 1621 (1846); *Frost & Co. v. Doyle*, 7 Smedes & M. (15 Miss.) 68, 1846 WL 1671 (1846); and *Berry v. Bland*, 7 Smedes & M. (15 Miss.) 77, 1846 WL 1672 (1846).

225. Miss. Laws, ch. 13, § 2 (1846).

226. Miss. Laws, ch. 13, §§ 3, 4 (1846).

227. Miss. Laws, ch. 13, §§ 4, 6 (1846).

228. Revised Code Mississippi Statutes, Section V, arts. 23–32 (1857).

229. Miss. Const. art.1, § 16 (1869).

230. *Staton v. New*, 49 Miss. 307, 309 (1873).

231. *Staton v. New*, 49 Miss. 307, 310 (1873).

232. Miss. Code, ch. 42, §§ 1167–1169; ch. 44, §1193 (1880). *See, e.g., Brantley v. Wolf*, 60 Miss. 420, 433 (1882) ("since by the adoption of the Code of 1880, all the disabilities of coverture have been swept away"); *Southworth v. Brownlow*, 84 Miss. 405, 36 So. 522 (1904) ("Since the 1st of November, 1880, when the Revised Code of 1880, went into effect, abolishing coverture with all its incidents and disabilities."); *Skehan v. Davidson Co.*, 164 Miss. 518, 145 So. 247, 248 (1933) ("since the Code of 1880, a married woman is fully emancipated from the disability of coverture.").

233. *See, e.g., Austin v. Austin*, 136 Miss. 61, 100 So. 591 (1924); *Tobias v. Tobias*, 225 Miss. 392, 83 So.2d 638 (1955).

234. *Burns v. Burns*, 518 So. 2d 1205 (Miss. 1988).

235. *See, e.g.,* "How to Make a Speculation," *Lynchburg Virginian*, and *Weekly Raleigh Register* (Raleigh, N.C.), Sat., May 18, 1839, page 2, Newspapers.com, https://www.newspapers.com /image/56879272; "The notorious Gordon D. Boyd. . . ," *Alton Telegraph* (Alton, Ill.) Sat., Feb. 19, 1842, page 3, Newspapers.com, https://www.newspapers.com/image/2496193.

236. "Richly Paid," *Carolina Watchman* (Salisbury, N.C.), Fri., Oct. 23, 1840), page 3, Newspapers.com, https://www.newspapers.com/image/59028588.

237. House Journal, page 97, 139 (1837).

238. "Death of Gordon D. Boyd," *Madisonian* (Canton, Miss.), Apr. 25, 1850.

239. "Indebted to the People," *Athens Post* (Athens, Tenn.), Fri., Dec. 17, 1852, page 1, Newspapers.com, https://www.newspapers.com/image/72149401.

240. William Shakespeare, *Julius Caesar*, act 3, scene 2, lines 80–81.

241. Last Will and Testament of Gordon D. Boyd, admitted to probate in Attala County, Mississippi, "in open court the 1st Monday of July 1850. /s/ E. M. Wells Judge Probate." *See* Attala County Will Book A-190. In 2016, James Boyd, an eighty-one-year-old descendant of Gordon's brother, A. P. Boyd, was still operating Boyd's Drug Store in downtown Kosciusko, Mississippi.

242. Last Will and Testament of Gordon D. Boyd, admitted to probate in Attala County, Mississippi, "in open court the 1st Monday of July 1850. /s/ E. M. Wells Judge Probate." *See* Attala County Will Book A-190.

243. The home that the Boyds built now fronts 823 North Jefferson Street and is the Oaks House Museum, title to which was held exclusively by Eliza Boyd and subsequently by her daughter, Mary Boyd McGaill and her children. *See* www.theoakshousemuseum.org. A block south, then to the right/west, on to the corner of George Street and North Street lies a large office building, which in 2016 was state headquarters for the Mississippi Department of Environmental Quality. Hadley's boardinghouse stood on that land in 1838 and 1839.

244. Deed to Lot 7 North, dated June 1, 1853, Deed Book 22, page 395, land records of Hinds County, Mississippi, in the office of the chancery clerk in Raymond, Mississippi.

245. Sandra Moncrief, "The Mississippi Married Women's Property Act of 1839," *Hancock County Historical Society*, http://www.hancockcountyhistoricalsociety.com/vignettes/the -mississippi-married-womens-property-act-of-1839.

246. See chapter 4 above.

247. Over the years, a handful of great works have been produced by perceptive scholars that address these questions. Some would say these begin and end with Holmes's *The Common*

Law (1881). They also range from Dean Roscoe Pound's *The Spirit of the Common Law* (1921) to Prof. Karl N. Llewellyn's *The Common Law Tradition: Deciding Appeals* (1960). A particularly thoughtful discussion—from historical and conceptual perspectives—may be found in Herbert Pope, *The English Common Law in the United States*, 24 Harv. L. Rev. 6–30 (1910). More locally, Justice Virgil A. Griffith's early chapter on the common law in his *Outlines of the Law: A Comprehensive Summary of the Major Subjects in American Law* [Mississippi Edition], at pages 4–9 (1940) merits reading and reflection.

248. "Edward Coke," https://en.wikipedia.org/wiki/Edward_Coke. *See also* "Institutes of the Lawes of England," https://en.wikipedia.org/wiki/Institutes_of_the_Lawes_of_England.

249. "Matthew Hale," https://en/wikipedia/org/wiki/Matthew_Hale_(jurist).

250. For a thoughtful summary exposition regarding the writing and approaches of these three great historical figures in Anglo-American law, see Mississippi native Evelyn Keyes's "The Common Law Tradition," in her *Hedgehogs and Foxes: The Case for the Common Law Judge*, 67 Hastings Law Journal 749, 760–769 (2016).

251. *Winn v. Cole's Heirs*, Walker (1 Miss.) 119, 124, 1822 WL 407 (1822).

252. *State v. Moor*, Walker (1 Miss.) 134, 135–136, 1823 WL 542 (1823).

253. *Kerr, Adm'r. v. Baker, Adm'r*, Walker (1 Miss.) 140, 141–142, 1823 WL 1097 (1823).

254. *State v. Johnson*, Walker (1 Miss.) 392, 394, 397, 1831 WL 542 (1831).

255. *Shaffer v. State*, 1 Howard (2 Miss.) 238, 242, 245, 1835 WL 1010 (1835).

256. *Porter's Heirs v. Porter*, 7 Howard (8 Miss.) 106, 108, 109, 112, 1843 WL 2001 (1843).

257. *Morgan v. Reading*, 3 Smedes & M. (11 Miss.) 366, 400–402, 1844 WL 3217 (1844).

258. *Commissioners of Homochitto River v. Withers*, 7 Cushm. (29 Miss.) 21, 34, 1855 WL 107 (1855).

259. *Yazoo & M. V. R. Co. v. G. W. Bent & Co.*, 94 Miss. 681, 47 So. 805, 809 (1908).

260. *Sinclair v. State*, 161 Miss. 142, 132 So. 581, 583–584 (1931).

261. *McLarty v. State*, 842 So.2d 590, 595 (¶21) (Miss. Ct. App. 2003) (citing Matthew Hale, *History of the Pleas of the Crown, Vol. 2*, 299 (1st Am. ed. 1847) (1671)).

262. *Dycus v. State*, 875 So.2d 140, 153 (¶34) (Miss. 2004).

263. William Blackstone, *Commentaries on the Laws of England*, 9th ed., book 2, page 363 (1783, reprinted 1978).

264. *Carpenter v. State*, 4 Howard (5 Miss.) 163, 166, 1839 WL 1414 (1839).

265. *Carpenter v. State*, 4 Howard (5 Miss.) 163, 166–167, 1839 WL 1414 (1839).

266. Very flimsy circumstantial evidence suggested that Mercer Byrd may have been an accessory to the murder of a prominent and wealthy planter, Joel Cameron. While not necessary to the present discussion, the story behind the prosecutions arising from Cameron's murder is further testament to the tenor of the times in the 1830s and 1840s in pre–Civil War Vicksburg and Warren County. The story gets interesting when it is borne in mind that Joel Cameron was the business and law partner of Alexander Gallatin McNutt, who served as governor between 1838 and 1842, and whose character is arguably in play. Adversary counsel (and future US senator [1847–1852]) and Mississippi governor (1852–1854) Henry S. Foote charged that McNutt was behind the murder of his partner, in order to gain control of Cameron's wealth. That charge is hotly disputed. No one questions that McNutt married Cameron's widow fairly shortly after the homicide. See chapter 4 above, where A. G. McNutt was a prominent player. For arguable details, see two articles by Stanley Nelson, editor of the *Concordia Sentinel*, published in Ferriday, Louisiana, viz., "The Murder of Joel Cameron," June 1, 2016, http://www.hannapub.com/concordiasentinel/the-murder-of-joel-cameron/article_ed5670c2-2823-11e6-ab9b-f3bc9563bb0.html; and "The Execution of Mercer Byrd," June 8, 2016, http://www.hannapub.com/concordiasentinel/the-execution-of-mercer-byrd/article_cfe94ecc-2d98-11e6-9955-ef064402df9e.html.

267. *Byrd v. State*, 1 Howard (2 Miss.) 163, 177, 1834 WL 1172 (1834), citing "4 Blackstone 302," and "Littleton, s. 464," which all lawyers of the times knew meant "Coke Upon Littleton."

268. *Jones v. State*, Walker (1 Miss.) 83, 85, 1820 WL 1413 (1821).

269. *Robinson v. Payne*, 58 Miss. 690, 708, 709, 1881 WL 4518 (1881).

270. *Mississippi Cent. R. Co. v. Ratcliff*, 214 Miss. 674, 59 So.2d 311, 314 (1953).

271. *Harvey v. State*, 207 So.2d 108, 111 (Miss. 1968).

272. *Coulter & Richards, Executors v. William Robertson, Trustee*, 2 Cushm. (24 Miss.) 278, 278, 321, 1852 WL 14 (1852).

273. *Yazoo & M. V. R. Co. v. Scott*, 106 Miss. 871, 67 So. 491, 492 (1915).

274. *See Dr. Bonham's Case*, 8 Co. 114a, 118a, 77 Eng. Rep. 646, 652 (1610), cited in *McGowan v. Mississippi State Oil & Gas Bd.*, 604 So. 2d 312, 315 (Miss. 1992).

275. *Griffin v. Mixon*, 9 George (38 Miss.) 424, 434 (1860).

276. *See McCluskey v. Thompson*, 363 So. 2d 256, 262–264 (Miss. 1978). Unfortunate statements to the contrary appear in *McBroom v. Jackson County* 154 So. 3d 827, 838 (¶30) (Miss. 2014); and *Reno v. Reno* 119 So. 3d 1154, 1156 (¶10) (Miss. Ct. App. 2013).

277. "James Kent," en.wikipedia.org/wiki/James_Kent.

278. *Yazoo & M. V. R. Co. v. Scott*, 106 Miss. 871, 67 So. 491, 492 (1915), quoting Kent's *Commentaries on American Law*, Vol. 1, 471 (1826–1830) (emphasis added in *Y. & M. V.* opinion).

279. *Yazoo & M. V. R. Co. v. Scott*, 106 Miss. 871, 67 So. 491, 492 (1915), quoting *Kansas v. Colorado*, 206 U.S. 46, 96–97 (1907) (emphasis added in *Y. & M. V.* opinion).

280. *Yazoo & M. V. R. Co. v. Scott*, 106 Miss. 871, 67 So. 491, 492 (1915), quoting *Murray v. C. & N. W. Ry. Co.*, 92 Fed. 868, 870 (8th Cir. 1899) (emphasis added in *Y. & M. V.* opinion). *Western Union Tel. Co. v. Allen*, 66 Miss. 549, 6 So. 461, 463 (1889) is another case where the court carefully explains that and why "the courts then, as the courts now, conscious of the needs of the public, expanded the principles of the law, [and] fitted them to the exigencies of the occasion . . . required for the safety and protection of the public." *Shingleur v. Western Union Tel. Co.*, 72 Miss. 1030, 18 So. 425, 427 (1895). After giving several examples, the *Western Union* court concluded that "[i]nstances might be multiplied in which courts pressed by the public necessities, and in the absence of legislative remedy, have afforded relief." *Western Union Tel. Co. v. Allen*, 66 Miss. 549, 6 So. 461, 463 (1899) *See* the discussion of the *Western Union* cases in *Y. & M.V.*, 67 So. at 493.

281. *Yazoo & M. V. R. Co. v. Scott*, 106 Miss. 871, 67 So. 491, 492 (1915). This would not be the last time Chief Justice Smith anchored a decision in the wisdom of Roscoe Pound. *See* Sydney McCain Smith, *The State and the Social Process*, 9 Miss. L. Journ. 147 (December 1936), relied on *sub silentio* in *Albritton v. City of Winona*, 181 Miss. 75, 178 So. 799 (1938), discussed in chapter 10 below.

282. Oliver Wendell Holmes, *The Essential Holmes*, Introduction, page x (Richard A. Posner ed., 1992).

283. *Mitchell v. State*, 179 Miss. 814, 176 So. 743, 745 (1937).

284. *See, e.g., Burns v. Burns*, 518 So. 2d 1205 (Miss. 1988) (abolishing common law interspousal tort immunity); *Pruett v. City of Rosedale*, 421 So.2d 1046 (Miss. 1982); *Presley v. Mississippi State Highway Commission*, 608 So.2d 1288 (Miss. 1992) (abolishing common law sovereign immunity to tort actions, though subsequently supplanted by Mississippi Tort Claims Act).

285. *Saunders v. Alford*, 607 So.2d 1214, 1219 (Miss. 1992). *See also Bradley v. State*, Walker 156, 157, 1 Miss. 156, 157, 1 Morr. St. Cas. 13, 1824 WL 631 (1824), discussed above.

286. Evelyn Keyes, *Hedgehogs and Foxes: The Case for the Common Law Judge*, 67 Hastings Law Journal 749, 779 (2016). Mississippi-born Justice Keyes's thoughtful work is worth a reflective reading, though she is a bit too judgmental regarding the work of judges who are doing

their best to read and apply the law faithfully and fairly, without fear or favor, only at times they see novel facts and nuances more readily than others.

287. *Ellis v. Doe*, 11 Smedes & M. (19 Miss.) 422, 431, 1848 WL 3132 (1848).

288. Oliver Wendell Holmes, *The Common Law* 35 (1881). This Holmes passage, give or take a few lines above or below, enjoys biblical authority. Richard A. Posner, *Divergent Paths: The Academy and the Judiciary* 41 n. 3 (2016).

289. *Noonan v. State*, 1 Smedes & M. (9 Miss.) 562, 573, 1844 WL 2016 (1844).

290. Oliver Wendell Holmes, *The Common Law* 1 (1881).

291. *Southern Pacific Co. v. Jensen*, 244 U.S. 205, 222 (1917) (Holmes, J., dissenting). Holmes was taken with the phrases he had turned here and was repeating those to his correspondents for years to come. *See, e.g., Holmes-Pollock Letters: The Correspondence of Mr. Justice Holmes and Sir Frederick Pollock, 1874–1932, Vol.* 2, page 215 (Mark de Wolfe Howe ed., 1942); *Holmes-Laski Letters: The Correspondence of Mr. Justice Holmes and Harold J. Laski, 1916–1935*, at pages 822 (Jan. 29, 1926) and 896 (Nov. 23, 1926) (Mark de Wolfe Howe ed., 1953).

292. *Vicksburg and Jackson Railroad Co. v. Patton*, 2 George (31 Miss.) 156, 185, 1856 WL 2591 (1856).

293. *Jones v. State*, Walker (1 Miss.) 83, 85–86, 1820 WL 1413 (1821).

294. *Gross v. State*, 135 Miss. 624, 100 So. 177, 178 (1924).

295. *Yazoo & M. V. R. Co. v. Scott*, 108 Miss. 871, 67 So. 491, 492 (1915), quoting *Murray v. C. & N. W. Ry. Co.*, 92 Fed. 868, 870 (8th Cir. 1899).

296. *Halcyon Lines v. Haenn Ship Ceiling & Refitting Corp.*, 342 U.S. 252 (1952) considered the question whether under the general maritime law there was a right of contribution between and among joint tortfeasors in a non-collision context. The court decided not to decide the question, for that would be making law. For decades, *Halcyon Lines* was cited for the proposition that there was no such right of contribution. By refusing to make law, the US Supreme Court unwittingly made law, and very bad law at that. This case and problem were highlighted to generations of law students by Profs. Henry M. Hart Jr. and Albert M. Sacks in Problem No. 18, "The Paradox of Making Law by Refusing to Make Law: The Halcyon Case," in their materials. *The Legal Process: Basic Problems in the Making and Application of Law* 515–541 (Tentative ed., 1958).

297. William Faulkner, *Requiem for a Nun* 35 (1950).

298. *Planters Oil Mill v. Yazoo & M. V. R. Co.*, 153 Miss. 712, 717, 121 So. 139, 140 (1929).

299. *Interstate Co. v. Garnett*, 154 Miss. 325, 347, 122 So. 373, 378 (1929).

300. *Burns v. Burns*, 518 So.2d 1205, 1298 (Miss. 1988).

301. *Presley v. Mississippi State Highway Commission*, 608 So.2d 1288, 196 (Miss. 1992).

302. *Clark v. Luvel Dairy Products, Inc.*, 731 So.2d 1098, 1105 (¶20) (Miss. 1998).

303. In chapter 4, we saw Justice Handy's outrageous decision in *McIntyre v. Ingraham*, 6 George (35 Miss.) 25, 1858 WL 4580 (1858), where he thumbed his nose at the US Supreme Court. In 1866, Justice Handy outdid himself, holding unconstitutional federal legislation from the Reconstruction Congress that gave civil rights and other protections to the former slaves. The context was review of the conviction of a former slave for carrying a weapon. Handy found this state prohibition unaffected by the Thirteenth Amendment, and more particularly by the act of April 9, 1866, ch. 31, § 1, 14 Stat. 27, codified as amended as 42 U.S.C. § 1981. *See Ex Parte Lewis, Weekly Clarion* (Jackson, Miss.), Oct. 4, 1866, at 2 (1866) (not officially reported). When federal troops came looking for him, Handy resigned his office and fled back to his native Maryland.

304. Miss. Const. art. 6, § 155 (1890).

305. I have explained this process more fully in my *Variations on a Theme by Posner: Facing the Factual Component of the Reliability Imperative in the Process of Adjudication*, 84 Miss.

L. Journ. 471, 483–497 (2015), and elaborated thereafter, including in my *Practical Benefits of Literature in Law, and Their Limits*, 35 Miss. Coll. L. Rev. 266, 282 (2016).

306. In the words of Justice Benjamin Cardozo, "A judgment by the highest court of a state as to the meaning and effect of its own constitution is decisive and controlling everywhere." *Highland Farms Dairy v. Agnew*, 300 U.S. 608, 613 (1937). Justice Cardozo served on the Court of Appeals of New York, the highest court of that state, for eighteen years, five as its chief justice. He is widely regarded as one of the great common law judges of the twentieth century.

307. Miss. Const. art. 6 (1890) and comparable judicial power clauses in prior constitutions.

308. Miss. Const. art. 1 (1890) and comparable separation-of-powers clauses in prior constitutions.

309. *See Planters Oil Mill v. Yazoo & M. V. R. Co.*, 153 Miss. 712, 717, 121 So. 139, 140 (1929) down through *Presley v. Mississippi State Highway Commission*, 608 So.2d 1288, 196 (Miss. 1992) and *Clark v. Luvel Dairy Products, Inc.*, 731 So.2d 1098, 1105 (¶20) (Miss. 1998).

310. *Norway Plains Co. v. Boston & Maine Railroad*, 1 Gray (67 Mass.) 263 (Mass. Sup. Jud. Ct. 1854). Chief Justice Shaw (1781–1861) is widely regarded as one of the great American common law judges of the nineteenth century. As a point of interest, if not consequence, Shaw was the father-in-law of novelist Herman Melville. "Lemuel Shaw," en.wikipedia.org/wiki/Lemuel Shaw; "Lemuel Shaw," *Britannica*, britannica.org/biography/Lemuel-Shaw. *See particularly* Brook Thomas, "Legal Fictions of Herman Melville and Lemuel Shaw," *Critical Inquiry*, Vol. 11 (Sept. 1984), pages 24–51.

311. Oliver Wendell Holmes, *The Common Law* 106 (1881).

312. *Stone v. Yazoo & M. V. R. Co.*, 62 Miss. 607, 636 (1885). See particularly chapter 6 regarding the Mississippi Railroad Commission created in 1884 and litigation regarding its constitutionality.

313. *Stone v. Natchez, Jackson & Columbus R. Co.*, 62 Miss. 646, 653 (1885). Again, see particularly chapter 6 regarding the creation and function of the Mississippi Railroad Commission.

314. *Blackledge v. Omega Ins. Co.*, 740 So. 2d 295, 297–98 (Miss. 1999).

315. *Shrader v. Shrader*, 119 Miss. 526, 81 So. 227, 235 (1919) (Ethridge, J., dissenting).

316. *Parker v. Benoist*, 160 So.3d 198, 206 (¶¶9, 11, 15) (Miss. 2015).

317. *Yazoo & M. V. R. Co. v. Scott*, 106 Miss. 871, 67 So. 491, 492 (1915), quoting *Murray v. C. & N. W. Ry. Co.*, 92 Fed. 868, 870 (8th Cir. 1899).

318. *Parker v. Benoist*, 160 So.3d 198, 206–207 (¶17) (Miss. 2015).

319. The problematics of an independent subjective "good faith" legal standard are discussed more fully in my *Variations on a Theme by Posner: Facing the Factual Component of the Reliability Imperative in the Process of Adjudication*, 84 Miss. L. Journ. 471, 580–592 (2015).

320. Nothing said above speaks to the quality of the court's lawmaking effort in *Parker*. In point of fact, there is much good that may be said of *Parker*. Following well-reasoned lawmaking efforts from other jurisdictions has long been a credible approach to a state's deciding a question of first impression. Equal credibility comes with a court's adopting standards set forth by the highly respected American Law Institute in its Restatements of the Law. *Parker* appropriately cites and relies on *Restatement (Third) of Property: Wills and Donative Transfers* § 8.5 (2003). *See Parker*, 160 So.3d at 205, 206, 209 (¶¶ 12, 15, 24). And it is proper for a court to cite learned treatises and law review articles. Purported reliance of the vague, general, and open-ended clauses of Miss. Const. art. 3, § 24, however, is a bit much. This no more undermines the legal enforceability of the law made in *Parker* than exposure of the actual grounds for legislation undermines the enforceability of statutes enacted by the legislature and signed by the governor.

321. There have always been a handful of strict liability torts such as libel and nuisance.

322. *See, e.g., State Stove Mfg. Co. v. Hodges*, 189 So.2d 113 (Miss. 1966); *Ford Motor Co. v. Matthews*, 291 So.2d 169 (Miss. 1974).

323. *Sperry-New Holland v. Prestage*, 617 So.2d 248 (Miss. 1993).

324. *Yazoo & M. V. R. Co. v. Scott*, 106 Miss. 871, 67 So. 491, 492 (1915), quoting *Murray v. C. & N. W. Ry. Co.*, 92 Fed. 868, 870 (8th Cir. 1899) (emphasis added in *Y. & M. V.* opinion); *Gross v. State*, 135 Miss. 624, 100 So. 177, 179 (1924). *Western Union Tel. Co. v. Allen*, 66 Miss. 549, 6 So. 461, 463 (1889) is another case where the court carefully explains that and why "the courts then, as the courts now, conscious of the needs of the public, expanded the principles of the law, [and] fitted them to the exigencies of the occasion. . . . required for the safety and protection of the public." *Shingleur v. Western Union Tel. Co.*, 72 Miss. 1030, 18 So. 425, 427 (1895). After giving several examples, the *Western Union* court concluded that "instances might be multiplied in which courts pressed by the public necessities, and in the absence of legislative remedy, have afforded relief." *Shingleur v. Western Union Tel. Co.*, 72 Miss. 1030, 18 So. 463 (1895). *See* the discussion of the *Western Union* cases in *Y. & M.V.*, 67 So. at 493.

325. Mississippi Tort Reform Act of 2004, H.B. 13, 2004 Miss. Laws 1st Ex. Sess., http://billstatus.ls.state.ms.us/20041e/pdf/history/HB/HB0013.htm; H.B. 2, 2002 Miss. Laws 3d Ex. Sess., http://billstatus.ls.state.ms.us/20023E/pdf/history/HB/HB0002.htm.; Mississippi Tort Claims Act, Miss. Code Ann. §§ 11-46-7, et seq.

326. Miss. Code Ann. § 11-7-15.

327. *See, e.g.*, the brief monograph by Anne Brunon-Ernst, *Bentham, Common Law and Codification*, Université Panthéon-Assas Paris 2 (January 2014), https://www.researchgate.net/publication/263007800.

328. Most prominent is the Mississippi Uniform Commercial Code, Miss. Code Ann. §§ 75-1-101, et seq. (co-sponsored by NCCUSL and the American Law Institute). *See, e.g.*, Mississippi Uniform Trade Secrets Act, Miss. Code Ann. §§ 75-26-1, et seq.; Mississippi Uniform Prudent Investor Act, Miss. Code Ann. §§ 91-9-601, et seq.; Mississippi Uniform Transfers to Minors Act, Miss. Code Ann. §§ 91-20-1, et seq.; and many more. Other invaluable model laws that have been enacted include the Mississippi Business Corporation Act, Miss. Code Ann. §§ 79-4-1.01, et seq., largely patterned after the American Bar Association's Model Business Corporation Act.

329. *See, e.g.*, *In re Estate of Anderson*, 541 So. 2d 423, 430 (Miss. 1989) (empowering courts to imply a savings clause where devise would violate rule against perpetuities).

330. Miss. Code Ann. §§ 89-25-1, -3(1)(b), -(2)(b), and -(3)(b), et seq.

331. That statutes are construed and applied by the same judicial techniques as common law rules, and all other rules satisfying the criteria for legal validity (CLV) is explained fully in James L. Robertson and David W. Clark, "An Interpretive Stratagem," in *The Law of Business Torts in Mississippi*, 15 Miss. Coll. L. Rev. 13, 24–57 (1994).

332. Miss. Const. art. 3, §§ 5–8 (1890).

333. *Parker v. Benoist*, 160 So.3d 198 (Miss. 2015).

334. *Restatement (Third) of Property: Wills and Donative Transfers* § 8.5 (2003). *See Parker*, 160 So.3d at 205, 206, 209 (¶¶ 12, 15, 24).

335. For a partial listing made in 1994, *see* Robertson & Clark, *The Law of Business Torts in Mississippi*, 15 Miss. Coll. L. Rev. 13, 21 n. 41 (1994).

336. *The Common Law* 45 (1881).

337. Holmes, *The Path of the Law*, 10 Harv. L. Rev. 470 (1897).

338. Letter from O. W. Holmes to Franklin Ford (Feb. 8, 1908), in *The Essential Holmes*, 201, n. 31 (Richard A. Posner ed., 1992).

339. See sources cited in my *Variations on a Theme by Posner: Facing the Factual Component of the Reliability Imperative in the Process of Adjudication*, 84 Miss. L. Journ. 471, 509–516, 539–564 (2015) and attendant discussion, and citations to supporting empirical evidence and patterns of research ongoing.

340. William Blackstone, *Commentaries on the Laws of England*, book 4, chapter 27, page 358 (1783, 9th ed. reprinted 1978); see also "Blackstone's Formulation," https://en.wikipedia.og/wiki

/Blackstone%27s_formulation. This sage truism is cited and quoted by the Supreme Court of the United States in *Coffin v. United States*, 156 U.S. 432, 456 (1895).

341. Benjamin Franklin, Letter to Benjamin Vaughan, March 14, 1785, *The Writings of Benjamin Franklin*, Vol. 9, page 293 (Albert H. Smyth, ed. 1906).

342. J. F. H. Claiborne, *Mississippi, as a Province, Territory, and State* 482 (1880, reprinted by Louisiana State University Press 1964).

343. See Genesis 18:23–32 (King James Version).

344. Holmes, "Law and the Court," Speech to the Harvard Law School Association of New York, February 15, 1913, in *The Essential Holmes*, at 147 (Richard A. Posner ed., 1992).

BIBLIOGRAPHY

Benson, Megan, "*Fisher v. Allen*: The Southern Origins of the Married Women's Property Acts," *Journal of Southern Legal History* 97–122 (1997–1998).

Blackstone, William, *Commentaries on the Laws of England* (9th ed., 1783, reprinted 1978)

Brown, Elizabeth Gaspar, *Husband and Wife—Memorandum of the Mississippi Woman's Law of 1839*, 42 Michigan L. Rev. 1110 (1944)

Brunon-Ernst, Anne, *Bentham, Common Law and Codification*, Université Panthéon-Assas Paris (Jan. 2014), https://www.researchgate.net/publication/263007800.

Cash, W. J., *The Mind of the South* (1941, 1991).

Claiborne, J. F. H., *Mississippi, as a Province, Territory, and State* (1880, reproduced by Louisiana State University Press, 1964).

Crowson, George M., "History of Alabama and Vicksburg R. R.," *Newton County Historical & Genealogical Society*, http://www.nchgs.org/html/history_of_a-v_r-r.html.

Davis, Jefferson, *The Papers of Jefferson Davis, June 1841–July 1846*, Vol. 2 (James T. McIntosh ed., 1974).

Faulkner, William, *Requiem for a Nun* (1950).

Fields, Cameron L., "Equity Law Consequences upon the Mississippi Married Women's Property Act of 1839," 77 *Journal of Mississippi History* 69–85 (2015).

Foote, Shelby, *The Civil War: A Narrative, Vol. 2, Fredericksburg to Meridian* (1963).

Fuller, Lon L., *The Morality of Law* (1964).

Gilmer, Robert, *Chickasaws, Tribal Laws, and the Mississippi Married Women's Property Act of 1839* (History 452, Dr. Tracy Rizzo, 11/21/03).

Griffith, Virgil A., "The Common Law," *Outlines of the Law: A Comprehensive Summary of the Major Subjects in American Law [Mississippi Edition]* 4–9 (1940).

Hale, Lord Matthew, *De Jure Maris*.

Hale, Lord Matthew, *De Portibus Maris*.

Handy, Alexander H., An AHGP Transcription Project, http://msmadison.genealogyvillage.com/Biography/Handy/AlexanderH.html.

Hart, Henry M., Jr., and Albert M. Sacks, *The Legal Process: Basic Problems in the Making and Application of Law* (Tentative ed., 1958).

Hoffheimer, Michael H., *Mississippi Courts: 1790–1868*, 65 Miss. L. Journ. 99 (Fall 1995).

Holmes, Oliver Wendell, *The Common Law* (1881).

Holmes, Oliver Wendell, *The Essential Holmes* (Richard A. Posner ed., 1991).

Holmes, Oliver Wendell, *The Path of the Law*, 10 Harv. L. Rev. 457 (1897).

Holmes, Oliver Wendell, *Holmes-Pollock Letters: The Correspondence of Mr. Justice Holmes and Sir Frederick Pollock, 1874–1932* (Mark de Wolfe Howe ed., 1942).

Holmes, Oliver Wendell, *Holmes-Laski Letters: The Correspondence of Mr. Justice Holmes and Harold J. Laski, 1916–1935* (Mark de Wolfe Howe ed., 1953).

Howe, LeAnne, "Betsy Love and the Married Women's Property Act of 1839," *Mississippi History Now* (Sept. 2005), http://www.mshistorynow.mdah.ms.gov/articles/6/betsy-love-and-the-married-womens-property-act-of-1839.

Keyes, Evelyn, *Hedgehogs and Foxes: The Case for the Common Law Judge*, 67 Hastings Law Journal 749 (2016).

Llewellyn, Karl N., *The Common Law Tradition: Deciding Appeals* (1960).

Magna Carta, cls. 39, 40 (Sir William Blackstone ed., 1215).

McCain, William D., *The Story of Jackson*, Vol. 1 (1953)

Moncrief, Sandra, "The Mississippi Married Women's Property Act of 1839," *Hancock County Historical Society*, http://www.hancockcountyhistoricalsociety.com/vignettes/the-mississippi-married-womens-property-act-of-1839.

Moynihan, Cornelius, *Introduction to the Law of Real Property* (West Group, 3d ed., 2002).

Pope, Herbert, *The English Common Law in the United States*, 24 Harv. L. Rev. 630 (1910)

Posner, Richard A., *Divergent Paths, The Academy and the Judiciary* (2016).

Posner, Richard A., ed., *The Essential Holmes* (1992).

Pound, Roscoe, *The Spirit of the Common Law* (1921).

Scalia, Antonin, and Garner, Bryan, *Reading Law* (2012)

Schmeller, Mark G., *Invisible Sovereigns: Imagining Public Opinion from the Revolution to Reconstruction* (2016).

Sheppard, Si, *The Partisan Press: A History of Media Bias in the United States* (2007).

Sims, Amanda K., *Patriarchy and Property: The Nineteenth-Century Mississippi Married Women's Property Acts*, Brigham Young University Scholars Archive (2007), Paper 1433

Smith, Sydney McCain. *The State and the Social Process*, 9 Miss. L. Journ. 147 (Dec. 1936).

Sydnor, Charles S., *The Development of Southern Sectionalism, 1819–1848* (1948).

Williams, Jack K., *Dueling in the Old South: Vignettes of Social History* (1980).

Younger, Judith T., *Marital Regimes: A Story of Compromise and Demoralization, Together w/ Criticism and Suggestions for Reform*, 67 Cornell L. Rev. 45–102 (1981).

CHAPTER 9

The Governor and
the "Gold Coast"

If when you say whiskey you mean the devil's brew,
the poison scourge, the bloody monster, that defiles
innocence, dethrones reason, destroys the home . . . ,
takes bread from the mouths of little children, . . . then
I am certainly against it. But, If when you say whiskey
you mean the oil of conversation, the philosophic
wine, the ale that is consumed when good fellows get
together, that puts a song in their hearts and laughter on
their lips, . . . , then I am certainly for it.

—NOAH S. "SOGGY" SWEAT. JR.[1] (1952)

It made news in Chicago, perhaps with a bit of exaggeration. But maybe not.
A lawman and the kingpin of a family prominent in vice, illegal liquor, and
gambling each emptied four or five bullets into the other. A "'WILD WEST' GUN
DUEL" the headline blared. The scene was the Shady Rest night club in "East
Jackson" or the "Gold Coast" or just "'cross the river," depending on who was
telling the story. All agree it happened on the Rankin County side of the once
quite navigable Pearl River, a little after midnight in late August 1946.

The Shady Rest was one of the more prominent of dozens of night spots
in the area, offering adult entertainment largely in small and outwardly undis-
tinguished or dilapidated buildings where men could, among other things,
purchase bonded whiskeys supplied by federally licensed vendors, though
Mississippi was legally "dry" and had been since 1908. The Jackson *Clarion-
Ledger* said, "The shooting occurred in the doorway off the crowded dance hall,
in the dining room."[2] The *Chicago Tribune* called it "a dance hall duel in the
notorious 'Gold Coast' district a mile from the Mississippi capitol" and said it
was "typical wild west style."[3]

There were no survivors in this one-on-one shootout. Rankin County constable Norris Overby, thirty-two years old, and vice lord Samuel Alvin Seaney,

forty-two, each died at the hands and gun of the other in the early minutes of Wednesday, August 28, 1946.

The practical point of beginning of the story that led to this twin killing was the repeal of Prohibition at the national level, in December 1933. The Congress quickly undid the federal Volstead Act, which had implemented the short-lived Eighteenth Amendment. The country had restored to the states the regulation of alcoholic beverages.[4] Until that time, the only choice available to thirsty Mississippians was corn liquor, moonshine whiskey, or white lightning—a choice greater in poetics than in substance. In short order, despite the State's decision to remain "dry," bonded liquid intoxicants became available in Mississippi, by and large brought in from accessible Louisiana venues such as Vidalia, Rayville, and Tallulah,[5] and not always so surreptitiously at all.

Sam Seaney was just turning thirty years of age when it all began. The story goes that Seaney was the second enterprising young man to sense a business opportunity near the intersection of the north/south US Highway 49 and the east/west US Highway 80—on the east side of the Pearl River.[6] This could become a prime location for a profitable approach to selling booze and providing related leisure activities such as dining, gambling, slot machines, music, dancing, good times, and sometimes more earthy endeavors. Seaney opened the Jeep, which in time "became wholesale liquor headquarters of the outlaw city,"[7] an area that has been taken into the southwest corner of what is now the still-growing city of Flowood, Mississippi.

But first a bit more background on the principals so intimately involved in what went down that fatal night in August of 1946.

SAM AND THE SEANEY CLAN

Sam was the fourth-oldest and the first son of ten children born to Alexander Alvin Seaney (1876–1953) and his wife, Minnie Ethel Highsmith (1879–1949), Illinois natives and longtime residents of East Jackson and western Rankin County. A. A. Seaney was a lumberman and mill operator first and later an entrepreneur in the East Jackson family businesses, living in the midst of them on Casey's Lane in what is now Flowood. The elder Seaneys' first three children, all daughters, died young. In 1918, Anna Belle, the third child, was shot to death on the back porch of the Seaney home by a jealous would-be suitor described in newspaper articles as an "Assyrian." The murder was cruel and gruesome and happened while the mother and daughter pleaded for her life as George Howie blasted her three times with a shotgun. This tragic story made headlines for years to come. Anna Belle was about sixteen years old when she was murdered. She was not the last Seaney to die violently, only the first.

Alexander Alvin and Minnie Ethel Seaney had three sons after Sam—Eugene, Joe, and Frank—and four more daughters—Ruby Dell, Mildred Nell, Doris, and Opal. Eugene was born about 1906, Joseph, 1910, and Frank, 1914. Sisters Ruby Dell, Nell, Doris, and Opal were born about 1908, 1913, 1916, and 1918, respectively.

During his early adulthood, Sam is believed to have worked in a Rankin County sawmill and creosote plant.[8] Sam married Zilpha C. Jones (whose younger brother, Woodrow, married Sam's sister, Nell Seaney). In 1930, Sam and Zilpha lived on US Highway 49 South, also known as 418 East Gulfport Road, East Jackson, in Rankin County, along with their daughter, Zell Frances, born in 1924. The 1939 Jackson City Directory listed Sam's business as the Jeep City Tourist Court. By 1940, the Seaney family had been joined by brother-in-law Robert C. Jones.

The Seaney family had more than a few run-ins with the law over their assorted lives and enterprises. A June 1931 news report stated, "The liquor traffic in Rankin County is not having a bed of roses at this time." The sheriff and several deputies announced the arrest of ten men and women for possession and sale of illegal liquor, including A. A. Seaney and his wife.[9] Five years later, Jackson city police won a chase down West Capitol Street early one Wednesday morning that netted "105 cases of taxed whiskey" and the arrest of a passenger "booked as A. A. Seaney of East Jackson and said to be the father of Sam Seaney, operator of an East Jackson 'soft drink' establishment." This led to a "bust it up" and "pouring out party" behind the Jackson police station, where officers and city employees destroyed nearly 2,500 bottles of said-to-have-been-illegal liquor. Sam's dad was charged with possession of outlawed whiskey and carrying concealed weapons.[10]

In 1937 alone, District Attorney—and future circuit judge and longtime state supreme court justice—Percy Mercer Lee filed at least seven complaints[11] charging one or more Seaneys with illegal-liquor offenses. These complaints demanded chancery-court-issued injunctions that in practical effect—and if enforced—could have shut the Seaneys down. Lee was proceeding under a statute that authorized the district attorney to go into chancery court and on proper proof obtain an order the effect of which supposedly was to "abate" a "common nuisance."[12]

That same year, Sam Seaney showed himself to be quite a hothead when it came to official proceedings against him.[13] At the conclusion of a chancery court hearing on two of the common nuisance cases, Seaney approached Charles M. Hupperich, a principal witness presented by the district attorney, and called Hupperich "a God dam lying son-of-a-bitch." He then turned to two other witnesses, Ernest Jackmore and Paul Stribling,[14] "and in a threatening and accusing manner stated, in effect, that what he had previously said to Hupperich applied equally to [them]." Later, Seaney withdrew his accusations and apologized to the witnesses and to the court. Judge A. B. Amis then announced that "the court accepts the apology and is of the opinion that no punishment should be imposed."[15]

In July of 1938, a National Guard officer procured a warrant to search the place of business of Alexander A. Seaney. The warrant pointed to "a building being very small, with windows close together and painted white," on the west side of Casey's Lane, about a mile north of US Highway 80 and only 200 yards northwest of son Eugene's residence. The guardsman making the search found "15 cases of whiskey and three cases of wine, 1 pistol and 3 rifles." He seized the guns and destroyed the wine and whiskey.[16]

In early 1939, Sam A. Seaney won a reversal and discharge after having been held in contempt of the Chancery Court of Rankin County.[17] The Supreme Court of Mississippi held that Seaney's place of business had been improperly padlocked.[18] The family was emboldened by this judicial success. On March 3, 1939, brother Eugene made an affidavit in federal court supporting the unsuccessful counterattack by two amusement equipment vendors who had supplied musical and less benign devices to Gold Coast proprietors who had been raided by the National Guard.[19] Eugene told the court that in his presence—at the intime fateful Shady Rest—"the Guard appeared . . . armed with pistols, rifles and axes and commenced to break up neon signs, tables chairs, counters and other articles." The Guard also destroyed a juke box that Eugene was "advised was worth about four hundred twenty-five dollars." The uniformed guardsmen proceeded to "turn over a gas stove in this building and break up furniture and pile on the lighter fluid, thus setting fire to the building" and "at the point of firearms forced your deponent to leave the building."[20]

Early in the summer of 1939, A. A. Seaney and Eugene Seaney were among those caught up in another National Guard raid of the Gold Coast.[21] An October 1939 survey of the color and costs of the Gold Coast noted that "Sam Seaney has paid whopping big fines."[22] The Seaneys had their run-ins with the state tax collector as well over taxes unpaid, late paid, short paid, and some taxes arguably not payable at all.[23]

CONSTABLE NORRIS OVERBY

The all-too-brief thirty-two-year life of Constable Norris Overby[24] could not have begun more differently. A news brief told of the then eighteen-year-old Overby transferring to the Brandon school, and having prior thereto "been attending the agricultural high school at Camden."[25] In the fall of 1933, Overby played on the Brandon football team. One of three players who had been injured early in the season, Overby was "back in form" for Brandon's mid-November

13–0 win over the Deaf School of Jackson.[26] Three months later, he became chairman of the program committee of the boys' Hi-Y Club.[27] A month later he was in a runoff election for most popular boy at Brandon High School.[28] Later that spring, Overby was a member of the school chorus in a regional school competition.[29] In the fall of 1934, he enrolled at the University of Mississippi, where he accepted a bid from the Pi Kappa Phi social fraternity.[30]

Back in Brandon after graduating from Ole Miss, Overby joined the "Thursday Nighters Club" for "young people who meet every Thursday night at the WPA Recreation Center" and was elected vice-president.[31] On Christmas Day 1938, Norris married Maureen Turner (1918–2009),[32] a Coahoma County girl and graduate of then Delta State Teachers College. The new Mrs. Overby became active in Brandon civic affairs, such as becoming recording secretary for the local Woman's Christian Service group.[33] A son, James Norris "Buddy" Overby Jr., came along on the Fourth of July 1941. Twin boys were born to the Overbys in early June of 1942,[34] Marvin Lane and Melvin Wayne. Sadly, Marvin Lane lived only six days. A little over three years later, a baby sister,[35] Lynne, joined the family. She had not yet celebrated her first birthday when her father died so violently, almost three years to the day from his election to a first term as second district constable for Rankin County.[36] Overby had been considering a run for sheriff in the 1947 county elections.

It is not reliably known why Overby, father of two small children, was hanging out in the Shady Rest Club as midnight approached on the evening of August 27, 1946. Or why he was both alone and armed. It should be noted that the day when constables had largely become process servers for the justice courts lay ahead. If Overby was there to enjoy the pleasures of the club, one would have thought he would have chosen more conventional hours. According to a latter-day investigator, "[o]ne of Constable Overby's brothers, Ruell Overby, believed the raid on another nightclub may have caused the shooting." Inevitably, the idea began to surface that, for whatever reason, Overby had become one of those officers of the law "on the take" and was there to suggest that Sam Seaney up his contribution, either in cash or free booze or both.[37] After all, the thirty-two-year-old Overby had a wife and two young children to support, rather a difficult job if one's resources were limited to the meager earnings legally available to a constable.

PEARL RIVER VENUES AND CELEBRITIES

Of course, there is much more to the story of the Pearl River than the Gold Coast era. In 1985, Sara Richardson penned a nice history of the river. Writing from the perspective of those who have lived and worked to the east of Jackson, and perhaps played as well, Richardson sets the tone with her opening line, "It would be difficult to name any one thing, natural or man-made, that has had a greater effect on Rankin County's development than the Pearl River."[38] Some have said it wasn't much of a river, but it flooded every spring and still does, often big-time. One such flood in February of 1939 sent waters "ominously near the backyards of South Jackson yesterday and threatened to drive more Rankin County residents from their homes along the now desolate Gold Coast."[39] The Pearl begins somewhere up in Neshoba County. Several hundred miles downstream, it provides the political boundary between Mississippi and Louisiana before it empties into the Gulf of Mexico.[40] Upstream where it separates Hinds and Rankin Counties, it has been called "A Mud Hollow Monte Carlo."[41]

Eudora Welty's fictitious William Wallace said, "There is nothing in the world as good as ... fish. The fish of the Pearl River."[42] But the river would never be the same after the legislature got through with it in the 1950s. "A team of wild horses could not have prevented the Barnett Reservoir coming into being" and damming up the Pearl River a little more than ten miles north and upstream from the Gold Coast area.[43] And so Richardson concludes insightfully as well, "Wide and slow-moving, the [no longer quite so] mighty Pearl makes its way to the Gulf of Mexico.... Sometimes it provides pleasure, sometimes pain and sorrow, often employment. It never does nothing."[44]

Rankin County was quite rural in the late 1930s, much more so than it has become three-quarters of a century later. Its capacity for local self-governance was meager at best, even had there been no extraordinary circumstances to deal with. Gold Coast goings-on tested officialdom of the county. It is a fair hypothesis that the sheer overwhelming number of joints and night spots was such that the county could barely cope, if at all. Perhaps illegal liquor and gambling and debauchery in this one small corner of the county were but the symptoms of an inability to cope. Supply-and-demand economics go a long way toward explaining the resilience of the Gold Coast.

There seem to have been times when a sort of peaceful coexistence prevailed between Brandon and Florence and towns farther to the east and south, on the one hand, and the Gold Coast on the other. The latter was Jackson's problem, or asset, depending on one's point of view. The area was, after all, known as East Jackson, not West Brandon or North Florence. To say that over the era there may have been close to fifty "places of business" packed into the Casey's Lane and Fannin Road corner of the county only partially sets the stage; the ambiance of the Gold Coast was as important as raw numbers.

People are still compiling lists of those that operated and were a source of such shady vibrance 'cross the river from Jackson during the decade that straddled the year 1940. Many have found the list of the venues invaded in National Guard raids as a good place to start.[45] The Blues Trail marker[46] on the east side of Crystal Lake is helpful but incomplete. One problem is that the venues were fluid; they came and they went. Others never had a formal name, much less neon lights out front that folk would remember. Any list should include Foy's Place,[47] Red Top,[48] Grace's Place, Dipsie Doodle, Oak Grove, Cedar Grove,[49] Brown Derby,"[50] Put & Take,[51] Gus Place,[52] White Horse Cellar,[53] Black and White Café, Grissett's Sandwich Shop,[54] Hotel Stamps Bros. (see below), Silver Moon,[55] New Colonial Club,[56] Gold Coast Café,[57] Casa Loma,[58] Bellew's Café,[59] DeLuxe Cleaners, Lone Star, the Maple Grove Club, Blue Peacock Club, Hood's (later known as Hoo's Place),[60] Eastside (or was it East Side?) Club and Club Royal, all said to have been operated by J. H. "Doc" Steed,[61] the Shady Rest noted above, The Jeep Tourist Club, and Bazooka, said to have been owned and operated by Sam Seaney,[62] The Oaks run by Ernest Rogers,[63] Owl's Nest,[64] The Spot, Bradley's Café or Bradley's Bat Shoppes, Woodland Club, East Jackson Club, Ace of Spades, The Buckhorn, Willie Stevens Night Club, Dunbar's Night Club, Hill Top Grocery, Rainbow Club, Carr's Place, the Green Lantern,[65] "and a place without a name at the site where the old 'Moon River' club formerly operated."[66]

The inventory of Gold Coast proprietors, nocturnally operating variety and otherwise, also included Pat Hudson, believed to have been the first to see "gold" in the area[67]; A. A., Sam, and the Seaney family; Guysell McPhail (1909–1966),[68] who became the lead raidee and defendant in the most important judicial contribution to the saga of the Gold Coast; N. E. Muse; Ed Garrett; Lee Graves; Joe Catchings and his Rocket Lounge, and also the Green Frog and the Wild Owl, which may or may not have been the enterprise called the Owl's Nest in the June 1937 lists compiled by the National Guard. A roll call of those taken into custody in a June 1939 "Raid-to-End-All Raids" comprises approximately twenty-five more, though some were mere employees, and a couple were customers.[69]

Doc Burnham is on several lists. After his 1939 arrest,[70] Marion Clifton "Doc" Burnham (1898–1996) moved to more tolerant environs in Cullen in northwest Louisiana. Residing in Cullen, "Doc Burnham fitted himself into the lively community," owned a drug store, and was mayor for a number of years.

Wayne Ray Queen (1909–1978) was one of the most attractive characters to make his mark on the Gold Coast. Early in life, Queen drew a term in prison for stealing a pair of mules. He earned parole but was soon in trouble again, when he turned up as a "bouncer" in a Gold Coast night club. Then Queen vanished. In time, he got his act together and resurfaced in Nashville, Tennessee, as a successful tree surgeon. Starting business with one helper, Queen's Tree Surgery had a hundred employees and was one of the largest such operations in Nashville when its proprietor died. In building his successful tree surgery service, Queen gained a reputation for giving hard-time job-seekers a chance by hiring them straight out of prison, boys straight out of reformatories and others whom most prospective employers would not give the time of day. Queen would tell each new worker, "Your past makes no difference. It's what you do from now that counts."[71] At the time of his death, Queen had been a longtime active member of the Hillsboro Church of Christ in Nashville.

In 1937, the Stamps brothers—Charlie, Clifton, and Bill, sons of a Baptist minister—opened the Stamps Brothers Hotel on Fannin Road. The hotel included a club and restaurant, catering to African American patrons from throughout the South. The hotel's large dancefloor and the Rankin Auditorium were attractive features not offered by other Gold Coast entrepreneurs. Another aspect of flourishing Gold Coast entertainment that at times created more controversy than not-so-free-flowing whiskey and gambling was its failure to observe then-prevalent racial separation mores.

Lists of entertainers who appeared on the Gold Coast in the years when it thrived are many and varied and may or may not have borne a similarity to names on respective birth certificates, and even less frequently correct spellings. Nationally prominent performers include Duke Ellington, Cab Calloway, Lena Horne, and Billie Holliday.[72] Lionel Hampton brought his famous band to the Gold Coast. Ella Fitzgerald, Ike and Tina Turner, and Holliday are said to have frequented the Gay Lady nightclub 'cross the River.[73] Later blues legends Elmore James, Sonny Boy Williamson, and a young B. B. King are said to have performed in clubs and joints. A Mississippi Blues Trail monument[74] lists "notable local artists" such as Sam Myers, King Mose, Cadillac George Harris, brothers Charles and Sammie Lee Smith, Jimmy King, Jesse Robinson, Charles Fairley, Willie Silas, Bernard "Bunny" Williams, brothers Kermit Jr., Bernard, and Sherrill Holly, brothers Curtis and J. T. Dykes, Milton Anderson, Booker Wolfe, Tommy Tate, Robert Broom, Joe Chapman, and Sam Baker Jr. These notables entertained and shared life at the Off-Beat Room at the Stamps Hotel, the Blue Flame, and the Travelers Home, with or without advance public notice.[75]

BLAME IT ON THE GOLD COAST

Part of the Gold Coast's notoriety derives from the way people blamed it for all kinds of bad things that happened, in order to try to get themselves out of trouble. In April of 1937, Charles Alonzo Tripp lost an eye in an accident and brought suit against a local bus company alleging that its driver had been negligent. The plaintiff's niece testified that on the evening in question, Tripp was brought to her uncle's home in a drunken condition saying he hurt his eye in a fall on some rocks "across the river" in an area "known as the 'Gold Coast.'"[76] Years later, Sherman Street stood trial in Jackson for allegedly raping a young girl who testified that in her struggles of resistance she had scratched the face of her assailant. Street denied everything and "said he got the scratches at the 'Gold Coast' in a fight with a negro girl."[77]

The saga of the homicidal demise of Roy Grant in March of 1938 captures important dimensions of the culture and humanity of the Gold Coast in those days.[78] Two groups got liquored up one night 'cross the river. The Fates brought these worthies together at Tom's Tavern, and in time a free-for-all broke out. At the end of the evening, Grant was dead, and in fairly short order Jack Hartfield was tried, convicted of murder, and sentenced to be hanged. Two state supreme court justices—Harvey McGehee, speaking for the court and reversal, and George H. Ethridge, speaking for himself and one other in dissent and for affirmance—collectively penned a fascinating true-crime short story.[79]

Understand that on the fateful evening Hartfield, a life-termer at Parchman but for ten years a trusty, had chauffeured the prison superintendent to Jackson on business. There, Hartfield met up with R. B. (Happy) Davis, another life-term convict and chauffeur, who had driven a prison sergeant to Mobile to assist in the recapture of an escaped convict. Their charges deposited at their hotel for the evening, Hartfield and Davis went out on the town, where they joined two old friends from their own Parchman days but who were by then released from custody. Both judicial tale tellers agree that the foursome made their way to the Gold Coast and acquired enough whiskey for the evening.[80] The deceased Ray Grant "had also visited the 'Gold Coast'" before he, a male friend, and three ladies made their way to Tom's Tavern for the fateful encounter.

Another Blues Trail marker notes the "frequent murders" on the Gold Coast. The altercation that got Woodworth McLaurin convicted of killing Hertisense Porter a few years later had its origin at Carr's Place . . . or was it the Green Lantern?[81] "Sometimes lives ended outside in the makeshift muddy parking lots near the clubs."[82] Bodies that were fished from the Pearl River were often not victims of rough waters during stormy weather or just leaky bass boats.[83] Nonfatal, liquor-accelerated fights were routine. One well-known altercation saw Sheriff J. V. Therrell smashed over the head with a beer bottle, rendering him unconscious and doubting the wisdom of seeking reelection in the fall of 1935.[84]

To this day, evidence, mostly anecdotal or apocryphal or both, abounds that law enforcement in Rankin County was not of one mind as to how the Gold Coast should be regarded. In 1939, Craddock Goins insisted, "It was nothing unusual for a police-court judge to swig liquor and gamble on the Coast one night and in court the next morning fine drunks who swigged at the same bar with him."[85] The best may have been when the husband of a lady named Bernice Mechatto lost his shirt gambling at Doc Steed's Eastside Club. Bernice not only sued Steed and his wife to get back the $17,399 she said her husband lost but also named Rankin County sheriff Troy Mashburn as a defendant. The charge was that the high sheriff knew all about Steed's profitable ways but refused to do anything about them.[86]

THE COMPLAINT TO ABATE A COMMON NUISANCE

Almost from the beginning, and certainly by the mid-1930s, an ongoing socioeconomic legal and political war raged between Rankin County's pro-Prohibition advocates and those who were not so ready to discourage the by-then flashy and flourishing Gold Coast. Many of the latter group had little or no say in the matter, as they hailed from environs outside of Rankin County, particularly in the capital city of Jackson.

Governor Hugh Lawson White[87] (1881–1965) took office in January of 1936 for the first of his two terms. Personally, politically, and sincerely, White was pro-"dry." In time, the new governor acceded to a plea from Rankin County residents to visit their westerly environs and see for himself the extent of illegal liquor and gambling operations. On December 6, 1936, White made his move. He marshaled the National Guard. In relevant part, White's executive order read,

> In view of the conditions existing in East Jackson, Rankin County, Mississippi, I . . . do hereby order the Adjutant General of Mississippi to order out such part of the Mississippi National Guard as he may deem necessary for the purpose of assisting in enforcing the criminal laws of the State of Mississippi in the county aforesaid. The number of troops used and the amount of expenditures shall be held to a minimum, compatible with the mission to be performed. The senior officer will be in direct command of the troops ordered out, and will use such force of arms as may be necessary in his opinion to accomplish the mission of the troops. . . .
>
> The officers and men ordered out will remain on duty until relieved by order from the Adjutant General of Mississippi.[88]

The yield of this effort was enough to pass the buck back to local District Attorney Percy M. Lee. At seemingly regular intervals, and following each raid, Lee began filing not-so-civil chancery court complaints to abate common nuisances. This less-than-garden-variety prosecutorial process merits a pause.

At least since 1918, when Mississippi became the first state to ratify the Eighteenth Amendment, state law authorized legal proceedings for the abatement of common nuisances,[89] not necessarily among "the criminal laws of the State of Mississippi," at least in the formal sense. Still, by legislative command, intoxicating liquor was one core element of such an offense. Gambling was another. The law then specified particular venues where common nuisances were likely to be practiced, viz., "any club, vessel or boat, place or room where liquors are found, kept or possessed." Also swept up in the cumbersome and legalistic text was "any person with intoxicating liquor in their possession or under their control." All in all, the simultaneous and continued existence of all of these facts and circumstances "in this state shall be deemed to be a common nuisance." In the same sentence the legislature said what should be done. Any prosecuting attorney—the attorney general, a district attorney, or a county attorney—was authorized to go to the local court of equity—more formally the chancery court—and upon proving his case, have the said "common nuisance . . . abated by writ of injunction."

By March of 1937, apparently so many common nuisances across the state had been found in need of abatement—and so frequently—that the prosecuting attorneys developed a two-page, small-print, legal-sized paper, fill-in-the-blanks, one-size-fits-all form that enjoyed the generic title of "Bill of Complaint."[90] After completing the names of parties, jurisdiction, and venue, the boilerplate form began to state the formal charge: "That defendants, in flagrant disregard and open defiance of the statutes of Mississippi...." One would have thought that enough wording to leave no doubt that illegal possession of "intoxicating and spirituous liquors" was being charged. Nothing in the statute said anything more was needed. The judge would issue the injunction if, of course, the state proved its case. Gilding the lily, however, the form's draftsmen added "and in detriment to the welfare, morals and well-being of the citizens of Mississippi."

Normally, a plaintiff is expected to prove the truth of the facts he alleges. In Mississippi in the late 1930s—and for many years thereafter—many would have thought no proof was needed regarding the morals or utility of booze. The good churchgoing teetotalers required no proof. On the other hand, many a good citizen saw no harm in a person engaging in moderate social drinking. The fact that alcoholism is a known and serious illness has never sensibly meant that intoxicating beverages should be banned altogether, the fervent wish of the Prohibitionists then and now to the contrary notwithstanding.[91]

More pragmatically, fourteen years of national Prohibition had not only failed. It had been a disaster. And so one can imagine a devilish defense lawyer challenging the state's attorney to prove what it had alleged, that the particulars of possessing whiskey were "detriment[al ...] to the welfare, morals and well-being of the citizens of Mississippi." And after the D.A. had made his speech sufficient until the next election, then moving the good chancery judge to dismiss for failure to prove an essential element of the charge it had brought. The legalistic answer from a good D.A. would have been that the law does not require that such a detrimental effect be established, and he would have been correct. Clever counsel for the defense would retort, "Of course, proof of this detrimental effect on morals is essential and must be shown, else the learned District Attorney would never have made this charge in his bill of complaint in the first place."

The same fun could have been had with the next clause in the printed form. The defendants "have on numerous occasions—fill in the dates—illegally kept and possessed large quantities of intoxicating and spirituous liquors in and on the premises hereinafter described." Again, nothing in Section 2007—the applicable code section in the 1930s, and Section 99–27–23 today—required anything beyond a simple showing of "possession" of "intoxicating liquor."

Many more lines of legalese followed with a blank then left for the premises to be described as though lands were being conveyed. Then it got better.

This (in)famous form said the defendants have—of all things—"kept the same [intoxicating and spirituous liquors] in open view and have allowed the general public to have free access to said premises." Then the form complaint to abate public nuisances charged that "the general public had congregated there and purchased from the defendants and drunk on said premises large quantities of intoxicating and spirituous liquors." The name of the accused was then typed into a blank space after which each was formally charged by form, viz., their actions "constitute an insult to the law, order and morals of Mississippi and if allowed to continue will weaken respect for law, order and morals, encourage violations of law, tend to promote breaches of peace and be detrimental to the general welfare of the public." And this does not even complete the first page of the form, but it is enough.

On March 31, 1937, District Attorney Lee filed thirteen such bills of complaint to abate common nuisances, the yield of a raid of Gold Coast nightspots.[92] Thirty or more defendants are named in these complaints, including members of the Seaney clan, who are named twice.[93] Another raid a couple of months later led to fifteen new common nuisance complaints being filed June 2, 1937.[94] Among the more than thirty new defendants were Pat Hudson,[95] the colorful "Doc" Steed and his wife,[96] and, of course, Sam A. Seaney.[97] A late-September raid netted fewer complaints—only nine.[98] A. A. Seaney and son Frank were among the guests of honor in a filing made by the district attorney on September 28, 1937.[99] Two months later came yet another raid, and another nine nuisances that needed abating.[100] "Historical documents indicate that Governor White alone ordered over a dozen raids on Gold Coast establishments between 1937 and 1939."[101] Sam Seaney kept up his consistent record.[102]

On December 26, 1938, Governor White issued another executive order mobilizing the National Guard, essentially the same as his first such order just over two years earlier.[103] Raids of area premises followed. "Wielding axes, more than sixty guardsmen smashed gambling equipment and liquor stores in their first descent upon the section," according to news reports.[104] "Additional whiskey stores were destroyed in several succeeding raids." "In a series of three raids in as many nights, the militia seized and destroyed liquor stocks and gambling equipment devices of an estimated value of several thousands of dollars."[105] But this is getting ahead of the story.

THE GENESIS OF THE GREAT CASE

In late 1937, Major T. B. Birdsong led some sixty-eight armed guardsmen as they invaded the Gold Coast. Large quantities of bonded though illegal liquors were seized. Gambling equipment and paraphernalia were destroyed. Many arrests followed. The next morning found a number of familiar nightclubs and other facilities padlocked.[106] One of the late-November 1937 defendants was Guysell McPhail (1909–1966), sued along with his brother Stanley McPhail (1913–1977).[107]

Guy McPhail was one of five brothers. He was only twenty years old when he and brother J. P. McPhail (1903–1978) were charged with possession of illegal liquor arising from a 1929 gun battle in Marion County "during the seizure of a large car containing a considerable amount of whiskey the night of May 23."[108] J. P. was acquitted, and charges against Guy were dropped.

Ten years later, this new charge against Guy McPhail came before Chancery Judge A. B. Amis (1867–1949) of Meridian.[109] Judge Amis was then in his second four-year term serving a seven-county district that stretched from the Alabama state line along Clarke and Lauderdale Counties across Highway 80 to its westernmost extension in Rankin County. A respected legal and judicial practitioner, Amis had published *Divorce and Separation in Mississippi* in 1934, reflecting scholarly and practical insights in a field at the heart of chancery court jurisdiction and practice. Perhaps Judge Amis was not as caught up in local passions of the times, because as the crow flies the Gold Coast was about as far away from Meridian as one could get and still be in that district as it was then configured.

On December 11, 1937, Judge Amis sent the State packing on its case against McPhail, on grounds that Governor White's use of guardsmen as police officers exceeded his authority.[110] In his ruling Judge Amis made clear his view of the "strictly limited" authority of the governor regarding the National Guard, adding that what Hugh White had done "strikes at the very foundation of our republican form of government."[111] The reference, of course, is to the guarantee in the Constitution of the United States art. 4, § 4, that each state shall enjoy "a republican form of government."

Two days later the State of Mississippi filed its notice of appeal. Two and a half months after that, Assistant Attorney General W. D. Conn Jr. argued that Judge Amis had committed legal and reversible error when he ruled "that evidence acquired by State Militia, ordered into active duty on proclamation of the Governor, . . . under search warrant, was incompetent because the search was unlawful."[112] This led to the second assigned error to the effect that the State had not produced enough evidence at trial to prove the charge of a common nuisance under Section 2007, which presumably the State could not do without the evidence the National Guard seized when it raided McPhail's premises. But while all of this was pending, the legislature came to town, to Jackson, that is, 'cross the river a few miles to the west. Always an adventure, then as now.

One can reasonably surmise that 1937's four waves of State-filed complaints to abate common nuisances on the Gold Coast—and the raids that preceded them—had become well known. There is little evidence elucidating how this law enforcement strategy came to be regarded, and, for that matter, what the public thought of the role the National Guard was playing, and what the costs might have been. Arguably, common nuisance proceedings in chancery were more efficient than individualized criminal grand juries, indictments, and prosecutions, and where those accused would have more extensive rights. For one thing, there was no presumption of innocence in chancery. Proof of guilt beyond a reasonable doubt was not required. Juries may or may not have been reluctant to convict. Put otherwise, a juror or two not prepared to deny all access to booze may have presented the district attorney with a serious practical obstacle. Without serious doubt, Judge Amis's ruling in the McPhail case—whatever else it may have said—raised questions about the common nuisance in chancery strategy and its viability going forward.

What we do know is that once—in January of 1938—the lawmakers had settled into their respective houses in the state capitol, Governor White—still flush with first fruits from his special session victory for his Balance Agriculture with Industry program[113]—was feeling his oats. He excoriated the prevalence of "gambling devices," particularly the "illegal operation and crooked construction of these slot machines, so called one-armed bandits," noting that in some communities

> they are operated on the morals of young people, even very small children being robbed and corrupted thereby. No gunman with his pistol pressed against the vitals of his intended victim is more certain of his booty than are these mechanical highwaymen that mercilessly extract from their victims money that in many instances should go to pay honest debts or to buy food and clothing for needy children.[114]

Representatives Gerald Chatham and N. A. Spencer, both of DeSoto County, introduced a series of bills aimed at strengthening the prosecution's hand in proceedings for abatement of common nuisances. On February 7, 1938, Chatham and Spencer moved to up the ante for those in the gambling or liquor trades. A prospective sanction would be an enhanced deterrent on the front end for those practicing a common nuisance. Upon a judicial finding for the prosecution, the nuisance practitioner "may be required by the court to enter into a good and sufficient bond in such amount as may be deemed proper by the court to be conditioned that he or they would not commit a similar offense for the next two years." Adding teeth to the bonding authority, the failure to make such a bond would be a contempt of court by reason of which the nuisance operator would be placed behind bars in the county jail until some of his associates came to the rescue and provided the bond, which of course would create an inference that such friends or relations might themselves be in the common nuisance business. House Bill No. 497 then tacked this sledgehammer onto the state's anti-gambling laws. House Bill No. 498 would so amend the laws condemning intoxicating liquors.[115]

On February 10, Chairman T. N. Gore of Quitman County quickly called up both bills, and each was passed unanimously by the house of representatives.[116] The senate soon followed suit. On February 21, and on motion by Senator Walter W. Capers of Jackson in Hinds County, the rules were suspended. H.B. 497 concerning the common nuisance of gambling passed thirty-five to four, with ten senators absent or not voting. In short order, Senator Capers also brought up H.B. 498, which concerned liquor prohibition, and it passed thirty-six to five, with eight senators abstaining or not voting.[117] On February 23, 1938, Governor White signed both bills into law.[118]

A bit of perspective may be needed here, and kept in mind throughout. Practically every article or other publication concerning the Gold Coast in its heyday mentions that legislators were among its patrons, in addition to many of the more prominent citizens of Jackson. In October of 1939, onetime Jackson journalist Craddock Goins reported, "It is generally understood that several legislators are financially interested in Gold Coast gambling joints; certainly many are frequent patrons."[119]

VIRGIL A. GRIFFITH, JURIST PAR EXCELLENCE

Virgil A. Griffith[120] (1874–1953) is one of the most recognized and respected names in Mississippi legal history, though most do not know the "A." is an abbreviation for Alexis. His *Mississippi Chancery Practice* was one of the most-used books in the library for at least two generations of lawyers throughout the state. The first edition was published in 1925. The second edition, published in 1950, lasted until the advent of the Mississippi Rules of Civil Procedure in 1982. Lawyers going to chancery court took their Griffith's like Christians took their Bibles to church. When citing it in written or oral argument, or merely in conversations among lawyers, few felt the need to go beyond "Griffith's says. . . ." or "Griffith's is the best explanation you will find on . . . [whatever the point of law might be]." Justice Griffith authored a less-known but at times equally valuable 700-page survey work entitled *Outlines of the Law: A Comprehensive Summary of the Major Subjects of American Law* [Mississippi Edition], published in 1949.

Virgil Griffith was born in 1874 in Lawrence County, the son of a planter and former slaveholder. He graduated from the University of Mississippi in 1897 and spent another year there studying law. As was the custom and practice of many at the time, Griffith then read law, in the office of A. C. McNair of Brookhaven. Upon admission to the bar, he soon moved to Harrison County, which remained home for the rest of his life. For almost ten years, he partnered with William Lyon Wallace in the private practice of law based in Gulfport. In 1920, Griffith was elected chancery judge for the Eighth District. In 1929, he was elevated to the Supreme Court of Mississippi, where he served for twenty years, the last two as chief justice. Though maintaining his residence in Gulfport, Griffith is known to have resided—while in Jackson on court business—in a brick house still standing at 814 North Jefferson Street. The circumstantial evidence shows this to be a straight shot about ten city blocks[121] south to Silas Brown Street, thence easterly across the Woodrow Wilson Bridge and only a hop, skip, and jump to the Fannin Road and Casey's Lane area. It is not unfair to suggest that Mississippi's legislators were hardly the only variety of state lawmakers who accessed the Gold Coast for liquid refreshments—the bonded bottled variety—during their public service in Jackson.

This is not the place to extol all of Griffith's judicial virtues, but one moment stands out. In 1935, he faced another case as politically explosive as those tendered by the Gold Coast. Three young African Americans had been tortured until they confessed to a murder they never committed. In the trial court, they were convicted and sentenced to be hanged. A week-kneed state supreme court affirmed.[122] But not unanimously. Virgil Griffith filed a powerful dissent. In time, Chief Justice Charles Evans Hughes spoke for a unanimous US Supreme Court and reversed, copying Griffith's words at considerable length.[123] The lead editorial in the *Washington Daily News* was entitled, "Here Is a Judge," praising Griffith's "breadth and clarity of intellect."[124] The same could be said of the opinion he released April 18, 1938, in *State of Mississippi vs. Guysell McPhail.*[125]

"THAT THE LAWS ARE FAITHFULLY EXECUTED"

Before the state supreme court, the appeal of Judge Amis's Gold Coast order teed up some fundamental premises—and practical realities—of state constitutional government. On the one hand was that grand and elegant command that the governor "shall see that the laws are faithfully executed."[126] Only slightly less weighty and general was the implementing premise that the governor "shall have power to call forth the militia to execute the laws," in which event he "shall be commander-in-chief of the militia."[127] In this context, of course, "the military shall be in strict subordination to the civil power."[128] How should these premises and powers play out when particular laws—quite constitutionally valid—become controversial and difficult for practical enforcement in some quarters?

On the other hand, there is the equally general and settled premise that "[n]o person shall be deprived of . . . liberty or property except by due process of law."[129] May a raiding guardsman take his ax or match to whatever personal property he finds on the premises and thinks may be an instrumentality of nuisance, illegality, or vice? More formally, is civil National Guard destruction of bonded whiskey or paraphernalia—reasonably believed susceptible of use in gambling—constitutionally permissible, without a prior judicial authorization that is itself preceded by reasonable advance notice to the property claimant and the opportunity to be heard? What about electronic music-making devices benign in and of themselves but used to entice the public to drink and gamble and make their experience more enjoyable? Are not these latter constitutional premises—once quantified—equally among the laws that the governor is charged to see are "faithfully executed"?

Rights and powers collide, and with legally protected interests. What is to be done when they do, and where quite arguably there has been in certain quarters a widespread disregard of some parts of the law? Make that in two or more conflicting quarters! When such cases arise, is there a practical role for the constitutional imperative expressed at the highest level of generality, but cited by Judge Amis in the court below, that we all enjoy "a republican form of government"?

A circle has no point of beginning, but to experience its utility one must start somewhere. The same is true of a case in court where the judge's goal is always coming as close as practicable to a reliable and official congruence of law and fact. In most court cases—civil or criminal—the judge is charged to find the facts, identify the law, and then apply the law to the facts as reliably as practicable to produce an adjudication. Oftentimes, the judge gets help from a jury in finding the facts, and juries play an all-important role in that most challenging third phase of any adjudication, the reliable application of the law to the facts, when jurors take the law given them in the judge's charge, apply it to the facts, and return a verdict. Those first two *desiderata* are and will ever remain a chicken-and-egg proposition. Understanding this assists in understanding the rather remarkable and quite commendable first two paragraphs of Griffith's *McPhail* opinion.

The reality is that within the realm of facts there are three conceptually distinct but practicably overlapping categories of facts that courts consider—and should consider—with varying levels of consciousness in deciding cases. Most familiar here are the adjudicative facts, sometime called evidentiary facts, which are often disputed, though sometimes not, or at least not seriously so. Whether the liquid contained in the bottles seized by guardsmen in November of 1937 was whiskey or some other watery substance would be a question of adjudicative fact. The same is true for whether a device was in fact a legally prohibited slot machine, though a question of law would arise in later cases whether it mattered that at the time of seizure the device was not being used as an instrumentality of chance. What about a deck of fifty-two playing cards? More problematic would be whether a Victrola machine that would play particular pieces of music in response to coins being deposited—commonly known later as a jukebox or a nickelodeon—was off-limits. And what about a pinball machine? These became important questions of law application.

On April 18, 1938, Justice Griffith reviewed the question whether the governor had exceeded his powers in ordering the National Guard to the Gold Coast. Judge Amis said that he had. Griffith began with a broader category of facts, those subject to what courts call judicial notice. In today's legal parlance, these are facts the accuracy of which is not subject to reasonable dispute.[130] Geophysical facts that might be identified by a surveyor using reliable surveying equipment, techniques, and principles are often susceptible of judicial notice. Ground-penetrating radar is a common instance today, but what about drones that can be manipulated? Justice Griffith began with a somewhat less precise description of the Gold Coast, but still largely geophysical, one certain and precise enough that it should suffice for the purposes at hand.

> Immediately across the Pearl River, adjacent to the municipal limits of the city of Jackson, there is situated an unincorporated community formerly known as East Jackson, but now more generally known by the name "The Gold Coast," as being more definitely descriptive. This area extends about half a mile eastward from the Farish bridge along Highway No. 80, and thence nearly the same distance along the Fannin road, and also along Highway No. 49 for a distance of about one-fourth of a mile from the underpass, which is near the junction of said highways. The area is in Rankin county.[131]

Craddock Goins added journalistic color with a complementary description in a nationally circulated article inspired in part by the *McPhail* case. "The Gold Coast is within a half mile radius. It consists of thirty-five or forty crude structures, outwardly like cheap tourist cabins, despite the carnival effect of floodlights." It is "separated from the capital city [of Jackson] only by a minor swamp stream called Pearl River. . . . There is no coast except the hogwallows of the river banks. . . . Jackson is connected with this glorified, mud-hollow Monte Carlo by the half-mile long Woodrow Wilson Memorial Bridge."[132]

These facts are made clear to today's Jackson-oriented old-timers by bearing in mind that one entered the Gold Coast from the west by making one's way to the once wonderful and well-patronized Dennery's Restaurant on the corner of Silas Brown and South Jefferson Streets—an area now occupied by WLBT Television—and thence easterly along the bridge 'cross the river. More recent highways, roadways, a new and considerably widened Woodrow Wilson Bridge, a levee on the east bank of the Pearl River, and the serene Crystal Lake—all more or less today within the city limits of Flowood—make some of the details less obvious than once they appeared. Of course, nothing affected the Pearl River like the Barnett Dam and Reservoir about ten miles to the North.[133] Fannin Road and Casey's Lane are sad shadows of their former selves. Still a casual drive-through investigator (who may even be a judge) today can easily gain a fair idea of where the Gold Coast was in the late 1930s.

There is a further dimension to what Griffith knew but mentioned nowhere, though it is quite important practically. For most of his adult life, he lived in Harrison County on the Mississippi Gulf Coast. It was and remains common knowledge that when it came to gambling and intoxicating liquors, eastern Harrison County, or just Biloxi, had long drawn many comparisons with East Jackson, the Gold Coast, 'cross the river, or whatever one wished to call that area of Rankin County geophysically depicted at the outset of the *McPhail* opinion. Past that, there is every reason to assume that the then sixty-two-year-old Virgil Griffith had a personal familiarity with at least the bonded-whiskey intoxicating-liquors aspect of both venues. Griffith was labeled in many ways by diverse persons over his long life. One label never applied to him during his adult years was teetotaler.

The geophysics set out, Griffith's statement of the facts of the Gold Coast then became more challenging. He stretched easily judicially knowable facts through the twilight zone and into the realm of legislative facts.[134] "In this area for some time, and in numerous places, intoxicating liquors have been openly displayed and sold in the manner as if in licensed saloons."[135] A bit loosey-goosey, but such descriptions remain common in judicial utterances today, and helpful to the reader[136]—though many might have to just imagine what things were like in "licensed saloons"—while working no harm to either party in the case.

Griffith then turned up the heat, adding the quite judgmental *pronunciamiento* that in this area "gambling in its most vicious forms has been carried on."[137] Eighteen months later Craddock Goins opined in a similar vein that "plenty of gold crosses those banks to the pockets of the most brazen clique of cutthroats and bootleggers that ever defied the law."[138] Back to Griffith for the conclusory claim

> The salient facts with reference to the general situation in the area in question have persisted for such a considerable length of time, have been of such glaring notoriety and have aroused such general public interest; have been the subject of such extensive public comment both in the daily and weekly press and of common conversation throughout the state; have been so open and flagrant and without dispute anywhere. . . .

These are legislative facts, purely and simply and properly so called. Their use is not governed by formal rules of evidence. Yet they are quite important and legitimately useful, particularly so in a case like *McPhail*. These are the sorts of facts and circumstances that—however general or imprecise may be the perception of reality and the form of expression—anybody would find most helpful in deciding upon a forwarding-looking course of regulation in the public interest. Griffith said as much when he added that "that the court may notice as a matter of current history the import of said facts. . . ."[139] Then without surprise he returned quickly to the case at bar and said these legislative facts are helpful "when taken in connection with the evidence before us dealing with those facts." Griffith told his reader that the case he was about to decide had arisen in the context of "what we consider to have amounted to a substantial breakdown in the enforcement of the law by the local executive officers in that law."[140] This is the reason it was important that the court make reference to these legislative facts and "at subsequent points in this opinion."

But not everyone saw it that way. Inescapably, Griffith's broad brush left no doubt that many persons found the Gold Coast and its activities and opportunities very much to their liking. In contrast, many of those offended by the Gold Coast are those who are unhappy that sin (as they define sin) is being practiced, albeit they suffer no injury or other harm aside from their self-inflicted unhappiness. Besides, "it was probably the damned grandest place our grandparents and great-grandparents ever snuck off to," according to writer David McCarty in 2011,[141] no doubt relying on multiple layers of hearsay testimony from declarants long since unavailable.[142]

Then the familiar format returned. Griffith noted the governor's executive order calling out the guard "for the purpose of assisting in the enforcement of the criminal laws of the state." He turned next to the warrant issued to search Guysell McPhail's premises "for intoxicating liquors," which warrant "was in an orderly manner duly executed." Griffith then tells us "a quantity of intoxicating liquors was found and seized, and much other evidence was obtained of violations of the law in keeping with the stated conditions in that area." Nonetheless, Judge Amis had sustained McPhail's view that on the facts the governor had exceeded his authority in calling out the National Guard, and the State had appealed.[143]

A FINE LEGAL ESSAY

And so we come to the core constitutional concern of this chapter—the proper understanding and application and effect of the command that "[t]he governor shall see that the laws are faithfully executed."[144] And its scope, once we have on the table all laws that might be implicated by the full facts, plus the practical limits of just what the governor could do and the powers conferred on other officers as authorized by the constitution.

In April of 1938, Justice Griffith penned a fine legal essay, persuasive as well as expository. He mentioned but three prior court decisions—only one from Mississippi—and none for a controlling point of law. In the end,

> we say that under the state of facts here presented the Governor was within his constitutional and statutory power in sending the militia to the area in question, and that in consequence the official members of the militia were lawful civil officers within that area.

Griffith cut a step-by-step path straight to this end. He expounded the law so well that few would remain unpersuaded. His words remain worthy of study and reflection, though that may expose a point or two where he may have missed the mark a tad. Then and now, people may differ on these facts as to just how much of a breakdown in law and order there really had been, and of what consequence to the people of the community concerned, and of their conflicting interests and points of view. He ended with an overview of other points of constitutional concern bound to arise, given what he did decide, other laws that the governor—and the courts—might think themselves just as bound to see faithfully executed as the laws regulating liquor and gambling.

McPhail added flesh to our understanding of the "powers of the Governor, and of the militia, in the execution of the laws." And in the context of what Griffith sincerely saw as "a substantial breakdown of local [law] enforcement." At three points in his opinion, he used variants on that "breakdown" image.[145] He was not talking about cases where the governor "may believe and have reason to believe that the laws are not being as diligently enforced as they ought to be."[146] The National Guard should never be sent to a community "merely because the [laws] are not at times being diligently executed or perfectly enforced.... A fair measure of deference should be accorded to the local authorities." Even then a second showing is required. The "substantial breakdown" must exist and persist "for that length of time which makes it clearly apparent that no dependence is to be placed upon the local executive officers and that they either cannot or will not enforce the laws." Only in this latter circumstance may the governor call out the National Guard, "not at all to supersede the law, but to enforce it." En route the activated guardsmen may serve and return warrants for the search and seizure of evidence under the same criteria as apply to ordinary local law enforcement authority "and with the same effect. The search warrant in this [Guy McPhail's] case was legally executed, and it was error to exclude the testimony obtained during its execution."[147]

This case of Guy McPhail and the constitution arose in the course of human events. It concerned practical aspects of social existence as they are affected by government and the rules it makes. That included the people who in a time long past lived and worked and visited and experienced life within the ambit of the Gold Coast and its environs. These interest us now because of the tensions—the sparks and barbs and passions, the pleasures and the pains—that were once generated by the activity of men and women in this now quiet if not obscure strip of land along the Rankin County side of the Pearl River penetrated by Old Brandon Road. Mississippi had laws on the books that on their face regulated that practical activity. The constitution told the governor to see that those laws were faithfully executed according to their tenor. Sections 123 and 217 and the statutes that implement them—in the late 1930s as today—"have no obscure or technical meaning, neither were they intended as a mere verbal adornment of [the] office [of governor]."

> Griffith was right when he insisted that the court was not talking about "an arbitrary enforcement by the executive of what he may consider the law to be, but the enforcement of judicial process that is, the enforcement of a right and remedy provided by the law and judicially determined to be enforced."[148]

And he was right to consider seriously and discuss a "permeating feature" of our constitution "that primary local authority shall be preserved." But questions remained. The governor's authority was grounded in what constitutional text and with what limits emanating from what sources and with what wiggle room when it came to practical decision making? "It was foreseen, however, by the framers of the constitution that for one cause or another, local conditions would sometimes arise which would render the local authorities powerless to enforce the laws, or unwilling or afraid to do so."[149] Fair enough, but keep ever in mind the distinction between what the framers may or may not have foreseen and what they then said.

The problem was and remains that there are times when at local levels the law goes unenforced. "For one cause or another local conditions would sometime arise that would render the local authorities powerless to enforce the laws, or unwilling or afraid to do so." Quoting from a Kentucky court, Griffith added that at times local authorities are "too weak" and at other times even "in sympathy with the forces who want to take the law into their own hands."[150] The constitution did not "leave any such loophole" as to permit local option when it came to "statutes enacted for general observance throughout the state.... Power to enforce the law is not left as a matter of finality to the discretion of local authorities or the local inhabitants."[151]

Griffith's premises seem familiar enough, and agreeable in the abstract or at least at the ten-thousand-foot level of generality. Yet questions remain. If the local authorities choose to allow motorists to exceed state speed limits, or get by with a warning, who is to say they shouldn't? This is particularly problematic where the sheriff has been on the job long enough to understand that his practical choice is between arbitrarily enforcing the law as to only one out of every fifty offenders or hiring so many additional patrol officers that the taxpayers or ideology-driven legislators will revolt. Who is to complain if today in a "dry" county the sheriff decides as a matter of policy and practice to make no arrest so long as the bottle of whiskey on the front seat is unopened, though it is in plain view in the vehicle of the motorist stopped for some other offense? Or just for a routine driver's license and proof-of-insurance check?

A wise future justice of the Supreme Court of the United States once said, "The life of the law has not been logic; it has been experience. The felt necessities

of the time, the prevalent moral and political theories, intuitions of public policy, avowed or unconscious, even the prejudices which judges share with their
fellow men" are the source of the norms of society that as a practical matter
courts consider, apply, and enforce.[152]

The point and its broader perspective were later well put by federal attorney
general Robert H. Jackson, who in time became a widely admired US Supreme
Court Justice, and just a few years after *McPhail*.

> Law enforcement is not automatic. It isn't blind. One of the greatest difficulties of
> the position of prosecutor is that he must pick his cases, because no prosecutor can
> even investigate all of the cases in which he receives complaints. . . . With the law
> books filled with a great assortment of crimes, a prosecutor stands a fair chance
> of finding at least a technical violation of some act on the part of almost anyone.

Jackson's insight is as true at the local county level in the states as at the federal
district level in the United States as a whole. It is even truer today than in 1940.

> We know that no local police force can strictly enforce the traffic laws, or it would
> arrest half the driving population on any given morning. What every prosecutor
> is practically required to do is to select the cases for prosecution and to select
> those in which the offense is the most flagrant, the public harm the greatest, and
> the proof the most certain.[153]

Governor White had the authority to act as he did on December 8, 1936,
issuing an executive order calling out the guard. But that authority reeked with
discretion. Little in the constitution and laws was helpful when it came to when,
how, and why he exercised that discretion. Robert Jackson's criteria for deciding
when to prosecute are about as close to precision as is practicably possible.

As sound as *McPhail* is in so many respects, Griffith's take on judicial review
of the governor's actions puts the cart before the horse. Make no mistake about
it, the governor's "decision whether the exigency is such as to authorize him" to
"call out the militia" is *not* "solely for his discretion."[154] "Official action, whether
the officer be of the highest or the lowest grade, must be within the Constitution
and laws." Griffith had it backward, however, when he moved to whether the
facts are such as to justify the executive's action. Enough was shown to merit
judicial review when Guy McPhail made a nonfrivolous claim that the executive had exceeded his authority. Only after the full exercise of the power and
prerogative of judicial review could the court take the next step and decide reliably whether it should order, to use Griffith's phrase, "remedial rectification."

In a follow-up paragraph, Griffith repeated his conceptual error, viz., "so long
as the officers or agents of the government act within the boundaries of their
appointed duties, their actions and decisions are not reviewable by the courts."

Again, this is backward. No court can reliably adjudge whether an executive officer or agent has acted within his authority without—first and foremost—reviewing fully and faithfully what the officer or agent has done or failed to do. Whether there should be a remedial rectification can be decided reliably only *after* there has been a full-fledged judicial review of all of the relevant facts and circumstances. It is devoutly to be wished that most official actions fully judicially reviewed should be found exemplary.

Griffith left another confused idea in his splendid but imperfect essay. He spoke of "certain features of official action which are of purely political concern . . . matters that are nonjusticiable in their nature."[155] This is talk that today is associated with what is commonly called the political question doctrine.[156] The idea is that courts ought to stay out of the political thicket. In Griffith's words, as in those of other jurists in more recent times, it is often overlooked that the political question doctrine is nowhere grounded in any overt constitutional text.[157] It states only a principle of practical prudence, far short of a jurisdictional command absolute. The obvious reason why this is the only practical way to understand the process is that so many adjudications that no one would doubt are proper for the courts nevertheless have great political consequences or effects. Any doubt on this score is removed when one gives a moment's thought to the political passions, prejudices, and pocketbooks brought to bear in judicial appointments at the federal level and in judicial elections at the state level.

Finally, Griffith provided an attractive but ultimately incomplete summary of the process of adjudication. "The courts will determine for themselves not only the law, but ultimately also whether there be justifying facts," and this "however much may be the weight, prima facie, which the judicial department will yield to the findings of fact by an executive or administrative officer as those upon which he has acted."[158] But adjudication is a three-step process, as noted above. Of course, the court must reliably identify and elaborate the relevant law and legal principles. And it must identify and assess the relevant facts, though this becomes a chicken-and-egg proposition when considered together with the court's law declaration duty. So often overlooked is the conceptually different and practicably more difficult and quite discrete third and final job of applying the law reliably to the facts, or as some might say, of finding the ultimate facts.[159]

Griffith took note, and quite correctly, that there may be some extent to which the court "will yield to the findings of fact by an executive or administrative officer." Sometimes others are in a better position to find the facts reliably than are judges and juries. "Scope of review" or sometimes "standard of review" are labels commonly used for this often critical and outcome-determinative dimension of the process of adjudication.[160] The difficulty and controversy of whether review should be *de novo*, deferential, and if so, how so, is easy to overlook—particularly by the uninitiated reader—given Griffith's skillful use of the King's English.

A NOBLE NOD TO MAGNA CARTA?

Virgil Griffith laid out the case that Governor White was within his authority when he sent the National Guard to the Gold Coast, and not just to raid the premises maintained by Guysell McPhail. His ruling was carefully limited to the facts—all three varieties—of the "conditions" on the Gold Coast at that time. The governor had probable cause to believe that for some time there had been an ongoing "substantial breakdown in the enforcement of the laws by the local executive officers in that area."[161]

Of considerable importance, the search warrant issued to the adjutant general "was in an orderly manner duly executed by him or under his directions." The powers and immunities of the office of governor in such circumstances were well laid out. Griffith could have stopped there, except for the formality of "reversed and remanded for further proceedings on the complaint to abate a common nuisance consistent with this opinion." Many justices would have stopped there. We will probably never know whether any of Griffith's colleagues on the state supreme court may have suggested as much, particularly when they read what followed "but whenever . . ." halfway down the third-to-last paragraph of the opinion.

Tried-and-true experience suggests a three-step process is required for a speaker to be sure his audience gets the point. You tell them what you are going to say, then you say it, and then you tell them what you just said. Griffith boldly took the first step, viz.,

> but whenever they [the governor, legislators or others in their "official capacity"],
> or any of them, or any other officer acting or assuming to act for the government,
> puts into action any agency which comes into collision with the private personal
> or private property rights of any person within the jurisdiction,[162]

the rules governing the other side of the coin come into play. After all "such personal and property rights of the citizen and their infringements are always subject to inquiry and redress by the courts. . . ."[163] Guysell McPhail had rights, too. So did every other Gold Coast operative who was raided and searched and had his property seized and often destroyed. Griffith's "but whenever" introduction prepares his audience for the point to come.

Those with a sense of history take to Griffith's next paragraph, the next-to-last paragraph in his *McPhail* opinion.[164] Note is taken in chapter 1 above.[165] It begins with the constitution's often misunderstood Section 24, a part of Article 3, the Mississippi Bill of Rights. Many label it only an Open Courts clause. Section 24, read together with Section 14 concerning due process and Section 21 regarding the writ of habeas corpus,[166] is nothing less than Mississippi's constitutional acceptance of the core ideas in what is left in England of Magna Carta,

Clauses 39 and 40, according to Blackstone's formulation. The social contract has been converted into the form of positive law: "Every person for an injury done him in his lands, goods [real and personal property in today's terminology], person or reputation, shall have a remedy by due course of law."[167]

One cannot read the assurance that "every unlawful power is subject to scrutiny by the courts, where it operates to the legal hurt of any citizen, however humble," without sensing that Griffith was likely thinking of what happened at Runnymede in the year 1215. He doesn't say so explicitly. Combining these three state constitutional clauses by accident seems highly unlikely, particularly for a judge as learned as Virgil Griffith. For the legal injury McPhail said was being done to his person and his property, Griffith said he was entitled to his day in court and a fair opportunity to prove or defend his case against the governor, the guard, and other officials. Griffith then repeated that upholding Governor White's executive order was proper because "there is no reason to apprehend irremediable danger to the citizen or his property by the exercise by the Governor of the power and duty, which we here sustain."

Step three. "We repeat, therefore, by way of summary." All that the governor and the National Guard may do "is subject to review by the courts at the suit, or other appropriate legal challenge, of any citizen who can show he has been unlawfully affected in his private person or private property rights."[168] At least this much of Magna Carta was and remains—by virtue of a collective reading of Sections 14, 21 and 24 of the Mississippi Bill of Rights[169]—among "the laws" that the governor "shall see . . . are faithfully executed."[170] Even if Guy McPhail, one of the Seaneys or Dick Farr (see below), or other person "however humble" should be the person claiming the benefit and protection of such laws. Of course, protecting the rights of persons however humble inevitably leads to the problematics of the rights and prerogatives of those not so humble, and even the arrogant, who in practical reality are nothing more than narcissistic bullies.

THE AFTERMATH FOR MCPHAIL AND MANY OTHERS

On March 22, 1939, Chancery Judge A. B. Amis entered an intriguing order. Its heading itemizes fifty pending cases brought by the district attorney against well over a hundred Gold Coast operatives to abate some fifty or more common nuisances. Most of the cases had been filed between late March and late November of 1937. Spell out the names of the "et al.'s" in the case styles, and you have a roll call of just about everyone doing business on the Gold Coast in 1937, and the trade names of most. Of course, some, like the Seaneys, make multiple appearances. In this order, Judge Amis found "that no action has been taken in any of the above entitled causes during the last two terms of court and that neither the complainant nor the defendants have appeared during this term to either prosecute or defend these causes." By this time, Percy M. Lee had moved on to the office of circuit judge. Tom Barnett of Carthage had become the new district attorney and had fresher fish to fry. Regular National Guard raids in the early weeks of 1939 had afforded Barnett more than enough new cases to prosecute, albeit the nuisances said in need of abatement were not unlike those of the past. In consequence, Judge Amis ordered

> that all of said causes be and the same hereby are passed to the files of this court and that no further action be taken thereon until and unless some person interested therein shall appear and move the court to restore the same . . . for action thereon.[171]

One of the cases passed to the files was No. 4203, *State vs. Guysell McPhail* on remand from the Supreme Court of Mississippi by virtue of its decision of April 1938. It does not appear that any of these fifty cases was ever restored to the court's active docket for any action thereon.

Guy McPhail was caught up in another National Guard raid of the Gold Coast in late February of 1939[172] and again in June of 1939.[173] It was hardly a consolation that McPhail's more famous case had been sent to that great judicial dustbin known as "passed to the files." As late as September of 1948, McPhail was named a defendant in a suit brought by the Rankin County Christian Citizens' League charging that he was illegally selling intoxicating liquor.[174]

In many ways, 1939 was the high-water mark for less-than-friendly interactions between the Gold Coast and the National Guard. Nine months after the Supreme Court had given the governor and the guard a green light to do what needed to be done, a headline appeared: "Gold Coast Hits New Peak after Brief Closures." On the third Sunday morning in 1939, the front-page story began, "The Hinds-Rankin 'gold coast' blazed with lights and thronged with customers as the doors swung wide open after the Christmas holiday closure." Much detail followed, including the positions of opposing parties in recent months, concluding with the report that newly sworn-in "District Attorney Tom Barnett had previously sent a chill up and down the 'coast' by making several casual 'inspections' of the district with a view to studying action by his office."[175]

Two weeks later, the worm had turned again. New justice of the peace H. H. Bullock "has let it become generally known that he doesn't like wide-open gambling and whiskey houses in his district." And so, "Yes, the 'Gold Coast' in Rankin County is again suffering from a lack of illumination. . . . The dazzling neon lights are taking another rest."[176] Ten days later, Major T. B. Birdsong led guardsmen on a surprise early-morning raid that "confiscated and destroyed" liquor, slot machines, dice tables, and other gambling equipment, a "$1,000 bar," and other paraphernalia.[177] Three days later, the guard was back. The subheadline read, "Guard Relentlessly Pounds at Doors of 'Gold Coast' Places." Major

Birdsong, acting under orders from Governor White, "commanding a squad of about 50 national guardsmen, continued sporadic raiding of the night club sectors outside of Jackson." "On successive nights," guardsmen have "destroyed liquor and gambling paraphernalia valued at thousands of dollars. A soldier was shot in the hand during one raid."[178]

On the last Saturday night in February 1939, Adjutant General John A. O'Keefe and Major Birdsong led another bevy of fifty guardsmen on raids. The Owl's Nest burned down, though it was disputed whether this was a result of faulty wiring or intentional actions of guardsmen. According to the news report, "[e]leven 'hot spots' along the 'Gold Coast' felt the heavy hand—or rather the destructive axes—of the soldiery last night."[179]

Late June of 1939 found the National Guard at its most active. "Raid-to-End-All Raids Destroys Much Property" was the headline on Friday, June 23.

> A miniature army, comprising 135 militiamen commanded by twelve officers, swooped down upon the area at four o'clock, and literally swept everything before it. When the retreat was sounded long after dark, the soldiers had wrecked thirty-one night spots and had confiscated and destroyed thousands of dollars worth of liquor, gambling equipment, slot machines and miscellaneous property used in the operation of the establishments.

The officers made some sixty arrests, including several women and a number of customers. One Jackson newspaper ran a headline claiming "Raid Wreckage at $100,000."[180] That's the equivalent of $1.677 million in 2015 dollars. Less exuberant reporters claimed only that the value of personal property seized or destroyed was said to exceed $50,000.[181] Not surprisingly, the next day's headline read, "Liquor Selling on Sly Resumed Following Raid."[182] The news story read

> First return to "normalcy" for the Coast has always been selling of liquor in bottles by establishments there—and thirsty Jackson patrons Saturday had been buying any whiskey they wanted for nearly three days.
>   What the next step will be is in the hands of the gambling overlords who say when the dice tables and roulette wheels can be returned to the clubs.
>   It took less than a month after the last Spring raid for the Gold Coast to blossom into its customary blatancy, going full blast and stripping Capital City visitors of their cash in familiar style.[183]

The following year featured an assault on the meal ticket *McPhail* had handed Governor White and the National Guard. April Fools' Day, 1940, however, brought another adverse adjudication for A. A. Seaney. Reasonably assuming that the Seaney family had hardly retired from its chosen profession, a National Guard officer had secured a search warrant for the premises of Daddy

Seaney. The place to be searched was on Casey's Lane. His client convicted of illegal possession, Seaney's lawyer tried to get around *McPhail*, arguing that there had been no showing that the sheriff or constable was unwilling or unable to act. The court—arguably unreliably if not irresponsibly—brushed the argument aside and gave a quick summary of the *McPhail* holding, adding, "It was not necessary for the Governor to await the request of the sheriff or the judge of the Circuit Court or any other local officer."[184] A. A. Seaney paid a $500 fine, arguably about right to reimburse Rankin County for his ninety days of food and lodging in the local jail.

MUSICAL EQUIPMENT SUPPLIERS HAVE RIGHTS TOO

"[T]wenty-one music boxes valued at $7,350" were among the inventory of items "destroyed or seized by the soldiers" led by Major Birdsong in the "raid-to-end-all raids" just reported.[185] This was not the first time amusement equipment vendors doing business with Gold Coast operators had felt the boot and ax of National Guard raiders. Unlike the raid that led to *McPhail*, this was not the first time when it could be denied with credibility that each search warrant "was in an orderly manner duly executed."[186]

We have seen that over the first weekend in February of 1939 guardsmen staged highly destructive raids of at least three nightspots—the Shady Rest, the East Jackson Club, and Bradley's Bat Shoppe.[187] Two men who had placed musical equipment in those clubs took big hits and decided to take the offensive. Their concern and their complaint was of the widespread and on-the-spot destruction of their property without a semblance of due process of law in which they could participate. It wasn't just that the guardsmen had a field day smashing bottles of whiskey. They were taking the immediate ax to almost everything in sight—slot machines, gaming tables, music makers, and other equipment. Scant attention was being paid to the Magna Carta–based last part of Virgil Griffith's *McPhail* opinion.[188] Governor White was not doing very much to assure that Sections 14 and 24 of the state constitution were being "faithfully executed."[189]

Richard Ansley (Dick) Farr (1907–1965) is not one of the well-known players in the Gold Coast drama, but his story added an important dimension to this constitutional encounter. Farr lived in Jackson. In many respects he was a taxpaying businessman and good citizen. Farr became active in the Royal Order of Moose, Lodge No. 1426, of which he was once governor. He ran an amusement equipment and vending machine company out of Jackson, known as the Dick Farr Amusement Co.[190] Nickelodeons, jukeboxes, electronic pianos, phonographs, pinball machines, and the like were among his stock in trade. Farr also owned and operated Dick Farr's Café at 327 South State Street in Jackson, about six blocks from the point where Silas Brown Street still connects up with the Woodrow Wilson Bridge, which then crosses the Pearl River and, voila! in the mid-1930s through the mid-1960s, you would be in the heart of the Gold Coast. In November of 1935, Farr had been fined $100 for operating a gambling device that he called a pinball machine.[191] Farr had argued that all you could win was a chance to play another game without putting another nickel in the machine, and that was hardly gambling. A week later, a circuit judge spurned Farr's challenge to Jackson's gambling ordinance.[192] The next day police found a "pin-ball marble machine" at Farr's place of business, and in short order "it was broken to bits."[193] In February of 1938, Farr was under siege again, this time for operating slot machines said to be gambling devices. Farr testified that the machines "were in a cabinet," and he "was planning on shipping them away." A Hinds County jury found Farr not guilty.[194]

Farr's obituary says he served in the US Army in World War II.[195] A news report in May of 1944 noted the Hinds County Grand Jury's consideration of slot machines—"three 'one-armed bandits'"—seized in a sheriff's raid on Mays Street in Jackson, adding "that the slot machines belong to Dick Farr who stays at a local hotel, the sheriff's deputy said."[196] While it is unclear whether Farr was providing slot machines to Gold Coast operatives in February of 1939, circumstantial evidence suggests he had the wherewithal to do so.

Slot machines and other gambling devices aside, Farr had placed music machines in many a Gold Coast night spot. Court papers refer to these as "music machines," "electric victrolas," "phonographs," and "electric pianos." Like as not, these were all some variant of what were commonly known as jukeboxes or nickelodeons. A patron would deposit a nickel in one of Farr's victrolas, which would then play a piece of music. At intervals, Farr would visit each club and remove the coins from the music machine. Farr would give the club owner a percentage as his commission for having allowed Farr to place and maintain the victrola in the particular venue. The value of these music machines was said to be approximately $425 each—in 1939 dollars.

Without doubt the early February 1939 National Guard raids had resulted in damage to or outright destruction of Farr's equipment. According to Farr, guardsmen were "armed with rifles, revolvers, axes and other implements and tearing down and burning buildings and breaking up and destroying" property, including a number of Farr's jukeboxes and an electric piano. Farr felt he had no choice but to go on the offensive. In doing so, he raised serious constitutional questions about pre-destruction property rights, running up against the rule that there can be no rights in illegal physical personal property.[197]

The initial petition to restrain the local officials and the guard was filed by J. D. Williams, a citizen of Hinds County but a property owner in Rankin County. Williams made strident charges arising out of the damage and destruction that the guard was said to have wrought that first week in February.[198] Dick

Farr then joined the fray. Farr made his plea to the Circuit Court of Rankin County and sought a writ of prohibition "to check further depredations by the National Guard in the area just east of Jackson." Farr charged that

> when property is seized under a search warrant the officer making the seizure is required to notify the owner where the property is sequestered in order that the owner may assert his rights in the proper court and have an adjudication of the question whether the property was seized legally.[199]

This was a reasonable proposition regarding pre-destruction due process rights. Williams and Farr were strongly opposed by the Briar Hills Baptist Church of Florence. The closest this church group came to making a legal defense was "If the national guardsmen in the discharge of their duties violated any property rights, it is indeed unfortunate and regrettable. We are of the opinion that the damage done was quite insignificant to the good accomplished."

The case came before Judge Percy M. Lee, who had recently ascended the circuit court bench, having resigned his position as district attorney. The case was heard "upon the plea of an estimated 50 property owners in Rankin County."[200] The request for a writ of prohibition against the guard, however, was denied.[201]

Time was of the essence. Farr never knew when another destructive raid would be staged. Rather than take a time-consuming appeal to the Supreme Court of Mississippi, Farr went straight to federal court in Jackson, claiming federal due process rights.[202] On March 2, 1939, he filed what his lawyer called a petition for injunction, naming State Adjutant General John A. O'Keefe as the defendant. Farr insisted that his musical equipment was not a part of any illegal activities. General O'Keefe, Major Birdsong, and other guardsmen were destroying Farr's personal property without affording him advance notice or the opportunity to be heard or any other semblance of due process of law. He asked the federal court to enjoin the National Guard from any further such harm to his property rights.[203] After all, the statute contained an exclusion for "music machines."[204]

Farr was fighting on another front as well. On or about March 1, 1939, City of Jackson police raided a garage he had rented and maintained on South President Street, "where the officers confiscated and destroyed three slot machines." The city had banned slot machines, including in the ordinance a clause providing, "It shall be the duty of all law enforcement officers to seize and destroy all such machines and devices."[205]

On March 14, Robert Bruce Grissett (1893–1964)[206] intervened as an additional plaintiff in Farr's case before the US District Court.[207] Grissett had long been operating what he referred to as a tourist camp on the south side of US Highway 80 near the Gold Coast. In early 1939, Grissett operated machines known as "mint vendors." A customer would put a coin in the machine and pull a lever. With every pull, the player would receive a package of mints. If the three dials lined up in a certain way, the customer would also receive a monetary prize.[208] This may have been a clever attempt at getting around the anti-gambling laws.

On February 6, 1939, Grissett's premises had been raided by the National Guard. He had three slot machines stored on the premises, which were not being used for gambling purposes at the time his premises were raided. The raiding guardsmen "with force and arms then and there destroyed machines with axes, that there was a quantity of money in one of the machines." Grissett said he "asked the sergeant who broke said machines for a receipt therefor, and that the sergeant rudely and peremptorily refused to give him a receipt for said money."[209] Supporting Farr and Grissett before the federal court, Eugene Seaney, Malcolm Foy, and Bill McCleave filed sworn factual statements elaborating the facts just summarized.[210]

The case was heard by newly appointed US District Judge Sidney Carr Mize (1888–1965).[211] Quite reasonably, Grissett claimed that he had a right, under the Constitution of the United States, to possess these slot machines. He argued that guardsmen in large numbers, armed with rifles, were—by denying him a pre-destruction hearing—depriving him of his personal property without due process of law. Judge Mize, however, dismissed the case twenty-two days after it was filed, on rather unpersuasive jurisdictional and equitable standing grounds, never formally reaching the merits of the claims made.[212] Grissett was said to have "unclean hands," because his mint vendors were gambling devices. At the time it was unlawful to possess "any slot machine which delivers . . . to the operator thereof anything of value in varying quantities, in addition to the merchandise received."[213] Farr and Grissett found little solace in Judge Mize's observation that in the protection of such due process rights, "the state courts are usually adequate to determine such rights, as he has an opportunity for ultimate review by the Supreme Court of the United States."[214] So much for federal question jurisdiction[215] and the rights of Farr and Grissett under the Due Process Clause of the Fourteenth Amendment and Civil Rights Act.[216]

In April of 1938, Justice Griffith had convincingly explained the rights of men like Farr and Grissett in the last part of his *McPhail* opinion. There is scant evidence that subsequent state or federal courts paid much mind.[217] To be sure, Judge Mize had acknowledged that "it is true that the federal courts may enjoin local peace officers from enforcing an illegal statute and destroying property when the acts are . . . exceptional and clear. . . ."[218] He saw no need to afford Farr and Grissett even temporary relief until they could be heard on whether they had bona fide rights in the claimed property at risk. In retrospect, Mize was surely wrong. It may be that the pre-destruction hearing would not have lasted very long, when it came to shot machines and other clearly outlawed gaming equipment. Jukeboxes and other music machines were another matter. Farr's fault may have been a function of guilt by association. Under the last part of *McPhail* and cases Judge Mize cited, the guard had no business seizing, much less destroying, music machines without Farr and Grissett and others similarly situated having first been given reasonable prior notice and the opportunity to be heard in opposition.

CRADDOCK GOINS'S MENCKENESQUE EFFORT

Eighteen months after the state supreme court decided *McPhail*, Craddock Goins published his article "Hooch and Homicide in Mississippi" in H. L. Mencken's monthly the *American Mercury*.[219] In short order, Goins's literary delight became the go-to source for insights about the Gold Coast for those who could not get there in person. Goins was a southerner, born and bred in Georgia. After a stint in Wisconsin circa 1926, he came to Mississippi and to Jackson in particular to edit "Mississippi Builder."[220] In 1935 and at the age of forty, Goins lived in rural Smith County, Mississippi, just below Rankin County. In 1940, he lived in Jackson.

His powerful and poignant "The Terror of the Mississippi" told of the tragedy of the Great Flood of 1927, and with unforgettable prose.[221] Time spent in Wisconsin informed his promotion of a cheese factory in Indianola, Mississippi.[222] In 1928, Goins served as director of publicity for the Mississippi State Board of Development. He brought his journalistic skills to bear as editor of the *Southland Dairy and Poultry Farmer*. He was a sought-after public speaker regarding and promoting Mississippi and the South.[223] Soon he was back in Wisconsin. In early 1933, the *Clarion-Ledger* reported that

> Craddock Goins, formerly city editor of The Clarion-Ledger, but now connected with the Olson Publishing Company of Milwaukee, is here in the interest of his publication, "The Ice Cream Review." Mr. Goins is a southern man and his home is in Atlanta, Ga.[224]

Goins made his mark with "Hooch and Homicide." His jabs at "Deacon Tom" Hederman,[225] editor of the *Clarion-Ledger*, are understood in the context of Goins having served as city editor of Hederman's, Jackson's, and the state's leading newspaper a few years earlier.[226] "Hooch" deserves a read in its entirety. But don't read too fast. Leave yourself open to the twinkle in Goins's eye as he penned his closing note. Doc Steed had emerged from another scrape with the law and resumed his "occasional ad in the Jackson papers. One such appeared recently next to an interview in which a leading dry official was quoted as being proud and happy 'that the city's moral life at last is safe.'"[227] Steed continued to live on the Gold Coast and in Pearl until his death in 1980.

But return to the time of the fateful clash between Sam Seaney and Norris Overby. Soon thereafter it was May of 1947. "Governor Closes Gold Coast, May Call Out Guard," the headline cried out on the front page of the *Clarion-Ledger*. Several stories followed. One was about an arrest made after "the decomposed body of . . . [a] prominent Jackson visitor was found in the Pearl River."[228] Another story featured Governor Fielding Wright's[229] "warn[ing] that if necessary he would call out the National Guard 'to restore law and order in that area,'"—"the notorious Gold Coast."[230]

Nine months earlier, Seaney and Overby had destroyed each other in the Shady Rest, all of which had supposedly shocked the Gold Coast, its patrons, and the public to their senses. But the Gold Coast had already begun its slow evolution into a home for garden-variety "drive-through" bootlegger operations. In 1944, the legislature enacted one of the most creative laws in its history. This bill became known as the "Black Market Tax."[231] A 10 percent sales tax was levied upon the sale of any "commodities whatsoever, the sale or distribution of which is prohibited by law."[232] In time the US Internal Revenue Service recognized that a bootlegger's 10 percent payments were deductible expenses the same as any other state-imposed tax.[233] This ingenious scheme accommodated three very different and conflicting interests. How can you improve on "the 'wets' have their whiskey, the Baptists have their law, and the state gets a healthy tax revenue"? Only the IRS took a hit, but without inequity, since it still got most of every person's taxes in support of good government. Most exemplary of all was 1946, when Rankin County was said to have been the largest contributor to the state's Black Market Tax coffers of any other of the eighty-two counties.[234] These numbers had plummeted by the late spring of 1947, reportedly as a result of evasive liquor distribution practices by Louisiana wholesalers and the ostensible closure of the Gold Coast under executive orders issued by Governor Wright.[235] Lingering aftereffects of Overby vs. Seaney likely played a part as well.

The era of the Gold Coast ended in 1966. The last chapter began in Mardi Gras season of that winter. The Jackson Country Club was the venue for a private soiree after the king and queen of Carnival had been crowned in a downtown hotel. Why the country club? Because it lay outside the city limits, and the crème de la crème of Jackson thought it only fitting that champagne, cocktails, and fine wines should flow freely and enhance the post-coronation celebration. Many prominent Jacksonians, civic leaders, the well-to-do, and many who never missed church on Sunday were all there having a jolly good time. Even the governor stopped by.

But an uninvited guest soon arrived. There was a new sheriff in town. Tom Shelton showed up with a host of deputies and rang down the curtain on the festivities. Outrage and consternation! Governor Johnson,[236] can't you do something?! A few months later, the legislature formally repealed prohibition, replacing it with a local-option liquor law that persists to this day. Hinds County sheriff Shelton was defeated in the next election.[237]

A FULL LIFE LIVED

There are those who have lived in central Mississippi who might raise eyebrows at the suggestion that Alexander Alvin Seaney was a good citizen. A few moments and minimal computer research skills yield the 1940 decision of the Supreme Court of Mississippi that begins "A. A. Seaney was convicted for the unlawful possession of intoxicating liquors, and he appeals." It takes a little longer to find the particulars of his most proficient son, Samuel Alvin Seaney, as vice kingpin on the Gold Coast, because there is so much to find. Second son Eugene's name shows up in court records on the side of those who made their living in the Gold Coast trade in the decade following the repeal of national Prohibition. But A. A. had become a great-grandfather by the time he died in 1963, at the age of seventy-six, a reasonably ripe age for the times. An appropriate Christian funeral service was held at Wright & Ferguson chapel, led by the Rev. L. S. Polk[238] and J. T. Chapman. A. A.'s resting place in Lakewood Memorial Park in Jackson is no different from those of many a good citizen of the area. His surviving good-citizen descendants are so numerous that they are hard to count.

But life had dealt A. A. Seaney a tough hand, with much tragedy and heartache over his years. The father's heartache began with the death of an infant in Illinois and then of a nine-year-old daughter, Millian, his second born, in 1909. This was bad enough, though those were the years when many still suffered the death of a young child. Not only was the brutal murder of daughter Anna Belle in 1918 horrible when it happened, the memory was resurrected time and again. Having survived threats of lynching, killer George Howie was first found guilty and sentenced to be hanged.[239] After a new trial because of the proverbial "technicality," venue variety, Howie was sent to the Mississippi State Penitentiary, supposedly for the rest of his life, a sentence later converted to ninety-nine years.[240] Whatever peace A. A. may have mustered over the years was shattered in 1930 when Howie escaped from Parchman, under sufficiently controversial circumstances to keep the story in the news for a while.[241] Twelve years later, A. A. no doubt had mixed emotions at the sudden news, dateline Seattle, Washington, July 1, 1942, that "George Howie, 57, picked up on a morals charge, is wanted by Mississippi authorities as an escaped murderer."[242]

A little more than four years later, in the latter part of August of 1946, A. A.'s eldest son Sam died violently in his twin shootout killing with Constable Norris Overby. We've told that story above.

In late January of 1949, following a brief illness, sixty-nine year old Minnie Ethel Seaney died in a Jackson area hospital. "Mrs. Seaney was a resident of East Jackson and had lived in Rankin County for the past 47 years."[243] Quite likely A. A. was relieved that the woman he married on March 19, 1899, died first, that she would have had a hard time living alone, though children and grandchildren survived. It goes without saying that there were gasps in A. A.'s heart that his wife's obituary did not list daughters Millian and Anna Belle or son Sam as being among the family survivors.

In mid-August of 1953, the seventy-six-year-old Alexander Alvin Seaney died unexpectedly while visiting one of his daughters in Galveston, Texas. His obituary noted his early years in Illinois followed by fifty years in the Jackson area: "He was a retired lumberman."[244] He had been spared experiencing the third violent death of a child. In late September of 1956, Eugene Seaney was in the midst of a heated telephone conversation with his ex-wife. A business partner at the Pic & Pay Grocery in Rankin County overheard Eugene's "voice rise in anger, and then heard Seaney say: 'Well, just listen to this.' Seaney then reached beneath the counter, Tharp said, got a .32 caliber pistol and fired a shot into his right temple."[245] Listed first among active pallbearers of Eugene's casket was G. W. Hydrick, by this time the most colorful bootlegger in Gold Coast history.

REFLECTIONS

This story opened with an excerpt from Soggy Sweat's Whiskey Speech, famous for more than half a century in Mississippi and environs. A more up-to-date introduction to the Gold Coast may have been the YouTube video of Crystal Lake,[246] a part of Flowood, Mississippi. Turn on to State Highway 468 North one exit and a few hundred feet north of Casey's Lane, and proceed westerly, curving toward the Pearl River. The serenity of the Crystal Lake area is as day-versus-night compared to the legislative facts that led to Governor White's December 1936 executive order. Twenty months later, Justice Griffith expounded on the constitution and en route the process of adjudication, with a moving caveat and conclusion grounded in Magna Carta. The only tangible evidence of what once was is a two-sided plaque posted near the lake by the Mississippi Blues Commission.[247]

> Mississippi state law prohibited the sale of liquor from 1908 to 1966, but humorist Will Rogers purportedly observed, "Mississippians will vote dry as long as they can stagger to the polls." By the 1930s bootleggers had set up shop openly here on the "Gold Coast," a name likely derived from the area's proximity to the Pearl River and the vast amounts of money that were made here from bootlegging, gambling and other vices. The Gold Coast soon became notorious for its

boisterous night life, frequent murders and official corruption, but customers continued to stream in from considerably stricter Jackson. On occasion the Mississippi National Guard was brought in to shut down the area, albeit with only temporary success, and the day-to-day operations and fortunes of bootleggers and clubs depended largely on the whims of local sheriffs. Infamous bootleggers included G. W. "Big Red" Hydrick[248] and Sam Heaney [sic], a club owner who was killed in a 1946 shootout that also claimed the life of Rankin County Constable Norris Overby.

The question that lingers from the tale of the Gold Coast is not whether the state can legislate morality. We've had enough experience with that one, the results overall a mixed bag. A better and more nuanced question is how—and why—We the People feel so compelled that we should try again and again and again to regulate the morality of the aggregate of humanity within a community and a country of lots of different people with many differing and conflicting interests, tolerances, and points of view. The question is tough enough before you add religion to the mixture.

Of course, any mention of legislating morality in Mississippi—or maybe just legislatin' of any kind—requires a nod to the late Justice George H. Ethridge (1871–1957) for his classic reflection regarding vending machines (likely not that different from the ones Dick Farr owned and dispensed over a decade later).

> But there are usually some 35 per cent to 40 per cent of the membership whose only excuse for being sent to the Legislature is to keep them out of the race for constables and justices of the peace. These men . . . are strong on midget legislation. . . . They introduce a bill to place jay birds under peace bonds, or to muzzle seed ticks, or to prohibit vending machines in stores,[249]. . . . These pigmy statesmen . . . attack small tasks. They are strong on moral questions or something that sounds well . . . for home consumption in future politics. They go around with a spiritual microscope searching for the germs of evils in trifles, while utterly ignoring the mountains of iniquity which stand out. . . . They hunt for earth worms.[250]

We are not aware that Justice Ethridge ever took to his bully pulpit around the time of Dick Farr's pinball machine wars. He would most surely have had a few choice words about Farr's "music machines," and likely his and Grissett's "one-armed bandits" as well. The worthies who would regulate these would be certain to feel the barbs of the justice's wicked pen.

But the other 60 or 65 percent of legislators proved quite creative when it came to dealing with sin on the Gold Coast. We saw above how they augmented the common nuisance statutes to authorize a form of sin-no-more guaranty bonds, backed by the threat of jail time if an acceptable bond were not filed.[251] That ingenious scheme remains in place, requiring of those found to have maintained one of those dreaded common nuisances—illegal liquor trafficking or illegal gambling—that they post a bond to assure that they will behave, at least for the next two years.[252]

The constitutional focus of this chapter began with that simple and familiar text, viz., the governor "shall see that the laws are faithfully executed."[253] Justice Griffith explained what that means about as well as can be, the bones picked above notwithstanding. But the truth is that *McPhail* did not go far enough. The idea of deference to local authorities is as sensible as it is practicable ordinarily. It is not, however, constitutionally commanded. The remedy for those offended that a governor may meddle too much in local affairs is at the ballot box and, ultimately, term limits. If the governor's use of the guard becomes unpopular, or even just too costly given other financial priorities, the legislature always has the power of the purse.[254]

The experience of the late 1930s and 1940s on the Gold Coast makes clear that the governor needs help when he tries to see that the laws are executed faithfully, help from others that he cannot constitutionally control. Of course, one would hope he could count on competent local law enforcement officials of integrity and good judgment. Even so, circumstances may suggest that the governor call out the National Guard and guide its mission. There he must count on competent guardsmen who can execute warrants and perform their duties with appropriate respect for the private personal and property rights of affected persons, guard officers who understand and respect all that Justice Griffith had to say in April of 1938. There can be no serious doubt—albeit with a bit of twenty-twenty hindsight—but that property owners like Dick Farr and R. B. Grissett at the very least were entitled to a pre-destruction due process hearing. In the case of music machines like those Farr had placed around the Gold Coast, raiding officers who destroyed first and asked questions later might even be liable for damages. As a practical matter, persons like Farr and Grissett might today proceed under the Mississippi Tort Claims Act.

The governor also needs prosecuting attorneys to take the evidence gathered in raids and bring proceedings to abate the common nuisance or, if they prefer, initiate conventional criminal prosecutions. If prosecuting attorneys fall short, there is not much the governor can do except mount the soapbox. It takes more than just the governor to see that some laws are faithfully executed. Recall the tales of the Mississippi Union Bank guaranty bonds and Planters' Bank guaranty bonds told in chapter 4 above.

The legislative power accepted and delegated in the constitution is never far from view. Who but the legislature has the primary job of legislating public morality? Courts have said that it's an element in the police power,[255] and the constitution declares that "the exercise of the police powers of the state shall never be abridged."[256]

Of course, the courts are always with us. Justice Griffith's grand legal essay—on the executive power and on the core teachings of Magna Carta more than seven hundred years after the fact—is one of the best discussed in this volume. It is so well written. Yet the Gold Coast continued to flourish—regular raids notwithstanding—until and past the shockwave of late August of 1946. The bootleg package stores continued without serious interruption until 1966, the State collecting its 10 percent sales tax on every half pint or fifth of Old Charter or Early Times a thirsty customer ever bought from a Gold Coast package store or anywhere else in Mississippi. A succession of governors beginning with Hugh White found their no-doubt faithful (albeit in part politically motivated) efforts to see that the laws regulating morality were executed became caught up in separation of powers and "checks and balances" and all of those other wonderful constraints that make the process of governing so cumbersome, maddening, and interesting.

In the end, we return to Holmes's insight from his famous *Abrams* dissent delivered in 1919, a time when fear was rampant, viz., "If you have no doubt of your premises or your power and want a certain result with all your heart you naturally express your wishes in law and sweep away all opposition." But the rest of us can answer, yes, for some results but by no means all. It becomes a matter of degree. Of course, by most any standard it is immoral to kill another person, or merely to injure another intentionally, or to steal from him or her. Many other such standards are found in criminal codes everywhere. But surely none of us has the prerogative of imposing on others our passions or our prejudices where no tangible objective harm is done to another. Mere awareness that others are engaging in practices or a lifestyle inconsistent with our strongly held beliefs is not a tangible objective harm to another, no matter how fervently some of us may wish it were. We the People, fearful or no, have not found a way to improve on the wisest thought that never made its way into the Judeo-Christian Bible—and that guides the more secular among us as well?—Live and let live.

ENDNOTES

1. I am not aware that there is an official citation for the late legislator, jurist, law professor Soggy Sweat's complete Whiskey Speech, the original 1952 version. I quoted it in full in 1986 in *City of Clinton v. Smith*, 493 So.2d 331, 336 fn. 13 (Miss. 1986), and accompanying text. *See* more recently Janice Branch Tracy, *Mississippi Moonshine Politics: How Bootleggers & the Law Kept a Dry State Soaked*, Appendix V, 173–174 (2015). Former Mississippi legislator turned author John Grisham reads it via YouTube at https://www.youtube.com/watch?v=qPzUcJcgXUA. *See also* "Noah S. Sweat," https://en.wikipedia.org/wiki/Noah_S_Sweat.

2. "Two Killed in Rankin Gun Battle, Sam Seaney and Constable Overby Die on Gold Coast," *Clarion-Ledger*, page 1 (Jackson, Miss.), Weds. morning, Aug. 28, 1946. Willie Mae Bradshaw has a slightly fictionalized account of this central event and its effects in her memoir

of the life of her father, the colorful bootlegger G. W. "Big Red" Hydrick, *Big Red* 127–131 (1977). Janice Branch Tracy has published a more recent account of the shootout in her *Mississippi Moonshine Politics: How Bootleggers & the Law Kept a Dry State Soaked* 105–106 (2015). This bit of history was featured on *Jackson Jambalaya* on Saturday, July 4, 2015, together with copies of press clippings from late August of 1946. *See* http://kingfish1935.blogspot.com/2015/07/rankin-constable-killed-in-gold-coast.html.

3. "Two Kill Each Other in Wild West Gun Duel, Shoot It Out on Floor of Crowded Dance Hall," *Chicago Tribune*, Aug. 29, 1946, page 4, columns 1–4.

4. *See, e.g.*, "Volstead Act," en.wikipedia.org/wiki/Volstead_Act.

5. According to a newspaper report in June of 1947, some 90 percent of all liquor shipments into Mississippi originated in Louisiana. "'Runners' Cause Drop in Liquor Tax Revenue," *Jackson Daily News* (Jackson, Miss.), June 5, 1947.

6. Sam Seaney was so recognized in Craddock Goins's 1939 article "Hooch and Homicide in Mississippi," *American Mercury*, Vol. XLVIII (Oct. 1939), pages 183–184. Goins was born in Georgia in 1896, is shown a resident of Jackson on the 1940 census, and was a frequent contributor to H. L. Mencken's periodical publication the *American Mercury*.

7. For other versions of the story of the emergence of the Gold Coast culture, *see* Del Stover, "Gold Coast; Rankin County's Infamous Past Is Recalled as Liquor Vote Nears," *Clarion-Ledger* (Jackson, Miss.), Sun., Oct. 23, 1983, page 1, Newspapers.com, https://www.newspapers.com/image/181242330; and more recently Janice Branch Tracy, *Mississippi Moonshine Politics: How Bootleggers & the Law Kept a Dry State Soaked* 91–94, 103–105 (2015).

8. Janice Branch Tracy, *Mississippi Moonshine Politics: How Bootleggers & the Law Kept a Dry State Soaked* 92–93 (2015).

9. "Arrest Ten," *Clarion-Ledger* (Jackson, Miss.), Thurs., June 25, 1931, page 7, Newspapers. com, https://www.newspapers.com/image/202688196.

10. "Truckload Whiskey Seized Here Broken by Policemen," *Clarion-Ledger* (Jackson, Miss.), Feb. 6, 1936, page 16, Newspapers.com, https://www.newspapers.com/image/202528222.

11. See civil Bills of Complaint to Abate a Common Nuisance shown on the docket and in the records of the Chancery Court of Rankin County for the year 1937 naming one or more Seaneys as defendants and bearing docket numbers 4025, 4112, 4113, 4138, 4182, 4199, 4209.

12. See Miss. Laws, ch. 189 (1918), then codified as Miss. Code §2007 (1930).

13. The cases were *State ex rel. Percy M. Lee, District Attorney, vs. Sam A. Seaney, et al.*, Chancery docket nos. 4025 and 4113.

14. Stribling was a member of the state National Guard who had taken part in raids on other establishments, as reflected in filings made in March of 1939 with the clerk of the US District Court, Southern District of Mississippi, Jackson Division, and styled *Dick Farr, etc., vs. John A. O'Keefe, Adjutant General of the State of Mississippi*, Docket No. 63. See *Farr v. O'Keefe*, 27 F. Supp. 216 (S. D. Miss. 1939).

15. Order of Chancery Court dated December 8, 1937, in Case No. 4209.

16. *A. A. Seaney v. State*, 188 Miss. 367, 194 So. 913, 914 (1940).

17. *Sam A. Seaney v. State ex rel. District Attorney*, 186 So. 312 (Mem.) (Miss. 1939). The Memorandum Order of the Supreme Court relied on *Redding v. State*, 184 Miss. 371, 185 So. 560 (1939), decided a month earlier, and also on *Pigford v. State ex rel. Broach, Dist. Atty.*, 184 Miss. 194, 183 So. 259 (1938).

18. "Two 'Gold Coast' Cases Dismissed by High Court," *Clarion-Ledger* (Jackson, Miss.), Feb. 7, 1939, page 12, Newspapers.com, https://www.newspapers.com/image/202594774. The same result was announced in *Dick Kent v. State ex rel. District Attorney*, 186 So. 312 (Mem.) (Miss. 1939).

19. *See Farr v. O'Keefe*, 27 F. Supp. 216 (S. D. Miss. 1939) for the order of US District Judge Sidney C. Mize dismissing on jurisdictional, standing, and traditional equity grounds the complaint for injunction that had been filed by area vending and amusement machine operators

Richard A. (Dick) Farr (1907–1965) and R. B. Grissett against the National Guard. See pages 396, 399–403, 407–408.

20. Sworn Statement of Eugene Seaney, made March 3, 1939, and filed with the clerk of the US District Court in proceedings leading to *Farr v. O'Keefe*, 27 F. Supp. 216 (S. D. Miss. 1939).

21. "Nearly . . ." *Clarion-Ledger* (Jackson, Miss.), June 23, 1939, page 5, Newspapers.com, https://www.newspapers.com/image/202702879.

22. Craddock Goins, "Hooch and Homicide in Mississippi," *American Mercury*, Vol. XLVIII (Oct. 1939), page 186.

23. *See* Rankin County Chancery Court Docket and Cases Nos. 4138, 4182, 4199, 4209, 4303, 4337, 4331, and 4342.

24. Norris Overby was born on June 20, 1914. *See* "Norris Overby," *Find A Grave*, Memorial #1108997846, https://www.findagrave.com/memorial/110899786/norris-overby.

25. *Clarion-Ledger* (Jackson, Miss.), Fri., Jan. 11, 1933, page 11, Newspapers.com, https://www.newspapers.com/image/202666144.

26. *Clarion-Ledger* (Jackson, Miss.), Tues., Nov. 21, 1933, page 7, Newspapers.com, https://www.newspapers.com/image/202643891.

27. *Clarion-Ledger* (Jackson, Miss.), Mon., Feb. 5, 1934, page 5, Newspapers.com, https://www.newspapers.com/image/203064896.

28. "Brandon School to Present Play," *Clarion-Ledger* (Jackson, Miss.), Weds., March 21, 1934, page 2, Newspapers.com, https://www.newspapers.com/image/202666144.

29. *Clarion-Ledger* (Jackson, Miss.), Sat., Apr. 7, 1934, page 2, Newspapers.com, https://www.newspapers.com/image/202656081.

30. "Ole Miss Fraternities Announce New Pledges," *Clarion-Ledger* (Jackson, Miss.), Sun., Sept. 23, 1934, page 8, Newspapers.com, https://www.newspapers.com/image/202645016.

31. "'Thursday Nighters' Elect New Officers," *Clarion-Ledger* (Jackson, Miss.), Thurs., June 16, 1938, page 4, Newspapers.com, https://www.newspapers.com/image/202533781.

32. "Miss Maureen Turner and Norris Overby to Be Wed Xmas Day," *Clarion-Ledger* (Jackson, Miss.) Tues., Dec. 13, 1938, page 4, Newspapers.com, https://www.newspapers.com/image/202636341.

33. "Brandon W.S.C.S. Names New Officers," *Clarion-Ledger* (Jackson, Miss.), Weds., Dec. 3, 1941, page 8, Newspapers.com, https://www.newspapers.com/image/202680543.

34. *Clarion-Ledger* (Jackson, Miss.), Sat., June 6, 1942, page 6, Newspapers.com, https://www.newspapers.com/image/202708158.

35. *Clarion-Ledger* (Jackson, Miss.), Fri., Aug. 3, 1945, page 8, Newspapers.com, https://www.newspapers.com/image/202680543.

36. On August 25, 1943, Overby won a runoff second Democratic primary election, defeating John White by 458 votes to 413 votes. *Clarion-Ledger* (Jackson, Miss.), Thurs., Aug. 26, 1943, page 9, Newspapers.com, https://www.newspapers.com/image/202690594.

37. *See* particularly Janice Branch Tracy's version set out in her *Mississippi Moonshine Politics: How Bootleggers & the Law Kept a Dry State Soaked* 105–106 (2015).

38. Sara Richardson, "The Pearl 'Never Does Nothing,'" Rankin County Historical Society, July 10, 1985, http://rankinhistory.com/site/?page_id=425.

39. "Rankin Squirms as Water Rises," *Clarion-Ledger* (Jackson, Miss.), Thurs., Feb. 16, 1939, page 146, Newspapers.com, https://www.newspapers.com/image/202605158.

40. "Pearl River (Mississippi-Louisiana)," en.wikipedia.org/wiki/Pearl_River _(Mississippi%E2%80%93Louisiana).

41. Janice Branch Tracy, *Mississippi Moonshine Politics: How Bootleggers & the Law Kept a Dry State Soaked* 92–93 (2015).

42. Eudora Welty, "The Wide Net," in *Collected Stories* 181 (1980), quoted in *Dycus v. Sillers*, 557 So.2d 486, 491 (Miss. 1990).

43. *Ryals v. Pigott*, 580 So.2d 1140, 1155, fn. 31 (Miss. 1991); *see also Pearl River Valley Water Supply District v. Hinds County*, 445 So.2d 1330 (Miss. 1984); *Culley v. Pearl River Industrial Commission*, 234 Miss. 788, 108 So.2d 390 (1959).

44. Sara Richardson, "The Pearl 'Never Does Nothing,'" Rankin County Historical Society, July 10, 1985, http://rankinhistory.com/site/?page_id=425.

45. One such list appeared in the *Clarion-Ledger* on Fri., June 23, 1939. "Nearly . . ." *Clarion-Ledger* (Jackson, Miss.), June 23, 1939, page 5, Newspapers.com, https://www.newspapers.com /image/202702879.

46. *See* "Gold Coast-Jackson," Mississippi Blues Trail, http://msbuestrail.org/blues-trail -markers/goldcoast.

47. On June 2, 1937, the State named Malcolm Foy as a defendant in a bill to abate a common nuisance, Chancery Court No. 4137. The rundown and apparently abandoned building that housed Foy's Grocery is found today on the north side of Old Brandon Road between Casey's Lane to the west and Fannin Road to the east.

48. The State named Red Top et al. as defendants in a bill to abate a common nuisance, Chancery Court No. 4016.

49. *McComb Daily Journal* (McComb, Miss.), Fri., Mar. 10, 1939, page 6, Newspapers.com, https://www.newspapers.com/image/249569117.

50. The State named Brown Derby et al. as defendants in a bill to abate a common nuisance, Chancery Court No. 4017.

51. The State named Put & Take et al. as defendants in a bill to abate a common nuisance, Chancery Court No. 4018.

52. The State named Gus Place as defendant in a bill to abate a common nuisance, Chancery Court No. 4019.

53. The State named White Horse Cellar as defendant in a bill to abate a common nuisance, Chancery Court No. 4020.

54. *See Farr v. O'Keefe*, 27 F. Supp. 216 (S. D. Miss. 1939), in which R. B. Grissett was an intervening plaintiff in a failed suit seeking to enjoin the National Guard from destroying his slot machines.

55. On June 2, 1937, the State named Silver Moon Night Club et al. as defendants in a bill to abate a common nuisance, Chancery Court No. 4140.

56. On June 2, 1937, the State named New Colonial Club et al. as defendants in a bill to abate a common nuisance, Chancery Court No. 4143.

57. On September 28, 1937, the State named Gold Coast Café et al. as defendants in a bill to abate a common nuisance, Chancery Court No. 4178.

58. On September 28, 1937, the State named Casa Loma et al. as defendants in a bill to abate a common nuisance, Chancery Court No. 4179.

59. On September 28, 1937, the State named Ballew's Café et al. as defendants in a bill to abate a common nuisance, Chancery Court No. 4185

60. *See* news report of National Guard raid in early February, 1939, "Guard Stages Surprise Raid on 'Gold Coast,'" *Clarion-Ledger* (Jackson, Miss.), June 23, 1939, page 5, Newspapers.com, https://www.newspapers.com/image/202593786.

61. Doc Steed was more colorfully recognized by Craddock Goins in his article "Hooch and Homicide in Mississippi," *American Mercury*, Vol. XLVIII (Oct. 1939), pages 184, 186. Steed becomes downright three-dimensional as a result of Gene Trimble's column "Illegal of the Day Mississippi," *The Chip Board*, http://www.thechipboard.com/archives/archives.pl/bid/399 /md/read/id/1269587/sbj/illega . . . ; *see also* Phil McCausland, "The Art of Distillation," *Oxford American Magazine*, http://oxfordamerican.org/magazine/item/92-the-art-of-distillation.

62. On November 29, 1937, the State named the Bazooka, Sam A. Seaney, et al. as defendants in a bill to abate a common nuisance, Chancery Court No. 4199.

63. On September 28, 1937, the State named the Oaks et al. as defendants in a bill to abate a common nuisance, Chancery Court No. 4184. Rogers was given a nod by Craddock Goins in "Hooch and Homicide in Mississippi," *American Mercury*, Vol. XLVIII (Oct. 1939), page 184.

64. On September 28, 1937, the State named Owl's Nest et al. as defendants in a bill to abate a common nuisance, Chancery Court No. 4186.

65. See *McLaurin v. State*, 205 Miss. 554, 566–567, 37 So.2d 8 (1948) (Carr's Place and the Green Lantern).

66. "Nearly ..." *Clarion-Ledger* (Jackson, Miss.), June 23, 1939, page 5, Newspapers.com, https://www.newspapers.com/image/202702879, provides a long list of venues and proprietors that the National Guard had recently raided.

67. Pat Hudson was recognized for his foresight only a few years after the fact by Craddock Goins in his article "Hooch and Homicide in Mississippi," *American Mercury*, Vol. XLVIII (Oct. 1939), page 183. On June 2, 1937, Hudson had been recognized for his activity in a Bill of Complaint to Abate a Common Nuisance filed by the district attorney in the Chancery Court of Rankin County, Case No. 4136.

68. "Guysell McPhail," *Find a Grave*, Memorial #86036804, https://www.findagrave.com /memorial/86036804?search=true.

69. "Raid-to-End-All Raids Destroys Much Property," *Clarion-Ledger* (Jackson, Miss.), June 23, 1939, page 1, Newspapers.com, https://www.newspapers.com/image/202702498.

70. *See* report in "Drives Continue on Weary Rankin," *Clarion-Ledger* (Jackson, Miss.), Feb. 10, 1939, page 20, Newspapers.com, https://www.newspapers.com/image/202598771.

71. *See* "Wayne Queen, Tree Surgery Owner, Dies," https://www.ancestry.com/mediaui-viewer /tree/104185934/person/160038407509/media/ ... ; "Motorist Mistakes Police for Thugs; Dares Bullet Hail," *Clarion-Ledger* (Jackson, Miss.), Fri., Mar. 18, 1938, page 7, Newspapers.com, https://www .newspapers.com/download/image/?id=202331937&height=2398&width=97 ... ; "Parole Violator Surrenders Voluntarily to Superintendent Thames," *Clarion-Ledger* (Jackson, Miss.), Newspapers .com, https://www.newspapers.com/download/image/?id=203061947&height=1597&width=86 ... ; Craddock Goins, "Hooch and Homicide in Mississippi," *American Mercury*, Vol. XLVIII (Oct. 1939), page 184; and more recently Janice Branch Tracy, *Mississippi Moonshine Politics: How Bootleggers & the Law Kept a Dry State Soaked* 98–99 (2015).

72. Janice Branch Tracy, *Mississippi Moonshine Politics: How Bootleggers & the Law Kept a Dry State Soaked* 99 (2015).

73. Janice Branch Tracy, *Mississippi Moonshine Politics: How Bootleggers & the Law Kept a Dry State Soaked*, 116 (2015). Tracy's source is Davie Ricardo Lindsey, son of Jimmy Lindsey, who owned and operated the Gay Lady.

74. See Mississippi Blues Trail, Gold Coast-Jackson, http://msbluestrail.org/blues-trail -markers/goldcoast.

75. Janice Branch Tracy, *Mississippi Moonshine Politics: How Bootleggers & the Law Kept a Dry State Soaked* (2015).

76. *Mississippi Power & Light Co. v. Tripp*, 183 Miss. 225, 183 So. 514, 516 (1938).

77. *Street v. State*, 200 Miss. 226, 229, 26 So.2d 678 (1946).

78. *See Hartfield v. State*, 186 Miss. 75, 189 So. 530 (1939). This one was remembered years later by David McCarty, in his "Welcome to East Jackson," *jackson obscura*, https:// jacksonobscura.wordpress.com/2011/06/28/welcome-to-east-jackson-part-I/.

79. *Hartfield v. State*, 189 So. at 531–534 (McGehee), and 534–541 (Ethridge) (Miss. 1939).

80. *Hartfield v. State*, 189 So. at 531 (McGehee), and 534 (Ethridge) (Miss. 1939).

81. *McLaurin v. State*, 205 Miss. 554, 37 So.2d 8 (1948).

82. Janice Branch Tracy, *Mississippi Moonshine Politics: How Bootleggers & the Law Kept a Dry State Soaked* 104 (2015).

83. *See* Jesse Yancy in his "Rankin County Redux," *Mississippi Sideboard*, Aug. 15, 2012.

84. *See* Craddock Goins, "Hooch and Homicide in Mississippi," *American Mercury*, Vol. XLVIII (Oct. 1939), page 184; and more recently Janice Branch Tracy, *Mississippi Moonshine Politics: How Bootleggers & the Law Kept a Dry State Soaked* 94 (2015).

85. Craddock Goins, "Hooch and Homicide in Mississippi," *American Mercury*, Vol. XLVIII (Oct. 1939), page 183.

86. "Sheriff Mashburn Raps Suit Filed for Gambling Loss," *Daily Herald* (Gulfport, Miss.), Feb. 21, 1951, reproduced in Gene Trimble's column "Illegal of the Day Mississippi," *The Chip Board*, http://www.thechipboard.com/archives/archives.pl/bid/399/md/read/id/1269587/sbj /illega . . .

87. *See* "Hugh Lawson White," in David G. Sansing, *Mississippi Governors: Soldiers, Statesmen, Scholars, Scoundrels: A Bicentennial Edition* 176–179 (2016); Hugh Lawson White, *Mississippi Encyclopedia* 1331–1332 (Ownby and Wilson eds., 2017).

88. See *State v. McPhail*, 182 Miss. 360, 182 So. 387, 389 (1938).

89. Miss. Laws, ch. 189 (1918), codified as Miss. Code §2007 (1930).

90. Many well-used exemplars of this form Bill of Complaint are gathering dust while in storage in the basement of the Rankin County Chancery Court building. *See, e.g.*, Bill of Complaint in *State of Mississippi and County of Rankin, Ex Rel. Percy M. Lee, District Attorney, Complainant, vs. A. A. Seaney, Frank Seaney, and Lee Jones, Defendants*, Chancery Court Docket No. 4182, dated September 27, 1937.

91. Regarding the varying points of view and experiences of men and women regarding intoxicating beverages, see *City of Clinton v. Smith*, 493 So.2d 331, 334–336 (Miss. 1986); and my *Practical Benefits of Literature in Law, and Their Limits*, 35 Miss. Coll. L. Rev. 266, 313–319 (2016).

92. These are cases Nos. 4107 through 4119 on the docket of the Chancery Court of Rankin County, Mississippi, kept in the office of the chancery clerk in Brandon, Mississippi.

93. Case Nos. 4112 and 4113 are each styled *The State of Mississippi, etc., vs. A. A. Seaney and others.*

94. These are cases Nos. 4129 through 4143 on the docket of the Chancery Court of Rankin County, Mississippi, kept in the office of the chancery clerk in Brandon, Mississippi.

95. Case No. 4136 is styled *The State of Mississippi, etc., vs. Pat Hudson, et al.*

96. Case No. 4139 is styled *The State of Mississippi, etc., vs. Annie Steed and "Doc" Steed.*

97. Case No. 4138 is styled *The State of Mississippi, etc., vs. S. A. Seaney, et al.*

98. These are cases Nos. 4178 through 4186 on the docket of the Chancery Court of Rankin County, Mississippi, kept in the office of the chancery clerk in Brandon, Mississippi.

99. Case No. 4182 is styled *The State of Mississippi, etc., vs. A. A. Seaney, et al.*

100. These are cases Nos. 4198 through 4205 on the docket of the Chancery Court of Rankin County, Mississippi, kept in the office of the chancery clerk in Brandon, Mississippi.

101. Janice Branch Tracy, *Mississippi Moonshine Politics: How Bootleggers & the Law Kept a Dry State Soaked* 98 (2015).

102. Case No. 4199 is styled *The State of Mississippi, etc., vs. "Bazooka," Sam A. Seaney, et al.*

103. A copy of this December 26, 1938, executive order is in the papers filed with the clerk of the US District Court, Southern District of Mississippi, Jackson Division, and styled *Dick Farr, etc., vs. John A. O'Keefe, Adjutant General of the State of Mississippi*, Docket No. 63, which appears to have been initiated on March 2, 1939.

104. "Gold Coast Action against Guard Supported," *Clarion-Ledger* (Jackson, Miss.), Mar. 15, 1939, page 14, Newspapers.com, https://www.newspapers.com/image/202605216.

105. "'Gold Coast' Leaps Back into the Legal Spotlight," *Clarion-Ledger* (Jackson, Miss.), Sun. Feb. 26, 1939, page 16, Newspapers.com, https://www.newspapers.com/image/202599505.

106. A few years later, Craddock Goins provided a journalist's version of this story in "Hooch and Homicide in Mississippi," *American Mercury*, Vol. XLVIII (Oct. 1939), 183–184.

107. Case No. 4203 is styled *The State of Mississippi, etc., vs. Guysell McPhail and Stanley McPhail.*

108. "M'Phail Freed in Rum Trial," *Clarion-Ledger* (Jackson, Miss.), Dec. 19, 1929, page 11, Newspapers.com, https://www.newspapers.com/image/202713470.

109. Chancellor Amis's full name was Alphonso Bobbet Amis. He practiced law in Meridian, where he was city attorney from 1912 until 1931, when he was elected to the first of three four-year terms as chancellor. He returned to the practice of law in the mid-1940s and remained active until December of 1948. He died in July of 1949. See "Judge A. B. Amis' Funeral Friday," *Clarion-Ledger* (Jackson, Miss.), July 8, 1949, page 10, Newspapers.com, https://www .newspapers.com/image/179697322.

110. Craddock Goins took note of Judge Amis's role in the story in "Hooch and Homicide in Mississippi," *American Mercury*, Vol. XLVIII (Oct. 1939), page 185.

111. Janice Branch Tracy, *Mississippi Moonshine Politics: How Bootleggers & the Law Kept a Dry State Soaked* 96–97 (2015).

112. Assignment of Error No. 1 filed by State of Mississippi in *State ex rel. Percy M. Lee, District Attorney*, No. 33,159, filed March 3, 1938. For reasons unknown, this Assignment of Error and McPhail's subsequent Suggestion of Error are the only documents found in what is supposed to be the complete appellate record in the McPhail case, kept by the Mississippi Department of Archives and History. After diligent search and inquiry, no further documents from this important court file have been found. The State's failure to have preserved the entire file of this historically important case is a matter of not inconsiderable concern.

113. See chapter 10, below.

114. Senate Journal, pages 26–27 (Reg. Sess. 1938); House Journal, pages 21–22 (Reg. Sess. 1938).

115. House Journal, page 402 (Reg. Sess. 1938).

116. House Journal, pages 441–442 (Reg. Sess. 1938).

117. Senate Journal, pages 307–308 (Reg. Sess. 1938).

118. See Miss. Laws, ch. 341 (1938), codified today as Miss. Code §§ 95-3-25 (with subsequent amendments) and 99-27-23.

119. Craddock Goins, "Hooch and Homicide in Mississippi," *American Mercury*, Vol. XLVIII (Oct. 1939), page 183. *See also* Bill Minor, "New Liquor Bill Revives Memory of Rankin Bootle," *Daily Journal* (Tupelo, Miss.), March 9, 2000, http://djournal.com/news/hedbill-minor-new-liquor-bill-revives-memory-of-rankin-bootle. Gold Coast establishments served "a ready-made clientele of fun starved folks out of the capital city, including state lawmakers."

120. John Ray Skates Jr., *A History of the Mississippi Supreme Court, 1817–1948* page 79 (1973); Robert Gillespie, "Virgil Alexis Griffith," Vol. XXXVII, *Journal of Mississippi History* 267 (1997).

121. A number of streets and city blocks in downtown Jackson, Mississippi, appear to have been modified from what they probably were in the 1930s.

122. *Brown v. State*, 173 Miss. 542, 161 So. 465, 470–471 (1935).

123. For the quoted parts of Justice Griffith's dissent, *see Brown v. Mississippi*, 297 U.S. 278, 281–285 (1936).

124. The story of Ed Brown, Arthur Ellington, Harry Shields, and Virgil A. Griffith is well told by Richard C. Cortner in his *A Scottsboro Case in Mississippi* (2005).

125. *State vs. McPhail*, 182 Miss. 360, 180 So. 360 (1938).

126. Miss. Const. art. 5, § 123 (1890); Miss. Code § 7-1-5(c) (1972).

127. Miss. Const. art. 9, § 217 (1890).

128. Miss. Const. art. 3, § 9 (1890).

129. Miss. Const. art. 3, § 14; U.S. Const. amend. XIV, § 1.

130. *See* Miss. R. Evid. 201; Fed. R. Evid. 201.

131. *State v. McPhail*, 182 Miss. 360, 180 So. 387, 388 (April 18, 1938).

132. Craddock Goins, "Hooch and Homicide in Mississippi," *American Mercury*, Vol. XLVIII (October 1939), pages 181–183.

133. *See, e.g., Pearl River Valley Water Supply District v. Hinds County*, 445 So.2d 1330 (Miss. 1984); *Culley v. Pearl River Industrial Commission*, 234 Miss. 788, 108 So.2d 390 (1959).

134. For a discussion of the proper and legitimate use of legislative facts in the process of adjudication, *see* my *Variations on a Theme by Posner: Facing the Factual Component of the Reliability Imperative in the Process of Adjudication*, 84 Miss. L. Journ. 471, 524–537 (2015).

135. *State v. McPhail*, 182 Miss. 360, 180 So. 387, 388 (April 18, 1938).

136. *See* my *Practical Benefits of Literature in Law, and Their Limits*, 35 Miss. Coll. L. Rev. 266 (2016).

137. *State v. McPhail*, 182 Miss. 360, 180 So. 387, 388–389 (April 18, 1938).

138. Craddock Goins, "Hooch and Homicide in Mississippi," *American Mercury*, Vol. XLVIII (Oct. 1939), page 182.

139. Did he thereupon adjudge once and for all time that the Gold Coast in its entirety was within the meaning and contemplation of Section 2007?

140. *State v. McPhail*, 182 Miss. 360, 180 So. 387, 389 (April 18, 1938).

141. David McCarty, "Welcome to East Jackson," *jackson obscura*, https://jacksonobscura .wordpress.com/2011/06/28/welcome-to-east-jackson-part-I/.

142. The reference is to what is now Miss. R. Evid. 804.

143. *State v. McPhail*, 182 Miss. 360, 180 So. 387, 389 (April 18, 1938).

144. Redundantly and as though the constitutional command were not self-executing, the legislature also enacted that the governor "shall see that the laws are faithfully executed." Miss. Code, § 48179(c) (1930).

145. *State v. McPhail*, 182 Miss. 360, 180 So. 387, 389, 391, 392 (April 18, 1938). Initially, Griffith refers to "a substantial breakdown in the enforcement of the laws by the local executive officers in that area." *McPhail*, 180 So. at 389. At another point, Griffith uses the phrase "where there is a breakdown of the enforcement of the laws." *McPhail*, 180 So. at 390.

146. *State v. McPhail*, 182 Miss. 360, 180 So. 387, 390 (April 18, 1938).

147. *State v. McPhail*, 182 Miss. 360, 180 So. 387, 391 (April 18, 1938).

148. *State v. McPhail*, 182 Miss. 360, 180 So. 387, 389–390 (April 18, 1938).

149. *State v. McPhail*, 182 Miss. 360, 180 So. 387, 390 (April 18, 1938).

150. *Franks v. Smith*, 142 Ky. 232, 134 S.W. 484, 488 (1912).

151. *State v. McPhail*, 182 Miss. 360, 180 So. 387, 390 (April 18, 1938).

152. Oliver Wendell Holmes Jr., *The Common Law* 1 (1881).

153. Robert H. Jackson, "The Federal Prosecutor," Address to Second Annual Conference of United States Attorneys page 3–4 (April 1, 1940).

154. *State v. McPhail*, 182 Miss. 360, 180 So. 387, 391 (April 18, 1938).

155. *State v. McPhail*, 182 Miss. 360, 180 So. 387, 391 (April 18, 1938).

156. James L. Robertson, "Political Questions," in *Subject Matter Jurisdiction,* § 1:35, in Mississippi Civil Procedure, Vol. 1, pages 128–136 (eds. Jackson, Campbell, & Matheny 2016); Robertson, "Political Questions," in *Constitutional Law,* § 19:216, in *Mississippi Constitutional Law,* Vol. 3 (2d ed., Jackson, Miller & Campbell, eds. 2018).

157. *Gunn v. Hughes*, 210 So.3d 969, 2017 WL 533802 (¶¶ 16, 17) (Miss. 2017) is a more recent decision on a so-called political question ostensibly controlled by the "absolute" separation of powers when no such absolute separation of powers has textual support in Article 1 or any other credible command of the constitution.

158. *State v. McPhail*, 182 Miss. 360, 180 So. 387, 392 (April 18, 1938).

159. For a more complete explanation of this three-step process so essential to the reliability of an adjudication, see my *Variations on a Theme by Posner: Facing the Factual Component of the Reliability Imperative in the Process of Adjudication*, 84 Miss. L. Journ. 471, 485–497 (2015).

160. For an extensive discussion of scope of review far beyond what is appropriate here, see my *Variations on a Theme by Posner: Facing the Factual Component of the Reliability Imperative in the Process of Adjudication*, 84 Miss. L. Journ. 471, 540–564 (2015).

161. *State v. McPhail*, 182 Miss. 360, 180 So. 387, 389 (April 18, 1938).

162. *State v. McPhail*, 182 Miss. 360, 180 So. 387, 391 (April 18, 1938).

163. *State v. McPhail*, 182 Miss. 360, 180 So. 387, 391 (April 18, 1938), quoting Miss. Const. art. 3, § 24 (1890).

164. The paragraph is found in *State v. McPhail*, 182 Miss. 360, 180 So. 387, 392 (April 18, 1938), and begins "By section 24 of the constitution of this state, . . ."

165. See chapter 1, "No Arbitrary Power," pages 7–8 above.

166. Sections 14, 21 and 24 noted above are all found within Article 3, Bill of Rights, of the Mississippi Constitution of 1890.

167. *State v. McPhail*, 182 Miss. 360, 180 So. 387, 392 (April 18, 1938), quoting from Miss. Const. art. 3, § 24 (1890).

168. *State v. McPhail*, 182 Miss. 360, 180 So. 387, 392 (April 18, 1938).

169. Miss. Const. art.3, §§ 14, 21 and 24 (1890).

170. Miss. Const. art. 5, § 123 (1890); Miss. Code § 7-1-5(c) (1972).

171. Order entered March 22, 1939, found in Minute Book 11, pages 124–127 in the records of the Chancery Court of Rankin County kept in the office of the chancery clerk.

172. "Saturday Night Sees 2 Attacks on Rankin Area," *Clarion-Ledger* (Jackson, Miss.), Feb. 26, 1939, page 1, Newspapers.com, https://www.newspapers.com/image/202598151.

173. "Nearly . . .," *Clarion-Ledger* (Jackson, Miss.), June 23, 1939, page 5, Newspapers.com, https://www.newspapers.com/image/202702879.

174. *See Melvin v. State*, 210 Miss. 132, 49 So.2d 837, 857–858 (1950).

175. "Gold Coast Hits New Peak after Brief Closures," *Clarion-Ledger* (Jackson, Miss.), June 15, 1939, page 1, Newspapers.com; https://www.newspapers.com/image/202576165.

176. "New Magistrate Turns Off Gold Coast Lights," *Clarion-Ledger* (Jackson, Miss.), Sat., Jan. 28, 1939, Newspapers.com; https://www.newspapers.com/image/202585388.

177. "Guard Stages Surprise Raid on 'Gold Coast,'" *Clarion-Ledger* (Jackson, Mississippi) page 2, Feb. 7, 1939, Newspapers.com; https://www.newspapers.com/image/202593786.

178. "Drives Continue on Weary Rankin," *Clarion-Ledger* (Jackson, Miss.), Feb. 10, 1939, page 20, Newspapers.com, https://www.newspapers.com/image/202598771.

179. "Saturday Night Sees 2 Attacks on Rankin Area," *Clarion-Ledger* (Jackson, Miss.), Feb. 26, 1939, page 1, Newspapers.com, https://www.newspapers.com/image/202598151.

180. "White Hints Martial Law as Next Gold Coast Move; Raid Wreckage at $100,000," *Jackson Daily News* (June 23, 1939), page 1.

181. "Raid-to-End-All Raids Destroys Much Property," *Clarion-Ledger* (Jackson, Miss.), June 23, 1939, page 1, Newspapers.com, https://www.newspapers.com/image/202702498. *See also* "Mop-Up Tactics Executed along Rankin Sectors," *Clarion-Ledger* (Jackson, Miss.), June 25, 1939, page 1, Newspapers.com, https://www.newspapers.com/image/202704466; and "Axes Used in Second Gold Coast Raid," *Clarion-Ledger* (Jackson, Miss.), June 25, 1939, page 1, Newspapers. com, https://www.newspapers.com/image/202704466.

182. "Liquor Selling on Sly Resumed Following Raid," *Clarion-Ledger* (Jackson, Miss.), June 24, 1939, page 1, Newspapers.com, https://www.newspapers.com/image/202703823.

183. *Clarion-Ledger* (Jackson, Miss.), June 25, 1939, page 10, Newspapers.com, https://www .newspapers.com/image/202705105.

184. *A. A. Seaney v. State*, 188 Miss. 367, 194 So. 913, 914–915 (1940).

185. "Raid-to-End-All Raids Destroys Much Property," *Clarion-Ledger* (Jackson, Miss.), June 23, 1939, page 1, Newspapers.com, https://www.newspapers.com/image/202702498.

186. *State v. McPhail*, 182 Miss. 360, 180 So. 387, 389 (April 18, 1938).

187. The depictions above are set out in three affidavits filed with the clerk of the US District Court, Southern District of Mississippi, Jackson Division, in a case styled Dick Farr, etc., vs. John A. O'Keefe, Adjutant General of the State of Mississippi, Docket No. 63. Eugene Seaney's affidavit was given on March 3, 1939, as was Malcolm Foy's affidavit. Bill McCleave's affidavit was given on March 8, 1939. All three affidavits were filed on March 9, 1939.

188. *State v. McPhail*, 182 Miss. 360, 180 So. 387, 391–392 (April 18, 1938).

189. Miss. Const. art. 5, § 123 (1890); Miss. Code § 7-1-5(c) (1972).

190. "Dick Farr Amusement Co.," *Clarion-Ledger* (Jackson, Miss.), Feb. 6, 1948, page 17, Newspapers.com, https://www.newspapers.com/image/202670206.

191. "Café Manager Fined $100 in Pin-Ball Machine Case," *Clarion-Ledger* (Jackson, Miss.), Nov. 13, 1935, page 8, Newspapers.com, https://www.newspapers.com/image/202529422.

192. "Judge Sustains City Demurrer against Writ of Prohibition in Pin Machine War," *Clarion-Ledger* (Jackson, Miss.), Nov. 21, 1935, page 14, Newspapers.com, https://www.newspapers.com/image/202591662.

193. "Punchboards Included in Police Drive on Gambling," *Clarion-Ledger* (Jackson, Miss.), Nov. 22, 1935, page 14, Newspapers.com, https://www.newspapers.com/image/202592499.

194. "Farr Exonerated by County Jury," *Clarion-Ledger* (Jackson, Mississippi) page 7, March 16, 1938, Newspapers.com; https://www.newspapers.com/image/202430944.

195. "STOP," *Clarion-Ledger* (Jackson, Mississippi) page 6, Jan. 15, 1959, Newspapers.com; https://www.newspapers.com/image/179700357; "Richard A. Farr," *Clarion-Ledger* (Jackson, Mississippi) page 5, Jan. 17, 1959, Newspapers.com; https://www.newspapers.com/image/180077156.

196. "Sheriff's Office to Present Slot Machine Case to Grand Jury," *Clarion-Ledger* (Jackson, Miss.) page 1, Fri., May 12, 1944, Newspapers.com; https://www.newspapers.com/image/203073176.

197. Miss. Laws, chapter 535, §2 (1938), later codified as Miss. Code Ann. § 97-33-7(2). See cases cited in the last paragraph of *Farr v. O'Keefe*, 27 F. Supp. 216, 217 (S. D. Miss. 1939); and, more recently, *Trainer v. State*, 930 So.2d 373 (Miss. 2006).

198. "Court Is Asked to Keep Guards off Gold Coast," *Clarion-Ledger* (Jackson, Miss.) page 1, Thurs. Feb. 16, 1939, Newspapers.com, https://www.newspapers.com/image/202604082.

199. "'Gold Coast' Leaps Back into the Legal Spotlight," *Clarion-Ledger* (Jackson, Miss.) page 16, Sun. Feb. 26, 1939, Newspapers.com, https://www.newspapers.com/image/202599505.

200. "Gold Coast Action Against Guard Supported," *Clarion-Ledger* (Jackson, Miss.) page 14, March 15, 1939, Newspapers.com, https://www.newspapers.com/image/202605216.

201. Numerous requests have been made to the Circuit Clerk of Rankin County for access to the court records regarding these proceedings in early 1939. All such requests have been met with the assertion that no court records prior to 1952 have been retained. The Mississippi Department of Archives and History does not have these records either. This is particularly disappointing, as substantial records exist in the Chancery Court of Rankin County and have been made readily available by the Chancery Clerk.

202. See "'Gold Coast' Is Appealing Case to U. S. Courts," *Clarion-Ledger* (Jackson, Mississippi) page 1, Fri. March 3, 1939, Newspapers.com; https://www.newspapers.com/image/202604610. As was the custom and practice at the time, Farr filed a sworn Petition for an Injunction, being dated March 1, 1939, and Farr's verifying oath having been made before Hinds County Justice of the Peace M. W. Sharp.

203. Petition for an Injunction filed by Dick Farr with the Clerk of the U.S. District Court, Southern District of Mississippi, Jackson Division, and styled Dick Farr, etc., vs. John A. O'Keefe, Adjutant General of the State of Mississippi, Docket No. 63.

204. Miss. Laws, ch. 353, § 1 (1938), today codified as Miss. Code Ann. §97-33-7(1).

205. "Farr Fined $100 in Police Court," *Clarion-Ledger* (Jackson, Mississippi) page 5, March 5, 1939, Newspapers.com; https://www.newspapers.com/image/202609022.

206. Grissett's name is misspelled "Gressitt" in the federal court records, and in some news reports thereof. He lived most of his life in the area that is now Flowood, Mississippi. "R. B. Grissett," *Clarion-Ledger* (Jackson, Miss.), May 2, 1964, page 5, Newspapers.com, https://www.newspapers.com/image/180457068.

207. Grissett's Intervening Petition was also sworn, being dated March 14, 1939, verified before Hinds County Justice of the Peace M. W. Sharp, and filed March 15, 1939, with the clerk of the US District Court, Southern District of Mississippi, Jackson Division, and styled Dick Farr, etc., vs. John A. O'Keefe, Adjutant General of the State of Mississippi, Docket No. 63. *See also* "New Plea Filed in Rankin Suit," *Clarion-Ledger* (Jackson, Miss.), March 15, 1939, page 14, Newspapers.com, https://www.newspapers.com/image/202629543.

208. A very similar machine is displayed on a YouTube video found at https://www.youtube.com/watch?v=MYIF8oQNh5s&t=3s.

209. Intervening Petition filed by R. B. Grissett with the Clerk of the U.S. District Court, Southern District of Mississippi, Jackson Division, and styled Dick Farr, etc., vs. John A. O'Keefe, Adjutant General of the State of Mississippi, Docket No. 63.

210. *See* Statements of Eugene Seaney and Malcolm Foy each dated March 3, 1939, filed with the Clerk of the U.S. District Court, Southern District of Mississippi, Jackson Division, and styled Dick Farr, etc. vs. John A. O'Keefe, Adjutant General of the State of Mississippi, Docket No. 63. The sworn statement of Bill McCleave was made March 8, 1939 and filed the next day.

211. *See* Sidney Carr Mize, en.wikipedia.org/wiki/Sidney Carr Mize.

212. *Farr v. O'Keefe*, 27 F. Supp. 216 (S. D. Miss. 1939); *see also* "Mize Denies Writ against Militia," *Clarion-Ledger* (Jackson, Miss.), July 1, 1939, page 7, Newspapers.com, https://www.newspapers.com/image/202711603.

213. Miss. Laws, ch. 353 (1938).

214. *Farr v. O'Keefe*, 27 F. Supp. 216, 271 (S. D. Miss. 1939).

215. 28 U. S. C., § 1331.

216. 42 U. S. C., § 1983.

217. Twelve years later Farr remained at war. A January 1951 news report said Farr "ha[d] filed a petition for temporary injunction to prevent the Jackson police department from breaking up confiscated pinball machines. Farr claimed the machines involved were not actually gambling devices, since the only payoff is in free games." "Pin Ball Operator Would Enjoin Police," *Delta Democrat-Times* (Greenville, Miss.), Jan. 9, 1951, page 1, Newspapers.com, https://www.newspapers.com/image/20288546. More than ten months after that, Farr was still in business. In late November, thieves stole an estimated $60 from two pinball machines in the Continental Trailways bus station in Jackson. The machines were owned and operated by the Dick Farr Amusement Co. "$72 Taken from Pin-Ball Machines," *Clarion-Ledger* (Jackson, Miss.), Tues., Nov. 27, 1951, page 1, Newspapers.com, https://www.newspapers.com/image/179628247.

218. *Farr v. O'Keefe*, 27 F. Supp. 216, 217 (S. D. Miss. 1939).

219. Craddock Goins, "Hooch and Homicide in Mississippi," *American Mercury*, Vol. XLVIII, 181–186 (October 1939).

220. *Clarion-Ledger* (Jackson, Mississippi), page 11, Fri. Sept. 10, 1926, Newspapers.com; https://www.newspapers.com/image/202627961.

221. Craddock Goins, "The Terror of the Mississippi," *Clarion-Ledger* (Jackson, Miss.), July 3, 1927, page 13, Newspapers.com, https://www.newspapers.com/image/202535553.

222. "Cheese Factory Sure Thing," *Indianola Enterprise*, Thurs., Sept. 29, 1927, page 2, Newspapers.com, https://www.newspapers.com/image/238463941.

223. *See, e.g.*, "Poultry Men Meet at Tinnin to Open Extensive and Intensive Drive over County for Development of Industry," *Clarion-Ledger* (Jackson, Miss.), Sun., Feb 5, 1928, page 24, Newspapers.com, https://www.newspapers.com/image/202458851; "Craddock Goins to Make Commencement Address," *Clarion-Ledger* (Jackson, Miss.), Sat., Apr. 28, 1928, page 2, Newspapers.com, https://www.newspapers.com/image/202535553.

224. *Clarion-Ledger* (Jackson, Miss.), Mon., Jan. 16, 1933, page 4 .

225. Craddock Goins, "Hooch and Homicide in Mississippi," *American Mercury*, Vol. XLVIII (Oct. 1939), pages 185, 186.

226. *Clarion-Ledger* (Jackson, Mississippi), Mon., Jan. 16, 1933, page 4, Newspapers.com, https://www.newspapers.com/image/202660499.

227. Craddock Goins, Hooch and Homicide in Mississippi, *American Mercury*, Vol. XLVIII (Oct. 1939), page 186.

228. "Suspect Is Moved to Rankin; Habeas Corpus Plea Set Today," *Clarion-Ledger* (Jackson, Miss.), Fri., May 2, 1947, page 1, Newspapers.com, https://www.newspapers.com /image/185056699.

229. See "Fielding Lewis Wright," in David G. Sansing, *Mississippi Governors: Soldiers, Statesmen, Scholars, Scoundrels: A Bicentennial Edition* 188–191(2016); Fielding L. Wright, *Mississippi Encyclopedia* 1363–1364 (Ownby and Wilson eds., 2017).

230. "Demands End to Illegal Activities," *Clarion-Ledger* (Jackson, Miss.), Fri., May 2, 1947, page 1, Newspapers.com, https://www.newspapers.com/image/185056699.

231. One version of the story of the Black Market Tax has been told by Janice Branch Tracy in her *Mississippi Moonshine Politics: How Bootleggers & the Law Kept a Dry State Soaked* 73–78, 109 (2015).

232. Miss. Laws, ch. 139 (1944), also known as House Bill No. 892 (Reg. Sess. 1944, effective March 31, 1944).

233. Schenck, William Frank, Estate of, TC Memo 1961–241, PH TCM ¶61241, 20 CCH TCM 1252 (1961).

234. The year 1946 was one such year according to Janice Branch Tracy in her *Mississippi Moonshine Politics: How Bootleggers & the Law Kept a Dry State Soaked* 105 (2015), and before that, Jesse Yancy in his "Rankin County Redux," *Mississippi Sideboard*" (August 15, 2012).

235. "'Runners' Cause Drop in Liquor Tax Revenue," *Jackson Daily News* (Jackson, Miss.), June 5, 1947; *Morning Star* (Greenwood, Miss., June 6, 1947).

236. See "Paul Burney Johnson, Jr.," in David G. Sansing, *Mississippi Governors: Soldiers, Statesmen, Scholars, Scoundrels: A Bicentennial Edition* 202–205 (2016); Paul B. Johnson Jr., *Mississippi Encyclopedia* 658 (Ownby and Wilson eds., 2017).

237. The story of Sheriff Shelton's crashing the party at the Jackson Country Club in February of 1966 has been often told. Longtime political columnist Bill Minor provided a colorful account in "Forty Years of Legal Liquor; It's Mostly Ho-hum," http://djournal.com/opinion /bill-minor-forty-years-of-legal-liquor-its-mostly-ho-hum/. Mississippi native Janice Branch Tracy has provided a more complete account at pages 141–145 in her *Mississippi Moonshine Politics: How Bootleggers & the Law Kept a Dry State Soaked* (2015)

238. Rev. L. S. Polk soon left his position as pastor at the Eastside Baptist Church in the Jackson area to become pastor at First Baptist Church of Pacolma, California.

239. See *Howie v. State*, 121 Miss. 197, 83 So. 158 (1919).

240. "George Howie Sent to Pen for 99 Years," *Union Appeal* (Union, Miss.), Thurs., March 30, 1922, page 1, Newspapers.com, https://www.newspapers.com/image/317496081.

241. *See, e.g., Winston County Journal* (Louisville, Miss.), Fri., Nov. 21, 1930, page 4, Newspapers.com, https://www.newspapers.com/image/3033327701.

242. *See, e.g.,* "Await Papers," *Hattiesburg American* (Hattiesburg, Miss.), Weds., July 1, 1942, page 9, Newspapers.com, https://www.newspapers.com/image/278284151; "State Agent Is

Enroute to Seattle," *Clarion-Ledger,* Jackson, Mississippi, Wed., July 8, 1942, page 8, https://www
.newspapers.com/image/203348308; "Notorious Convict from Mississippi Found in Seattle,"
Hattiesburg American (Hattiesburg, Miss.), Tues. July 7, 1942, page 10, Newspapers.com, https://
www.newspapers.com/image/278286733.

243. "Mrs. A. A. Seaney Funeral Set Monday," *Clarion-Ledger* (Jackson, Miss.), Sun., Jan. 23,
1949, page 2, Newspapers.com, https://www.newspapers.com/image/185441553.

244. "A. A. Seaney Dies at Daughter's Home," *Clarion-Ledger* (Jackson, Miss.), Sun., Aug. 16,
1953, page 12, Newspapers.com, https://www.newspapers.com/image/179678222

245. "Ends Life While Talking to Ex-Wife," *Hattiesburg American* (Hattiesburg, Miss.),
Weds., Sept. 26, 1956, page 1, https://www.newspapers.com/image/277238692; "Seaney Funeral
Held Wednesday," *Clarion-Ledger* (Jackson, Miss.), Thurs., Sept. 27, 1956, page 14,
Newspapers.com, https://www.newspapers.com/image/179739095

246. Roy Adkins, "Crystal Lake," YouTube, https://www.youtube.com/watch?v=iMbXa1mFG5Y.

247. The remainder of the information on the Blues Trail Marker is a partial version of the
description at pages 376–378 above. The marker reads

> Blues activity "cross the river" centered on Fannin Road, where dozens of venues
> ranging from elaborate clubs to informal juke joints were frequented and mostly
> owned by African Americans. Many businesses stayed open twenty hours a day,
> seven days a week. By the 1940s, many national blues and jazz acts were playing
> at the Blue Flame/Play House complex run by Joe Catchings, and at the Rankin
> Auditorium behind the Stamps Brothers Hotel, operated by brothers Char-
> lie, Clift, and Bill Stamps. The Auditorium advertised that its dancefloor could
> accommodate three thousand people, and other reports noted that white patrons
> were provided balcony seating. By the mid-fifties local clubs, including the Blue
> Flame, the Rocket Lounge, the Heat Wave, the Last Chance, and the Gay Lady
> featured mostly local artists. Among these were Sam Myers, King Mose, Cadillac
> George Harris, brothers Charley and Sammie Lee Smith, Jimmy King, Jesse Rob-
> inson, Charles Fairley, Willie Silas, Bernard "Bunny" Williams, brothers Kermit,
> Jr., Bernard, and Sherrill Holly, brothers Curtis and J. T. Dykes, Milton Ander-
> son, Booker Wolfe, Tommy Tate, Robert Broom, Joe Chapman and Sam Baker Jr.,
> whose parents ran the Heat Wave.

248. George Washington "Big Red" Hydrick (1906–1974) was more of a conventional
bootlegger, but that was the only thing conventional about him. After struggling to find a way
to support his burgeoning family of six, Big Red turned to selling whiskey in the late 1930s.
He was still in business in the early 1960s. In 1977, Hydrick's daughter, Willie Mae Bradshaw,
published an admiring and highly personal biography of Big Red. Bradshaw proudly proclaims
that her daddy "for twenty-seven years was a giant liquor dealer along the infamous Rankin
County Gold Coast." "This wonderful and provocative man helped to form an era of Mississippi history which has now vanished with time" and the legislative enactment of a local-
option liquor law in 1966. "His side of the bootlegging era had to be told!"

249. Placing vending machines in stores was the subject of the case at hand.

250. *Crippen v. Mint Sales Co.*, 139 Miss. 87, 103 So. 503, 505–506 (1925) (Ethridge, J., dissenting).

251. *See* Miss. Laws, ch. 341 (1938), codified today as Miss. Code §§ 95-3-25 (with subsequent
amendments) and 99-27-23.

252. House Journal, page 402 (Reg. Sess. 1938).

253. Miss. Const. art. 5, § 123 (1890); Miss. Code § 7-1-5(c) (1972).

254. *Alexander v. State by and through Allain*, 341 So.2d 1329, 1339–1341 (Miss. 1983) (budget
making power).

255. See footnote 9 and accompanying text in Robertson, "Police Powers," in *Constitutional Law*, § 19:133, *Mississippi Constitutional Law*, Vol. 3 (2d ed, Jackson, Miller & Campbell, eds. 2018).

256. Miss. Const. art. 7, § 190 (1890).

BIBLIOGRAPHY

Bradshaw, Willie Mae, and G. W. Hydrick, "Big Red," *Big Red* (1977).

Cortner, Richard C., *A Scottsboro Case in Mississippi* (2005).

Gillespie, Robert, "Virgil Alexis Griffith," *Journal of Mississippi History* 37 (1997), 267.

Goins, Craddock, "Hooch and Homicide in Mississippi," *American Mercury* 48 (Oct. 1939).

Holmes, Oliver Wendell, *The Common Law* (1881).

Jackson, Robert H., "The Federal Prosecutor," Address to Second Annual Conference of United States Attorneys (April 1, 1940).

Magna Carta (Blackstone ed., 1215).

Richardson, Sara, "The Pearl 'Never Does Nothing,'" Rankin County Historical Society, July 10, 1985, http://rankinhistory.com/site/?page_id=425.

Tracy, Janice Branch, *Mississippi Moonshine Politics: How Bootleggers & the Law Kept a Dry State Soaked* (2015).

CHAPTER 10

Balancing Industry
with the Constitution

If the state is to promote the happiness of its citizens, it must abandon laissez-faire—a doctrine that is an anachronism in a state that exists to make life good, and which the American states have already partially abandoned—and secure to all of its citizens an equal opportunity to obtain a fair share of economic fruits.[1]

—SYDNEY MCCAIN SMITH. CHIEF JUSTICE, SUPREME

COURT OF MISSISSIPPI (1936)

"One Fourth of a State Sold for Taxes" was the attention-getting title of an article published in 1932.[2] That state was Mississippi.[3] No other state suffered so much in the Great Depression, despite quips that its people were already so poor no one realized anything had changed.

It was not just that Mississippi had been at the bottom when it came to industrial jobs when the Depression began, and that more than half of those had disappeared.[4] Those jobs were not coming back. Pine forests had once been plentiful and everywhere, but now they were long gone. The disappearance of an extractive timber industry had left south Mississippi a wasteland of ragged stumps once graced by towering pines.[5] In 1930, lumber entrepreneurs like Pennsylvania tycoon Fenwick Lyman Peck (1854–1943) were telling one and all that the state's industrial outlook was good because, among other reasons, "labor is comparatively cheap." Nor did Peck make a secret of his view that things would be fine "in south Mississippi, if its own people will get down to work."[6] So much for the myth of hardworking Mississippians, which has never taken account of how each year oppressive humidity and hot summer sun saps the strength and energy of the most determined men and women.

The Delta area in northwest Mississippi had long looked to cotton for salvation. Yet that apocryphal region had no sooner emerged from the flood of 1927 than it plunged into the Great Depression.[7] The Cotton South faced definitive disaster as mortgages were foreclosed in great numbers and many banks just closed.[8] To make matters worse, the blasted boll weevil had been worming its way into young cotton bolls for a few years before the stock market crash of 1929.[9] By 1931, cotton sold at its lowest level since 1894.[10] Throw in depleted soils, rising costs of production, and too much water that did not end with The Flood, and the Delta had a recipe for what W. J. Cash would call "[i]mmediate disaster for farmer, planter, tenant and sharecropper."[11]

Hardest hit were the hill counties of northeast Mississippi. Their soils were the poorest, their terrain more rugged. Their people were more isolated than others from the rest of the South and of the country. In this largely white population area, more were unemployed, and with fewer options. Even picking up and leaving was next to impossible. And yet when a promising proposal came for economic relief, opposition was strongest in the hill country.[12] Fearful and suspicious white Mississippians—"rednecks" they are often called[13]—have a track record of voting against an objective and rational view of their own economic self-interests.

Reticence was also found in the Piney Woods, whence in the fullness of time there came a spark of hope. In 1929, Mayor Hugh L. White[14] (1881–1965) of Columbia in Marion County, led a community industry recruitment effort in the wake of substantial unemployment due to the decline of the lumber industry. White had been a lumberman. He had inherited money and made more from that and his lumber business. Others had depended on logging, sawmills, and related railroads for more meager livelihoods. White was determined that his town "would not disappear like other lumber mill towns; it would 'refuse to die.'"[15] Motivated Marion Countians attracted small industries to their community. People who had lost their jobs went back to work. Young folk found their first jobs.

Encouraged by this local success,[16] and after a false start in 1931, White ran for and was elected governor of Mississippi. He took office in January of 1936. Balancing agriculture with industry became law with White's leadership at a specially called legislative session in the last week of the summer of 1936.[17] The mountain had come to Mohammed.[18] Of course, "balance agriculture with industry" was never much more than a slogan. But it contained the kernel of an idea that held a potential for positive thinking, and the same for its acronym "BAWI." Sort of like "New Deal." The slightly more specific purpose of adding agriculture to industry was to enable communities to provide greater job opportunities and paychecks for their people.

TOWARD STATEWIDE PLANNING AND REGULATION

In a sense, BAWI's story and the constitutional challenges it survived are a sequel to chapter 7 above. Newman Lumber Company failed in its assault on the state's use of its police powers to limit the hours of work a manufacturer could require. Like that constitutional encounter, BAWI was about jobs for people who were struggling to make ends meet. Bettering the worker's quality of life was the legislative goal in each instance.

As has often been the case, Mississippi's foremost need in 1936 was "to create more wealth" within the state.[19] If this meant enticing outsiders to come here and bring their money, fine, well, and good. Without Hugh White's leadership, it may not have happened. Without the state's constitutional legislative power, it would not have happened. The policy goals behind the crop lien laws passed beginning in 1867 are an earlier but still instructive precedent. See chapter 5 above.[20] It was clear that simply piling more taxes on the backs of the people would not work, the politics of point aside. The modest sales tax enacted in 1932 under Gov. Mike Conner[21] had taken tax strategy about as far as was practicable.

In other ways, the encounters were the obverse of each other. The ten-hour workday law and the *Newman Lumber*[22] case were about manufacturing employers who came to Mississippi on their own and sought out and found fertile soil. The BAWI program and *Allbritton v. City of Winona*[23] were about luring manufacturing employers to the state, employers who never would have come here without substantial coaxing. Newman Lumber and the other sawmill companies centered on a large swath of forested lands across south Mississippi. The BAWI program and the *Allbritton* case were about the entire state, from Jackson County and the new Ingalls shipbuilding facilities on the Gulf Coast to as far north as Union County and the lesser-known I. B. S. Manufacturing Co. garment factory. Workers in sawmill and lumber industries, and their related "dummy line" railroad activities, were mainly men. Women made up most of the workforce at ten of the twelve BAWI industries, the exceptions being Ingalls and the Armstrong Tire & Rubber Co. in Adams County.[24] The unwritten plan and assumption were that "white women would accept low-paying mill jobs that would sustain small family farms and draw country people into the consumer society without upsetting patriarchal households."[25]

Newman Lumber and the other timber companies had provided their own capital. When, as in the case of Judson Jones Newman, private resources failed, other, better-heeled outsider entrepreneurs like Pennsylvanian Fenwick Peck stepped up to the plate. By the fall of 1936—after more than six years of the Depression—the state and local communities were at the threshold of becoming enabled to grant substantial financial subsidies and incentives to industries who would come to Mississippi and pay salaries to people for whom meager subsistence farming otherwise seemed their only hope.

The challenge was daunting. Hugh White and his advisers well knew that the Columbia strategy from back in 1929 would not work statewide.[26] Few Mississippi communities had a chamber of commerce. Few had civic leaders with the know-how or connections to identify and attract outside industrial capital to Mississippi, and with a specific plan that held a promise of profit for investors and a sustained payroll for local area people. And yet it was important that the people participate in and in the end support each new industry with their tax dollars, their purchasing power and their goodwill. Engendering a sense of local pride in the new plant seemed essential. Paychecks cashed—or, better still, deposited—at local banks, the monies soon to be spent with local merchants would help. A sense of empowerment would flow from popular participation in bringing a particular industry to a particular community. Each citizen and taxpayer would get an "annual reminder"[27] of his and his town's role in having created and nurtured this endeavor "for the promotion of the general welfare of the said municipality."[28]

The plan called for the community to own the land and bricks and mortar that would make up the physical plant where new goods would be produced. Formally, the city would be empowered to operate the new industry. No one expected that to happen in fact. The lease option would be available and was sure to be insisted upon by industrialists willing to bring their production lines to some theretofore unknown community in the largely unproven and more-than-somewhat financially suspect state of Mississippi. Of course, this local government ownership would become an onus if new industry in time became less than a sustained success. Obstacles loomed at many levels.

In early 1936, White struck a deal with legislative leaders that what would become the BAWI Act[29] would be withheld until a special session.[30] He had eight months to put the pieces together. The devil was in the details of White's grand idea. First, there was the practical chore of structuring a statewide program to bring new industrial capital and production to Mississippi. White's policy advisors conceived a state-level commission that would provide leadership, planning, recruiting, and quality control. The commission would set and enforce standards that both local communities and would-be new industries would have to meet. By what criteria would state officials decide to which communities to steer particular industrialists from other states that might show an interest in Mississippi? What if disparate communities sought the same prospect?[31]

A careful empirical inquiry whether the local community could sustain a contemplated enterprise was crucial. Was there an adequate pool of workers that the plant might produce efficiently and at profitable levels? What training would new workers need, and how would that training be provided? Were needed raw materials accessible? And what about marketing, transportation, and otherwise, as new industries sought to distribute their wares to friendly venues elsewhere? Did the community really have a tax base adequate to retire the bonds that would be issued on the full faith and credit of that community, and without undue hardship to its already strapped taxpayers? Financing, ownership, operation, or contract management of a specific new industry would be a local responsibility, but savvy advice and counsel would be needed. There was no way around the practical reality that—for there to be a realistic hope of success and endurance—BAWI enterprises would require statewide planning and regulation on a scale the state had never seen.

THE PROBLEMATIC LEGAL LANDSCAPE

There were potential constitutional impediments to the program Governor White proposed, and these were serious. Hurdles had to be cleared at both state and federal levels. In the summer of 1936, a discerning Mississippi lawyer would have had reason to fear for BAWI's prospects. This is particularly so given darker forces thought emanating from socialism. In February of 1938, a state supreme court justice would suggest that, if BAWI were tolerated, "that would indeed be giving Soviet Russia an approving handshake. Mississippi would be safe not for democracy but for communism. . . . We would have a commonwealth of serfs instead of freemen—parasites instead of patriots."[32] Otherwise sensible men and women thought that way, before and after the summer of 1936. Collectively, these premises gave the sense of what practical BAWI proponents saw themselves up against, and particularly in the six-day special legislative session that last week of summer.[33]

Hugh White asked six accomplished Jackson-area lawyers to draft legislation that would facilitate his economic recovery policy goals and do so within federal and state constitutional criteria. These lawyers were Hiram H. Creekmore, Garner W. Green and his partner, Forrest Butler Jackson, Louis Meredith Jiggitts,[34] William Hamilton Watkins, and W. Calvin Wells. Watkins later served as president of the Mississippi State Bar in 1939. Wells had so served in 1934–1935.[35] In the summer of 1936, the governor's blue-ribbon team had its work cut out for it. The consequences of a constitutional guess that did not pan out could be severe.

More than a few reports have these lawyers focusing upon "the general welfare clause of the constitution" or, more rhetorically, "the 'general welfare' clause that is so familiar to American law."[36] It is doubtful that the six painted with so broad a brush. To be sure, "We the People" in 1787 declared that one of the purposes of the US Constitution was to "promote the general Welfare."[37] More substantively, the "Congress shall have the Power to . . . promote the general Welfare of the United States."[38] These aspirational expressions are federal only and did not per se apply to the states. The Mississippi Constitution had no express "general welfare" clause. Section 5 came close when it declared that "all government of right . . . is instituted solely for the good of the whole."[39] So did Section 6 when it provided that "[t]he people of this state have the inherent, sole and exclusive right to regulate the internal government and the police thereof," and that the people could alter their constitution or form of government "whenever they deem it necessary to their safety and happiness."[40]

As we saw in chapter 7 above, the Supreme Court of Mississippi had construed the legislative power granted by Section 33 to include "the power to enact proper laws to regulate and provide for . . . 'the general welfare of the public.'"[41] And Section 190 made it clear that "the exercise of the police powers of the State shall never be abridged."[42] No lawyer worth shooting—and certainly none of the governor's special six—thought any of these constitutional clauses and constructions, even collectively, would have been enough to insulate the BAWI Act from a proficient substantive due process attack grounded in the Fourteenth Amendment[43] or Mississippi's Section 14,[44] or, for that matter, under Section 183's injunction that no municipality may "loan its credit in aid of . . . [a] corporation or association."[45]

Prudence and practice have long suggested that a state look first to its own constitution and laws, that points of federal constitutional law not be reached or decided where a case might be resolved on independent and adequate state grounds.[46] The nature and structure of the federal union has been and remains such that points of state law come first. In contexts like Hugh White's BAWI idea, Justice Holmes had explained fifteen years earlier that nothing in the Fourteenth Amendment "beyond the absolute compulsion of its words . . . prevent[s] the making of social experiments that an important part of the community desires, in the insulated chambers afforded by the several states, even though the experiments may seem futile or even noxious to me and to those whose judgment I respect."[47] Eleven years after that, Justice Brandeis had added, "It is one of the happy incidents of the federal system that a single courageous state may, if its citizens choose, serve as a laboratory; and try novel social and economic experiments without risk to the rest of the country."[48] To be sure, the Supremacy Clause of the US Constitution was what it always has been—a federal trump card when states go awry. Sections 6 and 7 of the Mississippi Constitution[49] left no doubt the state understood and accepted its duty to honor the supreme power of the federal constitution, but only in the event of conflicts. The Tenth Amendment—cited prominently and arguably problematically in the *Newman Lumber* case that was the centerpiece of chapter 7—has been a perennial favorite in Mississippi.

STATE HURDLES

Any state-supported endeavor that generated competition with private enterprise would be constitutionally suspect. The practical reality is that public subsidies, tax breaks, and the like afford their recipients an advantage over competitors. But would the public use of taxpayer-generated funds to enable private industry withstand scrutiny if a putative competitor not so favored should complain? Would it be held to be within the state's police power at all?

And how would such an industry promote the public welfare any more than a nonsubsidized industry would except that it would be there?

More specifically, neither state nor local government could lend its credit in aid of private enterprise.[50] Any BAWI-type program that contemplated public financing or other subsidies was certain to be scrutinized under Sections 183 and 258—local and state-level bans on government loaning its credit to private enterprises—with no way to know whether it would survive. But what about local communities buying the land, building the plant, and then leasing it to the new industry? To complicate matters, Mississippi's judiciary has had a long history of sanctimony in such contexts, refusing to help when other state officials need reliable advice before an important public undertaking. That's what attorney generals' opinions are for, except that's not what the statute says,[51] and even though the Supreme Court of Mississippi has plenary power to eschew following any such opinion not to its liking.[52] Even in the twenty-first century, when declaratory judgments are authorized by rule in the context of civil litigation,[53] the state supreme court often refuses to budge when its advice is needed most.[54]

The year 1936 found the State with a constitution manifesting a clear hostility to government at any level lending its credit for the benefit of private enterprise. The State had been burned by this one before—the Union Bank and Planters' Bank bond contretemps.[55] The credit extension hands of local government were tied about as tightly as the law and the English language could tie them. Three specific ties bind. First, no investing via the capital stock of "any railroad or other corporation or association." Second, no local governmental entity could "make [an] appropriation . . . in aid of such corporation or association." Third, and most important, every local governmental entity was forbidden to "loan its credit in aid of such corporation or association."[56] Separately and independently, Section 258 extended these preclusions to state government. "The credit of the State shall not be pledged or loaned in aid of any person, association or corporation."[57] This state-level preclusion need never be reached, given the thinking of Governor White's legal advisors.

On the other hand, the idea was that a city or town would provide the land and the manufacturing facility. Full faith and credit bonds would be sold to investors to secure funds needed to do all of this. Local property owners would be assessed annually at a level sufficient to pay the principal and interest on these bonds. The credit of the local entity would be pledged to secure timely retirement of this bonded indebtedness. But the locally owned physical facilities would be leased to the private corporate recruit that could operate the new industrial enterprise. If all of these were so, was there any way around the conclusion that—again as a practical matter—the local governmental entity would be loaning "its credit in aid of such corporation or association"?[58] Section 183 seemingly afforded no room for legal creativity.

The constitutional text began, "No county, city, town or other municipal corporation. . . ." How much "aid" must the local entity's credit afford "such corporation" before a constitutional offense would have been committed? Presumably, substantial aid would trigger a violation, while *de mininis* aid might not. Still, the phrase in Section 183 was "loan its credit," with no qualifiers or modifiers. And would not the Industrial Commission's certificate of public convenience and necessity serve as a state finding that the local financial aid was "necessary" and therefore substantial? Was there any way the governor's very good lawyers could avoid the conclusion that only where the municipality substantially operated the enterprise itself would Section 183 permit the municipality to extend its credit to buy the land and build the building?[59]

FEDERAL HURDLES

Lochner stood as the shadow over the ten-hour workday law passed in 1912 and considered in chapter 7 above. Any workplace reform legislation that seemed to favor workers at the expense of management was in danger of being held unenforceable. The force of Lochnerism had not been spent by the mid-1930s. If anything, it seemed stronger than ever, augmented not only by the latent fear of socialism. There were storm clouds emanating from its second-generation progeny, the US Supreme Court decisions—predictably and regularly—striking important parts of President Roosevelt's New Deal program.[60] Few could be rational when it came to the "Red Scare" in response to Joseph Stalin's Soviet Union. As if the text of state Section 183 weren't problem enough for Hugh White's lawyers.

In the summer and fall of 1936, the "Four Horsemen," plus one[61] or two,[62] were still riding high in Washington. One swath after another, legislation designed to alleviate the burdens of the Great Depression had been struck down—and more were at risk. Willis Van Devanter, James Clark McReynolds, George Sutherland, and Pierce Butler were quite competent US Supreme Court justices. Their opinions rested on seemingly sensible constitutional reasoning, if it were permissible to so reason in a world of never-never land where one was not expected to take into account that hard-pressed legislators were struggling as best they could to bring the police power to bear and alleviate human misery. The Fourteenth Amendment contained no text that condemned these federal and state legislative efforts. Nothing in the United States Constitution was—on its face—nearly so problematic as the third clause in Section 183 of the Mississippi Constitution.

There was a time when *Green v. Frazier*[63] provided an important US Supreme Court exposition of federal substantive due process, one that surely should have afforded solace for Mississippi's BAWI draftsmen. The *Green* decision must be understood in proper historical context. First, *Green* was hardly a fresh and thus likely controlling precedent. It had been decided back on June 1, 1920. Justice William R. Day spoke for a unanimous court. Day had dissented in *Lochner*. He often defended laws regulating large corporations and other forms of big business.[64] The Supreme Court had experienced a substantial turnover in personnel and persuasion since 1920. Van Devanter and McReynolds were the only justices joining *Green* who remained on the court, while Mississippi was politically contemplating BAWI. By the mid-1930s, Day was gone, and Holmes as well. Van Devanter and McReynolds had moved to the right and become consistent constitutional opponents of governmental social and economic reforms.

If *Green* had been the controlling federal constitutional precedent, BAWI draftsmen could have rested easily, at least as far as they needed to be concerned about federal Fourteenth Amendment substantive due process scrutiny of their work. This would have been because *Green* concerned a use of state power more problematic than anything Mississippi ever dreamt of. North Dakota's legislature had created a state-owned and state-operated bank and a building and loan association, and much more.[65] These entities were financed by state-issued negotiable bonds to be paid and redeemed by taxing the citizens of North Dakota. There appeared to be no state constitutional impediment to the program North Dakota adopted, but, of course, that did not pretermit a Fourteenth Amendment substantive due process analysis. The *Green* court took it as "settled that the authority of the states to tax does not include the right to impose taxes for merely private purposes." In the end, however, the US Supreme Court ruled that

> Under the peculiar circumstances existing in North Dakota, which are emphasized in the opinion of its highest court, if the state sees fit to enter upon such enterprises as are here involved, with the sanction of its Constitution, its Legislature and its people, we are not prepared to say that it is within the authority of this court, in enforcing the observance of the Fourteenth Amendment, to set aside such action by judicial decision.[66]

In a practical sense, it is easy to see how a non-lawyer, looking at the extensive powers North Dakota had granted to state-owned and state-controlled enterprises, would think the anticipated structure of the BAWI act secure from federal judicial scrutiny. Overlay the substantial post-*Green* shift to the right against social and economic innovations to address the seemingly intractable problems of the Great Depression, however, and the federal constitutional landscape seemed far more problematic. President Roosevelt had not yet been reelected. While BAWI was being drafted in the late summer of 1936, the best that could be said of *West Coast Hotel Co. v. Parrish*, decided in March of 1937,[67] and *Carmichael v. Southern Coal & Coke Co.*, decided two months later,[68] was that they were a collective "consummation devoutly to be wished," without which the authority of *Green* was more than a bit iffy.

THE LEGISLATURE'S SPECIAL SESSION

On September 14, 1936, the legislature convened pursuant to call. Hugh White addressed a joint session and stated his case. Mississippi was at the bottom rung of the national ladder in every relevant socioeconomic statistic. Annual per capita income was $212. The national average was $636 earned per person per year. The state's foremost industry of the first part of the twentieth century—the lumber mills—was by and large gone. The per capita value of industrial plants in Mississippi was $35, only a fourth of the average of other southern states. There was no measure by which Mississippi was not found at the bottom, often by a considerable margin.

The first important test came in the house of representatives regarding the structure of the state industrial commission that would oversee the new program. White recommended a three-person commission appointed by the governor. A number of house members demurred. An alternative proposal would have had the commission made up of the governor, the state tax commissioner—then a statewide elective office—and the commissioner of agriculture. At issue was whether the governor would have the practical control of the commission through his appointees, or whether three officials—each with his independent constituency and electoral base—would substantially dilute the governor's input. By a margin of seventy-four to fifty-eight, with eight not voting, gubernatorial control prevailed.[69]

House opponents then sought to require a statewide referendum—let the people decide. Rather than allow representative democracy to do its job, these legislators sought to have the state's eligible electors at large decide the fate of Hugh White's brainstorm. In 1990, legislator and future secretary of state Eric Clark analyzed the special session and reported that the referendum strategy "was a clear effort to kill the plan by indirect means when it became apparent that the Governor had the votes to win a straightup-or-down vote" in the legislature.[70] The referendum proposal was defeated eighty-five to forty-five, with ten not voting. This vote set the stage for final passage. The House of Representatives approved the governor's proposal by a vote of eighty-seven to forty-four, with nine not voting.

The senate passed the bill in two different forms. First, the senate approved it with an ex-officio commission. The governor, the secretary of state, and the state tax commissioner would so serve. That version passed thirty-two to ten, with seven senators not voting. Two days later, Governor White's preferred version passed, giving the governor the power to appoint all commission members. This bill passed twenty-two to twenty, with seven senators not voting.[71]

BAWI SPREADS ITS WINGS

On September 19, 1936, the special session adjourned. Governor White's signature effort to bring his state out of the Depression had become law. Under BAWI as enacted,[72] the initiative for a particular new industry was a chicken-and-egg endeavor. Formally, a local petition was required. Twenty percent of the qualified electors of the particular municipality or other local government entity had to ask that the local officials request the Mississippi Industrial Commission to bless its plan.[73] But these voters had no way of knowing whether they were buying a pig in a poke. They were certifying that they wanted a new industry for their community—almost any new industry—with little clue of the particulars of the proposed industry, or even what options were reasonably available.

The commission was charged to investigate fully and assess the practical viability of the plan.[74] If the commission found the new industrial plan viable, it would issue a certificate of public convenience and necessity to the applicant local entity. The certificate in hand, the local entity would then call a special referendum election. After substantial advance public notice, local electors would be asked to vote for or against the proposed industrial plan, with many details still unknown and hardly knowable. Qualified electors in the locality were then required to satisfy two conditions. First, more than half would have to vote. If fewer than half showed up at the polls to vote, the matter was at an end. Assuming the requisite 50 percent plus 1 registered electoral participation, the second requirement was that two-thirds of those casting ballots have voted for the new industrial plan.[75] As much as anything, these hurdles cleared assured a prospective industrialist of a warm political welcome.

Once the returns were in, the local governmental entity would adopt an ordinance that, among other things, would authorize the issuance of the industrial bonds to finance the development, including acquiring land meeting the Industrial Commission's requirements and the physical plant that would house the new industry. The bonds would be underwritten by the "good name, faith and credit" of the local government. When issued, the bonds would impress a lien on all taxable property in the community. The local government would then levy a tax on all property sufficient to pay the principal and interest on the bonds as payments fell due.[76] Once both the Industrial Commission and the local government found that all was in order,[77] the State's bond attorney would be required to investigate, consider independently all relevant matters, and render an opinion that the proposed bond issue was in all respects legally permissible and that it should be validated. Finally, the local governmental entity was expected to apply to the local chancery court for a decree that would formally adjudge the validity of the bonds. At that point, one and all with an interest—particularly taxpayers whose property would be assessed and charged to pay the bonds—would have the opportunity to approach the chancery court with any constitutional or other practical legal concerns. This was a speak-now-or-forever-hold-your-peace moment.

A REFLECTIVE INTERLUDE

Only eighteen days after Governor White signed the BAWI Act into law, something special happened. We met Chief Justice Sydney McCain Smith[78] (1869–1948) in chapter 7 above. Twenty-three years later, in October of 1936— two months into the twenty-fifth year of the longest chief justiceship of state history—Smith rose to speak at the University of Mississippi School of Law.[79] He could not have been unaware of what had just happened in the legislature. In those days, the state supreme court and the legislature had their chambers and offices in the same New Capitol Building between High and Mississippi Streets in Jackson. The politics of Hugh White's BAWI program had been the biggest news in the state for weeks. Nor could Smith have been unaware that there was certain to be a challenge to the constitutional validity of the BAWI Act. His October 7, 1936, engagement at the law school had likely been scheduled prior to the special legislative session.

What Sydney Smith said in the early fall of 1936 would have been remarkable in any setting. It was the more so that his state had just enacted a game-changing—albeit unproven—means to a better life for its citizens. Many Mississippi chief justices have addressed largely legal audiences over the decades. Perhaps there have been other such addresses as philosophical and prophetic and in tune with contemporary jurisprudence. But as proximate in temperament and text and timing, reflecting on the most fundamental principles of organized society at a time when those principles were being tested, and severely so? No such occasion is commonly known; it will be for others to scour the archives for another such chief justice address.

Smith began, "We are passing through one of the ever-recurring periods in which men strive to shake off the 'dead hand of the past,' and bring all their institutions into accord with social and economic facts, not as they once were, but as they are now." Before the many sensing that they had wandered into the wrong meeting room could make a move, the chief justice smote them between the eyes. "This is true in the field of law—the State's Primary Social Process." Few Mississippians thought of the law and the legal system in such terms. Even the majority who had favored the BAWI Act would have shrugged at the suggestion that the law was a social process, if for no other reason than that sounded too much like socialism, thought of which was anathema to so many at the time. Another quarter of a century would pass before the British legal scholar H. L. A. Hart would establish the premise that law is a social fact.[80] The core truth that Hart would teach could be found in Holmes,[81] though few then in Mississippi would have seen it so.

Sydney Smith followed with a ten-page lecture, grounded in the work of Dean Roscoe Pound of the Harvard Law School.[82] Pound had become one of the most influential legal scholars in the country, and in time of the entire twentieth century. He was the leading proponent of a pragmatic view of law that had become known as sociological jurisprudence.[83] The early years of Pound's deanship were controversial among the more staid of Harvard Law alums. Amidst one controversy, Holmes said, "If the law school should lose Pound and Frankfurter it would lose its soul," and that Pound was "a real focus of spiritual energy."[84] Sydney Smith had picked Pound's central work as his topic before a Mississippi law school audience in the wake of Pound's retirement after twenty years as law dean at Harvard. In doing so, he said more of himself than of Dean Pound.

"The state, of course, cannot confer happiness; but it can, and its duty is to, create institutions and promote conditions that will enable individuals to pursue and attain it." "Happiness" is posited alongside "safety" as among the goals of organized society in a seldom-read part of Mississippi's constitution.[85] Its pursuit is famously exalted in the Declaration of Independence. Smith had used it in an opinion he authored in early 1936.[86] Past these, happiness is not a word or a concept much thought of in legal gatherings, then or now. Sydney Smith put it out there, and in a sensible setting.

Smith then assessed the socioeconomic circumstances of the times. "On its productive side the system has been a complete success, producing sufficient material goods for all; on its distributive side, it has been, at least, a partial failure. It has permitted wealth, produced by the toil of many, to be largely accumulated in the hands of the few, resulting in poverty and suffering being the undeserved lot of many." Smith left no doubt he thought something should be done about this partial failure, and should be done through the state's primary social process—the activity of law. He made no mention that only days earlier, the Hugh White–led legislature had taken a stab at addressing this partial failure.

Continuing, Smith added, "But the trouble with us, and for that matter with all peoples, is that we have not fully accepted democracy as a way of life; and a mistaken view of self-interest sometimes prevents us from according to others their economic rights. When this occurs, it is the duty of the state . . . to protect the individual from economic injustice." Smith had tossed a stick of dynamite into the discussion. Of course, we have all—always and invariably—thought of ourselves as somewhat rational, self-interested wealth maximizers, but that does not mean we should accept blind selfishness in ourselves, much less in others. Smith carried the point a qualitative step further as he coun-seled the democratically elected powers that be. He had dived headlong into the economic dimension of the familiar Madisonian dilemma—the tensions inherent in respecting the right of the individual in a majoritarian democracy. Then Smith went deeper. He added, "The state has the negative duty of not itself abridging economic liberty, but it also has the positive duty of insuring that equality. . . . Freedom of one from economic restraint by another that subjects him economically to such other's will, is secured only by economic equality, without which, for the common man, economic liberty does not exist."

Surely some in his audience began thinking of fresh-in-mind BAWI as Smith became more concrete. Due process of law "means simply this: the state is with-out the right to deprive any person of life, liberty or property by an act which has no reasonable relation to any proper governmental purpose, or is so far beyond the necessities of the case as to be an arbitrary exercise of governmental power." The answer to this "question of fact and of inferences to be drawn from facts—political, economic, and social" was not to be found by looking to "the time our governments were organized, but at the time the act in question was committed."[87] This view of constitutional construction and application seems so obvious. It has had its proponents in every era. For reasons seldom severable from results sought, men of those same generations have taken refuge in such shibboleths as "strict construction," "originalism," and "original understanding." In a state and country where so much else is living, Smith saw the good sense of a constitution whose words and meaning are as alive and amenable as the people it governs. What "due process of law means" is not what men thought it meant in 1789, or in 1868, but what informed and deliberate men reasonably considered that those words should mean in 1936, or today for that matter. And when he spoke of a "question of fact and of inferences to be drawn from facts—political, economic, and social," there could be no doubt that Smith knew of and appreciated the power of what had become known as the Brandeis Brief.[88] And of the idea if not the substance of what would become the (in)famous footnote 11 in the US Supreme Court public school desegregation decision in 1954.[89]

Sydney Smith then took a shot at the "laws of nature" that had been so cen-tral a part of the thinking of Joshua G. Clarke,[90] whom we met in chapter 2 above. "Nor have we such a guide in the law of Nature, so dear to our Eighteenth Century forefathers, with its theory of inalienable rights pressed to the breaking point. Indeed, it is that school of jurisprudence which has steered us into the near *impasse* which now confronts us."[91] The idealism of our eighteenth-century forefathers notwithstanding, and our early nineteenth-century forebears as well, the better view is captured in several Holmesian jewels. "The common law is not a brooding omnipresence in the sky but the articulate voice of some sov-ereign or quasi-sovereign that can be identified."[92] "There is no mystic over law to which even the United States must bow."[93] Nor has there ever been a "mystic over law" or "a brooding omnipresence" enforceable in Mississippi, except it be subject to the common law and its processes and ultimately the will of the legislature, as explained in chapter 8 above.

Summing up, Smith saw that the task of achieving a just society—the Madisonian dilemma notwithstanding—

> can be discharged only by adopting the methods of thought and action of the sociological jurist who believes that 'the destinies of men are the most important objects of human interest'; whose thinking is empirical and pragmatic; who believes with the late Mr. Justice Holmes that 'The life of the law has not been logic; it has been experience'[94]; and who is not afraid to proceed by the method by which all good laws are made—trial and error.

He closed by endorsing wise words from Justices Benjamin Cardozo and Harlan Fiske Stone—both admirers of Holmes and Pound—"In short, the method of sociology is the method which the wise and competent judge uses in rendering the dynamic decision which makes the law a living force. . . . The weak and incompetent judge [to which I would add "and lawyer"] cannot use it and indeed in his hands it is a dangerous instrument."[95]

Seventeen months later, Sydney Smith would author the controlling opinion adjudging the constitutional enforceability of the BAWI Act.[96] Without surprise, en route there had been references in the briefs of counsel taking note of the chief justice's remarks made at the University of Mississippi back in early October of 1936.

THE INDUSTRIAL COMMISSION GOES TO WORK

Shortly after the BAWI Act took effect in late 1936, the governor appointed the members of the Mississippi Industrial Commission.[97] Harry O. Hoffman of Hattiesburg became chairman, who would serve full-time. Hoffman was a mid-level executive for the Mississippi Central, a short-line railroad. Two part-time commissioners were S. A. Klein, a retired merchant, civic leader, and philanthropist of Meridian in east Mississippi, and Frank A. England of Greenville in the Mississippi Delta along the River. England had been an industrialist in South Bend, Indiana. Once in Greenville, he opened a Ford dealership and became a civic leader and bank director.[98]

In time, the City of Winona's mayor and board of aldermen received a petition from more than 20 percent of the city's qualified electors, asking the board to take advantage of the opportunities offered by the new law.[99] Following the newly established procedures, Winona asked the Industrial Commission to "hold hearings and make investigations and to examine the conditions and opportunities presented in the ... City" and, thereupon, to issue a certificate of public convenience and necessity to that effect.[100] The commission followed the processes set forth, holding hearings and making investigations as required. It received "oral and documentary evidence" as well, to show whether and to what extent Winona would be a sensible locale for a new industrial activity.

On June 1, 1937, the commission found "as a matter fact that the natural resources readily and economically available and obtainable in the territory of the City of Winona, ..., the available labor supply, the property values and the financial condition of the city" were such that the city could support "some textile, hosiery, or other manufacturing plant that will employ not in excess of one hundred and fifty (150) operatives, and at an annual aggregate compensation for wages for said operatives of not less than sixty thousand dollars ($60,000.00) for said operations over a period of not less than twenty-five years." The commission found further that the assessed valuation of taxable property within the city was such that bonds may be issued in the sum not to exceed $35,000, which "was less than ten per centum of the total assessed valuation of all the property in the said city of Winona." The plan contemplated that the city would acquire land containing not less than 20,000 square feet, situated within the corporate limits of Winona, and buy that land for not more than $2,500. On this parcel of land, the city would construct a "municipal factory building" with not less than 14,000 square feet of floor space.[101] Accordingly, the certificate of public convenience and necessity was issued "for the promotion of the general welfare of the said municipality, and of the State of Mississippi, as declared in [the BAWI Act]."[102]

The commission unanimously approved the order on June 1, 1937.[103]

In due course, the mayor and board of aldermen called a special municipal referendum election for September 14, 1937. The qualified electors of Winona would vote a year to the day after Hugh White opened the special legislative session with a powerful account of the circumstances facing Mississippi and his thoughts of what should be done. Winona voters would be asked to approve a bond issue "for the purpose of acquiring, owning, operating and/or leasing to some reputable concern a textile, knitting, hosiery, or other manufacturing building."[104] Nothing further was known of the name of the "reputable concern" or the precise kind of manufacturing business it would be engaged in. That would come later, if the bond issue were ratified.

On the second Tuesday in September, 1937, some 377 of an eligible 579 registered electors appeared and voted. The industrial plan and bond issue were approved by a vote of 262 to 113, with two votes rejected. Percentagewise, a smidgeon fewer than 69.5 percent of those Winonans casting ballots favored the plan—barely clearing the two-thirds, or 66.7 percent, bar.[105] The issue was formally declared approved, more than two-thirds of those casting ballots having voted aye. The mayor and board of aldermen then certified all of the proceedings in the matter to G. Garland Lyell, the State's bond attorney, who on October 19, 1937, gave his "opinion that the proposed bonds are legal and should be validated."[106]

BAWI IN THE CHANCERY COURT

The City next applied to the Chancery Court of Montgomery County that the bonds be formally and finally validated.

It is no surprise that in the bond validation proceedings, the City of Winona would be represented by Forrest B. Jackson (1901–1970), then of the law firm of Green, Green and Jackson in the city of Jackson.[107] Or that the Green firm would be of counsel to the City. Forrest Jackson and Garner Green had served on Hugh White's six-lawyer special panel, charged to draft BAWI legislation designed to survive a constitutional challenge. Jackson served as lawyer for the BAWI Act–created Mississippi Industrial Commission. A brief perusal of the clients Jackson appeared for[108] suggests he was quite comfortable defending the public policy the BAWI program sought to promote and that he was more than competent to handle cases of the constitutional delicacy of *Allbritton*.[109]

In the mid-1930s, the constitutional climate was toxic when it came to legislative and other governmental efforts to plan and regulate contrary to traditional laissez-faire economics. Full faith and credit bonds issued to finance establishment of a BAWI industry in Mississippi were by no means a cinch to survive a competent constitutional challenge. By late September of 1937, no one had stepped forward to mount such a challenge. Ten days after Winona's bond issue squeaked by in the electoral referendum, a story appeared in the *Winona Times* making it clear that Governor White, the Industrial Commission, and many others wanted the issue litigated and settled. "We would be receptive to such a test, and would gladly cooperate to see that all the facts are brought out," according to Chairman Harry O. Hoffman of the Industrial Commission.[110] Four weeks later, another headline appeared: "Gov. White Urges Suit to Be Filed." Commission lawyer Forrest Jackson described the procedure that such a constitutional challenge would follow.[111]

A subheading in this latest article added a new dimension. "Plaintiff to be Represented by W. E. Morse of Jackson." Morse served as lawyer for "the bonding companies who are interested in the purchase of these municipal bonds throughout Mississippi."[112] Of course, those "bonding companies" and any potential objector who came forth would waive any conflict of interest, so that Morse could handle the constitutional challenge. It was in everyone's interest that the final adjudication have great credibility in all circles. Morse was the man to make sure that happened.

William Eugene Morse[113] (1891–1975) was a native of Gulfport. He spent his adult life in Jackson, dating back to his matriculation at Millsaps College. He served as president of the Mississippi State Bar in 1940. In time Morse became "noted for his legal writings, which are constantly used by his conferees."[114] He was a very smart, civic-minded lawyer. Before appearing for Allbritton and filing his objection, Morse had studied the issues. He was well aware that there were legally reasonable grounds why the BAWI Act in general—and the City of

Winona's proposed industrial bond issue in particular—should be held unenforceable. Professionally, he believed in the adversary system through which the courts would become as well advised as reasonably practicable before making an important decision. Morse could be counted on the play it straight, to present the case against BAWI as competently as could be.

CITIZEN ALLBRITTON APPEARS

For reasons not fully known, William Samuel Allbritton (1878–1958) decided to oppose the city of Winona in the bond validation proceedings.[115] As a resident and taxpayer of Winona, Allbritton formally appeared on November 2, 1937, and objected to the bond validation. W. E. Morse became his lawyer. The story was carried in the newspaper ten days later, with Morse explaining that on Allbritton's behalf he had filed the "friendly test" case that many had sought.[116]

In legalese, Allbritton had standing to object because he had a colorable interest in the subject matter of the litigation. Allbritton stood to experience an adverse effect from the full faith and credit bonds issue the city proposed. He would have to pay city *ad valorem* taxes that he would not otherwise have to pay. His taxes (along with the taxes paid by all others) would be used to retire the bonds Winona proposed to issue in order to finance the new "textile or hosiery or other manufacturing plant." Elsewhere in the Industrial Commission's order, it was called a "hosiery, knitting and wearing apparel manufacturing plant." One and all were in the dark as to just what kind of manufacturing enterprise—if any—would come to Winona, once all of the legal issues had been resolved. No one was about to contest Allbritton's standing to so proceed.

W. S. Allbritton was born in Choctaw County. He was living in West Point on July 24, 1918, when he registered for the draft four months before the end of the World War. He listed his employment as labor foreman for the J. G. White Engineering Company of Muscle Shoals, Alabama. Soon thereafter, Allbritton moved to Winona, residing at 34 Sterling Avenue. By occupation, he was a railroad worker in 1937. On the 1930 federal census, his employment had been listed as "section foreman, Steam RR." There is every reason to believe that in 1937 Allbritton was a public-minded citizen who wanted to do his part to make Winona a good place to live and work and raise a family.

On December 2, 1937, the City of Winona's bond validation case was called for hearing in the chancery court in Winona. On that day the Montgomery County Courthouse was, in Faulkner's words, a "repository and guardian of the aspirations and the hopes" of the men and women of the county.[117] More than a thousand people from the area had signed up for no more than 150 jobs likely to be available.[118] Chancellor L. A. Smith Sr.[119] of Holly Springs had been appointed special chancellor to hear the matter. The lawyers—Jackson for the City and Morse for Objector Allbritton—had provided the court with written briefs setting out their arguments, pro and con, including both the points of fact and law that each believed important. As was customary, Chancellor Smith convened court to hear oral argument, a proceeding open to the public and as many as could squeeze into the courtroom.

A few days later, Chancellor Smith delivered his decision denying Allbritton's objections and validating the City of Winona's bond issue.[120] Smith stated preliminarily, "When the validation proceedings in this case were started, the public press everywhere proclaimed that a friendly suit would be filed at Winona for the purpose of testing the constitutionality of the act . . . , and that an immediate appeal would be taken to the Supreme Court from the findings of this court."[121] In 1937, knowledgeable persons were aware that many governmental efforts to address the dire circumstances of the Depression would lead to constitutional litigation. Courts had struck down a number of such efforts at both federal and state levels.

As recently as 1934, the Supreme Court of Mississippi had found constitutional infirmities in the Town of Booneville's effort to secure a garment factory funded with bonds backed by the city's credit. "The act is one strictly in aid of a private corporation, and it is well settled in this state that taxes cannot be levied for private purposes."[122] Those supporting the BAWI program had high hopes that the governor's lawyers had navigated the legal shoals and crafted a bill that would withstand constitutional scrutiny. Two US Supreme Court decisions earlier that year had upheld federal regulatory legislation, giving hope to BAWI proponents that the winds were changing at that level. *Town of Booneville*, however, was still a fresh and unquestioned state constitutional precedent. Potential bond purchasers would be extra-cautious until the act was blessed in an authoritative court ruling.

Chancellor Smith then referred to the question of the constitutionality of Senate Bill No. 1 as "a momentous question of such far reaching importance, touching so many angles of public policy." Friendly suit or no, the court record suggests that the lawyers—particularly W. E. Morse for the taxpayer objector— went all out for their respective views of the law and sides of the case. Smith thanked the lawyers for their "voluminous and extensive briefs of a most careful and brilliant nature."

Few, if any, aspects of the constitutional points before the court were without precedent in one or more state or federal cases. Smith reviewed these in his bench opinion and then turned to the particulars of the BAWI Act. He noted counsel's description of the BAWI program as being "in effect the institution of a state-wide experimental laboratory to determine and demonstrate that Mississippi is capable of industrial development."[123] Further describing the act, he emphasized that "the State of Mississippi has adopted a public policy and in furtherance of development of that policy has set up a machinery applicable to the entire state and communities in the state."

Smith then put his finger on what he considered the nub of the issue; "the difficulty is in the application of the rule to determine what is a public purpose."[124] To survive under then-current substantive due process jurisprudence—at both federal[125] and state[126] levels—the state action was required to promote or serve a public purpose, as distinguished from merely affecting the private rights of discrete individuals. Harkening back to *Runnels v. State*, discussed in chapter 3 above, Chancellor Smith added that "the statement of a public policy expressed in a legislative enactment is entitled to weighty consideration and all reasonable doubt on the question should be resolved in favor of the legislative declaration thereon." All of this led to whether and to what extent there should be "flexibility of constitutional interpretations to keep pace reasonably with a changing world." Smith then explained that courts "must keep abreast of the times within the limitations of the law, and while not changing the terms of the Constitution . . . must recognize that what is a public purpose is a changing term."[127]

Next, Smith made clear his view of the BAWI Act.

> This statute, remedial in its nature and operation, is one of a number of legislative acts devised in the attempt to meet, so far as practicable, the unusual conditions brought about by the present economic depression, and in effect to salvage something in the general wreck of things. In considering legislation and administrative efforts at salvage and rehabilitation, in the distressing situation with which the country has been and is yet confronted, we must not permit ourselves to be maneuvered into positions which would view the Federal and State Constitutions as sculptured idols, frowning with changeless features upon a changing world.[128]

Chancellor Smith concluded with an insight from Holmes, that "the interpretation of constitutional principles must not be too literal. We must remember that the machinery of government would not work if it were not allowed a little play in the joints."[129]

The chancery court entered its final judgment, rejecting Allbritton's objections, and declaring the bonds fully and finally validated. Shortly thereafter, W. E. Morse gave notice of appeal on behalf of his client. Once the formal record was prepared and filed with the clerk of the Supreme Court of Mississippi in Jackson, the parties filed written briefs arguing their respective positions. Jackson lawyer Weaver E. Gore filed a brief as amicus curiae, arguing that the BAWI Act was unconstitutional.[130] This was followed by oral argument, held in the Supreme Court's open courtroom a floor below the senate chamber where the BAWI Act had finally been passed, back in September of 1936.

THE SUPREME COURT OF MISSISSIPPI DECIDES

In February of 1938, the Supreme Court rendered its decision. Speaking for the court,[131] Chief Justice Sydney Smith called upon one and all to "remember that the state's prime duty, the purpose for which it exists, is to promote the peace, prosperity, and happiness of its citizens."[132] He set forth at the outset "certain fundamental and accepted principles that underlie the American theory of government in the light of which the case must be decided."[133] More important, he explained how a constitution—to the extent it has been well crafted— should be used so that organized society not only works but progresses as well. A constitution is and certainly should be "made for people of fundamentally different views,"[134] that they may get along with one another. No one's particular view of economic theory or social order is embodied in a constitution unless the words unmistakably say so. Smith left no doubt of his view that the Mississippi Constitution had not said so, and that he thought it would have been a mistake had the constitution makers in 1890 done otherwise.

Allbritton was litigated in late 1937 and decided in early 1938. Many feared for lack of food to eat or clothes to wear. Others a bit more fortunate feared the isms of the times. Concurring Justice Virgil Griffith, whom we met in chapter 9 above, warned against "a communistic or soviet state."[135] Dissenting Justice Anderson argued that the "logic of the majority opinion" would lead to "giving Soviet Russia an approving handshake. Mississippi would be safe not for democracy but for communism."[136] Chief Justice Smith rose to the bait only enough to remark calmly, "Every intervention of any consequence by the state and national governments in the economic and social life of the citizens has been so branded." Facing the charge of "a step towards socialism," the chief justice replied firmly, "We must not permit ourselves to be subjected to the tyranny of symbols."[137]

The chief justice then noted different views of economic theory afoot and announced that "the due process provisions of our constitutions[138] do not enact Adam Smith's concept of the negative state." This was important if not imperative in Mississippi in the late 1930s, as "one of the main functions of [Adam Smith's views] would be to stand aloof from intervention in the social and economic life of its citizens."[139] To the extent it may ever have been "acted upon in the early history of this country [this approach] has long since discarded."[140]

Smith stated, "The purpose for which the state exists" with a generality approaching abstraction—is "to promote the general welfare of its citizens— their peace, happiness, and prosperity." Two more specific points follow. State government is the constitutionally created agency "charged . . . with the duty of accomplishing this purpose." This "duty rests with equal force on each of the departments into which the government is separated—the executive, the legislative and the judicial."

His preface completed, Smith turned first to the due process issues. W. E. Morse had articulated the view that substantive due process did not permit a man to be taxed to support a private enterprise. The chief justice answered with a comprehensive discussion of the growth of the law to meet changing times and circumstances, particularly where its terms were open textured, and an application consistent with present social and economic realities would do no violence to contemporary understandings of the constitutional language. "The due process clauses of our constitutions must not be construed so as to put the state and federal governments into a strait-jacket and prevent them from adapting life [and the positive law] to the continuous change in social and economic conditions."[141]

Applying premises that had come into general acceptance, Smith turned to the question that the Chancery Court had found controlling, whether the BAWI Act was committed to "a constitutionally valid public or governmental purpose." One purpose so legislated was "to promote the public welfare by providing an opportunity for laboring men to obtain employment."[142] Smith quoted all of the "Whereas" clauses of the act, followed by findings of legislative facts that supported what was to follow. Its foundation grounded in these public factual premises, the legislature had found "that the state public welfare demands and the state public power requires" that the state pursue six general goals. To accomplish these goals, certain "means and measures [were] herein authorized."[143]

> The question here then is: Has the method provided by the statute for these purposes a reasonable relation thereto, and is it not so far beyond the necessity of the case as to be an arbitrary exercise of governmental power?

The chief justice then explained that, and why, a municipality was allowed to own and operate manufacturing plants, and, as that was so, why it might contract with private parties via a lease to that same end. "The Legislature is entitled to its judgment" in such matters.[144]

Then and now many think of the facts that control a case as the product of witnesses taking the stand and exhibits being offered into evidence. In cases like *Allbritton*—and *McPhail* discussed in chapter 9 above and decided in the same year—there is so much more to the fact-gathering and assessing process. Courts necessarily enter the realm of legislative facts, that is, the sorts of facts that a competent lawmaking body ought to consider to the end of making good law.[145] The *Allbritton* majority opinion elaborated upon the kinds of facts the Legislature might rely on, and which the courts would be bound to respect. The relevant legislative facts were "of a social and economic character." An all-important premise followed.

> Some of these facts are set out in the preamble to, and section 1 of, the statute, but the Legislature was not confined thereto, and we must take into consideration

other rel[evant] sustaining facts which may reasonably be conceived to exist. If from these facts the reasonableness of the method adopted for accomplishing the desired purpose appears, the statute is valid, or, if different reasonable inferences can be drawn therefrom, the Legislature is entitled to its judgment.[146]

Smith had been thinking such thoughts for quite a while. He had said the same thing—though a bit more generally—in his law school address in October of 1936.[147]

The rest of this part of the opinion[148] is an eloquent response to the arguments against the BAWI Act, no small part of Smith's words having been foreshadowed by his law school address delivered seventeen months earlier. Though two of his colleagues would raise questions, the chief justice had carried the day in the court of common sense and sober judgment. The act offended neither state nor federal due process clauses.

But this did not end the case.

A POINT OVERLOOKED?

The majority opinion's analysis of the state Section 183 objection[149] was a bit tricky. Recall that this state constitutional clause enacts three prohibitions and that these are stated in the disjunctive. No municipality may become a shareholder in "any railroad or other corporation or association." Nor may it make an "appropriation . . . in aid of such corporation or association." But only the third proscription was really at issue: No municipality may "loan its credit in aid of such corporation or association."[150] Winona had complied with the BAWI Act. It proposed to issue bonds "and for the payment thereof the good name, faith and credit of the said municipality [was] pledged and a tax levied on all taxable property in the municipality, adequate to pay principal and interest on such bonds as the same fall due."[151] Was this not lending its credit in aid of a corporation that seemed someday likely to lease the city-owned facility and manufacture goods therein for distribution and sale for the corporation's profit?

Smith took note of the holding in *Carothers v. Town of Booneville*, decided less than four years earlier.[152] To secure a garment factory "and thereby increase employment in the town," Booneville had pledged its credit via a $10,000 bond issue authorized by a local and private bill approved by the legislature. The bonds were to be retired by a local tax levy. The Supreme Court of Mississippi held the bond issue invalid. "The act is one strictly in aid of a private corporation, and it is well settled in this state that taxes cannot be levied for private purposes." The problem in *Carothers*, according to the Justice George Ethridge, speaking for the Supreme Court of Mississippi, had been that the Town of Booneville "was not authorized to operate a manufacturing enterprise itself."[153]

But this premise in the *Carothers* opinion misled Chief Justice Smith to the view that *Allbritton* presented no such problem. The City of Winona retained power to require its lessee to use the publicly funded, constructed and owned plant for public purposes. "The statute there [in *Town of Booneville*] did not recognize that the lease of the property should retain in the municipality power to enforce the use of the property by the lessee for the purposes sought to be accomplished by leasing the property. *The statute here so requires.*"[154]

But the real concern with *Allbritton* lay in what it did not say. Winona may well have retained an appropriate enforcement power in the lease contract that it would make with the as yet unknown "textile, knitting, hosiery or other manufacturing" enterprise. That only begs the question whether Winona's bond issue was nonetheless "a loan of its credit in aid of such corporation." Both teacher and student in an eighth-grade English class would surely say what the city was doing was giving its credit to aid the bedspread company to come. Indeed, it seems fair to say that the company would never have agreed to the lease if the city had not provided the land and building, which in turn could not have been done had the city not made "a loan of its credit." It is one of those inexorable realities of our human-made and human-operated courts that at times murder convictions get affirmed without a judge understanding and deciding what ought to have been an outcome-determinative question of law application that should have led to reversal.[155]

Sydney Smith's *Allbritton* opinion has many virtues. It deserves continued praise. Whether the BAWI Act promoted "a legitimate public purpose"[156] was legally beside the point if in practical effect the city of Winona proposed to "loan its credit in [substantial] aid of such [private] corporation."[157] Instead, Smith found analogies in waterworks or gasworks that a city might operate and remain within its constitutional powers. No constitutional impediment could be found to leasing such enterprises "as a means of supplying the public needs."[158] The BAWI Act made sure that Winona's proposed lease was similarly dedicated, and the court said that was enough. Nonetheless, one cannot help but wonder how the justices would have dealt with the *Carothers* precedent had the lease with the bedspread company been signed, sealed, and delivered prior to the day of final adjudication in *Allbritton*.

JUSTICE ANDERSON DISSENTS

Justice William D. Anderson took exception to the majority view. He opened with the oft-quoted, "In my judgment the majority opinion drives a steam shovel though our Constitution."[159] Considerable bombast followed, including the charge noted above that the court was "giving Soviet Russia an approving handshake." Anderson concluded, "This is not a case of stretching the Constitution to meet new conditions, but it is a case of breaking it."[160] Several points merit mention.

William Dozier Anderson (1862–1952) was born in Cedar Grove in Pontotoc County in northeast Mississippi, while his father was away in service with the Confederate Army. Anderson was a combatant himself, though more of the political variety than his father. He practiced law and lived in Tupelo for many years. Anderson famously led the fight in 1910 to have Theodore G. Bilbo expelled from the senate, an effort that failed by one vote.

Anderson was from that part of the state that had been arguably most in need of—but was politically most hostile to—BAWI leading up to and during that last week of summer in 1936. He was seventy-four years old. In his dissenting opinion, Anderson never mentioned the Fourteenth Amendment or any other clause of the US Constitution, or any US Supreme Court decision. He came close to making the Section 183 argument that Sydney Smith overlooked but was so enmeshed in his mind-set of fear and outrage that he never nailed the point. Anderson's dissent is most useful as a reminder of an atmosphere of suspicion and retrenchment and self-righteousness that has had its way of clouding the minds of many Mississippians for so many years, long before February of 1938, and all too often ever since.

JUSTICE GRIFFITH'S SPECIAL CONCURRENCE

We met Justice Virgil A. Griffith above. He filed a concurring opinion in *Allbritton* that is worthy of note and reflection. Two points are discussed. Griffith concurred in the affirmance of the judgment of the chancery court, but he did not like the way Chief Justice Smith got there. Griffith said that Smith's majority opinion "goes too far as respects the grounds upon which the [BAWI] act is sustained, and not far enough in regards to the terms of the proposed lease" that the city would enter with the operator of the "hosiery, knitting and wearing apparel manufacturing plant."

Griffith began explaining why the State had the constitutional authority to act to alleviate unemployment with a nice touch.

> From the earliest times in our history it has been regarded as a public purpose and within the direct power of taxation to keep the poor from . . . starvation. . . . . . Ordinarily, a man will break in and take before he will starve, and all will do this for their families. They will do so singly and in groups. Thus the public duty and purpose to furnish food and necessaries to the famished is traceable directly to the police power of the state.

From this, Griffith reminded us that the constitutional power to perform this public duty and purpose "includes, by implication, the authority to avail of all the necessary and proper means for the accomplishment of the particular object."[161] He said the majority "goes too far," however, when it upholds BAWI "merely because the establishment of manufacturing or industrial enterprises will promote the public good or will benefit other occupations."

> [S]o to hold is to throw the door wide open to take over the wholesale and retail mercantile business, or the farms, or the publishing business, including the public newspapers, or any other business, and to establish a communistic or soviet state, or embark upon a boundless and uncharted sea without rudder or compass.

Griffith noted the legislative fact of "public statistics that the average of unemployment has run throughout several past years at about 10 per cent of the total population, and because of new inventions past and future, we can well estimate . . . the percentage of unemployment . . . throughout the years which are to come." The phenomenon of unemployment thus arguably cabined, Griffith accepted that the State might embark upon a program for the "public purpose of the alleviation of unemployment, but for that object only."

His general premise articulated, Griffith turned to his secondary concern. Since the alleviation of unemployment "is the only constitutional ground upon which" the proposed apparel manufacturing plant might go forward, its operations "must in a reasonable measure be under the control of the public authorities, as regards who shall be employed, and as to minimum wages, and maximum hours of work."[162] Fine, but has not Justice Griffith begun to circle back towards the "communistic or soviet state" that he said he was so worried about, and that Justice Anderson was positively terrified of? This aside, Griffith offered general guidance as to the sorts of terms the lease should include. Here he proceeded in the face of familiar judicial reluctance to "decide upon the details of an additional step proposed to be taken but not yet taken."

> Before this bond money is allowed to be spent, the municipal authorities, the commission, and the prospective lessee or lessees should know at least in general outline whether such a lease as they are willing to make would be approved by this court."[163]

This practical advice should be forthcoming from the normally reticent court, lest the parties run the risk that in the end "an empty and idle plant would stand as the mournful result of the taxpayers' money that has been spent."[164]

The judgment of the Supreme Court of Mississippi became final in February of 1938. The legislation enabling and regulating the BAWI program had survived federal and state constitutional attacks. Winona's industrial bonds had been finally validated. The city was authorized to proceed. One and all could finally get down to the business of identifying and recruiting a particular business to come to Winona.[165]

Without any order staying the final judgment, W. S. Allbritton and his lawyer, W. E. Morse, thought one last shot was expected. On March 23, 1938, they appealed to the Supreme Court of the United States.

Established procedure required that appealing parties file a jurisdictional statement explaining that the case presented a federal question and why the US Supreme Court should consider and adjudge that question. Such appeals had been common and included *Lochner*.[166] Allbritton and Morse cited the aging precedent of *Cole v. City of LaGrange*,[167] which provided facial support, and the then seventeen-year-old *Green v. Frazier*,[168] which supported jurisdiction but little else.

The federal constitutional premise that Allbritton and Morse pressed against BAWI—in general, and against the full faith and credit bonds Winona proposed to issue to finance its textile, knitting, hosiery, or other manufacturing plant in particular—was straightforward. Property owner Allbritton was to be taxed to help retire the debt on bonds to be issued primarily for the benefit of private enterprise. "This is the taking of property for a private individual or a private corporation and is in violation of the 14th Amendment of the Constitution of the United States."[169] The city could not operate such an enterprise, at least, not within the constitution. A textile or other like plant was not a public utility. Nor could the city lend its credit to provide financial support for such an endeavor. BAWI's leasing stratagem was authorizing the city to do indirectly that which it could not do directly.

The argument of Allbritton and Morse was as old as Shakespeare. What the state and its counties may not do directly, they are equally forbidden to achieve by indirection. The Georgia Court of Appeals once put the point, viz., what officials "may not do directly they cannot indirectly do, for 'indirection thereby grows direct.'"[170]

Two weeks later, the US Supreme Court entered a short order. "The appeal herein is dismissed for want of a substantial federal question."[171]

TIMING, FORTUITY, AND IRONY

BAWI had survived, not so much because of the prescience of the six Jackson lawyers who drafted the legislation as because of several fortuities. *W. S. Allbritton v. City of Winona, Mississippi*, 303 U.S. 627 (1938) reached the Supreme Court more than a year after "the switch in time that saved nine."[172] In March of 1937, otherwise largely forgotten Justice Owen Roberts stopped voting with the "Four Horsemen" who had been striking down one piece of New Deal legislation after another. Roberts's switch had made a new majority in *West*

Coast Hotel Co. v. Parish.[173] *Carmichael v. Southern Coal & Coke Co.* followed two months later.[174] Chief Justice Smith's opinion in *Allbritton* relied on *West Coast Hotel* and *Carmichael*,[175] neither of which had been available to Hugh White's six-lawyer panel back in 1936.

To be sure, the one-paragraph *per curiam* order cited *Green v. Frazier*, along with *Jones v. City of Portland*, which Justice Day had called "the nearest approach"[176] to the question for decision in *Green*. Willis Van Devanter had retired in 1937, and George Sutherland left the US Supreme Court in January of 1938. By April of 1938, only James Clark McReynolds and Pierce Butler remained of the original "Four Horsemen." A dismissal "for want of a substantial federal question" was not a decision on the merits and would have no precedential value. McReynolds and Butler likely saw no reason to signal any unhappiness they may have felt about allowing a relatively minor state supreme court decision such as *Allbritton* to stand. Back in September of 1936, Governor White and his legal team could only have hoped for such an eventuality.

The second and perhaps even more important fortuity was that Sydney Smith never objectively and in writing confronted, construed, or applied state Section 183's injunction that—public purpose and the general welfare of the people of Winona notwithstanding—the city simply could not loan its credit in substantial aid of a private corporation. In candor, how one gets around that third alternative injunction in Section 183 is not apparent.

A certain irony attended what happened next. Winona's long-unidentified new industry turned out be a chenille-bedspread manufacturing enterprise. Chenille is a tufted textile made of cotton fibers. It has always been a southern product. In the early part of the twentieth century, chenille bedspreads were handcrafted foremost in northern Georgia. That state's tufted textile production is associated with US Highway 41, the Dixie highway also known around Dalton, Georgia, as the "bedspread boulevard" along that southerly road leading to Florida.[177] By the late 1930s, handcrafting had surrendered to technology, and machine-produced chenille products were widely distributed, including chenille beach capes, jackets, and robes.

The industry coming to Winona produced and marketed chenille bedspreads. It was based in Jackson, Mississippi, at the time, with an affiliation with cotton cloth and bedspread plants in towns in Alabama and Mississippi.[178] In 1911, James W. Sanders (1865–1937), a native of Tuscaloosa, Alabama, had purchased his first cotton mill and operated in Kosciusko, Mississippi.[179] Sanders's success enabled him to acquire mills in the nearby communities of Starkville, Winona, and Yazoo City, and as far away as Natchez and Mobile. Sanders's son, Robert David Sanders (1898–1959), attended what was then known as Mississippi A & M College in Starkville and later served as a captain in the World War. In 1920, he had come back home and become general manager of his father's cotton mills. At his father's death in 1937, Robert inherited the business and expanded it.[180] He soon developed the slogan "What Mississippi Makes, Makes Mississippi."[181] The Sanders-controlled cotton mills continued in Winona and six other Mississippi communities.

By this time, the City of Winona—its bonds finally validated—had bought land enough and built a manufacturing plant. The new company secured a lease from the city and began production.[182] When fully operational, the new chenille concern planned to hire at least 150 workers. January 1, 1940, had been the target date for the grand opening. Just before Thanksgiving of 1939, the *Winona Times* reported that "contractors are rushing the completion of the building and it is expected that machinery will be set up and the factory will be ready to start operating by the first of January."[183] A training center for new workers was established in cooperation with the State Vocational Training Department of the Department of Education. The Winona Chamber of Commerce handled the paperwork and other logistics of accepting and processing employment applications.

On March 29, 1940, Winona Bedspread Company filed articles of incorporation with the secretary of state of Mississippi.[184] Incorporators included R. D. Sanders and two others, all listing addresses in Jackson, Mississippi. In short order, the company was operating chenille mills in Winona and nearby towns of Durant and Kosciusko, and in the southwest Mississippi community of Summit.[185]

As the year 1942 began, the world had turned upside down in many respects. World War II has become a reality for the United States. The people of Winona and Montgomery County, Mississippi, were no more exempted than anyone else. An announcement was made to the effect that the local chamber of commerce would cooperate with the American Federation of Labor in establishing an army camp in the Winona area. After two years of manufacturing bedspreads, the company announced that it would switch over to the production of chenille house robes. On March 6, 1942, it was reported that the company had "already received orders for 800 dozen chenille house robes. Fifty operators are scheduled to go to work next week."[186]

On April 22, 1943, the company changed its name to Aponaug Chenille Company, Inc. A little over four months later, the company changed its name again, this time to Delta Chenille Company, Inc. In time it hired more workers, no doubt much to the benefit of the people of Winona and the surrounding area. So much for any constitutional questions regarding taxing the people of Winona so that industrial wealth and entrepreneurship from other parts of the country might be lured to bring its capital and manufacturing know-how and invest in north central Mississippi. On the other hand, corporate by-laws provided that the Delta Chenille Company "may also have an office in the City of New York, State of New York." Likely this suggested a banking connection in New York and northern capital coming to Mississippi after all, albeit of the secured credit variety. Unofficial and incomplete "Minutes of First Meeting of

Directors—continued" include an entry authorizing a "factoring contract with Textile Banking Company of New York City," said to be dated "April 20, 1940."[187]

AFTERMATH OF BAWI

Hugh White made it happen. He had some luck along the way, but had White not stepped forward circa 1929 and 1930 as mayor of the old sawmill town of Columbia, there may never have been a BAWI program. Had he not shrugged off his gubernatorial defeat in 1931 and tried again four years later, Mississippi would have had no BAWI program. In time, of course, and after World War II, the state almost certainly would have developed some sort of a program for recruiting industry. Without Hugh White, the state would have been a follower, not a leader.

Still, White had his blind spots. Like other southern leaders seeking industry, White made it crystal clear that Mississippi was a friend to management and entrepreneurship, who had no truck with labor unions. Congress's enactment of the Fair Labor Standards Act of 1938 somewhat blunted management's efforts in the all-important area of wages, with the added advantage for Mississippi that competing southern states would be under the same federal law. Nothing suggests White gave much thought to improving the employment opportunities of African American workers. Nothing suggests he would have short of a similar across-the-board federal inducement, such as Title VII of the Civil Rights Act of 1964.

Surprisingly, White could not see the worth of a state workers' compensation law that, if properly crafted, carried as many advantages for management as for its workers. He consistently opposed such a law for Mississippi. In the course of negotiations with Ingalls Shipbuilding in 1938, company representatives tried to educate White about workers' compensation.[188] Alabama had just passed such a law. But not until 1948 did the legislature finally enact a workers' compensation law,[189] assuming Mississippi's all-too-familiar position of being last in the nation. It was a done deal well before January of 1952, when Hugh White was sworn in as governor for his second four-year term.[190]

The story of the chenille bedspread plant in Winona, Mississippi, adds humanity and practical reality to the rhetoric of the special chancellor who spoke in early December of 1937 and of the state supreme court justices who spoke in February of 1938. The social justice dimensions of Hugh White's idea of the BAWI program, its strengths and flaws, were laid bare, along with constitutional thinking of the times. It took a while before the Sanders-controlled chenille manufacturing concern became operational. Many otherwise eligible employees who badly needed jobs hesitated.[191] Was this really just a government handout? The proverb was proved yet again: pride goeth before a fall.[192]

Still there were more than enough workers grateful to have a job, any job, and a paycheck, however modest. And there was a war on.

All new industries established under the BAWI Act were required to give employment preferences to local workers.[193] As a practical matter, this included workers from nearby areas such as Carroll, Choctaw, and Webster Counties. For example, Willie Mae Randall (1893–1966) lived in the Blackmonton community in adjacent Carroll County, but a family post notes that she "worked . . . at the chenille bedspread factory in Winona."[194] Interestingly, the 1940 federal census for Winona lists Dewitt C. Whitmire, age twenty-three, as "mechanic bedspread plant," and his wife, Goldie, age twenty, as "chenille worker." Five years earlier, Dewitt and Goldie had lived in Dalton, Georgia. Albert Watkins, age twenty-seven, from just across the state line in South Carolina is listed as "mechanic," while his wife, Madge, age twenty-six, and her sister, Elzie Keller, age nineteen, are listed as "chenille workers." The census reflects that these young people had established their residence in Winona, though only a few years earlier they had lived in the heart of the traditional chenille-producing part of the southeastern United States.

The plant's first full year of production was 1940, with one hundred employees. This number of workers had more than doubled by 1941, dropped to 176 in 1942, but was on pace to have 330 employees by 1943.[195] Published data suggest that the total wages paid by the chenille bedspread company were $254,814 for the first three and a half years of operation.[196] The city's bond issue was $35,000, to be retired over twenty-five years. By 1943, the project seemed on track and keeping pace consistent with the targets that had been set by the Industrial Commission in its certificate of public convenience and necessity issued June 1, 1937.

Of course, World War II had an effect here, but no studies have been found to quantify this effect and isolate it from other influences. A Federal Reserve Bank study cautioned against assuming too much about cause and effect: "[A] subsidy is an inducement, not an investment, and the causative effect of that inducement can never, in the nature of things, be satisfactorily proved."[197] Likely, it may never be known if Delta Chenille would have come to Winona without inducements.

As fate would have it, the Delta Chenille Company is no more. Chenille-bedspread manufacturing ended, and the plant closed in the 1950s.[198] R. D. Sanders, for years one of the most active industrialists in Mississippi and who led Delta Chenille and a number of related companies, died unexpectedly on September 25, 1954. News reports and company records show an October 3, 1955, contract to sell "the plant site, buildings and machinery" to the Joe L. Moore & Company, Inc. of Gadsden, Alabama. The deal was finally approved on January 4, 1956.[199] New officers and directors were named on July 3, 1956. No further entries appear in the corporate minute book. The Mississippi secretary of state's office lists the status of the corporation as "Dissolved."

In 1958, the Winona Chamber of Commerce announced a Hometown Development Program, listing ten primary objectives. Number eight was "Expansion of industry. Reactivating the old Delta Chenille plant buildings by some industry."[200] Nine months later, the chamber listed among its accomplishments of the past year rental of the old Delta Chenille plant for use as a warehouse and shipping center. Also announced was a plan to expand the present plant with twenty-five additional sewing facilities.[201]

In August of 1960, Kimco Auto Products of Memphis announced that it had acquired rights to the 35,000-square-foot facility and would begin operations of the Kimco Brake Shoe Factory, an altogether different kind of manufacturing enterprise.[202] Kimco said it expected to employ between fifty and a hundred workers.[203] Twenty years later, Kimco reported a stable employment with an annual payroll of some $600,000, bettering the economy of Winona and Montgomery County. All seemed well in June of 1981,[204] but in 1986 the business was sold. A year later, the new owners shut down Kimco's thirty-year run in the old BAWI-approved Delta Chenille plant.[205] The economic fates were done with Kimco.

In the summer of 2008, a Notice of Sale appeared in the Winona Times.

The Montgomery County Board of Supervisors will sell by public auction one vacant lot located on NW corner of South Union Street and Republican Street in Winona, Mississippi, formerly known as the Kimco Brake Shoe Factory Lot at 9:00 a.m. on Monday, the 21st day of July, 2008 at the front steps of the Montgomery County Courthouse in Winona, MS.

In the 1940s and 1950s, the chenille plant property at the southwest corner of South Union Street and Republican Avenue was improved with a main building, sheds, and a café on about two and a half acres of land. The building built with Winona's BAWI-authorized and approved bonds lay empty for years after Kimco left and was finally demolished altogether, leaving but a few slabs of concrete. In March of 2016, this large tract of land was a meadow of clover, wildflowers, weeds, and grass—a lonely magnolia tree in one corner of the lot—with no apparent evidence anything of interest had ever happened there. A sign read, "For Sale By Owner."[206]

Not even "an empty and idle plant . . . was left stand[ing] as the mournful result of the taxpayers' money that ha[d] been spent."[207] Yet the case can be made that Winona got its money's worth. Forty-plus years of jobs and money infused into the community are not to be sneezed at. By the fall of 2017, the last vestiges of industry were gone, and, like the rest of the near neighborhood, the real estate was residential again, with two new brick residences, as of that time unoccupied but with hope for more.

REFLECTIONS

Takeaways from this BAWI-generated constitutional encounter include updates of many of the reflections at the end of chapter 7. Foremost, the legislature again actualized its forward-looking prerogative, given the social and economic needs of the people. Governor White was the force, but his powers were limited to persuasion and leadership and an occasional veto. Remember, Hugh White was a 250-pounder back when that size really did make one a force.

Then there are the tensions between the substantive overlays on the due process clauses of federal and state constitutions, on the one hand, and the state's Section 6 declaration that "[t]he people of this state have the inherent, sole, and exclusive right to regulate the internal government and police thereof,...."[208] This aspiration is augmented by the more specific (but still quite general) command found in Article 7 that "the exercise of the police powers of the State shall never be abridged."[209] Ordinarily, an act will "survive under the constitution" if it is shown to be within the police power of the state, that is, if it bears "a reasonable relation to a governmental purpose" such as the promotion of the public convenience and prosperity, the general welfare, the public health, or the public safety.[210] Before and after the *Newman Lumber* case, and before and since *Allbritton*, the legislature has given flesh to the constitution's grant of the legislative power in ways and means as varied as the needs of the people and legislators' perception of those needs, and seemingly feasible strategies for satisfying those needs.[211]

No one doubts that the legislature has every prerogative—if not responsibility—to engage in pragmatic socioeconomic analyses of economic development proposals. The governor and the executive department are similarly charged in making their recommendations. On judicial review, is not the court charged to do its own socioeconomic analyses (whether informed by a Brandeis Brief or two or three, or not)? How else may the court adjudge reliably whether a given program is justified by credible legislative facts or is an arbitrary and capricious exercise of governmental power? How else would the court learn with reasonable confidence whether—and to what practical extent—this new enactment or that affects reasonable reliance interests of persons or firms? Or has packed within it too great a risk of more harm than good? And what should the court do where the work of the other two branches is found wanting?

There are more than a few parallels between Sydney Smith's opinion in *Allbritton* and his public address at the University of Mississippi School of Law some seventeen months earlier. In *Allbritton* he cited Holmes's swipe at laissez-faire economics in his famous *Lochner* dissent.[212] If anything, Holmes was softer than Smith's own take.[213] Chief Justice Smith cited and quoted Roscoe Pound again, albeit for a different point from a different article,[214] to take a poke at natural-law thinking. He had made the same point in his address to the legal community, though citing other legal philosophers on that occasion. This suggests only that Smith was more than an occasional student of writings and thinking of Dean Pound and his contemporaries.[215] Smith's understanding of the crucial role of social facts was set forth in his law school address in October of 1936.[216] That understanding was made only slightly more specific and particular-case-oriented in *Allbritton* in February of 1938.[217] The constitution and laws of a community enjoy great value—and enhanced humanity and social utility—when its judges read widely in the philosophy of law and of economics and the other social sciences, and then think deeply, and talk to one another, and beyond particular cases. And are open to new insights, such as those being afforded by the emerging discipline of behavioral economics, which has garnered three Nobel Prizes in economics in the past fifteen years.[218]

A more specific and quite noteworthy aspect of *Allbritton* is the full and considered approach to constitutional construction and application set out over a full six pages of the opinion.[219] Borrowing liberally from constitutional literature and legal philosophy, Sydney Smith articulated a practical and contemporary approach to the way people should think of and enjoy the benefits and protections of their constitution. Dean Pound's sociological jurisprudence was only a part of that approach. Smith went back to John Marshall's view that a constitution is "intended to endure for ages to come, and, consequently to be adapted to the various crises of human affairs."

Of course, any constitution can be amended, as any contract can be amended. If, for example, it were thought desirable, in the era when people live a lot longer than on average they did in 1787, that the minimum age for the office of president might be upped to forty, the matter might be achieved by amendment. Past that, Smith quotes Marshall's compliment to those at the 1787 convention for not giving the Constitution "the properties of a legal code." Smith did his part to assure that his state did not succumb to the prejudice that—where the court was confronted with construing and applying one of the great general phrases of the federal or state constitution—a formal amendment would be needed before the court could take full account of changing social and economic circumstances of living in the here-and-now and the reasonably foreseeable future.

It would have been a mistake the constitutional draftsmen did not make in Philadelphia in 1787 "to [have] provided, by immutable rules, for exigencies which, if foreseen at all, must have been dimly, and which c[ould] be best provided for as they occur."[220] By and large, the draftsmen of the Mississippi Constitution of 1890 avoided that mistake as well.[221] After all, a constitution is not "a temporary document . . . incapable, in a healthful and uniform manner, of any expansion or development or movement with the living current of the times."[222] "It is a mistake to suppose that a constitution is to be interpreted only in the light of things as they existed at the time of its adoption."[223] To repeat, because it cannot be said too often, "the due process clauses of our constitutions must not be construed to put the state and federal governments into a straight-jacket and prevent them from adapting life to the continuous change in social and economic conditions."[224]

The way in which the *Allbritton* litigation came about may raise eyebrows. It is hard to imagine a case where interested and affected parties were more public about inviting litigation. Champerty and maintenance have long been frowned upon in Mississippi.[225] Inducing litigation for gain is thought contrary to public policy. The circumstances that evolved through the summer and fall of 1937 throw an important light on this traditional no-no familiar to all lawyers. More broadly, courts have long frowned on feigned or collusive cases.[226]

Decisions by the US Supreme Court and the Supreme Court of Mississippi in the mid-1930s had cast doubts on any state-level planning and regulation of a social or economic nature. Governor White had taken the prudent step of engaging six very good lawyers and charging them to draft as best as they could a BAWI bill that would survive constitutionally. The *West Coast Hotel* and *Carmichael* decisions handed down by the US Supreme Court in early 1937 were unforeseeable blessings. Still, the September 1937 first anniversary of BAWI came and went, uncertainty and its attendant anxieties remaining in the minds of both industrial recruits and potential municipal bond purchasers. This uncertainty imperiled the entire program. At the very least, a merits decision by the Supreme Court of Mississippi was needed to settle the matter—one way or the other—and there seemed no route to such a decision short of stirring up litigation of the point.

Then as now, and for reasons confusing the familiar with the necessary, the Supreme Court ordinarily will not consider giving an advisory opinion. Given its constitutional power as the state court of last resort with ultimate expository responsibilities regarding the state constitution, it seems only sensible that the state supreme court should have looked the other way, had anyone in 1937 raised a question about the bona fides of the *Allbritton* parties and their litigation. No evidence suggests anyone formally questioned the propriety of the *Allbritton* proceedings.

W. E. Morse was one of the unsung heroes of the BAWI wars. On the merits, there can be no doubt that Morse presented the case against the constitutional enforceability of the BAWI Act as well as any lawyer reasonably could. To be sure, we have no access to Morse's oral arguments. From his written briefs in the chancery court and before the Supreme Court of Mississippi, Morse pulled no punches. He even tried an appeal to the US Supreme Court. He was surely aware that, by the late winter of 1938, the tide had turned in the long-running war against Lochnerism, but it was not his fault that the *Allbritton* case could not have been appealed before the "switch in time that saved nine."[227]

From the time Hugh White started soliciting someone to sue, the question was whether a case such as *Allbritton* would settle the constitutional questions.

Some might wonder whether justiciability defenses should have been raised. A lawyer with proper cunning and zeal to win through any legally permissible strategy could have questioned W. S. Allbritton's standing to sue. Or whether the case presented a political question such that the judiciary should stay its hand. Or argued that this was a feigned lawsuit, and that this undermined the professed desire of everyone from Hugh White on down for a reliable and authoritative ruling by the state supreme court. This, of course, was not a concern W. E. Morse was in a position to address. And the last thing White and the Industrial Commission wanted was for the case to be thrown out on some "technicality." It was to the collective credit of all participants that *Allbritton* was not allowed to get bogged down in such faux issues.

Lawyers, concerned citizens, and other informed persons debated another constitutional concern of consequence. Assume *arguendo* that a given manufacturing or service industry that provides jobs and payroll enhances the well-being of a community. And assume further that such an industry might not fare so well without public support, whether in the form of low-rent leases of publicly owned property, tax exemptions, fees in lieu of taxes, subsidies, free auxiliary services, whatever. Is that enough, when challenged in the courthouse, to satisfy the substantive due process precept that a governmental or other public purpose must be shown before the enterprise may proceed? Or need more be shown, as the estimable Justice Griffith would argue in time?[228]

Even if substantive due process were satisfied, is there not another elephant in the room? What happens if another person or firm offering the same or substantially similar credentials had approached the City of Winona and the Industrial Commission claiming the right to compete with the Delta Chenille Company? Is there an equal protection question there? Or was BAWI just another form of garden-variety competitive bidding? To the point, do not such public support stratagems always provide an unfair advantage to competitors, notwithstanding the good that might otherwise be done for the community?

Some have refined the *Allbritton* argument into a factual inquiry—whether "the essentiality of a given public facility to the welfare of a given area is a question of fact for the court to decide in each case, rather than a question of law, and [whether] that essentiality in fact may vary from time to time and place to place."[229] Are regular paychecks in the hands of working men and women such a social necessity that a local government might issue bonds "under a simple state enabling act, without the apparatus of certification found necessary in Mississippi in 1936?[230] Of course, when you think about it, each of these is a third kind of question, one of law application that the court is charged reliably to adjudge.[231] And this means accessing and assembling the facts, whether the legislative variety or more traditional forms of evidence produced in the courthouse or, more likely, both.

Does not Mississippi at some point have to deal with the problem long embedded in the text of state constitutional Section 183 that a municipality really may not "loan its credit in [substantial] aid of such corporation or association"?[232] Where a project is funded by a local full faith and credit bond issue, is not any sort of BAWI-type lease arrangement such a loan of local government credit? To what extent may it be said that other forms of publicly afforded value are "credit" within Section 183? When that moment comes, there will be every good reason why the substantiality of that "aid" should be measured by its causative effects assuming those can reliably be measured. Remember, "a subsidy is an inducement, not an investment, and the causative effect of that inducement can never, in the nature of things, be satisfactorily measured."[233]

To be sure, causative effect may be subject to empirical investigation and shown with more clarity than the Federal Reserve Bank thought possible in 1949. That has been done of late, as new and more sophisticated approaches to measurement and analysis have become known.[234] For example, a recent empirical investigation of the BAWI program and its effects has shown that

> counties benefiting from BAWI investment not only experienced an immediate rise in female labor force participation. . . . The results imply that even short-lived industrial policies may interact in subtle ways with social norms to give rise to enduring economic impacts.[235]

Still, the burden rests with the party trying to establish the substantiality proposition. Resort to legislative facts or Brandeis Briefs may be allowable. The court should allow and defer to the regulators where—but only where—on the face of the matter they have done their job.[236]

But does any of this satisfy the concerns of a competitive bidder with substantially similar credentials seeking a city subsidy? Where that competing bidder says, Give us a similar inducement and watch what we can do for your community and its people? Leave aside who makes the decision and through what process. Do these public questions not ultimately boil down to which applicant would be the best corporate citizen of the community? Or does the thought of such a question merely cause the local chamber of commerce to smile, If only we had the luxury of multiple qualified entities bidding against one another?

As a practical matter, BAWI faded away when new governor Paul Johnson[237] took office in January of 1940. In those days, Mississippi's governor was constitutionally barred from serving consecutive terms. Hugh White served a second term, but from 1952 to 1956, and in a considerably different Mississippi than the one he began to lead in January of 1936.

BAWI had produced few tangible results by 1940. With hindsight, the three-year time frame from the fall of 1936 was probably not long enough so that substantial positive results should have been expected. The Delta Chenille Company in Winona and the I. B. S. Manufacturing Company in New Albany were not even open for business before 1940 when the legislature consolidated the Industrial Commission with two other commissions and effectively dropped the curtain on BAWI.[238] In the early 1940s, Mississippi's economy improved. Raw numbers suggest some progress and success stories among most of the twelve BAWI plants.[239] But so much was changing on other fronts—World War II being front and center—that no one could measure reliably the extent to which BAWI should get the credit.

Time and more sophisticated research may tell a different and more positive story. Ten BAWI plants primarily employed women. In the aggregate the counties in which these plants were located experienced an approximate 23 percent increase in female labor force participation. Noteworthy as well, these positive effects lingered long after 1963, by which time the majority of the original BAWI plants had closed. Female labor force participation faded only gradually through the end of the twentieth century. Moreover, there is less-tangible evidence that BAWI counties and surrounding areas experienced "impacts that operate[d] more subtly by influencing social and cultural norms and expectations within regions." For example, "there is some evidence that female educational attainment . . . rose in communities where BAWI investment occurred."[240] Though this research remained forty-five years in the future, it was fitting that the plant manager of the chenille plant was a woman. Some fifteen years after the company was sold, and almost ten years after Kimko began operations, former chenille plant manager Mary Patey Evans was the guest of honor at a November 1969 reunion of those who had been associated with the original BAWI-sanctioned plant. Among the memories shared was that Evans had "trained the first women employees in the operation of the machines and the making of spreads and robes."[241]

There remained another elephant in the room—perhaps larger than all others—along the road to the chenille-bedspread manufacturing company that opened in Winona in 1940. No mention was made that poor and unemployed black persons needed work as much as anyone else. The Atlanta Federal Reserve Bank's 1949 report on BAWI just may be one of the most comprehensive and thoughtful ever produced.[242] African Americans are never mentioned. These were years of strict racial segregation in Mississippi and the rest of the Deep South. Industrial Commission promotional literature emphasized the plentiful number of "Anglo-Saxon" men and women who were hungry, able, and available for hire.[243]

A perusal of the *Winona Times* for 1937 yields many a front-page story about the city's need for job-creating industry. Those front pages make clear the racial climate of the times as well. Foremost, there is the April 1937 story of a brutal lynching of two black men near Duck Hill, just north of Winona, for the alleged murder of a white man. Other stories of less proximate lynchings appear as well, along with many other reports of criminal charges against black persons. There is an editorial congratulating the state's congressional delegation for its successful efforts (with those of other southern congressmen) in defeating federal anti-lynching legislation.

Agriculture is one context in which Sydney Smith's *pronunciamento* regarding laissez-faire economics has been fulfilled. Since the days of the New Deal, Mississippi's farmers have never tired of reminding Washington of its obligations to support agriculture. Ironically, farmers who were not even a gleam in their parents' eyes at the time recall the spring of 1952. Then-recent Nobel laureate William Faulkner addressed the Delta Council's annual meeting. James C. Cobb captured the moment: "Faulkner delivered an eloquent indictment of the growing dependence of Americans on federal assistance," for which "he received a standing ovation from Delta Council members, who assumed that the famous author was aiming his remarks not at them but at the poor and the black (who, if they heard Faulkner's speech that day, did so only as they served food or washed dishes)."[244] The shoe was a better fit closer to home—with the applauding Delta Council members themselves.

Recruiting industry has remained a function of state-level planning, equally at odds with pure laissez-faire economic theory. Consider the incentives Mississippi afforded Nissan for its automobile production plant south of Canton in Madison County, and for Toyota for its Wellspring manufacturing establishment in Blue Springs in northeast Mississippi. More recently, the legislature has enacted the "fee-in-lieu" program. If an industrialist will establish a plant in Mississippi, he will not have to pay *ad valorem* taxes for ten years. Instead, he may be required to pay a "fee-in-lieu" of taxes computed the same as taxes, only he is promised that fee will not exceed one-third of what he would have to pay if he were on the same footing as other *ad valorem* taxpayers.[245] Again the idea is to induce outside capital to Mississippi to create jobs. No one mounts substantive due process challenges to such a legislative exercise of the police power. The sad outcome of *Carothers v. Town of Booneville* has been forgotten.

Another question for serious reflection at the end of *Allbritton* is, What do we do with the lessons from Holmes's *Lochner* dissent?[246] Children whose families have limited means remain in underfunded, inadequately staffed, and otherwise substandard public schools. People of all ages and stations in life lack the health care they reasonably need. Infrastructure fails.[247] Smaller towns across the state— Winona and other BAWI towns, and particularly once relatively thriving communities in the Delta—have eased into socioeconomic decay. Industry expects major financial concessions before it will consider coming to Mississippi. Not even that can lure cutting-edge technologies. As a middle class has emerged and struggled, individually and in the aggregate, Mississippians have extended their lengthy track record for voting against apparent rational and objective views of their economic self-interests, but, again, is this not their right?[248]

Once more, the legislature has every prerogative—if not responsibility—to engage in pragmatic socioeconomic analyses of economic development proposals. But may not the legislative responsibilities of the state's senate and house of representatives appropriately be limited by the aggregate will of the majority of those who elect their members? No legislature has come up with a means of ameliorating the Madisonian dilemma. Are we not once again free to become a G. T. T. (Gone To Texas) state if enough of us so choose? And as for those who decide to stay, taxes are still the price we pay for civilization, but may not the majority say when we have been civilized enough? And that tax breaks may be traded for jobs as long as we want, and as the courts will let us. Past that, do not Sections 12 and 18 of our constitution say we can put guns and Bibles ahead of all else? Others, and particularly outsiders, are free to call us fearful people, even to suggest the only thing we have to fear is fear itself, but this does not strip us of the right to say what we are afraid of, and how we may ward off those fears. After all, we can refuse to reelect any judge who tries to say otherwise.

ENDNOTES

1. Sydney McCain Smith, *The State and the Social Process*, 9 Miss. L. Journ. 147, 149 (December 1936).

2. "One Fourth of a State Sold for Taxes," *Literary Digest*, May 7, 1932; *see also* Connie Lester, "Balancing Agriculture with Industry: Capital, Labor, and the Public Good in Mississippi's Home-Grown New Deal," *Journal of Mississippi History* 70 (Fall 2008), pages 235, 239; and Matthew Freedman, "Persistence in Industrial Policy Impacts: Evidence from Depression-Era Mississippi," (Sept. 2015), https://belkcollegeofbusiness.uncc.edu/ . . . /wp/Freedman_UNCC.pdf.

3. Gene Dattel, *Cotton and Race in the Making of America* 359 (2009).

4. *See, e.g.*, Connie L. Lester, "Balancing Agriculture with Industry: Capital, Labor, and the Public Good in Mississippi's Home-Grown New Deal," *Journal of Mississippi History* 70 (Fall 2008), pages 235, 239 fn. 4.

5. Connie L. Lester, "Balancing Agriculture with Industry: Capital, Labor, and the Public Good in Mississippi's Home-Grown New Deal," *Journal of Mississippi History* 70 (Fall 2008), 235, 243–244.

6. Gilbert H. Hoffman quoting Fenwick L. Peck in *Steam Whistles in the Piney Woods*, Vol. 1, page 99 (1998). See chapter 7 above.

7. James C. Cobb, *The Most Southern Place on Earth* 185 (1992). In the first part of his chapter 8, "We Are at the Crossroads," pages 184–201, Cobb provides a vivid and at times individualized depiction of the Delta's struggle though the 1930s.

8. David L. Cohn, *The Life and Times of King Cotton* 252 (1956). Cohn was born and raised in Greenville in the Mississippi Delta.

9. David G. Sansing, *Mississippi: Its People and Culture* 288 (1981); Connie Lester, "Balancing Agriculture with Industry: Capital, Labor, and the Public Good in Mississippi's Home-Grown New Deal," *Journal of Mississippi History* 70 (Fall 2008), 235, 240.

10. W. J. Cash, *The Mind of the South* 360–361 (1941). Gene Dattel, who was born and raised in Ruleville in the Mississippi Delta, made the same report in his *Cotton and Race in the Making of America* 359 (2009).

11. W. J. Cash, *The Mind of the South* 360 (1941).

12. See Eric C. Clark, "Legislative Adoption of BAWI, 1936," *Journal of Mississippi History*, Vol. 52 (Nov. 1990), pages 283, 295; Connie L. Lester, "Balancing Agriculture with Industry: Capital, Labor, and the Public Good in Mississippi's Home-Grown New Deal," *Journal of Mississippi History* 70 (Fall 2008), 235, 252.

13. For a perceptive commentary of these people ending before the period in which this chapter is centered, see Albert D. Kirwan, *Revolt of the Rednecks, Mississippi Politics 1875–1925* (1951).

14. See "Hugh Lawson White," in David G. Sansing, *Mississippi Governors: Soldiers, Statesmen, Scholars, Scoundrels: A Bicentennial Edition* 176–179 (2016); Hugh Lawson White, *Mississippi Encyclopedia* 1331–1332 (Ownby and Wilson eds., 2017).

15. Connie Lester, "Economic Development in the 1930s: Balance Agriculture with Industry," *Mississippi History Now* (May 2004), http://mshistorynow.mdah.state.ms.us/articles/224 /economic-development-in-the-1930s.

16. The story of Hugh White and the Columbia Plan has been told often as the springboard for the BAWI program (September of 1936 through June of 1940 and beyond). *See* Ernest Hopkins, "Mississippi's BAWI Plan," at pages 11–16 (1944), published by Federal Reserve Bank of Atlanta in its Thirty-Fifth Annual Report (1949), http://fraser.stlouisfed.org/; James C. Cobb, *The Selling of the South* 8–10 (2d ed., 1993); "Balance Agriculture with Industry Program," *Mississippi Encyclopedia*, 63 (Ownby and Wilson eds., 2017). *See also* the story of Gov. Hugh White's role in the saga of the Gold Coast chronicled in chapter 9 above.

17. Proclamation of Governor Hugh White, made September 9, 1936, Miss. Laws, page 2 (Ex. Sess. 1936).

18. Historian Ralph J. Rogers is credited with calling forth—in the present context—the converse of a familiar saying attributable to Francis Bacon's *Essays* (1625). Rogers, "The Effort to Industrialize," in *A History of Mississippi, Vol. II* 241 (McLemore ed., 1973).

19. See Eric C. Clark, "Legislative Adoption of BAWI, 1936," *Journal of Mississippi History* 52 (Nov. 1990), pages 283, 284.

20. The organization of the Mississippi Union Bank in the late 1830s and the sale of state-guaranteed bonds was also an effort to attract northern and other out-of-state investors, and their big bank rolls undergird an ambitious state-authorized commercial venture. See chapter 4 above.

21. *See* William F. Winter, "Governor Mike Conner and the Sales Tax, 1932," *Journal of Mississippi History* 41 (August 1979); Connie L. Lester, "Balancing Agriculture with Industry: Capital, Labor, and the Public Good in Mississippi's Home-Grown New Deal," *Journal of Mississippi History* 70 (Fall 2008), 235, 247; *see* "Martin Sennet Conner," in David G. Sansing, *Mississippi Governors: Soldiers, Statesmen, Scholars, Scoundrels: A Bicentennial Edition* 172–175 (2016); "Martin Sennet Conner," *Mississippi Encyclopedia* 276 (Ownby and Wilson eds., 2017).

22. *State v. J.J. Newman Lumber Co.*, 102 Miss. 802, 59 So. 923, 928 (1912), suggestion of error overruled, 103 Miss. 263, 60 So. 215 (1913).

23. The reference is to the decision of the Supreme Court of Mississippi handed down on February 7, 1938, commonly cited as *Albritton v. City of Winona*, 181 Miss. 75, 178 So. 799 (1938). On his tombstone, the appellant's name is chiseled in as "William Samuel Allbritton." *Find a Grave*, http://forums.findagrave.com/cgi-bin/fg.cgi?page=gr&GRid=21389568. This gentleman's last name is spelled with two "l's" in every other proceeding in his case. As best can be determined, the only place his last name is spelled with a lone "l" is in the Supreme Court of Mississippi, where in time more substantive minutiae would be overlooked to a substantive end seen in the public interest.

24. Ernest Hopkins, "Mississippi's BAWI Plan," at page 30 (1944), published by Federal Reserve Bank of Atlanta in its Thirty-Fifth Annual Report (1949), http://fraser.stlouisfed.org/.

25. Connie L. Lester, "Balancing Agriculture with Industry: Capital, Labor, and the Public Good in Mississippi's Home-Grown New Deal," *Journal of Mississippi History* 70 (Fall 2008), pages 238, 247.

26. James C. Cobb has provided a well-written, once-over-lightly report of the BAWI story in his *The Selling of the South: The Southern Crusade for Industrial Development, 1936–1990*, pages 5–34 (2d ed., 1993), albeit treating the legal issues a bit superficially.

27. "Mississippi's BAWI Plan," at pages 10–11, published by Federal Reserve Bank of Atlanta in its Thirty-Fifth Annual Report (1949), http://fraser.stlouisfed.org/.

28. Order Granting Certificate of Public Convenience and Necessity entered by Mississippi Industrial Commission on June 1, 1937, in Application No. 8. "[I]ndustrial expansion for the promotion of the general public welfare" was the raison d'être of the whole BAWI Act, the enacting part of which began with a "declar[ation] that the state public welfare demands and the state public policy requires. . . ." Miss. Laws, ch. 1, §1 (Senate Bill No. 1, Ex. Sess. 1936); *see also* the final "Whereas" paragraph in the Preamble, just before the "Now, Therefore" beginning of the enactment.

29. Senate Bill No. 1, enacted and approved on September 19, 1936, Miss. Laws, ch. 1 (Senate Bill No. 1, Ex. Sess. 1936) was called by some the Mississippi Industrial Act. *See* "Mississippi's BAWI Plan," passim, published by Federal Reserve Bank of Atlanta in its Thirty-Fifth Annual Report (1949), http://fraser.stlouisfed.org/. It has long been more commonly known as the BAWI program or the BAWI Act. That acronym is used here.

30. *See* Eric C. Clark, "Legislative Adoption of BAWI, 1936," *Journal of Mississippi History* 52 (Nov. 1990), page 284 fn. 5, and accompanying text.

31. "Mississippi's BAWI Plan," at page 27, published by Federal Reserve Bank of Atlanta in its Thirty-Fifth Annual Report (1949), http://fraser.stlouisfed.org/. "Some communities found themselves bidding against rival communities."

32. *See* dissenting opinion of Justice William D. Anderson of Pontotoc County delivered in *Allbritton v. City of Winona*, 181 Miss. 75, 178 So. 799, 812 (1938) (Anderson, J., dissenting).

33. Former legislator and future Mississippi secretary of state Eric C. Clark has provided a thoughtful analysis of the special session held from September 14 to September 19, 1936. Eric C. Clark, "Legislative Adoption of BAWI, 1936," *Journal of Mississippi History* 52 (Nov. 1990), pages 283–299, and particularly pages 284–285.

34. Louis Jiggitts has been recognized for his service in World War I, as a Rhodes Scholar, for an essay on legal ethics in 1924, and for his service in founding the *Mississippi Law Journal* in 1928. *See The Mississippi Bar's Centennial: A Legacy of Service*, at 43, 50, 109 (Melanie H. Henry comp. and ed., 2006).

35. *See The Mississippi Bar's Centennial: A Legacy of Service*, at 81 (Melanie H. Henry comp. and ed., 2006).

36. *See, e.g.*, Connie L. Lester, "Balancing Agriculture with Industry: Capital, Labor, and the Public Good in Mississippi's Home-Grown New Deal," *Journal of Mississippi History* 70 (Fall 2008), 235, 249; "Mississippi's BAWI Plan," at page 45, published by Federal Reserve Bank of Atlanta in its Thirty-Fifth Annual Report (1949), http://fraser.stlouisfed.org/.

37. Preamble, U.S. Const.

38. U.S. Const. art. 1, §8, cl. 1.

39. Miss. Const. art. 3, §5 (1890).

40. Miss. Const. art. 3, §6 (1890); *see* construction and application of Section 6 in State v. J. J. Newman Lumber Company, 102 Miss. 802, 59 So. 923, 925 (1912).

41. *State v. J. J. Newman Lumber Company*, 102 Miss. 802, 59 So. 923, 925 (1912).

42. Miss. Const. art. 7, §190.

43. U.S. Const. amend. XIV, § 1 (1868).

44. Miss. Const. art. 3, §14 (1890).

45. *See Carothers v. Town of Booneville*, 169 Miss. 511, 153 So. 670, 671–672 (1934).

46. *See, more recently*, Jean v. Nelson, 472 U.S. 846, 848, 854 (1985).

47. *Truax v. Corrigan*, 257 U.S. 312, 344 (1921) (Holmes, J., dissenting).

48. *New State Ice Co. v. Liebmann*, 285 U.S. 262, 311 (1932) (Brandeis, J., dissenting).

49. Miss. Const. art. 3, §§ 6, 7 (1890).

50. Miss. Const. art. 7, §183; Art. 14, §258.

51. Miss. Code Ann. §7-5-25.

52. *See, e.g., Dupree v. Carroll*, 967 So. 2d 27, 31 (¶21) (Miss. 2007); *City of Durant v. Laws Constr. Co.*, 721 So. 2d 598, 604 (Miss. 1998); *Maynard v. City of Tupelo*, 691 So. 2d 385, 389 (Miss. 1997); *Meeks v. Tallahatchie County Democratic Executive Comm.*, 513 So. 2d 563, 568 (Miss. 1987).

53. *See* Rule 57, Mississippi Rules of Civil Procedure. *Alexander v. State by and through Allain*, 441 So. 2d 1329, 1347 (Miss. 1983) is the most prudent use of declaratory judgment practice. If only latter-day judges would so practice.

54. *See, e.g., Hughes v. Hosemann*, 68 So.3d 1260 (Miss. 2011); *Speed v. Hosemann*, 68 So.23d 1278 (Miss. 2011); *Burgess v. City of Gulfport*, 814 So.2d 149 (Miss. 2002).

55. *See* Miss. Const. art. 14, § 258; *see* more generally chapter 4, above.

56. Miss. Const. art. 7, § 183 (1890).

57. Miss. Const. art. 14, § 258 (1890).

58. Miss. Const. art. 7, § 183 (1890).

59. *See, e.g., Brister v. Leflore County*, 156 Miss. 240, 125 So. 816, 818–819 (1930); *Carothers v. Town of Boonville*, 169 Miss. 511, 153 So. 670, 671–672 (1934).

60. *See, e.g., Panama Refining Co. v. Ryan*, 293 U.S. 388 (1935), striking the National Industrial Recovery Act of 1933 [NIRA]; *Schecter Poultry Corp. v. United States*, 295 U.S. 495 (1935), the so-called sick chicken case invalidating a live poultry code; and *Carter v. Carter Coal Co.*, 298 U.S. 238 (1936), holding the Bituminous Coal Conservation Act constitutionally unenforceable.

61. Justice Owen J. Roberts was most prone to join the "Four Horsemen."

62. Chief Justice Charles Evans Hughes was another "swing vote." In 1936, only the aging Louis D. Brandeis, the already legendary Benjamin N. Cardozo, and future chief justice Harlan Fiske Stone could be counted on to bring an open mind and an awareness of the real world to the task of constitutional adjudication.

63. *Green v. Frazier*, 253 U.S. 233 (1920).

64. "William R. Day," https://en.wikipedia.org/wiki/William_R._Day.

65. The facts of the North Dakota banking legislation are set out in full in *Green*, 253 U.S. at 240–241.

66. *Green*, 253 U.S. at 238, 242–243.

67. On March 29, 1937, the Supreme Court split five to four and upheld a Washington state minimum wage law from a federal due process attack. *West Coast Hotel Co. v. Parrish*, 300 U.S. 379 (1937).

68. On May 24, 1937, the Supreme Court split five to four and upheld an Alabama unemployment compensation law from a federal due process and equal protection attacks. *Carmichael v. Southern Coal & Coke Co.*, 301 U.S. 495 (1937).

69. Mississippi House Journal, 1936 Extraordinary Session, at pages 799, 810–811; Eric C. Clark, "Legislative Adoption of BAWI, 1936," *Journal of Mississippi History* 52 (Nov. 1990), 285, 288.

70. Eric C. Clark, "Legislative Adoption of BAWI, 1936," *Journal of Mississippi History* 52 (Nov. 1990), 288.

71. Mississippi Senate Journal, 1936 Extraordinary Session, at pages 813–914, 816–817, 830–831.

72. The BAWI Act in its entirety, as made effective September 19, 1936 through and including April 1, 1940, may be found at Miss. Laws, ch. 1, including its title, Preamble, and §§ 1–23 (Senate Bill No. 1, Ex. Sess. 1936, pages 1–17).

73. Miss. Laws, ch. 1, §8(a) (Senate Bill No. 1, Ex. Sess. 1936). The formal and practical aspects of the process of certification are described fully in "Mississippi's BAWI Plan," at pages 24–26, published by Federal Reserve Bank of Atlanta in its Thirty-Fifth Annual Report (1949), http:// fraser.stlouisfed.org/.

74. Miss. Laws, ch. 1, §8(a) (Senate Bill No. 1, Ex. Sess. 1936).

75. Miss. Laws, ch. 1, §9 (Senate Bill No. 1, Ex. Sess. 1936).

76. Miss. Laws, ch. 1, §12 (Senate Bill No. 1, Ex. Sess. 1936).

77. Miss. Laws, ch. 1, §§10, 11 (Senate Bill No. 1, Ex. Sess. 1936).

78. See "Sydney McCain Smith," Mississippi Encyclopedia 1167–1168 (Ownby and Wilson eds., 2017).

79. Sydney McCain Smith, The State and the Social Process, 9 Miss. L. Journ. 147 (December 1936).

80. H. L. A. Hart, The Concept of Law (1961).

81. Oliver Wendell Holmes, The Common Law (1881); Oliver Wendell Holmes, The Path of the Law, 10 Harvard L. Rev. 457 (1897).

82. The lecture was published in short order thereafter. Sydney McCain Smith, The State and the Social Process, 9 Miss. L. Journ. 147–156 (December 1936).

83. Sydney Smith cites Pound, Scope and Purpose of Sociological Jurisprudence, 25 Harvard L. Rev. 516 (1912).

84. Holmes letter to Harold Laski, June 1, 1919, quoted in The Essential Holmes, at 110 (Richard Posner ed., 1992). A few years later, in a typical comment, Holmes wrote to a frequent correspondent that he was about to "turn to the learned Pound's The Spirit of the Common Law (1921) and improve my mind." Holmes letter to Lewis Einstein, Feb. 13, 1922, Holmes-Einstein Letters 204 (Peabody ed., 1964).

85. Miss. Const. art. 3, § 6 (1890).

86. Notgrass Drug Co. v. State ex rel. Rice, 175 Miss. 358, 165 So. 884, 885 (Feb. 17, 1936) (". . . when we remember that the state's prime duty, the purpose for which it exists, is to promote the peace, prosperity, and happiness of its citizens").

87. Sydney McCain Smith, The State and the Social Process, 9 Miss. L. Journ. 147, 149–154 (December 1936).

88. See Brief for Defendant in Error, Muller v. Oregon, 208 U.S. 412 (1908) (No. 107). The reference is to the brief filed by then lawyer Louis D. Brandeis in Muller v. Oregon, 208 U.S. 412 (1908). You would never know much of a brief had been filed from the parallel cite, 52 L. Ed. 551, 553. The story is briefly told in Samuels v. Mladineo, 608 So. 2d 1170, 1185–86 (Miss. 1992) (quoting K. C. Davis, An Approach to Problems of Evidence in the Adminitrative Process 55 Harvard L. Rev. 364, 403–404 [1942]). The Brandeis Brief was enough of a landmark event that the Supreme Court Historical Society staged a reenactment of the oral argument in Muller v. Oregon on its hundreth anniversary. Justice Ruth Bader Ginsburg, Muller v. Oregon: One Hundred Years Later, 45 Willamette L. Rev. 359 (2009); see also First Frank C. Jones Reenactment Revisits the Case of Muller v. Oregon, 31 Sup. Ct. Hist. Soc'y Q., no. 2, 2009 at 1; Tony Mauro, "Re-Envisioning Muller v. Oregon," Blog Legal Times (Dec. 16, 2008, 10:14 AM), http://legaltimes. typepad.com/blt/2008/12/reenvisioning-muller-v-oregon.html.

89. See, e.g., Brown v. Board of Education, 347 U.S. 483, 494 fn. 11 (1954), citing social science work highly regarded in its day, including Gunnar Myrdal's two-volume work An American Dilemma (1944).

90. Harry and Others v. Decker & Hopkins, Walker (1 Miss.) 36, 42–43 **1, 1818 WL 1235 (1818). See chapter 2 above.

91. Sydney McCain Smith, The State and the Social Process, 9 Miss. L. Journ. 147, 155 (December 1936).

92. Southern Pacific Co. v. Jensen, 244 U.S. 205, 222 (1917) (Holmes, J., dissenting).

93. *The Western Maid*, 257 U.S. 419, 432 (1922) (Holmes, J.); *see also* Oliver Wendell Holmes, "Natural Law," reprinted in *The Essential Holmes* at 180–183 (Posner ed., 1992); *see, e.g., Holmes-Pollock Letters: The Correspondence of Mr. Justice Holmes and Sir Frederick Pollock, 1874–1932*, Vol. 2, page 215 (Mark de Wolfe Howe ed., 1942); *Holmes-Laski Letters: The Correspondence of Mr. Justice Holmes and Harold J. Laski, 1916–1935*, at 822 (Jan. 29, 1926) and 896 (Nov. 23, 1926) (Mark de Wolfe Howe ed., 1953).

94. Oliver Wendell Holmes, *The Common Law* 1 (1881).

95. Sydney McCain Smith, *The State and the Social Process*, 9 Miss. L. Journ. 147, 155–156 (December 1936).

96. *Allbritton v. City of Winona*, 181 Miss. 75, 178 So. 799 (decided February 7, 1938).

97. The Mississippi Industrial Commission was authorized and governed by Miss. Laws, ch. 1, §§2–8 (Senate Bill No. 1, Ex. Sess. 1936).

98. "Mississippi's BAWI Plan," at pages 21–22, published by Federal Reserve Bank of Atlanta in its Thirty-Fifth Annual Report (1949), http://fraser.stlouisfed.org/; Lester, "Balancing Agriculture with Industry: Capital, Labor, and the Public Good in Mississippi's Home-Grown New Deal," *Journal of Mississippi History* 70 (Fall 2008), page 235, 250, 258–259.

99. Minutes of Mayor and Board of Aldermen of City of Winona, Book 11, pages 33–34 (May 4, 1937), found in record of proceedings re Validation of $35,000 City of Winona Industrial Bonds, before the Chancery Court of Montgomery County, Case No. 5806, and also a part of appellate record before Supreme Court of Mississippi, at pages 5, 6, in Case No. 33,074, filed December 9, 1937.

100. Minutes of Mayor and Board of Aldermen of City of Winona, Book 11, pages 33–34 (May 4, 1937), found same.

101. Order Granting Certificate of Public Convenience and Necessity entered by Mississippi Industrial Commission on June 1, 1937, in Application No. 8, found same, at page 11.

102. Miss. Laws, ch. 1, §12 (Senate Bill No. 1, Ex. Sess. 1936).

103. Order Granting Certificate of Public Convenience and Necessity entered by Mississippi Industrial Commission on June 1, 1937, in Application No. 8, found same, at page 14.

104. "Sept. 14th. Set for Citizens to Vote on Industrial Issue," *Winona Times*, Aug. 6, 1937, page 1; *see also Winona Times*, Sept. 10, 1937, page 1.

105. *See* "Mayor and Board Given Permission to Issue Bond," *Winona Times*, Sept. 17, 1937, front page; see also Miss. Laws, ch. 1, §9 (Senate Bill No. 1, Ex. Sess. 1936).

106. Appellate record before Supreme Court of Mississippi, at pages 5, 6, in Case No. 33,074, filed December 9, 1937, at pages 19–23, 40.

107. Back in late 1912, Garner Green of the firm of Green & Green in Jackson had been counsel on rehearing for the J. J. Newman Lumber Company, opposing the State's use of its police powers to regulate daily hours of work for those hired by employers engaged in "manufacturing or repairing." See chapter 7 above, and proceedings leading to *State vs. J. J. Newman Lumber Co.*, 103 Miss. 263, 60 So. 215 (1913). That in 1938 Green Green and Jackson were arguably on the other side of the constitutional law issues before the court in 1912 and 1913 should be taken only as confirming that the Greens were considered very good lawyers at both points in time.

108. Ten years later, Jackson fought for Willie McGee and secured a reversal at one stage in an infamous, racially charged, and ultimately tragic capital rape case. *McGee v. State*, 200 Miss. 350, 26 So.2d 680 (1946); *see also* Patricia Michelle Boyett, *Right to Revolt: The Crusade for Racial Justice in Mississippi's Central Piney Woods* 37 (2015). He was more successful for a client charged with assault with intent to ravish. *Lee v. Mississippi*, 332 U.S. 742 (1948), reversing *Lee v. State*, 201 Miss. 403, 30 So.2d 74 (1947).

109. In addition to his criminal constitutional cases handled in the late 1940s, see *Mississippi Power & Light Co. v. City of Jackson*, 116 F.2d 924 (5th Cir. 1941).

110. "Industrial Test Wanted in State," *Winona Times*, Sept. 24, 1937, page 1.

111. "Gov. White Urges Suit to Be Filed," *Winona Times*, Oct. 22, 1937.

112. "Constitutionality of Industrial Law Argued," *Winona Times*, Nov. 26, 1937, page 1.

113. For a brief biography of William Eugene Morse, *see* Francis Fontaine, *The Builder, 1721–1785, Hubert Horton McAlexander, et al.* 142 (2009); *see also* William D. McCain, *The Story of Jackson, Vol. II* 68–69 (1953); and *The Mississippi Bar's Centennial: A Legacy of Service*, at 101 (Melanie H. Henry comp and ed., 2006).

114. William D. McCain, *The Story of Jackson, Vol. II* 68 (1953).

115. In the present context, and likely others throughout his life, Allbritton had to live with his last name often being misspelled. On his tombstone in Oakwood Cemetery in Winona, we find "WILLIAM SAMUEL ALLBRITTON, JULY 24, 1878—JULY 29, 1958." Two "l's" was correct, not one as with most people bearing the name as "Albritton," https://forums.findagrave.com /cgi-bin/fg/cgi?page=gr&GRid=21389568. In the bond validation proceedings before the Chancery Court of Montgomery County in 1937, his name appears as "W. S. Allbritton." Before the Supreme Court of Mississippi, his last name is misspelled "W. S. Albritton." *See Albritton v. City of Winona*, 181 Miss. 75, 178 So. 799 (1938). Before the Supreme Court of the United States, his last name is spelled correctly: *W. S. Allbritton v. City of Winona, Mississippi*, 303 U.S. 627 (1938).

116. "Friendly Test Industrial Bonds Be Made," *Winona Times*, Nov. 12, 1937, page 1.

117. William Faulkner, *Requiem for a Nun* 35 (1950).

118. "1000 Registered Here Wednesday in Labor Survey," *Winona Times*, May 28, 1937, page 1.

119. Lemuel Augustus Smith Sr. served as chancellor in the Third Mississippi District from 1935 until 1944, when he was elected to the Supreme Court of Mississippi from the Northern District. Justice Smith died on October 10, 1950. *See* John Ray Skates Jr., *A History of the Mississippi Supreme Court, 1817–1948*, pages 94–95 (1973). Lemuel Augustus Smith Sr. was a distant cousin of Sydney McCain Smith. Their mothers, both born with the last name West, were first cousins.

120. *See* "Chancellor Smith, Court Cites Reasons for Opinion—Suit to Be Appealed to Supreme Court at Once," *Winona Times*, December 1937.

121. "Opinion of the Court" in appellate record before Supreme Court of Mississippi, at pages 5, 6, in Case No. 33,074, filed December 9, 1937, at page 52. Prof. Connie L. Lester reports that "[c]ommissioners and industrialists informally encouraged a test case to settle the [constitutional] issue and promote further investment." Connie Lester, "Balancing Agriculture with Industry: Capital, Labor, and the Public Good in Mississippi's Home-Grown New Deal," *Journal of Mississippi History* 70 (Fall 2008), 235, 249.

122. *Carothers v. Town of Booneville*, 169 Miss. 511, 153 So. 670, 671–672 (1934).

123. "Opinion of the Court" in appellate record before Supreme Court of Mississippi, at pages 5, 6, in Case No. 33,074, filed December 9, 1937, at pages 52–53, 64. Smith did not but certainly could have called to mind the insights of Holmes and Brandeis. *Truax v. Corrigan*, 257 U.S. 312, 344 (1921) (Holmes, J., dissenting), and *New State Ice Co. v. Liebmann*, 285 U.S. 262, 311 (1932) (Brandeis, J., dissenting).

124. "Opinion of the Court" in appellate record before Supreme Court of Mississippi, at pages 5, 6, in Case No. 33,074, filed December 9, 1937, at page 64.

125. The meaning and effect of federal constitutional substantive due process was a function of authoritative US Supreme Court constructions and applications of the Due Process Clause of Section 1 of the Fourteenth Amendment. This area of the law had been much debated and highly controversial at least since the *Lochner* decision in 1904.

126. The meaning and effect of state constitutional substantive due process was a function of authoritative state supreme court constructions and applications of the due process clause of Article 3, Section 14 of the Mississippi Constitution. On April 4, 1934, *Carothers v. Town of Booneville*, 169 Miss. 511, 153 So. 670, 671 (1934) had held that Booneville's proposed full faith and credit industrial bond issue was "in violation of . . . the due process clause of the state Constitution."

127. "Opinion of the Court" in appellate record before Supreme Court of Mississippi, at page 5, 6, in Case No. 33,074, filed December 9, 1937, at page 66.

128. "Opinion of the Court" in appellate record before Supreme Court of Mississippi, at page 5, 6, in Case No. 33,074, filed December 9, 1937, at page 67, quoting *Dunn v. Love*, 172 Miss. 342, 155 So. 331, 333 (1934).

129. *Bain Co. v. Pinson*, 282 U.S. 449, 501 (1931) (Holmes, J.). quoted in "Opinion of the Court" in appellate record before Supreme Court of Mississippi, at page 5, 6, in Case No. 33,074, filed December 9, 1937, at page 67, where Smith in turn quoted *Dunn v. Love*, 172 Miss. 342, 155 So. 331, 333 (1934) and *City of Jackson v. Deposit Guaranty Bank & Trust Co.*, 160 Miss. 752, 133 So. 195, 198 (1931).

130. "Mississippi's BAWI Plan," at page 45, published by Federal Reserve Bank of Atlanta in its Thirty-Fifth Annual Report (1949), http://fraser.stlouisfed.org/; see also *Allbritton v. City of Winona*, 181 Miss. 75, 178 So. 799, 801 (1938). A brief of *amicus curiae* is sometimes called a "friend of the court" brief filed by a third person, someone not a formal party to the case. Such briefs are usually filed only with the permission of the court, and only by persons who are likely to experience an effect from the decision and who informs the court of points of fact or circumstance that the court might otherwise overlook. Today the practice is formally regulated by Rule 29 of the Mississippi Rules of Appellate Procedure. The practice in 1937 and 1938 was substantially similar to today's procedure.

131. The six justices of the supreme court were Chief Justice Smith; George H. Ethridge, whom we met in the preface and then in chapters 1, 8, and 9 above; Virgil A. Griffith, whom we met in chapter 9 above; and W. D. Anderson, James G. McGowan, and Harvey McGehee. *See* John Ray Skates Jr., *A History of the Mississippi Supreme Court, 1817–1948*, at pages 60–61, 75, 78, 82–83, 95 (1973).

132. *Notgrass Drug Co. v. State ex rel. Rice*, 175 Miss. 358, 165 So. 884, 885 (1936).

133. *Allbritton v. City of Winona*, 181 Miss. 75, 178 So. 799, 803 (1938).

134. *Allbritton v. City of Winona*, 181 Miss. 75, 178 So. 799, 806 (1938), from Holmes' oft-quoted language, in *Lochner v. New York*, 198 U.S. 45, 75 (1904) (Holmes, J., dissenting).

135. *Allbritton v. City of Winona*, 181 Miss. 75, 178 So. 799, 811 (1938) (Griffith, J., specially concurring).

136. *Allbritton v. City of Winona*, 181 Miss. 75, 178 So. 799, 812 (1938) (Anderson, J., concurring).

137. *Allbritton v. City of Winona*, 181 Miss. 75, 178 So. 799, 805 (1938).

138. Miss. Const. Art. 3, § 14 (1890); U.S. Const., Amndt. XIV, § 1. The due process clause in the Fifth Amendment is similarly worded but applies only to restrain the federal government.

139. *Allbritton v. City of Winona*, 181 Miss. 75, 178 So. 799, 805 (1938).

140. *Allbritton v. City of Winona*, 181 Miss. 75, 178 So. 799, 805 (1938). Compare Smith's thoughts in a similar vein as he addressed the law school community in early October of 1936. Sydney McCain Smith, *The State and the Social Process*, 9 Miss. L. Journ. 147, 149 (December 1936).

141. *Allbritton v. City of Winona*, 181 Miss. 75, 178 So. 799, 803, 805–806 (1938).

142. *Allbritton v. City of Winona*, 181 Miss. 75, 178 So. 799, 803–804 (1938).

143. Miss. Laws, ch. 1, Preamble and §1 (Senate Bill No. 1, Ex. Sess. 1936); See footnote 1 in *Allbritton v. City of Winona*, 181 Miss. 75, 178 So. 799, 804 (1938).

144. *Allbritton v. City of Winona*, 181 Miss. 75, 178 So. 799, 804–805 (1938).

145. See discussion in chapter 9 above wherein Justice Virgil A. Griffith considered and relied on legislative values in *State v. McPhail*, 182 Miss.360, 180 So. 387, 388–389 (1938). Justice Griffith did so as well in his concurring opinion, *Allbritton*, 178 So. at 310.

146. *Allbritton v. City of Winona*, 181 Miss. 75, 178 So. 799, 805–806 (1938).

147. Sydney McCain Smith, *The State and the Social Process*, 9 Miss. L. Journ. 147, 154 (December 1936).

148. *Allbritton v. City of Winona*, 181 Miss. 75, 178 So. 799, 806–809 (1938).

149. *See Allbritton v. City of Winona*, 181 Miss. 75, 178 So. 799, 809 (1938).

150. Miss. Const. Art. 7, §183 (1890).

151. Miss. Laws, ch. 1, §12 (Senate Bill No. 1, Ex. Sess. 1936).

152. *Carothers v. Town of Booneville*, 169 Miss. 511, 153 So. 670, 671–672 (1934).

153. *Carothers*, 153 So. at 670–671.

154. *Allbritton*, 178 So. at 809 (emphasis supplied).

155. *See, e.g.,* the decision in *Galloway v. State*, 122 So. 2d 614 (Miss. 2013), the fatal flaw in which is explained by the author in *Variations on a Theme by Posner: Facing the Factual Component of the Reliability Imperative in the Process of Adjudication*, 84 Miss. L. Journ. 471, 649–660 (2015); *see also* Petition for a Writ of Certiorari filed in David W. Parvin v. State of Mississippi, filed June 21, 2017 in Supreme Court of the United States, No. 16–1472.

156. *Allbritton*, 178 So. at 809.

157. Miss. Const. art VII, §183.

158. *Allbritton*, 178 So. at 810.

159. *Allbritton*, 178 So. at 812 (Anderson, J., dissenting).

160. *Allbritton*, 178 So. at 814; see, e.g., "Supreme Court Decides White's Program Constitutional, INDUSTRY SOUGHT, Winona Now Ready To Entertain Proposition For Industry," *Winona Times* February 11, 1938, page 1.

161. *Allbritton*, 178 So. at 810. (Griffith, J., concurring).

162. *Allbritton*, 178 So. at 811. (Griffith, J., concurring)

163. *Allbritton*, 178 So. at 812. (Griffith, J., concurring).

164. *Allbritton*, 178 So. at 810. (Griffith, J., concurring).

165. "Supreme Court Decides White's Program Constitutional, INDUSTRY SOUGHT, Winona Now Ready to Entertain Proposition for Industry," *Winona Times*, February 11, 1938, page 1.

166. *Lochner v. New York*, 198 U.S. 46 (1904).

167. *Cole v. City of LaGrange*, 113 U.S. 1 (1885).

168. *Green v. Frazier*, 253 U.S. 233 (1920).

169. Allbritton Jurisdictional Statement, filed in U.S. Supreme Court on March 25, 1938, page 2.

170. *Associates Financial Services Company v. Johnson*, 197 S.E.2d 764, 766 and fn. 1 (Ga. App. 1973), citing Shakespeare, *King John*, act III, scene 1, line 276. More fully, "Nor can a 'sham' sale to a third party be upheld, it appearing that in fact the third party bid off the property and bought it for the sheriff or his deputy. What the sheriff or his deputy may not do directly they cannot indirectly do, for 'indirection thereby grows direct.'"

Several years later, the Georgia court wrote, "There is a sizable quantum of evidence that tended to impeach appellant's disclaimers of having made or placed the signs, and otherwise to implicate him to such an extent as to permit a rational trier of fact to (as Shakespeare's Polonius expressed it) 'by indirections find directions out.'" *Snipes v. Mack*, 318 S.E.2d 318, 319 (Ga. App. 1989), quoting Shakespeare, *Hamlet*, act II, scene 1, line 66.

171. *Allbritton v. City of Winona*, 303 U.S. 627 (April 4, 1938).

172. "The switch in time that saved nine," https://en.wikipedia.org/wiki/The_switch_in_time _that_saved_nine.

173. *West Coast Hotel Co. v. Parish*, 300 U.S. 329 (1937).

174. On May 24, 1937, the Supreme Court split five to four and upheld an Alabama unemployment compensation law from a federal due process and equal protection attacks. *Carmichael v. Southern Coal & Coke Co.*, 301 U.S. 495 (1937).

175. *Allbritton*, 178 So. at 804–807.

176. *Green v. Frazier*, 253 U.S. 233, 242 (1920).

177. *See* Ashley Callahan, *Southern Tufts: The Regional Origins and the National Craze for Chenille* (2015).

178. "Mississippi's BAWI Plan," at page 45, published by Federal Reserve Bank of Atlanta in its Thirty-Fifth Annual Report (1949), http://fraser.stlouisfed.org/.

179. The rags-to-riches life of James William Sanders, including the advent of the Kosciusko Cotton Mill, is summarized admiringly in William D. McCain, *The Story of Jackson, Vol. II*, pages 66–67 (1953).

180. For an effusive description of the life and career of Robert D. Sanders, industrialist and philanthropist, *see* William D. McCain, *The Story of Jackson, Vol. II*, pages 64–66 (1953). No mention is made of the Delta Chenille Company in Winona, but George E. Shaw is identified as a co-owner with Sanders of certain properties in the Jackson area. George E. Shaw is one of the incorporators of Delta Chenille Company in papers filed with the secretary of state of Mississippi.

181. *See* William D. McCain, *The Story of Jackson, Vol. II*, page 64 (1953). For a more complete story of the rise of the Sanders mills, *see The MS Gen Web Project*, chapter 5, "Twentieth Century Mills: 1898–1953," msgw.org.

182. The BAWI manufacturing business in Winona at other times continued to be referred to as the Winona Bedspread Company. *See* "Mississippi's BAWI Plan," at pages 32, 39, 45, 57 published by Federal Reserve Bank of Atlanta in its Thirty-Fifth Annual Report (1949); http://fraser.stlouisfed.org/. The Federal Reserve report leaves little doubt that this is one and the same enterprise as the Sanders-owned and Sanders-controlled Delta Chenille Company when it refers, at page 45 to the "tenant in the new Winona plant . . . [as] a Jackson, Mississippi, concern loosely affiliated with a group of cotton cloth and bedspread plants in Mississippi and Alabama towns."

183. "Opening Jan. 1," *Winona Times*, Fri., Nov. 17, 1939, page 1, Newspapers.com, https://www.newspapers.com/image/305030352.

184. See records on file at Secretary of State of Mississippi, www.sos.ms.gov; also Corporate Minute Book for Delta Chenille Company, Inc., f/k/a Aponaug Chenille Company, Inc., f/k/a Winona Bedspread Company.

185. *The MS Gen Web Project*, chapter 5, "Twentieth Century Mills: 1898–1953," msgw.org.

186. "A Glance from the Past . . .," March 6, 1942," *Winona Times*, Thurs., Mar. 5, 1992, page 5, Newspapers.com, https://www.newspapers.com/image/278911551.

187. Corporate Minute Book for Delta Chenille Company, Inc., f/k/a Aponaug Chenille Company, Inc., f/k/a Winona Bedspread Company, contains much of the formal business side of the textile, hosiery, or other manufacturing plant headquartered in Jackson, Mississippi, that the BAWI program had yielded for Winona and Mississippi.

188. Connie Lester, "Balancing Agriculture with Industry: Capital, Labor, and the Public Good in Mississippi's Home-Grown New Deal," *Journal of Mississippi History* 70 (Fall 2008), 235, 250, 259–260. *See* John R. Bradley and Linda A. Thompson, *Mississippi Workers Compensation*, §§1:1, 1:2, pages 1–3 (2018).

189. Miss. Laws, ch. 412 (Reg. Sess. 1948) (effective January 1, 1949).

190. As late as 1954, Mississippi was still fighting off attacks on the constitutional enforceability of its workers' compensation law. *Walters v. Blackledge*, 220 Miss. 485, 71 So.2d 433 (1954). *See* John R. Bradley and Linda A. Thompson, *Mississippi Workers Compensation*, §1:3, pages 3–4, fn. 4 (2018), and accompanying text.

191. "Mississippi's BAWI Plan," at page 45, published by Federal Reserve Bank of Atlanta in its Thirty-Fifth Annual Report (1949), http://fraser.stlouisfed.org/.

192. Proverbs 16:18.

193. "Mississippi's BAWI Plan," at page 31, published by Federal Reserve Bank of Atlanta in its Thirty-Fifth Annual Report (1949), http://fraser.stlouisfed.org/.

194. Ken Gower, Noah—Randall Family, The Carroll County, Mississippi, Genealogical website (1998), sponsored by MSGenWeb Project, copyright John Hansen (2010).

195. See Table 2 in "Mississippi's BAWI Plan," at page 32, published by Federal Reserve Bank of Atlanta in its Thirty-Fifth Annual Report (1949), http://fraser.stlouisfed.org/.

196. See Table 6 in "Mississippi's BAWI Plan," at page 57, published by Federal Reserve Bank of Atlanta in its Thirty-Fifth Annual Report (1949), http://fraser.stlouisfed.org/.

197. "Mississippi's BAWI Plan," at page 56, published by Federal Reserve Bank of Atlanta in its Thirty-Fifth Annual Report (1949), http://fraser.stlouisfed.org/.

198. Matthew Freedman reports that the chenille bedspread plant was one of three BAWI-sponsored enterprises that closed in the 1950s. Freedman, Persistence in Industrial Policy Impacts: Evidence from Depression-Era Mississippi, at page 8 (September 2015). https://belk-collegeofbusiness.uncc.edu/ … /wp/Freedman_UNCC.pdf.

199. Corporate Minute Book for Delta Chenille Company, Inc., f/k/a Aponaug Chenille Company, Inc., f/k/a Winona Bedspread Company, Minutes of Special Stockholders' Meeting held January 4, 1956.

200. *Winona Times*, Fri., Apr. 12, 1957, page 1, Newspapers.com, https://www.newspapers.com /image/317410363.

201. *Winona Times*, Fri., Jan. 31, 1958, page 1, Newspapers.com, https://www.newspapers.com /image/317476733.

202. Chamber Tells of New Events," *Winona Times*, Fri., Sept. 22, 1960, page 1, https://www .newspapers.com/image/317491774.

203. Business notice, *Delta Democrat-Times* (Greenville, Miss.) Aug. 18, 1960, page 15; *Stone County Enterprise* (Wiggins, Miss.), Aug. 18, 1960, page 2.

204. "Management Looks Things Over," *Winona Times*, Thurs., June 18, 1981, page 1, News-papers.com, https://www.newspapers.com/image/317898793.

205. "Kimco Changes Ownership," *Winona Times*, Thurs., Jan. 9, 1986, page 1, *Newsapers. com*, https://www.newspapers.com/image/318158388; "Kimco Folds, Winona Escapes," *Winona Times*, Thurs., May 21, 1987, page 16, Newspapers.com, https://www.newspapers.com/image /317866320.

206. One relatively recent conveyance filed in the land records kept in the office of the chancery clerk of Montgomery County is a warranty deed dated September 5, 2008. By that deed, Montgomery County conveyed the land to Maurice Ferguson.

207. *Allbritton*, 178 So. at 812 (Griffith, J. concurring).

208. Miss. Const. art. 3, §6.

209. Miss. Const. art. 7, §190.

210. *Moore v. Grillis*, 205 Miss. 865, 39 So. 2d 505, 508 (1949); *see also Columbia Land Development LLC v. Secretary of State*, 868 So.2d 1006, 1017 (¶33) (Miss. 2004) ("reasonable relation to … governmental purpose"); *State v. Jones*, 726 So.2d 572, 574 (¶10) (Miss. 1998) ("reasonable relation to any proper governmental purpose," quoting *Allbritton v. City of Winona*, 181 Miss. 75, 97, 178 So. 799, 804 (1938)).

211. *See, e.g., In Interest of B. D.*, 720 So. 2d 476, 478 to 479 (Miss. 1998); *Mississippi Pub. Serv. Comm'n v. Alabama Great S. R.R.*, 294 So. 173, 176 (Miss. 1974); *Hattiesburg Firefighters Local 184 v. City of Hattiesburg*, 263 So. 2d 767, 772 (Miss. 1972); *Wheeler v. Shoemake*, 213 Miss. 374, 57 So. 2d 267, 279 to 281 (1952).

212. *Allbritton*, 178 So. at 806.

213. See epigram at beginning of article from Sydney McCain Smith, *The State and the Social Process*, 9 Miss. L. Journ. 147, 149 (December 1936).

214. In *Allbritton* at 806, Smith cited Pound, *The Theory of Judicial Decision*, 36 Harvard L. Rev. 641, 656, while seventeen months earlier he had cited Pound, *Scope and Purpose of Sociological Jurisprudence*, 25 Harvard L. Rev. 516 (1912).

215. One of those contemporaries (albeit a generous generation younger) was Prof. Myres S. McDougal (1906–1998) of the Yale Law School. Together with his regular collaborator, Prof. Harold D. Lasswell, McDougal early on made original contributions in the fields of legal realism and public policy science. Prof. McDougal was a native of Prentiss County in northeast Mississippi and had a substantial association with the University of Mississippi as a student, joined the Yale Law faculty in 1934, but for life was a counselor and friend of Ole Miss. Sydney Smith makes no mention of McDougal in his law school address in October of 1936, but there is little doubt that he was acquainted with McDougal and his early work.

216. Sydney McCain Smith, *The State and the Social Process*, 9 Miss. L. Journ. 147, 154 (December 1936).

217. *Allbritton*, 178 So. at 806.

218. Daniel Kahneman was awarded the Nobel Memorial Prize in Economic Sciences in 2002. Robert J. Shiller took the prize in 2013. Robert H. Thaler won in 2017. *See, e.g.*, Jeff Sommer, "Finding Deep Meaning, Even in Cashews," *New York Times*, Oct. 15, 2017, Business Section, page 3.

219. *Allbritton*, 178 So. at 803–809.

220. *Allbritton v. City of Winona*, 181 Miss. 75, 178 So. 799, 806 (1938) (quoting from *McCulloch v. Maryland*, 4 Wheat. 316, 415 (1819)).

221. But *see, e.g.*, Rules of Procedure, Miss. Const. art. 4, §§ 54–77, which are far more detailed than they need to be.

222. *Moore v. General Motors Acceptance Corp.*, 155 Miss. 818, 823 to 824, 125 So. 411, 413 (1930) (quoted in *Alexander v. State by and through Allain*, 441 So. 2d 1329, 1334 (Miss. 1983).

223. *Stepp v. State*, 202 Miss. 725, 729, 32 So. 2d 447, 447 (1948) (quoted in *Pro-Choice Mississippi v. Fordice*, 716 So. 2d 645, 651 (Miss. 1998).

224. *Mississippi State Department of Health v. Baptist Memorial Hospital-DeSoto, Inc.*, 984 So.2d 967, 984 (¶33) (Miss. 2008), citing and quoting cases.

225. For champerty and maintenance cases close in time to the *Allbritton* litigation, see *Whelchel v. Stennett*, 192 Miss. 241, 5 So.2d 418 (1942); *Harrell v. Daniel & Greene*, 151 Miss. 761, 118 So. 899 (1928).

226. *Smith v. Citizens' Bank & Trust Co.*, 125 Miss. 139, 87 So. 488 (1921).

227. "The switch in time that saved nine," https://en.wikipedia.org/wiki/The_switch_in_time_that_saved_nine.

228. *Allbritton*, 178 So. at 810 (Griffith, J., concurring).

229. "Mississippi's BAWI Plan," at page 62, published by Federal Reserve Bank of Atlanta in its Thirty-Fifth Annual Report (1949), http://fraser.stlouisfed.org/.

230. "Mississippi's BAWI Plan," at page 62, published by Federal Reserve Bank of Atlanta in its Thirty-Fifth Annual Report (1949), http://fraser.stlouisfed.org/.

231. *See Boardman v. United Services Auto Ass'n*, 470 So.2d 1024, 1029 (Miss. 1985). *Cf.* Rule 702(d), Miss. R. Evid.

232. Miss. Const. art. 7, § 183 (1890). *Carothers v. Town of Booneville*, 169 Miss. 511, 153 So. 670, 671–672 (1934).

233. "Mississippi's BAWI Plan," at page 56, published by Federal Reserve Bank of Atlanta in its Thirty-Fifth Annual Report (1949), http://fraser.stlouisfed.org/.

234. *See, e.g.*, Matthew Freedman, *Persistence in Industrial Policy Impacts: Evidence from Depression-Era Mississippi* (2015).

235. Matthew Freedman, *Persistence in Industrial Policy Impacts: Evidence from Depression-Era Mississippi*, at 24 (2015).

236. Regrettably the courts have been excessively permissive regarding summary and short form agency orders. See footnote 7 and accompanying text in Judge Leslie H. Southwick's chapter entitled Administrative Law, 1 MS Prac Encyclopedia MS Law, 2:66 (2018 ed.).

237. *See* "Paul Burney Johnson, Sr." in David G. Sansing, *Mississippi Governors: Soldiers, Statesmen, Scholars, Scoundrels: A Bicentennial Edition* 180–183 (2016); "Paul B. Johnson, Sr.," *Mississippi Encyclopedia* 658–659 (Ownby and Wilson eds., 2017).

238. "Mississippi's BAWI Plan," at page 52, published by Federal Reserve Bank of Atlanta in its Thirty-Fifth Annual Report (1949), http://fraser.stlouisfed.org/.

239. *See* "Mississippi's BAWI Plan," Tables 2, 4, 5, and 6, at pages 32, 55, 56, and 57, published by Federal Reserve Bank of Atlanta in its Thirty-Fifth Annual Report (1949), http://fraser.stlouisfed.org/.

240. Matthew Freedman, *Persistence in Industrial Policy Impacts: Evidence from Depression-Era Mississippi*, at 2, 3, 11, 13–16, 20, 24 (2015).

241. "Chenille Plant Reunion Draws Large Crowd," *Winona Times*, Thurs., Nov. 20, 1969, page 6, https://www.newspapers.com/image/317926289.

242. "Mississippi's BAWI Plan," published by Federal Reserve Bank of Atlanta in its Thirty-Fifth Annual Report (1949), http://fraser.stlouisfed.org/.

243. Connie Lester, "Balancing Agriculture with Industry: Capital, Labor, and the Public Good in Mississippi's Home-Grown New Deal," *Journal of Mississippi History* 70 (Fall 2008), 235; Matthew Freedman, *Persistence in Industrial Policy Impacts: Evidence from Depression-Era Mississippi*, at 8, fn. 13 (2015), and accompanying text; https://belkcollegeofbusiness.uncc.edu/ . . . /wp/Freedman_UNCC.pdf.

244. James C. Cobb, *The Most Southern Place on Earth* 254 (1992).

245. Miss. Code Ann. §27-31-104(4), (5).

246. Justice Holmes's *Lochner* dissent would in time be dubbed as "possibly the most famous and influential of all of his opinions." Richard A. Posner, *The Essential Holmes*, page xvii (Posner ed., 1992). Judge Posner later provided an extended analysis and critique of Holmes's dissent, concluding, "It is merely the greatest judicial opinion of the last hundred years." Richard A. Posner, *Law and Literature* 346 (3d ed., 2009).

247. On August 29, 2018, the governor signed the Mississippi Infrastructure Modernization Act, Senate Bill 2002 (Special Sess. 2018), the adequacy and effects of which will only be known in time.

248. Compare takeaway thoughts from the *Newman Lumber* constitutional experience during the calendric hump of late 1912 and early 1913. See chapter 7.

BIBLIOGRAPHY

Callahan, Ashley, *Southern Tufts: The Regional Origins and the National Craze for Chenille* (2015).

Cash, W. J., *The Mind of the South* (1941).

Clark, Eric C., *Industrial Development and State Government Policy in Mississippi, 1890–1980*, Ph.D. dissertation, History, Mississippi State University (May 1989).

Clark, Eric C., "Legislative Adoption of BAWI, 1936," *Journal of Mississippi History* 52 (Nov. 1990).

Cobb, James C., *The Most Southern Place on Earth* 185 (1992).

Cobb, James C., *The Selling of the South* (2d ed., 1993).

Cohn, David L., *The Life and Times of King Cotton* (1956).

Dattel, Gene, *Cotton and Race in the Making of America* (2009).

Freedman, Matthew, Persistence in Industrial Policy Impacts: Evidence from Depression-Era Mississippi (September 2015). UNC https://belkcollegeofbusiness.uncc.edu/ . . . /wp /Freedman_UNCC.pdf.

Hopkins, Ernest, "Mississippi's BAWI Plan" (1944), published by Federal Reserve Bank of Atlanta in its Thirty-Fifth Annual Report (1949), http://fraser.stlouisfed.org/.

Kirwan, Albert D., *Revolt of the Rednecks, Mississippi Politics 1875–1925* (1951).

Lester, Connie L., "Balancing Agriculture with Industry: Capital, Labor, and the Public Good in Mississippi's Home-Grown New Deal," *Journal of Mississippi History* 70 (Fall 2008).

Pound, Roscoe, *Scope and Purpose of Sociological Jurisprudence*, 25 Harvard L. Rev. 516 (1912).

Rogers, Ralph J., *A History of Mississippi*, Vol. II (McLemore ed., 1973).

Sydney McCain Smith, *The State and the Social Process*, 9 Miss. L. Journ. 147 (Dec. 1936).

Winter, William F., "Governor Mike Conner and the Sales Tax, 1932," *Journal of Mississippi History* 41 (August 1979).

Epilogue

We have now navigated nine general slices of social history in which locals and people passing through Mississippi encountered one aspect or another of the state's constitution du jour. These experiences have spanned roughly 130 years, from the advent of statehood up through World War II. While discrete and not exactly fungible, the tales we have shared have involved a great variety of people from many walks of life, in all of their humanity encountering two or three or more of the foremost dimensions of constitutional practice. We outlined these in the Preface. An interesting pop test question becomes, How many constitutional encounters has each reader had—say, in the last twenty-four hours?

Yes, the mundane count as well as the annoying. You submitted to the police power of the state when you put your seatbelt on before driving to the grocery, though maybe you claimed your right to be let alone[1] when you didn't "click it" because you were focused on what later in the day your doctor might say about some ache or pain that had you worried. Suddenly you see flashing blue lights behind you. Your car did not "rock back" at that stop sign, or so you were told. You are getting a ticket that says you have to appear in municipal court or pay a fine. Rattled, you took what seemed like forever to fish from the bottom of your purse the insurance card the legislature said you have to carry, only to have the polite officer say, "I'm sorry, ma'am, but this card expired twelve days ago."

Finally, at the grocery store, you paid a sales tax the state legislature had enacted under its constitutional authority. While waiting in the checkout line, you could hardly miss the tabloid headlines that may have pressed the limits of Mississippi's long-standing constitutional view that freedom of the press be held "sacred."[2]

If you were headed to your doctor's office, the first thing you did when you checked in was sign away your common law right to be free of tortious assault and battery, though in your mind you were there not to consent to anything but to request that the doctor exercise his state-licensed and regulated skills and help you through the days ahead. Likely as not, you never noticed the fine print where you may have waived your constitutional right to trial by jury in the unlikely event of a malpractice dispute. If it took the form of an arbitration clause, you waived more than that. Perhaps the video screen on the wall was peppering you with promos of how wonderful the doc is, how many services her clinic provides, a few health-care tips, or the talking heads on Fox News. First Amendment issues of Mississippi's "sacred press" variety are everywhere.

Were you carrying a small pistol in your purse in exercise of your right to do so under state[3] and federal constitutions?[4] What about those large letters on the entrance: "This Is a Healthcare Facility. Firearms and Other Dangerous Weapons Are Expressly Prohibited." Can they do that?

In the next ten minutes, how many constitutional encounters of your last twenty-four hours can you list? Then think through your last twenty-four years.

A FEW OF MY ENCOUNTERS

I began and now finish with that common denominator that connects us all. As with Jane and John Q. Public, I am a child of all that I have met. I grew up in Greenville, Mississippi, but before that, without my knowledge or consent, an arbitrary exercise of state judicial power exposed me to great risk in making the grand entrance that my parents had anticipated for some nine months. I was their first born. An encounter with the judicial power of the state caused me to be born fifty-five miles to the east in a hospital in Greenwood, Mississippi, rather than in the hospital eleven blocks from where my parents lived in Greenville. I have told this story before.[5] None other than Chief Justice Sydney Smith, whom I have venerated for his efforts in *Allbritton*, if not *Buckeye Cotton Oil*, said my mother's obstetrician could not practice in Greenville, primarily to protect the profit level of an established medical clinic run by Dr. Hugh Gamble.

Make no mistake about it. In late July of 1940, though an unborn viable fetus, I was possessed of an abundance of rights even then, and my parents had their own rights. Those wielding the constitutional judicial power—leading up to their decision on December 6, 1937—should have been bound to consider that bundle of rights, or at least so it seems, even at this late date. Consider what was reasonably foreseeable back in 1937 when, in one superficial paragraph,[6] Sydney Smith gave the back of his hand to the relationship that my mother and many other loyal patients had with young Dr. John Lucas that arguably rose to the level of a common law professional contract. The problem became another contract, a written one between young Dr. Lucas and old Dr. Gamble that the constitution said could not be impaired.[7] And so my mother and I experienced great risks that hot summer afternoon via my father's ninety-mile-an-hour mad dash in that not-so-new Chrysler easterly along Highway 82 so that Dr. Lucas could assist in the birth.

Of course, if Dr. Lucas and his partner, Dr. John Wilson, had refused to close their Greenville medical clinic, the judicial power would have been brought to bear to tell them they had no choice, and the executive power stood ready to make sure they complied. More broadly, the legislative power could have played its trump card if the young married women in the area and their families had been able to out-politick established medical practitioners like old Dr. Gamble and the state medical association. As early as 1932, the American Medical Association was considering whether the Dr. Gambles of the country were improperly interfering with the right of the people to "the free choice of a physician."[8] Lawyers have long regarded noncompetition clauses as unethical, and the judiciary respects that view.[9] Constitutional legislative, executive, and judicial authorities and their powers are inherently available to help decide little questions like where I and others might be born, if only mothers, families, and brave young doctors can bring their persuasive influences to bear at any or all of those levels. I have often wondered whether in deciding *Wilson* the good Chief Justice Sydney Smith may have been influenced by knowing of the high probability that two very good doctors might move to his neighboring county and enhance the quantity and quality of medical services there. In point of fact, that's what happened. Dr. Lucas and Dr. Wilson moved to Greenwood, nearby to Smith's rural home area of adjacent Holmes County.

Of course, over my growing-up years, I had many constitutional encounters. For twelve years, I attended public schools that were authorized, funded, and operated under various constitutional authorities. As a teenager, I and a number of my running mates had several encounters with the Youth Court of Washington County, unaware that once there had been quite a dispute whether such courts were constitutionally permitted.[10]

In the fullness of time, I became licensed under the authority of the legislative department, administered by the judicial department, so that I practiced law in Mississippi, and I did so in Greenville from 1965 to 1979. Another constitutional encounter and many more after the license rested on the wall in my small office in the law firm then known as Keady, Campbell & DeLong. I was a child of *Gideon*, meaning that I and every other lawyer in the county were routinely appointed to represent indigent criminal defendants to vindicate their then recently articulated constitutional right to counsel.[11] Before that, in the summer after my second year in law school, I had a considerable constitutional encounter, helping an older lawyer defend a young African American man charged with capital rape.[12]

I have spent lots of time in Oxford, Mississippi. I attended the University of Mississippi[13] in those four very interesting years ending with my graduation in June of 1962. Earlier that year the US Court of Appeals for the Fifth Circuit— ex cathedra from a grand old courthouse in New Orleans—had talked of our living "here in the eerie atmosphere of never-never land" en route to ordering that we endure a very important encounter with the US Constitution, one in which state constitutional officers—from governor[14] to the board of trustees of Institutions of Higher Learning[15] (some knew better) and university administrators (all of whom knew better)—were forcibly taught the meaning and effect of the federal Supremacy Clause.[16] During those years, Jim Silver spoonfed W. J. Cash's *The Mind of the South* (1941) into my curious mind and those of others similarly situated.

I do not recall having read much Faulkner prior to the evening in the spring of 1962 when Professor Silver walked into our seminar classroom and said, "I don't feel much like teaching this evening." It was one of those spring eessorvenings that were and still are so special in the South. "Bill Faulkner is in town. How would you like to go out [to Rowan Oak] and meet Bill Faulkner?" I have since not only read a bit of Faulkner but am guilty of that cardinal sin in the environs of Yoknapatawpha County of thinking his predecessor American Nobel laureate Eugene O'Neill may have been better.

Before and after those years when I grew up and lived and practiced law in Greenville over by the River, I was exposed to the legends and lore of the Percys and the Carters and, of course, David L. Cohn. I'm sure I was well shy of graduating from high school when I learned that "the Mississippi Delta begins in the lobby of the Peabody Hotel in Memphis and ends on Catfish Row in Vicksburg." I wasn't quite sure about the Catfish Row part, as every field trip my school class took to Vicksburg ended in the National Military Park with its utter lack of Delta flat lands. Nor did I realize that the levee was constitutionally authorized,[17] engineered, and maintained like our lives depended on it. By that time I had heard Cohn's sage observation that "folk in the Delta fear God and the Mississippi River."

I sensed the awe and omnipresence of the courthouse long before I read *Requiem for a Nun* and stumbled across the passages presented back on page 1 of chapter 1. The Washington County Courthouse was dark, brooding, center stage on a huge city block—the obligatory Confederate memorial on the right front lawn—surrounded by just enough trees to make sure you knew it had been there a long time. Every now and then back in the 1940s, my parents would drive me past it on the way to the railroad station to meet the train that would bear my maternal grandfather, and in those short two blocks between the C & G Railway tracks and the Illinois Central station, my eyes would fixate on the courthouse. Both of those railroad companies and their stations—terminals, they were sometimes called—operated under the constitutional police power, and legislative authority and supervision of the Mississippi Railroad Commission, whose constitutional trials and tribulations in its period of gestation we learned all about in chapter 6.

One memory stands out. Maybe it was the local newspaper practicing the freedom of the press made constitutionally sacred,[18] or just talk on the school grounds or among the kids in the neighborhood, probably both. I knew there was a trial going on. In the small town of Leland, a few miles east of Greenville, a lady named Dickins had brutally killed her mother with hedge shears, but she said a Negro broke in and did it. The jury found her guilty and some even said she should go to the chair.[19] I was nine years old, and prone to fantasies and nightmares. A constitutional encounter of the gravest kind, though it was a few more years before I had that perspective.

Some twenty-five years later my law office was just across Washington Avenue from the courthouse. I was in the (constitutionally authorized[20]) circuit clerk's office for some reason long forgotten when a nicely dressed, rather petite (as I recall), gray-haired lady walked in. She had a smile on her face, and everyone seemed to know her, but I didn't. She presented her pardon papers and said she was there to register to vote. The pardon is a constitutional act, within the authority of the governor.[21] Registering to vote after pardon from a criminal conviction is constitutionally regulated by the legislature.[22] It was the only time I ever laid eyes on Ruth Dickins, and it was in the courthouse.

Courthouses anchored each county in the Delta where I was born and raised, but Rosedale had one almost forty miles north of Greenville with a special ambiance about it, the River just a short distance to the west. It was said that once they put a man on trial for murder on Monday, convicted him on Thursday, hanged him on Friday, and had a grand ball on Saturday evening attended by everybody who was anybody in the Delta, with the ten-piece band within the rail, their booze stashed away behind the bench, the last revelers leaving just in time so the trusties brought in from the county jail early Sunday could get the courtroom cleaned up in time for a community-wide church service at eleven o'clock that morning. All in the very same cavernous courtroom. I never heard who said it, never knew if it was so. Not sure whether I heard of such before or after—as a fourteen-year-old—I attended my first dance there. But it was said. You didn't dare doubt the courthouse.

No later than the fifth grade I'm sure, I knew the country had something called a constitution that was pretty important and that there was some sort of bill of rights. I'd had sporadic exposures. By the seventh grade, we had all read the Gettysburg Address, but the real point there was Abe Lincoln's feat of rising from circumstances far worse than we lived in, and he became president of the United States. America was the wonderful land of opportunity. It welcomed the tired and the poor from all over the world, and those who longed to breathe free.

And then it happened. May 17, 1954.[23] Soon school let out for the summer. I had just finished the eighth grade. It was time to gather our baseballs and bats and gloves and head for the sand lots. But none of my white buddies could or would play. For years, much of the summer months in Washington County and most other Mississippi communities had been consumed with racially mixed baseball games. I had grown rather naturally to the view that a fellow's dignity and worth were a function of how far he could hit a baseball. Two of the black guys we played with—brothers as I recall—were mighty men. I'm sure at some point my father explained that the US Supreme Court had said we had to start going to school with the black kids. He never said there was anything wrong with that. He certainly never said I could not play ball that June as we had always done. But none of us did. Something had changed. And in time I learned that it had changed because some judges in a magnificent courthouse in Washington, DC, had said we had to change. The US Constitution had one of its greatest encounters in the country's greatest courthouse. Of course, as I have reflected back, I've wondered if the change among my friends who had theretofore been were pretty darn sure God made summer so you could play baseball was that we had all reached an age when girls had become a lot more interesting.

The pace quickened, though in many ways the life of teenagers in Greenville was normal. I heard about meetings at the courthouse when white men had gotten lathered up over their view that our Tenth Amendment constitutional rights were being trampled on. I slipped into one such meeting with a year-older friend. It had been his idea that we needed to check it out. Congressman John Bell Williams was ranting and raving about "Black Monday" and how those nine black-robed judges in Washington had raped the Constitution, though there was nothing in the Constitution saying there was anything wrong with "separate but equal" schools for white and black kids. Mississippi and the rest of the South were going to fight back. My friend and I were not sure what to make of it all. We sensed something serious was going on—he was a bit more politically savvy than I was at the time, and we were both a bit more interested in a young and upcoming rock 'n' roll performer named Elvis Presley and then Jerry Lee Lewis and a number of others who recorded for Sun Records in Memphis. And rhythm 'n' blues stars like Fats Domino, Ray Charles, and Ruth Brown.

Then came the autumn of 1957 and Little Rock.[24] In Greenville, we were only a stone's throw from Arkansas just across the River. Some judge in a federal courthouse had said *Brown v. Board of Education* really was constitutionally controlling and that racial integration in the public schools should proceed. Nine black children prepared to enter Central High School in September of 1957. The governor and the State of Arkansas said, No! Then federal forces arrived. President Eisenhower had ordered troops to see that the laws were faithfully executed. He federalized the Arkansas National Guard for good measure. Central High School at Little Rock would be racially desegregated.

Thanks to Little Rock and its proximity—and the several years before—by the time I graduated from high school, the symbiotic relationship between the courthouse and the Constitution had become a part of my worldview. It wasn't so much that this was good or bad. This was the way things were. I'm not sure I took very seriously the so-called difference between the federal government and the states. Of course, we were all white "southern boy[s] fourteen years old" who knew the stakes and the story of Gettysburg on July 3, 1863, that Faulkner wrote about with his inimitable poetry.[25] But Faulkner was talking about the great and fateful decisions one must make in this life, like crossing the Rubicon that we had learned about in Latin class. *Alea iacta est!* Anyway, the South lost the Civil War. Didn't that decide the question? We were all one country, weren't we? Hadn't we fought within our lifetimes as one people in World War II and then in Korea?

I have reflected often on what happened in Mississippi along the constitutionally bumpy calendar leading up to September 30, 1962.[26] In a sense it was anticlimactic. Inevitable. Gains had been fought for and progress made on basic human dignity fronts, like breaking down barriers in interstate transportation and at a handful of lunch counters. So much of the constitutional compliance issues during my college years concerned voting rights, the US Constitution and the courthouse functioning together on that oh-so-important front. My opening passages in chapter 1, and references to Cash and Faulkner—and Baldwin—are but a natural maturing of a sense of the marriage between the Constitution and the courthouse that has been with me since before my coming of age, before I was born. If I discern accurately, my thinking on this score has changed in only two ways. I've learned a bit more about the distinction between federal and state constitutions and courthouses. And I have gained a greater and more mature appreciation of the enormous effect that constitutions and courthouses have on our social existence, indeed, our everyday lives.

WHENCE THESE NINE TALES?

Prior to embarking on this venture, I had a passing familiarity with each of the encounters presented above. My knowledge of each courthouse constitutional encounter had been superficial, incomplete, and at points just plain wrong. Teachers learn more than their students every time out. More than two years after my fumbling beginnings with this work, I have learned much that I had not known. I cannot persuade another of the importance of these constitutional encounters, sort of like when Holmes said that "you cannot argue a man into liking a glass of beer."[27] I've tried to tell the stories reasonably well, given time and space, adding a few details and insights I had not found in the work before. If I've tried your patience, well, most of these stories tried mine until I got past my tenth or twelfth go at it, when fascination and concern began to set in, and I was hooked, torn between still further research and the opportunities for learning from partially told tales. Two years later, I marvel at the power in these incomplete stories. I've tried to leave enough citations, clues, and rabbit trails for those who might think it worthwhile to stretch some of the yarns a bit further. Or to correct my errors.

Except in the general sense just explained regarding the whole project, none of the nine chapters above was inspired by my past experiences. I was in gestation—as they say—as the tales of the Gold Coast and the BAWI program were playing out. Thinking about and writing each chapter did lead to memories and reflections. Judge Mike Mills's seventeen-year-old article about slavery law taught me of *Harry and Others* that in the summer of 1818, at its very first term, the Supreme Court of Mississippi decided a *Dred Scott*-type case and got it right. But I did not then know that twenty-eight slaves had been freed by an Adams County jury, not just three. Soon I was remembering growing up in a racially segregated society, many friends of both races working hard to break down the barriers in the 1960s and after. Sort of a second Emancipation. And particularly of those whose efforts were focused on the constitution and the courthouse. With bicentennial talk so in the air as the calendar turned toward December 10, 2017, how could we not pick a time in the summer of 1818 to commemorate the remarkable blow for freedom struck by the Supreme Court of Mississippi in its very first term!

Of course, the idea for a chapter on judicial review came from my professional involvement in *Alexander v. Allain*,[28] but soon I was recalling federal judicial review of all sorts of laws passed by the Mississippi legislature to preserve racial segregation.[29] There is still something wonderful about arch-segregationist Justice Tom P. Brady's twice-published confession first uttered in 1965 in a case arising in my hometown of Greenville.[30] "Irrespective of how erroneous it may appear, or how odious it is, a decision of the United States Supreme Court is still the ultimate in judicial determination and is binding on the tribunals and citizens of the respective states."[31]

Then there was the time ten years later when the Supreme Court of Mississippi exercised its power of judicial review to clean up its own mess in the area of *ad valorem* taxation, enforcing that special state constitutional equal protection clause.[32] Along with my good friend John Maxey, I was privileged in that case to represent a coalition of state business, labor, and education leaders seeking property tax equalization,[33] a worthy end in and of itself but for the greater purpose of assuring adequate funding for the by-then racially well-integrated public schools of Mississippi. Alas, that one may be more problematic today than back in 1980.

Article 7, § 9 of the constitution of 1832 was front and center in chapter 4 about the Union Bank bond embarrassment and the State's more general war on banks. I remembered my youth, when the presidents of the three banks were respected citizens and civic leaders. As a young lawyer, I was privileged to represent two banks in substantial secured lending in agriculture, in the river transportation business, and then in catfish farming and in financing such businesses as a honey farm. Of course, the paperwork was crucial, but first and foremost, all of these ventures thrived on trust. I became ashamed as I came to understand my state's blatant breach of trust, particularly after it lost the *Hezron Johnson* case. Do we not live in a state governed by the rule of law?

Chapter 5 concerning the crop lien laws presents almost a century's earlier dimension of that same experience I was having in the late 1960s and into the 1970s. Every standard form land deed of trust or security agreement on personal property waived priority or subordinated altogether the landlord's lien and many others. Now I know where those practices began, and I have an idea why. I did enough inland waterways law practice to learn of maritime liens for necessaries for a voyage, and of the primacy and priority of the crew member's wage lien. Again, another effort to attract outside capital into Mississippi, and with some modest albeit temporary successes, and in the end creating almost as many problems as were solved.

The advent of the regulatory state just may be the most important development in constitutional life in America since the Bill of Rights was added in 1789. It makes hash of rigid separation-of-powers thinking that some have conjured and to this day cling to so woodenly. Taking a look at Mississippi's maiden voyage was a natural. Then I recalled that this story began with railroad regulation. I mentioned above that my maternal grandfather was a railroad man. Those monthly widow's benefit Railroad Retirement Fund checks my grandmother received for many years always evoked memories of going down to the station in Greenville to greet the trains backing in from Leland, and of a retirement system everyone said was better than Social Security.

I settled early on the idea of a chapter about ten-hour workday law in the Piney Woods area. It was Mississippi's first encounter with—and evasion of—the (in)famous *Lochner* decision I learned about in law school. And then I recalled the first case I had argued and lost before the Supreme Court of Mississippi. It concerned a seventeen-year-old boy who had been injured while working long hours in a cotton gin during harvest and ginning season. My client, the gin company, was outraged at the suggestion it should have to pay workers' compensation benefits, and double benefits for having hired a minor.[34]

For years I thought of the common law as ranging between outdated and archaic. Early on, it struck me that the canon of construction that statutes in derogation of common law should be strictly construed was utter nonsense. I came to appreciate Justice Bob Sugg's opinion in *McCluskey v. Thompson*[35] several years before January of 1983, when I succeeded him on the Supreme Court of Mississippi. Through my law practice on the inland waterways and, in time, teaching admiralty and maritime law, I came to see that the reason-based general maritime law had evolved as the common law was said to have,[36] only there was not nearly so much political interference and influence by powerful and narrowly focused interest groups. After teaching in that area for seven years, I went back and started plowing through Holmes's *The Common Law* and other great works about the common law. Combine this with the massive misunderstanding among We the People concerning the constitutional origins and practice of judicial law-making, and a chapter on common law, its evolution, the process of adjudication at its core, and its enduring and dynamic status in Mississippi became a must. The insights of that chapter enhance a fair understanding of all else.

I wrote the chapter focused on *McPhail v. State* last. The country had its Roaring Twenties. Mississippi had the Gold Coast and then Soggy Sweat. I had enjoyed the general subject before in the *City of Clinton* beer case.[37] This chapter was essential to what I hoped to achieve, as the powers and prerogatives of the governor had become more important since the state constitution had been amended so that the governor could serve a second term. The *Alexander* case in 1983 had removed many legislative shackles from the governor's office. Gov. Haley Barbour's leadership in the wake of Hurricane Katrina added to the aura. Then, as he was walking out the door at the end of his second term, Barbour pardoned some 135 (give or take) felons. All hell broke loose.[38] Recalling as well the problematic and quixotic role alcoholic beverages have played in the life of this state, I returned to *McPhail* and more than with any other chapter learned just how superficial, incomplete, and erroneous my thinking had been. It hit me that Justice Virgil Griffith's last three paragraphs were nothing less than an elegant affirmation of the core of Magna Carta as a part of Mississippi constitutional law and practice. To be sure, Griffith never claimed as much. That combination of three sections of the state bill of rights could not have been made by accident. Besides, I loved coming across David McCarty's line that the Gold Coast "was probably the damned grandest place our grandparents and great-grandparents ever snuck off to."[39]

Chapter 10 focuses on a theme that has been a part of Mississippi history for as long as anyone can remember. In 1838, the Mississippi Union Bank was supposed to entice rich Yankees and foreigners to invest their money in Mississippi. In 1867, as just noted above, the act for the improvement of agriculture was expressly designed to attract supply merchants to come to Mississippi and bring money with them and lend it to farmers. With dozens of fits and starts, the State is still at it, with the payments "in lieu" statutes that are supposed to lure out-of-state (and out-of-country) entrepreneurs to invest big bucks in Mississippi in exchange for huge tax breaks. Gov. Hugh White's Balance Agriculture with Industry program was planned to pull the state out of the Great Depression. It was a well-meaning effort, as sincerely implemented as we have seen in Mississippi, except that no regard was had for the needs of nonwhite persons. Still, there was reason enough to tell the story set out in chapter 10. But another dimension of the BAWI story is timely as well. The specter of socialism from afar and in parts of America, coupled with the economic desperation of so many, had spawned a fear-based society the likes of which—once desegregation was survived—had seemed to fade away. Until recently!

THE PEOPLE WE ENCOUNTER AND
THE CONSTITUTIONS THEY ENCOUNTERED

There is a dimension to all of these stories that I had not anticipated. I disdain historians who begin with a thesis, a purpose, a conclusion, and then bend the facts accordingly, excluding the inconvenient ones. I thought you had to have a law degree to become licensed to do that. Taking off that part of my lawyer hat, I began with the intention of doing the research and telling the stories, letting the chips fall where they may. Such storytelling as a vehicle for explaining and understanding what a state constitution is all about seemed enough of a thesis, if you must have one at all. There is so much misunderstanding afoot about the function of a state constitution and about the powers and rights and ideals enshrined therein, and the role of all of these in our federal Union. Digging out the facts, trying to get inside the minds and skins of so many flawed and yet hopeful people over such an expanse of time, seemed the proper focus, and an interesting one as well.

I suggest there is something enriching, even ennobling, about the constitutional encounters chronicled above, beyond what I may have been expected a couple of years ago. Particularly this is so when all are considered in the aggregate. Front page after front page in the *Winona Times* in 1938 leading up to the referendum on seeking a new and reputable textile, knitting, hosiery, or other manufacturing plant told of hope and belief that a small town in north central Mississippi could come out of the poverty and hardships of the Great Depression. A similar theme runs through the many stories of the legislatively spawned crop-lien laws, as We the People struggled to climb from the depths and desperation of the folly that had led to Civil War. There was something wonderful, exciting, and uplifting about those great iron horses that roared down man-laid rails, particularly as the technologies and dreams of the post-Reconstruction era unfolded and made us a mobile people beyond our wildest imaginations.

Then there were the characters. Casey Jones was as much of a hero as men who had given their last full measure of devotion in the Civil War, and everyone knew that without R. T. Wilson and Edward H. Harriman, none of it may have happened. Fenwick L. Peck never became another Carnegie or Rockefeller, as he so longed to be. But he brought his money and entrepreneurship to the Piney Woods area of Mississippi around the turn of the twentieth century and for thirty years created jobs, real jobs with real paychecks. Hugh White shook the spirit of a small-town success and through dint of will put a state on his broad back and gave hope to so many. Before the War a bull-headed woman like Piety Smith Hadley and a conniving rascal like Gordon Boyd rose to the occasion and cajoled legislators until they began to undo the social injustice that the common law disabilities of coverture had inflicted on married women. A flawed ne'er-do-well grandson of a signer of the Declaration of Independence unwittingly conjoined with the resolve of the least accomplished of the four sons of the Kingfish of Lawrence County. By 1825, they had established judicial review as a core dimension of constitutional practice in Mississippi. If only I could have found more about Harry and the others around the time of statehood, about the unknown slave for whose murder Isaac Jones was hanged, about Sylvia Brooks and Jesse Kitchens and Bohlen Lucas and Drew Whitley and the freedmen with whom they labored after the War, and so, so many more.

Many lawyers were unsung heroes. Men like Lyman Harding and George S. Yerger and J. W. C. Watson and W. E. Morse and numbers of others seized the time and through their practice set examples that young lawyers of today would do well to reflect upon.[40] Yerger's family was remarkable. Together with younger brothers Jacob and William and George's brother-in-law Charles Scott, they set a standard made possible by the legal system enabled by the constitution. Great judicial contributions were made—nay, required—as well, and so we think back on the roles played by Powhatan Ellis, William L. Sharkey, C. Pinckney Smith, Josiah A. P. Campbell, Richard F. Reed, and George H. Ethridge who left their special mark on state constitutional law and practice. Without denigrating others, the State would benefit far into the future were its young people schooled in those special moments of Joshua Clarke, Sydney Smith, and Virgil Griffith, so that they could remind their elders of lessons they, too, should recall and revere. A last day of class on the constitutional encounters of that ever clever and patient latter-day Chief Justice Neville Patterson would be appropriate icing on the cake.[41]

Foremost are the ideas and ideals, made real and enjoyable and enforceable by the constitution *du jour*, expounded and made practicable by Clarke and William Yerger and two Smiths and Griffith. One cannot read too often those overarching paragraphs articulating our social compact that vary in location from one constitution to the next. Nor reflect too often on the meaning and application of the Madisonian dilemma and its economic variant—protecting individual rights in a majoritarian democracy and one's fair minimum share without unduly retarding the dynamic growth of the economic pie more commonly called the gross national product.

Sometimes it is enough just sitting on a bench on the courthouse lawn and reading Faulkner's passages that you've half memorized anyway from *Requiem for a Nun*, and maybe his words about the Constitution taken from *The Town* and quoted in chapter 1 above. Only then can you put into context the last rant you heard on Fox News. And enjoy a proper silent chuckle as you reflect upon Joseph G. Baldwin's passage penned back in 1853 in *Flush Times* about the constitution's chief excellency in the minds of those of us who are opinionated objectors, being that it doesn't allow "the government to do anything" we don't like, or has turned to "being a regular prize fighter that knocked all laws and legislators into a cocked hat, except those of the objector's party." [42]

ENDNOTES

1. For textual grounding for a right to be let alone, you may have to look to Miss. Const. art. 3, § 32 (1890).

2. Miss. Const. art. 3, § 13 (1890) ("freedom of ... the press shall be held sacred"); see also Miss. Const. art. 1, § 4 (1869) (same); Miss. Const. art. 1, § 7 (1832) ("No law shall ever be passed to curtail or restrain the liberty of ... the press"); Miss. Const. art. 1, § 7 (1817) (same). *See, e.g.,* Jeffrey Toobin's timely reminder in "Feeding the Beast," *New Yorker 38* (July 3, 2017).

3. Miss. Const. art. 3, § 12.

4. U.S. Const. amend. II.

5. *See* "A Case in Point from My Distant Past," in my article, *Variations on a Theme by Posner: The Factual Component of the Reliability Imperative in the Process of Adjudication,* 84 Miss. L. Journ. 471, 618–625 (2015), centered on *Wilson v. Gamble,* 177 So. 363 (1937). Dr. Lucas had a partner, Dr. John Wilson, a pediatrician, who was in the same boat and whose name became fixed to the case, normal regard for alphabetical order notwithstanding.

6. *Wilson v. Gamble,* 177 So. 363, 365–366 (1937).

7. Miss. Const. art. 3, § 16.

8. American Medical Association, *1846–1958 Digest of Official Actions* (1959).

9. Miss. R. Prof. Cond. 5.6.

10. See my §19:198 *Youth Courts* in Vol. 3 of the *Encyclopedia of Mississippi Law* (Jackson, Campbell & Miller eds., 2018).

11. *See Gideon v. Wainwright,* 372 U.S. 335 (1963).

12. See my "An August Memory," *CABA Newsletter,* 2013, http://caba.ms/articles/features/an-august-memory.html.

13. See Miss. Const. art. 8, § 213-A; Miss. Code §37-115-1.

14. Miss. Const. art. 5, §§ 116, 123.

15. Miss. Const. art. 8, § 213-A; Miss. Code § 37-115-1.

16. *Meredith v. Fair,* 298 F.2d 696, 701 (5th Cir. 1962) (Wisdom, J.).

17. Miss. Const. art. 11, §§ 227–239.

18. Miss. Const. art. 3, § 13 (1890) ("freedom of ... the press shall be held sacred"); *see also* Miss. Const. art. 1, § 4 (1869) (same); Miss. Const. art. 1, § 7 (1832) ("No law shall ever be passed to curtail or restrain the liberty of ... the press"); Miss. Const. art. 1, § 7 (1817) (same).

19. *Dickins v. State,* 208 Miss. 69, 78, 43 So. 2d 366 (1949) (that the jury "was unable to agree upon the punishment" means that one or more jurors, but less than all, voted that Mrs. Dickins should be sentenced to death).

20. Miss. Const. art. 6, § 168.

21. Miss. Const. art. 5, § 124.

22. Miss. Const. art. 12, § 253.

23. *See Brown v. Board of Education of Topeka,* 347 U.S. 483 (1954).

24. The story of the desegregation of the Little Rock schools was told by the Supreme Court of the United States in *Cooper v. Aaron,* 358 U.S. 1 (1958). *See also Aaron v. Cooper,* 163 F. Supp. 13 (E. D. Ark. 1958), and *Aaron v. Cooper,* 143 F.Supp. 855 (E. D. Ark. 1956).

25. William Faulkner, *Intruder in the Dust* 190 (1948).

26. See my "Of September 30, 1962 and 2012," *CABA Newsletter*, posted August 2012.caba. ms/articles/features/of-september-30–1962-and-2012.html.

27. Holmes, *Natural Law*, 32 Harv. L. Rev. 40 (1918), reprinted in *The Essential Holmes* 18 (Richard Posner ed., 1992).

28. *Alexander v. State by and through Allain*, 441 So.2d 1329 (Miss. 1983). I was a justice on the Supreme Court of Mississippi when *Alexander* was decided. I worked closely with Chief Justice Neville Patterson and others as that decision was experiencing its period of judicial gestation.

29. *See* my *Judge William C. Keady and the Bill of Rights*, 68 Miss. L. Journ. 1 (Fall 1998).

30. *See* my "The Confession of Justice Thomas Pickens Brady," *CABA Newsletter*, posted December 2015, http://caba.ms/articles/features/confessions-justice-thomas-pickens-brady. html.

31. *Bolton v. City of Greenville*, 178 So.2d 667, 672 (Miss. 1965); *Watts v. State*, 196 So.2d 79, 82–83 (Miss. 1967).

32. Miss. Const. art. 4, § 112 (as it read in 1980).

33. *State Tax Commission v. Fondren, Redd and others*, 387 So.2d 712 (Miss. 1980).

34. *Lopanic v. Berkeley Cooperative Gin Company*, 191 So.2d 108 (Miss. 1966).

35. *McCluskey v. Thompson*, 363 So.2d 256, 262–264 (Miss. 1978); see chapter 8 above.

36. Long ago, the maritime law imposed on all vessel owners a simple general tort duty of reasonable care toward all on board, *see Kermarec v. Compagnie Generale Transatlantique*, 358 U.S. 625 (1959), while Mississippi justices squabble and squabble over whether and to what extent to preserve the problematic and arbitrary common law distinctions among invitees, licensees, and trespassers when enforcing a landowner's tort duty of care. *See, e.g., Doe v. Jameson Inn, Inc.*, 56 So.3d 549 (Miss. 2011) and *Little v. Bell*, 719 So.2d 757 (Miss. 1998).

37. *See City of Clinton v. Smith*, 493 So.2d 331 (Miss. 1986), the story of which I have told in my *Practical Benefits of Literature in Law, and Their Limits*, 35 Miss. Coll. L. Rev. 266, 313–319 (2016).

38. *See* my op-ed article, "I Beg Your Pardon?," *CABA Newsletter*, posted June 2012, http:// caba.ms/articles/features/beg-pardon.html.

39. David McCarty, "Welcome to East Jackson," *jackson obscura*, https://jacksonobscura. wordpress.com/2011/06/28/welcome-to-east-jackson-part-I/.

40. I think of these and many more like them as I recall a soapbox I once mounted with no doubt monotonous regularity. *See* my *The Lawyer as Hero*, 53 Miss. L. Journ. 431 (Sept. 1983).

41. See my *Neville Patterson: A Remembrance*, 57 Miss. L. Journ. 417 (August 1987).

42. Joseph G. Baldwin, *The Flush Times of Alabama and Mississippi* 55 (1843, 1974); see chapter 1, note 7 above.

Index

Abrams v. United States, XI, 13, 299, 409
Ace of Spades, Gold Coast, 377
Adams, Charles Francis, Sunshine Commission, 210, 235
Adams, Daniel W., 316, 356; killing of James Hagan, 311, 314, 354; murder trial, 103, 104, 144, 315, 355
Adams, George, 311, 354
Adams, William Wirt, 316
Agricultural Bank, 115, 314
Agricultural lien legislation: Act for encouragement of, February 18, 1867, 154, 159–60, 164, 169, 179; Act to receive payment of wages for labor and liabilities for supplies, April 5, 1872, 157, 177, 195–97; Act for encouragement of (including landlord's lien), April 17, 1873, 197, 198; Act for encouragement of (including landlord's lien), April 14, 1876, 158–60, 190–91
Agricultural economics, 41, 116, 152, 156, 161, 166–67, 187–91, 193–95
Alcorn, James L., 158
Alexander v. State by and through Allain, XVI, 13, 59, 63, 89, 92, 297, 421, 473, 484, 486, 490
Allain, Bill: *Alexander* case, XVI, 13, 58, 63, 89, 92, 297, 421, 473, 490; draft constitution of 1986, VIII; *Papasan v. Allain*, 361
Allbritton, William S., XIII, XVIII, 425, 439–47, 449–50, 455–58, 463, 468–69
Allbritton v. City of Winona, 297, 365, 425, 439, 443–50, 455–58, 461, 463–64, 467–70, 472–73, 478
Allen, Elizabeth "Betsy" Love, 326–27, 336
Allen, James, 326–28, 359
Amis, A. B., 374, 383–84, 386–87, 390, 396–97, 415
Anderson, Milton, 378, 421
Anderson, William D., 343–44, 443, 446–48, 464
Angola State Penitentiary, Louisiana, XI

Anthony, a slave, XIII, 17, 28, 48, 55
Armstrong, Richard, 74
Armstrong Tire & Rubber Co., 425
Articles of Confederation, 39
Augustus, W. B., 214

Badgett, W. P., 167
Baker, Sam, Jr., 378, 421
Balance Agriculture with Industry Act (BAWI), XIII, XVIII, 187, 282, 384, 424–31, 433–34, 436–42, 444–49, 452–55, 457–61, 463–67, 469, 471–75, 480, 484, 486; Federal Reserve Bank study, XVIII, 453, 460; women's long-range benefit study, 460
Baldwin, Joseph G., XVI, 6, 14, 95, 97, 110, 112, 149, 483, 488, 490
Banks, Fred, 341
Barbour, Haley, 486
Barnett, Tom, 397
Barry, A. P., 154, 156–57
Barry, Frederick George, 210–11
Bazooka, Gold Coast, 377, 412
Behavioral economics, 183, 190–91, 456
Bellew's Café, Gold Coast, 377
Biddle, Nicholas, 95–96, 100, 110, 113–15, 118, 121, 127, 132, 140
Big Black River, 106
Bill of Rights, Mississippi, 59, 149, 395–96, 417, 486
Bill of Rights, US, XV, 7, 15, 64, 296, 481, 485, 490
Birdsong, T. B., 382, 397–99, 401
Bissell, J. W., 168
Black & White Café, Gold Coast, 377
"Black market tax," 404, 409–10, 420
Blackstone, William: common law, 312, 337–39, 348–49; Magna Carta, 14, 396; Rule in Shelley's Case, 318
Blatchford, Samuel, 232, 234
Blue Flame, Gold Coast, 378, 421

Blue Peacock, Gold Coast, 377

Bob, a slave, XIII, 17, 28, 48, 55

Bootleggers, 389, 404, 406–7, 409–11, 413–15, 420–22

"Bottom rail on top," 261, 264, 292

Bowman, L. W., 262

Boyd, Eliza Ellis, 336

Boyd, Gordon D., XVIII, 100, 330–36, 360–63, 488; House speech, 119; Senate speech, 332; US government judgment, 331

Boyd, James H., 336

Boyd, John, 267

Boyd, Rebecca Francis Williams, 361

Bradley, Calvin, 65

Bradley's Bat Shoppes, Gold Coast, 377, 399

Bradley's Café, Gold Coast, 377

Bradley v. State, 65, 90, 309–10, 352, 365

Bradstreet, John M., Co., 163, 194

Brady, Thomas P., 296, 299, 484

Brady, Tom, Jr., 275, 296

Brandeis, Louis D., 147, 257, 295, 428, 465

Brandeis Brief, 257, 271, 295, 436, 455, 459, 466

Brandon, Gerald, 318

Brandon Republican, 194, 222, 249

Breaux, Mrs. W. E., 238

Brewer, David Josiah, 270, 340

Brewer, Earl Leroy, 262–65

Breyer, Stephen, 39

Briggs, Joseph L., 73–76, 79, 83–84, 88, 91

Brooks, Sylvia, XIII, 173–74, 178–80, 198, 488

Broom, Robert, 378

Brown, Albert G., 158, 311

Brown, Ruth, 482

Brown Derby, Gold Coast, 377, 412

Bruin, Peter Bryan, 25

Bryant, Joseph, 106

Buckeye Cotton Oil Co., 275

Buckeye Cotton Oil Co. v. State, 275–77, 478

Buckhorn, The, Gold Coast, 377

Bullock, H. H., 397

Burnett, Daniel, 73

Burnham, Marion Clifton "Doc," 377

Butler, Pierce, 430, 450

Butterfield Lumber Co., 275, 277, 289, 294, 296–97

Butterfield Lumber Co., State v., 291, 294, 296–97

Calloway, Cab, 378

Cameron, Joel, 101, 143, 364

Campbell, John A., 219, 249

Campbell, John Beasley, 96–97, 103, 123–26, 131

Campbell, Josiah A. P., XVIII, 224–26, 250, 488; crop lien legal practice, 162–63, 171, 173, 184–86, 190, 195; railroad regulation, 193, 203, 227–29, 241, 251

Campbell v. Mississippi Union Bank, XIII, 98–99, 102, 127–28, 131–32, 139–47, 149

Canemount Plantation, near Lorman, 88, 92

Cannonball Express, 237

Canton, Aberdeen & Nashville Railroad, 215–18, 235, 247, 249, 250, 252

Capers, Walter W., 385

Cardozo, Benjamin, 367, 437, 465

Carothers v. Town of Booneville, 445–46, 461, 465, 468, 470, 473

Carpetbaggers, 150, 157, 161, 189, 226, 258

Carr's Place, Gold Coast, 377, 379, 413

Casa Loma, Gold Coast, 377, 412

Casey's Lane, Rankin County, 372, 374, 376, 386, 388, 399, 406, 412

Cash, Johnny, 238

Cash, W. J.: cheap labor, 288; courthouse, 3–4, 483; crop lien laws, XVII, 160–63, 165; The Mind of the South, XVI, 4, 6, 14, 152, 168, 192, 200, 254, 299, 300, 355, 424, 480; supply merchants, 167, 181, 190

Catchings, Joe, 377, 421

Catfish Row, Vicksburg, 174, 204, 480

Cedar Grove, Gold Coast, 377

Cedar Grove, Mississippi, 447

Cedar Hill Cemetery, Vicksburg, 315, 356

Chalmers, Hamilton H., 158, 172–73, 184–86, 338

Chance, John, 262

Chancery Court, Hinds County, 229

Chancery Court, Madison County, 215, 228

Chancery Court, Monroe County, 215, 228

Chancery Court, Montgomery County, 439–44, 447, 457, 467–68

Chancery Court, Rankin County, 373–74, 410–14, 418

Chancery courts, Mississippi: abate common nuisance, 373, 379–84, 396–97; court of equity, 9, 55, 302–3, 306, 320, 357, 362, 380, 434; jurisdiction and practice, 383–85; Superior Chancery Court, 95, 98, 127

Chapman, Joe, 378, 421

Chapman, J. T., 405

Charles, Ray, 482

Chatham, Gerald, 384

Chenille manufacturing, 450–53, 460, 471; Aponaug Chenille Co., 451, 471–72; Delta Chenille Co., 451, 453–54, 458, 460, 471; Winona Bedspread Co., 451, 471

Cherokee Indians, 98

Chicago Tribune, 371

Chickasaw Indians, 105, 325–28, 331, 359–61, 369; Elizabeth "Betsy" Love, 326–28, 336, 359; *Fisher v. Allen*, 327–28, 359; *Papasan v. Allain*, 361; Sally Colbert Love, 326; Thomas Love, 326; Treaty of Pontotoc Creek, 105, 331, 359

Choctaw Nation, 88, 105, 108, 328, 331, 359; Treaty of Dancing Rabbit Creek, 88, 105, 331, 359

Christian, Jesse, XIII, 173, 178–80

Circuit Court, Adams County, 48

Circuit Court, Claiborne County, 59, 73–75, 77, 83–84

Circuit Court, Lamar County, 269

Circuit Court, Lincoln County, 275

Circuit Court, Rankin County, 97, 123, 399, 401

Circuit courts, Mississippi, 7, 9–10, 81, 87; *Farrar v. State*, 14, 352; *State ex rel. Knox v. Speakes*, 14, 352

Claiborne, J. F. H., 48, 140, 141, 349, 356, 360

Claremont, Port Gibson, 24

Clarion, Jackson, 222, 230

Clarion-Ledger, Jackson, 371, 403–4

Clark, Charles, 162

Clark, Eric C., 432, 464

Clarke, J. Calvitt, III, 54

Clarke, Martha "Patsy" Calvit, 24

Clarke, Joshua Giles, XVI, 24–25, 67, 320, 488; *Harry and Others*, 15, 18, 21, 26–47, 50; *Jones v. State*, 36–49; natural law, 43–45, 436; political philosophy of Rousseau, 30, 33–35, 46–47, 52, 281; power of reason, 309; reliance on English law, 338, 343

Clayton, Alexander M., 135, 334, 338

Cleveland, Grover, 234

Club Royal, Gold Coast, 377

Cobb, James C., 162, 461–62, 464

Cochrane, George, 72, 90

Cochrane, Robert, 72–73, 90

Cochrane & Murdock, 73–75, 78, 83–84

Cochrane & Murdock v. Kitchens, 59–60, 70, 72–88, 91, 257, 272, 280, 359

Cogan, Thomas, M., 75

Cohens v. Virginia, 10, 47, 53–54, 309, 352

Cohn, David L., XVI, XVII, 480; *The Life and Times of King Cotton*, 151–52, 160–61, 165, 168, 171, 181, 183, 190; *Mississippi Delta and the World*, 89, 189; *Where I Was Born and Raised*, 174

Coke, Edward, 36, 52, 309, 314, 337–39, 352, 364

Coker, William L., XVII, 145, 149

Commerce Clause, 218–19, 221, 223–24, 227–28, 233–34

Common law, x, 8–10, 16, 65, 102, 123, 134, 178, 416; agricultural liens, 155–56, 158, 164, 175; case of first impression, 29–30, 50, 322, 340, 345, 367; case of *Harry and Others*, 27, 36–38, 40–44; coming of common law in Mississippi, 301–49; corporate governance, 129; disabilities of coverture, 225, 310, 328–33, 488; Justice Holmes, XVIII, 51, 192, 301, 340–41, 436–37, 486; liberty of contract, 277–80, 477–78; railroad regulation, 212, 229, 231, 235–36, 241; reason practiced, 344; restatements of law, 348, 356–57, 367; rule of precedent, XIII, 30, 32, 79, 85–86, 92, 98, 127, 135, 239, 278, 309, 325, 333, 339, 341, 343–44, 347, 425; statutes in derogation, 333, 339, 485

Conn, W. D., Jr., 383

Conner, Martin S. "Mike," 425, 463

Contract clauses: contrary to public policy, 277–78; *Dartmouth College Case*, 211, 221, 245; liberty of/freedom of contract, 224, 268–69, 272, 277–80, 284, 286; Mississippi Constitution, 77, 84–85, 103, 132–33, 139, 142, 177, 224, 228, 239, 250, 268; US Constitution, 77, 84–85, 103, 132–39, 142, 149, 177, 211, 219, 221, 224, 228, 239, 250

Cook, Sam C., 263–65, 272–77, 280–82, 285–86, 293, 343

Cooper, Tim E., 156–57, 190, 192, 250

Copiah County Agricultural Association, 154

Cortner, Richard C., 415, 422

Cotton South, 152, 170, 189–91, 423

Coulter, E. Merton, 168

Coulter, George, 311, 313, 354

Coverture, disabilities of, 187, 225, 310, 326–30, 333–35, 337, 354, 359, 361, 363, 488

Creekmore, Hiram H., 427

Crystal Lake, Rankin County, 376, 388, 406, 421

Dabney, Mayre, 158

Dalton, Georgia, 205, 450, 453

Dantzler, Adolph, 275

Dartmouth College, Trustees of, v. Woodward, 70–71, 90, 147, 221

Dattel, Gene, 163, 186, 188, 191, 193, 462

Davis, Alfred H., 208, 244

Davis, Jefferson, 78, 354, 355, 369

Davis, Joseph Emory, 78

Davis, Kenneth Culp, 358, 466

Davis, R. B. (Happy), 379

Davis, Ronald L. F., 21, 54

Davis, Thomas D., 291, 300

Davis, William C., 52, 54, 93, 144, 149

Dawson, A. B., 308

Day, William R., 431, 450, 465

Debtors' Relief Act of 1824, 74, 75, 77, 79, 83, 84, 187

Debt peonage, 169, 171, 191

Decker, Abraham, 22

Decker, Hiram, 19, 22, 26–28, 32, 40–43, 48

Decker, Isaac, 17

Decker, John, 16–19, 22–26, 29, 31, 40

Decker, Luke, 16–19, 21, 22, 26–29, 32, 38, 40–45, 48, 51, 55

Decker, Moses, 18, 40

Decker family of Indiana, XIII, 16–19, 21, 29, 30, 35, 40–43, 48, 50, 53

Declaration of Independence, 18, 35, 43, 58, 66–67, 71, 80, 87, 89, 92, 186, 333, 435, 488

Delta State Teachers College (now University), 375

DeLuxe Cleaners, Gold Coast, 377

Denkmann Lumber Co., 289

Dennery's Restaurant, Jackson, 388

Depression, Great, VII, 288, 423, 425, 430–31, 433, 441–42, 486–87

DeSoto National Forest, 288

Deto, Mrs. Wm., 238

Dewitt, Hicks, 262

D'Iberville, Pierre le Moyne, 265

Dickens, Ruth, 481

Dipsy Doodle, Gold Coast, 377

Domino, Fats, 482

Dorsey, Bates, 74

Dred Scott v. Sanford, XVI, 16, 25, 40, 43, 45, 48, 50–51, 53, 55, 138, 484

Driver, Eli Moore, 173–74, 188

Driver, Giles L., 173

Driver Plantation, 173–74, 178

Dun, R. G., Co., 163, 194

Dunbar's Night Club, Gold Coast, 377

Dyche, Isaac R., 164–65

Dyche, John T., 158–59, 165

Dykes, Curtis, 378, 421

Dykes, J. T., 378, 421

East Jackson Club, Gold Coast, 377, 399

Eastside Club, East Side Club, Gold Coast, 377, 379

Economics: analyses, 199–201, 212, 227, 240–42, 271, 280–81, 283, 376, 434–35; economic liberty, 269, 436; "fallacy of static pie," 191, 242, 283, 488; "finance is amoral," 163, 186, 188; laissez-faire, XIV, 240, 261, 268–69, 284, 439, 455, 461; law and, 188, 200, 254, 257, 284, 295, 298, 300, 423, 427–28

Edward Hines Yellow Pine Trustees, 289

Eisenhower, Dwight D., 482

Elijah, a slave, 83

Ellington, Duke, 378

Ellis, Powhatan, 24, 48–50, 61–65, 68–72, 76, 79, 81–82, 85–91, 93, 272, 309, 320, 337, 488

Emancipation, XVII, 27, 32, 152–55, 161, 190–95, 201, 319, 484

Eminent domain, IX, X, 40, 297, 303, 306, 311

England, Frank A., 437

Equal Footing Doctrine, 50, 261, 303–5, 327, 333

Equitable remedies, 130, 302, 320, 357; abate nuisance, 373, 379–85, 395–96, 407–8; indemnity, 115, 121, 130, 147, 167; rescission, 118, 120–21, 146

Ethridge, George H., 469, 488; *Carothers v. Town of Booneville*, 445; *Crippen v. Mint Sales Co.*, 296, 407; *Hartfield v. State*, 379; *Mississippi Constitutions*, VII; *Shrader v. Shrader*, 367; *Sinclair v. State*, 338

Evans, Mary Patey, 460

Executive power: laws faithfully executed, 102, 131, 142, 153, 223, 386–87, 390–91, 396, 399, 408, 416, 482; Mississippi Constitutions, IX, X, 7, 9, 58, 60, 79, 223, 240, 351, 409, 479

Fairley, Charles, 378, 421

Fannin Road, Rankin County, 376, 378, 386, 388, 412, 421

Farmers' Loan & Trust Co., 215, 219–20
Farmers' Loan & Trust Co. v. Stone, 219, 222,
    230–34, 240, 247
Farr, Richard Ansley "Dick," 396, 399–403,
    407–8, 419; Dick Farr's Amusement Co.,
    399; Dick Farr's Café, Jackson, 399
Farrar v. State, 14, 352
Farrington & Howell, 174, 196
Faulkner, William, XVI, 3, 263, 290, 461, 480;
    "Barn Burning," 195, 200; characters, 166,
    170, 181, 195; constitution, 6, 483, 488;
    courthouses, 3–6, 13, 180, 307, 352, 440,
    483, 488; *The Hamlet*, 200; *Intruder in the
    Dust*, 489; *Light in August*, XVII, 290, 299;
    Requiem for a Nun, 3–4, 13, 14, 197, 200,
    247, 488; *The Town*, 6, 14
Fede, Andrew, 28, 47, 49–52, 54
Federal Reserve Bank, Atlanta, XVIII, 453,
    459–60, 463–66, 471, 475
Fentress, James, 215–17, 247–48
Fickle, James E., XVII, 260, 291–92, 294,
    299–300
Field, Stephen J., 232, 234
Finkelman, Paul, 50
Finnis, John, 53
Fish, Stuyvesant, 204, 207, 211
Fisher, Ephraim S., 128, 136, 139, 147
Fisher, John, 326–27
Fisher v. Allen, 327–28, 359
Fitzgerald, Ella, 378
Foote, Henry S., 101, 143, 149, 364
Foote, Shelby, 356, 369
Ford, R. A., 238
Forest Lawn Cemetery, Buffalo, New York,
    259
"Four Horsemen", 430, 449, 450, 465
Foy, Malcolm, 402, 412
Foy's Place, Gold Coast, 377
Franklin, Benjamin, 349, 369
Freedmen's Bureau, 174
Freedom-by-residence, XVI, 15–19, 22, 29–33,
    40, 50
Freund, Ernst, 281
Front Street, Memphis, 167, 174–75, 188, 196

Gamble, Hugh, 478
Gardner, Philip S., 260
Garner, Lou, 265
Garrett, Ed, 377

Gates, Gillespie & Co., New Orleans, 158–59,
    164–67
Gay Lady nightclub, Gold Coast, 378, 413
George, James Z., 158, 184–86, 188, 193, 226,
    250
Georgia Compact of 1798, 27, 304, 307, 350, 358
Gibson, T. C., 262
Glenn, David C., 100
Glenwood Cemetery, Houston, 333, 362
Goins, Craddock, XVIII, 379, 385, 388–89, 403,
    410–16, 419–20, 422
Gold Coast, XIV, XVIII, 371–422, 484, 486;
    frequent murders, 379, 404, 407; raids,
    374–77, 380, 382–83, 395, 397–402, 408–9;
    Seaney-Overby gun duel, XIV, 372, 375, 409
Gold Coast Café, 377
Goodman, Steve, 238
"Good of the whole," 269, 271, 280–81, 283,
    298, 427
Gore, T. N., 385
Gore, Weaver E., 442
Grace's Place, Gold Coast, 377
Grand Gulf Railroad & Banking Co., 136–37
Granger movement, 210, 245
Grant, Roy, 378–79
Grant, Ulysses S., 157
Grateful Dead, 238
Graves, James, 338
Graves, Lee, 377
Graves, Richard S., 354
Gray, Horace, 234
"Great commercial highway," 221, 232
Great Depression, VII, 288, 423, 425, 430–31,
    433, 441–42, 486–87
Greeley, Horace, 157
Green, Charles B., 62
Green, Garner W., 427, 439, 467
Green, John J., 170
Green Frog, Gold Coast, 377
Green & Green law firm, 272; Green, Green &
    Jackson, 439, 467
Green Lantern, Gold Coast, 377, 379, 413
Green v. Frazier, 430–32, 449–50, 465, 470–71
Greenwood Cemetery, Jackson, 101, 316, 358
Griffith, Virgil A., 385–86, 415, 422, 469, 488;
    Allbritton v. City of Winona, 443, 447–48,
    458, 469; *Brown v. State of Mississippi*,
    386, 415; common law, 341, 364; *Farrar v.
    State*, 14; Magna Carta, XIV, XVIII, 7–8, 396,

406, 469–70, 486; *McPhail, State v.*, 352,
386–96, 399, 402, 408–9, 416, 469; *Missis-
sippi Chancery Practice*, 55, 385; *Mississippi
Reports & Reporters*, 55; *Outlines of the
Law*, 146, 364
Griffith, William B., 82–83
Griffith v. Fanny, 51
Grissett, Robert Bruce, 401–3, 407–8, 412, 419
Grissett's Sandwich Shop, Gold Coast, 377
Gus Place, Gold Coast, 377, 412
Guthrie, Arlo, 238

Habeas corpus, writ of, 311–12, 354, 395, 420
Hadley, Piety Smith, 329, 333, 336, 488
Hadley, Thomas B. J., 329, 332–33, 360
Hadley boarding house, 329, 336, 360, 363
Hagan, James, 311, 314–15, 354–56
Haile, William, 76–77, 81
Hale, Matthew, 305, 337–39, 353, 364, 369
Hall, Toxey, 262–63
Hamilton, Alexander, 107; Hamiltonian, 110,
118
Hamilton, Peter, 220
Hammond, M. B., 183
Hampton, John P., 24, 49, 50, 55, 61, 68–70,
76, 91
Hampton, Lionel, 378
Hand, Learned, 46, 54
Handy, Alexander H., 136–39, 306, 308, 321–25,
338, 342–43, 350, 357, 366
Handy, W. C., 204
Hanging, XIII, XIV, 16, 36, 43, 101, 140, 309, 315,
343, 379, 386, 405, 481, 488
Harding, Lyman, 21, 22, 488
Harlan, John Marshall, 232–34, 270, 295
Harriman, Edward Henry "Ned," 207–8, 236,
244, 487
Harris, Buckner C., 124, 139
Harris, Cadillac George, 378, 421
Harris, Wiley P., 217, 248
Harris, William L., 136, 339
Harrison, Benjamin, 226
Harrison, Peter, 170
Harrison, William Henry, 17–19
Harry, a slave, XIII, 15–55
Harry and Others v. Decker & Hopkins, XI,
XVI, XVIII, 15–55, 298, 466, 484, 488
Hart, H. L. A., 53, 435
Hartfield, Jack, 379

Harvard College, 242, 311
Harvard Law School, 369, 435
Hawkins, Armis E., 343
Haynen, W. J., 262–63, 293
Hederman, Tom, 403
Hickey, Ex parte, 199, 311–14, 354–55
Hickey, Walter, 311, 313–16, 354–55
Hickman, Nollie W., XVII, 260
Hill, James J., 236
Hill, Robert Andrews, 219–22, 227, 230, 232,
234, 249
Hiller & Co., 168
Hill Top Grocery, Gold Coast, 377
Hinds v. Terry, 49–50
Hinton Brothers Mill, 289
Hoffheimer, Michael H., 48–50, 53, 55, 93, 350
Hoffman, Gilbert H., XVII, 266, 288–91,
293–94, 296, 299
Hoffman, Harry O., 437
Holliday, Billie, 378
Holly, Bernard, 378, 421
Holly, Kermit, Jr., 378, 421
Holly, Sherrill, 378, 421
Holmes, David, 25, 49, 64, 73, 93
Holmes, James G., 338
Holmes, Oliver Wendell, Jr., 57–58, 240, 270,
281, 296, 298, 300, 318, 344, 349, 365–66,
368–69, 428, 431, 435, 442, 466–68, 483,
490; *Abrams v. United States*, XI, 13, 299,
409; *The Common Law*, XVIII, 51, 54, 192,
323, 340–42, 357–58, 363–64, 366–67, 369,
416, 422, 437, 466, 486; criminal law, 38,
348; *Frank v. Mangum*, 312–13, 354; *Int'l
News Serv. v. Associated Press*, 53; *Law in
Science and Science in Law*, 253, 254; *Lochner v. New York*, XVII, 270–71, 274, 284–85,
295, 298, 445, 461, 469, 474; *New York Trust
Co. v. Eisner*, 145, 320, 357; *Olmstead v.
New York*, 38, 52; *Path of the Law*, IX, XVIII,
298, 300, 356, 368–69, 466; *Rock Island,
A. & L. R. Co. v. United States*, 147; *South-
ern Pacific Co. v. Jensen*, 52, 301, 306, 351,
366, 436, 466; *The Western Maid*, 53, 467
Homochitto Lumber Co., 259
Homochitto River, 301–6, 308, 337, 350
Homochitto River, Commissioners of, v. Withers,
144, 301–11, 320–21, 323, 338, 342–43, 349–51
Hood's Place, Hoo's Place, Gold Coast, 377
Hopkins, Francis, 19–23, 26, 28, 38, 42–43, 48, 55

Hopkins, John L., 20
Hopkinson, Francis, 71, 93
Hopkinson, Joseph, 70–71
Horne, Lena, 378
Houston v. Royston, 14, 87, 352
Howard, Volney E., XIV, 97, 100–101, 103, 123, 142–43
Howerton, Huey B., *Yesterday's Constitution Today*, VII
Howie, George, 372, 405
Hudson, Pat, 377, 382, 413
Hughes, Charles Evans, 385
Hume, David, 46, 186
Humphreys, Benjamin G., 153, 165, 192
Humphreys, W. W., 211
Hunt, William R., 173–74
Hunt v. Wing, 173–81, 185, 188, 195–97, 199
Hupperich, Charles M., 373–74
Hurt, John, 238
Hydrick, George W. "Red," 406, 421

I. B. S. Manufacturing Co., 425, 460
Illinois Central Historical Society, 238
Illinois Central Railroad Co., XVII, 204–7, 215–16, 236–38, 243–44, 246, 249, 251–54, 480
Indiana Constitution, 18, 31, 32, 35, 44, 47
Indian Removal Act, 105, 144
Industrial Revolution, 105, 240
In favorem vitae et libertatis, 35–36, 38, 44–45
Ingalls Shipbuilding, 425, 452
Ingraham & Lindsay, 136
Ingraham & Read, 136
Interstate Commerce Act of 1887, 220, 222, 234, 241, 251

Jackmore, Ernest, 373
Jackson, Andrew, 150; Age of Jackson, 100, 110, 150, 241, 331; association with Powhatan Ellis, 63–64, 88; feud with banks, 96, 105, 107, 109–12; Indian removal, 325, 328; Jacksonian Democracy, 45, 96, 102, 109, 328, 333; other supporters of, 77, 98, 330–31; Second Bank of the United States,, 107, 109–10; War of 1812, 360
Jackson, Forrest B., 427, 439, 467
Jackson, Robert H., 393
Jackson & Brandon Railroad & Bridge Co., 321

Jackson Country Club, 404, 420
James, Elmore, 378
Jayne, Joseph M., 169, 182
Jeep City Tourist Court, Gold Coast, 373
Jiggitts, Louis Meredith, 427, 464
Johnson, Andrew, 153, 219
Johnson, Henry, 78
Johnson, Hezron A., 95, 97–101, 104, 126–31, 138–40, 147
Johnson, Hezron A. v. State of Mississippi, XIII, XVIII, 39, 95, 98–100, 104, 131, 138–41, 485
Johnson, Isaac, 78
Johnson, Joseph, 78–80, 91
Johnson, Paul B., 404, 420, 459
Johnson, William, 78
Johnston, Oscar Goodbar, 262, 292
Jones, Isaac, XIII, XVI, 16, 36, 41, 55, 341, 488
Jones, John Luther "Casey," 236–38, 241, 253, 487; "Ballad of Casey Jones," 238; Casey Jones Railroad Museum, 236
Jones, Robert C., 373
Jones, Woodrow, 373
Jones & Tyler, 275, 296
Jones v. State, 28, 36, 37, 45, 50, 52–53, 366
Judicial power, IX, 9, 60; circuit court has residual jurisdiction, 10, 309; no matter beyond state judicial power, 10, 14, 57, 87, 352; not to decide is to decide, 10, 87, 187, 343, 366
Judicial review, IX, X, XVI, 21, 24, 57–94, 218, 350, 393–394, 455, 484, 488

Kahneman, Daniel, 191, 473
Keady, Campbell & Delong, 479
Keady, William C., XV, 298, 490
Keller, Elzie, 453
Kennedy, Anthony, 39
Kent, James, 339–40, 365
Keyes, Evelyn V., XVIII, 28, 46, 50, 54–55, 341, 351–52, 364–65
Kimbrough, B. T., 157–58, 171, 177
Kimco Auto Products of Memphis, 454; Kimco Brake Shoe Factory, 454, 472
King, B. B., 378
King, Jimmy, 378, 421
Kitchens, Ben Earl, 246, 254
Kitchens, Benjamin, 72–75, 78–79, 83–84, 88, 90, 92
Kitchens, Jesse, 488

Klein, S. A., 437
Knox, State ex rel., v. Speakes, 14, 352
Kyle, Christopher H., 22
Kyle, John C., 214

La Cache Plantation, 73, 90
Lackawanna Lumber Co., 259
Lafayette, Marquis de, 80
Lake, George, 75
Lakewood Memorial Park, Jackson, 40
Lamar, L. Q. C., 246
Lang, Meredith, XVII, 51, 90, 93, 148
Langsford, supply merchant, 169, 181–86
Laselle, State v., 47
Leake, Walter, 21, 48, 55, 64, 66, 74–76, 81, 84
Lee, Percy Mercer, 373, 380, 382, 397, 401, 410, 414–15
Lee, Robert E., surrender of, 156, 161
Lehman Abraham & Co., 168
Lewis, Furry, 238
Lewis, Jerry Lee, 482
Lincoln, Abraham, XII, 138, 154, 233, 481
Lochner v. New York, XVII, 268–71, 274, 277, 284–86, 298, 430–431, 449, 455, 461, 468, 474, 485
Locke, John, 60, 89, 93
Loggins, Will, 262
Lombard, John, 72
Lone Star, Gold Coast, 377
Longino, Andrew H., 263
Louisville, New Orleans & Texas Railroad, 204, 207
Louisville & Nashville Railroad, 215, 218–19, 247, 251
Love, Elizabeth "Betsy," 326–28, 336, 359
Love, Sally Colbert, 326
Love, Thomas 326
Lowry, Robert, 169, 209, 211–12, 214–15, 218, 239
Lucas, Bohlen, XIII, 181–82, 185–86, 188, 488
Lucas, John, 478–79, 489
Lunsford v. Coquillon, 51
Lynch, Charles, 67, 68, 101, 106, 111–15, 142, 145
Lynch, James Daniel, 25, 49, 64, 66, 91, 147

Madison, James, 47, 51, 68, 278
Madisonian dilemma, 141, 285, 436–37, 462, 488
Magna Carta, XIV, 7, 8, 14, 186, 199, 309, 311–13, 316, 325, 327, 352, 354–55, 395–96, 399, 406, 409, 486

Mallory, John H., 111–12
Mansfield, Lord, 35, 52
Maple Grove, Gold Coast, 377
Marbury v. Madison, 59, 68–69, 79, 89, 92, 249, 350
Married Women's Property Law: disabilities of coverture, 187, 225, 310, 325–36, 361, 488; Senator Boyd's speech, XVIII, 332–33, 360; Senator Hadley's bill, 329, 332
Marshall, John, 10, 47, 57, 59, 68–69, 79, 98, 352, 456
Martin, Luther, 71
Marye, Mary P., 159, 164–65
Marye v. Dyche, 165, 175, 180, 193–97
Mashburn, Troy, 379, 414
Matthew, St., Gospel According to, 7, 14
Matthews, John, 265
Matthews, Stanley, 234
Matthews v. State, 294
Maxey, John L., II, 484
Mayes, R. B., 263–65
Mayott, Thomas, 267
McCarty, David, 390, 413, 486
McCleave, Bill, 402, 418–19
McCluskey v. Thompson, 362, 365, 485, 490
McCraw, Thomas K., XVII, 150, 242, 245, 252, 254
McCulloch v. Maryland, 71, 473
McFarland, Baxter, 215, 218, 247
McGehee, Harvey, 379, 469
McIntosh, McQueen, 20
McIntyre and Bridges, 136
McKaskey, R. E., 262, 278
McLaurin, Anselm J., 261
McLaurin, Woodworth, 379
McLean, John, 25, 43, 48, 53
McNair, A. C., 385
McNutt, Alexander G., 101, 181, 364; agricultural bank, 314–15; bank wars, 95–97, 100, 104, 113–32, 141–43, 146–48; Married Women's Property Act, 333; Repudiator, XIII, 355
McPhail, Guysell, 377, 383, 390, 393, 395–97, 413
McPhail, Guysell, v. State of Mississippi, XIV, XVI, XVIII, 8, 13, 199, 352, 383–99, 402–3, 408, 414–17, 444, 486
McPhail, J. P. 383
McPhail, Stanley, 383
McReynolds, James Clark, 430–31, 450
McWillie, William, 214

Mechatto, Bernice, 3

Merchants, supply and furnish, 154–63, 165–72, 174, 177, 179–85, 189–91, 197–99, 486

Meyer, Weis & Co., 182, 185, 199

Mill, John Stuart, 188

Miller, Samuel F., 233–34

Miller, T. Marshall, 234

Miller, William, 238

Mills, Michael P., XVI, 19, 46, 49, 55, 65, 484

Millsaps College, 439

Mississippi A & M College, 450

Mississippi & Tennessee Railroad, 216

Mississippi Central Railroad, 216, 259, 437

Mississippi College School of Law, VIII, 250

Mississippi Constitution, 1817, XI, 34, 44, 50–53, 59–60, 67–69, 85–86; slavery, 27, 29, 40–43, 52–53. *See also specific clauses, powers, and rights*

Mississippi Constitution, 1832, XI, 8, 87–88, 98–99, 102, 108, 140–41, 350, 484; Art. 7, sec. 9, guaranty, 126; Art. 7, sec. 18, liberty of contract, 277. *See also specific clauses, powers, and rights*

Mississippi Constitution, 1869, XI, 13–14, 88

Mississippi Constitution, 1890, XI, 10, 13–14, 88, 138, 158, 236, 239, 258, 277, 456; separation of powers, X, XVI, 60, 61, 89, 94, 367, 409, 416, 485

Mississippi Hall of Fame, XIV, 193

Mississippi Industrial Commission, 430, 432–33, 437–40, 453, 458, 460, 464, 467

Mississippi Railroad Co. Bank, 136

Mississippi Railroad Commission, 204, 212–14, 217–18, 221–24, 226, 228–30, 232–34, 240, 243–46, 249, 480

Mississippi River, 105, 115, 152, 173, 178, 189, 259, 301, 480; navigation, 20–21, 32, 305, 351; sold down river, 19, 41, 51

Mississippi Union Bank, XIII, XIV, XVII, 39, 62–63, 88, 95–112, 187, 486; *Beasley Campbell* case, 122–26; bonds, 114–15, 408, 429, 463, 484; Gordon Boyd, 331–32, 335; *Hezron Johnson* case, 126–29; legislative wrangling, 113–22; repudiation, 115–22, 130–32, 138–40

Mississippi Workers' Compensation Act, 274, 452, 471

Mize, Sidney Carr, 402–3, 410

Mobile & Ohio Railroad Co., 209, 215, 218, 230, 247

Monroe, James, 25

Montgomery, Andrew, 20

Montesquieu, Baron de, 60, 89

Moon River Club, Gold Coast, 377

Moor, State v., 64–65, 89, 364

Moore, Lee, 262

Moorhead, Mississippi, 203, 243

Morgan, Albert T., 157–58, 171, 177, 192

Morgan, Carrie Highgate, 157

Morgan, Charles, 157

Morgan, Daniel, 63

Morgan v. Reading, 5, 13, 143, 304–5, 350–51, 364

Morrison, Toni, 28

Morse, William E., 439–40, 442, 449

Morton, Elijah, 20

Mose, King, 378, 421

Moyses & Co., 168

Munn v. Illinois, 210, 222–24, 245, 250

Murdock, John, 72–73, 88, 90

Murray, Billy, 238

Muse, N. E., 377

Myers, Sam, 378

Nashville Tennessean, 143–44, 330, 355, 361

Natchez, Jackson & Columbus Railroad ("Little J"), 215, 218, 222–24, 229, 235, 246, 251

Natchez Courier, 330

Natchez slave market, 19–23

National Conference of Commissioners on Uniform State Laws, 348, 368

National Guard a.k.a. State Militia, 5, 131, 148, 374, 376–77, 380, 382–83, 386–87, 390–91, 393, 395–402, 404, 407–8, 410–13, 482

Natural law, 29, 37, 43–45, 53, 312, 339, 455, 467; John Finnis, 53; laws of nature, 35, 45, 436

New Colonial Club, Gold Coast, 377, 412

New Deal, 290–91, 300, 424, 430, 449, 461–64, 467–68, 471, 474–75

Newman, C. B. "Buddie," 203, 243

Newman, Edmund, 259

Newman, Flora, 259

Newman, H. & C., Co., 168

Newman, J. J., Lumber Co., 258–75, 278–79, 287–91, 293, 424–25, 467

Newman, J. J., Lumber Co., State v., 53, 264, 270, 273–77, 280–83, 285–87, 289–90, 425, 428, 455, 467

Newman, Judson Jones, 259, 285

Newman v. Bank of Greenville, 156–57, 190, 192–93, 219, 224
New Orleans & Northeastern Railroad Co., 215, 218–19, 222, 249
Noel, Edmund F., 263
Norris, Leseray, 287
Northwest Ordinance of 1787, 337; Article 1, 18; Article 2, 8, 41, 50, 304, 310, 325, 352, 358; Article 3, 325; Article 6, 15, 17, 18, 23, 27, 31, 35, 38–41, 44, 350
Nugent, William L., 151, 182, 192

Oak Grove, Gold Coast, 377
Oaks, The, Gold Coast, 377, 413
Oaks House Museum, Jackson, 363
Obama, Barack, xi
Obergefell v. Hodges, 38–39, 52
Ohio River, 16–18, 20, 31–32, 40, 51–52, 209, 220, 222
O'Keefe, John A., 398, 401
Old River, 301–5, 321
Ole Miss, University of Mississippi, xviii, 242, 263–64, 292, 375, 434, 437, 455, 473, 479
Olmstead v. United States, 38, 52
O'Neill, Eugene, 480
Overby, James Norris "Buddy," 375
Overby, Lynne, 375
Overby, Marvin Lane, 375
Overby, Maureen Turner, 375
Overby, Melvin Wayne, 375
Overby, Norris, xiv, 374, 411; gun duel with Sam Seaney, xiv, 371–72, 375, 404–7
Overby, Ruell, 375
Owl's Nest, Gold Coast, 377, 398

Panic of 1837, 96, 101, 111–14, 119–20, 144, 329, 360
Panic of 1839, 119, 134
Panic of 1873, 162, 191, 194, 200–201
Panic of 1893, 162
Panic of 1907, 260
Parchman state penitentiary, 192–93, 200, 379, 405
Pardee, Don A., 219, 249
Parson, John P., 82
Patterson, Neville, 59, 488, 490
Patton, William Lee, 321–25, 357–58
Paxton, Andrew J., 169, 181–83
Peabody Hotel, Memphis, 174, 480

Pearl River, 106, 180, 351, 371–72, 411; Pearl River Country, 62; Pearl River venues, celebrities, 375–79; Gold Coast, 388, 400, 403–6
Peck, Fenwick Lyman, 259–62, 268, 272–73, 285, 288–89, 291, 423, 425, 487
Percy, LeRoy, 261, 292, 480
Percy, Will, 261
Percy & Yerger, lawyers, 182
Pettit, J. N., & Co., 174
Peyton, Ephraim G., 158–59, 164, 175, 193, 225, 247
Peyton, E. G., chancellor, railroad lawsuits, 215, 218, 222, 225, 229
Phillips, James, 95, 126, 131
Phillips, Sarah, 265
Pierce, Merrily, 55
Piney Woods, 257, 259–60, 288–89, 424
Planters Bank: banking practices, 106–10, 113, 315; bonds, xviii, 14, 96–99, 104, 111–12, 116–21, 336, 408, 429; failure of, 332
Pledge of faith, credit, 14, 95, 98–99, 104, 108, 111–16, 336, 429, 433, 439–40, 445, 449, 468; guaranty, 116–19, 121–27, 139, 141, 408
Plessy v. Ferguson, 13
Pocahontas, 63
Police power, ix, 151–201, 203–55, 257–300, 371–422, 423–75; Article 7, § 190, x, 7, 30, 239, 266, 289, 306, 408, 422, 424, 427–30, 447, 455, 461, 477, 480; petty larceny of, 30, 279–80, 298; never be abridged, 7, 239, 266, 289, 408, 428, 455. *See also* Mississippi Constitutions
Polk, L. S., 404, 420
Porter, Hertisense, 379
Positive law, 7, 15, 29, 35, 37, 39–41, 43–45, 176, 277–78, 342, 396, 444
Posner, Richard A., xv, xvii, 14, 50–52, 200, 253, 295, 298–300, 358, 365–70, 466–67, 474, 490
Pound, Roscoe, 281, 340, 365, 435, 437, 455–56
Powell v. Brandon, 318–19, 333
Prather, Lenore, 343
Prentiss, Seargent S., 134
Presley, Elvis, 482
Probate court, Lawrence County, 67–68
Probate courts, Mississippi, 67–68
Progressive era, 261, 263–64, 274, 285

Prohibition, 372, 379, 381, 401, 404–5

Pruitt, J. N., 175

Put & Take, Gold Coast, 377, 412

Queen, Wayne Ray, 377, 413

Quinn, W. W., 267

Quitman, John A., 140–41

Rachel, a slave, XIII, 17

Railroad Regulation Act of 1884, 187, 203–55, 212–14

Rainbow Club, Gold Coast, 377

Randall, Willie Mae, 453, 472

Rankin v. Lydia, a Pauper, 51

Ransom, Roger L., XVII, 192, 194–95, 201

Raymond Gazette, 230

Red Top, Gold Coast, 377

Reed, Richard F., 39, 53, 264–65, 269–72, 279, 285–87, 293–95, 488

Rencher, Guy Jack, 261–62, 292

Repudiation, XIV, XVII, 96–99, 102–3, 117, 119–21, 125, 128–29, 132

Richardson, Sara, 375

Riparian owners, rights, lands, 5, 143, 304, 305, 338, 351, 353

Roberts, Owen, 449

Robinson, Jesse, 378, 421

Robinson, Marylyne, XI

Robinson, Tully, 21–22

Rocket Lounge, Gold Coast, 377, 421

Roe v. Wade, 38, 52

Rogers, Ernest, 377

Rogers, Henry Lee, 339

Rogers, Will, 406

Roosevelt, Franklin D., 430–31

Ross, Alison, 82

Rousseau, Jean-Jacques, XI, 30, 33–35, 46–47, 52, 281

Routh, John, 22, 55

Rowland, Dunbar: counties and towns, 93; on Joshua G. Clarke, 25, 55; judges and lawyers, 150, 250, 254; *Mississippi, Heart of the South*, 89, 93; Mississippi legislature, 292–93; Railroad Commission, 243–46, 249; on William L. Sharkey, 143

Rundell, Joshua, 75

Runnels, Hardin, 63

Runnels, Harmon M., 58, 62

Runnels, Harmon M., Jr., 62, 67–69, 72

Runnels, Hiram George, 62–63, 88, 93, 100–101, 103, 115, 130, 140, 147, 360

Runnels, Howell W., 63

Runnels v. State, 59, 63, 75, 88, 249, 257, 272, 280, 442

Russell, E. L., 220

Russell, John, 267, 294

Russell, Lee Maurice, 261–62, 292

Sanders, James W., 450, 471

Sanders, Robert David, 450–53, 471

Sansing, David: Mississippi governors, 55, 93, 150, 201, 254; Mississippi people and culture, 150

Saunders, Wallace, 236, 238

Scalawags, 189

Scalia, Antonin, 39, 362, 370

Schumpeter, Joseph, 242, 254

Scott, Charles, XIV, 103–4, 123, 127, 139, 147, 488

Scott, Sally Meriwether, 104, 144

Seaney, Alexander Alvin, XIV, 372–74, 382, 398, 405–6, 414

Seaney, Anna Belle, 372, 405–6

Seaney, Doris, 373

Seaney, Eugene, 373–74, 377, 402, 406, 411, 418–19

Seaney, Frank, 373, 382, 414

Seaney, Joseph, 373

Seaney, Mildred Nell, 373

Seaney, Millian, 405–6

Seaney, Minnie Ethel Highsmith, 372–73, 406

Seaney, Opal, 373

Seaney, Ruby Dell, 373

Seaney, Samuel Alvin, XIV, 371–75, 377, 382, 409–12; gun duel with Norris Overby, XIV, 371–72, 375, 404–7

Seaney, Zell Frances, 373

Seaney, Zilpha C. Jones, 373

Second Bank of the United States, 107, 109–10

Seeger, Pete, 238

Select legislative committee, Union Bank bonds, 104, 118–23, 128

Sessions, J. F., 214

Shady Rest nightclub, Gold Coast, XIV, 374–75, 377, 399; Seaney-Overby gun duel, XIV, 371, 375, 404

Shakespeare, William, 4, 46, 449; *Hamlet*, 11, 14, 47, 54, 142, 252, 470; *Julius Caesar*, 336, 363; *King John*, 470; *Merchant of Venice*, 263–64, 293

Sharkey, William L., 14, 39; bank wars, 100, 102, 124–29, 133–34, 139, 143, 145; common law, 304–5, 310, 327–28, 337–38, 341; judicial contribution, 488

Shaw, Lemuel, 270, 344, 367

Shelley's Case, Rule in, 310, 317–19, 333, 356–57

Shelton, Tom, 404–5, 420

Sherman Anti-Trust Act, 269

Shewbrooks v. A. C. & S., Inc., 54

Shields, William Bayard, 25–26

Shiller, Robert J., 191, 473

Silas, Willie, 378, 421

Silver, Jim, 480

Silver Moon, Gold Coast, 377, 412

Simrall, Horatio F., xiv, 155–56, 158, 166, 172–73, 195, 309

Skates, John Ray, Jr., 52, 89, 91–92, 147, 193, 247, 250, 297, 415

Sloan, Peter, 82

Smith, Adam, 186, 443

Smith, B. H., 163, 170

Smith, Charles, 378

Smith, Cotesworth Pinckney, 100, 102, 127–29, 136, 139, 143, 327–28, 488

Smith, James, 171–73

Smith, Lemuel A., Sr., 440–42, 468

Smith, Mark, 171–73

Smith, Sammie Lee, 378, 421

Smith, Sydney McCain, xiii, xviii, 240, 253, 469; common law, 339–40, 350, 365; constitution and industry, 423, 434–37, 443, 446–56, 461–62, 468, 473; sociological jurisprudence, 434–37; state police power, 263, 275, 277, 281, 288, 293, 297

Social compact, contract, order, x, xi, 6, 30, 33–35, 52, 96, 100, 157, 396, 488

Social Darwinism, 268, 284–85

Somerset v. Stewart, 35, 52

Southern Cross the Dog, 203, 243

Southern Pacific Railroad, 207

Southern Railroad Co., 247, 321

Southwick, Leslie H., xvi, 89, 240, 250, 253–54, 338, 474

Specie, hard currency, 97, 107, 111, 115, 119, 123–24, 142; specie currency statute, 123–25, 132, 142, 146

Specie Circular, 96, 110–11, 134, 142

Spencer, N. A., 384

Spot, The, Gold Coast, 377

Stamps, Bill, 378, 421

Stamps, Charlie, 378, 421

Stamps, Clifton, 378, 421

Stamps Bros. Hotel, Gold Coast, 377–78, 421

St. Clair, Arthur, 18–19

Steed, J. H. "Doc," 377, 379, 382, 403, 412

Stockton, Richard, grandfather, signer, 66–67, 87, 89

Stockton, Richard, Jr., 21, 61, 66–72, 75–94; duel with John Parson, 82

Stockton, Richard, Jr. (Old Duke), 66–67, 71, 87

Stockton, Robert Field, 87, 89

Stone, Harlan Fiske, 437, 465

Stone, James, 263, 264

Stone, John Marshall, 158, 210–11, 214–15, 222, 226, 246, 254

Stone, Phil, 263, 293

Stone v. Illinois Central RR Co., 232

Stone v. New Orleans & Northeastern RR Co., 232

Storm, John, 170

Stovall, Charles, 82

Stovall's Springs, 82

Stribling, Paul, 373, 410

Sugg, Robert P. "Bob," 362, 485

Sullivan, Michael D., 343–44

Summers & Brannin, 167

Sun Records, 482

Sutch, Richard, xvii, 192, 194

Sutherland, George, 430, 450

Sweat, Noah S. "Soggy," 371, 405, 409

Sykes, Eugene O., 276, 286, 297

Taft, William Howard, 271

Tallahatchie River, 106

Taney, Roger B., 40

Tarbell, Jonathan, 154–58, 226

Tate, Tommy, 378, 421

Tatum, Frank, 290

Tatum Lumber Co., 289–90

Taylor, John, 23–25, 49

Ten-hour workday law, 187, 258, 260–63, 266, 268, 270–86, 289–90, 296, 425, 430, 495

"Texas, Gone To," "G. T. T.," 147, 333, 462

Thacher, Joseph Stevens B., 8, 311–14, 342, 354–55

Thaler, Richard H., 191, 200, 473

Therrell, J. V., 379

Thies, Clifford, xvii, 138–39, 145

Thompson, H. E., 262, 278
Tilden, Samuel, 165
Titanic, 257
Tombigbee River, 101, 106, 180
Tom's Tavern, Gold Coast, 378
Toney, a slave, 326–28
Tracy, Janice Branch, XVIII, 409–11, 413, 420
Travelers Home, 378
Travis, S. E., 263, 266, 293
Tripp, Charles Alonzo, 378
Trotter, James F., 124, 139
Tucker, Tilghman M., XVII, 100–102, 123, 143, 145, 354
Turnbull, Andrew, 82
Turner, Edward, 61–62, 76, 91, 124, 139
Turner, George, 18, 50
Turner, Ike and Tina, 378

Union Pacific Railroad, 207
Union Station, Chicago, 242
United States Lumber Co., 259
Universal planter, 157
US Constitution: Commerce Clause, 218–19, 221, 223–24, 227–28, 233–34; Contracts Clause, 77, 84–85, 133, 135–36, 139, 142, 149, 177, 219, 221, 224, 228, 239; Double Jeopardy Clause, 64–65; Due Process Clause, 40, 64, 177, 224, 269, 271, 278, 401–2, 428, 430–31, 436, 442–45, 455–58, 461, 468; Eighteenth Amendment, 372, 380; Fourteenth Amendment, 64, 218, 224, 228, 278, 428, 430–31, 447; republican form of government, 4, 51, 58, 358, 383, 387; Supremacy Clause, 44, 103, 149, 286, 303, 428, 480; Tenth Amendment, 12, 258, 269, 271, 287, 428, 482
US Highway 49, 372–73, 203–4
US Highway 61, 203–4
US Highway 80, 372, 374, 383, 401
US Highway 82, 203–4, 478

Van Buren, Martin, 64, 111, 331
Vanderbilt University, 264
VanderVelde, Lea, XVI, 50, 55
Van Devanter, Willis, 430–31, 450
Vardaman, James K., 261, 264, 285, 292
Vaughan, Thomas C., 20
Vicksburg & Jackson Railroad Co., 321
Vicksburg & Meridian Railroad Co., 215, 218

Vicksburg Evening Post, 212, 222, 233
Vicksburg Railroad Case, 322
Vicksburg Sentinel, 311, 315, 355–56
Volstead Act, repeal of, 372, 410

Wabash, St. Louis & Pacific RR Co. v. Illinois, 233, 252
Wabash Cannonball, 233
Wabash River, 17, 40
Wadlington, James M., 164–65
Waite, Morrison Remick, 222, 230–34, 251
Walker, Clitus Bordeaux, 261, 292
Walker, Robert J., 28, 45, 52, 54, 69, 88, 91
Wallace, William Lyon, 385
Walters, John, 267
Warren, Robert Penn, XVII, 257, 300
Washington, George, 16, 39
Washington & Lee University, 63, 101
Washington Daily News, 386
Washington Monument, 356
Watkins, Albert, 453
Watkins, Madge, 453
Watkins, William H., 427
Watson, John William Clark, 217, 222–23, 248, 488
Weathersby, A. E., 263
Webb, Simon T., 237–38
Webster, Daniel, 66, 70–71, 90, 122, 134
Wells, W. Calvin, 427
Welty, Eudora, 376
West & East Railroad, 216
West Feliciana Railroad, 78, 106, 209
Westmoreland, J. G., 171
Whiskey Speech (Soggy Sweat's), 371, 406, 409
White, Hugh Lawson: BAWI program, XIII, XVIII, 282, 424–39, 450, 452, 455, 457–59, 463, 486–87; National Guard to Gold Coast, 380–85, 393–96, 398–99, 406, 409
White & Billingsley, 174–76, 179, 196
White Horse Cellar, Gold Coast, 377, 412
Whiteside, W. L., 238
Whitfield, McNeill and Whitfield, 272
Whitley, Drew, xiii, 181, 185–86, 488
Whitmire, Dewitt C., 453
Whitmire, Goldie, 453
Wild Owl, Gold Coast, 377
Wilkie, Curtis, 14
Williams, Bernard "Bunny," 378, 421

Williams, Christopher H., 77
Williams, J. D., 400–401
Williams, John Bell, 482
Williams, J. P., 332
Williamson, Sonny Boy, 378
Willie Stevens Night Club, Gold Coast, 377
Wilson, John, 479, 489
Wilson, Richard T., 205–8, 236, 243–45, 487
Wilson, Woodrow, XII, 286
Winchester, George, 83
Wing, Cox & Co., 173–76, 178–79
Winkle, John W., III, VII
Winn, George, 319
Winny v. Whitesides Alias Prewitt, 51
Winston, Louis, 61, 68, 70, 76, 91
Withers, David D., 301–7, 337, 349
Withers Case, 144, 301–11, 320–21, 323, 338,
    342–43, 349–51
Wolfe, Booker, 378, 421
Woodbury, Levi, 134–35
Woodland Club, Gold Coast, 377
Woodman, Harold D., XVII, 193, 195, 197, 201
Woodrow Wilson Bridge, Jackson, 386, 388,
    400
Woods, William B., 234
Woodward, C. Vann, 160, 215, 246
Wooten, Andrew Jackson, 171–73
Workman, Noel, XVII, 243, 254–55
Wright, Fielding, 404, 420

Yalobusha River, 106
Yazoo & Mississippi Valley (Y&MV)
    Railroad, XVI, 203–9, 215–18, 222–29, 231,
    234–35, 243–51
Yazoo River, 106, 192, 204–5
Yellow Dog Café, 203
Yellow fever epidemic of 1898, 207, 244
Yerger, George Shall, XIV, 100, 103, 123, 135,
    350, 488
Yerger, Jacob Shall, XIV, 100, 104, 118–23, 128,
    145, 147
Yerger, Sarah Meriwether Scott, 104, 144
Yerger, William, XIV, 100, 104, 127–30, 136,
    138–40, 147, 318, 350, 488
Yocknapatafa River, 106
Yoknapatawpha County, 13, 170, 195, 215, 480